FAMILIES & CHANGE

Fifth Edition

This book is dedicated to Sharon J. Price and Patrick C. McKenry (1949–2004),
our mentors and role models.

FAMILIES & CHANGE

Coping With Stressful Events and Transitions

Fifth Edition

Edited by

Christine A. Price
Montclair State University

Kevin R. Bush
Miami University of Ohio

Sharon J. Price
University of Georgia, Athens

Los Angeles | London | New Delhi
Singapore | Washington DC

Los Angeles | London | New Delhi
Singapore | Washington DC

FOR INFORMATION:

SAGE Publications, Inc.

2455 Teller Road

Thousand Oaks, California 91320

E-mail: order@sagepub.com

SAGE Publications Ltd.

1 Oliver's Yard

55 City Road

London, EC1Y 1SP

United Kingdom

SAGE Publications India Pvt. Ltd.

B 1/I 1 Mohan Cooperative Industrial Area

Mathura Road, New Delhi 110 044

India

SAGE Publications Asia-Pacific Pte. Ltd.

3 Church Street

#10–04 Samsung Hub

Singapore 049483

Acquisitions Editor: Kassie Graves

Editorial Assistant: Carrie Montoya

Production Editor: Bennie Clark Allen

Copy Editor: Michelle Ponce

Typesetter: Hurix Systems Pvt. Ltd.

Proofreader: Wendy Jo Dymond

Indexer: Wendy Allex

Cover Designer: Janet Kiesel

Marketing Manager: Shari Countryman

eLearning Editor: Lucy Berbeo

Printed in the United States of America

Library of Congress Cataloging-in-Publication Data

Families & change : coping with stressful events and transitions / edited by Christine A. Price, Kevin R. Bush, Sharon J. Price— Fifth edition.

pages cm

Includes bibliographical references and index.

ISBN 978-1-4833-6675-3 (pbk. : alk. paper) 1. Families—United States. 2. Social problems--United States. 3. Social change—United States. I. Price, Christine A. II. Title: Families and change.

HQ536.F332 2017

306.850973—dc23   2015029687

This book is printed on acid-free paper.

15 16 17 18 19 10 9 8 7 6 5 4 3 2 1

Brief Contents

The companion website at study.sagepub.com/pricefamchnge5e provides password-protected instructor resources to accompany this book, including a test bank, PowerPoint® slides, chapter exercises, and discussion questions.

Note: PowerPoint is a registered trademark of Microsoft Corporation in the United States and/or other countries.

Detailed Contents

3 Conceptualizing Parental Stress With Family Stress Theory 53

GARY W. PETERSON

4 Families With Special Needs: A Journey From Coping and Adaptation to Resilience and Hope 79

BRIANA S. NELSON GOFF, JESSICA HIGH, ADAM CLESS, KELSEY KOBLITZ, NATIRA STAATS, AND NICOLE SPRINGER

8 Stress and Resilience in Stepfamilies Today   161

CHELSEA GARNEAU AND KAY PASLEY

9 Adaptation Among Immigrant Families: Resources and Barriers   179

KEVIN R. BUSH, BERTRANNA A. ABRAMS-MURUTHI, STEPHANIE A. BOHON, AND HYOUN K. KIM

10 The Newest Generation of U.S. Veterans and Their Families 203

KYUNG-HEE LEE AND SHELLEY McDERMID WADSWORTH

SECTION V: VIOLENCE IN A FAMILY AND COMMUNITY CONTEXT 221

11 Promoting Pathways to Resilient Outcomes for Maltreated Children 223

MARGARET WRIGHT AND LUCY ALLBAUGH

12   Stress and Coping With Intimate Partner Violence   249

LYNDAL KHAW

13   Family Responses to School and Community Mass Violence   269

AMITY NOLTEMEYER, COURTNEY L. MCLAUGHLIN, AND MARK R. MCGOWAN

List of Tables and Figures

Preface to the Fifth Edition

The fifth edition of *Families & Change: Coping With Stressful Events and Transitions* presents the vast literature that has emerged in recent years detailing families' responses to various transitions and stressful life events. Scholarly interest in family stressors is not new. The social and behavioral sciences evolved during the Progressive Era (1890–1920) out of an interest in social problems facing families as a result of industrialization and urbanization. The primary interest at that time was in social reform and the use of research to help in solving these problems. During the 1920s and 1930s, scholars started focusing on the internal dynamics of families. Because of the disillusionment with the effects of social reform programs and the growing depersonalization of mass society, there was an increasing interest in the well-being and personal adjustment of families and individuals. Researchers became interested in healthy lifestyles, mental health, and child development. Both family sociology and family therapy started developing at this time (Cole & Cole, 1993).

Two major societal disruptions—the Great Depression and World War II—prompted further attention on how families cope with unprecedented change. Angell (1936) and Cavan and Ranck (1938) identified various family characteristics that mediated the impact of the effects of the depression—that is, family organization, integration, and adaptability. These findings remain largely unchallenged today (Boss, 1987). Hill (1949), in his study of wartime family separations, developed a framework for assessing family crisis: the ABC-X Model. This framework, with its emphasis on family resources and definitions that mediate the extent of the stress or crisis response, serves today as the basis for most stress and coping theoretical models. The 1950s represented a focus on both the integrity of the American family as an institution and traditional family patterns. The social and political revolution of the 1960s, and the technological changes accompanying the greater industrialization and urbanization of the 1970s, 1980s, and 1990s, resulted in a proliferation of research on families' coping and adaptation to a multitude of changes and new problems.

In the 22 years between the publication of the first and fifth editions (1994–2016), our society has witnessed significant familial, social, and global changes. Today, families often live in a context of time demands, insecurity, and stress. They are experiencing the consequences of an economic recession, including loss of jobs; serious threats to pensions, investments, savings, and benefits; and the involvement of the United States in multiple crises around the globe. Technology has advanced to the point of being nonstop and often invasive. Life has become more impersonal as human connections are replaced by virtual relationships. Industrialization and urbanization have expanded, leading to denser living environments and the associated stressors of expensive housing, traffic congestion, and increased cost of living. Extended longevity is offering the benefit of more time with family members yet there are added costs (e.g., chronic and degenerative illness, caregiving demands, health care costs).

Based on multiple indications, the stress and change that families are experiencing appear to be intensifying. Stressors inherent to daily life include the discrimination families often face based on race, religious beliefs, gender, and sexual orientation as well as the unpredictable yet stressful events of ongoing natural disasters including hurricanes, tornadoes, storms, floods, and earthquakes. With the blurring of gender roles and the increased diversity in family structure, the basic conceptualization of "family" has evolved. Although the family system may still be viewed as a "haven" from external stressors, families are also challenged to meet their increasingly complicated needs.

It is evident that many academic and social service professionals are involved in developing knowledge, as well as teaching classes and offering outreach programs in areas that focus on the stressors confronting families. This emphasis on family stress continues to grow. Before the development of the first edition of *Families & Change,* Pat McKenry and Sharon Price (the original editors) conducted an extensive review of more than 400 randomly selected undergraduate and graduate college and university catalogs. These institutions ranged from small, private, liberal arts colleges to large, land-grant/research universities. They found that more than 60% of these institutions offered courses that dealt with family problems, stress, and/or change. These courses were found in departments of social work, home economics/human ecology, sociology, human services, psychology, human development, family science, family relations, child and family development, health, professional studies, and criminology. They also surveyed instructors of those courses and discovered that texts representing a compilation of recent research findings in this area were almost nonexistent. As a result, the first edition of *Families and Change* (1994) was published to address this void. Since that time, and via the subsequent editions, Sharon and Pat worked to provide a text appropriate for the study of various family problems, stressors, and changes in today's society.

In light of this goal, each edition has reflected contemporary issues and transitions taking place in the larger society as well as in families. This has been achieved by including updated research findings, introducing new chapter subjects, and adding new topics in selected chapters. For example, in this edition, there is updated research in every chapter, and most chapters contain new substantive content (e.g., elder abuse in the *Stress and Coping in Later Life,* characteristics of resilience in stepfamilies in *Stress and Resilience in Stepfamilies Today*). Additionally, we have introduced chapters on the impact on families of school and community mass violence and the circumstances of families raising children with special needs. Finally, the chapter on family violence in the 4th edition has been divided into two chapters addressing child maltreatment and intimate partner violence, respectively, while the chapters on mental and physical illness have been combined.

In the 5th edition of *Families and Change,* as with previous editions, not all family stressors could be reviewed because of page constraints. The topics chosen represent contemporary issues that many families face today and that have received considerable social, professional, and research attention. Each chapter presents an overview of our current understanding of selected family transitions and stressors, real-life scenarios meant to illustrate content specific stressors families face, and most include possible mechanisms of intervention. However, each author was afforded the opportunity to present his or her area of expertise in the manner that he or she viewed as appropriate.

The topics in this book represent both predictable and unpredictable problems and stressors. Predictable family problems would include those stressors that are inherently stressful even though they are foreseen. We take the position that all abrupt or disjunctive changes, although moderated or buffered by the family's coping resources, are likely to be stress producing. Such predictable or normative changes include marriage, parenting, aging, death, and dying. Other problems are potentially more traumatic because they cannot be predicted. These would include physical or mental illness, death, substance abuse, war, violence, economic insecurity, divorce, and remarriage. We take the position that many of these problems are interrelated and often combine to produce stress-related responses. For example, stress related to economic issues may lead to marital problems, including violence; they may then initiate a cycle of divorce, personal and economic disorganization, and remarriage.

We also assume that family problems, change, and stress responses are not always "bad" for a family. The disequilibrium that develops requires new methods for handling problems. Out of stressful situations new and creative solutions may arise that are superior to those that were present when the problem occurred. This experience may enable the family to handle future crises in a superior manner, and it may result in greater individual and group satisfaction with family life.

This text represents an integration of research, theory, and application, drawing on the interdisciplinary scholarship in each topic area. It is intended to serve as a basic or supplementary text for undergraduate and introductory graduate courses on family or social problems. This edition will also be useful to professionals, novices, and those with considerable experience, especially in social work, education, and public health, who increasingly work with families who are confronting a multitude of problems.

OVERVIEW OF CHAPTERS

We begin this text (Chapter 1) with an updated overview of the research on family problems, stressors, change, and coping. The nature and origin of the problems and changes facing families today are discussed, noting that while many of today's problems are not new, the degree of change in American society is unprecedented. The history of systematic inquiry into family problems and change is traced to individual physiological stress studies in the late 17th century; these studies of individuals have evolved in today's focus on whole-family interaction and an increased emphasis on resilience. An ecological or systems approach is presented as the integrating framework for studying families under stress. These perspectives facilitate an understanding of families as dynamic mechanisms, always in the process of growth and adaptation as they deal with change and stress over time.

In Chapter 2, Heather Helms, Natalie Hengstebeck, and David Demo discuss everyday hassles and family stress. Specifically, they examine how daily stress and hassles are associated with family functioning, paying particular attention to the variability in family members' experiences and the invisible dimensions of family work.

A stress-vulnerability-adaptation model is introduced as a way to frame the research on daily hassles and family stress. The authors emphasize the diversity that exists across and within families as well apply a feminist perspective when examining the gendered meanings applied to routine family activities. Finally, they discuss how the existing policies and practices in the United States fail to mesh with the daily life of American families and propose policy interventions.

Gary Peterson, in Chapter 3, focuses on parenthood as a stressor. He emphasizes a "realistic" approach that integrates research on parental stress with family stress theory and recognizes that caring for and socializing children involves challenges and hassles as well as satisfactions and fulfillment. Dr. Peterson addresses (a) why parental stress is so common, (b) why parental stress varies within mothers and fathers, (c) why parents vary in their capacities to cope with and adapt to stress, (d) what linkages exist between parental stress and the adjustment (or maladjustment) of parents and children, and (e) what strategies exist for controlling and reducing adverse parental stress. This approach helps one understand the wide range of circumstances varying from highly disruptive crises, to chronic stress, to normative challenges, and increases our understanding about how parental stress applies to both individuals and families.

In Chapter 4, Briana S. Nelson Goff, Jessica High, Adam Cless, Kelsey Koblitz, Natira Staats, and Nicole Springer present the varied challenges facing families who have a member with special needs. Because of the complex terminology associated with this area of research, the authors first present an overview of terms used to describe individuals and families with special needs. Nelson Goff and her coauthors go on to discuss relevant theoretical frameworks that can be used to better understand these families in their unique contexts. They also examine both internal and external contextual factors that impact families with special needs. Finally, several external resources available to families with special needs members are shared.

Abbie Goldberg, in Chapter 5, discusses the challenges confronting lesbian, gay, bisexual, and queer (LGBQ) individuals as well as LGBQ-parent families. Using an ecological or systems approach, she reviews the situational and contextual forces that impact these populations as they move through the life course. These include issues surrounding "coming out," forming and maintaining intimate relationships, barriers faced in becoming parents, and the stressors related to relationships with their families of origin, schools, and the legal system. Finally, she presents implications for professionals with regard to supporting LGBQ-parent families.

Áine Humble and Christine Price, in Chapter 6, focus on individual and family challenges that result from aging. They frame the chapter around the concept of an "aging family" which pertains to the relationships, transitions, and social support networks of older family members. Using both ecological systems theory and the ABC-X model of family stress, the authors examine stressful events commonly associated with aging. Specifically, they focus on the unfortunate experience of elder abuse as well as two major transitional events that occur in later life, retirement and caregiving. Adaptive and coping strategies applied by individuals and their families in later life are also reviewed.

In Chapter 7, David Demo and Mark Fine provide a comprehensive overview of current research on divorce and its consequences for individuals and families. They use the divorce variation and fluidity model, an integrated process model, to illustrate the variability in which families experience divorce but also to explore how adjustment to divorce changes over time. Dr. Demo and Dr. Fine review historical trends and sociocultural factors to provide a current context for divorce as well as review current literature on predictors and causes of divorce. Finally, interventions (i.e., parent education, mediation) that may facilitate divorce adjustment are presented.

In Chapter 8, Chelsea Garneau and Kay Pasley discuss the stressors associated with remarriage and stepfamily life. They provide definitions of stepfamilies and present the prevalence and demographic characteristics of stepfamilies in general. Using a family systems perspective, they identify sources of stress within the various stepfamily subsystems (i.e., couples, parent, parent–child, sibling subsystems) as well as the most common characteristics of resilient stepfamilies. Finally, Dr. Garneau and Dr. Pasley discuss psychoeducational and clinical approaches to easing stepfamily adjustment.

In Chapter 9, Kevin Bush, Bertranna Abrams-Muruthi, Stephanie Bohon, and Hyoun Kim discuss the resources and barriers to immigrant families who are adapting to their new environments. Using the family systems framework, they highlight the importance of interactions among individuals and family subsystems during the immigration process. They outline how families are deeply involved from the time the decision to migrate is made through the complex stages involved in acculturation and adaptation. The barriers and stressors that exist at the societal, community, family, and individual levels are examined (i.e., limited language proficiency, diminished social support networks, intergenerational conflict, marital conflict, poor housing, discrimination, inadequate public policies, and lack of economic resources). Finally, the varied resources that can facilitate an immigrant family's adaptation to their adopted country are presented and discussed.

Kyung-Hee Lee and Shelly McDermid Wadsworth, in Chapter 10, use the life course perspective to examine the impact of military life on individuals and families. By employing this framework, concepts such as *historical time*, *transitions*, *timing*, and *linked lives* are used to help facilitate an understanding of the stressors experienced by, and the resources available to, veterans and their families. The authors first situate current wars and veterans in historical context followed by a discussion of the individual and family transitions that veterans, their spouses, and their children encounter. Finally, three interventions that target the challenges veterans and their families often encounter are introduced.

In Chapter 11, Margaret Wright and Lucy Allbaugh discuss child maltreatment from an ecological and systems perspective placing considerable emphasis on adaptation and resilience of maltreated children. Data from longitudinal studies are used to examine both risk and protective factors that result in the diversity of outcomes found among maltreated children. Specifically, the chapter highlights what is known about factors that heighten risk for psychopathology and behavioral dysfunction following child maltreatment, as well as factors that promote positive adaptation and that protect against adverse, enduring effects. Promising interventions to foster resilience and recovery following child maltreatment are also reviewed.

Lyndal Khaw, in Chapter 12, provides a comprehensive overview of intimate partner violence (IPV). She describes types of IPV recognizing the disparities that exist in the definitions, measures, and methods researchers employ to study this dimension of domestic violence. In an attempt to facilitate a better understanding of IPV, Dr. Khaw presents several theoretical explanations for why this violence takes place and effectively applies a simplified version of the contextual model of family stress to illustrate its complexity. Additional topics of importance to this area of research, such as, same-sex relationships, male victimization, and the process of leaving an abusive partner are also addressed.

In Chapter 13, Amity Noltemeyer, Courtney McLaughlin, and Mark McGowan discuss the impact on families of mass violence in schools and communities. They begin the chapter by reviewing the trends of mass violence in the United States and providing a context for discussing both adaptive and maladaptive responses. They outline a theoretical framework to explain how this type of stressor can impact families and, more specifically, how resilience takes place at both the individual and family level. Finally, they describe risk and protective factors that can influence family resilience, exploring implications for professionals working with families.

Jeremy Yorgason and Kevin Stott, in Chapter 14, discuss both physical and mental illness in the context of the family. They integrate aspects of the Double ABC-X, family resilience, and the vulnerability-stress adaptation models to examine the characteristics of physical and mental illnesses as well as the stressors families encounter and the resilience they display. By employing this approach, they recognize how health stressors are connected to individual and family outcomes through adaptive processes and enduring vulnerabilities. Research findings relating to three situations, including childhood physical/mental illness, physical/mental illness in marriage, and physical/mental illness of aging parents, are discussed.

In Chapter 15, Kevin Lyness and Judith Fischer present challenges faced by families coping with alcohol and substance abuse. Specifically, their focus is on the experiences of children and adolescents (and their parents) as they struggle with this issue. Dr. Lyness and Dr. Fisher employ a biopsychosocial model, which includes biological, psychological, and social influences and combine this with the family stress and coping model. They place particular emphasis on the mediating and moderating effects that intervene between two variables, that is, variables that mediate or modify the associations between parent and offspring substance abuse. Finally, they search for explanations of resilience in families coping with substance abuse and discuss issues relating to prevention and treatment.

In Chapter 16, Suzanne Bartholomae and Jonathan Fox address the impact of economic stress on families using the family economic stress model as a framework. The authors acknowledge the impact of the recent and severe economic downturn known as the Great Recession and review economic conditions and indicators of a family's financial status and economic stress. They discuss outcomes associated with economic stress, including a review of the research on economic stress and its interaction with resources and problem solving. Finally, using a family economic life cycle, they examine family financial planning as a coping strategy to combat negative economic events.

In Chapter 17, Colleen Murray discusses family experiences with death, dying, and grief. She notes that death is a normative and often predictable event, yet it is not viewed as normal and instead is frequently avoided by society. She reviews several theories of grieving to illustrate the complex process of loss that individuals and families endure. Family adaptation to loss is described in terms of family vulnerability, belief systems, definitions, and appraisal with gender, culture, and religion identified as important mediating factors in the grief process. The developmental nature and the unique challenges of children's grief are examined with an emphasis on factors that influence this evolving process. Finally, the death of specific family members (i.e., children, spouse, sibling, parent) and the associated stressors relating to interpersonal and contextual factors are described.

REFERENCES

Angell, R. C. (1936). *The family encounters the depression.* New York, NY: Scribner.

Boss, P. (1987). Family stress. In M. B. Sussman & S. K. Steinmetz (Eds.), *Handbook of marriage and the family* (pp. 695–724). New York, NY: Plenum.

Cavan, R. S., & Ranck, K. H. (1938). *The family and the depression.* Chicago. IL: University of Chicago Press.

Cole, C. L., & Cole, A. L. (1993). Family therapy theory implications for marriage and family enrichment. In P. G. Boss, W. J. Doherty, R. LaRossa, W. R. Schumm, & S. K. Steinmetz (Eds.), *Sourcebook of family theories and methods: A contextual approach* (pp. 525–530). New York, NY: Plenum.

Hill, R. (1949). *Families under stress.* New York, NY: Harper & Row.

Acknowledgments

As editors of the fifth edition of *Families & Change,* we would like to acknowledge the "passing of the torch" that has taken place. As many of you are aware, the first, second, and third editions of this book were the product of two well-respected and prolific scholars in the field of family science, Dr. Patrick McKenry and Dr. Sharon Price. At the time the third edition was being completed, Pat McKenry died. Pat and Sharon had been friends and coauthors for almost 30 years. They had a remarkable friendship, one that involved both hard work and unceasing humor. When SAGE requested a fourth edition of this book, Sharon approached Christine Price (her niece) to join her in the editorial responsibilities. She felt the passing of this legacy was appropriate not only because of their family relationship but also because Pat had been a senior faculty friend and mentor to Christine during her years as an assistant professor at the Ohio State University. When discussions of a fifth edition took place, Sharon (who retired from the University of Georgia in 2000) decided that it was time to hand over the editorial responsibilities entirely to the next generation. Sharon and Christine were both thrilled when Kevin Bush, a former student of Pat McKenry's at the Ohio State University, a former faculty member at the University of Georgia, and a current associate dean at Miami University accepted.

Because this book was the original creation of Sharon and Pat's combined efforts and their fingerprints are still present, we want to recognize and pay tribute to them both. We felt honored to take on the editorial responsibilities for the fifth edition of *Families & Change* and understood that we had big shoes to fill. The suggestions and advice we received from those who used the fourth edition of this book were appreciated and important to the changes made in the content and format of the fifth edition. Also, the quality of the authors' contributions, their timely responses, and their enthusiasm were invaluable to this updated version. Some of the authors were colleagues of both Sharon and Pat for many years and have contributed to multiple editions. Following in the tradition that Sharon and Pat practiced in previous editions, we sought out both "senior" and "young" scholars to collaborate and contribute to this volume. We were very pleased that "senior" authors involved junior colleagues or students to be coauthors, and some former second authors moved into the position of senior authors. In addition, several new senior authors were asked to contribute. We would like to extend a special thank you to all of the authors; your efforts and contributions are greatly appreciated. Finally, we would like to send a sincere thank you to the anonymous external reviewers who read chapter drafts and provided constructive feedback.

Christine A. Price
Kevin R. Bush

Theoretical Foundations

CHAPTER 1

Families Coping With Change: A Conceptual Overview

Kevin R. Bush, Christine A. Price, Sharon J. Price, and Patrick C. McKenry

Families increasingly experience a wide variety of stressors associated with both positive and negative events. Advances in technology, industrialization, urbanization, increased population density (including housing, traffic, and demand on the infrastructures), terrorism, and economic issues are frequently identified as making daily life more complicated and impersonal. Family roles are more fluid and diverse than the past, resulting in fewer social norms and supports. Families have become more diverse as a result of changing family structures (e.g, divorce, single-parent families, LGBTQ families, remarriage, cohabitation, intergenerational reciprocity), immigration, economics (e.g., increased cost of living and two earner families), geographic mobility, and other macro level factors. In addition to natural disasters (e.g., hurricanes, tornadoes, earthquakes) and everyday stressors (e.g., accidents, discrimination based on race, religious beliefs, gender, and sexual orientation), U.S. families are facing the reality of wars involving American troops overseas. Additionally, contemporary families are experiencing economic insecurity and stress due to the Great Recession and the severe economic downturn in the global economy (see Bartholomae & Fox, this volume). Fluctuating unemployment rates, sobering financial losses in pensions, investments, and savings accounts, and the disappearance of benefits contribute to the financial struggle of individuals and families. Consider the accumulation of these events and it quickly becomes apparent that stress is a part of everyday life.

Families, which were once viewed as havens for individuals, are increasingly challenged to meet the emotional needs of members. This may be complicated because many still hold the myth that happy families are (or should be) free from stress. Many believe it is acceptable to experience stress from external sources, that is, environment and work-related stress, but not stress from within the family system.

Families are often faced with many unique problems, not because of any one identifiable crisis, event, or situation but because of continuous everyday societal change. For example, technology, which has facilitated an increasing life span, has also brought about a growing aged population with whom already overextended and geographically mobile families must cope. Young family members are contending with the realization that there might be fewer opportunities and resources available for them as compared to their parents and grandparents. In addition, the fluidity of family structures requires most families to deal with several family structural transitions during the life course (Price, McKenry, & Murphy, 2000; Teachman, Tedrow, & Kim, 2013; Walsh, 2013b).

All families experience stress as a result of change or pressure to change, whether or not change is "good" or "bad." The impact of change or pressure to change is dependent on the family's perception of the situation as well as coping ability (Boss, 2013; Lavee, 2013; L. D. McCubbin & McCubbin, 2013). Boss (1988, 2002, 2006) defines *family stress* as pressure or tension on the status quo; it is a disturbance of the family's steady state. Life transitions and events often provide an essential condition for psychological development, and family stress is perceived as inevitable and normal or even desirable since people and, therefore, families, must develop, mature, and change over time. With change comes disturbance in the family system and pressure–what is termed *stress* (Boss, 2002; Lavee, 2013). Changes affecting families also occur externally (e.g., unemployment, natural disasters, war, acts of terrorism), and these also create stress in family systems. Change becomes problematic only when the degree of stress in a family system reaches a level at which family members and/or the family system becomes dissatisfied or show symptoms of decreased functioning (i.e., ability to carry out regular routines and interactions that maintain the stability of family system).

THE STUDY OF FAMILY STRESS AND CHANGE

In comparison with the long history of research in the general area of stress and coping, theoretical and clinical interest in family stress, problems, and coping is a rather recent phenomenon. Research on family stress and coping gradually evolved from various disciplines that have examined stress and coping from more than an individualistic perspective.

According to the *Oxford English Dictionary,* the term *stress* can be traced back to the early 14th century when *stress* had several distinct meanings, including hardship, adversity, and affliction (Rutter, 1983). Even among stress researchers today, *stress* is variably defined as a stimulus, an inferred inner state, and an observable response to a stimulus or situation (e.g., Oken, Chamine, & Wakeland, 2015); also there is debate concerning the extent to which stress is chemical, environmental, or psychological in nature (Frankenhaeuser, 1994, 2002; Lazarus, 2006; Lazarus & Folkman, 1984; Sarafino, 2006).

In the late 17th century, Hooke used *stress* in the context of physical science (e.g., "Hooke's Law," 2015). The usage was not made systematic until the early 19th century when stress and strain were first conceived as a basis of ill health (Lazarus & Folkman, 1984). In the 20th century, Cannon (1932) laid the foundation for systematic research on the effects of stress in observations of bodily changes. He showed that stimuli associated with emotional arousal (e.g., pain, hunger, cold) caused changes in basic physiological functioning (Dohrenwend & Dohrenwend, 1974). Selye (1978) was the first researcher to define and measure stress adaptations in the human body.

He defined *stress* as an orchestrated set of bodily defenses against any form of noxious stimuli (general adaptation syndrome). In the 1950s, social scientists became interested in his conceptualization of stress, and Selye's work has remained influential in the stress and coping literature (e.g., Hatfield & Polomano, 2012; Lazarus & Folkman, 1984).

Meyer, in the 1930s, taught that life events may be an important component in the etiology of a disorder, and that the most normal and necessary life events may be potential contributors to pathology (Dohrenwend & Dohrenwend, 1974). In the 1960s, Holmes and Rahe (1967) investigated life events and their connection to the onset and progression of illness. Through their schedule of recent events, which includes many family-related events, Holmes and Rahe associated the accumulation of life changes and those of greater magnitude to a higher chance of illness, disease, or death.

In the social sciences, both sociology and psychology have long histories of study related to stress and coping. Sociologists Marx, Weber, and Durkheim wrote extensively about "alienation," which was conceptualized as synonymous with powerlessness, meaninglessness, and self-estrangement, clearly under the general rubric of stress (Lazarus & Folkman, 1984). In psychology, stress was implicit as an organizing framework for thinking about psychopathology, especially in the theorizing of Freud and later psychologically oriented writers. Freudian psychology highlighted the process of coping and established the basis for a developmental approach that considered the effect of life events on later development and gradual acquisition of resources over the life cycle. Early psychologists used anxiety to denote stress, and it was seen as a central component in psychopathology through the 1950s. The reinforcement-learning theorists (e.g., Spence, 1956) viewed anxiety as a classically conditioned response that led to unserviceable (pathological) habits of anxiety reduction. Existentialists (e.g., May, 1950) also focused on anxiety as a major barrier to self-actualization (Lazarus & Folkman, 1984). Developmentalists (e.g., Erikson, 1963) proposed various stage models that demand a particular crisis be negotiated before an individual can cope with subsequent developmental stages. Personal coping resources accrued during the adolescent-young adult years are thought to be integrated into the self-concept and shape the process of coping throughout adulthood (Moos, 1986). Crisis theorists (e.g., Caplan, 1964) conceptualized these life changes as crises, with the assumption that disequilibrium may provide stress in the short run, but can promote the development of new skills in the long run.

The study of family stress began at the University of Michigan and the University of Chicago during the 1930s and the upheavals of the Depression (Boss, 2002). Reuben Hill, referred to as the father of family stress research (Boss, 2006), was the first scholar to conceptualize family stress theory (Hill, 1949, 1971), when he developed the ABC-X model of family stress and his model of family crisis (Boss, 1988, 2002, 2006; Lavee, 2013). Subsequent generations of family stress researchers have made major contributions to this basic model (e.g., Boss, 1988, 2002, 2013; H. I. McCubbin, 1979; H. McCubbin & McCubbin, 1988; L. D. McCubbin & McCubbin, 2013). Developments in family stress theory include emphases on (a) family strengths or resilience (e.g., Henry, Morris, & Harrist, 2015); (b) culture, race, or ethnicity (e.g., Emmen et al., 2013; L. D. McCubbin & McCubbin, 2013); (c) spirituality and faith (Boss, 2006; Walsh, 2013a); and (d) ambiguous loss (Boss, 2002, 2013).

FAMILY STRESS THEORY

Ecological/Systems Perspective

Family theorists typically have used an ecological or systems approach (e.g., Bronfenbrenner, 1979) in their conceptualization of families under stress. As a result, families are viewed as living organisms with both symbolic and real structures. They have boundaries to maintain and a variety of instrumental and expressive functions to perform to ensure growth and survival (Anderson, Sabatelli, & Kosutic, 2013; Boss, 1988, 2013). As any social system, families strive to maintain a steady state. Families are the products of both subsystems (e.g., individual members, dyads) and suprasystems (e.g., community, culture, nation).

Although most general stress theories have focused only on the individual, the primary interest of family stress theory is the entire family unit. Systems theory states that the system is more than the sum of its parts (Anderson et al., 2013; Boss, 2006; Hall & Fagan, 1968). In terms of families, this means that the collection of family members is not only a specific number of people but also an aggregate of particular relationships and shared memories, successes, failures, and aspirations (Anderson et al., 2013; Boss, 1988, 2002). However, systems theory also involves studying the individual to more completely understand a family's response to stress.

An ecological/systems approach allows the researcher to focus beyond the family and the individual to the wider social system (suprasystem). Families do not live in isolation; they are part of the larger social context. This external environment in which the family is embedded is referred to as the "ecosystem," according to ecological theory. This ecosystem consists of historical, cultural, economic, genetic, and developmental influences (Anderson et al., 2013; Boss, 1988, 2002). Thus, the family's response to a stressor event is influenced by living in a particular historical period, its cultural identification, the economic conditions of society, its genetic stamina and resistance, and its stage in the family life cycle.

ABC-X MODEL

The foundation for a systemic model of family stress lies in Hill's (1949) classic research on war-induced separation and reunion. Although his ABC-X formulation has been expanded (e.g., Boss, 1988, 2002, 2013; Burr & Klein, 1994; L. D. McCubbin, & McCubbin, 2013; H. I. McCubbin & Patterson, 1982; Patterson, 1988; Walsh, 2013a), it has withstood careful assessment and is still the basis for analyzing family stress and coping (Boss, 2002, 2006; Darling, Senatore, & Strachan, 2012; Lavee, 2013). This family stress framework may be stated as follows: A (the provoking or stressor event of sufficient magnitude to result in change in a family)-interacting with B (the family's resources or strengths)-interacting with C (the definition or meaning attached to the event by the family)-produces X (stress or crisis). The main idea is that the X factor is influenced by several other moderating phenomena. Stress or crisis is not seen as inherent in the event itself, but conceptually as a function of the response of the disturbed family system to the stressor (Boss, 1988, 2002, 2006; Burr, 1973; Hill, 1949; Lavee, 2013; Walsh, 2013a). (See Figure 1.1.)

Figure 1.1   ABC-X Model of Family Crisis

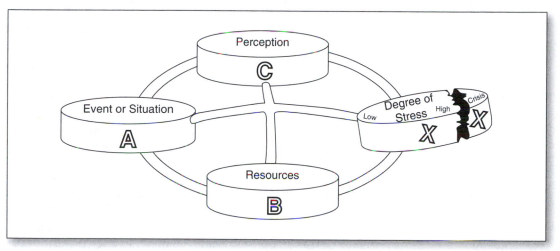

Source: Reprinted with permission from *Families in Society* (www.FamiliesInSociety.org), published by the Alliance for Children and Families.

Stressor Events

A stressor event is an occurrence that provokes a variable amount of change in the family system. Anything that changes some aspect of the system such as the boundaries, structures, goals, processes, roles, or values can produce stress (Boss, 2002; Burr, 1973; Lavee, 2013; Walsh, 2013a). This variable denotes something different than the routine changes within a system that are expected as part of its regular, ordinary operation. This variable is dichotomous; that is, an event either changes or does not change (Burr, 1982). The stressor event by definition has the potential to raise the family's level of stress. However, the degree of stress is dependent on the magnitude of the event as well as other moderating factors to be discussed. Also, both positive and negative events can be stressors. Life events research has clearly indicated that normal and/or positive changes can increase an individual's risk for illness. Finally, stressor events do not necessarily increase stress levels to the point of crisis; the family's stress level can be managed and the family can return to a new equilibrium.

Researchers have attempted to describe various types of stressor events (e.g., Boss, 1988, 2002; Hansen & Hill, 1964; L. D. McCubbin & McCubbin, 2013). Lipman-Blumen (1975) described family stressor events in terms of eight dimensions, which we have updated by adding two additional dimensions based on the research literature: (1) internal versus external, (2) pervasive versus bounded, (3) precipitate onset versus gradual onset, (4) intense versus mild, (5) transitory versus chronic, (6) random versus expectable, (7) natural generation versus artificial generation, (8) scarcity versus surplus, (9) perceived insolvable versus perceived solvable (e.g., ambiguous loss), and

(10) substantive content (see Table 1.1 for definitions). The type of event may be highly correlated with the family's ability to manage stress. Other researchers (e.g., H. I. McCubbin, Patterson, & Wilson, 1981; Pearlin & Schooler, 1978) have classified stressor events in terms of their intensity or hardship on the family.

One dichotomous classification that is often used by family stress researchers and clinicians is normal or predictable events versus nonnormative or unpredictable events. Normal events are part of everyday life and represent transitions inherent in the family life cycle, such as birth or death of a family member, child's school entry, and retirement. Normative stressor events by definition are of short duration. Although predictable and normal, such life-cycle events have the potential of changing a family's level of stress because they disturb the system equilibrium (Anderson et al., 2013; Henry et al., 2015). These events lead to crisis only if the family does not adapt to the changes brought about by these events (Carter & McGoldrick, 1989).

Nonnormative events are the product of some unique situation that could not be predicted and is not likely to be repeated. Examples of nonnormative events would include natural disasters, loss of a job, or an automobile accident. Unexpected but welcome events that are not disastrous may also be stressful for families, such as a promotion or winning the lottery. Although these events are positive, they do change or disturb the

Table 1.1   Ten Dimensions of Family Stressor Events

(1) *Internal versus External* refers to whether the source of the crisis was internal or external to the social system affected.
(2) *Pervasive versus Bounded* refers to the degree to which the crisis affects the entire system or only a limited part.
(3) *Precipitate onset versus Gradual onset* marks the degree of suddenness with which the crisis occurred, that is, without or with warning.
(4) *Intense versus Mild* involves the degree of severity of the crisis.
(5) *Transitory versus Chronic* refers to the degree to which the crisis represents a short- or long-term problem.
(6) *Random versus Expectable* marks the degree to which the crisis could be expected or predicted.
(7) *Natural generation versus artificial generation* connotes the distinction between crises that arise from natural conditions and those that come about through technological or other human-made effects.
(8) *Scarcity versus Surplus* refers to the degree to which the crisis represents a shortage or overabundance of vital commodities—human, material, and nonmaterial.
(9) *Perceived insolvable versus Perceived solvable* suggests the degree to which those individuals involved in the crisis believe the crisis is open to reversal or some level of resolution.
(10) *Substantive content*: (This dimension differs from the previous nine in that it subsumes a set of subject areas, each of which may be regarded as a separate continuum graded from low to high.) Using this dimension, one can determine whether the substantive nature of the crisis is primarily in the political, economic, moral, social, religious, health, or sexual domains or any combination thereof.

Source: Adapted from Lipman-Blumen, J. (1975). A crisis framework applied to macrosociological family changes: Marriage, divorce, and occupational trends associated with World War II. *Journal of Marriage and Family, 27,* 889–902.

family's routine and thus have the potential of raising the family's level of stress (Boss, 1988; Lavee, 2013).

There has been much interest in the study of isolated versus accumulated stressors. Specifically, life event scholars (e.g., Holmes & Rahe, 1967; H. I. McCubbin et al., 1981; L. D. McCubbin & McCubbin, 2013) suggest that it is the accumulation of several stressor events rather than the nature of one isolated event that determines a family's level of stress. The clustering of stressor events (normative and/or nonnormative) is termed *stress pileup*. An event rarely happens to a family in total isolation. Normal developmental changes are always taking place and nonnormative events tend to result in other stressors; for example, loss of job may result in a family having to move or marital disruption. By focusing only on certain events or stressors, researchers may fail to capture the complexity in the range and clustering of stressors (Pearlin, 1991; Yeh, Arora, & Wu, 2006).

Researchers have also offered alternative perspectives on stressor events. One such alternative is focusing on daily stressors or hassles and ongoing strains and their relationship to stress outcomes (e.g., Darling et al., 2012; Serido, Almeida, & Wethington, 2004; for a review, see Helms, Hengstebeck, & Demo, Chapter 2, this volume), rather than solely assessing major life events which tend to be extreme in nature and are fairly low in base-rate occurrence (Fisher, Fagot, & Leve, 1998). Daily hassles not only parallel major life events in their potential to engender stress but also have an even stronger relationship than traditional life events measures in predicting physical health (Derogatis & Coons, 1993; Gruen, 1993).

Not all stressor events, however, are clear-cut. As a result, a state of ambiguity is created. Boss (1999, 2006, 2013) addressed the issue of *ambiguous loss* resulting from incongruency between physical and psychological/emotional presence/absence. There are two major types of *ambiguous loss*: (a) a person being physically absent but psychologically or emotionally present (missing children, divorce, a family member in prison, soldiers missing in action, immigrants) and (b) when a person is physically present but psychologically/emotionally absent (a person that has Alzheimer's disease or a chronic mental illness, chronic substance abuse, a spouse preoccupied with work or another issue) (Boss, 1999, 2013). Ambiguous loss not only disrupts family functioning, it results in a lack of clarity regarding who is "in" and who is "outside" the family, as well as appropriate roles for family members. This type of ambiguity is the most stressful situation a person or family can experience. Boss attributed this high level of stress to (a) people being unable to problem-solve because they do not know whether the problem is final or temporary, (b) the ambiguity prevents people from adjusting by reorganizing their relationship with the loved one, (c) families are denied society rituals (e.g., funerals, death certificate) that usually support a clear loss, (d) friends/neighbors tend to withdraw rather than give support, and (e) ambiguous loss may continue for a long time; therefore, those who experience it become physically and emotionally exhausted (Boss, 1999, pp. 7–8).

Resources

The family's resources buffer or moderate the impact of the stressor event on the family's level of stress. Hansen (1965) uses the term *vulnerability* to denote the difference in families' physical and emotional responses to stressful stimuli (Gore & Colten, 1991). This moderator denotes variation in a family's ability to prevent a stressor event or change from creating disruptiveness in the system (Burr, 1973; Henry et al., 2015). When family members have sufficient and appropriate resources, they are less likely to view a stressful situation as problematic. H. I. McCubbin and Patterson (1985) defined *resources* as traits, characteristics, or abilities of (a) individual family members, (b) the family system, and (c) the community that can be used to meet the demands of a stressor event. Individual or personal resources include financial (economic well-being), educational (problem solving, information), health (physical and emotional well-being), and psychological resources, which include self-esteem, optimism, sense of coherence, sense of mastery, and a positive family schema or ethnic identity (Everson, Darling, & Herzog, 2013; Lavee, 2013; L. D. McCubbin & McCubbin, 2013).

The term *family system resources* refers to internal attributes of the family unit that protect the family from the impact of stressors and facilitate family adaptation during family stress or crisis. Family cohesion (bonds of unity) and adaptability (ability to change) (Olson, Russell, & Sprenkle, 1979, 1983; Patterson, 2002) have received the most research attention (Lavee, 2013). These two dimensions are the major axes of the circumplex model (Olson et al., 1979). This model suggests that families who function moderately along the dimensions of cohesion and adaptability are likely to make a more successful adjustment to stress (Olson, Russell, & Sprenkle, 1980). However, it should be noted that the family literature contains studies and writings that qualify or refute the curvilinear interpretation of the relationship between adaptability and cohesion and effective functioning; instead, these studies support a linear relationship between these two dimensions and effective outcomes (Anderson & Gavazzi, 1990).

Community resources refer to those capabilities of people or institutions outside the family upon which the family can draw for dealing with stress. Social support is one of the most important community resources, such as informal support from friends, neighbors, and colleagues, as well as formal support from community institutions (Lavee, 2013). Social support may be viewed as information disseminated to facilitate problem solving and as development of new social contacts that provide help and assistance. Social support offers information at an interpersonal level that provides (a) emotional support, (b) esteem support, and (c) network support (Cobb, 1976). In general, social support serves as a protector against the effects of stressors and promotes recovery from stress or crisis. Increasingly, the concept of community resources has been broadened to include the resources of cultural groups; for example, ethnic minority families are thought to be characterized by more elaborate and efficient patterns of social support (Emmen et al., 2013; Hill, 1999; H. I. McCubbin, Futrell, Thompson & Thompson, 1998; L. D. McCubbin & McCubbin, 2013; Yeh et al., 2006)

Definition of the Event/Perceptions

The impact of the stressor event on the family's level of stress is moderated by the definition or meaning the family gives to the event. This variable is also synonymous with family appraisal, perception, and assessment of the event. Thus subjective definitions can vary from viewing circumstances as a challenge and an opportunity for growth, to the negative view that things are hopeless, too difficult, or unmanageable (Lavee, 2013; H. I. McCubbin & Patterson, 1985). Empirical findings suggest that an individual's cognitive appraisal of life events strongly influences the response (Lazarus & Launier, 1978) and may be the most important component in determining an individual's or family's response to a stressor event (Boss, 2002; Hennon et al., 2009).

This concept has a long tradition in social psychology in terms of the self-fulfilling prophecy that, if something is perceived as real, it is real in its consequences (Burr, 1982). Families who are able to redefine a stressor event more positively (i.e., reframe it) appear to be better able to cope and adapt. By redefining, families are able to (a) clarify the issues, hardships, and tasks to render them more manageable and responsive to problem-solving efforts; (b) decrease the intensity of the emotional burdens associated with stressors; and (c) encourage the family unit to carry on with its fundamental tasks of promoting individual members' social and emotional development (Lavee, 2013; H. I. McCubbin & Patterson, 1985; L. D. McCubbin & McCubbin, 2013).

Lazarus and Launier (1978) discussed the impact of an individual's learned cognitive attributional style on the stress response; this work has been applied to the study of families as well (e.g., Benedetto & Ingrassia, 2013; Boss, 1988). For example, a family may respond to an event in terms of "learned helplessness," thereby increasing their vulnerability due to low self-esteem and feelings of hopelessness. Such a family would react to the unemployment of a spouse by failing to look for another job or by not supporting that family member in the search for another job.

With regard to gender or sex differences in response to stress, relevant research suggests that these differences are often modest at best and likely only present in particular contexts (e.g., Brody, 1999), for example, when individuals experience stress or negative emotions (Gottman & Levenson, 1988; Schulz, Cowan, Cowan, & Brennan, 2004; Taylor et al., 2000). Examination of the fairly consistent results from laboratory based research on couple interaction suggests that gender differences exist in how husbands and wives respond to negative emotional arousal in martital interactions regarding conflict (e.g., Gottman & Levenson, 1988). More specifically, during marital conflict husbands are more likely to withdraw emotionally and behaviorally while wives are more likely to be verbally confrontational and critical and to engage in conflict (Gottman & Levenson, 1988; Schulz et al., 2004).

Researchers investigating biological influences (e.g., cortisol levels) of gender differences in stress response report preliminary evidence for sex differences in biobehavioral stress responses—with men's stress response being fight or flight, while the stress response of women is better described as "tending and befriending" behavior (e.g., Smeets, Dziobek, & Wolf, 2009; Taylor et al., 2000). Taylor and colleagues (2000) propose that this biobehavioral sex difference is related to the attachment-caregiving system where nurturant activities to protect themselves and their offspring lead women to focus on relationship development and maintenance that may aid in their survival.

Additional factors which could influence families' perceptions in a stressful situation include *spirituality, values and beliefs, culture,* and *stage of the family life cycle* (e.g., Emmen et al., 2013; L. D. McCubbin & McCubbin, 2013; Walsh, 2013a; Yeh et al., 2006).

As earlier noted, there has been an increased emphasis on the role of spirituality, beliefs, and faith on family stress. Boss (2002, 2006) discussed several cases where a strong sense of spirituality resulted in a more positive attitude, hope, and optimism when families were confronted with a stressful situation. Faith can be a major coping mechanism resulting in families turning to their religious institutions and communities more than cognitive problem solving (Tix & Frazier, 1998; Walsh, 2013a). Of course, spirituality can be experienced within or outside formal religious institutions. Regardless of the source, spiritual associations can bring a sense of meaning, wholeness, and connection with others. For example, religious communities provide guidelines for living and scripted ways to make major life transitions, as well as congregational support in times of need (Walsh, 2006, 2013a).

The belief system and value orientation of families may also influence their perceptions of stressful events. For example, families with a *mastery orientation* may believe they can solve any problem and control just about anything that could happen to them. For example, a recent study found that adolescent mastery orientation served to increase health promotion behaviors in teens despite family stress (Kwon & Wickrama, 2014). In contrast, families with a *fatalistic orientation* are more likely to believe that everything is determined by a higher power; therefore, all events are predetermined and not under their control. As a consequence, a highly *fatalistic orientation* could be a barrier to coping because it encourages passivity, and active coping strategies have been found to be more effective than passive strategies (e.g., Boss, 2002; Yeh et al., 2006). Belief and value orientations such as these are also related to culture (L. D. McCubbin & McCubbin, 2013; Yeh et al., 2006).

Culture influences the family stress process through (1) values or value orientations and (2) minority and immigrant status, both of which in turn influence perceptions, coping strategies, and resources (Emmen et al., 2013; Folkman & Moskowitz, 2004; Walsh, 2013a; Yeh et al., 2006). Researchers of individual models of coping have made some strides in identifying how cultural values and social norms influence one's coping strategies. Scholars in this area have asserted that coping is not dualistic (e.g., Lazarus & Folkman, 1984) with only action-oriented coping strategies resulting in positive outcomes but rather moderated by cultural context (Folkman & Moskowitz, 2004; Lam & Zane, 2004; Yeh et al., 2006). For example, while taking direct action (confronting others, standing up for oneself, etc.) is a preferred and effective strategy in individualist cultural contexts, in collectivistic contexts, the emphasis on group harmony and interdependence leads individuals to enact coping strategies that focus on changing themselves to meet the needs of the group instead of attempting to change the situation (Lam & Zane, 2004; Yeh et al., 2006). Scholars examining the cultural context of stress and family stress have focused on models that account for the depth and complexity of cultural and ethnic influences on family systems related to family stress and resilience. For example, Linda McCubbin and Hamilton McCubbin (2013) recently presented the relational and resilience theory of ethnic family systems (R&RTEFS), which was designed to identify and validate competencies among ethnic/cultural families that facilitate successful adaption in the context of family stress.

The *stage of the family life cycle* that the family is currently in can also influence a family's perceptions during a stressful event. Stage of the family life cycle points to the variation in structure, composition, interaction (between family members as well as between the family and the outside culture), and resources in families (Henry et al., 2015; Price et al., 2000; Walsh, 2013b). Consequently, families at different stages of the life cycle vary in their response to stressful situations. This is particularly relevant as families move from one stage of development to another during normative transitions. It is during these periods of change (a child is born, children leave home, a family member dies) that families are likely to experience high levels of stress as they adjust rules, roles, and patterns of behavior (Aldous, 1996). This stress is also impacted by whether the transition is "on time" or "off time" as well as expected or unexpected (Rodgers & White, 1993). In general, "off time" (e.g., a child dies before a parent dies) and unexpected (a family member dies in an accident) transitions create periods of greater stress. This greater stress could, at least partially, be attributed to the family members' perception of the stressful situation as being overwhelming or unfair.

Stress and Crisis

According to systems theory, stress represents a change in the family's steady state. Stress is the response of the family system to the demands experienced as a result of a stressor event. Stress is not inherently bad; it becomes problematic when the degree of stress in the family system reaches a level at which the family becomes disrupted or individual members become dissatisfied or display physical or emotional symptoms. The degree of stress ultimately depends on the family's definition of the stressor event as well as the adequacy of the family's resources to meet the demands of the change associated with the stressor event.

The terms *stress* and *crisis* have been used inconsistently in the literature. In fact, many researchers have failed to make a distinction between the two. Boss (1988, 2006) makes a useful distinction as she defines crisis as (a) a disturbance in the equilibrium that is so overwhelming, (b) pressure that is so severe, or (c) change that is so acute that the family system is blocked, immobilized, and incapacitated. When a family is in a crisis state, at least for a time, it does not function adequately. Family boundaries are no longer maintained, customary roles and tasks are no longer performed, and family members are no longer functioning at optimal physical or psychological levels. The family has thus reached a state of acute disequilibrium and is immobilized.

Family stress, on the other hand, is merely a state of changed or disturbed equilibrium. Family stress therefore is a continuous variable (degree of stress), whereas family crisis is a dichotomous variable (either in crisis or not). A crisis does not have to permanently break up the family system. It may only temporarily immobilize the family system and then lead to a different level of functioning than that experienced before the stress level escalated to the point of crisis. Many family systems, in fact, become stronger after they have experienced and recovered from crisis (Boss, 1988, Walsh, 2013b).

Coping

Family stress researchers have increasingly shifted their attention from crisis and family dysfunction to the process of coping. Researchers have become more interested in explaining why some families are better able to manage and endure stressor events rather than documenting the frequency and severity of such events (e.g., Henry et al., 2015). In terms of intervention, this represents a change from crisis intervention to prevention (Boss, 1988; H. I. McCubbin et al., 1980; L. D. McCubbin & McCubbin, 2013).

The study of family coping has drawn heavily from cognitive psychology (e.g., Lazarus, 2006; Lazarus & Folkman, 1984) as well as sociology (e.g., Pearlin & Schooler, 1978; L. McCubbin, 2006). *Cognitive coping strategies* refer to the ways in which individual family members alter their subjective perceptions of stressful events. Sociological theories of coping emphasize a wide variety of actions directed at either changing the stressful situation or alleviating distress by manipulating the social environment (H. I. McCubbin et al., 1980; L. D. McCubbin & McCubbin, 2013). Thus family coping has been conceptualized in terms of three types of responses: (a) direct action (e.g., acquiring resources, learning new skills), (b) intrapsychic (e.g., reframing the problem), or (c) controlling the emotions generated by the stressor (e.g., social support, use of alcohol) Lazarus & Folkman, 1984; Pearlin & Schooler, 1978). These responses can be used individually, consecutively, or, more commonly, in various combinations. Specific coping strategies are not inherently adaptive or maladaptive; they are very much situation specific (e.g., Folkman & Moskowitz, 2004; Yeh et al., 2006). Flexible access to a range of responses appears to be more effective than the use of any one response (Moos, 1986; Yeh et al., 2006).

Coping interacts with both family resources and perceptions as defined by the "B" and "C" factors of the ABC-X model. However, coping actions are different than resources and perceptions. Coping represents what people do, that is, their concrete efforts to deal with a stressor (Folkman & Moskowitz, 2004; Pearlin & Schooler, 1978). Having a resource or a perception of an event does not imply whether or how a family will react (Boss, 1988; Lazarus & Folkman, 1984; Yeh et al., 2006).

Although coping is sometimes equated with adaptational success (i.e., a product), from a family systems perspective, coping is a process, not an outcome per se. *Coping* refers to all efforts expended to manage a stressor regardless of the effect (Lazarus, 2006; Lazarus & Folkman, 1984). Thus the family strategy of coping is not instantly created but is progressively modified over time. Because the family is a system, coping behavior involves the management of various dimensions of family life simultaneously: (a) maintaining satisfactory internal conditions for communication and family organization, (b) promoting member independence and self-esteem, (c) maintenance of family bonds of coherence and unity, (d) maintenance and development of social supports in transactions with the community, and (e) maintenance of some efforts to control the impact of the stressor and the amount of change in the family unit (H. I. McCubbin et al., 1980). Coping is thus a process of achieving balance in the family system that facilitates organization and unity and promotes individual and family system growth and development (L. D. McCubbin & McCubbin, 2013). This is consistent with systems theory, which suggests that the families that most effectively cope with stress are strong as a unit as well as in individual members (Anderson et al., 2013; Buckley, 1967).

Boss (1988) cautions that coping should not be perceived as maintaining the status quo; rather, the active managing of stress should lead to progressively new levels of organization as systems are naturally inclined toward greater complexity. In fact, sometimes it is better for a family to fail to cope even if that precipitates a crisis. After the crisis, the family can reorganize into a better functioning system. For example, a marital separation may be very painful for a family, but it may be necessary to allow the family to grow in a different, more productive direction.

In addition to serving as a barrier to change and growth, maladaptive forms of coping serve as a source of stress. There are three ways that coping itself may be a source of additional hardship (Roskies & Lazarus, 1980). One way is by indirect damage to the family system. This occurs when a family member inadvertently behaves in such a way as to put the family in a disadvantaged position. For example, a father may overwork to ease his family's economic stress but then become ill from the lack of sleep and related consequences of overworking. The second way that coping can serve as a source of stress is through direct damage to the family system. For example, family members may use an addictive behavior or violence to personally cope, but this will be disruptive to the family system. The third way that coping may increase family stress is by interfering with additional adaptive behaviors that could help preserve the family. For example, denial of a problem may preclude getting necessary help and otherwise addressing the stressor event (Lavee, 2013; H. I. McCubbin et al., 1980).

Adaptation

Another major interest of family stress researchers has been the assessment of how families are able to recover from stress or crisis. Drawing from Hansen's (1965) work, Burr (1973) described this process in terms of a family's "regenerative power," denoting a family's ability to recover from stress or crisis. Accordingly, the purpose of postcrisis or post-stress adjustment is to reduce or eliminate the disruptiveness in the family system and restore homeostasis (Lavee, 2013; H. I. McCubbin & Patterson, 1982; L. D. McCubbin & McCubbin, 2013). However, these authors also note that family stress has the potential of maintaining family relations and stimulating desirable change. Because system theorists (e.g., Anderson et al., 2013; Buckley, 1967) hold that all systems naturally evolve toward greater complexity, it may be inferred that family systems initiate and capitalize on externally produced change in order to grow. Therefore, reduction of stress or crisis alone is an incomplete index of a family's adjustment to crisis or stress.

H. I. McCubbin and Patterson (1982) use the term *adaptation* to describe a desirable outcome of a crisis or stressful state. *Family adaptation* is defined as the degree to which the family system alters its internal functions (behaviors, rules, roles, perceptions) or external reality to achieve a system (individual or family) environment fit (Henry et al., 2015). Adaptation is achieved through reciprocal relationships in which (a) system demands (or needs) are met by resources from the environment and (b) environmental demands are satisfied through system resources (Hansen & Hill, 1964; L. D. McCubbin & McCubbin, 2013).

Demands on the family system include normative and nonnormative stressor events as well as the needs of individuals (e.g., intimacy), families (e.g., launching of children), and social institutions and communities (e.g., governmental authority) (Lavee, 2013; H. I. McCubbin & Patterson, 1982). Resources include individual (e.g., education, psychological stability), family

(e.g., cohesion, adaptability), and environmental (social support, medical services) attributes. Adaptation is different than adjustment. Adjustment is a short-term response or modification by a family that changes the situation only momentarily. Adaptation implies a change in the family system that evolves over a longer period of time or is intended to have long-term consequences involving changes in family roles, rules, patterns of interaction, and perceptions (Henry et al., 2015; H. I. McCubbin, Cauble, & Patterson, 1982).

H. I. McCubbin and Patterson (1982) expanded Hill's (1949) ABC-X model by adding postcrisis/poststress factors to explain how families achieve a satisfactory adaptation to stress or crisis. Their model consists of the ABC-X model followed by their "Double ABC-X" configuration. (See Figure 1.2.)

H. I. McCubbin and Patterson's (1982) "Double A" factor refers to the stressor pileup in the family system, and this includes three types of stressors. The family must deal with unresolved aspects of the initial stressor event, the changes and events that occur regardless of the initial stressor (e.g., changes in family membership), and the consequences of the family's efforts to cope with the hardships of the situation (e.g., intrafamily role changes). The family's resources, the "Double B" factor, are of two types. The first are those resources already available to the family and that minimize the impact of the initial stressor. The second are those coping resources (personal, family, and social) that are strengthened or developed in response to the stress or crisis situation. The "Double C" factor refers to (a) the

Figure 1.2 Double ABC-X Model

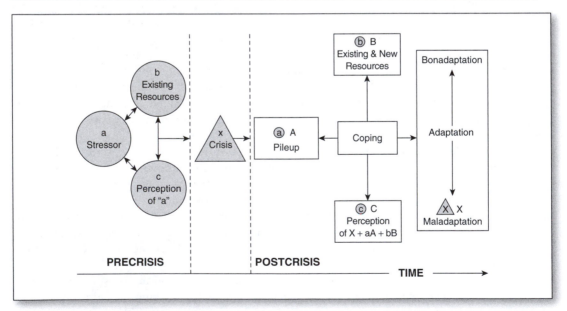

Source: McCubbin,, H. I., Cauble, A. E., & Patterson, J. M. (1982). *Family stress, coping, and social support.* Courtesy of : Charles C. Thomas Publisher, Ltd., Springfield, IL.

perception of the initial stressor event and (b) the perception of the stress or crisis. The perception of the stress or crisis situation includes the family's view of the stressor and related hardships and the pileup of events as well as the meaning families attach to the total family situation. The family's postcrisis/poststress perceptions involve religious beliefs, redefining (reframing) the situation, and endowing the situation with meaning.

The "Double X" factor includes the original family crisis/stress response and subsequent adaptation. The xX factor represents a continuum ranging from maladaptation (family crisis/stress) on one end to bonadaptation (family adjustment over time) on the other and illustrates the extent of fit between individual family members, the family system, and the community in which they are imbedded (Lavee, 2013).

Boss (1988, 2002) has cautioned against the use of the term *adaptation* to describe the optimal outcome of a stressful or crisis state. She contends that the family literature appears to assume that calm, serenity, orderliness, and stability are the desired ends for family life. Like Hoffman (1981), Boss maintains that systems naturally experience discontinuous change through the life cycle in the process of growth. If adaptation is valued over conflict and change, then families are limited to a perspective that promotes adjustment to the stressor event at the expense of individual or family change. Boss contends that sometimes dramatic change must occur for individual and family well-being, including breaking family rules, changing boundaries, and revolution within the system. For example, an abused wife may need to leave or at least dramatically change her family system to achieve a sense of well-being for herself and perhaps for other family members. Therefore, in order to avoid circular reasoning, Boss prefers use of the term *managing* to refer to the coping process that results from the family's reaction to stress or crisis. Specifically, "unless crisis occurs, the family is managing its level of stress. Managing high stress and being resilient are indeed the alternative outcome to falling in crisis" (Boss, 2002, p. 89).

Patterson (1988) revised the Double ABC-X model to include the community system as well as the individual and family system. This complex form of analysis requires that the (a) stressors, (b) resources, and (c) meanings/definitions of the individual, family, and community systems as well as their interactions be considered. Patterson's extension of the Double ABC-X model is consistent with biopsychosocial systems models that attempt to deal with the complex interplay and multiplicative interactions among biological, psychological, and social phenomena regarding health and illness (e.g., Masten & Monn, 2015; Repetti, Robles, & Reynolds, 2011). A few examples include research on domestic violence that has noted the role of testosterone and alcohol use as it interacts with other variables in increasing the risk of men's abuse of a female partner (e.g., Hillbrand & Pallone, 1994) and a recent study that highlighted links between marital conflict, children's stress reactivity (e.g., cortisol and alpha-amylase), and children's emotional and behavioral regulation strategies (Koss et al., 2014).

Resilience

Resilience has its roots in family stress and is both an individual and family phenomena. It has been defined as "the capacity to rebound from adversity strengthened and more resourceful . . . an active process of endurance, self-righting, and growth in response to crisis and challenges" (Walsh, 2006, p. 4). In addition, Boss (2006) described resiliency as the ability to stretch (like elastic) or flex (like a suspension bridge) in response to the pressures and strains of life. In general, resiliency refers to the coping strengths of those families that seem to benefit from the challenges of adversity; the ability to successfully deal with a stressor event actually results in outcomes as good or better than those that would have been obtained in the absence of the adversity (Cicchetti & Garmezy, 1993; Hawley & DeHaan, 2003; Henry et al., 2015; Rutter, 1987).

While early research and theorizing about the impact of stress on families focused mainly on the adverse effects of stressor events of families, more recent scholarship and theorizing have emphasized family resilience (Bonanno, 2004; Henry et al., 2015; Lavee, 2013). Scholars have moved beyond viewing resiliency as a characteristic of an individual to providing a framework for viewing resiliency as a quality of families (Hawley & DeHaan, 2003; Henry et al., 2015). Following the family resilience model (FRM), when family risk interacts with family protection and vulnerability in such ways that result in short-term and long-term family system adaptation, family resilience is present (Henry et al., 2015). Henry and colleagues (2015) describe the FRM as consisting of four key elements: (1) family risk, (2) family protection, (3) family vulnerability, and (4) short-term adjustment and long-term adaptation. Several key principles from individual resilience theories are applied, including variables that serve as protective or promotive functions in one circumstance, may serve as risks or vulnerabilities in other circumstances (e.g., across cultural contexts).

Rather than a pathological view, or deficient model of families, the emphasis is on family wellness and strengths (Hawley & DeHaan, 2003; H. McCubbin & McCubbin, 1988; L. D. McCubbin & McCubbin, 2013; Walsh, 2006, 2013b). In contrast to Hill's (1949) original model which hypothesized that, following a crisis, families would return to functioning at a level below or above their previous level, resilient families are expected to return to a level at or above their previous level (Henry et al., 2015). A valuable conceptual contribution from the family resilience literature has been the recognition of a family ethos (i.e., a schema, world view, or sense of coherence) that describes a shared set of values and attitudes held by a family unit that serves as the core of the family's resilience (Hawley & DeHaan, 2003; L. McCubbin, 2006; L. D. McCubbin & McCubbin, 2013).

CONCLUSION

Families today are being challenged with an unbelievable number of changes and problems that have the capacity to produce stress and crisis. After many years of focusing on individual stress responses, researchers have begun systematic assessments of whole family responses, often by focusing on resiliency. Major theoretical paradigms that have been used to study family responses to stressor events include human ecology models (e.g., Bronfenbrenner, 1979) and family systems models (e.g., Anderson et al., 2013). Developing from Hill's (1949) work on the effect of wartime separation, various characteristics of stressor events as well as the mediating effects of perceptions and resources have been studied, suggesting that there is nothing inherent in the event per se that is stressful or crisis producing. More recently, family stress research has moved beyond the linear relationship of stressor, buffer/moderator, and response to look at coping and adaptation as a process that continues over time, that is, how families actually manage stress or crisis. Coping is conceptualized as an ongoing process that facilitates family organization but also promotes individual growth. Increasingly, the outcome of interest is adaptation, that is, the ability of a family to make needed changes and ultimately recover from stress and crisis. Adaptation, like coping, however, should not be perceived as a definitive end product because families are always growing and changing. Further, the serenity and stability synonymous with adaptation are not always functional for family members, and for some families the response to a stressor event may result in a higher level of functioning. Finally, emphasis on the resilience of families has received increasing attention. By acknowledging the ability of families to successfully manage stressful events, scholars are broadening our understanding of how some families thrive in the face of adversity.

REFERENCES

Aldous, J. C. (1996). *Family careers: Rethinking the developmental perspective*. Thousand Oaks, CA: Sage.

Anderson, S. A., & Gavazzi, S. M. (1990). A test of the Olson Circumplex Model: Examining its curvilinear assumption and the presence of extreme types. *Family Process, 29*, 309–324.

Anderson, S.A., Sabatelli, R. M., & Kosutic, I. (2013). Systemic and ecological qualities of families. In G. W. Peterson, K R. Bush (Eds.), *Handbook of marriage and the family (3rd ed.;* pp. 121–138). New York, NY: Springer

Benedetto, L., & Ingrassia, M. (2013). Parent perceived control and stress in families of children with attention-deficit/hyperactive disorder. *Life Span and Disability, 16*(1), 39–55.

Bonanno, G.A. (2004). Loss, trauma, and human resilience: Have we underestimated the human capacity to thrive after extremely aversive events? *American Psychologist, 59*(1), 20–28.

Boss, P. (2006). *Loss, trauma, and resilience: Therapeutic work with ambiguous loss*. New York, NY: W. W. Norton and Company.

Boss, P. (2013). Resilience as tolerance for ambiguity. In D. S. Becvar. (Ed.), *Handbook of family resilience* (pp. 285–297). New York, NY: Springer.

Boss, P. G. (1988). *Family stress management*. Newbury Park, CA: Sage.

Boss, P. G. (1999). *Ambiguous loss*. Cambridge, MA: Harvard University Press.

Boss, P.G. (2002). *Family stress management: A contextual approach* (2nd ed.). Thousand Oaks, CA: Sage.

Brody, L. (1999). *Gender, emotion and the family*. Cambridge, MA: Harvard University Press.

Bronfenbrenner, U. (1979). *The ecology of human development*. Cambridge, MA: Harvard University Press.

Buckley, W, (1967*). Sociology and modern systems theory*. Englewood Cliffs, NJ: Prentice Hall.

Burr, W.R. (1973). *Theory construction and the sociology of the family*. New York, NY: John.

Burr, W. R. (1982). Families under stress. In H. I. McCubbin, A. E. Cauble, & J. M. Patterson (Eds.), *Family stress, coping, and social support* (pp. 5–25). Springfield, IL: Charles C Thomas.

Burr, W. R., Klein, S. R. (1994). *Reexamining family stress: New theory and research*. Thousand Oaks, CA: Sage.

Cannon, W. B. (1932). *The wisdom of the body*. New York, NY: Norton.

Caplan, G. (1964). *Principles of preventive psychiatry*. New York, NY: Basic Books.

Carter, B., & McGoldrick, M. (1989). Overview: The changing family life cycle-A framework for family therapy. In B. Carter & M. McGoldrick (Eds.), *The changing family life cycle: A framework for family therapy* (pp. 3–28). Boston, MA: Allyn & Bacon.

Cicchetti, D., & Garmezy, N. (1993). Prospects and promises in the study of resilience. *Developmental and Psychopathology, 5,* 497–502.

Cobb, S. (1976). Social support as a moderator of life stress. *Psychosomatic Medicine, 38,* 300–314.

Darling, C. A., Senatore, N., & Strachan, J. (2012). Fathers of children with disabilities: Stress and life satisfaction. *Stress and Health: Journal of The International Society for the Investigation of Stress, 28*(4), 269–278. doi:10.1002/smi.1427

Derogatis, L. R., & Coons, H. L. (1993). Self-report measures of stress. In L. Goldberger & S. Breznitz (Eds.), *Handbook of stress: Theoretical and clinical aspects* (pp. 200–233). New York, NY: Free Press.

Dohrenwend, B. S., & Dohrenwend, B. P. (1974). *Stressful life events: Their nature and effects.* New York, NY: John Wiley.

Emmen, R. G., Malda, M., Mesman, J., van IJzendoorn, M. H., Prevoo, M. L., & Yeniad, N. (2013). Socioeconomic status and parenting in ethnic minority families: testing a minority family stress model. *Journal of Family Psychology, 27*(6), 896–904. doi:10:1037/a003493

Erikson, E. H. (1963). *Childhood and society.* New York, NY: Norton.

Everson, R. B., Darling, C. A., & Herzog, J. R. (2013). Parenting stress among U.S. Army spouses during combat-related deployments: The role of sense of coherence. *Child and Family Social Work, 18*(2), 168–178.

Fisher, P. A., Fagot, B. I., & Leve, C. S. (1998). Assessment of family stress across low-, medium-, and high-risk samples using the family events checklist. *Family Relations, 47,* 215–219.

Frankenhaeuser, M. (1994). A biopsychosocial approach to stress in women and men. In V. J. Adesso, D. M. Reddy, & R. Fleming (Eds.), *Psychological perspectives on women's health* (pp. 39–56). Philadelphia, PA: Taylor and Francis.

Frankenhaeuser, M. (2002). Ancient humans in the newborn millennium: Stress and gender perspectives. In L. Backman, C. von Hofsten (Eds.), *Psychology at the turn of the millennium, Vol. 1: Cognitive, biological, and health perspectives* (pp. 307–318). Hove, England: Psychology Press/Taylor and Francis (UK).

Folkman, S., & Moskowitz, J. T. (2004). Coping: Pitfalls and promise. *Annual Review of Psychology, 55,* 745–774.

Gore, S., & Colten, M. E. (1991). Gender, stress and distress: Social-relational influences. In J. Eckenrode (Ed.), *The social context of coping.* New York, NY: Plenum.

Gottman, J. M., & Levenson, R. W. (1988). The social psychophysiology of marriage. In P. Noller & M. A. Fitzpatrick (Eds.), *Perspectives on marital interaction* (pp. 182–200). Clevedon, England: Multilingual Matters.

Gruen, R. J. (1993). Stress and depression: Toward the development of integrative models. In L. Godlberger & S. Breznitz (Eds.), *Handbook of stress: Theoretical and clinical aspects* (pp. 550–569). New York, NY: Free Press.

Hall, A. D., & Fagan, R. E (1968). Definition of system. In W. Buckley (Ed.), *Modern systems research for the behavioral scientist* (pp. 81–92). Chicago, IL: Aldine.

Hansen, D. A. (1965). Personal and positional influence in formal groups: Propositions and theory for research on family vulnerability to stress. *Social Forces, 44,* 202–210.

Hansen, D. A., & Hill, R. (1964). Families under stress. In H. Christensen (Ed.), *Handbook of marriage and the family* (pp. 215–295). Chicago, IL: Rand McNally.

Hatfield, L. A., & Polomano, R. C. (2012). Infant distress: Moving toward concept clarity. *Clinical Nursing Research: An international Journal, 21*(2), 164–182

Hawley, D. R., & DeHaan, L. (2003). Toward a definition of family resilience: Integrating life-span and family perspectives. In P. Boss (Ed.), *Family stress: Classic and contemporary readings* (pp. 57–70). Thousand Oaks, CA: Sage.

Hennon, C. B., Newsome, W. S., Peterson, G. W., Wilson, S. M., Radina, M. E., & Hildenbrand, B. (2009). Poverty, stress, resiliency: Using the MRM model for understanding poverty related family stress. In C. A. Broussard & A. L. Joseph (Eds.), *Family poverty in diverse contexts* (pp. 187–202). New York, NY: Routledge.

Henry, C. S., Morris, A. S., & Harrist, A. W. (2015). Family resilience: Moving into the third wave. *Family Relations: An Interdisciplinary Journal of Applied Family Studies, 64*(1), 22–43.

Hill, R. (1949). *Families under stress.* Westport, CT: Greenwood.

Hill, R. (1971). *Families under stress.* Westport, CT: Greenwood. (Original work published in 1949).

Hill, R. (1999). *The strengths of African American families: Twenty-five years later.* New York, NY: University Press of America.

Hillbrand, M., & Pallone, N. J. (1994). *The psychobiology of aggression: Engines, measurement, control.* New York, NY: Haworth.

Hoffman, L. (1981). *Foundation of family therapy: A conceptual framework for systemic change.* New York, NY: Basic Books.

Holmes, T. H., & Rahe, R. H. (1967). The social readjustment rating scale. *Journal of Psychosomatic Research, 11,* 213–218.

Hooke's law. (2015). In *Encyclopedia Britannica.* Retrieved from http://www.britannica.com/science/Hookes-law

Koss, K. J., George, M. R. W., Cummings, E. M., Davies, P. T., El-Sheikh, M., & Cicchetti, D. (2014). Asymmetry in children's salivary cortisol and alpha-amylase in the context of martial conflict: Links to children's emotional security. *Developmental Psychobiology, 56,* 836–849.

Kwon, J. A., & Wickrama, K. S. (2014). Linking family economic pressure and supportive parenting to adolescent health behaviors: Two developmental pathways leading to health promoting and health risk behaviors. *Journal of Youth and Adolescence, 43*(7), 1176–1190. doi:10.1007/s10964-013-0060-0

Lam, A. G., & Zane, N. W. S. (2004). Ethnic differences in coping with interpersonal stressors. *Journal of Cross-Cultural Psychology, 35,* 446–459.

Lavee, Y. (2013). Stress processes in families and couples. In G. W. Peterson and K. R. Bush (Eds.), *Handbook of marriage and family* (3rd ed.), (pp. 159–176). New York, NY: Springer

Lazarus, R. S. (2006).Emotions and interpersonal relationships: Toward a person-centered conceptualization of emotions and coping. *Journal of Personality, 74*(1), 9–46.

Lazarus, R. S., & Folkman, S. (1984). *Stress, appraisal, and coping.* New York, NY: Springer.

Lazarus, R. S., & Launier, R. (1978). Stress-related transactions between person and environment. In L. A. Pervin & M. Lewis (Eds.), *Perspectives in interactional psychology* (pp. 360–392). New York, NY: Plenum.

Lipman-Blumen, J. (1975). A crisis framework applied to macrosociological family changes: Marriage, divorce, and occupational trends associated with World War II. *Journal of Marriage and the Family, 27,* 889–902.

Masten, A. S., & Monn, A. R. (2015). Child and family resilience: Parallels and multilevel dynamics. *Family Relations, 64,* 5–21.

May, R. (1950). *The meaning of anxiety.* New York, NY: Ronald.

McCubbin, H., & McCubbin, M. (1988).Typology of resilient families: Emerging roles of social class and ethnicity. *Family Relations, 37,* 247–254.

McCubbin, H. I. (1979). Integrating coping behavior in family stress theory. *Journal of Marriage and the Family, 41,* 237–244.

McCubbin, H. I., Cauble, A. E., & Patterson, J. M. (1982). *Family stress, coping, and social support.* Springfield, IL: Charles C Thomas.

McCubbin, H. I., Joy, C. B., Cauble, A. E., Comeau, J. K., Patterson, J. M., & Needle, R. H. (1980). Family stress and coping: A decade review. *Journal of Marriage and the Family, 42,* 125–141.

McCubbin, H. I., Futrell, J. A., Thompson, E. A., & Thompson, A. I. (1998). Resilient families in an ethnic and cultural context. In H. I. McCubbin, E. A. Thompson, A. I. Thompson, & J. A. Futrell (Eds.), *Resiliency in African-American families* (pp. 329–351). Thousand Oaks, CA: Sage.

McCubbin, H. I., & Patterson, J. M. (1982). Family adaptation to crisis. In H. I. McCubbin, A. E. Cauble, & J. M. Patterson (Eds.), *Family stress, coping, and social support* (pp. 26–47). Springfield, IL: Charles C Thomas.

McCubbin, H. I., & Patterson, J. M. (1985). Adolescent stress, coping, and adaptation: A normative family perspective. In G. K. Leigh & G. W. Peterson (Eds.), *Adolescents in families* (pp. 256–276). Cincinnati, OH: Southwestern.

McCubbin, H. I., Patterson, J. M., & Wilson, L. (1981). *Family inventory of life events and changes (FILE): Research instrument.* St. Paul: University of Minnesota, Family Social Science.

McCubbin, L. (2006). The role of indigenous family ethnic schema on well-being among Native Hawaiian families. *Contemporary Nurse, 23*(2), 170–180.

McCubbin, L. D., & McCubbin, H. I. (2013). Resilience in ethnic family systems: A relational theory for research and practice. In D. S. Becvar (Ed.), *Handbook of family resilience* (pp. 175–195). New York, NY: Springer

Moos, R. H. (1986). *Coping with life crises: An integrated approach.* New York, NY: Plenum.

Olson, D. H., Russell, C. S., & Sprenkle, D. H. (1979). Circumplex model of marital and family systems cohesion and adaptability dimensions, family types, and clinical applications. *Family Process, 18,* 3–28.

Olson, D. H., Russell, C. S., & Sprenkle, D H. (1980). Marital and family therapy: A decade review. *Journal of Marriage and the Family, 42,* 239–260.

Olson. D. H., Russell, C. S., & Sprenkle, D. H. (1983). Circumplex model of marital and family systems: VI. Theoretical update. *Family Process. 22,* 69–81.

Oken, B. S., Chamine, I., & Wakeland, W. (2015). A systems approach to stress, stressors and resilience in humans. *Behavioural Brain Research. 282,* 144–154. doi:10.1016/j.bbr.2014.12.047

Patterson, J. M. (1988). Families experiencing stress. *Family Systems Medicine, 6,* 202–237.

Patterson, J.M. (2002). Integrating family resilience and family stress theory. *Journal of Marriage and the Family, 64,* 349–360.

Pearlin, L. (1991). The study of coping: An overview of problems and directions. In J. Eckenrode Ed., *The social context of coping* (pp. 261–276). New York, NY: Plenum.

Pearlin, L., & Schooler, C. (1978). The structure of coping. *Journal of Health and Social Behavior, 19,* 2–21.

Price, S. J., McKenry, P. C., & Murphy, M. (2000). *Families across time: A life course perspective.* Los Angeles, CA: Roxbury.

Repetti, R. L., Robles, T. F., & Reynolds, B. (2011). Allostatic processes in the family. *Development and Psychopathology, 23,* 921–938. doi:10.1017/ S095457941100040X

Rodgers, R. H., & White J. M. (1993). Family developmental theory. In P. G. Boss, W. J. Doherty, R. LaRossa, W. R. Schumm, & S. K. Steinmetz (Eds.), *Sourcebook of family theories and methods: A contextual approach* (pp. 225–254). New York, NY: Plenum.

Roskies, E., & Lazarus, R. (1980). Coping theory and the teaching of coping skills. In D. Davidson & S. Davidson (Eds.), *Behavioral medicine: Changing health lifestyles* (pp. 38–69). New York, NY: Brunner/Mazel.

Rutter, M. (1983). Stress, coping, and development: Some issues and questions. In N. Garmezy & M. Rutter (Eds.), *Stress, coping, and development* (pp. 1–41). New York, NY: McGraw-Hill.

Rutter, M. (1987). Psychosocial resilience and protective mechanisms. *American Journal of Orthopsychiatry, 57,* 316–331.

Sarafino, E. P. (2006). *Health psychology: Biopsychosocial interactions* (5th ed.). Hoboken, NJ: John Wiley & Sons.

Schulz, M. S., Cowan, P. A., Cowan, C. P., & Brennan, R. T. (2004). Coming home upset: Gender, marital satisfaction, and the daily spillover of workday experience into couple interactions. *Journal of Family Psychology, 18*(1), 250–263.doi:10.1037/0893-3200.18.1.250

Selye, H. (1978). *The stress of life.* New York, NY: McGraw-Hill.

Serido, J., Almeida, D. M., & Wethington, E. (2004). Chronic stressors and daily hassles: Unique and inter-active relationships with psychological distress. *Journal of Health and Social Behavior, 45,* 17–33.

Smeets, T., Dziobek, I., & Wolf, O.T. (2009). Social cognition under stress: Differential effects of stress-induced cortisol elevations in health young men and women. *Hormones & Behavior, 55*(4), 507–513.

Spence, K. W. (1956). *Behavior therapy and conditioning.* New Haven, CT: Yale University Press.

Taylor, S. E., Klein, L. C., Lewis, B. P., Gruenewald, T. L., Gurung, R. A. R., & Updegraff, J. A. (2000). Biobehavioral responses to stress in females: Tend-and-befriend, not fight-or-flight. *Psychological Review, 107*, 411–429.

Teachman, J., Tedrow, L., & Kim, G. (2013). The demography and families. In G. W. Peterson & K. R. Bush (Eds.), *Handbook of marriage and the family* (3rd ed., pp. 39–62). New York, NY: Springer.

Tix, A. P., & Frazier, P. A. (1998).The use of religious coping during stressful life events: Main effects, moderation, and mediation. *Journal of Consulting and Clinical Psychology, 66,* (2), 411–422.

Walsh, F. (2006). *Strengthening family resilience.* New York, NY: Guilford Press.

Walsh, F. (2013a). Religion and spirituality: A family systems perspective in clinical practice. In K. I. Pargament, A., Mahoney, & E. P., Shafranske (Eds.), *APA handbook of psychology religion, and spirituality (Vol 2): An applied psychology of religion and spirituality* (pp. 189–205). Washington, DC: American Psychological Association.

Walsh, F. (2013b). Community-based practices of a family resilience framework. In D. S. Becvar. (Ed.), *Handbook of family resilience* (pp. 65-82). New York, NY: Springer.

Yeh, C. J., Arora, A. K., & Wu, K. A. (2006). A new theoretical model of collectivistic coping. In P. P. Wong & L. J. Wong (Eds.), *Handbook of multicultural perspectives on stress and coping* (pp. 55–72). New York, NY: Springer.

General Family Stress

CHAPTER 2

Everyday Hassles and Family Relationships

Heather M. Helms, Natalie D. Hengstebeck, and David H. Demo

For many American families, daily life involves negotiating a maze of activities that includes cooking; cleaning; running errands; paying bills; dropping off and picking up children; commuting to and from work; tending to pets; scheduling appointments; attending events (community, religious, and school related); returning phone calls, e-mails, and text messages; caring for aging family members; and remembering birthdays—often while parents fulfill the duties of full- or part-time jobs. These routinized experiences define the rhythm of family life, and family members can experience them at some times as rewarding and at other times as hassles. Whether family members perceive a particular event to be a hassle, a pleasure, or both can depend on any number of factors. For example, women and men define and react to hassles differently; socioeconomic resources, cultural context, and work schedules make it easier for some families and harder for others to deal with daily hassles, and differences in personality characteristics and coping resources influence how individual family members experience and respond to everyday hassles.

In this chapter, we discuss the everyday hassles that researchers have examined in studies of daily stress and family life. We first define the kinds of events that constitute such hassles and then describe the methods researchers use to study them, including the means by which researchers explore invisible dimensions of family life. We then examine how everyday hassles are associated with family functioning, paying particular attention to the variability in family members' experiences. We present Karney and Bradbury's (1995) vulnerability-stress-adaptation (VSA) model as a helpful way to frame the research on daily hassles and family relationships, focusing on the diversity that exists both across and within families in each of the three domains proposed in the model. Because elements of context such as socioeconomic factors, workplace policies, and macrosocietal patterns (e.g., institutionalized discrimination based on race, gender, and sexual orientation) potentially introduce differential opportunities and constraints for family members that are likely to affect the links between each element of the model, we adapt Karney and Bradbury's model by nesting it within the ecological niches that families inhabit. In so doing, we underscore how contextual factors moderate the associations between vulnerability, stress, and adaptation. Furthermore, given the gendered meanings attached to many routinized family activities and the often divergent experiences of women and men in families, our approach is necessarily feminist. We conclude the chapter with a discussion of how existing social policies in the United States fail to mesh with the daily reality of most American families and thus contribute to family members' experiences of everyday hassles. We close with implications and suggestions for family policy interventions.

WHAT ARE EVERYDAY HASSLES?

Everyday hassles are the proximal stressors, strains, and transactions of day-to-day life that can be viewed as common annoyances. These events are relatively minor and arise out of routinized daily activities, such as the tasks involved in maintaining a home, caring for family members, working at a paid job, and participating in community activities (e.g., Serido, Almeida, & Wethington, 2004). Both anticipated and unanticipated events constitute daily hassles (Wheaton, 1999). For example, commuting to work in morning traffic, chauffeuring children to and from school and activities, and working longer hours at particular times of the year (e.g., holiday season for retailers, tax season for accountants) are all daily hassles that families routinize and anticipate. Unanticipated daily hassles, in contrast, are distinct in their episodic nature. Examples of such hassles include an argument with a spouse, a reprimand from a boss, a midday phone call or text concerning a sick child who needs to be picked up from a child-care center, or a flat tire on the way to work. Although many unexpected daily hassles are relatively minor, they often disrupt the flow of everyday life and thus add to family stress.

Whether anticipated or unanticipated, everyday hassles are distinct from other daily stressors that are severe in nature (e.g., micro aggressions, discrimination, racism) and the major life events or transitions discussed in other chapters of this book (e.g., death of a loved one, divorce, job loss, immigration). First, everyday hassles represent a more frequent and continuous form of stress than the relatively rare events that constitute major life changes. Because of their frequency, everyday hassles may be more important determinants of family stress than major, but less frequent, life events (Repetti & Wood, 1997b; Serido et al., 2004). Accordingly, the aggregate effects of everyday hassles have the potential to compromise family and individual well-being and even increase vulnerability to major life events. Second, hassles are characterized by relatively minor ongoing stressors that occupy daily living. Although they may contribute to a major life stressor or co-occur with other more toxic forms of daily stress, everyday hassles are viewed as conceptually distinct from other forms of daily stress (Serido et al., 2004). These conceptually distinct forms of stress may interact; families experiencing major life changes also confront daily hassles and continuous toxic stressors. For example, a family member who is adjusting to a major life event, such as immigration to the United States, may feel heightened stress if he or she misses an appointment or has to pick up a sick child from school. The stress from a relatively minor everyday hassle is likely to be heightened for a recent immigrant who may also be exposed to more severe chronic stressors related to English competency, legal status, or discriminatory practices at work.

METHODS FOR STUDYING EVERYDAY HASSLES AND FAMILY RELATIONSHIPS

Researchers who study the links between everyday hassles and family relationships have used a variety of methods to assess family members' experiences of daily stress. In early studies, researchers defined hassles as "those irritating, frustrating, distressing demands and troubled relationships that grind on us day in and day out" (Miller & Wilcox, 1986, p. 39). Participants in these studies were presented with lists of various kinds of hassles and were asked to rate the frequency and severity with which they had experienced each hassle in the past month (Kanner, Coyne, Schaefer, & Lazarus, 1981). One criticism of this method is that it does not take into account the complexity of individuals' experiences of daily hassles. For example, Lazarus (1999) argued that the likelihood that an individual perceives or experiences a particular event as a hassle depends on the person's appraisal of the event as well as his or her coping resources. To account more fully for individual differences in appraisals of daily hassles, DeLongis, Folkman, and Lazarus (1988) revised Kanner et al.'s (1981) measure of daily hassles to enable respondents to rate how much of a hassle or an uplift they found each category (e.g., work, health, family, friends) to be on a particular day. DeLongis et al.'s revised checklist demonstrates an important shift in scholars' thinking about daily hassles, from viewing hassles as inherently stressful events to viewing them as experiences that individuals might appraise as hassles, uplifts, or both.

Feminist scholars who have used qualitative methods to study everyday, routinized experiences within families have also emphasized the multidimensional nature of daily hassles. Focusing on the routine, gendered experiences of everyday family life, feminist researchers have conducted in-depth, face-to-face interviews to uncover valuable insights regarding daily hassles. These studies provide rich sources of information about the nuances of daily family life that include participants' own, often quite complex, appraisals of their experiences. Through the use of these methods, feminist scholars have learned that although women may label many of the routinized tasks of daily life as essential and often unpleasant hassles, they also view these tasks as expressions of care for the people they love. For example, caring for an elderly partner or parent may include providing transportation to activities and doctor's appointments, grocery and clothes shopping, cleaning, and help with personal care. Women are more often responsible for carrying out these types of tasks than are men and, on average, experience them as more stressful than do men, yet regardless of the stress that accompanies the added responsibilities of caregiving, many women derive meaning and satisfaction from attending to the needs of their loved ones (Walker, Pratt, & Eddy, 1995).

In addition to underscoring the complex and sometimes contradictory nature of family members' experiences of daily hassles, a rich history of qualitative research has uncovered routinized aspects of daily family life previously overlooked by researchers. This body of work directs our attention beyond the activities typically identified in survey studies to include (a) emotion work (Dressel & Clark, 1990), (b) kin work (DiLeonardo, 1987), (c) marriage work (Oliker, 1989), (d) the scheduling of family time (Daly, 1996; Roy, Tubbs, & Burton, 2004), (e) the feeding of the family (DeVault, 1991), (f) the enactment of family rituals (Oswald, 2000), (g) household labor (Coltrane, 2000), (h) child care and care for aging or sick family members (Abel & Nelson, 1990), and (i) volunteer or service work (Hunter, Pearson, Ialongo, & Kellam, 1998).

At the start of the 21st century, researchers began to examine whether and how fluctuations in daily hassles affected daily interactions in families. The methods used in these labor-intensive studies generally feature precise temporal sequencing of daily stressors and subsequent interactions with family members. The development of innovative research tools such as time diaries and experience sampling permitted researchers to obtain detailed accounts of daily hassles and resolved problems associated with retrospective recall that limited earlier research. Perhaps the greatest benefit of this body of research is that the methods allow for a within-person examination of the day-to-day or even hourly fluctuations in everyday hassles and their links with family relationships and functioning (Almeida, Stawski, & Cichy, 2010).

Influenced by family systems and stress transmission literatures as well as ecological and psychobiological perspectives, contemporary scholars have conducted daily experience studies focusing on how one family member's daily stress is linked to another family member's affect or behavior, as well as the reactivity of men versus women to daily stressors, and—most recently—family members' physiological arousal. Reed Larson's seminal work in the area of emotional transmission across family relationships is noteworthy in its use of the experience sampling method (ESM; Larson & Almeida, 1999)—an approach in which family members carried preprogrammed alarm watches throughout the day for 7 consecutive days and were signaled at random moments. When signaled, family members completed brief questionnaires about their activities, companions, and emotional states at those moments. In addition, researchers have coupled multiple methods (i.e., observations of marital and parent–child interactions, daily diary self-report data of mood and workload) with self-collected saliva samples gathered by each family member at multiple time points on each day of the study (Saxbe, Repetti, & Nishina, 2008; Seltzer et al., 2009; Stawski, Cichy, Piazza, & Almeida, 2013). In combination, these time-intensive and comprehensive methods have allowed researchers to examine the complex associations between family members' everyday hassles, their physiological arousal, and subsequent marital and family functioning in multiple contexts throughout the day.

Early work in this area was criticized for its reliance on relatively small, nonrepresentative samples (Perry-Jenkins, Newkirk, & Ghunney, 2013), the use of self-administered checklists to assess daily hassles and stressors, and the time-intensive demands placed on respondents, which often lead to attrition or missing data (Almeida, Wethington, & Kessler, 2002). To address these concerns, researchers have begun to examine the links between everyday hassles and family functioning in understudied populations, including same-sex couples, older adults, cohabiters, families with children, military families, and families of color (Cinchy, Stawski, & Almeida, 2012; Doyle & Molix, 2014; Lara-Cinisomo et al., 2012; Totenhagen, Butler, & Ridley, 2012; Totenhagen & Curran, 2011; Villeneuve et al., 2014). Informing this body of work is the Daily Inventory of Stressful Events (DISE), a semistructured telephone interview designed for use with a nationally representative sample of 1,483 adults (i.e., the National Study of Daily Experiences; Almeida et al., 2010). The DISE methodology involves eight consecutive daily telephone interviews in which participants respond to a series of semistructured, open-ended questions about the occurrence of daily stressors across several domains, including arguments or disagreements, work or school, home life, discrimination, and issues involving close friends or relatives. Participants are asked to provide narrative descriptions of all the daily stressors they mention as well as the perceived severity of the stressors. All interviews are recorded, transcribed, and coded. Almeida's methodology is unique in that rather than relying on participants' self-reported appraisals of stressors, it uses investigator ratings of objective threat and severity to determine the type of threat each stressor poses (i.e., loss, danger, disappointment, frustration, and opportunity) as well as its severity. Participants' highly specific, brief narratives provide detailed explanations about the types of events that men and women typically experience as daily hassles, and the investigator ratings reduce some of the bias associated with self-reported appraisals of stressors. Almeida's methodology reflects scholars' calls for studying the intensity, duration, and source of stress in understanding daily hassles (Randall & Bodenmann, 2009). In addition, interviewing participants over 8 consecutive days enables researchers to examine within-person fluctuations in daily hassles and well-being over time as well as the cumulative effects of hassles rather than relying on single reports about particular days or subjective estimates of hassles over several days.

UNDERSTANDING THE LINKS BETWEEN EVERYDAY HASSLES AND FAMILY WELL-BEING

In this section, we examine how family members manage daily hassles and discuss the links between everyday hassles and individual and family functioning. We begin with a discussion of Karney and Bradbury's (1995) VSA model, and then use this model to frame a review of the literature on the effects of everyday hassles for families and their members.

The Vulnerability-Stress-Adaptation Model

The application of theory to the study of everyday hassles and family relationships is as varied as the methodologies used. Studies range from the theoretical to research grounded in life course theory (e.g., Almeida & Horn, 2004; Moen, 2003), the ecological perspective (e.g., Repetti & Wood, 1997a, 1997b), feminist perspectives (e.g., Daly, 2001; DeVault, 1991), emotional transmission paradigms (e.g., Larson & Almeida, 1999), and, most recently, biopsychosocial approaches (e.g., Charles & Almeida, 2007; Saxbe et al., 2008; Slatcher, 2014). Originally designed to provide an integrative framework for understanding the empirical research on marital quality and stability, Karney and Bradbury's (1995) VSA model is helpful in that it parsimoniously integrates and expands principles from various social and behavioral theoretical perspectives to explain the ways in which family members' experiences of potentially stressful events may be linked to relational outcomes. In our application of Karney and Bradbury's model, we treat everyday hassles as stressful events and explore how they interact with enduring vulnerabilities and adaptive processes to predict family well-being. In addition, the opportunities and constraints afforded by the ecological niches that family members inhabit are viewed as central to each element of the model, and we illustrate the adapted model in Figure 2.1.

Figure 2.1 Adapted Vulnerability-Stress-Adaptation Model

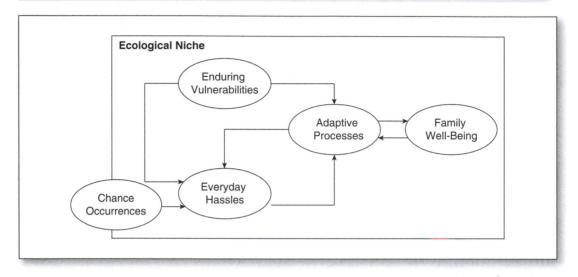

At the most basic level of their model, Karney and Bradbury (1995) identified three elements that contribute to our understanding of the links between everyday hassles and family relationships. Adaptive processes, which play a central role in the model, are the ways in which individuals and families cope with everyday hassles. They are critical to our application of the model because they moderate the associations between daily hassles and family well-being. Family well-being and functioning changes as a function of the way family members behave in response to everyday hassles, and, in turn, family well-being can affect how family members appraise daily hassles. For example, some studies suggest that employed spouses and parents withdraw from family interaction following workdays characterized by interpersonal difficulties and high work demands (Repetti & Wood, 1997a; Schulz, Cowan, Cowan, & Brennan, 2004). This type of social withdrawal has short-term benefits, in that solitary time can rejuvenate spouses and parents and buffer children and partners from the transmission of negative emotions. Rejuvenated parents and protected children are then better able to deal with additional hassles as they unfold. However, the short-term benefits of emotional withdrawal for the individual and the family may be offset over time as repeated instances of withdrawal may erode feelings of closeness in the family, leading to negative interactions, resentment, and more hassles which ultimately decrease family functioning and overall well-being (Story & Repetti, 2006).

The model also proposes a reciprocal relationship between adaptive processes and daily hassles. The level of stress is partially determined by the number, severity, and centrality of daily hassles that the family and its members encounter (Almeida et al., 2002; Randall & Bodenmann, 2009). Interpersonal tensions or arguments have been linked with both physical symptoms and psychological distress, whereas everyday hassles that disrupt daily routines, threaten physical health, or generate feelings of self-doubt are rated as highly psychologically distressing by adults (Almeida, 2005; Stawski et al., 2013). Furthermore, the manner in which family members deal with hassles can exacerbate or alleviate family stress. To put it simply, certain days, weeks, and months are better than others; some hassles are easier to manage than others; and some people cope with everyday hassles better than others (Almeida, 2005).

In a study of divorced single mothers, Hodgson, Dienhart, and Daly (2001) found that careful planning, scheduling, and multitasking were important coping strategies for mothers of young children. To the extent that the mothers in their study were able to navigate daily hassles, they maintained a sense of control over their family routines. For example,

> I have a certain amount of minutes allotted to get in and out of the daycare center . . . then I have half an hour to get to work so I have it timed to about, I have like 6 minutes to get them in and out. . . . I can't always, things don't always go that way, smoothly, you know those 6 minutes to get him dropped off in the morning, I can't guarantee that that happens 5 days a week, 52 weeks of the year. . . . if I didn't leave the daycare right at the right minute then there's a school bus that I follow all the way down [Highway] 21 . . . there was construction last fall on 21, you know, and there have been situations where I've forgotten things or (child) hasn't settled into daycare. . . . He needed a few extra minutes of comforting. . . . I drop him off the minute it opens and the minute it closes is the minute I'm there to pick him up. (Hodgson et al., pp. 14–15)

This mother's words illustrate that, as the model suggests, even with the most careful planning around rigid work and child-care schedules, chance events (e.g., bad weather, road construction, forgetfulness, an upset child) can lead to unanticipated hassles, disrupted plans, and the need for additional adaptation. For single mothers with young children, backup plans and the anticipation of the unexpected are essential coping strategies for dealing with daily hassles.

A family's ability to adapt to daily hassles is also influenced by the enduring vulnerabilities that the family and its members possess. Karney and Bradbury (1995) defined enduring vulnerabilities as family members' relatively stable intrapersonal characteristics (e.g., personality, child temperament) and family background variables (e.g., structural and behavioral patterns in family of origin). In her seminal research using daily diary methods, Rena Repetti and her colleagues (e.g., Repetti & Wood, 1997a) documented that the extent to which parents are able to refrain from engaging in negative interaction with their children following high-stress depends, in part, on the parents' own general level of psychological functioning. Using mood data collected at the end of study participants' workdays as well as self-report and observational data collected in the first few minutes of mother–child interaction at a work-site child-care center, Repetti and Wood found that mothers with higher levels of type A behaviors, depression, and anxiety were more likely than other mothers to engage in aversive interactions with their preschoolers on days during which they had experienced either overloads or negative interpersonal interactions at work. Such enduring vulnerabilities can both contribute to family members' appraisals of daily hassles and affect how they adapt to those hassles.

In the VSA model, adaptive processes are hypothesized to be positively associated with family well-being; that is, families and their members function better to the extent that they deal with daily hassles in constructive ways. In addition, the model proposes an inverse association between family well-being and enduring vulnerabilities and family well-being and daily hassles. High levels of enduring vulnerabilities and daily hassles are linked with low levels of family well-being. However, adaptive processes are expected to moderate this link in such a way that families with average levels of enduring vulnerabilities and daily hassles have lower levels of family well-being when adaptive processes are poor and higher levels of family well-being when adaptive processes are average or good.

A strength of the VSA model is that it provides an integrative framework that scholars can apply to gain a better understanding of everyday hassles and family stress. The components of the applied model—daily hassles, enduring vulnerabilities, and adaptive processes—and the general paths in the model can help us understand the complex and reciprocal processes operating among the model's components. The model is limited by its inattention to the ecological niches and sociocultural characteristics that families and their members inhabit, which leads it to ignore the potential variability that may exist in model paths based on between- and within-family differences. For example, contemporary American families are likely to work evenings, nights, rotating hours, or weekends, and some have access to workplace policies, such as telecommuting and flextime that may enhance their ability to manage everyday hassles (Berg, Kossek, Misra, & Belman, 2014). However, low-income families are disproportionately more likely to work nonstandard shifts with little access to family-supportive workplace policies than are their high-income counterparts who are disproportionately more likely to use and have access to these policies and also the associated gains to well-being (Mills & Täht, 2010). Furthermore although workplace flexibility may benefit family well-being, technology-enabled flexibility (e.g., via cell phones, tablets, home-accessible e-mail, etc.) may also increase the potential of work to impede on family life for those "fortunate" enough to have it (e.g., Heijstra & Rafnsdottir, 2010). Though some parents may organize nonstandard shift work to reduce daily hassles (e.g., working opposite shifts to allow one parent to be home with the children), constraints created by a work schedule that is "out of sync" with family life and compounded by limited financial resources pose significant challenges for managing everyday hassles:

> We interviewed Betty Jones, a low-income solo African American mother who worked the late afternoon and evening shift as a custodian in an Oakland hospital. Her car had broken down months before and she couldn't afford repairs, so her 11-year-old son Tyrone (all names have been changed) took responsibility for bringing himself and his 6-year-old sister to school on a city bus. After school, Tyrone picked up his younger sister and they walked to a bus stop to begin an hour-long daily ride, including a transfer, from Oakland to San Leandro where their grandmother lived. The grandmother took them with her to her evening job as a custodian in an office building. After she got off work at 10 or 11pm, she drove the kids back to their apartment in a low-income area of Oakland. This scheduling exhausted all of them, and Betty, the children's mother, was concerned about her own mother's willingness to continue watching after grandchildren while cleaning

offices at night. Like others we interviewed with very tight budgets, Betty wanted to send her kids to the after-school program located at the public school but she found the fees exorbitant; her income was more than used up by basics like food, rent, and utilities. Betty's swing shift job as a hospital custodian precluded the presence of her children. (Thorne, 2004, pp. 168–169)

In other words, just as the "out-of-sync" nonstandard work schedule has the potential to undermine family well-being, providing families some degree of flexibility and autonomy in their work is related to higher well-being. It is beyond the scope of this chapter to develop a comprehensive model that can better account for variability in the ecological niches that families inhabit, but we suggest that the current model should be expanded to consider contextual factors to better reflect the growing body of research on everyday hassles and family relationships.

Everyday Hassles

A growing number of researchers using widely varying methodologies have explored the everyday hassles that family members typically experience as well as the different meanings that men and women ascribe to these hassles. With a sample of 1,031 adults, each of whom completed an average of seven daily phone interviews, Almeida and Horn (2004) found that women reported experiencing everyday hassles more frequently than did men. However, they found no differences in the numbers of days that men and women reported experiencing multiple hassles. In addition, a negative relationship between age and reports of everyday hassles was found, with a decrease in reports of hassles occurring in old age (i.e., ages 60 to 74). Compared with older adults, young and midlife adults reported experiencing a hassle or multiple hassles on more days, and they perceived their hassles to be more severe.

The content of the everyday hassles that individuals reported included arguments or tensions, overloads (i.e., having too little time or resources), and hassles regarding respondents' social networks, health care, home management, and work or school. Arguments or tensions accounted for half of all daily stressors reported by men and women, and most of these tensions involved spouses or partners. Overload and network hassles were much less common, occurring on 6% and 8% of the study days, respectively. Women were more likely than men to report hassles involving their social networks (i.e., relatives or close friends), whereas men reported more overloads related to work or school than did women (Almeida, 2005). Compared with older adults, the younger and midlife adults in Almeida and Horn's study experienced a greater proportion of overloads and reported that hassles caused greater disruption in their daily routines.

Feminist scholars have focused on gender differences in family members' experiences and the subjective meanings that family members ascribe to routinized hassles. For example, feminist researchers have demonstrated that women perform the bulk of family labor (e.g., cooking, housecleaning, laundry), parenting, and caregiving, and this work has multiple and sometimes contradictory meanings for the individuals who perform it. Studies involving national surveys and time diaries confirm a "gender gap" in household labor but suggest that it may be narrowing somewhat (Sayer, 2005). These results show that men are spending more time on routine household chores and child care than in the past. Women, however, continue to perform about twice the amount of housework as their husbands (Bianchi, Sayer, Milkie, & Robinson, 2012), and mothers spend substantially more solo time caring for children than do fathers (Bianchi & Raley, 2005). Furthermore, even though men's and women's time allocation has become more similar, the types of activities performed remain strongly gendered. Women spend a greater percentage of total time in unpaid labor on routine, time-consuming, and less optional housework (e.g., laundry, cooking), whereas men spend a greater percentage of time on occasional household tasks that require less time and regularity (e.g., mowing the lawn, car maintenance). Relative to fathers, mothers experience child care as more stressful and tiring, which may reflect the fact that mothers do more multitasking and physical care, provide care on a more rigid timetable, spend more time alone with children, and have more overall responsibility for managing care (Connelly & Kimmel, 2014; Offer & Schneider, 2011). In addition, gender disparities in free time have increased, with women reporting almost 4 hours less free time each week than men (Sayer, 2005). When paid and unpaid work hours are combined, married mothers work more total hours per week than married fathers (Bianchi & Raley, 2005; Sayer, 2005). The gendered nature of family work is not without costs, as evidenced in findings demonstrating that women report more stress from both external daily hassles and internal (relationship) daily hassles, and, relative to men's, women's internal and external hassles place both partners' relationship satisfaction at risk (Falconier, Nussbeck, Bodenmann, Schneider, & Bradbury, 2014).

Even in situations where couples define their division of family work as equal, inequalities abound when examining the management of everyday hassles. Regarding the everyday hassles associated with organizing family members' schedules, Jeannie (a mother of two children ages 9 and 12) observed, "I mean the thing is it generally falls on the woman. It's really kind of hard to expect (this to happen) and maybe it's just because of . . . nature. When I first got married and had kids I thought [we should share child care] fifty-fifty because everything else was fifty-fifty" (Kaplan, 2010, pp. 598–599). Inequalities may also manifest in the degree of worry mothers and fathers express about their children. For example, Eleanor, a mother of a 12- and 14-year-old, commented, "[My husband] doesn't worry as much as I about my daughter. . . . Sometimes I say to him, 'Don't you know when she's coming home?' And he's sort of, 'Oh, she'll be home.' So we have a different standard of worry" (Kaplan, 2010, pp. 603–604). These mothers' experiences of tending to the everyday needs of their children underscore feminist characterizations of the often "invisible" nature of the work required to care for children and maintain a home and suggest that if this type of family work were measured directly in large-scale survey studies, gender differences may be even more pronounced.

To understand the links between everyday hassles and family relationships, one must recognize that family labor is multidimensional and time intensive, involves both routine and occasional tasks, and is highly variable across and within households. Furthermore, because much of the "worry-shift" is mundane, tedious, boring, and generally performed without pay, most women and men report that they do not like doing it (DeVault, 1991; Kaplan, 2010; Robinson & Milkie, 1998). The sheer volume of family labor and caregiving, as well as the ongoing and relentless nature of many of these responsibilities, requires planning, preparation, scheduling, and multitasking—tasks that often fall disproportion-ately on the shoulders of women. Thus, although caring for family members includes enjoyable aspects, the work itself often creates hassles that impact family relationships (Connelly & Kimmel, 2014). Peg, a school psychologist working 45 hours per week and a married mother of three young children, explains the division of family labor in her home and her frustrations with the arrangement:

> He's not a morning person. He has coffee and sits. That's one of the biggest gripes. When I've had a tough morning, I'll say, "Am I the only one who hears people say, 'more orange juice?' . . . Things build to a head and then I have what you call a meltdown. "I can't do this anymore. This isn't fair. This isn't right. I'm not the only adult in the house!" Then for a few days he'll try to make lunch. It's generally when I'm feeling pressured . . . and the stress level just gets to me and then I let it all out. It changes for a short period of time but then reverts right back to the same. (Deutsch, 1999, pp. 50, 53)

Ethan, Peg's husband who works 60 hours per week in the biotechnology business, recognizes the inequality but explains it differently: "[Peg] just naturally jumps in where I kind of wait for her to take the initiative. . . . Maybe I'm not helping as much as I could because I feel like that" (Deutsch, 1999, p. 51). Ethan's response implies that "helping" with the children in the morning is an option for him—something he can opt out of if he does not feel like participating.

One explanation for the differences between women and men in the ways they experi-ence everyday hassles focuses on the extent to which individuals interpret their involve-ment in family labor to be freely chosen or voluntary. In an exploration of the contextual conditions surrounding family members' experience of emotions, Larson, Richards, and Perry-Jenkins (1994) were the first to discover how married spouses' perceptions of choice played a key role predicting fluctuations in their moods throughout the day. Their rich data on the contrasting moods of husbands and wives at work and at home highlighted how differently men and women experience these contexts and the everyday hassles they encounter. For example, employed wives recorded their most positive moods while at work and an emotional decline at home during the evening hours, which were filled with house-work and child care. In contrast, husbands recorded their most negative emotions in the workplace; at home their moods lightened, in part, because nonwork time included leisure activities. However, even when men performed housework or child care, their moods while doing these tasks were more positive than were those of their wives when they performed the same activities. Further analyses revealed that performing housework and child-care tasks elicited more positive reactions from husbands than from wives because the hus-bands perceived that they had more choice regarding their involvement in these domains than did the wives.

The reverse is true for paid work. Husbands in Larson et al.'s (1994) study reported low levels of choice while at work, potentially related to constraints associated with gendered expectations for men to be providers. Employed wives reported more positive moods at work than did employed husbands. For many (but not all) women, an unhurried work pace and a friendly work environment contributed to their positive moods while on the job, demonstrating the importance of social support in the workplace for women's mental health. Collectively, these findings suggest that the transfer of women's and men's routinized experiences in the workplace or at home to emotional distress is a gendered process. The translation of work and family experiences into emotional health or distress may depend, in part, on the degree to which the individual perceives the activity to be freely chosen and whether it provides opportunities for positive social interaction, rather than the characteristics of the activity per se.

In sum, the studies reviewed earlier suggest that scholars may achieve a better understanding of everyday hassles by considering the ecological contexts in which the hassles occur. A family's construction of gendered expectations is one such context (Allen & Walker, 2000) and contributes to differences in women's and men's perceptions of and reactions to daily hassles. In addition, research has shown that a family's socioeconomic status (Grzywacz, Almeida, Neupert, & Ettner, 2004; Maisel & Karney, 2012), exposure to chronic stressors at work or at home (Serido et al., 2004), nonstandard work schedules (Almeida, 2004), and minority stress linked to individuals' race, ethnicity, sexual orientation, and/or immigration status (Lincoln & Chae, 2010; Riggle, Rostosky, & Horne, 2010; Trail, Goff, Bradbury, & Karney, 2012) may exacerbate (or buffer) the impact of everyday hassles on family well-being. For example, a consistent theme to emerge in a study of over 600 gay and lesbian partners conducted in California prior to the state's 2008 Supreme Court ruling was the sentiment that the legal recognition of same-sex marriage would enable same-sex couples to "have much more ease and security going through our daily life" and to be "more secure and more confident in every single area of life" (Shulman, Gotta, & Green, 2012, p. 170 and 172). As spoken in the words of one participant in a domestic partnership who longed for the opportunity to marry her partner,

> I worry about whether they will call me if she gets in an accident, and I worry that if there came a time to make an end of life decision, that it won't be me; and always I worry, when she dies, am I going to have to fight to be able to keep the things that we have shared together, amongst other worries. (Shulman et al., 2012, p. 172)

For same-sex couples whose unions are not legally recognized, everyday hassles are embedded in a larger context that amplifies the impact that seemingly minor irritations are likely to have on family and personal well-being. Laws that institutionalize discrimination, including legal marital status, are an important dimension of context that scholars are just beginning to examine (e.g., Riggle et al., 2010).

Adaptive Processes

According to the VSA, the processes that family members use to cope with everyday hassles have important implications for how those hassles affect family interactions. In general, two different patterns of responses have been identified following workdays characterized by heavy workloads or negative interactions with coworkers: (1) increases in marital or parent–child conflict and (2) social withdrawal. These patterns, however, vary across studies, within couples, and by reporter.

In one of the first daily diary studies of married couples with children, Bolger, DeLongis, Kessler, and Wethington (1989) found that on days when husbands experienced an argument at work with a coworker or supervisor, they were more likely to return home from work and argue with their wives but not with their children. For wives, however, the researchers found no significant associations between arguments at work and subsequent arguments with spouses or children. In contrast, a more recent diary study, Story and Repetti (2006) found that wives, but not husbands, reported more marital anger toward their spouse and were more withdrawn from family interaction following workdays characterized by heavy workloads and unpleasant social interactions. In an interesting twist, husbands' reports of their wives' behavior suggested that husbands did not notice their wives' displays of anger or withdrawal on these same days. This may be partially explained by the finding that everyday hassles at work were found to contribute to wives' negative moods, which in turn colored wives' perceptions of their interactions at home. Although husbands did not perceive their wives to be more angry or withdrawn following difficult days at work, wives perceived that they were more irritable and less emotionally available, in part, due to their negative moods. For some families, daily stressors experienced at work may also spill over into interactions with children. For example, Repetti's (1994) early work demonstrated that fathers engaged in more expressions of anger toward children and more harsh discipline following days characterized by negative social interactions at work. In addition, both mothers and fathers have been shown to be less behaviorally and emotionally engaged with their children following busy workdays (Repetti, 1994; Repetti & Wood, 1997a).

Daily relationship stress—or hassles related to the sharing of housework, different goals, and partners' annoying habits—may also be important in understanding the link between everyday hassles (e.g., at work) and couple functioning (Falconier et al., 2014; Ledermann, Bodenmann, Rudaz, & Bradbury, 2010). For example, a study of 345 married and unmarried Swiss couples found that the everyday hassles that partners experienced impacted their overall relationship quality and communication effectiveness via elevations in daily relationship stressors (Ledermann et al., 2010). In a second Swiss study of 110 couples, Falconier et al. (2014) found that women's daily hassles predicted their own physical well-being and anxiety and both partners' relationship stress. Women's relationship stress, in turn, was related to women's depression and both partners' relationship satisfaction. Men's daily hassles were related to their own relationship stress, depression, anxiety, and physical well-being. Men's relationship stress predicted their own depression and relationship satisfaction. Taken together, these findings suggest that although daily hassles are inherently beyond couples' control, couples who adopt effective strategies to reduce relationship stress may be able to protect their relationship quality and satisfaction from the negative effects of everyday hassles.

How might family members buffer others from the effects of the everyday hassles they encounter? Repetti and Wood's (e.g., 1997b) early research suggested that parents' behavioral and emotional withdrawal may actually protect children from the transmission of their parents' negative work experiences. Another early study (Bolger et al., 1989) found that when husbands experienced greater-than-usual demands at the workplace, they performed less household labor and child care when they returned home, and their wives compensated for their withdrawal by performing more of the work at home. The parallel pattern did not occur when wives experienced overloads at work. When wives experienced overloads at work, they too performed less work at home (i.e., behavioral withdrawal), but their husbands did not reciprocate by performing more. Bolger et al. (1989) label this an "asymmetry in the buffering effect" (p. 182) and suggest that, in the short term, wives' stepping in for husbands may alleviate husbands' stress and avoid the transmission of stress from husbands' daily hassles to children. However, this short-term adaptive process may prove harmful over time for families—most particularly for wives. Coping in this manner in repeated instances over time may be one factor in explaining the consistent finding that marriage benefits the emotional health of men more than that of women (Amato, Johnson, Booth, & Rogers, 2003). To the extent that women's emotional health plays a key role in child well-being (Demo & Acock, 1996), a pattern of asymmetrical buffering may be detrimental for children in families as well.

More recently, several researchers have inquired as to how patterns of emotional transmission from daily hassles in the workplace to home vary based on the quality of the marital relationship (Schulz et al., 2004; Story & Repetti, 2006). Story and Repetti (2006) found that both husbands and wives in higher conflict marriages were more likely than their peers in less conflicted marriages to express anger toward their spouse and withdraw from family interaction on evenings following stressful days at work. Similarly, Schulz et al. (2004) found that husbands in more satisfying marriages were less likely than maritally dissatisfied husbands to express anger or criticism toward their wives following emotionally upsetting days at work. Taken together, this research suggests that husbands and wives in higher conflict families are more likely to express negative feelings toward their spouses following high-stress days. Spouses in these families also frequently withdraw from family interaction following difficult workdays, perhaps in an attempt to disengage from further negative interactions.

One unexpected finding indicated that some wives in more satisfying marriages actually withdraw more and express more anger following demanding days at work than do wives in less satisfying marriages (Schulz et al., 2004). The authors suggest that a more satisfying marital relationship may create a context in which husbands encourage wives to express their frustrations as a way of coping. It may be that more maritally satisfied husbands facilitate wives' temporary withdrawal from family interactions by increasing their own involvement with child care and housework so that their wives can recuperate (e.g., "Mommy needs some time to relax and unwind because she had a hard day at work."). In turn, wives in more satisfying marital relationships may feel freer than their maritally dissatisfied counterparts to express anger and withdraw from family interaction after difficult workdays because their husbands are willing to hear their complaints and increase their supportive behavior. This research suggests that the nature of the marital relationship may affect the extent to which everyday hassles at work spill over into family interactions and that these patterns may vary by gender. Similarly, the results of other studies suggest that additional family vulnerabilities or strengths (e.g., child conduct problems, overly controlling parenting) may influence the extent to which daily hassles transfer to family stress (Larson & Gillman, 1999; Margolin, Christensen, & John, 1996).

Research from a 10-year, multisite qualitative study suggests that buffering children from the effects of parents' everyday hassles may be a luxury afforded to only middle-class and more affluent families (Dodson & Dickert, 2004). In their study of low-income families, Dodson and Dickert (2004) found that parents engaged children, most typically eldest daughters, in child care and housework tasks as a strategy to compensate for the inflexible work hours, low wages, and nonstandard shifts of working-poor parents. Whereas studies of both working- and middle-class families have found that girls, more than boys, assume household labor responsibilities when mothers' work demands are high (e.g., Crouter, Head, Bumpus, & McHale, 2001), low-income families differ in that girls' contributions to family labor are essential for family survival because the demands of parents' work render mothers and fathers unavailable to attend to even the most basic everyday hassles of family life. In this way, parents' workplace demands have direct impacts on eldest daughters' daily experiences in that these girls must contend with the everyday hassles and responsibilities customarily assigned to parents. As a teacher of the low-income adolescent girls participating in Dodson and Dickert's (2004) study observed, "They have to take their little brother to the bus stop in the morning and sometimes that means getting to school late or they are babysitting . . . they are like little mothers" (p. 326). One 15-year-old daughter's own words illustrate that the girls themselves are keenly aware of their responsibilities as child-care providers and assistant housekeepers: "I have to take care of the house and take care of the kids and I don't go outside. I have to stay home. They have to go to work so I take over" (p. 324).

The results of Dodson and Dickert's (2004) study suggest that although this adaptive strategy has both short-term benefits (e.g., children are cared for and housework is completed) and long-term benefits (e.g., family cohesion or loyalty, higher levels of social responsibility for adolescents), families use it at considerable cost to eldest daughters. When eldest daughters assume responsibility for the everyday hassles associated with family care, their own education and goals are secondary to the needs of the family. In Dodson and Dickert's study, teachers, parents, and the girls themselves described lost opportunities for education and extracurricular involvement and, perhaps most disconcerting, lost hope for the eldest daughters' futures.

Enduring Vulnerabilities

Individual differences or enduring vulnerabilities in personality and emotional functioning can both contribute to everyday hassles and affect how family members adapt to them. For example, enduring vulnerabilities play an important role in determining how family members process, interpret, and react to the everyday hassles they encounter. In addition, the extent to which individuals possess relatively stable traits can render them resilient or vulnerable to the transfer of stress from everyday hassles. For example, studies have found exaggerated stress responses to hassles among individuals with higher levels of negative affectivity, neuroticism, type A personality traits, depression, and introversion (e.g., Almeida, McGonagle, Cate, Kessler, & Wethington, 2002; Falconier et al., 2014) and lower levels of mastery and self-esteem (Almeida, McGonagle, et al., 2002; Pearlin, 1999).

Gender differences may influence the extent to which enduring vulnerabilities moderate the links between daily hassles, and family stress may differ for men and women. Almeida, McGonagle, et al. (2002) asked 166 married couples to complete daily diaries for

42 consecutive days. In each diary entry, participants responded to a short questionnaire about a variety of daily stressors, including arguments with their spouse, as well as a questionnaire designed to assess psychological distress. The analyses addressed the moderating effects of psychological characteristics (i.e., neuroticism, mastery, self-esteem, and extraversion) on the link between marital arguments and psychological distress. They found that the extent to which wives felt distressed following marital arguments was exacerbated by high levels of neuroticism and attenuated by high levels of mastery, self-esteem, and extraversion. In contrast, self-esteem alone moderated the link between marital arguments and psychological distress for husbands. Almeida, McGonagle, et al. (2002) suggested that because personality has been shown to be particularly salient for coping with stressors that are highly threatening or uncontrollable, the different patterns that emerged for husbands and wives in their sample imply that wives may perceive marital arguments as more threatening than do husbands.

INTERVENTION: TOWARD A NEW FAMILY-RESPONSIVE POLICY AGENDA

Feminists argue for gender equity in daily tasks as a solution to the disproportionate burdens that mothers, wives, and daughters carry in families (Allen, Walker, & McCann, 2013), but they also warn that even with gender equity, many contemporary families would still have too many hassles to manage on their own (Coontz, 2015). In contrast, those ascribing to structural-functionalist views suggest that families function best when women focus on children and home management and men focus on breadwinning (Popenoe, 2009). Rare among scholars but quite prevalent in popular culture are self-help perspectives that frame the link between everyday hassles and family well-being as a private matter that individuals can solve by using time more efficiently. Still others emphasize government- or employer-subsidized child- and elder-care services as mechanisms for outsourcing many of the everyday hassles associated with caregiving while also acknowledging that government and workplace policies may actually amplify sources of hassles if ineffectively administered (Bogenschneider, 2000, 2014).

We argue that contemporary American families need better opportunities both at home and in the workplace to meet family members' diverse needs without inadvertently creating additional stressors for individuals already living in chronically stressful situations (Perry-Jenkins et al., 2013; Roy et al., 2004). We support Moen's (2003) conclusion that we must "re-imagine and reconfigure work hours, workweeks, and occupational career paths in ways that address the widening gaps between the time needs and goals of workers and their families at all stages of the life course on the one hand and the time available to them on the other" (p. 7). For example, some families may want to devote more time to paid work outside the home and therefore need ways to simplify aspects of their daily home lives and outsource everyday tasks to readily available, high-quality substitutes. As Valcour and Batt (2003) note, for parents who want to focus more of their time on family obligations, flexibility in the workplace is of paramount importance. They quoted a mother of three children (including 4-year-old twins) who has been married to a business administrator for 15 years:

I was lucky to work out a job sharing arrangement because there was another woman in my department who did the same thing as me and was also struggling after she had her second baby. So we went to the human resource person and she was supportive but said the company doesn't have this in place. So we did the research and went to the president of the division and we went through a couple of struggles, but eventually they accepted it. I'm so glad it worked out, because it has been great for me and my family. (p. 320)

As this woman's experience illustrates, workplace policies that enable family members to care for the needs of their members without jeopardizing their financial security or jobs are likely to be particularly beneficial for families caring for young children or sick or aging family members.

Although the needs and desires of family members in diverse family forms are likely to change over the life course, they exist in a sociohistorical context that has seen little development in family-responsive workplace policies (Perry-Jenkins et al., 2013). For example, the everyday hassles that today's families encounter are situated in a society that is still predicated on a breadwinner-husband, homemaker-wife script in which the breadwinner is assured an adequate wage for family provision and a full-time, linear rise up the occupational ladder, and the homemaker manages the everyday nonwork aspects of her husband's life as well as the daily hassles of managing a home and family (Coontz, 2000; Moen, 2003). This outdated script contrasts starkly with the contemporary reality that the majority of American families (e.g., single-parent and dual-earner families) experience as they work in an economy where family-wage jobs are reserved for the highly educated, secure manufacturing jobs are few, job growth is limited to low-wage 24/7 service-sector positions with little security or hope for advancement, and income gains are disproportionately situated among more advantaged individuals (Autor & Dorn, 2013). Furthermore, relative to high-wage workers, low-wage workers are less likely to be employed at firms large enough to entitle them to health insurance and family leave and also less likely to be able to afford the insurance premiums and 12 weeks of unpaid leave (Perry-Jenkins et al., 2013). In addition, existing government and workplace policies have been slow to recognize that working family members have legitimate family demands on their time that may require greater flexibility in the workplace. As long as the culture of the workplace equates work commitment with overwork and fails to recognize the legitimacy of family caregiving as an employee right, those seeking a reasonable balance between work and family life are likely to be penalized (Jacobs & Gerson, 2005). This point is documented by a father of two children (ages 8 and 14) who is employed as a manufacturing production supervisor and married to a part-time educational coordinator:

I wish there were more flexibility, especially in our production environment. I've worked all my life around a rotating-work schedule, but this year alone I lost three excellent employees. They had each become single parents for one reason or another, and there's no way you can get child care in off hours and weekends. It just breaks my heart. Traditionally production has been a male-oriented thing, where one partner stays home with the children and the other one works crazy schedules. . . . the world is changing and the schedule is not. (quoted in Valcour & Batt, 2003, p. 310)

The mismatch between the work environments that family members inhabit and the needs of contemporary families creates a context in which everyday hassles emerge and multiply (Perry-Jenkins et al., 2013). The policies most effective at improving family well-being take a holistic approach by integrating service delivery, prevention programs, universal high-quality services, and programs that are flexible to families' needs (Hengstebeck, Helms, & Crosby, in press).

Valcour and Batt (2003) suggest that employers first adopt and promote a family-responsive attitude toward employees and then demonstrate support for this attitude through company policy. A primary objective of this approach is to reduce the often unspoken costs to employees who choose nonstandard work arrangements or take advantage of family-friendly policies (Jacobs & Gerson, 2005). Such an attitude recognizes that all employees, regardless of whether they have spouses, partners, children, or other kin at home, are members of families and experience everyday hassles and demands from personal involvements outside the workplace (Perry-Jenkins et al., 2013). Valcour and Batt (2003) note that family-responsive employers must offer employees the following: (a) a broad range of work-life programs that provide employees with control over their working time and support in meeting their family and personal needs; (b) adequate pay, benefits, and employment security; (c) work designed to provide employees with discretion and control in meeting work and life demands; and (d) a workplace culture, transmitted formally by organizational policies and informally by supervisors and coworkers that values and supports the work-life integration of all employees (Thompson & Prottas, 2005; Valcour & Batt, 2003, pp. 312–313). Jacobs and Gerson (2005) further emphasize that family responsive reforms must uphold two essential principles: (1) gender equality in opportunity structures and (2) support for employees regardless of socioeconomic location.

Moen (2003) argues that it is not enough for corporations to list such policies on the books. Employers must make continuous efforts to enforce these policies to cultivate a corporate climate that is truly responsive to the needs of families. Moen also suggests that employers and government officials need to keep better records of the variations (and the reasons for them) in employees' work-hour and career-path arrangements in order to track the implications of these variations for employees and corporations. The information gained through such tracking may help to convince employers and policy makers of the heterogeneity in employees' experiences both at work and at home and thus persuade them to change outdated workplace policies based on the breadwinner-homemaker template. Finally, and perhaps most important for families' experiences of everyday hassles and stress, employers and policy makers must view employees' vulnerabilities and family circumstances as key human resource, workforce, and labor issues. For family members struggling in uncertain economic times and working in low-wage jobs with inflexible work schedules, everyday hassles such as minor car accidents, sick children, and parent–teacher conferences scheduled during work hours can add strains that they may find hard to manage. Policies that focus on the risks, vulnerabilities, and family lives of workers are likely to attenuate the transfer of stress from everyday hassles to family relationships.

REFERENCES

Abel, E. K., & Nelson, M. K. (Eds.). (1990). *Circles of care: Work and identity in women's lives.* Albany: State University of New York Press.

Allen, K. R., & Walker, A. J. (2000). Constructing gender in families. In R. M. Milardo & S. Duck (Eds.), *Families as relationships* (pp. 1–17). Chichester, England: John Wiley.

Allen, K. R., Walker, A. J., & McCann, B. R. (2013). Feminism and families. In G. W. Peterson & K. R. Bush (Eds.), *Handbook of marriage and the family* (pp. 139–158). New York: Springer.

Almeida, D. M. (2004). Using daily diaries to assess temporal friction between work and family. In A. C. Crouter & A. Booth (Eds.), *Work-family challenges for low-income parents and their children* (pp. 127–136). Mahwah, NJ: Lawrence Erlbaum.

Almeida, D. M. (2005). Resilience and vulnerability to daily stressors assessed via diary methods. *Current Directions in Psychological Science, 14*(2), 64–68.

Almeida, D. M., & Horn, M. C. (2004). Is daily life more stressful during middle adulthood? In C. D. Ryff & R. C. Kessler (Eds.), *A portrait of midlife in the United States* (pp. 425–451). Chicago, IL: University of Chicago Press.

Almeida, D. M., McGonagle, K. A., Cate, R. C., Kessler, R. C., & Wethington, E. (2002). Psychological moderators of emotional reactivity to marital arguments: Results from a daily diary study. *Marriage and Family Review, 34,* 89–113.

Almeida, D. M., Stawski, R. S., & Cichy, K. E. (2010). Combining checklist and interview approaches for assessing daily stressors: The Daily Inventory of Stressful Events. In R. J. Contrada & A. Baum (Eds.), *The handbook of stress science: Biology, psychology, and health*, 583–596. New York, NY: Springer.

Almeida, D. M., Wethington, E., & Kessler, R. C. (2002). The daily inventory of stressful events: An interview-based approach for measuring daily stressors. *Assessment, 9,* 41–55.

Amato, P. R., Johnson, D. R., Booth, A., & Rogers, S. J. (2003). Continuity and change in marital quality between 1980 and 2000. *Journal of Marriage and Family, 65,* 1–22.

Autor, D. H., & Dorn, D. (2013). The growth of low-skill service jobs and the polarization of the US labor market. *The American Economic Review, 103*(5), 1553–1597.

Berg, P., Kossek, E. E., Misra, K., & Belman, D. (2014). Work-Life flexibility policies: Do unions affect employee access and use? *Industrial & Labor Relations Review, 67*(1), 111–137.

Bianchi, S. M., & Raley, S. B. (2005). Time allocation in families. In S. M. Bianchi, L. M. Casper, & R. B. King (Eds.), *Work, family, health, and well-being* (pp. 21–42). Mahwah, NJ: Lawrence Erlbaum.

Bianchi, S. M., Sayer, L. C., Milkie, M. A., & Robinson, J. P. (2012). Housework: Who did, does or will do it, and how much does it matter? *Social Forces, 91*(1), 55–63.

Bogenschneider, K. (2000). Has family policy come of age? A decade review of the state of U.S. family policy in the 1990s. *Journal of Marriage and the Family, 62,* 1136–1159.

Bogenschneider, K. (2014). *Family policy matters: How policymaking affects families and what professionals can do.* New York, NY: Routledge.

Bolger, N., DeLongis, A., Kessler, R. C., & Wethington, E. (1989). The contagion of stress across multiple roles. *Journal of Marriage and the Family, 51,* 175–183.

Charles, S. T., & Almeida, D. M. (2007). Genetic and environmental effects on daily life stressors: More evidence for greater variation in later life. *Psychology and Aging, 22,* 331–340.

Cinchy, K. E., Stawski, R.S., & Almeida, D.M. 2012. Racial differences in exposure and reactivity to daily family stressors. *Journal of Marriage and Family, 74*(3), 572–586.

Coltrane, S. (2000). Research on household labor: Modeling and measuring the social embeddedness of routine family work. *Journal of Marriage and the Family, 62,* 1208–1233.

Connelly, R., & Kimmel, J. (2014). If you're happy and you know it: How do mothers and fathers in the US really feel about caring for their children? *Feminist Economics.* doi:10.1080/13545701.2014.970210

Coontz, S. (2000). Historical perspectives on family studies. *Journal of Marriage and the Family, 62*(2), 283–297.

Coontz, S. (2015). Revolution in intimate life and relationships. *Family Theory & Review, 7,* 5–12.

Crouter, A. C., Head, M. R., Bumpus, M. F., & McHale, S. M. (2001). Household chores: Under what conditions do mothers lean on daughters? In A. J. Fuligini (Ed.), *Family obligation and assistance during adolescence* (pp. 23–41). New York, NY: John Wiley.

Daly, K. J. (1996). *Families and time: Keeping pace in a hurried culture.* Thousand Oaks, CA: Sage.

Daly, K. J. (2001). Deconstructing family time: From ideology to lived experience. *Journal of Marriage and Family, 63,* 283–294.

DeLongis, A., Folkman, S., & Lazarus, R. S. (1988). The impact of daily stress and health on mood: Psychological and social resources as mediators. *Journal of Personality and Social Psychology, 54,* 486–495.

Demo, D. H., & Acock, A. C. (1996). Family structure, family process, and adolescent well-being. *Journal of Research on Adolescence, 6,* 457–488.

Deutsch, F. M. (1999). *Halving it all: How equally shared parenting works.* Cambridge, MA: Harvard University Press.

DeVault, M. L. (1991). *Feeding the family: The social organization of caring as gendered work.* Chicago, IL: University of Chicago Press.

DiLeonardo, M. (1987). The female world of cards and holidays: Women, families, and the work of kinship. *Signs, 12,* 440–453.

Dodson, L., & Dickert, J. (2004). Girls' family labor in low-income households: A decade of qualitative research. *Journal of Marriage and Family, 66,* 318–332.

Doyle, M., & Molix, L. (2014). Love on the margins: The effects of social stigma and relationship length on romantic relationship quality. *Social Psychological and Personality Science, 5*(1), 102–110.

Dressel, P., & Clark, A. (1990). A critical look at family care. *Journal of Marriage and the Family, 52,* 769–782.

Falconier, M. K., Nussbeck, F., Bodenmann, G., Schneider, H., & Bradbury, T. (2014). Stress from daily hassles in couples: Its effects on intradyadic stress, relationship satisfaction, and physical and psychological well-being. *Journal of Marital and Family Therapy.* Advanced online publication. doi:10.1111/jmft.12073

Grzywacz, J. G., Almeida, D. M., Neupert, S. D., & Ettner, S. L. (2004). Socioeconomic status and health: A micro-level analysis of exposure and vulnerability to daily stressors. *Journal of Health and Social Behavior, 45,* 1–16.

Hengstebeck, N. D., Helms, H. M., & Crosby, D. A. (in press). Family policies. In C. Shehan (Ed.), *Encyclopedia of family studies.* Hoboken, NJ: Wiley-Blackwell.

Heijstra, T. M., & Rafnsdottir, G. L. (2010). The internet and academics' workload and work–family balance. *The Internet and Higher Education, 13*(3), 158–163. doi:10.1016/j.iheduc.2010.03.004

Hodgson, J., Dienhart, A., & Daly, K. J. (2001). Time juggling: Single mothers' experience of time-press following divorce. *Journal of Divorce and Remarriage, 35,* 1–28.

Hunter, A. G., Pearson, J. L., Ialongo, N. S., & Kellam, S. G. (1998). Parenting alone to multiple caregivers: Child care and parenting arrangements in black and white urban families. *Family Relations, 47,* 343–353.

Jacobs, J. A., & Gerson, K. (2005). *The time divide.* Cambridge, MA: Harvard University Press.

Kanner, A. D., Coyne, J. C., Schaefer, C., & Lazarus, R. S. (1981). Comparisons of two modes of stress measurement: Daily hassles and uplifts versus major life events. *Journal of Behavioral Medicine, 4,* 1–39.

Kaplan, E. B. (2010). Doing care on the run: Family strategies for the contested terrain of gender and institutional intransigence. *Journal of Contemporary Ethnography, 39,* 587–618.

Karney, B. R., & Bradbury, T. N. (1995). The longitudinal course of marital quality and stability: A review of theory, method, and research. *Psychological Bulletin, 118,* 3–34.

Lara-Cinisomo, S., Chandra, A., Burns, R. M., Jaycox, L. H., Tanielian, T., Ruder, T., & Han, B. (2012), A mixed-method approach to understanding the experiences of nondeployed military caregivers. *Maternal and Child Health Journal, 16*(2), 374–384.

Larson, R. W., & Almeida, D. M. (1999). Emotional transmission in the daily lives of families: A new paradigm for studying family process. *Journal of Marriage and the Family, 61,* 5–20.

Larson, R. W., & Gillman, S. (1999). Transmission of emotions in the daily interactions of single-mother families. *Journal of Marriage and the Family, 61,* 21–37.

Larson, R. W., Richards, M. H., & Perry-Jenkins, M. (1994). Divergent worlds: The daily emotional experiences of mothers and fathers in the domestic and public spheres. *Journal of Personality and Social Psychology, 67,* 1034–1046.

Lazarus, R. S. (1999). *Stress and emotion: A new synthesis.* New York, NY: Springer.

Ledermann, T., Bodenmann, G., Rudaz, M., & Bradbury, T.N. (2010). Stress, communication, and marital quality in couples. *Family Relations, 59*(2), 195–206.

Lincoln, K. D., & Chae, D. H. (2010). Stress, marital satisfaction, and psychological distress among African Americans. *Journal of Family Issues, 31,* 1081–1105.

Maisel, N.C., & Karney, B. R. (2012). Socioeconomic status moderates associations among stressful events, mental health, and relationship satisfaction. *Journal of Family Psychology, 26*(4), 654–660.

Margolin, G., Christensen, A., & John, R. S. (1996). The continuance and spillover of everyday tensions in distressed and nondistressed families. *Journal of Family Psychology, 10,* 304–321.

Miller, M. J., & Wilcox, C. T. (1986). Measuring perceived hassles and uplifts among the elderly. *Journal of Human Behavior and Learning, 3,* 38–45.

Mills, M., & Täht, K. (2010). Nonstandard work schedules and partnership quality: Quantitative and qualitative findings. *Journal of Marriage and Family, 72*(4), 860–875.

Moen, P. (Ed.). (2003). *It's about time: Couples and careers.* Ithaca, NY: Cornell University Press.

Offer, S., & Schneider, B. (2011). Revisiting the gender gap in time-use patterns: Multitasking and well-being among mothers and fathers in dual-earner families. *American Sociological Review, 76*(6), 809–833.

Oliker, S. J. (1989). *Best friends and marriage.* Berkeley: University of California Press.

Oswald, R. (2000). A member of the wedding? Heterosexism and family ritual. *Journal of Social and Personal Relationships, 17(3),* 349–368.

Pearlin, L. I. (1999). Stress and mental health: A conceptual overview. In A. V. Horwitz & T. L. Scheid (Eds.), *A handbook for the study of mental health: Social contexts, theories, and systems* (pp. 161–175). New York, NY: Cambridge University Press.

Perry-Jenkins, M., Newkirk, K., & Ghunney, A. K. (2013). Family work through time and space: An ecological perspective. *Journal of Family Theory & Review, 5,* 105–123.

Popenoe, D. (2009). *Families without fathers: Fathers, marriage and children in American society.* New Brunswick, NJ: Transaction.

Randall, A. K., & Bodenmann, G. (2009). The role of stress on close relationships and marital satisfaction. *Clinical Psychological Review, 29*(2), 105–15.

Repetti, R. L. (1994). Short-term and long-term processes linking job stressors to father-child interaction. *Social Development, 3,* 1–5.

Repetti, R. L., & Wood, J. (1997a). The effects of daily stress at work on mothers' interactions with preschoolers. *Journal of Family Psychology, 11,* 90–108.

Repetti, R. L., & Wood, J. (1997b). Families accommodating to chronic stress. In B. H. Gottlieb (Ed.), *Coping with chronic stress* (pp. 191–220). New York, NY: Plenum.

Riggle, E. D., Rostosky, S. S., & Horne, S. G. (2010). Psychological distress, well-being, and legal recognition in same-sex couple relationships. *Journal of Family Psychology, 24*(1), 82–6.

Robinson, J. P., & Milkie, M. A. (1998). Back to the basics: Trends in and role determinants of women's attitudes toward housework. *Journal of Marriage and the Family, 60,* 205–218.

Roy, K. M., Tubbs, C. Y., & Burton, L. M. (2004). Don't have no time: Daily rhythms and the organization of time for low-income families. *Family Relations, 53*(2), 168–178.

Saxbe, D. E., Repetti, R. L., & Nishina, A. (2008). Marital satisfaction, recovery from work, and diurnal cortisol among men and women. *Health Psychology, 27,* 15–25.

Sayer, L. C. (2005). Gender, time and inequality: Trends in women's and men's paid work, unpaid work and free time. *Social Forces, 84,* 285–303.

Schulz, M. S., Cowan, P. A., Cowan, C. P., & Brennan, R. T. (2004). Coming home upset: Gender, marital satisfaction, and the daily spillover of workday experience into couple interactions. *Journal of Family Psychology, 18,* 250–263.

Seltzer, M. M., Almeida, D. M., Greenberg, J. S., Savla, J., Stawski, R. S., Hong, J., & Taylor, J. L. (2009). Psychosocial and biological markers of daily lives of midlife parents of children with disabilities. *Journal of Health and Social Behavior, 50*(1), 1–15.

Serido, J., Almeida, D. M., & Wethington, E. (2004). Chronic stressors and daily hassles: Unique and interactive relationships with psychological distress. *Journal of Health and Social Behavior, 45,* 17–33.

Shulman, J. L., Gotta, G., & Green, R.-J. (2012). Will marriage matter? Effects of marriage anticipated by same-sex couples. *Journal of Family Issues 33,* 158–181.

Slatcher, R. B. (2014). Family relationships and cortisol in everyday life. In C. Agnew & S. South (Eds.), *Interpersonal relationships and health: Social and clinical psychological mechanisms* (pp. 71–88). New York, NY: Oxford.

Story, L. B., & Repetti, R. (2006). Daily occupational stressors and marital behavior. *Journal of Family Psychology, 20,* 690–700.

Stawski, R. S., Cichy, K. E., Piazza, J. R., & Almeida, D. M. (2013). Associations among daily stressors and salivary cortisol: Findings from the National Study of Daily Experiences. *Psychoneuroendocrinology, 38*(11), 2654–2665.

Thompson, C. A., & Prottas, D. J. (2005). Relationships among organizational family support, job autonomy, perceived control, and employee well-being. *Journal of Occupational Health Psychology, 11*(1), 100–118.

Thorne, B. (2004). The crisis of care. In A. C. Crouter & A. Booth (Eds.), *Work-family challenges for low-income parents and their children* (pp. 165–178). Mahwah, NJ: Lawrence Erlbaum.

Totenhagen, C. J., Butler, E. A., & Ridley, C. A. (2012). Daily stress, closeness, and satisfaction in gay and lesbian couples. *Personal Relationships, 19*(2), 219–233.

Totenhagen, C. J., & Curran, M. A. (2011). Daily hassles, sacrifices, and relationship quality for pregnant cohabitors. *Family Science, 2*(1), 68–72.

Trail, T. E., Goff, P. A., Bradbury, T. N., & Karney, B. R. (2012). The costs of racism for marriage: How racial discrimination hurts, and ethnic identity protects, newlywed marriages among Latinos. *Personality & Social Psychology Bulletin, 38*(4), 454–65.

Valcour, P. M., & Batt, R. (2003). Work-life integration: Challenges and organizational responses. In P. Moen (Ed.), *It's about time: Couples and careers* (pp. 310–331). Ithaca, NY: Cornell University Press.

Villeneuve, L., Dargis, L., Trudel, G., Boyer, R., Préville, M., & Bégin, J. (2014). Daily hassles, marital functioning and psychological distress among community-dwelling older couples. *European Review of Applied Psychology*. *64*(5), 251–258.

Walker, A. J., Pratt, C. C., & Eddy, L. (1995). Informal caregiving to aging family members: A critical review. *Family Relations, 44,* 402–411.

Wheaton, B. (1999). Social stress. In C. S. Aneshensel & J. C. Phelan (Eds.), *Handbook of the sociology of mental health* (pp. 277–300). New York, NY: Kluwer Academic/Plenum.

Developmental Family Forms

Conceptualizing Parental Stress With Family Stress Theory

Gary W. Peterson

Around the globe, adults and youth who soon will reach maturity are strongly encouraged by a variety of influences to become parents, value children, and view the young as sources of life satisfaction. Females, in particular, are traditionally pressured to view motherhood as a primary source of fulfillment, and men are identifying with fatherhood to a greater extent than in the past (Bigner, 2010; Holden, 2015; Marsiglio & Roy, 2013). Partly based in pronatalist and religious norms, cultural images of parenthood often focus on the positive meanings associated with raising children.

A current example is the viewpoint of the Quiverfull fundamentalist sect, a contemporary religious group of conservative evangelical couples, located within the United States and internationally in moderate numbers. Quiverfull Christians promote procreation and parenthood by believing strongly that children are blessings given by God and reject all forms of contraception, including natural family planning, sterilization, and abortion. Any form of birth control is wrong because it involves disobedience by married couples to the word of God captured in the biblical phrase, "Be fruitful and multiply" (Kaufmann, 2011; Pride, 1985). Happiness and reduced stress are supposed to result, especially for Quiverfull women, when they reject any form of birth control and accept their biblically mandated roles as parents. Husbands are ordained by God as primary family authorities and are also strongly encouraged to function as parents within these families (Pride, 1985).

Other positive views of parenting are based in secular beliefs that children make parents' lives complete and more meaningful. Raising children is seen as a source of fun, novelty, stimulation, and a means of solidifying ties among parents, grandparents, kin, and parental surrogates. Parenthood provides a socially defined marker of mature status, a sense of permanence, and feelings of personal efficacy (Bigner, 2010; Holden, 2015). Recent evolutionary views also reinforce pronatalist perspectives by proposing that, due to natural selection processes, our genetic heritage provides a significant tendency for adults to assume parental roles. Although these natural tendencies to become parents can be changed, considerable effort is needed to become conscious of and alter such predispositions (Buss, 2005).

As illustrated earlier, pronatalist views highlight the positive aspects of parenting often without realistic assessments of the challenges and stresses involved. Consequently, the purpose of this chapter is to apply concepts from family stress theory to provide a more realistic and balanced conception of parenting, which includes the pervasive but variable presence of both normative and nonnormative stress.

PRAGMATIC REALISM: CONCEPTIONS OF PARENTAL STRESS

Alternative views include the idea that parenthood is not inherently either an exclusively negative or a positive experience. Instead, newer conceptions are more realistic and recognize that caring for, disciplining, and socializing children involves both positive and negative consequences. Varied parental experiences include powerful attachments, personal fulfillment, satisfaction with children's achievements as well as daily hassles, tension, anxiety, distress, depression, and severe trauma. In fact, child rearing can be characterized as the most deeply meaningful and yet difficult challenge in the lives of adults!

Parenthood is increasingly being examined through a lens of pragmatic realism, or a more balanced view of what is involved, a key component of which is varying degrees of stress. Occupying and performing parenting roles are not homogenous experiences for mothers and fathers. A growing segment of the U.S. population, for example, appears to be choosing voluntary childlessness, or a child-free lifestyle, and feeling comfortable with this choice. Recent evidence indicates that a child-free lifestyle can have few psychological costs for many who choose this option (Bures, Koropeckyj-Cox, & Loree, 2009; Koropeckyj-Cox, Pienta, & Brown, 2007; Nomaguchi & Milkie, 2003; Umberson, Pudrovska, & Reczek, 2010). Feminist thought also questions the normative imperative for women to bear children as a primary means for defining meaningful identities. Parenthood is increasingly a matter of choice, and voluntary childlessness is becoming more normative (Kelly, 2009). Pragmatic realism also is reflected in the work of economists who seek to establish the monetary value of children as either assets or liabilities rather than simply viewing parenthood through idealized conceptions of inevitable happiness (Folbre, 2008).

A key source of parents' stresses is their social cognitions or mental models of themselves as parents that lead them to evaluate the challenges and benefits of parenting in realistic ways. These mental models of themselves are shaped by their own self-perceptions, how they perceive others (e.g., their children and youth) as well as attitudes, attributions, and expectations they endorse within particular cultural contexts that shape their concepts of parenthood. How parents appraise themselves in terms of such social meanings is decisive for the onset, continuity, intensity, and management of parenting stress (Deater-Deckard, Smith, Ivy, & Petrill, 2005; Hawk & Holden, 2006). Stressful experiences occur and require management throughout the life course, often on a daily basis. Such everyday experiences of parental stress can occur during the intense time of childbirth, the parents' sleepless nights caused by an infant's sleep-awake patterns, a toddler who bites a classmate in child care, a teenage daughter who demands later curfew hours for dating, when facing the difficult behavior of an autistic child, or when a teenage son gets arrested for marijuana possession.

Parents become stressed by difficult job circumstances compelling them to spend less positive time, be less supportive, and to use less effective discipline with their children (Kremer-Sadlik & Paugh, 2007). In fact, parental stress can result from variability in several external circumstances including socioeconomic resources, family structural characteristics, work and career-related factors, as well as child care arrangements. Recent findings make clear that the multiple roles of parents often influence the stress they experience in the parent–child relationship (Deater-Deckard, 2004; Umberson et al., 2010). Ethnic minority and immigrant parents often experience continuing or periodic stress, especially when confronting the challenges of balancing the demands of the dominant and minority cultures (Hennon, Peterson, Hildenbrand, & Wilson, 2008; Hennon, Peterson, Polzin, & Radina, 2007).

The point of all these diverse examples is that some degree of parental stress is likely to be a universal experience for parents and their surrogates, including grandparents, aunts, uncles, stepparents, foster parents, and others who perform parental roles. The ubiquitous nature of these experiences underscores the importance of understanding how stress contributes to effective or ineffective functioning of parents and other caregivers (Crnic, Gaze, & Hoffman, 2005; Crnic & Low, 2002; Hennon et al., 2008; Letiecq, Bailey, & Porterfield, 2008). In contrast, despite its universality, the precise manner and degree that parental stress is experienced may vary greatly from parent to parent depending upon many factors (Deater-Deckard, 2004). Individuals, in certain social circumstances, for example, some single parents and families of lower socioeconomic status, are more likely to experience parental stress because they encounter complicated life strains resulting from resources that are stretched to the limit or difficult to access (e.g., limited time and money). These resource deficiencies leave parents more vulnerable to typical stressors (Crouter & Booth, 2004) and illustrate further that parental stress may be both omnipresent but vary widely in intensity, depending upon diverse circumstances.

Consistent with these ideas, the primary purpose of this chapter is to integrate the research on parental stress with concepts central to family stress theory and provide greater understanding to this aspect of the parent–child relationship (Hennon et al., 2009; Hennon & Peterson, 2007; Hill, 1949; Lavee, 2013; McCubbin & Patterson, 1986; Patterson, 2002). Key concepts from family stress theory, consisting of stress and crisis, stressor event (or stressor), resources, definition of the stressor (or perception), coping, and adaptation, are used to accomplish this integration. A case study is presented and used to illustrate points throughout the chapter. Addressing these issues and concepts will provide greater understanding about (a) why the experience of parental stress is so common, (b) why the degree of stress varies widely within the population of parents, (c) why parents vary in their capacities to cope with and adapt to stress, (d) what linkages exist between parental stress and the adjustment (or maladjustment) of parents and children, and (e) what strategies exist for controlling and reducing adverse parental stress.

Rethinking the research literature on parental stress in terms of family stress theory also provides a more systemic or family systems view of this work. Previous research and the conceptualization of parental stress has been largely an application of psychological theory (Crnic & Low, 2002; Deater-Deckard, 2004) by emphasizing the internal dynamics of individuals (e.g., parents) who experience psychological "distress" (or similar forms of affect such as anxiety, depression, trauma, strain, uneasiness), while limited attention has been devoted to "relationship" or "systemic" conceptions. In contrast, this chapter seeks to reinterpret parental stress more extensively in terms of changes in family relationships or in the systemic contexts of parent–child relationships without ignoring the individual psychological experience of stress (Lavee, 2013).

Case Study: Tiffany

Tiffany is a 40-year-old divorced mother of three, Matt (17), Joey (10), and Pamela (3). She has full legal and physical custody of all three children, who only see their father on holidays and sometimes during the summer, as he lives in another state. Tiffany works one 40-hour per week job as a custodian on the third shift (11 p.m. to 7 a.m.). She prefers the third shift as it allows her to get the older two children off to school in the morning and be there in the afternoon when they return. She also has as second job on weekends that is part-time, just to be able to afford the necessities. The family is currently living in a mobile home that Tiffany is purchasing. Her previous mobile home was destroyed by a flood from a nearby stream during an extended rain storm. Luckily, neither her family nor Tiffany were at home at the time of the flood, but they lost most of their belongings. Tiffany often feels exhausted and overwhelmed by her parental responsibilities on top of being the sole financial provider. Fortunately, she is able to rely on her oldest son, Matt, to care for the two younger children on the weekends when she works. Also, her great aunt is a retired special education teacher who loves to spend time with the family and usually comes over during the day to watch Pamela (who was diagnosed with autism recently), while Tiffany sleeps in preparation for her night shift.

CONCEPTUALIZING FAMILY STRESS THEORY AND PARENTAL STRESS

The "Systemic" X Factor

Reuben Hill (1949) in his classic work on the ABC-X model, the foundation of family stress theory, proposes that family crisis or stress (the X factor) results from a complex three-way interaction (or combination) among (1) the stressor event (the A factor), (2) the resources that families have available (the B factor), and (3) the definition or meaning that families assign to the stressor (the C factor). Stressful or crisis situations are not simply the direct result of the event itself but a product of the event plus the interpretations of family members about changing or disruptive circumstances and the extent to which family systems have capabilities for coping (Boss, 2002; Lavee, 2013; Patterson, 2002). Originally, family stress theory examined only the circumstances of a "crisis" in which sudden, dramatic events occur (e.g., the flood that destroyed Tiffany's previous home or a child's diagnosis of life threatening cancer occurs) that incapacitates the family. In contrast, more recent conceptualizations of the X factor have dealt with more normative, cumulative, long-term changes, and, in particular, the systemic quality of parental stress within families can now be added to these evolving interpretations (Crnic & Low, 2002; Crnic et al., 2005; Hill, 1949; Lavee, 2013).

Family stress scholars view change in family systems as the essence of stress and tension within families and parent–child relationships (Boss, 2002; Hennon et al., 2008; Patterson, 2002; Serido, Almeida, & Worthington, 2004). Various life transitions and events provide essential ingredients for normal psychosocial development but do so as disturbances and pressures for change to occur in the roles and expectations that shape family life. Because family members and family systems are subject to persistent developmental change, stress in the form of systemic change becomes inevitable during everyday life, both within families and parent–child relationships (Lavee, 2013). An important contribution of family stress theory, therefore, is to move the construct of "stress" solely from psychological levels to both relationship (e.g., the parent–child relationship) and family systems levels of analysis (Boss, 2002; Hennon et al., 2009; Lavee, 2013; see Bush, Price, Price, & McKenry, Chapter 1, this volume).

At the psychological level, parental stress (or "distress") is an aversive emotional reaction by an individual parent to the demands of occupying child-care and socialization roles (Crnic et al., 2005; Crnic & Low, 2002; Deater-Deckard, 2004). In contrast, stresses at relationship or family systems levels are defined as pressure or tension for development within a relationship system that is synonymous with change (Boss, 2002; Lavee, 2013). Depending on how parents view such pressures for change, this may contribute either to psychological distress or to positive psychological feelings of individuals. Consequently, both family and parental stress involve changes in the structure, role relationships, and corresponding expectations that affect either the stability of family systems or family members' personal assessments of these changes. Changes that may evoke such stressful reactions include dramatic crisis events, changes in family members' behavior, mundane daily hassles, alteration in the family's authority structure, and the accumulation of several challenging circumstances at the same time (i.e., strain) (see Chapter 1; Lavee, 2013).

From a systems perspective, parental stress also must be viewed in terms of *reciprocal* or even *multidirectional* processes (Kuczynski & De Mol, 2015). Stress experienced by parents is both a *product* of connections with others (e.g., relationships with coworkers or with a person's spouse/partner) and an *activator* of parental behavior and other responses that have consequences for other family members such as children and youth (Deater-Deckard, 2004; Deater-Deckard et al., 2005). Children themselves are another primary source of parental stress that shapes the responses of parents to the young in a cyclical and bidirectional manner (Bush & Peterson, 2013). For example, Matt's high level of maturity, respect, and love that he displays within the family allows Tiffany to trust him to provide social support in the form of watching his siblings. Moreover, this trust leads to Tiffany's willingness to grant him more responsibility and privileges, including the use of the family car. Parental stress is a product of mothers' and fathers' circumstances based on their bidirectional connections with children and with other individuals, both inside and beyond family boundaries. Such system-based conditions include sudden job loss, severe spousal conflict, parental divorce or remarriage, disengagement from families, or intrusions by extended family members to name just a few (Gerard, Krishnakumar, & Buehler, 2008; Peterson & Bush, 2015).

As a "systemic activator," in turn, parental stress operates within parent–child relationships by fostering changes in parents' socializing behavior, sometimes leading to dysfunctional parenting (Baker et al., 2003; Crnic & Low, 2002; Deater-Deckard et al., 2005; Deater-Deckard, 2004). Stressful responses by parents may then have consequences for the social, emotional, and cognitive development of children (Buehler & Gerard, 2002; Bush & Peterson, 2008; Cappa, Begle, Conger, Dumas, Conger, 2011; Gerard et al., 2008; Jones, Rowe, & Becker, 2009). For example, highly stressed compared to less stressed parents are more inclined to be anxious, emotionally reactive, preoccupied with adult-centered goals, less inclined to maintain effective child rearing, and less likely to supervise their young. Thus, parental stress tends to *spill over* systemically into parent–child relationships by contributing to parental behaviors that are less responsive and affectionate as well as being more neglectful, punitive (authoritarian) and even abusive toward children (Buehler & Gerard, 2002; Bush & Peterson, 2008; Gerard et al., 2008). For example, Tiffany reports feeling very stressed with financial obligations toward the end of the month. During these times, she is more focused on providing food for her family and ensuring their rent is paid instead of being patient and affectionate toward her children. Declines in quality parenting may lead to negative outcomes in the young such as noncompliance, less effective social skills, problems with peer adjustment, feelings of rejection, lowered self-esteem, aggressive behavior, social withdrawal, and distressed psychological experiences (Bush & Peterson, 2013; Crnic et al., 2005; Crnic & Low, 2002; Deater-Deckard, 2004; Deater-Deckard et al., 2005; Gerard et al., 2008). In contrast, parents who have lower stress and perceive positive changes within the family system tend to be responsive, warm, rational, and use moderate control (e.g., firm control, reasoning, consistent rule enforcement, and monitoring rather than more punitive or intrusive forms of control) with children (Bush & Peterson, 2013; Crnic et al., 2005; Deater-Deckard, 2004; Deater-Deckard et al., 2005; Gerard et al., 2008; Shumow & Lomax, 2002). Child outcomes associated with positive parental behaviors include high self-esteem, effective school achievement, competent social skills, effective peer adjustment, as well as a balance between conforming to parents and making progress toward autonomy. All of these child and adolescent qualities are key aspects of social competence, or what a variety of cultures often view as adaptive attributes of the young (Bush & Peterson, 2013; Peterson & Bush, 2015).

The systemic *connections* between parental stress and child characteristics are not limited to circumstances where social influence is viewed as flowing only from parent to child. Instead, children and their perceived attributes have considerable influence on the stress experienced by parents (Bush & Peterson, 2013; Cappa et al., 2011; Deater-Deckard, 2004; Gerard et al., 2008). The existing literature generally supports the family systems hypothesis that relationships, such as those between parents and children, are extensively interdependent (Kuczynski & De Mol, 2015). Moreover, parents who report greater intimacy and communication in their marriages tend to be less stressed as well as more responsive, affectionate, and moderately controlling with children (Bush & Peterson, 2013; Gerard et al., 2008; Stone, Buehler, & Barber, 2002). Clearly, the parent–child relationship is systemic in nature by having reciprocal or multidirectional qualities, with parental stress being both a "product" and an "activator" of changes within the family system (Deater-Deckard, 2004; Kuczynski, & De Mol, 2015).

STRESSORS OR STRESSOR EVENTS FOR PARENTS: FACTOR A

Stressors or stressor events (the A factor) consist of occurrences that may be of sufficient magnitude to bring about changes within the larger family system, the parent–child subsystem and feelings of tension for parents. However, because many stressful circumstances for parents do not occur as discrete events, the general term *stressor* is preferred because parents may be dealing with circumstances that develop gradually over an extended period. Moreover, multiple stressors can accumulate to an extent that several stressors combine to determine the overall level of parental stress (see Chapter 1; McCubbin & Patterson, 1986).

Although a stressor has the *potential* to evoke systemic change and psychological responses, the occurrences that impinge on parent–child relationships are not equivalent to the onset of stress. Instead, stressors threaten the status quo of families and parent–child relationships, but they are *not solely capable* of fostering stress by imposing demands on individuals (e.g., parents) and relationships. By themselves, stressors (a) do not have all the necessary ingredients (i.e., the B factor, *resources,* and the C factor, *definitions*) for parental stress, (b) have no inherent positive or negative qualities, and (c) may never immobilize the parent–child relationship and bring about individual stress by parents. Instead, stressors are neutral phenomena involving pressures that range from developing quickly to unfolding over long periods. Rather than always being sudden aversive disruptions, many stressors are of moderate strength and accumulate as demanding circumstances in the form of "stressor pile up" over time (Buehler & Gerard, 2013; McCubbin & Patterson, 1986; Patterson, 2002).

Despite the fact that stressors have no inherent meaning, scholars have developed classification systems to identify common ways that parents and families tend to define and respond to them (see Chapter 1). A number of stressors often receive fairly common individual definitions that provide a rationale for classification that approximately captures their common qualities. Most of these classification systems include three common categories: normative stressors, nonnormative stressors, and chronic stressors. Because specific stressors can sometimes fit within more than one of these categories, any such classification system inherently has imperfections and often fail to be mutually exclusive in the purist sense.

Normative Stressors

Normative stressors are part of everyday life (i.e., daily hassles) or are longer-term developmental transitions that occur normally during the family life course (see Chapter 1).

Daily Hassles

Parents' daily hassles include constant caregiving demands and pressures from everyday tasks involved in caring for and socializing children (see Helms, Hengstebeck, & Demo, Chapter 2, this volume). Many everyday child-rearing experiences are sources of self-defined competence and satisfaction for parents as they engage in playful activities with children, solve parent–child challenges, and enjoy the developmental progress of their young (Bush & Peterson, 2008, 2013; Peterson & Bush, 2015; Shumow & Lomax, 2002). In contrast, other parenting experiences are less positive, such as when Tiffany reports dealing with her children's whining, their annoying conduct due to underdeveloped self-control, endless cleaning-up activities, loss of sleep, toilet training, constant interruptions, lack of personal time, and seemingly endless errands. Some hassles are infrequent and situational, whereas others occur repeatedly as part of everyday life (Crnic et al., 2005; Crnic & Low, 2002; Kalil, Dunifon, Crosby, & Houston Su, 2014). By itself, each hassle may have limited consequences, but the cumulative impact of daily hassles may result in substantial amounts of parental stress (Almeida, 2005; Hennon et al., 2009; Sepa, Frodi, & Ludvigsson, 2004).

Single-parent families may be particularly prone to stress resulting from daily hassles and stressor accumulation because adult partners are not available to share the everyday tasks of child rearing and to buffer the challenges of change and stress. For example, although Tiffany's ex-husband pays child support, he is not involved with the children regularly and thus not available to share in everyday tasks. The daily hassles that single parents face may be complicated by economic disadvantage, employment demands, and minimal social support to which many of these parents must adjust, which may accumulate and lead to feelings of isolation, exhaustion, depression, distress, and a lack of parental efficacy (Kremer-Sadlik & Paugh, 2007; Ontai, Sano, Hatton, & Conger, 2008; see Chapter 2). Although many single parents provide positive environments for their children, many daily hassles or accumulated stressors can occur repeatedly because of unrelenting demands that structure their circumstances. Consequently, the cumulative nature of daily hassles faced by parents may push parent–child relationships gradually into problematic directions over time (Ontai et al., 2008). When daily hassles occur with regularity, parents who once were satisfied and dealt with their circumstances competently may gradually become increasingly fatigued, dysfunctional, and experience growing stress (Dunning & Giallo, 2012). These evolving circular processes eventually may produce less competent, unresponsive, and less satisfied parents, along with children who further elicit such responses by becoming more aggressive and acting out (Crnic et al., 2005; Crnic & Low, 2002).

Developmental Transitions

Other sources of normative stress are the developmental transitions of the young, the social meanings associated with these changes, and the resulting need for modifications within parent–child relationships. Developmental transitions have the potential to result in stressors that accumulate and can be perceived collectively as disruptive change, psychological distress, or as a growing sense of competence.

One of these pivotal times of change and possible stress occurs in the earliest phase of the parent–child relationship referred to as the transition to parenthood. Newborns require almost constant care through feeding, cleaning, changing, and dealing with an infant's sleeping patterns. A persistent responsibility of parents is to be vigilant about their infant's health through both preventative measures and arranging treatment for problematic health issues (Medina, Lederhos, & Lillis, 2009). Parents who cope effectively with these increased demands are more adept at soothing newborns when they cry and providing other forms of sensitive responsiveness that often contribute to the establishment of secure parent-child attachment. Sensitive responsiveness involves managing stress so that parenting is attentive and empathic and reads the infant's cues accurately. Sensitive parents also establish a balance that avoids high intrusiveness and practices emotional availability (Solomon & George, 2008).

The birth of an infant means that the routine patterns of parents must change substantially overnight and become concentrated on the newborn. Sleep disturbances are experienced by parents because newborns often wake up every few hours for feeding. Because new mothers may leave the workplace, families with newborns often sustain decreases in income, which may increase the stress of fathers as they take second jobs or work more hours to supplement family resources (Medina et al., 2009). The decreased time and energy experienced by marital partners often result in decreased marital satisfaction, less mutual expressions of love, and greater conflict between spouses (Lawrence, Rothman, Cobb, Rothman, & Bradbury, 2008). How parents manage these potential sources of stress involves a variety of factors, with perhaps the most important accomplishments being the maintenance of positive marital relationships and successful coparenting (or establishing a parental alliance). Current research indicates that maintenance of high-quality marital relationships is predictive of effective coparenting, or the extent to which parents work together in performing child care and child socialization roles (Bouchard, 2014). Working together involves agreeing to provide support, resolve child-rearing disagreements, divide duties, and manage interaction patterns. Coparenting provides mutual social support and helps to reduce stress while increasing the likelihood that parents will respond to infants with sensitivity (Feinberg, 2002; Schoppe-Sullivan & Mangelsdorf, 2013). Coparenting is not only supportive of infants but is also associated with greater couple satisfaction and diminished parental stress (McHale & Lindahl, 2011).

Another example of a developmental transition is during the adolescent years, when stress may be experienced by parents during the process of granting increased autonomy to their young as the parent–child relationship changes in accordance with the teens' development (Collins & Steinberg, 2006; Kagitcibasi, 2013). Most parents in the United States who grant autonomy in a normative fashion often engage in a gradual process of allowing adolescents greater self-determination as relationship rules about power and control are renegotiated (Bush & Peterson 2008; Collins & Steinberg, 2006; Kagitcibasi, 2013; Peterson & Bush, 2015). This process of "letting go" in Western, individualistic cultures is not a sudden transfer of authority to the young. Instead, competent parents and their developing teenagers engage in renegotiation processes that are necessary, mutual, originate in childhood, accelerate during adolescence, and continue until the eventual transition to adulthood is accomplished (Collins & Steinberg, 2006; Kagitcibasi, 2013;

Peterson & Bush, 2013). This letting-go process presents many potential stressors, especially when parents are reluctant to grant their children autonomy. Some parents have difficulty accommodating to these changes and resist the need to gradually conclude their roles as authority figures for dependent children. This effort to delay youthful autonomy may erupt into heightened conflict and stress between adolescents and parents (Bush & Peterson, 2008; Collins & Steinberg, 2006; Peterson & Bush, 2015). Consequently, an adolescent's desire for autonomy may involve feelings of distress and separation anxiety by parents who resist this loss of control (Collins & Steinberg, 2006). At least moderate levels of parent–adolescent conflict and parental distress may be a normative energizer of developmental change for the letting-go process as relationship rules are renegotiated. In contrast, conflict between parents and adolescents that escalates to very high levels may be associated with problematic emotional distance, unmanaged conflict, and greater stress for parents during a malfunctioning autonomy-granting process (Collins & Steinberg, 2006; Peterson & Bush, 2015; Shumow & Lomax, 2002). Many families experience multiple developmental transitions simultaneously, for example, when Tiffany gave birth to Pamela, she was also going through the transition to adolescence with Matt.

Nonnormative Stressors

Parents also face stressor events that are nonnormative in the sense that they are unpredictable occurrences that are substantially disruptive to the everyday pattern of parent–child relationships (see Chapter 1). Nonnormative stressor events are often sudden, dramatic occurrences that have considerable potential to disrupt the lives of parents. Most often, these stressors are products of unique situations that are unlikely to be repeated. Examples include a natural disaster (e.g., Tiffany's flood), the sudden death of a child, a severe injury to a family member, an unexpected job promotion, and winning the state lottery. All are unexpected circumstances and have the potential to evoke substantial disruptions for parents in the daily rhythms of parent–child and family relationships. Moreover, the disrupted family relationships and structural changes evoked by these occurrences have the potential to increase the psychological stress of parents (see Chapter 1). These events, however, are not inherently stressful in exactly the same way for all parents; rather, such stressors vary in their disruptive qualities depending on the parents' subjective interpretations and their available resources (or vulnerabilities). Types of nonnormative stressors consist of off-time developments (e.g., premarital pregnancies, delayed developmental milestones in children), the diagnosis of unexpected conditions, and the sudden awareness of changes (e.g., childhood leukemia, being suddenly laid off from work).

Off-Time Developments

People generally anticipate that certain circumstances, such as retirement, the death of an elderly family member, and the advent of grandparenthood, will occur as part of normal family transitions at expected times of the life course (Boss, 2002; Carter & McGoldrick, 1999; Hennon et al., 2009; Hennon & Peterson, 2007). However, when seemingly normal events occur at unanticipated times, they can become sources of disruptive distress for parents. For example, during the school-age years of children, the death of a parent or the death of a child is an off-time event and often is very traumatic for surviving family members (Murray, Toth, Larsen, & Moulton, 2010). In similar fashion, parents often experience considerable upheaval when learning about their teenage daughter's pregnancy and the need to become grandparents much earlier than originally anticipated. By confronting families with sudden demands, such off-time, unanticipated events can disrupt family functioning and affect the stress and subjective experiences of parents (Devereux, Weigel, Ballard-Reisch, Leigh, & Cahoon, 2009; Huang, Costeines, Kaufman, & Ayala, 2014).

Initial Awareness or Diagnosis

Another type of nonnormative stressor for parents may result from acute situations involving the initial awareness or diagnosis of unexpected circumstances and deviant or abnormal child characteristics. Examples include initial awareness or diagnosis of delinquency, conduct disorders, attention deficit behavior, autism, physical illness, poor mental health, and birth defects (Ambert, 1997; Baker et al., 2003; Ben-Sasson, Soto, Martínez-Pedraza, & Carter 2013; Hennon & Peterson, 2007; Lambek et al., 2014; Ryan, Miller-Loessi, & Nieri, 2007). The initial diagnosis that Pamela has Autism, for example, was defined by Tiffany as an acute stressor that disrupted her life and the lives of her family members (i.e., her children as well as her aunt and other extended family members who contribute to the family's well-being). Likewise, parents have greater tendencies to experience acute stress or crisis when their son phones home from jail stating that he has been arrested for shoplifting. When parents are initially confronted with their child's delinquency, they often experience distress, worry, edginess, and feelings of devastation (Ambert, 1997, 1999; Caldwell, Horne, Davidson, & Quinn, 2007; Gavazzi, 2011). Parents' subsequent experience with severe, nonnormative stressors may be converted gradually into chronic stressors (see below), perhaps of more moderate strength, as the parents become more accustomed (or adapted) to these challenges.

Chronic Stressors

Chronic stressors are atypical circumstances that may be initiated by either the characteristics of children and youth or by other circumstances in the social environment. Stressors that are chronic occur over extended periods, are difficult to amend, and can accumulate over time.

Chronic Stressors From the Social Environment

As just indicated, some of these continuing stressors result from aspects of the social environment such as parental roles that may compete with child socialization and child care as well as from socioeconomic circumstances faced by families. Chronic stressors from the social environment such as work roles, poverty, immigration to a new culture, and marital conflict may have stressful effects, both for parents and their young.

Included among such stressors are parents' daily employment demands that compete with parenting at a level beyond the norm, including long work hours, shift work, and unusually dangerous or stressful jobs (e.g., police work or combat military personnel) that contribute to parental stress and spillover into the parent–child relationship (Barnett, Garreis, & Brennan, 2008; Bianchi & Milkie, 2010; Haines, Marchand, & Harvey, 2006). Another source of chronic stress for parents from ethnic-minority families, *generational dissonance,* results from differential rates of immigrant acculturation as the younger generation accepts the new culture more rapidly than their parents (Berry, Phinney, David, Sam, Vedder, & 2005; Gonzales, Fabrett, & Knight, 2009). Difficulties often arise when the cultural changes practiced by the younger generation prompt parents to begin viewing their youthful children as betraying their culture of origin. An unfortunate result is that accelerated levels of acculturative stress and parent–adolescent conflict may lead to greater distance between the generations (Berry et al., 2005).

Both persistent family poverty and prolonged marital conflict also can foster chronic stress that leads to consequences for the parent–child relationship. Both of these continuing problems can function as chronic stressors that spill over into the parent–child relationship and increase parental stress as well as have detrimental consequences for the social psychological outcomes of children and youth (Buehler, Benson, & Gerard, 2006; Gerard et al., 2008; Scarmella, Neppl, Ontai, & Conger, 2008; Stone et al., 2002).

Chronic Stressors: Child Effects

Other sources of chronic stress, specific child characteristics, are often identified as contributing to the stressful experience of parents (Ambert, 1997). This is particularly true where the shock of an initial diagnosis or recognition has passed and the realities of the long-term challenges faced by parents have set in. This conception, commonly referred to as *child effects,* underscores the impact of children's health, physical handicaps, and well-being on the social-emotional lives of parents (Ambert, 1997; Bush & Peterson, 2013; Moreland & Dumas, 2007). For example, children who have congenital birth defects, physical discrepancies, long-term illnesses, problematic behavior patterns (e.g., aggressiveness and disruptive behavior), social-emotional problems, attention-deficit/hyperactivity disorder (ADHD), autism, or schizophrenia, can bring about stressful circumstances for parents (Ambert, 1997; Baker et al., 2003; Beernink, Swinkels, Van der Gaag, & Buitelaar, 2012; Deater-Deckard, 2004; Hastings, 2002; Silva & Schalock, 2012; Singer, Ethridge, & Aldana, 2007). These circumstances can exert highly negative influences, even throughout the parents' later years of life. Accumulating stressors associated with these child effects include such things as treatment costs, social stigma, demanding supervision requirements, distrust of the young, and the constant need to provide care. These difficult circumstances create considerable potential for parents to experience stress, anger, embarrassment, guilt, despair, and a diminished sense of parental efficacy (Ambert, 1997, 1999; Caldwell et al., 2007; Singer et al., 2007).

PARENTS' RECOVERY FACTORS: RESOURCES, COPING, AND ADAPTATION: FACTOR B

The level of disruptive change within parent–child relationships, the psychological experience of parents, and the length of stress or crisis may partially be determined by Factor B's recovery factors, referred to as *parental resources*, *coping*, and *adaptation*. Parental resources are the *potential* strengths of mothers, fathers, and families that may be drawn upon as the possible basis for progress toward renewal. In contrast, parental coping involves actually *taking direct actions* (e.g., acquiring resources, learning new skills, and asking for assistance), *altering one's interpretations* (e.g., reframing circumstances), and *managing one's emotions* (e.g., positively through social support or negatively through substance abuse). Finally, *adaptation* refers to the ability of parents and other family members to recover from stress and crisis and establish a new level of functioning.

Parental Resources

The first aspect of the B factor, parental resources, identifies *potential* factors that may contribute to pressures for change and foster distress as well as potential sources of recovery (Boss, 2002; Hennon et al., 2007, 2009; Hill, 1949; Patterson, 2002). *Positive resources* are the traits, qualities, characteristics, and abilities of parents, parent–child relationships, family systems, and the larger social context that may possibly be brought to bear on the demands of stressors. These characteristics of individuals or the social context have the potential or *latent* capability of buffering stress by decreasing the negative effects of stressors. The concept of resources also includes *negative resources,* or the potential or latent vulnerabilities of parents and parent–child relationships to stressors and crisis events. Resources at individual and relationship levels have the possibility or latent capacity to accentuate stress by increasing the negative effects of stressors (McCubbin & Patterson, 1986; Patterson, 2002).

A distinguishing characteristic of resources (both positive and negative) is their *potential* rather than *actual* nature (Hennon et al., 2007; McCubbin & Patterson, 1986; Patterson, 2002). This is illustrated by the observation that parents with seemingly equivalent resources often vary in the extent to which they are capable of implementing these reserves within the parent–child relationship. Variability in resource accessibility underscores the idea that resources are simply capacities that are only possibly available but may or may not be *actualized,* or placed into action, for particular circumstances. Resources are often classified based on their origins, such as within the person, within the familial environment, or from other social contexts.

Personal Resources of Parents

The individual or personal resources of parents include economic well-being, knowledge (e.g., of child development), interpersonal skills, and physical health. Other personal resources are those that define positive or negative mental health and tendencies toward psychopathology (e.g., depression). Illustrative of individual resources are psychological and emotional qualities that are components of parents' competence or incompetence as they socialize and care for children. Parental competence, a complex array of individual resources (among other resources), is composed of such qualities as psychological maturity, empathy, warmth, secure self-image, parental self-efficacy, parental satisfaction, capacity to express affection, and ability to exercise firm control (Bush & Peterson, 2008, 2013; Katsikitis, Bignell, Rooskov, Elms, & Davidson, 2013; Liu, Chen, Yeh, & Hsieh, 2012;

Peterson & Bush, 2013, 2015; Purssell & White, 2013; Shumow & Lomax, 2002). Such personal competencies function as potential resources that may empower parents to marshal their resources and manage stressful circumstances.

The inverse personal qualities, or negative resources, also apply to the psychological experiences of parents. Adults who have psychological or emotional problems, such as extensive depression, anger, and anxiety, often have the potential for personal issues to become manifest within the parent–child relationship and increase vulnerability to the consequences of parenting stress. Parents who are self-preoccupied, depressed, highly anxious, distant, hostile, or abusers of substances are less capable of dealing effectively with stressors or crisis events (Delvecchio et al., 2014; Gavazzi, 2011; Hanington, Heron, Stein, & Ramchandani, 2012; Holden, 2015). They are also less likely to demonstrate the necessary patience, sensitivity, and responsiveness to raise children effectively (Bush & Peterson, 2008; Crnic et al., 2005; Deater-Deckard, 2004).

Familial and Social Resources

Parents also draw on resources and experience vulnerabilities that are situated both within the family system and the larger social-ecological context (Hennon et al., 2009; Hennon & Peterson, 2007). Concerning the larger social-ecological context, parental efficacy (or a sense of being confident as a parent) may be influenced by the quality of neighborhoods that encompass families. These immediate social environments can provide either the capacities for social support or offer potentially dangerous environments that diminish parental competence and increase parental stress (Henry, Merten, Plunkett, & Sands, 2008; Ontai et al., 2008; Shumow & Lomax, 2002). The potential to acquire assistance or social support from social networks has been associated with a variety of positive mental health outcomes for parents, including lower psychological distress (McHale et al., 2002) and better capacity to deal with stressful events (Henry et al., 2008; Shumow & Lomax, 2002). Supportive partners, extended kin, friends, church members, and neighbors all have the potential to assist parents in dealing with stressors and crises by providing advice, emotional support, material assistance, and encouragement. Potential for this kind of assistance leads to the belief that there is someone for parents to turn to when stressors arise, which, in turn, fosters feelings of being valued and a sense of security (Hennon et al., 2007).

Scholars differ in the types of social support they identify, but most distinguish between capacities to provide *emotional support,* or behavior that communicates caring, and *instrumental support,* or concrete assistance that reduces parents' tasks and responsibilities (Hennon et al., 2008, 2009). Although conceptualized as separate phenomena for the purposes of clarification, emotional and instrumental support are not always mutually exclusive. Indeed, the two types of support often overlap, as when Tiffany's aunt quickly cancels her cherished plans to play golf with her friends to assist Tiffany and her children. Her niece needs her help to babysit Pamela and Joey because she needs to deal with emergency circumstances at her workplace, and Joey is at a school event. The child care she provides is instrumental support, while this aunt's selfless actions to postpone her golf plans on short notice may also provide emotional support to her niece.

The parents' marital relationship is a critical, immediate aspect of the social network that is a potential source of support and may function to increase or decrease the vulnerability of parents (Boss, 2002; Crnic et al., 2005; Crnic & Low, 2002; Gerard et al., 2008; Ontai et al., 2008). Scholars have frequently concluded that, in the majority of circumstances, the role of potential social support beyond family boundaries is of secondary importance to the role of marital relationships. A key feature of marital relationships that may prevent stress is the extent to which parents have the potential to support each other (usually studied as fathers supporting or not supporting mothers) (Lamb, 2013). Research indicates that maternal stress is reduced when a spouse is valued for their potential to use humor for smoothing over difficult moments and for listening to the partner's frustrations. Parental stress also is reduced when marital satisfaction is high, marital conflict is low, and spouses are willing to share housework/child care responsibilities. The importance of husbands providing support to wives cannot be overstated, as recent evidence indicates that mothers continue to have more responsibility, more involvement, and experience greater parental stress from parenting (Crnic et al., 2005; Hennon et al., 2007; Lamb, 2013). Marriages characterized by a lack of shared caregiving, low support from fathers, marital dissatisfaction, marital hostility, and high marital conflict function as negative resources that add to parental stress (Deater-Deckard et al., 2005; Gerard et al., 2008; Grych, Oxtoby, & Lynn, 2013; Stone et al., 2002).

Social support from outside the family also has the potential to ameliorate parental depression and increase coping abilities during times of stress (Hennon et al., 2008; Lamb, 2013). Support from outside family boundaries becomes especially important when parents are not married, the involvement of partners in caregiving is inadequate, or alternative significant others (e.g., older siblings) are not available (Ontai et al., 2008). Moreover, social support has the potential to affect the quality of parenting indirectly by enhancing, maintaining, or impairing the emotional well-being of mothers and fathers (Lamb, 2013). Support that reduces parental distress assists parents to be more nurturant and rational and to use more moderate forms of control, while avoiding harsh or rejecting forms of discipline (Crnic et al., 2005; Deater-Deckard, 2004).

Consistent with conceptions of resources and vulnerabilities, an important idea is that social networks are not always supportive and may instead accentuate parental stress. For example, Tiffany's mother is good at providing instrumental support in emergencies (e.g., picking up the children, helping out with bills between pay days). In contrast, her mother was not in favor of divorce and tended to take the side of Tiffany's ex-husband concerning issues about their coparenting relationship. Because Tiffany can't rely on her mother for consistent emotional support or advice and feels that her mother just wants her to return to her ex-husband, things had often become stressful when her mother was involved. This idea also is illustrated by the stress, conflict, frustration, and disappointment that families of unmarried teenage mothers may demonstrate (Devereux et al., 2009; Huang et al., 2014). The social support conveyed by parents and extended kin may potentially be judgmental and restrictive to an extent that the stress of new parents is increased. For teenage mothers, effective social support involves the potential to provide assistance while also maintaining the inclination to foster autonomy that acknowledges the young parent's viewpoints, accepts the teen's feelings, and refrains from excessive control over the young person's activities (Devereux et al., 2009; Huang et al., 2014). Such an approach may have the potential to reduce stress, provide assistance for the daily demands of parenting, and encourage the long-term psychosocial maturity of youthful parents.

Parental Coping

From a family stress and crisis perspective, coping goes beyond being a potential resource by referring to how parents manage, endure, and recover from stressors (Patterson, 2002). Instead of being a potential ability, the process of coping involves actively seeking to maintain the status quo or to achieve new levels of family organization. Coping by parents involves *making actual responses to or redefining* the circumstances at hand (Jones et al., 2009). Specific coping strategies are not inherently adaptive or maladaptive but are useful to a degree that depends on the precise nature of the circumstances at hand (Hennon et al., 2009; Patterson, 2002).

The process of coping that involves using available resources and the parents' perceptions are conceptually distinct phenomena but often are indistinguishable in many circumstances. The types of coping responses that parents use can vary with the specific stressor or crisis (Hennon et al., 2007, 2008). For example, for parents and families who face serious financial stress that can add to child-rearing distress, parents who sustain positive self-evaluations, beliefs of mastery, and abilities to take charge of financial difficulties are better prepared to avoid the accumulation of stress from economic stressors. Coping strategies for chronic economic problems include financial problem solving, receiving social support (e.g., from a relative or financial counselor), acceptance of the situation, positive thinking, finding supplemental employment, and seeking distractions at select times to diminish the accumulation of parental stress (Morse, Rojahn, & Smith, 2014)

Several additional strategies for coping with parental stress can be found in the literature on parent–child relationships, such as cognitive coping. Cognitive strategies include passive approaches like denial or avoidance, as well as active approaches involving positive reappraisal and problem-focused strategies (Crnic et al., 2005; Crnic & Low, 2002). Parents who face economic problems or children with mental health issues can cope (i.e., reduce their stress) through positive reframing, problem solving, communication, affective responsiveness, and behavioral control (Morse et al., 2014). These active coping strategies are more successful in reducing stress and restoring constructive parental behaviors than are passive cognitions involving a fatalistic acceptance of one's circumstances. Other coping strategies involve drawing on or orchestrating resources from the social environment, perhaps in the form of parent education, to learn more about high-quality parenting, child development, and how stress can be managed (Hennon et al., 2007; Hennon, Radina, & Wilson, 2013; Moran & Ghate, 2005).

Parents are more likely to become less stressed when they can become more capable of practicing better parenting through the actual use of social support that is available. Moreover, exposure to parent education that provides knowledge of child development, realistic expectations for the young, and the development of quality parenting skills can provide effective coping. Subsequently, these parents are likely to be more capable of accessing resources, managing their responses, and developing the necessary social support networks to buffer stress levels and maintain quality parenting (Hennon et al., 2007). Critical attributes for parental coping are the willingness and ability to take advantage of potential parenting resources and available social support (Hennon et al., 2013; Moran & Ghate, 2005). For example, a single mother who is struggling to supervise a delinquent teenage son might gain assistance from her social network of parents, siblings, neighborhood friends, local social service agencies, and family life educators. Similarly, Tiffany is fortunate to have the social and instrumental support from her aunt, who not only provides emotional support and direct assistance through child care but also helps Tiffany to connect to community resources (e.g., parental groups and agencies that specialize in autism). However, failure to actually use potential resources may occur if parents' feelings of pride, embarrassment, personal responsibility, or exhaustion prevent the use of these supports.

Parental Adaptation

Another family stress recovery factor is *adaptation,* or the ability of parents and other family members to recover from stress and crisis. Recovery in the family system and parent–child relationships may occur either through the elimination of disruptions in relationships and a return to preexisting patterns or by moving to new levels of relationship organization and stability (Hill, 1949; McCubbin & Patterson, 1986).

A prominent example of parental adaptation research is the work on the experiences of parents following marital separation or divorce (Braver & Lamb, 2013; Demo & Buehler, 2013; Hetherington & Stanley-Hagan, 2002). Stress is a common result in custodial mothers' lives when role transitions are forced on them as ex-marital partners withdraw and become less involved in parental roles. Subsequently, many custodial mothers shoulder new responsibilities as providers, must build new support networks, and incorporate aspects of the father's role into their parenting repertoires. Such changes often occur under difficult economic circumstances that contribute to psychological problems such as distress, anxiety, and depression. Subsequently, these negative mental health conditions place mothers at risk for declines in the quality of their performance as parents. During early phases of separation and divorce, custodial mothers who experience increased irritability and stress often become (a) less capable of monitoring children, (b) more permissive in their parenting, (c) more punitive in their parenting, and (d) more inclined to engage in coercive exchanges with children. Fortunately, in the majority of cases, the stressful circumstances for these mothers subside over time as they engage in active coping efforts (Hetherington & Stanley-Hagan, 2002). The most frequent outcome of a divorce initiated stressor or crisis, therefore, is that parents eventually begin to define their situation as manageable, actively cope and manage stress, and restore the quality of their child-rearing behavior approximately 1 to 2 years following the onset of the divorce stressor (Braver & Lamb, 2013; Demo & Buehler, 2013; Hetherington & Stanley-Hagan, 2002).

PARENTAL DEFINITIONS: FACTOR C

As noted earlier, events or phenomena by themselves do not create the experience of stress or crisis. Instead, parents and other family members impose subjective definitions on their circumstances that involve personal cognitive appraisals. These definitions are shaped, in part, by varied cultural scripts for parenting that are prevalent within different cultures and ethnic groups (Hawk & Holden, 2006; Holden & Hawk, 2003; Jones et al., 2009; Marsiglio & Roy, 2013; Peterson & Bush, 2013). Consequently, the meanings that individuals and families attribute to phenomena (the C factor) help to determine whether they experience stressor or crisis events as positive, negative, or neutral definitions (Boss, 2002; McCubbin & Patterson, 1986; see Chapter 1).

Although the appraisals of each person or family are at least somewhat unique, a typology of these appraisals has been developed from the approximate patterns identified in these conceptions (Hennon et al., 2009). *Benign* appraisals, for example, signify that a stressor situation is not hazardous, whereas *challenges* are demanding appraisals that are viewed as being likely to be handled appropriately, though with some difficulty. Appraisals classified as *threatening,* in turn, are circumstances believed to have the potential to cause considerable harm or loss to the family, though such outcomes have not yet happened (e.g., growing financial difficulties that may lead to bankruptcy or a child's first signs of disruptive behavior in school). If managed appropriately, however, a threatening form of appraisal can be avoided, whereas, if the threatening definition cannot be dealt with effectively, harm can result for a family or parent–child relationship. Finally, a fourth category, *harm/loss,* represents situations appraised as having already resulted in damage within the family system (e.g., a child's health has been compromised severely, a teenage son's delinquent behavior results in incarceration).

The overall significance of appraisal categories is that virtually identical events may evoke varied responses from different parents and other family members. Subjective appraisals of similar circumstances either increase or decrease parental stress associated with changes and challenging events through such diverse feelings as hopelessness, denial of reality, or acceptance in the face of unpredictable circumstances (Boss, 2002; Jones et al., 2009; Marsiglio & Roy, 2013; McCubbin & Patterson, 1986). Variability in definitions or appraisals leading to disparate stress levels is rooted in many sources, including differences in previous life experiences, diversity in ethnic, cultural, and/or religous background and values, variations in family traditions, and a person's available resources (Boss, 2002).

These ideas from family stress theory are reinforced by research findings concerning the subjective experiences of parents. Of special importance are findings indicating that parental beliefs, values, attitudes, expectations, and "developmental scenarios" provide meaning for parents' relationships with their children and help to determine how they will respond to the young. Specifically, parents make attributions about their children's moods, motives, intentions, responsibilities, and competencies that shape the parents' emotional responses (e.g., positive stress or distress) as well as their subsequent child-rearing approaches (Bush & Peterson, 2013; Marsiglio & Roy, 2013; Peterson & Bush, 2013). Parents tend to hold their children accountable for negative behavior when they believe that children intend to misbehave and could choose to exercise self-control. Parents who make such attributions are more likely to be distressed and to use punitive behavior with their children, partly because they perceive children as being able to "know better." In contrast, parents who view younger children (e.g., infants and toddlers) as being immature, not yet fully competent, or lacking intention or responsibility for their actions are more inclined toward positive feelings and less inclined to experience stress that can, in turn, lead to punitive and rejecting behavior. Diminished parental stress, in turn, often translates into the expression of greater nurturance and moderate forms of control such as reasoning, monitoring, and consistent rule enforcement. Consequently, awareness of parental beliefs and subjective definitions are critical for understanding the varied intensity of both parental distress and more positive feelings as factors that influence how parents respond to their children (Deater-Deckard, 2004, Deater-Deckard et al., 2005; Peterson & Bush, 2013).

A closely related means of conceptualizing how subjective interpretations lead to parenting stress is the degree to which parents view their children's characteristics as deviating from broadly accepted standards about what is normality within a specific culture or ethnic group (Goodnow, 2005; Jones et al., 2009; Richman & Mandara, 2013). Parents can define their children as deviating from their expectations in either positive or negative directions, with greater deviations from accepted norms possibly leading to greater distress or satisfaction by parents (Goodnow, 2005; Jones et al., 2009; Richman & Mandara, 2013). The most frequent parental responses to perceived negative deviations (e.g., aggressive or conduct disorder behavior) are (a) adverse subjective experiences (e.g., psychological distress) and (b) communication of parent's negative feelings to children (e.g., through punitive, withdrawn, or rejecting behavior). In contrast, some parents may experience satisfaction or positive feelings (positive stress) regarding specific developmental changes (e.g., successful school achievement), which is viewed as affirming both their own sense of competence and their interpretations of what is viewed as youthful competence (Peterson & Bush, 2013, 2015). Common responses to positive interpretations include parental supportive behavior and moderate control strategies, such as the use of reasoning and rule-based supervision. The specific responses of parents to children tend to be shaped not simply by children's actual characteristics but also by the parents' subjective attributions and expectations, which may or may not reflect objective standards (Goodnow, 2005).

CONCLUSION

As proposed in this chapter, the scholarship on parental stress can be conceptualized in terms of general constructs from family stress theory that can add to our understanding of both the individual and relationship levels of family systems. When faced with demanding situations, parental stress or crisis is a complex product of several factors: (a) the nature of the stressor or crisis event; (b) the potential recovery factors in the form of resources, coping styles, and adaptive abilities available to parents; and (c) the subjective definitions or appraisals that parents assign to the stressor events. These separate ideas are actually extensively interrelated in ways that make them virtually indistinguishable as they function together in real time.

The application of family stress concepts to the research on parental stress helps bring greater understanding to a wide range of circumstances, varying from highly disruptive (nonnormative) crises to chronic stress and more normative challenges. A major contribution of family stress theory is the insight it provides into how parental stress applies to both the individual and relationship/systemic levels of families. Although parental stress is virtually a universal phenomenon, parents' experiences of stress varies widely in intensity. Applying family stress theory concepts to the scholarship on parental stress helps to show more clearly (a) how parental stress is such a universal experience, (b) why the intensity of parental stress and family system stress varies across parents and parent–child relationships, (c) how parents and families cope with and adapt to stress differently, and (d) how individual parenting stress and systemic stress influences parents' child-rearing performances and the psychosocial well-being of the young. Parental stress can function to disrupt, inhibit, or energize mothers and fathers, depending on numerous individual and social-environmental factors.

REFERENCES

Almeida, D. M. (2005). Resilience and vulnerability to daily stressors assessed via diary methods. *Current Directions in Psychological Science, 14*, 64–68.

Ambert, A. (1997). *Parents, children, and adolescents: Interactive relationships and development in context.* Binghamton, NY: Haworth.

Ambert, A. (1999). The effect of male delinquency on mothers and fathers: A heuristic study. *Sociological Inquiry, 69,* 368–384.

Baker, B. L., McIntyre, L. L., Blacher, J., Crnic, K., Edelbrock, C., & Low, C. (2003). Pre-school children with and without developmental delay: Behaviour problems and parenting stress over time. *Journal of Intellectual Disability Research, 47,* 217–230.

Barnett, R. C., Garreis, K. C., & Brennan, R. T. (2008). Wive's shift work schedules and husbands' and wives' well-being in dual-earner couples with children: Within-couple analysis. *Journal of Family Issues, 29,* 396–422.

Beernink, A. E., Swinkels, S. H. N., Van der Gaag, R. J., & Buitelaar, J. K. (2012). Effects of attentional/hyperactive and oppositional/aggressive problem behaviour at 14 months and 21 months on parenting stress. *Child and Adolescent Mental Health, 17*(2), 113–120.

Ben-Sasson, A., Soto, T. W., Martínez-Pedraza, F., & Carter, A. S. (2013). Early sensory over-responsivity in toddlers' autism spectrum disorders as a predictor of family impairment and parenting stress, *Journal of Child Psychology and Psychiatry, 54*(8), 846–853.

Berry, J. W., Phinney, J. S., Sam, D. L., & Vedder, P. (2005). Immigrant youth: acculturation, identity, and adaptation. *Applied Psychology: An International Review, 55*(3), 303–332.

Bianchi, S. M., & Milkie, M. A. (2010). Work and family research in the first decade of the 21st century. *Journal of Marriage and the Family, 72,* 705–725.

Bigner, J. (2010). *Parent-child relations: An introduction to parenting.* Upper Saddle River, NJ: Merrill-Pearson Education.

Boss, P. (2002). *Family stress management* (2nd ed.). Thousand Oaks, CA: Sage.

Bouchard, G. (2014). The quality of the parenting alliance during the transition to parenthood. *Canadian Journal of Behavioral Science, 46,* 20–28.

Buehler, C., Benson, M. J., & Gerard, J. M. (2006). Interparental hostility and early adolescent problem behavior: The mediating role of specific aspects of parenting. *Journal of Research on Adolescence, 16*(2), 265–292.

Buehler, C., & Gerard, J. (2002). Marital conflict, ineffective parenting, and children's and adolescent's maladjustment. *Journal of Marriage and the Family, 64,* 78–92.

Buehler, C., & Gerard, J. M. (2013). Cumulative family risk predicts increases in adjustment difficulties across early adolescence. *Journal of Youth Adolescence, 42,* 905–920.

Braver, S., & Lamb, M. E. (2013). Marital dissolution. In G. W. Peterson & K. R. Bush (Eds.), *Handbook of marriage and the family* (3rd ed., pp. 487–516). New York, NY: Springer.

Bures, R. M., Koropeckyj-Cox, T., & Loree, M. (2009). Childlessness, parenthood, and depressive symptoms among middle-aged and older adults. *Journal of Family Issues, 30,* 670–687.

Bush, K. R., & Peterson, G. W. (2008). Family influences on childhood development. In T. P. Gullotta (Ed.), *Handbook of childhood behavioral issues* (pp. 43–67). New York, NY: Taylor & Francis.

Bush, K. R., & Peterson, G. W. (2013). Parent-child relationships in diverse contexts. In G. W. Peterson & K. R. Bush (Eds.), *Handbook of marriage and the family* (3rd ed., pp. 275–302). New York, NY: Springer.

Buss, D. M. (2005). *The handbook of evolutionary psychology.* New York, NY: Wiley.

Caldwell, C. L., Horne, A. M., Davidson, B., & Quinn, W. H. (2007). Effectiveness of multiple family group intervention for juvenile first offenders in reducing parenting stress. *Journal of Child and Family Studies, 16,* 443–459.

Cappa, K. A., Begle, A., Conger, J. C., Dumas, J. E., & Conger, A. J. (2011). Bidirectional relationships between parenting stress and child coping competence: Findings from the pace study. *Journal of Child and Family Studies, 20*, 334–342.

Carter, B., & McGoldrick, M. (Eds.). (1999). *The expanded family life cycle: Individual, family, and social perspectives* (3rd ed.). Needham Heights, MA: Allyn & Bacon.

Collins, W. A., & Steinberg, L. A. (2006). Adolescent development in interpersonal context. In W. Damon & R. M. Lerner (Eds.), *Handbook of Child Psychology, Volume 3: Social, emotional, and personality development* (6th ed., pp. 1003–1068). New York, NY: Wiley.

Crouter, A. C., & Booth, A. (2004). *Work-family challenges for low-income parents and their children.* Mahwah, NJ: Erlbaum.

Crnic, K., Gaze, C., & Hoffman, C. (2005). Cumulative parenting stress across the preschool period: Relations to maternal parenting and child behavior at age 5. *Infant & Child Development, 14*, 117–132.

Crnic, K., & Low, C. (2002). Everyday stresses and parenting. In M. H. Bornstein (Ed.), *Handbook of Parenting: Vol. 5. Practical issues in parenting* (2nd ed., pp. 243–267). Mahwah, NJ: Lawrence Erlbaum.

Deater-Deckard, K. D. (2004). *Parenting stress.* New Haven, CT: Yale University Press.

Deater-Deckard, K., Smith, J., Ivy, L., & Petrill, S. A. (2005). Differential perceptions of and feelings about sibling children: Implications for research on parenting stress. *Infant and Child Development, 14*, 211–225.

Delvecchio, E., Di Riso, D., Chessa, D., Salcuni, S., Mazzeschi, C., & Laghezza, L. (2014). Expressed emotion, parental stress, and family dysfunction among parents of nonclinical Italian children. *Journal of Child & Family Studies, 23*, 989–999.

Demo, D. H., & Buehler, C. (2013). Theoretical approaches to studying divorce. In M. A. Fine & F. D. Fincham (Eds.), *Handbook of family theories: A content-based approach* (pp. 263–279). New York, NY: Routledge.

Devereux, P. G., Weigel, D. J., Ballard-Reisch, D., Leigh G. K., & Cahoon, K. L. (2009). Immediate and longer-term connections between support and stress in pregnant/parenting and non-pregnant/non-parenting adolescents. *Child and Adolescent Social Work Journal, 26*, 431–446.

Dunning, M. J., & Giallo, R. (2012). Fatigue, parenting stress, self-efficacy and satisfaction in mothers of infants and young children. *Journal of Reproductive and Infant Psychology, 30*(2), 145–159.

Feinberg, M. (2002). Co-parenting and the transition to parenthood: A framework for prevention. *Clinical and Family Psychology Review, 5*, 173–195.

Folbre, N. (2008). *Valuing children: Rethinking the economics of the family.* Cambridge, MA: Harvard University Press.

Gavazzi, S. M. (2011). *Families with adolescents: Bridging the gaps between theory, research, and practice.* New York, NY: Springer.

Gerard, J. M., Krishnakumar, A., & Buehler, C. (2008). Marital conflict, parent–child relations, and youth adjustment: A longitudinal investigation of spillover effects. *Journal of Family Issues, 27*, 951–975.

Gonzales, N. A., Fabrett, F. C., & Knight, G. P. (2009). Psychological impact of Latino youth acculturation and enculturation. In F. A. Villaruel, G. Carlo, M. Azmitia, J. Grau, N. Cabrera, & J. Chahin (Eds.), *Handbook of U.S. Latino psychology* (pp. 115–134). Thousand Oaks, CA: Sage.

Goodnow, J. J. (2005). Family socialization: New moves and next steps. *New Directions for Child and Adolescent Development, 109*, 83–90.

Grych, J. H., Oxtoby, C., & Lynn, M. (2013). The effects of interparental conflict on children. In M. A. Fine & F. D. Fincham (Eds.), *Handbook of family theories: Content-based approach* (pp. 228–245). New York, NY: Routledge, Taylor Francis Group.

Haines, V. Y., Marchand, A., & Harvey, S. (2006). Crossover of workplace aggression experiences in dual-earner couples. *Journal of Occupational Health Psychology, 11*, 305–314.

Hanington, L., Heron, J., Stein, A., & Ramchandani, P. (2012). Parental depression and child outcomes—Is marital conflict the missing link? *Child Care, Health & Development, 38*(4), 520–529.

Hastings, R. P. (2002). Parental stress and behaviour problems of children with developmental disability. *Journal of Intellectual and Developmental Disability, 27,* 149–160.

Hawk, D., & Holden, G. W. (2006). Meta-parenting: An initial investigation into a new parental social cognition construct. *Parenting: Science & Practice, 6,* 21–42.

Hennon, C. B., Newsome, W. S., Peterson, G. W., Wilson, S. M., Radina, M. E., & Hildenbrand, B. (2009). Poverty, stress, resiliency: Using the MRM Model for understanding and abating poverty-related family stress. In C. A. Broussard & A. L. Joseph (Eds.), *Family poverty in diverse contexts* (pp. 187–202). New York, NY: Routledge.

Hennon, C. B., & Peterson, G. W. (2007). Estrés parental: Modelos teóricos y revisión de la literatura [Parenting stress: Theoretical models and a literature review]. In R. Esteinou (Ed.), *Fortalezas y desafíos de las familias en dos contextos: Estados Unidos de América y México* [Strengths and challenges of families in two contexts: The United States of America and Mexico] (pp. 167–221). México, DF: Centro de Investigaciones y Estudios Superiores en Antropología Social (CIESAS) y Sistema Nacional para el Desarrollo Integral de la Familia (DIF).

Hennon, C. B., Peterson, G. W., Hildenbrand, B., & Wilson, S. M. (2008). Parental stress amongst migrant and immigrant populations: The MRM and CRSRP models for interventions [Stress Parental em Populações Migrantes e Imigrantes: Os Modelos de Intervenção MRM e CRSRP]. *Pesquisas e Práticas Psicossociais, 2,* 242–257.

Hennon, C. B., Peterson, G. W., Polzin, L., & Radina, M. E. (2007). Familias de ascendencia mexicana residentes en Estados Unidos: recursos para el manejo del estrés parental [Resident families of Mexican ancestry in United States: Resources for the handling of parental stress]. In R. Esteinou (Ed.), *Fortalezas y desafíos de las familias en dos contextos: Estados Unidos de América y México* [Strengths and challenges of families in two contexts: The United States of America and Mexico] (pp. 225–282). México, DF: Centro de Investigaciones y Estudios Superiores en Antropología Social (CIESAS) y Sistema Nacional para el Desarrollo Integral de la Familia (DIF).

Hennon, C. B., Radina, M. E., & Wilson, S. M. (2013). Family life education: Issues and challenges in professional practice. In G.W. Peterson & K. R. Bush (Eds.), *Handbook of marriage and the family* (3rd ed., pp. 815–843). New York, NY: Springer.

Hetherington, E. M., & Stanley-Hagan, M. (2002). Parenting in divorced and remarried families. In M. H. Bornstein (Ed.), *Handbook of Parenting: Vol. 3. Being and becoming a parent* (2nd ed., pp. 287–316). Mahwah, NJ: Lawrence Erlbaum.

Henry, C. S., Merten, M. J., Plunkett, S. W., & Sands, T. (2008). Neighborhood, parenting, and adolescent factors and academic achievement in Latino adolescents from immigrant families. *Family Relations, 57,* 579–590.

Hill, R. (1949). *Families under stress.* New York, NY: Harper.

Holden, G. W. (2015). *Parenting: A dynamic perspective* (2nd ed). Thousand Oaks, CA: Sage.

Holden, G. W., & Hawk, D. (2003). Meta-parenting in the journey of child rearing: A cognitive mechanism for change. In L. Kuczynski (Ed.), *Handbook of dynamics in parent-child relationships* (pp. 189–210). Thousand Oaks, CA: Sage.

Huang, C. Y., Costeines, J., Kaufman, J. S., & Ayala, C. (2014). Parenting stress, social support, and depression for ethnic minority adolescent mothers: Impact on child development. *Journal of Child and Family Studies, 23,* 255–262.

Jones, L., Rowe, J., & Becker, T. (2009). Appraisal, coping, and social support as predictors of psycho-logical distress and parenting efficacy in parents of premature infants. *Children's Health Care, 38,* 245–262.

Kagitcibasi, C. (2013). Adolescent autonomy-relatedness and the family in cultural context: What is optimal? *Journal of Research on Adolescence, 23*(2), 223–235.

Kalil, A., Dunifon, R., Crosby, D., & Houston Su, J. (2014). Work hours, schedules, and insufficient sleep among mothers and their young children. *Journal of Marriage and Family, 76*(5), 891–904.

Katsikitis, M., Bignell, K., Rooskov, N., Elms, L., & Davidson, G. (2013). The family strengthening pro-gram: Influences on parental mood, parental sense of competence and family functioning. *Advances in Mental Health, 11*(2), 143–151.

Kaufmann, E. (2011). *Shall the religious inherit the earth: Demography and politics in the twenty-first century.* London, England: Profile.

Kelly, M. (2009). Women's voluntary childlessness: A radical rejection of motherhood? *Women's Studies, Gender, and Sexuality, 37*(3&4), 157–172.

Koropeckyj-Cox, T., Pienta, A. M., & Brown, T. H. (2007). Women of the 1950s and the "normative" life course: The implications of childlessness, fertility timing, and marital status for psychological well-being in late midlife. *International Journal of Aging and Human Development, 64,* 299 – 330.

Kuczynski, L., & De Mol, J. (2015). *Theory and method.* In W. F. Overton & P. C. Molenaar (Eds.), *Handbook of child psychology and developmental science* (7th ed., Vol. 1, pp. 323–368). Hoboken, NJ: Wiley.

Kremer-Sadlik, T., & Paugh, A. L. (2007). Everyday moments—Finding 'quality time' in American working families. *Time & Society, 16,* 287–308.

Lamb, M. E. (2013). The changing faces of fatherhood and father-child relationships: From fatherhood as status to dad. In M. A. Fine & F. D. Fincham (Eds.), *Handbook of family theories: Content-based approach* (pp. 87–102). New York: Routledge, Taylor Francis Group.

Lambek, R. Sonuga-Barke, E., Psychogiou, L., Thompson, M., Tannock, R., David Daley, Damm, D., & Thomsen, P. (2014). The parental emotional response to children index: A questionnaire mea-sure of parents' reactions to ADHD, *Journal of Attention Disorders, 3,* 1–14.

Lavee, L. (2013). Stress processes in families and couples. In G. W. Peterson & K. R. Bush (Eds.), *Handbook of marriage and the family* (3rd ed., pp. 159–176). New York, NY: Springer.

Lawrence, E., Rothman, A. D., Cobb, R. J., Rothman, J. T., & Bradbury, T. N. (2008). Marital satisfaction across the transition to parenthood. *Journal of Family Psychology, 22,* 41–50.

Letiecq, B. L., Bailey, S. J., & Porterfield, F. (2008). "We have no rights, we get no help": The legal and policy dilemmas facing grandparent caregivers. *Journal of Family Issues, 29*(8), 995–1012.

Liu, C., Chen, Y., Yeh, Y., & Hsieh, Y. (2012). Effects of maternal confidence and competence on maternal parenting stress in newborn care. *Journal of Advanced Nursing, 68*(4), 908–918.

Marsiglio, W., & Roy, K. (2013). Fathers' nurturance of children over the life course. In G. W. Peterson & K. R. Bush (Eds.), *Handbook of marriage and the family* (3rd ed., pp. 353–376). New York, NY: Springer.

McCubbin, H. I., & Patterson, J. M. (1986). Adolescent stress, coping, and adaptation: A normative family perspective. In G. K. Leigh & G. W. Peterson (Eds.), *Adolescents in families* (pp. 256–276). Cincinnati, OH: Southwestern.

McHale, J., Kazan, I., Erera, P., Rotman, T., DeCourcey, W., & McConnell, M. (2002). Coparenting in diverse family systems. In M. H. Bornstein (Ed.), *Handbook of Parenting, Vol. 3: Being and becom-ing a parent* (2nd ed., pp. 75–108). Mahwah, NJ: Lawrence Erlbaum.

McHale, J., & Lindahl, K. (2011). *Co-parenting: Theory, research, and clinical applications.* Washington, DC: American Psychological Association.

Medina, A. M., Lederhos, C. L., & Lillis, T. S. (2009). Sleep disruption and decline of marital satisfaction across the transition to parenthood. *Families, Systems, & Health, 27*, 153–160.

Moran, P., & Ghate, D. (2005). The effectiveness of parenting support. *Children & Society, 19*, 329–336

Moreland, A. D., & Dumas, J. E. (2007). Evaluating child coping competence: Theory and measurement. *Journal of Child and Family Studies, 17*, 437–454.

Morse, R., Rojahn, J., & Smith, A. (2014). Effects of behavior problems, family functioning, and family coping on parent stress in families with a child with Smith-Magenis Syndrome. *Journal of Developmental & Physical Disabilities, 26*(4), 391–401.

Murray, C. I., Toth, K., Larsen, B. L., & Moulton, S. (2010). Death, dying and grief in families. In C. Price, S. Price, & P. C. McKenry (Eds.), *Families and change: Coping with stressful events and transitions* (4th ed., pp. 73–95). Thousand Oaks, CA: Sage.

Nomaguchi, K. M., & Milkie, M. (2003). Costs and rewards of children: The effects of becoming a parent on adults' lives. *Journal of Marriage and Family, 66*, 413–430.

Ontai, L., Sano, Y., Hatton, H., & Conger, K. J. (2008). Low-income rural mothers' perceptions of parental confidence: The role of family health problems and partner status. *Family Relations, 57*, 324–334.

Patterson, J. M. (2002). Integrating family resilience and family stress theory. *Journal of Marriage and Family, 64*, 349–360.

Peterson, G. W., & Bush, K. R. (2013). Conceptualizing cultural influences on socialization: Comparing parent-adolescent relationships in the U.S. and Mexico. In G. W. Peterson & K. R. Bush (Eds.), *Handbook of marriage and the family* (3rd ed., pp. 177–208). New York, NY: Springer.

Peterson, G. W., & Bush, K. R. (2015). Families and adolescent development. In T. P. Gullotta & G. R. Adams (Eds.), *Handbook of adolescent behavioral problems: Evidence-based approaches to prevention and treatment* (2nd ed., pp. 44–69). New York, NY: Springer.

Pride, M. (1985). *The way home: Beyond feminism, back to reality*. Wheaton, IL: Good News.

Purssell, E., & White, A. (2013). The family strengthening program: Influences on parental mood, parental sense of competence and family functioning. *Journal of Clinical Nursing, 22*(9/10), 1487–1494.

Richman, S. B., & Mandara, J. (2013). Do socialization goals explain differences in parental control between black and white parents? *Family Relations 62*, 625 – 636.

Ryan, L. G., Miller-Loessi, K., & Nieri, T. (2007). Relationships with adults as predictors of substance use, gang involvement, and threats to safety among disadvantaged urban high-school adolescents. *Journal of Community Psychology, 35*, 1053–1071.

Scarmella, L. V., Neppl, T. K., Ontai, L. I., & Conger, R. D. (2008). Consequences of socioeconomic disadvantage across three generations: Parenting behavior and child externalizing problems, *Journal of Family Psychology, 18*, 725–753.

Schoppe-Sullivan, S. J., & Mangelsdorf, S. C. (2013). Parent characteristics and early co-parenting behavior at the transition to parenthood. *Social Development, 22*, 363–383.

Sepa, A., Frodi, A., & Ludvigsson, J. (2004). Psychosocial correlates of parenting stress, lack of support and lack of confidence/security. *Scandinavian Journal of Psychology, 45*, 169–179.

Serido, J., Almeida, D. M., & Worthington, E. (2004). Chronic stressors and daily hassles: Unique and interactive relationships with psychological distress. *Journal of Health and Social Behavior, 45*, 17–33.

Shumow, L., & Lomax, R. (2002). Parental efficacy: Predictor of parenting behavior and adolescent outcomes. *Parenting Science and Practice, 2*, 127–150.

Silva, L. M. T., & Schalock, M. (2012). Autism parenting stress index: Initial psychometric evidence, *Journal Autism Development Disorder, 42*, 566–574.

Singer, G. H. S., Ethridge, B. L., & Aldana, S. I. (2007). Primary and secondary effects of parenting and stress management interventions for parents of children with developmental disabilities: A meta-analysis. *Mental Retardation and Developmental Disabilities Research Reviews, 13*, 357–369.

Solomon, J., & George, C. (2008). The measurement of attachment security and related constructs in infancy and early childhood. In J. Cassidy & P. R. Shaver (Eds.), *Handbook of attachment* (2nd ed., pp. 383–416). New York, NY: Guilford.

Stone, G., Buehler, C., & Barber, B. K. (2002). Interparental conflict, parental psychological control, and youth problem behavior. In B. K. Barber (Ed.), *Intrusive parenting: How psychological control affects children and adolescents* (pp. 53–95). Washington, DC: American Psychological Association.

Umberson, D., Pudrovska, T., & Reczek, C. (2010). Parenthood, childlessness, and well-being: A life course perspective. *Journal of Marriage & Family 72(3)*, 612–629.

CHAPTER 4

Families With Special Needs: A Journey From Coping and Adaptation to Resilience and Hope

Briana S. Nelson Goff, Jessica High, Adam Cless,
Kelsey Koblitz, Natira Staats, and Nicole Springer

_____ **Vignette** _____

Jared and Ashley had been married for 8 years when they learned they were expecting a child. They were completely overjoyed since they had difficulty conceiving, undergoing various fertility treatments and previous disappointments over the last several years. Upon learning about the pregnancy, Jared and Ashley immediately called their families to relay the good news. Over the next several months they prepared for the birth of their firstborn. Once they found out it was a girl, Ashley began preparing the nursery and shopping for girl clothes and toys. With their daughter's birth fast approaching, Jared and Ashley found themselves talking more and more about the activities they would enjoy and the memories they would create with their daughter. At the start of labor contractions, Jared and Ashley rushed to the hospital. At the end of an exhausting 8 hours, Ashley gave birth to a beautiful girl. It was immediately clear that something was wrong. After some consultation, a doctor returned to give Jared and Ashley the news: Their baby girl had indicators of Down syndrome. It was at this moment they realized their lives would never be the same.

• • •

According to the U.S. Department of Health and Human Services (2008), in the United States, 21.8% of households with children have a child with a special health care need. Here, *special health care need* is defined as those children who "have or are at an increased risk for a chronic physical, developmental, behavioral, or emotional condition and who also require health and related services of a type or amount beyond that required by children generally" (McPherson et al., 1998). Additionally, the prevalence of families with a member who has special needs is increasing. With autism spectrum disorder diagnoses alone, prevalence statistics have increased from 1 in 150 children in the year 2000 to 1 in 68 children in 2010 (Baio, 2014). Families with a member who has special needs may encounter numerous challenges, including, but not limited to, developmental, medical, educational, social, and financial issues. Coping with the diagnosis, the uncertainty of the condition, understanding what physical or developmental limitations may exist, identifying and accessing specialized services, dealing with chronic and sometimes severe health problems, engaging in community resources and support, and planning for the future are strains described by these families (Flaherty & Masters Glidden, 2000; Glidden, Billings, & Jobe, 2006). Although having a member with special needs may result in greater demands on family resources, social support, community resources, and family coping strategies can effectively reduce the stress associated with having a loved one with a disability (Asberg, Vogel, & Bowers, 2007). In this chapter, we present an overview of terms used to describe individuals and families with special needs, as well as relevant theoretical frameworks that can be used to understand these families in their unique contexts. We also provide a discussion of the various subsystems in families, as well as several external resources available to families with a member with special needs or disability.

DEFINITION OF TERMS

As the term implies, *disability* is a wide-ranging social construct of an individual's varying abilities. The term can describe a limitation in the ability to perform certain roles or functions within the larger context of society (DePloy & Gilson, 2004). Rather than applying the term *disability* to an individual, those with limitations often are identified as *exceptional* or as individuals with *special needs*. For instance, for children, the term *exceptional* represents one who is "different in some way from the typical child" (Turner & Welch, 2011, p. 240). It is this distinguishing idea that presents children and adults within the context of their environments. It has long been a problem for professionals working with individuals and their families to bridge the gap of understanding in reference to the special needs of individuals within a given population.

The social construct of disability and special needs has evolved from a person-oriented approach to a more inclusive approach, shifting from a description of a personal limitation or deficit to a characteristic that originates from an organic or social factor (DePloy & Gilson, 2004). This change has occurred in part to incur a wider acceptance from a sociological perspective and also to allow a clearer explanation of the impact disability has on an individual and on the family. Disability is therefore not considered to be an invariant trait of the person but instead focuses on the interaction between an individual and his or her environment, which can be further strengthened by the resources and support available to that person (Schalock, Luckasson, & Shogren, 2007).

Acknowledging the changing landscape of disabilities and special needs gives researchers the chance to further define these terms. Clear terminology allows for further research into ways families can effectively cope and adapt to the inevitable changes that will take place as one cares for a loved one with special needs as well as creates more inclusive services for individuals with disabilities and their families (Gargiulo, 2005). Although the importance of defining and classifying the terminology associated with disability is paramount to researching effective coping and adaptive strategies, it is challenging and complex in nature. There is a level of ambiguity common with defining disabilities, as well as placing individuals within a specific category. There is also difficulty due to individual development over time (Hallahan & Kauffman, 2014).

Despite the challenges of defining disability, there is significant research and explanation to portray similar approaches to disabilities by providing accurate definitions for the purpose of providing "universal application" to health-related concerns (Chapireau, 2005). According to the World Health Organization (2001), the components that define a disability for an individual are a response toward how an individual interacts with his or her environment. In other words, the needs of an individual are based on how functional that person is in the context of society. For example, if the condition is limiting the functionality of that person then the likelihood an individual is experiencing a specific disability or exceptionality is increased. In this way, disability is defined through social contexts contrasting the individual's needs with the abilities and needs of others. While there are a variety of conditions that can be defined by the term *disability*, for our purposes, we will limit our review to primarily intellectual and developmental disability research and literature. Additional chapters in the text provide an overview of other types of special needs, including physical and mental health issues that may be classified as a disability or special need. (For a description of intellectual and developmental disabilities, see National Institutes of Health, 2010.)

In addition to the variation that may occur in the types of special needs or disabilities experienced, there are changes that the family may encounter as an individual with a disability transitions into different life stages. The functionality of the person as well as available social supports are key predictors for the overall health, stability, and well-being of the individual and the family. As with many of life's challenges, having a member with special needs often is stressful, but the experiences of families are varied based on multiple contextual and biopsychosocial factors (World Health Organization, 2001).

THEORETICAL FRAMEWORKS: FAMILIES WITH SPECIAL NEEDS AS COMPLEX SYSTEMS

Literature suggests that families with special needs may experience unique stressors due to the nonnormative and chronic challenges they face. While all families experience stress as a result of change, families with special needs are at greater risk for experiencing this stress due to extended caregiving roles members must assume, navigating multiple systems of care, demands on resources, as well as the increased emotional issues that may come with a special needs diagnosis. Theoretical frameworks can assist researchers and practitioners in better understanding the stressors experienced by families with special needs as well as the coping strategies employed in response to this stress. Two specific theories will be applied to understand the experiences of families with special needs: ambiguous loss (Boss, 1999, 2002) and the contextual model of family stress (Boss, 2002). Before describing these theories, we provide some relevant historical background related to families experiencing stress, like a disability or special needs diagnosis. Also, because much research focuses on the individual, not addressing the experiences or contexts of the family, it is important to recognize the systemic theories as they apply to individuals and families with special needs.

As outlined in Hill's (1958) ABC-X model, the impact of any challenge faced by a family is determined by the nature of the stressor event within the family (component A), the resources and positive attributes available to the family (component B), the family's perception of the crisis event (component C), and other variables that affect the family's ability to cope or adapt to the stressor event thus contributing to the crisis itself (component X). A variety of factors related to stressor events have been identified that indicate the potential impact those events may have on the family, including: the source (internal vs. external to the family), timing (on-time/expected vs. off-time), duration of the stressor (chronic to acute), the amount of stressors experienced (isolated event vs. cumulative pileup of stressors), family resources (tangible vs. intangible), life-cycle stage of the family, level of ambiguity of the stressor, and resolution of the stressor (Weber, 2011).

One of the first theoretical perspectives developed specific to families with special needs identified five crisis stages these families experience: impact, denial, grief, focusing outward, and closure (Fortier & Wanlass, 1984). Although this theory was not meant to be a linear model, the stages and characteristics within each stage provide a tangible description of the initial experiences of families facing a special needs diagnosis. Because families with special needs often encounter specific and unique challenges that other families may not experience, having a family member with special needs may be considered a potential stressor or crisis for the family system. The chronic nature of the condition may contribute not only to the initial stress but also exacerbate daily or chronic stress, including caregiver burden and compassion fatigue (O'Brien, 2007). One approach to conceptualizing the effects of special needs on families is through the concept of ambiguous loss, particularly the early experiences of families facing the stressors that accompany a special needs diagnosis.

Ambiguous Loss

Ambiguous loss (Boss, 1999, 2002) is defined as an incongruence between the psychological and physical family. In families with special needs, the ambiguous loss would be the family's experience of having a family member who is both physically present yet psychologically absent, compared to those who are typically developing. A significant component of Boss's (2006) *ambiguous loss* is the concept of *boundary ambiguity*, which refers to the experience of not knowing who is in or out of the family or relationship. The ambiguity that stems from a special needs diagnosis primarily exists on two levels: the uncertainty of the level of impairment, which leaves future abilities and functioning unknown, and the family's grief of the loss of the more typical child and the life path they were anticipating. The uncertainty and grief that accompany this ambiguity can be paralyzing for some families, as it complicates both the loss and the processes of mourning (Boss, 1999). Like an ambiguous loss, a disability or special needs diagnosis represents a long-term, often permanent change in life's trajectory. It includes a number of unknown elements and requires the family to adapt to the incongruence that is present between the psychological (expected) and physical (present) family.

Consider the opening vignette about Jared and Ashley. It is clear that the excited parents-to-be spent time preparing for their new baby only to be confronted with the unexpected reality of a Down syndrome diagnosis. Their experience is an illustration of ambiguous loss in that they had planned to welcome a typically developing child, only to learn that the family they expected was going to be different. Although the couple's physical family still consists of two parents and their newborn child, their psychological family has changed.

Contextual Model of Family Stress

Boss's (2002) contextual model of family stress provides another conceptualization tool for considering families with special needs. Based on the original ABC-X model (Hill, 1958), in this model, the stressor, A, can be seen as the point of the special needs or disability diagnosis. Resources, the B component, are defined as helpful coping mechanisms available to the family on individual, family, and community levels. For Jared and Ashley, identifying resources to assist them and accessing services to support their daughter will be necessary in helping to adjust well and manage the unexpected challenges the family now faces. As described previously, the contextual model extends perceptions, C, to include the concepts of boundary ambiguity and socially constructed perceptions and meanings. Families with special needs may experience ambiguity in different settings and at various times across the life span, as their family member with special needs continues to change and develop. In addition, elements of the external context (i.e., culture, historical, economic, developmental, and heredity) and internal context (i.e., structural, psychological, and philosophical factors that are part of the family) are additional factors that accumulate to determine the degree of stress the family may experience (Boss, 2002). Furthermore, the internal and external context components may create conflict that contributes to the family stress. This theoretical model brings the various contextual factors into consideration to better understand a family's experiences when encountering a disability or special needs diagnosis. The internal and external contextual factors associated with the contextual model of family stress are described in the next sections.

Internal Context: Subsystems of Families With Special Needs

Some studies have shown that specific stressors that families with special needs experience may negatively affect the marital relationship (Stoneman & Gavidia-Payne, 2006) and have been associated with poorer family adjustment and higher levels of child behavioral problems (McGlone, Santos, Kazama, Fong, & Mueller, 2001). Conversely, higher marital quality, as well as higher family functioning, have been shown to be protective factors against stress in families with special needs (Kersh, Hedvat, Hauser-Cram, & Warfield, 2006). The following sections provide a description of the impact of a disability or special needs diagnosis on the various internal family subsystems.

Siblings of Children With Special Needs

The sibling relationship may by the longest, most dynamic, and influential relationship individuals experience, most likely because siblings spend vast amounts of time together in childhood, and their life spans can significantly overlap (Cicirelli, 1995; McHale & Crouter, 1996). This relationship, however, may be different when there is a family member with a special need or disability. Research regarding the impact on siblings living with a child with a special need has been mixed—showing that siblings experience a variety of effects (Schuntermann, 2007; Stoneman, 2005). Graff and colleagues (2012) explored the experiences, both positive and negative, of adolescent siblings of children with disabilities. Most participants reported growing up with their sibling was a positive experience; however, challenges associated with living with a sibling with a disability were also described, including difficult behaviors of the sibling with special needs and stress experienced by all family members. Research by Bayat (2007) indicated that siblings of children diagnosed with autism were emotionally close as siblings, with some siblings making personal choices to provide care for their sibling with autism. Other researchers found no differences in the psychosocial adjustment and social support for siblings of children with autism compared to siblings of children with Down syndrome or siblings of typically developing children (Kaminsky & Dewey, 2002).

When exploring issues of gender, Hastings (2007) found that siblings of a brother with developmental disabilities displayed more behavior problems than siblings of a sister with developmental disabilities. Furthermore, the level of behavior problems reported in the child with developmental disabilities was a significant predictor of behavior problems in the siblings (without special needs). Comparatively, a study by Gottfried and McGene (2013) indicated a positive effect on academic achievement for the siblings of those with special educational needs. Clearly, the impact of a special needs diagnosis on siblings is mixed, with both negative and positive effects represented.

Grandparents of Children With Special Needs

Very little special needs and disability research has focused on extended family members, specifically the experiences of grandparents, aunts, uncles, and other family roles. Extended family members, particularly grandparents, can provide a significant element of support, assistance, information, and other resources (e.g., child care, money) in very substantial and meaningful ways (Seligman & Darling, 2007). The effect that grandparents can have on the parents' ability to cope and a family's adjustment following the entrance of a child with a disability is significant (Trute, 2003). Schilmoeller and Baranowski (1998) found that grandparents provided support to their children and grandchildren in one of three primary ways: providing money when needed, taking time to do things with their grandchild, and doing activities with their adult sons or daughters that were fun or relaxing. Trute (2003) found that emotional support from maternal grandmothers was significantly related to mothers' higher self-esteem and lower symptoms of depression. Participants also indicated that maternal grandmothers tended to provide the most support as compared to paternal grandparents. Thus, it is necessary to recognize the important roles and contributions made by grandparents and other extended family members, in both tangible and intangible ways.

Parents of Children With Special Needs

Caring for a child can be demanding, but when a child has a special needs diagnosis, parental responsibilities increase in complexity and often are combined with a need to manage feelings of grief and loss. One area of study focuses on parental reactions to an initial special needs diagnosis and the evolution of parental response over time. Joosa and Berthelsen (2006) found that although participants' initial responses to having a child with special needs were more negative, their attitudes became more positive over time as they realized the deeper meaning and satisfaction they gained in their lives. Similarly, Nelson Goff and colleagues (2013) found parental reactions to a child's initial diagnosis involved a variety of emotions, for example, "having every emotion there is all at one time," "the full range of emotions," and "a complete rollercoaster of emotions" (p. 451). Often parents reported a process of adjustment, beginning with their original feelings of grief and loss to a more general acceptance and understanding of the diagnosis.

Research on children with special needs has predominantly included mothers as the primary participants. When comparing mothers of children with disabilities and mothers of typically developing children, researchers have found that the former group spends more time engaged in physical care of the child, less time socializing with other adult parents, and less time engaged in activities away from the home (Crowe, 1993; Johnson & Deitz, 1985; Smith et al., 2010). Helitzer, Cunningham-Sabo, VanLeit, and Crowe (2002) found that mothers of children with disabilities often reported feeling overwhelmed and isolated, lacking social support, and a reduced sense of identity and expectations for their future. Mothers of children with special needs also may experience higher daily stress and greater stress across time as compared to fathers (Crnic, Pedersen y Arbona, Baker, & Blacher, 2009). Ricci and Hodapp (2003) found that fathers of children with Down syndrome reported less stress and more positive perceptions of their children than did fathers of children with other types of special needs, but their involvement with their children did not differ across groups of fathers or between mothers and fathers.

One area that has received considerable attention is the impact of having a child with special needs on the marital/couple relationship of the parents. Some literature indicates that the presence of a child with disabilities has a negative impact on marriages; however, this effect may be less pronounced than expected (Risdal & Singer, 2004). Urbano and Hodapp (2007) were among the first to conduct an epidemiological study of divorce in families of children with Down syndrome. Their results suggested that parents of children with Down syndrome had a lower chance of divorce than did other parent groups (parents of children with and without disabilities). Freedman, Kalb, Zablotsky, and Stuart (2012) conducted a population-based study on divorce in children with autism spectrum disorders and found no evidence that these parents were more at risk for divorce compared to the general population. In a meta-analysis on marital adjustment in parents of children with various disabilities, Risdal and Singer (2004) found a detectable, but small, negative impact (an average of 5.97% more divorces) in parents of children with a disability. In general, data are mixed but not as severe as is often reported or presumed.

In addition to the internal contextual elements of the family system, there also are a number of external components that are important to recognize. As Boss (2002) described, these external contextual factors may include cultural and historical factors, as well as external systems in which the family is embedded. For families with special needs, these external systems may include health care, schools, social services, and other systems that families with typically developing children do not encounter to the same degree. The more common external contextual factors for families with special needs are described next.

EXTERNAL CONTEXT: RESOURCES AND SUPPORT SYSTEMS IN COPING, ADAPTATION, AND BUILDING RESILIENCE

Families of children with special needs often require a variety of resources to assist them in dealing with stressors associated with having a special needs child. Van Riper (2007) reported that family demands, family resources, and family problem solving were key elements in the adaptation process of families with special needs. Grant, Ramcharan, and Flynn (2007) described three primary elements that operate to enhance the resilience of these families: establishing a sense of meaning, gaining a sense of control over the situation, and maintaining personal identities for each family member (separate from the disability), as well as boundary maintenance within the family system (e.g., having a clear structure and defined roles and rules within the family).

High demands often are placed on families with special needs during times of crisis or medical emergencies; at the same time, parents must consistently deal with transitional changes at each level of development. Successfully navigating the health system, social services, and school system, as well as accessing personal support, becomes necessary to ensure the proper resources are available for individual family members as well as the family as a whole. Each of these external systems is described; however, it is important to emphasize that while these external systems are critical components of all children's developmental experiences, they play a unique role in the lives of children and families with special needs. Successfully mastering these systems is a complex task with many components, including interventions, policies, legal issues, structural barriers, and other elements. It is not possible to fully describe all the components and aspects of each external system, but this review emphasizes the key areas that relate to having a child with special needs.

Health Systems

Families with special needs often spend a significant amount of time in medical facilities, interacting with a plethora of health care professionals during their life span. Because of this, the attitudes and practices of these medical professionals can have a significant effect on parents' perspectives about their child's condition and their caregiving abilities. One of the primary themes in the Nelson Goff et al. (2013) study involved negative experiences with medical personnel relating to their child's Down syndrome diagnosis, including pressure by medical professionals to have prenatal testing or to terminate the pregnancy, negative and misinformation about Down syndrome, and a general lack of compassion. In fact, the participants in their study reported over twice as many negative to positive experiences with medical professionals. A possible implication of this study's finding is the need for compassion, understanding, and honesty in the medical sphere.

Skotko and colleagues (Skotko, Capone, et al., 2009; Skotko, Kishnani, et al., 2009) identify a variety of recommendations for health care professionals to incorporate into the delivery of a special needs diagnosis. Examples of recommendations include providing up-to-date and accurate information and materials on local support groups, as well as disclosing the news in a private setting. To improve the adjustment and to support the well-being of a family with special needs, continual, specific, and coordinated services need to be provided (Lefebvre & Levert, 2012). Interventions that promote more positive developmental outcomes for families with special needs, particularly during life-cycle transitions, can help build family resilience through the creation of therapeutic collaboration (Shapiro, 2002). Specifically, collaborative efforts that help parents to increase their use of resources to better meet the diverse demands of caring for a child with special needs are warranted. Naar-King, Siegel, Smyth, and Simpson (2003) identified the importance of providing integrated care (i.e., medical and behavioral health services) for families with children with special needs. Caregivers often indicate a need for better information about their health care concerns or problems related to the special needs diagnosis, including prognosis, rehabilitation, care, services, and other relevant issues (Lefebvre & Levert, 2012).

Educational Systems

Navigating the educational system can be an especially difficult task for families with special needs, as schools are primarily designed to provide educational services to typically developing children. Schools operate on the premise that children will fully participate in the classroom on a consistent and independent basis. There are some services available to children with special needs, but services can be limited or inadequate to meet the range of needs sometimes required. Children with special needs often benefit from having schools that will allow for flexibility in order to meet the child's unique needs (Libow, 2006), which often require extra administrative, social, and educational support during the child's transition to and immersion in school (Janus, Kopechanski, Cameron, & Hues, 2008). Parents and school personnel are faced with finding the best methods to educate a child with special needs, which can be a difficult task, sometimes resulting in conflicting interests and intentions. It is important for parents and school personnel to establish clear expectations and work collaboratively to ensure mutually beneficial outcomes.

Parental Employment

Parents of children with special needs face the difficult task of trying to balance both parenting and employment demands. Reducing work hours or terminating employment may be viewed by these families as their only option. There are a number of factors, however, that influence parental choice to alter employment, including the type and severity of the special needs diagnosis, the level of caregiving burden on family members, the family structure (e.g., dual parents or single parents), and family income levels. Accessibility to supportive resources (e.g., regular health care advice, routine preventative care, coordination of services, and receiving necessary referrals) can prevent a parent from having to change their employment situation (DeRigne & Porterfield, 2010). Parents of children with special needs that are more severe and who have their care provided by family members often report more financial and employment problems (DeRigne & Porterfield, 2010; Looman, O'Conner-Von, Ferski, & Hildenbrand, 2009).

Social Support Systems

An initial period of social withdrawal may occur for families of children with disabilities that is often due to the competing demand of multiple commitments. Eventually, these families may reintegrate into social networks particularly as they relate to specific special needs groups (Divan, Vajaratkar, Desai, Strik-Lievers, & Patel, 2012). Contributing to a sense of isolation is how society reacts to individuals with special needs; for example, families may encounter negative experiences, including discrimination and marginalization. At the same time, they may enter into new social support networks as they become involved with other families with special needs and the multitude of professionals that are involved in caring for a child with disabilities (Divan et al., 2012).

Parents have cited social, emotional, instrumental, and network support systems as being the most important factors of coping with their children's needs (Kapp & Brown, 2011). Families often seek support from friends, grandparents, faith-based groups, other families, teachers, medical professionals, and support groups. Acquiring social support is a coping strategy frequently reported by parents of children with special needs (Luther, Canham, & Cureton, 2005; Nelson Goff et al., 2013; Twoy, Connolly, & Novak, 2007). Parents who do not use social supports are encouraged to seek out social and community resources to assist in their adjustment and daily functioning (Martin, Wolters, Klaas, Perez, & Wood, 2004; Taanila, Syrjala, Kokkonen, & Jarvelin, 2002).

While some external systems described here may both positively and negatively impact the family with special needs, the importance of these external components cannot be ignored. These external systems provide necessary treatments, interventions, services, information, and support for families, which is critical to adjusting to a disability or special needs diagnosis and starting on a path toward positive family outcomes. Providing families with accurate information regarding the disability or special needs diagnosis, connecting them with effective resources and sources of support, and encouraging the development of a positive perspective are important in developing resilience in families with special needs.

IMPLICATIONS FOR RESEARCH AND PROFESSIONAL PRACTICE

There are a number of research topics that require further exploration in the area of families with special needs. Acknowledging both positive and negative aspects of having a child with special needs is important as are longitudinal studies that address family functioning at all developmental levels (Carr, 1988; Keogh, Bernheimer, & Guthrie, 2004). Further development and testing of theoretical models as they apply to families and children with special needs are required. While the current models of family stress and crisis described here are relevant, research applying theoretical frameworks to the experiences of families with special needs is limited.

Further research is needed to explore the experiences of families with special needs from more diverse populations, including greater socioeconomic, ethnic, and demographic diversity (Cuskelly, Hauser-Cram, & Van Riper, 2009; Hodapp, 2007). Additional research also is needed to understand differences in the adjustment process of families across different types of special needs/disability diagnoses, as well as longitudinally across the life span. Finally, most research on families with special needs continues to focus primarily on mothers with limited emphasis on the experiences of fathers or the broader impact on the couple and family system, including both internal and external contextual factors (Boss, 2002). Because a special needs diagnosis often brings with it implications for caregiving and needs of social resources, expansion of research to include the relationship of extended family members including fathers with a child with special needs is especially needed to gain a more complete understanding and shaping of professional recommendations and available support services. A greater understanding of how whole family systems interact both internally and with external services may speak not only to those developing and providing services to these families but also to those who have the power to shape policies relevant to the rights of individuals and families.

In addition to the research implications, there are several practice implications for working with parents of children with special needs. It is critical that professionals provide accurate and current information to families facing a disability diagnosis in a supportive, compassionate, and well-informed manner (Skotko, 2005). This initial contact with the health care community may significantly influence familial adjustment and is critical to connecting families to necessary support systems and resources. Families also should be provided with specific and practical information that target their unique needs (e.g., medical or educational issues) as well as with referrals for additional specialized services.

Further awareness of the life span needs of families with disabilities or special needs is an important next step. Some research indicates greater reports of behavioral and social problems in adults with developmental disabilities (Keogh et al., 2004). However, since the turn of the 21st century, more children with disabilities are being educated in fully integrated classrooms in public schools (Data Accountability Center, 2011). In addition, individuals with special needs are now living longer, are better educated, and are experiencing more life achievements, like employment and marriage, bringing a new set of demographics and experiences for families. These advancements require further understanding by researchers, professionals, and family members to fully recognize the impact of these changes on families and on the systems of care providing services to individuals with special needs and disabilities.

CONCLUSION

This chapter focused on understanding the unique experiences of families with a child with special needs, as well as how these families relate to external contexts. It is critical for professionals to not only recognize the specific ways in which these families may differ from families without a member with special needs or a disability diagnosis but also to understand the many ways these families are more alike than different (Bower, Chant, & Chatwin, 1998; National Down Syndrome Congress, 2014). Despite the potential stressors related to the diagnosis, families with special needs often report that they are content and see their lives as including both challenges and satisfying experiences (Asberg et al., 2007; Nelson Goff et al., 2013). It is important for professionals to understand and address the unique stressors of families with special needs as well as the positive experiences and resilience of these families. By exploring specific problems and challenges, as well as the coping strategies and resilience these families display, it is possible to develop interventions, establish professional practices, and provide greater opportunities for families with special needs to thrive and exceed all expectations.

Here are some recommended readings:

1. Grant, G., Ramcharan, P., & Flynn, M. (2007). Resilience in families with children and adult members with intellectual disabilities: Tracing elements of a psycho-social model. *Journal of Applied Research in Intellectual Disabilities, 20*(6), 563–575. doi: 10.1111/j.1468-3148.2007.00407.x

2. Ricci, L. A., & Hodapp, R. M. (2003). Fathers of children with Down's [*sic*] syndrome versus other types of intellectual disability: Perceptions, stress and involvement. *Journal of Intellectual Disability Research, 47*(4/5), 273–284. doi: 10.1046/j .1365-2788.2003.00489.x

3. Risdal, D., & Singer, G. (2004). Marital adjustment in parents of children with disabilities: A historical review and meta-analysis. *Research & Practice for Persons with Severe Disabilities, 29*(2), 95–103. doi:10.2511/rpsd.29.2.95

4. Seligman, M., & Darling, R. B. (2007). *Ordinary families, special children: A systems approach to childhood disability* (3rd ed.). New York, NY: Guilford

REFERENCES

Asberg, K. K., Vogel, J. J., & Bowers, C. A. (2007). Exploring correlates and predictors of stress in parents of children who are deaf: Implications of perceived social support and mode of communication. *Journal of Child and Family Studies, 17*(4), 486–499. doi:10.1007/s10826-007-9169-7

Baio, J. (2014). Prevalence of autism spectrum disorder among children aged 8 years: Autism and developmental disabilities monitoring network, 11 Sites, United States, 2010. *Surveillance Summaries, 63*(SS02), 1–21. Atlanta, GA: Centers for Disease Control and Prevention.

Bayat, M. (2007). Evidence of resilience in families of children with autism. *Journal of Intellectual Disability Research, 51*(9), 702–714. doi:10.1111/j.1365-2788.2007.00960.x

Boss, P. (1999). *Ambiguous loss: Learning to live with unresolved grief.* Cambridge, MA: Harvard University Press.

Boss, P. (2002). *Family stress management: A contextual approach.* Thousand Oaks, CA: Sage.

Boss, P. (2006). *Loss, trauma, and resilience: Therapeutic work with ambiguous loss.* New York, NY: W.W. Norton.

Bower, A., Chant, D., & Chatwin, S. (1998). Hardiness in families with and without a child with Down syndrome. *Down Syndrome Research and Practice, 5*(2), 71–77. doi:10.1007/BF01408072

Carr, J. (1988). Six weeks to twenty-one years old: A longitudinal study of children with Down's [*sic*] syndrome and their families. *Journal of Child Psychology and Psychiatry, 29*(4), 407–431. doi: 10.1111/j.1469-7610.1988.tb00734.x

Chapireau, F. (2005). The environment in the international classification of functioning, disability and health. *Journal of Applied Research in Intellectual Disabilities, 18*(4), 305–311. doi:10.1111/j.1468-3148.2005.00269.x

Cicirelli, V. G. (1995). *Sibling relationships across the life span.* New York, NY: Plenum.

Crnic, K., Pedersen y Arbona, A., Baker, B., & Blacher, J. (2009). Mothers and fathers together: Contrasts in parenting across preschool to early school age in children with developmental delays. *International Review of Research in Mental Retardation, 37,* 3–30. doi:10.1016/S0074-7750(09)37001-9

Crowe, T. K. (1993). Time use of mothers with young children: The impact of a child's disability. *Developmental Medicine and Child Neurology, 35*(7), 621–630. doi:10.1111/j.1469-8749.1993.tb11700.x

Cuskelly, M., Hauser-Cram, P., & Van Riper, M. (2009). Families of children with Down syndrome: What we know and what we need to know. *Down Syndrome: Research & Practice, 12*(3), 202–210. doi:10.3104/reviews/2079

Data Accountability Center (2011). *Population and enrollment data.* Retrieved from www.ideacenter.org/PopulationData.asp#2011

DePloy, E., & Gilson, S. F. (2004). *Rethinking disability: Principles for professional and social change.* Belmont, CA: Thompson Brooks/Cole.

DeRigne, L., & Porterfield, S. (2010). Employment change and the role of the medical home for married and single-mother families with children with special health care needs. *Social Science & Medicine, 70*(4), 631–641. doi:10.1016/j.socscimed.2009.10.054

Divan, G., Vajaratkar, V., Desai, M. U., Strik-Lievers, L., & Patel, V. (2012). Challenges, coping strategies, and unmet needs of families with a child with autism spectrum disorder in Goa, India. *Autism Research, 5*(3), 190–200. doi:10.1002/aur.1225

Flaherty, E., & Masters Glidden, L. (2000). Positive adjustment in parents rearing children with Down syndrome. *Early Education and Development, 11*(4), 407–422. doi:10.1207/s15566935eed1104_3

Fortier, L. M., & Wanlass, R. L. (1984). Family crisis following the diagnosis of a handicapped child. *Family Relations, 33*(1), 13–24.

Freedman, B. H., Kalb, L. G., Zablotsky, B., & Stuart, E. A. (2012). Relationship status among parents of children with autism spectrum disorders: A population-based study. *Journal of Autism and Developmental Disorders, 42*(4), 539–548. doi:10.1007/s10803-011-1269-y

Gargiulo, R. M. (2005). *Special education in contemporary society.* Florence, KY: Wadsworth.

Glidden, L. M., Billings, F. J., & Jobe, B. M. (2006). Personality, coping style and well-being of parents rearing children with developmental disabilities. *Journal of Intellectual Disability Research, 50*(12), 949–962. doi:10.1111/j.1365-2788.2006.00929.x

Gottfried, M. A., & McGene, J. (2013). The spillover effects of having a sibling with special educational needs. *The Journal of Educational Research, 106*(3), 197–215. doi:10.1080/00220671.2012.667011

Graff, C., Mandleco, B., Dyches, T. T., Coverston, C. R., Roper, S. O., & Freeborn, D. (2012). Perspectives of adolescent siblings of children with Down syndrome who have multiple health problems. *Journal of Family Nursing, 18*(2), 175–199. doi:10.1177/1074840712439797

Grant, G., Ramcharan, P., & Flynn, M. (2007). Resilience in families with children and adult members with intellectual disabilities: Tracing elements of a psycho-social model. *Journal of Applied Research in Intellectual Disabilities, 20*(6), 563–575. doi:10.1111/j.1468-3148.2007.00407.x

Hallahan, D., & Kauffman, J. (2014). *Exceptional learners* (13th ed.). Boston, MA: Allyn & Bacon.

Hastings, R. P. (2007). Longitudinal relationships between sibling behavioral adjustment and behavior problems of children with developmental disabilities. *Journal of Autism and Developmental Disorders, 37*(8), 1485–1492. doi:10.1007/s10803-006-0230-y

Helitzer, D. L., Cunningham-Sabo, L., VanLeit, B., & Crowe, T. K. (2002). Perceived changes in self-image and coping strategies of mothers of children with disabilities. *The Occupational Therapy Journal of Research, 22*(1), 25–33.

Hill, R. (1958). Generic features of families under stress. *Social Casework, 49,* 139–150.

Hodapp, R. M. (2007). Families of persons with Down syndrome: New perspectives, findings, and research and service needs. *Mental Retardation and Developmental Disabilities Research Reviews, 13*(3), 279–287. doi:10.1002/mrdd.20160

Janus, M., Kopechanski, L., Cameron, R., & Hughes, D. (2008). In transition: Experiences of parents of children with special needs at school entry. *Early Childhood Education Journal, 35*(5), 479–485. doi:10.1007/s10643-007-0217-0

Johnson, C. B., & Dietz, J. C. (1985). Time use of mothers with pre-school children: A pilot study. *American Journal of Occupational Therapy, 39*(9), 578–583.

Joosa, E., & Berthelsen, D. (2006). Parenting a child with Down syndrome: A phenomenographic study. *Journal on Developmental Disabilities, 12*(1), 45–58.

Kaminsky, L., & Dewey, D. (2002). Psychosocial adjustment in siblings of children with autism. *Journal of Child Psychology and Psychiatry, 43*(2), 225–232. doi:10.1111/1469-7610.00015

Kapp, L., & Brown, O. (2011). Resilience in families adapting to autism spectrum disorder. *Journal of Psychology in Africa, 21*(3), 459–463. doi:10.1080/14330237.2011.10820482

Keogh, B. K., Bernheimer, L. P., & Guthrie, D. (2004). Children with developmental delays twenty years later: Where are they? How are they? *American Journal on Mental Retardation, 109*(3), 219–230.

Kersh, J., Hedvat, T. T., Hauser-Cram, P., & Warfield, M. E. (2006). The contribution of marital quality to the well-being of parents of children with developmental disabilities. *Journal of Intellectual Disability Research, 50*(12), 883–893. doi:10.1111/j.1365-2788.20

Lefebvre, H., & Levert, M. (2012). The close relatives of people who have had a traumatic brain injury and their special needs. *Brain Injury, 26*(9), 1084–1097. doi:10.3109/02699052.2012.666364

Libow, J. A. (2006). Children with chronic illness and physical disabilities. In L. Combrinck-Graham (Ed.), *Children in family contexts: Perspectives on treatment* (pp. 223–241). New York, NY: Guilford.

Looman, W. S., O'Conner-Von, S. K., Ferski, G. J., & Hildenbrand, D. A. (2009). Financial and employment problems in families of children with special health care needs: Implications for research and practice. *Journal of Pediatric Health Care, 23*(2), 117–125. doi:10.1016/j.pedhc.2008.03.001

Luther, E. H., Canham, D. L., & Cureton, V. Y. (2005). Coping and social support for parents of children with autism. *The Journal of School Nursing, 21*(1), 40–47. doi:10.1177/10598405050210010901

Martin, S. C., Wolters, P. L., Klaas, P. A., Perez, L., & Wood, L. V. (2004). Coping styles among families of children with HIV infection. *AIDS Care, 16*(3), 283–292. doi:10.1080/09540120410001665295

McGlone, K., Santos, L., Kazama, L., Fong, R., & Mueller, C. (2001). Psychological stress in adoptive parents of special-needs children. *Child Welfare, 81*(2), 151–171.

McHale, S., & Crouter, A. (1996). The family contexts of children's sibling relationships. In G. H. Brody (Ed.), *Sibling relationships: Their causes and consequences* (pp.173–195). Westport, CT: Ablex.

McPherson, M., Arango, P., Fox, H., Lauver, C., McManus, M., Perrin, J. M., Shonkoff, J. P., Strickland, B. (1998). A new definition of children with special health care needs. *Pediatrics, 102*(1), 137–140.

Naar-King, S., Siegel, P. T., Smyth, M., & Simpson, P. (2003). An evaluation of an integrated health care program for children with special needs. *Children's Health Care, 32*(3), 233–243. doi:10.1207/S15326888CHC3203_4

National Down Syndrome Congress (2014, December 4). More alike campaign headquarters [Web site]. Retrieved from http://www.ndsccenter.org/resources/more-alike-campaign-headquarters/

National Institutes of Health (2010). *Fact sheet – Intellectual and developmental disabilities*. Retrieved from http://report.nih.gov/nihfactsheets/ViewFactSheet.aspx?csid = 100

Nelson Goff, B. S., Springer, N., Foote, L. C., Frantz, C., Peak, M., Tracy, C., Veh, T., Bentley, G. E., & Cross, K. A. (2013). Receiving the initial Down syndrome diagnosis: A comparison of prenatal and postnatal parent group experiences. *Intellectual and Developmental Disabilities, 51*(6), 446–457. doi:10.1352/1934-9556-51.6.446

O'Brien, M. (2007). Ambiguous loss in families of children with autism spectrum disorders. *Family Relations, 56*(2), 135–146. doi:10.1111/j.1741-3729.2007.00447.x

Ricci, L. A., & Hodapp, R. M. (2003). Fathers of children with Down's [*sic*] syndrome versus other types of intellectual disability: Perceptions, stress and involvement. *Journal of Intellectual Disability Research, 47*(4/5), 273-284. doi:10.1046/j.1365-2788.2003.00489.x

Risdal, D., & Singer, G. (2004). Marital adjustment in parents of children with disabilities: A historical review and meta-analysis. *Research & Practice for Persons with Severe Disabilities, 29*(2), 95–103. doi:10.2511/rpsd.29.2.95

Schalock, R. L., Luckasson, R. A., & Shogren, K. A. (2007). The renaming of mental retardation: Understanding the change to the term intellectual disability. *Intellectual and Developmental Disabilities, 45*(2), 116–124. doi:10.1352/1934-9556(2007)45[116:TROMRU]2.0.CO;2

Schilmoeller, G. L., & Baranowski, M. D. (1998). Intergenerational support in families with disabilities: Grandparents' perspectives. *Families in Society, 79*(5), 465–476. doi:10.1606/1044-3894.714

Schuntermann, P. (2007). The sibling experience: Growing up with a child who has pervasive developmental disorder or mental retardation. *Harvard Review of Psychiatry, 15*(3), 93–108. doi:10.1080/10673220701432188

Seligman, M., & Darling, R. B. (2007). *Ordinary families, special children: A systems approach to childhood disability* (3rd ed.). New York, NY: Guilford.

Shapiro, E. R. (2002). Chronic illness as a family process: A social-developmental approach to promoting resilience. *Journal of Clinical Psychology, 58*(11), 1375–1384. doi:10.1002/jclp.10085

Skotko, B. (2005). Mothers of children with Down syndrome reflect on their postnatal support. *Pediatrics, 115*(1), 64–77. doi:10.1542/peds.2004-0928

Skotko, B. G., Capone, G. T., Kishnani, P. S., & Down Syndrome Diagnosis Study Group. (2009). Postnatal diagnosis of Down syndrome: Synthesis of the evidence on how best to deliver the news. *Pediatrics, 124*(4), e751–e758. doi:10.1542/peds.2009-0480

Skotko, B. G., Kishnani, P. S., Capone, G. T., & Down Syndrome Diagnosis Study Group. (2009). Prenatal diagnosis of Down syndrome: How best to deliver the news. *American Journal of Medical Genetics, 149A*(112361–2367. doi:10.1002/ajmg.a.33082

Smith, L. E., Hong, J., Seltzer, M. M., Greenberg, J. S., Almeida, D. M., & Bishop, S. L. (2010). Daily experiences among mothers of adolescents and adults with autism spectrum disorder. *Journal of Autism and Developmental Disorders, 40*(2), 167–178. doi:10.1007/s10803-009-0844-y

Stoneman, Z. (2005). Siblings of children with disabilities: Research themes. *Mental Retardation, 43*(5), 339-350. doi:10.1352/0047-6765(2005)43[339:SOCWDR]2.0.CO;2

Stoneman, Z., & Gavidia-Payne, S. (2006). Marital adjustment in families of young children with disabilities: Associations with daily hassles and problem-focused coping. *American Journal on Mental Retardation, 111*(1), 1–14. doi:10.1352/0895-8017

Taanila, A., Syrjälä, L., Kokkonen, J., & Järvelin, M. R. (2002). Coping of parents with physically and/or intellectually disabled children. *Child: Care, Health and Development, 28*(1), 73–86. doi:10.1046/j.1365-2214.2002.00244.x

Trute, B. (2003). Grandparents of children with developmental disabilities: Intergenerational support and family well-being. *Families in Society, 84*(1), 119–126. doi:10.1606/1044-3894.87

Turner, P. J., & Welch, K. J. (2011). *Parenting in contemporary society* (5th ed.). Upper Saddle River, NJ: Pearson.

Twoy, R., Connolly, P. M., & Novak, J. M. (2007). Coping strategies used by parents of children with autism. *Journal of the American Academy of Nurse Practitioners, 19*(5), 251–260. doi:10.1111/j.1745-7599.2007.00222.x

Urbano, R. C., & Hodapp, R. M. (2007). Divorce in families of children with Down syndrome: A population-based study. *American Journal on Mental Retardation, 112*(4), 261–274. doi:10.1352/0895-8017(2007)112[261:DIFOCW]2.0.CO;2

U.S. Department of Health and Human Services, Health Resources and Services Administration, Maternal and Child Health Bureau. (2008). *The national survey of children with special health care needs chartbook 2005–2006*. Rockville, MD: U.S. Department of Health and Human Services. Retrieved from http://mchb.hrsa.gov/cshcn05/

Van Riper, M. (2007). Families of children with Down syndrome: Responding to 'a change in plans' with resilience. *Journal of Pediatric Nursing, 22*(2), 116–128. doi:10.1016/j.pedn.2006.07.004

Weber, J. G. (2011). *Individual and family stress and crises*. Thousand Oaks, CA: Sage.

World Health Organization. (2001). *International classification of functioning, disability, and health—ICF*. Geneva, Switzerland: Author. Retrieved from http://www.who.int/classifications/icf/en/

CHAPTER 5

LGBQ-Parent Families: Development and Functioning in Context

Abbie E. Goldberg

(Continued)

returning to her former career as a lawyer, a job she hated. This change would enable the couple to relocate to a more urban, progressive, and diverse community that might more readily accept their family.

• • •

An ecological or systems approach to human development recognizes that individuals exist within, are influenced by, and interact with multiple intersecting contexts, including their families, friends, neighborhoods, communities, and workplaces, as well as broader societal institutions, ideologies, and discourses (Bronfenbrenner, 1977; Whitchurch & Constantine, 1993). Such interactions shift throughout the life cycle, as individuals develop, establish relationships, and create families and communities. This approach is particularly useful in the study of lesbian, gay, bisexual, and queer (LGBQ) individuals, whose lives, relationships, and families are increasingly visible in society and yet who continue to encounter stigma and discrimination in a range of contexts (Goldberg, 2010; Savin-Williams, 2008). Indeed, continual and pervasive exposure to stigma and lack of access to equal rights may lead LGBQ persons and their families to experience psychosocial stress (also termed *minority stress;* Meyer, 2003). Such stress arises from the stigmatization that minorities tend to experience, as well as the power imbalance that exists between minorities and the broader systems with which they interact (e.g., families, schools, health care, the legal sphere) and places minorities at risk for adverse mental health outcomes, such as depression and anxiety (Goldberg & Smith, 2011; Meyer, 2003).

This chapter discusses research on various aspects of LGBQ individuals' experiences. Special attention is paid to the situational and contextual forces that impact LGBQ people's experiences as they move through the life course, particularly those that may pose challenges for sexual minorities and their families. Topically, this chapter begins with a discussion of LGBQ people's *coming out experiences,* as well as their experiences *forming and maintaining intimate relationships*, with attention to the barriers they face in doing so (e.g., lack of recognition and stigma). Next, the multiple barriers that LGBQ people face in *becoming parents* is discussed (e.g., challenges in accessing fertility treatments; discrimination in the adoption process) with attention to the resourcefulness that they display in the face of such barriers. The research on *LGBQ parents and their children* is also highlighted, with a focus on the stressors that LGBQ-parent families experience in relation to three major overlapping contexts: their families of origin, schools, and the legal system. A discussion of the *implications of this research*, along with suggestions for teachers, therapists, social workers, health care providers, and other professionals with regard to supporting LGBQ-parent families, concludes the chapter.

COMING OUT AND BEING OUT

The process of coming out is one that is unique to the life experience and life cycle of sexual minorities. According to Cass's (1979) stage model, which is perhaps the most widely known framework for understanding the coming out process, individuals move from a state of questioning and confusion ("could I be gay?") to acceptance of one's non-heterosexual identity ("I am gay, and I will be okay") to pride and synthesis of their LGBQ identity ("This is a part of who I am and I need to let people know who I am"). Thus, the coming-out process is conceptualized as one that is relatively linear and proceeds according to a series of predefined and continuous stages. Contemporary scholars, however, have asserted that coming out is an ongoing process for sexual minorities that is not necessarily linear but is often marked by contradiction and change and both pride and shame (Dindia, 1998; Orne, 2011). Furthermore, scholars have increasingly argued for a conceptual distinction between individual sexual identity and group membership identity (McCarn & Fassinger, 1996), noting that, for example, a woman may come to terms with her same-sex erotic feelings and intimacy (and may ultimately identify as a lesbian) without identifying with or becoming active within the lesbian community. Thus, failure to disclose one's sexual orientation in diverse contexts should not necessarily be interpreted as implying an incomplete sexual identity (Cohen & Savin-Williams, 2012; Orne, 2011).

Scholars have also increasingly emphasized the importance of considering the varied situational and contextual forces that impact individual decisions to come out (Orne, 2011). In deciding whether to disclose their sexual orientation, LGBQ people must consider their immediate social contexts and potential threats associated with disclosure (e.g., verbal or physical harassment, social humiliation and rejection, loss of housing or employment), how well they know the individual at hand, and the ease of concealment (Cohen & Savin-Williams, 2012). Broader contextual factors, such as characteristics of one's family, friendship network, workplace, neighborhood, and community will also influence the coming out processes; indeed, as we saw in the opening vignette, LGBQ individuals who find themselves in settings that are not LGBQ-affirming may in turn be more hesitant to disclose their sexuality. Individuals from highly religious or politically conservative families, for example, may be particularly fearful of rejection and social alienation (Cohen & Savin-Williams, 2012) and may resist or delay coming out to family members. Social class and occupation may also impact the degree to which individuals are out in various aspects of their lives (Moore, 2011; Nixon, 2011). For example, working-class sexual minorities, who are often employed in male-dominated, blue-collar workplaces, may experience less freedom to be "out" at work than their middle-class counterparts (McDermott, 2006). As illustrated in the opening vignette, geographic location may also shape sexual minorities' negotiations around outness, insomuch as there may be fewer visible (i.e., out) LGBQ persons in rural and nonmetropolitan areas than urban areas (Kinkler & Goldberg, 2011). In turn, in the absence of a visible LGBQ community or role models, sexual minorities may experience greater hesitation or anxiety surrounding disclosure (Goldberg, 2010; Tiemann, Kennedy, & Haga, 1998).

Race and ethnicity may also shape coming out. LGBQ racial/ethnic minorities may face multiple forms of marginalization, in that they are vulnerable to racism in the LGBQ community and may also be vulnerable to heterosexism and homophobia within their own families and their racial/ethnic communities (Green, 2007; Nadal & Corpus, 2012). For example, LGBQ racial/ethnic minorities are often aware of hostile attitudes regarding homosexuality within their immediate and extended families and thus may conceal their sexual orientation because they do not wish to lose the emotional and material support that family members provide (Green, 2007; Malebranche, Fields, Bryant, & Harper, 2009), particularly if they depend on their family for financial resources (Moore, 2011). They may also hesitate to come out because of strong cultural restrictions on sexuality and gender roles (Bridges, Selvidge, & Matthews, 2003) or because they do not wish to show disrespect for their cultural upbringing (Nadal & Corpus, 2012). For example, Merighi and Grimes (2000) found that African, Mexican, and Vietnamese American gay men struggled with wanting to establish their own gay identity while also respecting certain cultural norms and ideals. They were aware their families would respond to their coming out as the "end to the family lineage" and as a source of shame and embarrassment, and thus they were cautious about making their sexual identity widely known.

Social class and geographic location may also intersect with individuals' racial and sexual identities in key ways that have implications for outness. Moore (2011) studied a sample of Black lesbians in New York and found that the middle-class and upper middle-class lesbians in her sample tended to reside in economically stable and safer communities, which facilitated their outness. In contrast, working-class women tended to reside in urban areas where "strangers . . . may be more menacing, and safety in these communities is a sobering concern—not just around sexuality but around any visible identity that targets one as an easy mark," which had the effect of limiting their ability to live open lives (Moore, 2011, p. 202).

There are a number of benefits associated with outness. First, being out may reduce self-stigma and facilitate a sense of pride in one's identity (Vaughan & Waehler, 2010). Second, failure to come out may restrict individuals' ability to meet potential partners as well as their ability to maintain healthy relationships (Vaughan & Waehler, 2010). Third, closeting (i.e., hiding one's sexual orientation) necessarily limits the amount of support that sexual minorities have available to them, which may create feelings of isolation and intrapersonal conflict and contribute to mental health problems (Lane & Wegner, 1995; Vaughan & Waehler, 2010). At the same time, closeting oneself is a protective and adaptive strategy in certain contexts, individuals who are not "out" in all areas of their lives are not necessarily less psychologically healthy than those who are (Orne, 2011). Furthermore, sexual minorities who closet themselves in certain situations do not necessarily experience ambivalence or inner conflict but recognize that such closeting is often necessary to survival (Anderson & Holliday, 2004; Moore, 2011). Indeed, it is important to recognize the function, meaning, and implications of outness will vary depending on situational contexts, such that, individuals who are very out in unsupportive or homophobic contexts may suffer mental health consequences (Goldberg & Smith, 2013a; Legate, Ryan, & Weinstein, 2012).

SAME-SEX RELATIONSHIPS

Coming out may precede or occur alongside the formation of same-sex relationships. Same-sex unions share many characteristics with heterosexual unions but are also defined by certain unique characteristics, including the partners' shared sex, the stigmatized nature of nonheterosexuality, and the absence of legal, structural, and social supports to protect and maintain these relationships (Goldberg, 2010). And yet, despite the stigmatized nature of these relationships and in contradiction to stereotypes of LGBQ individuals as incapable of forming lasting relationships (Baker, 2005), many sexual minorities are in fact members of committed same-sex relationships. According to the 2010 U.S. Census, 646,464 same-sex couples reported sharing a household. Of those couples, 131,729 reported being married, while 514,735 reported being unmarried (Gates & Cooke, 2011). These estimates are probably conservative, in that some same-sex couples likely chose to conceal their relationships on the Census.

Studies have begun to compare the quality of same-sex relationships and heterosexual relationships (e.g., in terms of perceived relationship quality and satisfaction) and have found few differences between the two groups (Goldberg, Smith, & Kashy, 2010; Kurdek, 1998; Mackey, Diemer, & O'Brien, 2004). Several studies have found that female same-sex couples report higher relationship quality than heterosexual couples (Balsam, Beauchaine, Rothblum, & Solomon, 2008; Kurdek, 2001; Meuwly, Feinstein, Davila, Nunez, & Bodenmann, 2013), a finding that may in part reflect the absence of structural barriers that have historically governed heterosexual (but not same-sex) relationships; that is, in the absence of fundamental relationship "constraints" such as legal support, family support, and children, relationships that are not highly rewarding are perhaps more easily terminated (Goldberg & Kuvalanka, 2012). Indeed, a study by Kurdek (2006) found that male and female same-sex married couples were more likely to separate than were heterosexual married couples with children (i.e., couples with multiple institutionalized barriers to leaving).

On the other hand, same-sex *parents* may be no more likely to separate than their heterosexual counterparts. For example, a study of 73 lesbian couples with children found that 30 couples had split up by the time than their children were 10 years old (Gartrell, Deck, Rodas, Peyser, & Banks, 2005; Gartrell, Rodas, Deck, Peyser, & Banks, 2006), which is comparable to rates among heterosexual couples (national survey statistics indicate that at least one third of heterosexual couples terminate their first marriages within 10 years: Bramlett & Mosher, 2001). Likewise, a longitudinal study of 150 lesbian, gay, and heterosexual adoptive couples found that by 6 years postadoptive placement, similar numbers of lesbian and heterosexual couples had separated (15% and 11%, respectively), with gay male couples showing the lowest separation rate (3%; Goldberg, Moyer, Black, & Henry, 2015). Thus, children may serve as a relationship constraint for all types of couples (i.e., they help keep couples together, regardless of parents' sexual orientation).

Characteristics of Healthy Relationships: Same-Sex Couples

Of interest are the characteristics of healthy or stable relationships among same-sex couples. That is, what factors appear to promote relationship quality? And, by extension, what variables appear to contribute to instability in same-sex relationships?

Equality

Some scholars suggest that perceptions of egalitarianism in the relationship—that is, the extent to which partners perceive themselves as sharing decision-making power, household management, and so on—may be particularly important in same-sex couples, in that both partners may be particularly sensitive to power imbalances due to their stigmatized status in society (Blumstein & Schwartz, 1983; Goldberg, 2013). Female same-sex partners in particular may be especially likely to value equality in their intimate relationships, given their common socialization as women, and, therefore, their exposure to inequity in a variety of interpersonal and institutional contexts (Blumstein & Schwartz, 1983; Goldberg, 2013). Indeed, research suggests that women in female same-sex couples tend to place a greater valuing of equality in their appraisals of "ideal" relationships (Kurdek, 1995) and are more likely to perceive equal power in their relationships, compared to heterosexual and male same-sex couples (Kurdek, 1998). Both female and male same-sex couples also tend to share housework more equitably than heterosexual couples (Goldberg, 2013; Solomon, Rothblum, & Balsam, 2005). Importantly, such sharing appears to be facilitated by financial, educational, occupational, and social resources (Goldberg, Smith, & Perry-Jenkins, 2012). For example, Carrington (2002) studied the division of labor among gay and lesbian couples and found that equal sharing of domestic labor was most common among financially comfortable couples who relied on paid help and among couples in which both partners had flexible schedules.

Perceptions of equality have in turn been linked to relationship outcomes in same-sex couples. For example, Kurdek (1998) found that higher perceived equality was associated with higher relationship satisfaction among same-sex couples. Furthermore, Kurdek (2007) found that lesbian and gay partners' satisfaction with the division of labor affected relationship satisfaction and stability over time, via the mediating influence of perceived equality in the relationship. Increasing discrepancies between ideal and actual levels of equality over time have also been linked to declines in relationship quality for both lesbian and gay partners (Kurdek, 1995).

Conflict and Difference

Few couples can avoid any conflict or disagreement in their relationships. Indeed, lesbian, gay, and heterosexual couples tend to report a similar frequency of arguments in their relationships (Peplau & Fingerhut, 2007) and to disagree about similar topics, such as finances, sex, and household tasks (Kurdek, 2006). Likewise, research suggests that higher levels of conflict are associated with lower levels of relationship quality in both heterosexual and same-sex relationships (Balsam et al., 2008; Goldberg & Sayer, 2006).

Some sources of conflict may be specific to same-sex couples, however. Given the unique relational context of same-sex relationships (e.g., partners' shared sex and shared status as stigmatized minorities), same-sex couples may encounter certain unique interpersonal patterns and challenges with regard to conflict management. Mackey, O'Brien, and Mackey (1997) found that gay men in long-term committed relationships tended to avoid discussing their thoughts, feelings, and frustrations until difficulties threatened their relationships. Perhaps such dynamics arise from the "double dose" of male socialization that characterizes gay men's relationships (i.e., men are socialized to mask or avoid emotional distress and vulnerability). Female same-sex couples struggled in other areas (Mackey et al., 1997). For example, in the early stages of their relationships, women often avoided confronting interpersonal differences in an effort to maintain relational harmony.

As their relationships progressed, however, they became less avoidant of these differences and were increasingly likely to address them. The authors suggest this change might have been facilitated by women's declining fears of being abandoned by their partners and, therefore, their greater sense of security in their current relationships. Notably, though, female same-sex couples may also benefit, in some ways, from the presence of two women, or the "double dose" of female socialization that characterizes their relationships. Indeed, Meuwly et al. (2013) compared women in same-sex and heterosexual relationships and found that women in same-sex relationships reported receiving more support from and experiencing less conflict overall with their female partners, as compared to women in heterosexual couples.

Partners within same-sex couples may differ from one another in important ways that may cause conflict. For example, racial/ethnic differences between partners may create the potential for stress and misunderstanding. Racial/ethnic minority LGBQ individuals with White partners may experience alienation within their relationships if they feel that their partners cannot empathize with the intersecting forces of sexism, heterosexism, and racism that they face on a daily basis (Balsam, Molina, Beadnell, Simoni, & Walters, 2011; Pearlman, 1996). Likewise, White partners may feel guilty about internalized or institutional racism and attempt to compensate for their privilege, a strategy that may leave both partners feeling frustrated. Furthermore, interracial same-sex couples—such as Vivian and Anya, the couple in the opening vignette—may be more identifiable than two women or men of the same ethnic group, thereby eliciting strong homophobic and racist reactions from outsiders (Rostosky, Riggle, Savage, & Gilbert, 2008; Steinbugler, 2005) and possibly placing them at risk for victimization. This perceived risk may lead couples to avoid racially homogeneous settings and to prefer diverse racial atmospheres (Rostosky et al., 2008; Steinbugler, 2005). Despite the challenges that interracial same-sex couples face, however, they often maintain healthy committed relationships. For example, Peplau, Cochran, and Mays (1997) found that, on average, interracial couples did not differ from same-race couples in terms of relationship satisfaction. Thus, many interracial same-sex couples are able to successfully navigate their differences and the stigma their relationships endure to create satisfying and lasting unions.

Social Support and Recognition

The intimate relationships of LGBQ individuals are necessarily impacted by their social networks. The support (or lack of support) they receive from their families of origin, their friends, their communities, their workplaces, and from their state and national governments has profound implications for their individual and relational health (Goldberg & Smith, 2011). Individuals in same-sex couples have been found to perceive less social support from family members compared to heterosexual couples (Goldberg & Smith, 2008; Kurdek, 2001), which may have implications for their intimate relationship quality (Goldberg et al., 2010) and mental health (Goldberg & Smith, 2008, 2011). Certain sexual minorities are particularly at risk for diminished familial support, including LGBQ racial/ethnic minorities and sexual minorities in interracial relationships (Rostosky et al., 2008). In addition, gay male couples in which one or both partners are diagnosed with HIV/AIDS may be more likely to experience rejection by and alienation from their families (Paul, Hays, & Coates, 1995), which may have negative implications for their mental health and sexual risk behaviors (Hoff, Chakraverty, Beougher, Neilands, & Darbes, 2012).

Sexual minorities also face legal nonsupport and lack of recognition. Their relationships have historically been denied many of the legal protections and securities that are routinely afforded to heterosexual couples (Goldberg & Kuvalanka, 2012; Shapiro, 2013). That is, before the Supreme Court decision on June 26, 2015, which ruled that state bans on same-sex marriage are unconstitutional (a decision that, as of this writing, continues to be protested by some law makers as well as religious officials; Gryboski, 2015), many same-sex couples were denied the right to marry. Denial of this right disallowed them of automatic financial decision-making authority on behalf of a spouse, the ability to make medical decisions for an incapacitated partner, and the ability to file joint income tax returns, among numerous other benefits (Shapiro, 2013). The legal and social recognition that marriage provides to same-sex couples arguably has the capacity to strengthen these relationships and, in turn, individual well-being (Herek, 2006). Solomon and colleagues (2005) studied couples that had obtained civil unions in Vermont and found that 54% of same-sex couples reported positive changes in their love and commitment for each other as a result of having had a civil union. Other studies have also documented the positive effects of getting married on same-sex partners' sense of security, recognition as a couple, and mental health (Lannutti, 2011; Shulman, Gotta, & Green, 2012; Wight, LeBlanc, & Badgett, 2013), although some qualitative research suggests that some sexual minorities demonstrate ambivalence about the idea of marriage (e.g., they hold concerns about "assimilating" to a heterosexual way of life; Lannutti, 2011).

BECOMING PARENTS, FORMING FAMILIES

Many sexual minorities may become parents in the context of heterosexual relationships: That is, they become parents before coming out as LGBQ, and then, in some cases, enter same-sex relationships, wherein their children may ultimately be raised in LGBQ-parent stepfamilies (Tasker, 2013). Other LGBQ people become parents in the context of same-sex committed relationships,[1] a phenomenon that has become increasingly common due in part to advancements in reproductive technology and increasingly tolerant attitudes regarding same-sex parenting and adoption (Goldberg, 2010; Savin-Williams, 2008). An estimated 3 million LGBTQ Americans have had a child, and as many as 6 million American children and adults have an LGBTQ parent (Gates, 2013). Furthermore, as of 2013, among those individuals under age 50 who are living alone or with a spouse or partner, nearly half of LGBTQ women (48%), and one fifth of LGBTQ men, are raising a child under 18 (Gates, 2013). Of note is that LGBQ parents currently represent a sizable minority of *adoptive* parents, specifically. Among couples with children, same-sex couples are four times more likely than heterosexual couples to be raising an adopted child, with 16,000 same-sex couples raising more than 22,000 adopted children in the United States (Gates, 2013).

Alternative Insemination

Same-sex couples who wish to become parents may consider several potential routes to parenthood: alternative insemination (among lesbian couples); adoption; surrogacy; or more complex parenting arrangements (e.g., a female couple and a male couple may choose to coparent). The most common routes to parenthood among intentional LGBQ-parent families are alternative insemination and adoption.[2] Each of these presents unique challenges. Female couples that choose insemination must decide who will carry the child, a decision that may have profound legal implications, in that the biological mother is automatically the legal parent, and less than half of U.S. states allow the nonbiological mother to become a legal parent to her child via pursuing a second-parent adoption[3] (Human Rights Campaign [HRC], 2014; Shapiro, 2013).[4] Lesbian couples also confront legal anxieties in the context of deciding whether to use sperm from a known or unknown donor. Indeed, women who choose unknown donors often do so out of a desire to avoid unclear or fuzzy boundaries, or potential custody challenges (Chabot & Ames, 2004; Goldberg, 2006; Haimes & Weiner, 2000). Women who pursue insemination via known donors may also experience legal worries but feel strongly that their child deserves access to their biological heritage (Goldberg & Allen, 2013; Haimes & Weiner, 2000; Touroni & Coyle, 2002). They may also choose known donors because they wish to avoid interfacing with official, potentially heterosexist institutions such as sperm banks and fertility clinics (Touroni & Coyle, 2002).

Social change, combined with the increasing visibility of female same-sex couples with children, has gradually facilitated greater awareness and more sensitive treatment of sexual minority women who seek out donor insemination; however, reports of insensitive and inappropriate treatment by health care providers continue to appear in the literature (Goldberg, 2006; Spidsberg, 2007). For example, doctors may refuse to inseminate based on moral or ethical grounds (Goldberg, 2006). In addition, some insurance carriers have historically justified their decision to only cover married women on the basis that they treat infertility, and when a woman in a married couple seeks to inseminate it is because of a medical problem "within the couple" (e.g., genetic risk) or because of infertility "within the couple" (e.g., the husband is infertile; Agigian, 2004). Sexual minority women also routinely encounter clinic forms that are inappropriate for LGBQ patients (e.g., they assume a heterosexual two-parent family), as well as health care providers who fail to acknowledge the nonbirthing partner at office visits and prenatal classes (Goldberg, 2006; Goldberg, Downing, & Richardson, 2009).

Adoption

Some same-sex couples pursue adoption as a means of becoming a parent. Specifically, couples may pursue international adoption, public domestic adoption (through the child welfare system), and private domestic adoption (e.g., through a lawyer or agency). Private domestic adoptions may in turn be "open" or "closed." Open adoption (which is increasingly common in U.S. private domestic adoptions) refers to a continuum of openness that allows birth parents and adoptive parents to have information about and to communicate with each other before and/or after placement of the child. Closed adoptions refer to arrangements in which the birth parents and adoptive parents do not exchange identifying information and there is no contact whatsoever between the birth parents and the adoptive parents.

Same-sex couples may choose private domestic open adoption because they are attracted to the possibility of maintaining contact with birth parents and/or being able to provide their child with (possibly ongoing) information about their birth parents (Goldberg, Downing, & Sauck, 2007; Goldberg, Kinkler, Richardson, & Downing, 2011). They may also be drawn to open adoption because of the greater likelihood of adopting an infant compared to international or public adoption (Downing, Richardson, Kinkler, & Goldberg, 2009). On the other hand, prospective adoptive parents may select international adoption to avoid the long wait associated with domestic private adoptions of healthy infants (Hollingsworth & Ruffin, 2002). Sexual minority prospective parents may be particularly drawn to international adoption for this reason: That is, many sexual minorities suspect that birth mothers (who often choose the adoptive parents in open adoption arrangements) are unlikely to choose them because of their sexual orientation, and they worry they will end up waiting "forever" (Goldberg, 2012; Goldberg et al., 2007). Such concerns are not unrealistic: Some birth parents specifically protest the placement of their child with LGBQ parents (Brodzinsky, 2003).

However, same-sex couples who pursue international adoption must weigh such considerations against the reality that if they choose to adopt internationally, they must closet their relationship (no country allows same-sex couples to adopt, and therefore, same-sex couples who choose this route must choose one partner to pose as a single parent). This situation can create intra- and interpersonal tension and stress, in that one partner is virtually invisible in the adoption process (Goldberg, 2012; Goldberg et al., 2007). The nonlegal partner may in turn experience feelings of inadequacy, invisibility, anxiety, or jealousy, whereas the legal partner may feel burdened with feelings of guilt and/or overresponsibility. Finally, same-sex couples who seek to adopt through the child welfare system are typically in part motivated by finances and/or altruistic reasons (e.g., the wish to give a child a permanent family; Goldberg, 2012); indeed, as described in the opening vignette, it was important to Vivian to "adopt a child of color . . . and there are so many in the foster care system that it seemed irresponsible not to choose that route." Additionally, sexual minorities may also choose to adopt via the child welfare system because they believe that they have the best chance of adopting through this route, in that the number of children in foster care far exceeds the number of heterosexual prospective adoptive parents. And yet, while it is true that sexual minorities may be welcomed by some child welfare workers and social service agencies, reports of insensitive practices by child welfare workers do continue to appear in the literature (Goldberg, 2012; Goldberg et al., 2007; Matthews & Cramer, 2006).

Upon settling on an adoption route, prospective adoptive parents must then choose an agency and/or lawyer, a process that can be particularly challenging and time-consuming for same-sex couples. Given their vulnerability in the adoption process, it is not surprising that many same-sex couples expend significant time and effort researching potential adoption agencies for evidence that they are open to working with sexual minorities (Goldberg, 2012; Goldberg et al., 2007). Furthermore, even if same-sex couples select agencies that they believe to be accepting and affirming, they may still encounter heterosexism further into the adoption process. Sexual minorities often encounter forms, materials, and support groups that seem to focus on heterosexual couples only (e.g., they presume a history of infertility; Goldberg et al., 2007, 2009; Matthews & Cramer, 2006). They may also confront adoption professionals who hold discriminatory stereotypes and attitudes toward LGBQ people and who therefore sabotage potential adoptive placements. And, because of their vulnerability in the adoption process, LGBQ prospective parents may be silent about such incidents, so as not to "make waves" and further jeopardize their chances of adopting (Goldberg, 2012). Sexual minorities with few resources (e.g., social, financial, geographic) may be particularly careful about "making waves"; indeed, same-sex couples who have few financial resources, or who live in rural areas, for example, may have few choices in terms of what agency or lawyer to work with (Kinkler & Goldberg, 2011).

Other Challenges

Sexual minorities, regardless of what route to parenthood they choose, are typically vulnerable to additional challenges as they make their way toward parenthood. For example, LGBQ people do not benefit from the societal support that heterosexual couples receive when they become parents: They may face nonsupport from other (heterosexual) parents, as well as resistance from their families of origin (Goldberg, 2010). Female same-sex couples who become parents via insemination also encounter the unique challenge of negotiating various asymmetries in their relationship (i.e., during pregnancy, with regard to breastfeeding, and in the partners' genetic relatedness to the child; Goldberg & Perry-Jenkins, 2007). Such asymmetries may create feelings of jealousy on the part of the non-biological mother, and/or conflicts over who the child "belongs" to (Goldberg, Downing, & Sauck, 2008). Such issues are initially negotiated during the transitional stage of becoming parents but likely continue to be relevant as sexual minorities shape their lives as parents and families.

There is evidence that many LGBQ people adopt transracially and/or transculturally, as was the case of Anya in the opening vignette (Gates, Badgett, Macomber, & Chambers, 2007; Goldberg, 2009). Specifically, national survey data suggest that 47% of adopted children of same-sex couples are non-White, compared to 37% of adopted children of married heterosexual couples (Gates et al., 2007). In turn, same-sex transracial adoptive households may face additional challenges related to their multiply stigmatized and highly visible family structure, in that these families are vulnerable to the stresses associated with both heterosexism *and* racism (Goldberg, 2009, 2012). For example, both parents and children may experience discrimination and rejection on the basis of their family's racial/ethnic makeup as well as on the basis of parents' sexual orientation. Because of their visibility, they may also be faced with intrusive questions about the why's and how's of their family's creation (Gianino, Goldberg, & Lewis, 2009).

LGBQ-PARENT FAMILIES: EXPERIENCES AND CHALLENGES

Next, the experiences of LGBQ parents and their children is explored. Findings related to parent, family, and child functioning and well-being is discussed. Then, the challenges that LGBQ-parent families encounter in several interrelated contexts (namely, the family, school, and legal spheres) are examined.

Parent and Child Functioning

Despite concerns that the sexual orientation of LGBQ parents will negatively affect children in both indirect and direct ways, research is consistent in indicating that sexuality is not relevant to men and women's parenting capacities and parent–child relationships. Specifically, studies that have compared lesbian, gay, and heterosexual parents in terms of mental health, parenting stress, parenting skills, and parental warmth and involvement have found few differences according to family structure (Bos, van Balen, & van den Boom, 2007; Goldberg & Smith, 2011, 2014; Golombok et al., 2003; Leung, Erich, & Kanenberg, 2005; Shechner, Slone, Lobel, & Schecter, 2013). Some studies have found that sexual minorities may have less conventional parenting values than heterosexual women and men. Specifically, lesbian mothers appear to be less interested in fostering conformity in their children (Bos et al., 2007) and may also be more accepting of a range of sexualities in their children (Tasker & Golombok, 1997).

Similarly, studies suggest that children who grow up with LGBQ parents do not appear to differ remarkably from children of heterosexual parents in terms of their emotional and behavioral adjustment. Studies have found few differences between the two groups in terms of self-esteem, depression, behavioral problems, or social functioning (Goldberg & Smith, 2013b; Golombok et al., 2003; Tasker & Golombok, 1997; van Gelderen, Bos, Gartrell, Hermanns, & Perrin, 2012; Wainright, Russell, & Patterson, 2004). In fact, some studies point to potential strengths associated with a planned LGBQ-parent family. In a study of 17-year-olds raised by lesbian mothers from birth, adolescents were rated significantly higher in social competence and significantly lower in social problems and aggressive behavior, compared to an age- and gender-matched group of adolescents with heterosexual parents (Gartrell & Bos, 2010). Other studies have found that young adults cite various strengths associated with growing up with LGBQ parents, including resilience and empathy toward marginalized groups (Goldberg, 2007). Finally, although Tasker and Golombok (1997) found that young adults with lesbian mothers were more likely to express openness to and acceptance of same-sex relationships, they were no more likely to *identify* as gay as compared to young adults with heterosexual mothers. Other research has also found that children of LGBQ parents are no more likely to assume a homosexual identification compared to children of heterosexual parents (e.g., Bailey, Bobrow, Wolfe, & Mikach, 1995).

That LGBQ parents and their children demonstrate such positive outcomes suggests remarkable resilience, given that they develop in a heterosexist society and are exposed to stigma and nonsupport in multiple intersecting, overlapping contexts (Goldberg, 2010). Specifically, LGBQ parents and their children are vulnerable to nonsupport and alienation from their *families of origin*. They are also vulnerable to misunderstanding and mistreatment in the *school context*. Finally, they also confront lack of recognition and support in the *legal sphere*. LGBQ-parent families' experiences navigating challenges in these domains are discussed next.

The Family Context

LGBQ parents may perceive less support from members of their family of origin than heterosexual parents (Goldberg & Smith, 2008) but tend to report greater support from family members than LGBQ nonparents (DeMino, Appleby, & Fisk, 2007). It seems that family members may become more supportive once a child enters the picture. Goldberg (2006) found that lesbian women's perceptions of support from their own and their partners' families increased across the transition to parenthood. Thus, some family members may push their feelings about nonheterosexuality aside and seek to repair problematic or damaged relationships in the interest of developing a relationship with a new grandchild (or niece, or nephew; Goldberg, 2012). In fact, in some cases, family ties may actually be strengthened by the arrival of a child, such that LGBQ parents enjoy closer ties to their parents after becoming parents themselves (Goldberg, 2012; Sullivan, 2004). Indeed, as Anya and Vivian experienced, Anya's family went from having a "distant" relationship to the couple "begging to babysit." Of course, not all family members become more supportive or involved across the transition to parenthood. Some LGBQ parents confront reduced support from their families upon announcing their intention to parent. For example, their families may express opposition to their decision to parent on moral or religious grounds or because they believe that life as an LGBQ-parent family will simply be too difficult (Goldberg, 2012; Sullivan, 2004).

The level of support that LGBQ-parent families receive may depend on whether the child is biologically related to the family of origin. Some research suggests that biological mothers' families may be more involved in children's lives than nonbiological mothers' families (Patterson, Hurt, & Mason, 1998). Importantly, the establishment of *legal* ties has been found to foster greater investment and involvement by extended family members: Hequembourg and Farrell (1999) observed that when nonbiological lesbian mothers secured second-parent adoption rights (thereby legally validating their relationship with their children), their own parents often became more willing to acknowledge them as parents and to emotionally invest in their grandchildren.

Families' level of support can also vary depending on the racial-ethnic match between parent and child, such that LGBQ parents who adopt across racial lines may encounter particular resistance and nonsupport from family members—as we saw in the case of Anya, in the opening vignette (Johnson & O'Connor, 2002). Family members may be uncomfortable acknowledging their new grandchild (or niece, or nephew) based upon their own racist beliefs. They may also find it difficult to embrace a child that looks different from them (Goldberg, 2012). Additionally, family members may experience (and express) concerns about the many challenges and vulnerabilities that the children might be exposed to because of their multiple marginalized statuses (Johnson & O'Connor, 2002).

The School Context

As illustrated in the opening vignette, both LGBQ parents and their children are also vulnerable to alienation and stigma within the school setting (Goldberg & Smith, 2014). A recent study conducted by the Gay, Lesbian, and Straight Education Network (GLSEN) that focused on LGBT families' experiences in education found that more than half (53%) of over 500 LGBT parents described various forms of exclusion from their children's school communities (i.e., being excluded or prevented from fully participating in school activities and events, being excluded by school policies and procedures, and being ignored; Kosciw & Diaz, 2008). For example, parents were told that they could not be aids in their children's classrooms, that only one parent was allowed to attend a school event, and that their offers to assist with creating a more inclusive classroom were not welcome or needed. Furthermore, 26% of LGBT parents reported being mistreated by other parents (e.g., being stared at or ignored). Importantly, parents whose children's schools had comprehensive safe school policies (i.e., policies that protected both students and their parents from harassment or exclusion based on actual or perceived sexual orientation or gender) reported lower levels of mistreatment than did parents whose children's schools did not have such policies.

The GLSEN survey also found that 40% of the 154 students surveyed reported being verbally harassed in school because of their family (e.g., being called names such as "fag" and "lesbo"). Furthermore, although the vast majority of students in the study identified as heterosexual, 38% reported being verbally harassed at school because of their real or perceived sexual orientation; thus, they were assumed to be gay because their parents were gay (Kosciw & Diaz, 2008). Such data would appear to suggest that peer teasing and bullying are quite common; however, it is important to recognize that such experiences tend to be relatively prominent at certain developmental periods and relatively minimal at others, as illustrated in Keisha's case in the opening vignette. Gartrell et al. (2000) found that 18% of lesbian mothers reported that their 5-year-old children had experienced some type of homophobia from peers or teachers. However, by the age of 10, almost half of children had reportedly experienced some form of homophobia (e.g., in the form of teasing; Gartrell et al., 2005). Similarly, a study of LGBQ parents and their children in Australia found that no children in kindergarten through second grade had experienced bullying; 44% of children in Grades 3 through 6 had experienced bullying related to their parents' sexual orientation; 45% of children in Grades 7 through 10 had experienced bullying or harassment; and 14% of children in Grades 11 through 12 had experienced bullying (Ray & Gregory, 2001). Those who did not encounter bullying attributed it to the geographical area that they lived in or the type of school that they attended (e.g., progressive private schools). Thus, middle- and upper middle-class LGBQ parents may be at an advantage with regard to protecting their children from bullying: Their social and financial resources allow them some choice in where they live, and they may therefore favor areas and schools that are known to be more inclusive and progressive (Goldberg & Smith, 2014). Indeed, in the case of Anya and Vivian, both were considering career changes that would allow them to move to a more progressive area where their family and child would be better received.

It is notable that despite their potential vulnerability to teasing and stigma, the academic progress and performance of children of LGBQ parents appears to be on par with that of children of heterosexual parents (Potter, 2012; Rosenfeld, 2010). Growing up with LGBQ parents is not related to delayed progression through elementary school (Rosenfeld, 2010), nor is it related to lower academic achievement (Gartrell & Bos, 2010; Wainright et al., 2004).

The Legal Context

The legal sphere also presents challenges for LGBQ parents and their families. Historically, LGBQ parents have lacked legal recognition of their relationships—although again, with the 2015 Supreme Court decision on gay marriage, the legal landscape for same-sex relationship recognition has changed (although continues to be contested at the time of this writing). Second, they may also lack legal recognition of their parental status. Specifically, prior to the Supreme Court decision, many states did not allow openly same-sex couples to co-adopt their children—that is, to adopt their child jointly—on the basis that couples had to be married in order to adopt.[5] Thus, same-sex couples living in these states have historically had to select one partner to perform the official adoption; and then, in some states, same-sex partners were able to complete a second-parent adoption, thereby enabling their child to have two legal parents (HRC, 2014). Similarly, female same-sex couples that create their families via donor insemination have historically sought to obtain a second-parent adoption for the nonbiological, nonlegal parent (again, when available in their state of residence).

Research has shown that inequalities in parents' legal relationships to their children can have devastating consequences if couples dissolve their relationships. In such situations, the parental status of the legal parent (who is often also the biological parent) is virtually always affirmed (Goldberg & Allen, 2013). For example, in one study of 77 lesbian couples that consisted of a biological mother and a nonbiological mother, 30 couples had separated by the time that their children were 10; of these 30 couples, custody was shared after 13 separations, and the biological mother retained sole or primary custody in 15 cases (Gartrell et al., 2006). Couples in which the nonbiological mother had obtained a second-parent adoption were more likely to share custody, highlighting the importance of legal supports for family stability and, in turn, child well-being.

CONCLUSION AND SUGGESTIONS FOR PRACTITIONERS

LGBQ parents and their children are vulnerable to social and legal challenges at multiple stages of the life course and in multiple settings. For example, Anya, Vivian, and Keisha encountered nonsupport from their family, school, and community at various points during their lives. Such challenges undermine the integrity of sexual minorities' family relationships and threaten their emotional and physical well-being. And yet, LGBQ parents and their children demonstrate remarkable resilience in the face of such challenges. This resilience is likely facilitated by the formation of strong and stable relationships that are characterized by equality, mutuality, and compassion (Connolly, 2005; Kurdek, 1998); access to and engagement with an active and/or visible LGBQ community (Russell & Richards, 2003); and perceptions of support and affirmation from one's family and/or friendship network (Goldberg, 2012; Russell & Richards, 2003). Of course, the fact that LGBQ parents and their children demonstrate remarkable resilience by no means legitimates the heterosexism that they face in their everyday lives. Scholars, practitioners, educators, and policy makers are urged to work on behalf of LGBQ persons and families to identify and ameliorate the conditions that underlie and perpetuate the social stress and oppression that sexual minorities must endure. By destabilizing systems of oppression and inequality, we can begin to improve the social conditions in which sexual minorities live.

Therapists and practitioners who work with same-sex couples should be attentive to the unique dimensions of their relationships as compared to heterosexual relationships but at the same time should remain cognizant of the ways in which same-sex couples' relational difficulties may reflect "universal" relationship conflicts. Furthermore, therapists should be sensitive to the many variables and contexts that impact the formation, nature, and stability of same-sex relationships, such as similarities/differences between partners in terms of outness, race, and so on. Finally, and perhaps most importantly, therapists should maintain a heightened awareness of the ways in which both subtle and overt forms of societal stigma and exclusion may contribute to existing individual and relational problems. For example, in treating a socially isolated lesbian couple, a therapist should recognize the potential systemic causes of their isolation and should resist blaming the couple for their lack of social connectedness.

Practitioners (e.g., gynecologists, social workers) and institutions (e.g., fertility clinics, adoption agencies) that work with LGBQ individuals and couples during the transitional stage of becoming parents should strive to communicate a philosophy of inclusion and acceptance. Pink triangles, rainbow decals, and other symbols of LGBQ affirmation can be posted inconspicuously in hospitals, offices, and waiting rooms. Facilitators of prenatal education classes and adoption support groups can strive to use inclusive language (e.g., terms such as "partner"; Goldberg, 2006, 2012). In addition, practitioners (e.g., lawyers, social workers) who work with prospective LGBQ parents should aim to educate couples *in advance* about the legal barriers that they may face (e.g., in obtaining coparent or second-parent adoptions) and should assist them in (a) understanding the consequences of such barriers (e.g., the fact that their child will have one legal parent) and (b) considering other legal safeguards (e.g., living wills, medical powers of attorney, financial powers of attorney, hospital visitation authorizations) to offset the challenges posed by these barriers (Shapiro, 2013).

School educators and personnel are encouraged to take steps to reduce stigmatization of LGBQ-parent families by actively creating a climate of acceptance and inclusion of these families within schools and classrooms (Goldberg & Smith, 2014). School educators and administrators, for example, may choose to seek ongoing training and education about diverse families (e.g., via organizations such as the Gay, Lesbian, and Straight Education Network: www.glsen.org). Such training will support them in advocating for diverse families and actively fighting discrimination and prejudice against children resulting from their parents' sexual orientations.

Finally, at the policy/legal level, greater protections are clearly needed for LGBQ-parent families. State laws that discriminate against LGBQ-parent families (e.g., by allowing adoption and foster care agencies to refuse to place children with LGBQ indivdiuals or couples) render families vulnerable to stigma and serve to legitimate treatment of children and families as second-class citizens. Laws that protect the parenting rights of LGBQ parent-families will help to (a) foster acceptance, (b) ensure the protection of these families via the provision of standard rights and benefits, and (c) promote the stability and security of LGBQ parent-families and their children, thereby contributing to their health and well-being.

REFERENCES

Agigian, A. (2004). *Baby steps: How lesbian alternative insemination is changing the world*. Middletown, CT: Wesleyan University Press.

Anderson, S. C., & Holliday, M. (2004). Normative passing in the lesbian community: An exploratory study. *Journal of Gay & Lesbian Social Services, 17*, 25–38.

Bailey, J. M., Bobrow, D., Wolfe, M., & Mikach, S. (1995). Sexual orientation of adult sons of gay fathers. *Developmental Psychology, 31*, 124–129.

Baker, P. (2005). *Public discourses of gay men*. London, England: Routledge.

Balsam, K. F., Beauchaine, T. P., Rothblum, E. D., & Solomon, S. (2008). Three-year follow-up of same-sex couples who had civil unions in Vermont, same-sex couples not in civil unions, and heterosexual married couples. *Developmental Psychology, 44*, 102–116.

Balsam, K. F., Molina, Y., Beadnell, B., Simoni, J. M., & Walters, K. (2011). Measuring multiple minority stress: The LGBT People of Color Microaggressions Scale. *Cultural Diversity and Ethnic Minority Psychology, 17*, 163–174.

Berkowitz, D. (2013). Gay men and surrogacy. In A. E. Goldberg & K. R. Allen (Eds.), *LGBT-parent families: Innovations in research and implications for practice* (pp. 71–85). New York, NY: Springer.

Blumstein, P., & Schwartz, P. (1983). *American couples: Money, work, sex*. New York, NY: William Morrow.

Bos, H. M. W., van Balen, F., & van den Boom, D. C. (2007). Child adjustment and parenting in planned lesbian-parent families. *American Journal of Orthopsychiatry, 77*, 38–48.

Bramlett, M. D., & Mosher, W. D. (2001). *First marriage, dissolution, divorce and remarriage: United States: Advance data from vital and health statistics, No. 323*. Hyattsville, MD: National Center for Health Statistics.

Bridges, S. K., Selvidge, M. M. D., & Matthews, C. R. (2003). Lesbian women of color: Therapeutic issues and challenges. *Journal of Multicultural Counseling and Development, 31*, 113–130

Brodzinsky, D. M. (2003). *Adoption by lesbians and gay men: A national survey of adoption agency policies, practices and attitudes*. Retrieved on March 27, 2008 from http://www.adoptioninstitute.org/whowe/Gay%20and%20Lesbian%20Adoption1.html

Bronfenbrenner, U. (1977). Toward an experimental ecology of human development. *American Psychologist, 32*, 513–31.

Carrington, C. (2002). *No place like home: Relationships and family life among lesbians and gay men*. Chicago, IL: University of Chicago Press.

Cass, V. C. (1979). Homosexual identity formation: Testing a theoretical model. *Journal of Homosexuality, 4*, 219–235.

Chabot, J. M., & Ames, B. D. (2004). "It wasn't 'let's get pregnant and go do it'": Decision-making in lesbian couples planning motherhood via donor insemination. *Family Relations, 53*, 348–356.

Cohen, K., & Savin-Williams, R. (2012). Coming out to self and others: Developmental milestones. In P. Leyounis, J. Drescher, & M. Barber (Eds.), *The LGBT casebook* (pp. 17–33). Arlington, VA: American Psychiatric Publishing.

Connolly, C. M. (2005). A qualitative exploration of resilience in long-term lesbian couples. *The Family Journal, 13*, 266–280.

DeMino, K. A., Appleby, G., & Fisk, D. (2007). Lesbian mothers with planned families: A comparative study of internalized homophobia and social support. *American Journal of Orthopsychiatry, 77*, 165–173.

Dindia, K. (1998). "Going into and coming out of the closet": The dialectics of stigma disclosure In B. M. Montgomery & L. A. Baxter (Eds.), *Dialectical approaches to studying personal relationships* (pp. 83–108). Mahwah, NJ: Erlbaum.

Downing, J. B., Richardson, H. B., Kinkler, L. A., & Goldberg, A. E. (2009). Making the decision: Factors influencing gay men's choice of an adoption path. *Adoption Quarterly, 12,* 247–271.

Gates, G. (2013). *LGBT parenting in the United States.* Los Angeles, CA: The Williams Institute. Retrieved from http://williamsinstitute.law.ucla.edu/wp-content/uploads/LGBT-Parenting.pdf

Gates, G., Badgett, M. V. L., Macomber, J. E., & Chambers, K. (2007). *Adoption and foster care by gay and lesbian parents in the United States.* Washington, DC: The Urban Institute.

Gates, G., & Cooke, A. (2011). *United States Census snapshot: 2010.* Los Angeles, CA: The Williams Institute. Retrieved from http://williamsinstitute.law.ucla.edu/wp-content/uploads/Census2010Snapshot-US-v2.pdf

Gartrell, N., Banks, A., Reed, N., Hamiliton, J., Rodas, C., & Deck, A. (2000). The National Lesbian Family Study: 3. Interviews with mothers of five-year-olds. *American Journal of Orthopsychiatry, 70,* 542–548.

Gartrell, N., Deck, A., Rodas, C., Peyser, H., & Banks, A. (2005). The National Lesbian Family Study: 4. Interviews with the 10-year-old children. *American Journal of Orthopsychiatry, 75,* 518–524.

Gartrell, N., Rodas, C., Deck, A., Peyser, H., & Banks, A. (2006). The USA National Lesbian Family Study: Interviews with mothers of 10-year-olds. *Feminism & Psychology, 16,* 175–192.

Gartrell, N. K., & Bos, H. M. W. (2010). US National Longitudinal Lesbian Family Study: Psychological adjustment of 17-year-old adolescents. *Pediatrics, 126,* 28–36.

Gianino, M., & Goldberg, A. E., & Lewis, T. (2009). Family outings: Disclosure practices among adopted youth with gay and lesbian parents. *Adoption Quarterly, 12,* 205–228.

Goldberg, A. E. (2006). The transition to parenthood for lesbian couples. *Journal of GLBT Family Studies, 2,* 13–42.

Goldberg, A. E. (2009). Lesbian and heterosexual preadoptive couples' openness to transracial adoption. *American Journal of Orthopsychiatry, 79,* 103–117.

Goldberg, A. E. (2010). *Lesbian and gay parents and their children: Research on the family life cycle.* Washington, DC: American Psychological Association.

Goldberg, A. E. (2012). *Gay dads: Transitions to adoptive fatherhood.* New York, NY: NYU Press.

Goldberg, A. E. (2013). "Doing" and "undoing" gender: The meaning and division of housework in same-sex couples. *Journal of Family Theory and Review, 5,* 85–104.

Goldberg, A. E., & Allen, K. A. (2013). Same-sex relationship dissolution and LGB stepfamily formation: Perspectives of young adults with LGB parents. *Family Relations. 62,* 529–544

Goldberg, A. E., Downing, J. B., & Richardson, H. B. (2009). The transition from infertility to adoption: Perceptions of lesbian and heterosexual preadoptive couples. *Journal of Social and Personal Relationships, 26,* 938–963.

Goldberg, A. E., Downing, J. B., & Sauck, C. C. (2007). Choices, challenges, and tensions: Perspectives of lesbian prospective adoptive parents. *Adoption Quarterly, 10,* 33–64.

Goldberg, A. E., Downing, J. B., & Sauck, C. C. (2008). Perceptions of children's parental preferences in lesbian two-mother households. *Journal of Marriage and Family, 70,* 419–434.

Goldberg, A. E., Kinkler, L. A., Richardson, H. B., & Downing, J. B. (2011). Perceptions and experiences of open adoption among lesbian, gay, and heterosexual couples: A qualitative study. *Journal of Marriage and Family, 73,* 502–518.

Goldberg, A. E., & Kuvalanka, K. A. (2012). Marriage (in)equality: The perspectives of adolescents and emerging adults with lesbian, gay, and bisexual parents. *Journal of Marriage and Family, 74,* 34–52.

Goldberg, A. E., Moyer, A, Black, K., & Henry, A. (2015). Lesbian and heterosexual adoptive mothers' experiences of relationship dissolution. *Sex Roles.* doi:10.1007/s11199-014-0432-2

Goldberg, A. E., & Perry-Jenkins, M. (2007). The division of labor and perceptions of parental roles: Lesbian couples across the transition to parenthood. *Journal of Social & Personal Relationships, 24,* 297–318.

Goldberg, A. E., & Sayer, A. G. (2006). Lesbian couples' relationship quality across the transition to parenthood. *Journal of Marriage and Family, 68,* 87–100.

Goldberg, A. E., & Smith, J. Z. (2008). Social support and well-being in lesbian and heterosexual preadoptive parents. *Family Relations, 57,* 281–294.

Goldberg, A. E., & Smith, J. Z. (2011). Stigma, social context, and mental health: Lesbian and gay couples across the transition to adoptive parenthood. *Journal of Counseling Psychology, 58,* 139–150.

Goldberg, A. E., & Smith, J. Z. (2013a). Work conditions and mental health in lesbian and gay dual-earner parents. *Family Relations, 62,* 727–740.

Goldberg, A. E., & Smith, J. Z. (2013b). Predictors of psychological adjustment among early-placed adopted children with lesbian, gay, and heterosexual parents. *Journal of Family Psychology, 27,* 431–442.

Goldberg, A. E., & Smith, J. Z. (2014). Preschool selection considerations and experiences of school mistreatment among lesbian, gay, and heterosexual adoptive parents. *Early Childhood Research Quarterly, 29,* 64–75.

Goldberg, A. E., Smith, J. Z., & Kashy, D. A. (2010). Pre-adoptive factors predicting lesbian, gay, and heterosexual couples' relationship quality across the transition to adoptive parenthood. *Journal of Family Psychology, 24,* 221–232.

Goldberg, A. E., Smith, J. Z., & Perry-Jenkins, M. (2012). The division of labor in lesbian, gay, and heterosexual new adoptive parents. *Journal of Marriage and Family, 74,* 812–828.

Golombok, S., Perry, B., Burston, A., Murray, C., Mooney-Somers, J., Stevens, M., & Golding, J. (2003). Children with lesbian parents: A community study. *Developmental Psychology, 39,* 20–33.

Green, A. I. (2007). On the horns of a dilemma: Institutional dimensions of the sexual career in a sample of middle-class, urban, Black, gay men. *Journal of Black Studies, 37,* 753–774.

Green, E. (2015, June 26). How will the U.S. Supreme Court's same-sex marriage decision affect religious liberty? *The Atlantic.* Retrieved from http://www.theatlantic.com/politics/archive/2015/06/how-will-the-us-supreme-courts-same-sex-marriage-decision-affect-religious-liberty/396986

Gryboski, M. (2015, July 29). Texas lawmaker tells county clerks to ignore Supreme Court's gay marriage ruling. *Christian Post.* Retrieved from http://www.christianpost.com/news/tennessee-lawmaker-tells-county-clerks-to-ignore-supreme-courts-gay-marriage-ruling-142047

Haimes, E., & Weiner, K. (2000). 'Everybody's got a dad . . . : Issues for lesbian families in the management of donor insemination. *Sociology of Health & Illness, 22,* 477–499.

Herek, G. M. (2006). Legal recognition of same-sex relationships in the United States: A social science perspective. *American Psychologist, 61,* 607–621.

Hequembourg, A., & Farrell, M. (1999). Lesbian motherhood: Negotiating marginal-mainstream identities. *Gender & Society, 13,* 540–55.

Hoff, C., Chakraverty, D., Beougher, S., Neilands, T., & Darbes, L. (2012). Relationship characteristics associated with sexual risk behavior among MSM in committed relationships. *AIDS Patient Care & STDs, 26,* 738–746.

Hollingsworth, L., & Ruffin, V. M. (2002). Why are so many U. S. families adopting internationally? A social exchange perspective. *Journal of Human Behavior in the Social Environment, 6,* 81–97.

Human Rights Campaign. (2014). *Parenting laws: Second-parent or stepparent adoption.* Retrieved from http://s3.amazonaws.com/hrc-assets//files/assets/resources/parenting_second-parent-adoption_2-2014.pdf

Johnson, S. M., & O'Connor, E. (2002). *The gay baby boom: The psychology of gay parenthood.* New York: New York University Press.

Kinkler, L. A., & Goldberg, A. E. (2011). Working with what we've got: Perceptions of barriers and supports among same-sex adopting couples in non-metropolitan areas. *Family Relations, 60,* 387–403.

Kosciw, J. G., & Diaz, E. M. (2008). *Involved, invisible, ignored: The experiences of lesbian, gay, bisexual, and transgender parents and their children in our nation's K-12 schools.* New York, NY: GLSEN.

Kurdek, L. A. (1995). Developmental changes in relationship quality in gay and lesbian cohabiting couples. *Developmental Psychology, 31,* 86–94.

Kurdek, L. A. (1998). Relationship outcomes and their predictors: Longitudinal evidence from heterosexual married, gay cohabiting, and lesbian cohabiting couples. *Journal of Marriage & the Family, 60,* 553–568.

Kurdek, L. A. (2001). Differences between heterosexual non-parent couples and gay, lesbian, and heterosexual parent couples. *Journal of Family Issues, 22,* 727–754.

Kurdek, L. A. (2006). Differences between partners from heterosexual, gay, and lesbian cohabiting couples. *Journal of Marriage and Family, 68,* 509–528.

Kurdek, L. A. (2007). The allocation of household labor by partners in gay and lesbian couples. *Journal of Family Issues, 28,* 132–148.

Lane, J. D., & Wegner, D. M. (1995). The cognitive consequences of secrecy. *Journal of Personality and Social Psychology, 69,* 237–253.

Lannutti, P. J. (2011). Security, recognition, and misgivings: Exploring older same-sex couples' experiences of legally recognized same-sex marriage. *Journal of Social & Personal Relationships, 28,* 64–82.

Legate, N., Ryan, R., & Weinstein, N. (2012). Is coming out always a 'good thing'? Exploring the relations of autonomy support, outness, and wellness for lesbian, gay, and bisexual individuals. *Social Psychology & Personality Science, 3,* 145–152.

Leung, P., Erich, S., & Kanenberg, H. (2005). A comparison of family functioning in gay/lesbian, heterosexual and special needs adoptions. *Children & Youth Services Review, 27,* 1031–1044.

Mackey, R. A., Diemer, M. A., & O'Brien, B. A. (2004). Relational factors in understanding satisfaction in the lasting relationships of same-sex and heterosexual couples. *Journal of Homosexuality, 47,* 111–136.

Mackey, R. A., O'Brien, B. A., & Mackey, E. F. (1997). *Gay male and lesbian couples: Voices from lasting relationships.* Westport, CT: Praeger.

Malebranche, D. J., Fields, E. L., Bryant, L. O., & Harper, S. R. (2009). Masculine socialization and sexual risk behaviors among Black men who have sex with men: A qualitative exploration. *Men and Masculinities, 12,* 90–112.

Matthews, J., & Cramer, E. (2006). Envisaging the adoption process to strengthen gay- and lesbian-headed families: Recommendations for adoption professionals. *Child Welfare, 85,* 317–340.

McCarn, S. R., & Fassinger, R. E. (1996). Revisioning sexual minority identity formation: A New model of lesbian identity and its implications for counseling and research. *The Counseling Psychologist, 24,* 508–534.

McDermott, E. (2006). Surviving in dangerous places: Lesbian identity performances in the workplace, social class, and psychological health. *Feminism & Psychology, 16,* 193–211.

Merighi, J. R., & Grimes, M. D. (2000). Coming out to families in a multicultural context. *Families in Society, 81,* 32–41.

Meuwly, N., Feinstein, B., Davila, J., Nunez, D., Garcia, D., & Bodenmann, G. (2013). Relationship quality among Swiss women in opposite-sex versus same-sex romantic relationships. *Swiss Journal of Psychology, 72,* 229–233.

Meyer, I. (2003). Prejudice, social stress, and mental health in lesbian, gay, and bisexual populations: Conceptual issues and research evidence. *Psychological Bulletin, 129,* 674–697.

Moore, M. R. (2011). *Invisible families: Gay identities, relationships, and motherhood among Black women.* Berkeley: University of California Press.

Nadal, K. L., & Corpus, M. J. H. (2012). "Tomboys" and "baklas": Experiences of lesbian and gay Filipino Americans. *Asian American Journal of Psychology*, 1–14.

National Center on Lesbian Rights (NCLR). (2015). *Legal recognition of LGBT families.* Retrieved from http://www.nclrights.org/wp-content/uploads/2013/07/Legal_Recognition_of_LGBT_Families .pdf

Nixon, C. A. (2011). Working-class lesbian parents' emotional engagement with their children's education: Intersections of class and sexuality. *Sexualities, 141*, 78–99.

NeJaime, D. (in press). Marriage equality and the new parenthood. *Harvard Law Review*.

Orne, J. (2011). "You will always have to 'out' yourself": Reconsidering coming out through strategic outness. *Sexualities, 14*, 681–703.

Patterson, C. J., Hurt, S., & Mason, C. D. (1998). Families of the lesbian baby boom: Children's contact with grandparents and other adults. *American Journal of Orthopsychiatry, 68,* 390–399.

Paul, J., Hays, R., & Coates, T. (1995). The impact of the HIV epidemic on U.S. gay male communities. In R. Savin-Williams & C. Patterson (Eds.), *Lesbian, gay and bisexual identities over the lifespan: Children to adults* (pp. 436-561). New York, NY: Harcourt Brace.

Pearlman, S. F. (1996). Loving across race and class divides: Relational challenges and the interracial lesbian couple. *Women & Therapy, 19*, 25–35.

Peplau, L. A., Cochran, S. D., & Mays, V. M. (1997). A national survey of the intimate relationships of African American lesbians and gay men: A look at commitment, satisfaction, sexual behavior, and HIV disease. In B. Greene (Ed.), *Ethnic and cultural diversity among lesbians and gay men* (pp. 11–38). Thousand Oaks, CA: Sage.

Peplau, L. A., & Fingerhut, A. W. (2007). The close relationships of lesbians and gay men. *Annual Review of Psychology, 58,* 373–408.

Potter, D. (2012). Same-sex parent families and children's academic achievement. *Journal of Marriage and Family, 74*, 556–571.

Ray, V., & Gregory, R. (2001). School experiences of the children of lesbian and gay parents. *Family Matters, 59*, 28–35.

Rosenfeld, M. J. (2010). Nontraditional families and childhood progress through school. *Demography*, *47*, 755–775.

Rostosky, S., Riggle, E., Savage, T., Roberts, S., & Gilberg, S. (2008). Interracial same-sex couples' perceptions of stress and coping: An exploratory study. *Journal of GLBT Family Studies, 4*, 277–299.

Russell, G. M., & Richards, J. A. (2003). Stressor and resilience factors for lesbians, gay men, and bisexuals confronting antigay politics. *American Journal of Community Psychology, 31,* 313–328.

Savin-Williams, R. C. (2008). Then and now: Recruitment, definition, diversity, and positive attributes of same-sex populations. *Developmental Psychology, 44,* 135–138.

Shechner, T., Slone, M., Lobel, T., & Schecter, R. (2013). Children's adjustment in non-traditional families in Israel: The effect of parental sexual orientation and the number of parents on children's development. *Child: Care, Health, & Development, 29,* 178–184.

Shapiro, J. (2013). The law governing LGBT-parent families. In A. E. Goldberg & K. R. Allen (Eds.), *LGBT-parent families: Innovations in research and implications for practice* (pp. 291–304). New York, NY: Springer.

Shulman, J., Gotta, G., & Green, R-J. (2012). Will marriage matter? Effects of marriage anticipated by same-sex couples. *Journal of Family Issues, 33,* 158–181.

Solomon, S. E., Rothblum, E. D., & Balsam, K. F. (2005). Money, housework, sex, and conflict: Same-sex couples in civil unions, those not in civil unions, and heterosexual married siblings. *Sex Roles, 52*, 561–575.

Spidsberg, B. D. (2007). Vulnerable and strong: Lesbian women encountering maternity care. *Journal of Advanced Nursing, 60,* 478–486.

Steinbugler, A. C. (2005). Visibility as privilege and danger: Heterosexual and same-sex interracial intimacy in the 21st century. *Sexualities, 8,* 425–443.

Sullivan, M. (2004). *The family of woman: Lesbian mothers, their children, and the undoing of gender.* Berkeley, CA: University of California Press.

Tasker, F. L. (2013). Lesbian and gay parenting post-heterosexual divorce and separation. In A. E. Goldberg & K. R. Allen (Eds.), *LGBT-parent families: Innovations in research and implications for practice* (pp. 3–20). New York, NY: Springer.

Tasker, F. L., & Golombok, S. (1997). *Growing up in a lesbian family: Effects on child development.* London, England: Guilford Press.

Tiemann, K., Kennedy, S., & Haga, M. (1998). Rural lesbians' strategies for coming out to health care professionals. In C. M. Ponticelli (Ed.), *Gateways to improving lesbian health and health care: Opening doors* (pp. 61–75).

Touroni, E., & Coyle, A. (2002). Decision-making in planned lesbian parenting: An interpretative phenomenological analysis. *Journal of Community & Applied Social Psychology, 12,* 194–209.

van Gelderen, L., Bos, H. M. W., Gartrell, N. K., Hermanns, J., & Perrin, E. C. (2012). Quality of life of adolescents raised from birth by lesbian mothers: The U.S. National Longitudinal Lesbian Family Study. *Journal of Developmental & Behavioral Pediatrics, 33,* 1–7.

Vaughan, M. D., & Waehler, C. A. (2010). Coming out growth: Conceptualizing and measuring stress-related growth associated with coming out to others as a sexual minority. *Journal of Adult Development, 17,* 94–109.

Wainright, J., Russell, S., & Patterson, C. (2004). Psychosocial adjustment, school outcomes, and romantic relationships of adolescents with same-sex parents. *Child Development, 75,* 1886–1898.

Whitchurch, G. G., & Constantine, L. L. (1993). Systems theory. In P. G. Boss, W. J., Doherty, R., LaRossa, W. R. Schumm, & S. K. Steinmetz (Eds.), *Sourcebook of family theories and methods: A contextual approach* (pp. 325–352). New York, NY: Plenum.

Wight, R. G., LeBlanc, A., & Badgett, M. V. L. (2013). Same-sex legal marriage and psychological well-being: Findings from the California Health Interview Survey. *American Journal of Public Health, 103,* 339–346.

NOTES

1. These families are often referred to as "planned" or "intentional" LGBQ-parent families.
2. For a review of the limited research on surrogacy by LGBQ people, see Berkowitz (2013).
3. Second-parent adoptions allow nonlegal parents to adopt their partners' children without requiring the biological parents to give up their parental rights. These adoptions have historically been used by heterosexual stepparents to adopt their wives'/husbands' children. Some courts have interpreted the second-parent adoption to apply in same-sex couples, whereas others have not (Shapiro, 2013).
4. With the supreme court decision on same-sex marriage, many people have assumed that parental rights issues for same-sex couples will disappear (NeJaime, in press). In fact, parentage is (generally) not conclusively established through marriage for same-sex or different-sex couples, although there is a marital presumption that applies: namely, the husband of a woman who gives birth is presumed to be the father of child (although this presumption can be rebutted in certain circumstances, through, for example, evidence of nonbiological connection). Hence, in some states, nonbiological married fathers who are the intended parents in different-sex marriages are also technically just as vulnerable to questions of parentage as nonbiological parents in same-sex marriages. In turn, the

recommendation that nonbiological lesbian mothers continue to complete second-parent (or step-parent) adoptions still stands (despite the reality that most husbands in different-sex marriage do not complete these). Advocacy is currently being focused on ensuring that marital presumptions of parentage apply equally regardless of whether marriage is same-sex or different-sex (National Center on Lesbian Rights, 2015).

5. Although same-sex couples living in states that formerly prohibited same-sex couples from adopting on the basis of the fact that they were not married should theoretically now be able to co-adopt, it is not yet clear whether efforts to do so will meet resistance. Indeed, some states have passed laws allowing adoption agencies—even those that are publically funded—to refuse to place children with same-sex couples if they have religious objections to doing so (Green, 2015).

CHAPTER 6

Stress and Coping in Later Life

Áine M. Humble and Christine A. Price

Vignette

Alfonso and Malena Gomez live in a small town, and their two children, Carmen and Eduardo, and four grandchildren live nearby. Alfonso, 68, retired from construction, and Malena, 61, retired from teaching. They both retired this year, although Malena would have preferred to keep working a few more years. Alfonso loves to fish and take long walks when the weather is good. Malena reads and does crossword puzzles and draws strength from her religious faith. Alfonso has big plans for retirement; he wants to travel in a newly purchased RV and go fishing as often as he can. They feel they are healthy; however, Alfonso has macular degeneration and difficulty sleeping, and Malena has arthritis. In recent years, she has also showed some short-term memory loss. Carmen has been pushing to get her mother's memory checked, but Alfonso is resistant. He is afraid of what they may find, and being a caregiver for his wife is not something he wants to consider. Carmen provides most of the assistance to her parents and knows this will only increase. She feels frustrated that Eduardo is not "stepping up to the plate" and doing more to help out their parents. Because Carmen works full-time and has a family of her own, she also worries her responsibilities will eventually overwhelm her and negatively affect her marriage.

• • •

As illustrated in the vignette, aging takes place within the context of families. Yet, it is often viewed primarily from a human development perspective, with little recognition given to the importance of family relationships or the impact that family roles and responsibilities have on the aging process. In response to this situation, the field of *family gerontology* emerged to draw attention to the intersection between aging, family systems, and the life course (Roberto, Blieszner, & Allen, 2006). This intersection can be conceptualized from the perspective of the aging individual or from the family system, with emphasis on the experiences of older family members (Blieszner & Bedford, 1995). A bidirectional approach enables researchers and practitioners to consider the influences that family members have on individual responses to the processes of aging as well as older adults' impacts on their families.

In this chapter, we discuss individual and family challenges that can coincide with aging. We emphasize the concept of the "aging family" as it pertains to later life family relationships, transitions, and the social support networks of older family members. We discuss the demographic changes taking place in the United States that have profoundly affected the structure of American society. Using both ecological systems theory and the ABC-X model of family stress, we explore stressful events commonly associated with aging, focusing on elder abuse, retirement, and caregiving. Finally, models of coping and adaptation applied in later life are reviewed.

THE AGING FAMILY

From a family development perspective, an *aging family* consists of primary members who are middle aged (at least 40 years old) and older (Silverstein & Giarrusso, 2010) and who are experiencing later-life events and transitions such as retirement, widowhood, later-life divorce and/or marriage, grandparenthood, caregiving, and end-of-life issues. The study of aging families pertains to entire family systems, with emphasis on relationships, transitions, and social support networks of older family members.

Everyone ages within a family context, regardless of family size or whether all members are biologically related. Not all older adults, however, follow a traditional life course (i.e., marry, have children, launch children, retire). Factors such as high rates of divorce, increased cohabitation and remarriage, same-sex marriage, and reduced fertility "have altered the microcontext in which intergenerational, spousal, and sibling relationships function" (Silverstein & Giarrusso, 2010, p. 1039). Because of the family diversity in the United States today, scholars need to recognize the many types of families that impact individual aging experiences. In this chapter, we employ a broad definition of family, recognizing the diversity that exists, and we focus on aging family systems rather than individual aging family members.

Aging families can vary in ways such as family size and structure, emotional connection, geographic distance, and family roles. Aging families include opposite-sex and same-sex couples in cohabiting, common-law, or long-term marriages, with or without children; and those who are newly married (e.g., Humble, 2013), divorced, or widowed. Some have four or more living generations, whereas others have only one or two generations. Some families have emotionally close ties with members interacting on a regular basis, whereas others display conflicted interaction styles, feelings of ambivalence, or infrequent interaction due to personal reasons or geographic distance. Regardless of such differences, however, many face similar later-life transitions and age-related changes, and it is by focusing on these similarities that scholars can better understand how aging families function.

Two factors set aging families apart from younger families. The first factor relates to the extended family history that members share. How members of aging families communicate with one another and how they respond to anticipated changes (e.g., retirement) or family crises, for example, are influenced by interactional patterns and coping strategies established in earlier years (Connidis, 2010). A long family history can be a source of strength for family members or, alternatively, a painful barrier difficult to overcome.

Another factor that sets aging families apart from families earlier in their development is the likelihood that they will experience coinciding joyful and painful events. At no other life stage is the family system more likely to encounter growth and loss in such close proximity. For example, the loss of a spouse or partner can have a profound impact on the well-being of the surviving individual as well as challenge the stability and functioning of an entire family system. At the same time, a grandchild's birth can be a life-altering event for a new grandparent and an opportunity for increased family cohesion. These later-life transitions can contribute to both joyful and painful emotions, making for complex and bittersweet family dynamics. In fact, *ambivalence*—the "simultaneously held opposing feelings or emotions that are due in part to countervailing expectations about how individuals should act" (Connidis & McMullin, 2002, p. 558)—can be a common response to transitions and complex intergenerational relationships occurring later in life (Silverstein & Giarrusso, 2010).

DEMOGRAPHIC TRENDS

Families exist within a larger social and cultural context, and scholars can gain a better understanding of aging families by recognizing the many demographic changes that are currently taking place in the United States and globally. These shifting trends directly affect how aging families evolve and how they respond to the demands of later life.

Demographic changes that took place in the United States during the 20th century have had profound effects on the structure of American society. The average life expectancy of an infant born in the United States, for example, increased from 47.3 years in 1900 to 78.7 years today (U.S. Census Bureau, 2014). This is the greatest increase in longevity ever documented in human history, and it has resulted in the rapid growth of the older adult population. In 2012, 43 million Americans, or 13.7% of the population, were over the age of 65 (Ortman, Velkoff, & Hogan, 2014). Given these dramatic changes in longevity combined with the aging of the Baby Boom population (individuals born between 1946 and 1964), U.S. Census Bureau predictions indicate that growth in the older adult population will continue at a relatively rapid rate. For instance, the older population (65 +) is projected to increase to 71.4 million people in 2029, making up 20% of the U.S. population (Colby & Ortman, 2014).

Gerontologists frequently differentiate individuals over 65 years old into three categories: *young-old* (65 to 74), *middle-old* (75 to 84), and *oldest-old* (85 and above) (Hooyman & Kiyak, 2011). Those in the oldest-old population are the fastest-growing segment of older adults, increasing from under 4% between the years of 1900 and 1940 to 13.6% of the aging population in 2010 (U.S. Census Bureau, 2014). This segment is more likely than younger elders to have health and/or mobility limitations (Ferrini & Ferrini, 2013), experience the death of a spouse, or require instrumental assistance. Included among the oldest-old are centenarians (those living 100+ years), who are demanding more attention as a result of their expansion. From an estimated 37,000 in 1990 to over 53,000 in 2010, this population is a direct result of decreased mortality and access to better health care (U.S. Census Bureau, 2014).

In addition to cohort differences in the older adult population, gender differences also exist with regard to longevity as well as marital and living status. Life expectancy for a female child born today in the United States is estimated at 81 years; for a male child it is 76 years (U.S. Census Bureau, 2014). As a result of men's higher mortality rates across the life span and differences in "attitudes, behaviors, social roles and biological risks between men and women," women outnumber men in later life (He, Sengupta, Velkoff, & DeBarros, 2005, p. 36). However, as American women increasingly enter the workforce, experience higher stress levels, and adopt unhealthy lifestyle habits, it is expected they will lose their longevity advantage over men (U.S. Census Bureau, 2014). Related to longevity is the common experience of widowhood in later life; particularly for heterosexual women who frequently outlive their spouses. Higher widowhood rates for older women contribute significantly to the likelihood they will live alone. In fact, in 2010, of those 65 and over living alone, 71% were women and 29% were men (U.S. Census Bureau, 2014).

The older adult population in the United States is racially and ethnically diverse, and the level of diversity in this group is predicted to dramatically increase. In 2010, 86% of the aging population was non-Hispanic White; this population is expected to decrease to 77% by 2050 (U.S. Census Bureau, 2014). In comparison, the Hispanic population is expected to grow the most dramatically, increasing from 7% of the total aging population in 2010 to 18% by 2050. Overall, members of minority groups (Hispanics, African Americans, and Asian Americans) constitute 14% of the aging population and this percentage is expected to increase as this population expands (U.S. Census Bureau, 2014). Contributing to this expansion is growth in the aging immigrant population. In 2010, elder immigrants were comprised of 4.6 million individuals (Ortman et al., 2014). This group includes both foreign-born older adults who have lived in the United States for many years as well as those who recently migrated to the United States to join family or were admitted as refugees (Leach, 2009).

Finally, it is difficult to estimate the number of older lesbian, gay, bisexual, and transgendered (LGBT) individuals in the United States primarily due to their reluctance to identify as such often for fear of rejection or retribution. However, it is estimated that there are between 1 to 3 million older gay, lesbian, and bisexual individuals currently and that this will increase to 2 to 6 million by 2030 (Fredriksen-Goldsen & Muraco, 2010).

STRESS IN LATER LIFE

Scholars recognize the different types of stressful experiences older adults encounter, such as chronic role strains, daily hassles, and lifetime trauma (Krause, 2007). They emphasize the effects of such stress on health and well-being (Aldwin, Yancura, & Boeninger, 2007), with some even suggesting that stress can accelerate the aging process (Yancura & Aldwin, 2010). Research often focuses on the coping strategies of aging individuals rather than how aging families experience and adapt to later life challenges, yet these stressors are often experienced within the context of a family system with multiple generations affected.

In accordance with ecological systems theory (Bronfenbrenner, 1979), aging individuals and their families confront stressors at multiple systemic levels. At the macrosystem level (i.e., the cultural contexts influencing how people live), families must deal with government policies (i.e., Medicare, Social Security), economic realities, and social expectations surrounding care. At the exosystem level (i.e., the community environment), formalized health care, insurance companies, care facilities, and other professional agencies are involved. At the meso- and microsystem levels, respectively, aging families manage their home environments, neighborhood resources, transportation accessibility, and renegotiate family roles and responsibilities.

Knowledge about stress and aging has centered primarily on two assumptions. First, there is a critical difference between stress encountered in early or middle adulthood and that experienced in later life. Earlier in life, individuals are more likely to encounter stressors associated with growth that occur in a context of excitement and future potential such as marriage and parenthood as well as educational and professional opportunities. In later life, seniors often face changes that take place within a context of physical decline and the contraction of social and family interaction patterns. These decisions can be more difficult because they relate to relinquishing power and changing levels of independence. Examples of these later life decisions can include accepting assistance from family or service professionals, relocating to a new city to be closer to one's adult children, placing a spouse in a nursing home, or relinquishing one's driver's license.

A second assumption related to stress and aging pertains to the economic and social resources available to older adults. These are assumed to decrease with age as a result of restricted financial reserves, geographic distance from family, and limited community assistance. Yet, although many stressors associated with aging may be challenging, aging itself is not only about decline and disability. Getting older can involve personal growth and development, a sense of satisfaction with one's accomplishments, and enthusiasm for new experiences and transitions. Researchers use the terms *stress-related growth* and *post-traumatic growth* (Aldwin & Igarashi, 2012) to refer to positive outcomes emerging from stress such as resilience. Resilience is not just an individual characteristic, however. In accordance with the ecological model, communities and broader contexts can contribute to resilience; they "do not *cause* individual resilience; rather, they provide an *opportunity* to use resources" (Aldwin & Igarashi, 2012, p. 118).

According to the ABC-X model of family stress, the perception of an event as stressful (the C factor) is the most powerful variable in explaining family stress (Boss, 1987). Thus, it is critical that scholars understand what older adults identify as stressful life events. Older adults report experiences in three stressor areas: (a) health and physical functioning, (b) personal and social problems, and (c) difficulties faced by family members (Aldwin, 1990; Aldwin, Sutton, Chiara, & Spiro, 1996). Events that appeared to cause the highest stress ratings included the death of a child, institutionalization of a spouse, or death of a spouse. The least stressful life events were a spouse's retirement, the individual's own retirement, and an increase in paid or volunteer responsibilities. A common assumption is that the circumstances individuals identify as stressful are those that affect them directly. In fact, research indicates that older adults spend considerable time worrying about other people's problems (e.g., a spouse's health, an adult child's marriage, a grandchild's life choices). Aldwin (1990) and others refer to this as *nonegocentric stress* (Sutin, Costa, Wethington, & Eaton, 2010).

There are competing perceptions regarding how much stress is experienced in old age. On one hand, seniors encounter fewer life events and transitions than do younger adults (Aldwin et al., 2007; Stawski, Sliwinski, Almeida, & Smyth, 2008). Later life is frequently characterized as a time of fewer responsibilities than young adulthood, less salient social roles, decreased time demands, and therefore greater flexibility and freedom. On the other hand, aging can be considered a stressful life process (Lawrence & Schigelone, 2002). A sense of trepidation about future events later in life is pervasive among Americans, many of whom fear difficulties such as increased illness and disability and dependence on others for care. Moreover, many simply fear the physical aging process, intensified in recent years by the pervasive influence of the *antiaging industry*, which claims to be able to reduce, hide, or even reverse the signs of physical aging (Flatt, Settersten, Ponsaran, & Fishman, 2013).

Stress may vary among older adult age groups. For example, stressors encountered during the young-old years can differ significantly from those encountered during the middle-old years and oldest-old years. During the young-old years, a majority of seniors are making their own decisions, engaging with family and community activities, and experiencing anticipated and normative life events (e.g., retirement). These transitions can be stressful because they involve role changes and family adjustments, but they also offer opportunities for growth and development. However, as age increases, the likelihood of an individual encountering unanticipated, nonnormative life events increases dramatically, especially with regard to physical frailty, disability, and cognitive impairment. As a result, stressors experienced in late life, especially age 85 and beyond, are associated with greater stress.

STRESSFUL EVENTS IN LATER LIFE

Many later-life events can test the adaptability and coping resources of aging families. Two major transitions that may be stressful are retirement and caregiving, while elder abuse is another stressful experience that can happen to a minority of older adults. In this section, we briefly discuss these three stressors and the implications they have for aging families.

Retirement

Retirement traditionally refers to a person's withdrawal from the paid labor force. It is a normative affair currently experienced by the majority of older adults, both men and women. Retirement can be a long-anticipated event that provides new opportunities for personal growth and development (Fehr, 2012), the discovery of new interests and relationships, and a release from demanding time constraints. At the same time, it can pose unique challenges, including the loss of a work role identity, decreased social contact with peers, a reduced sense of personal achievement, and loss of economic stability (Szinovacz, 2003). There are a variety of outcomes with regard to retirement well-being.

In the U.S. Health and Retirement Study, a national longitudinal study over 8 years, 25% of the respondents experienced negative changes in their psychological well-being, 70% experienced little change, and 5% experienced a positive change (Wang, 2007).

Financial stress is a key consideration for retirees, not only in terms of one's eligibility to retire but also in relation to one's future economic security. The volatile financial sector, with regard to stock market trends, the solvency of pension plans, and the need for more personal savings, has resulted in greater financial uncertainty for current and future retirees. Combined with extended longevity and increased divorced rates, rising poverty rates for older women are of considerable concern. In fact, in spite of women's increased labor force participation, women are still financially disadvantaged in retirement compared to men, specifically in terms of their lower life-time earnings and limited financial preparation and the impact of their marital status (Butrica & Smith, 2012).

Many retirees may return to work for financial reasons. However, individuals with low incomes and few savings may not leave the workforce—rather, these individuals may have no choice but to work into later life provided their health permits. Indeed, the U.S. Bureau of Labor Statistics (Toossi, 2012) notes that more older workers are remaining in the paid labor force, choosing full-time work over part-time work, and this trend is expected to continue. In 2010, for example, 17% of the 65 and above population were still working (up from 11.7% in 1990). Demographers project that by 2020, 22% of those over 65 will remain in the labor force (Toossi, 2012).

The fact that many people still work "in retirement" raises the question of whether the traditional definition of retirement still makes sense. In the past, retirement typically meant leaving a full-time job and no longer working for pay, but there is increasing diversity in how people view and experience retirement (Denton & Spencer, 2009) and deal with the associated stressors. New definitions of retirement are emerging as reflected in the multiple pathways individuals choose, for example, transitioning to a new job or career, reducing employment hours but continuing to work, or finding recreational employment that is less stressful and more enjoyable. Furthermore, people can "unretire" by reentering the workforce or "reretire" by choosing to retire more than once (Shultz & Wang, 2011).

People experience stress in retirement for many reasons. In addition to finances, the reasons for and the timing of retirement are related to retirement stress. Individuals typically assume their retirement will occur voluntarily, at a time of their choosing. Unfortunately, this is not the case for many people. Szinovacz and Davey (2005a) found that one third of retired individuals viewed their retirement as involuntary. Involuntary retirement contributes to negative attitudes about retirement, but its relationship to long-term adjustment is less clear (Shultz & Wang, 2011). Reasons for retiring earlier than planned can include poor health, job displacement, or family reasons (e.g., pressure from one's spouse or caregiving responsibilities). Gay and bisexual men may look toward a life beyond and outside of employment if they are unable to open about their sexual orientation in the work force (Mock, Sedlovskaya, & Purdie-Vaughns, 2011).

Retirement is a significant life transition therefore its repercussions impact not only the individual but the entire family system, including one's spouse, children, and extended kin (Solinge & Henkens, 2005; Szinovacz & Davey, 2005b). With regard to marriage, retirement may reinforce preretirement marital quality. That is, those with good marriages prior to retirement will experience increased marital quality, whereas those in unhappy marriages will experience a decline in marital quality (Dew & Yorgason, 2010). For couples who jointly retire, especially those who share mutual interests and have effective communication skills, retirement can be a time of increased marital satisfaction and renewed intimacy. For other couples, however, extended free hours together with limited structure can result in greater conflict or may reveal an indisputable lack of common interests. Retirement may impact spouses differently as well, depending on the timing. When couples experience *dysynchronized retirement* (retiring at different times), retirement satisfaction can be negatively affected; this is particularly true when wives continue to be employed after their husbands retire (Davey & Szinovacz, 2004). However, women who are pressured by their husbands to retire at the same time as their husbands and before they are ready to retire—such as Malena Gomez in the vignette at the start of this chapter—can experience difficulties (Zimmerman, Mitchell, Wister, & Gutman, 2000).

The retirement transition can also affect adult children and grandchildren. Those who are expecting financial assistance or child-care support from their retired parents may experience disappointment or conflict when retirees choose to spend their money on traveling and fill their time with new hobbies. Alternatively, retirees who expect adult children and grandchildren to fill their days may encounter feelings of resentment or increased emotional distance from them.

As illustrated in the vignette at the beginning of the chapter, retirement is clearly a complex life event with the potential for increasing the stress of multiple generations. A multilevel approach to studying the retirement processes and experiences of individuals and families is needed (Szinovacz, 2013). Such an approach takes into consideration not only macrolevel (e.g., economic climate, Social Security eligibility) and exo level (e.g., workplace policies) factors but also microlevel (e.g., reciprocal influences between the retiree and family members) and individual level factors (such as one's desire to retire and how much money has been saved).

Caregiving

Because the risk of experiencing chronic illness and/or disability is associated with advancing age (Ferrini & Ferrini, 2013), older adults and their families frequently encounter increased caregiving responsibilities. According to the National Alliance for Caregiving and AARP (2009), 19% of the adult population (approximately 43 million people) is providing care to an adult over 50 who is in poor health. The typical age of a caregiver is 50 years, an increase of 2 years from 2004.

A *caregiver* is anyone who provides assistance to someone physically or psychologically impaired and therefore dependent on others. Caregiving can be *informal* (i.e., provided by unpaid volunteers, family members, or friends) or *formal* (i.e., provided by paid care workers) and can take the form of different types of assistance. *Instrumental support* (hands-on assistance with daily functioning) and *emotional support* (actions and gestures expressing affection and encouragement) are two general types of assistance that researchers have frequently explored (Pearlin, Aneshensel, Mullan, & Whitlatch, 1995). *Care management* (e.g., arranging for paid care and seeking out information and resources) is a care activity seldom studied (Rosenthal, Martin-Matthews, & Keefe, 2007) but increasingly experienced, particularly for individuals providing assistance from a distance.

Family caregiving is provided by spouses, adult children, extended family members, and fictive kin, and the motivation to provide care is what sets it apart from assistance supplied by more formal sources. Family members provide care because of feelings of love and affection, intergenerational solidarity (Silverstein & Bengtson, 2001), or filial responsibility (Silverstein, Gans, & Yang, 2006). However, in some cases, care is provided because of family pressure to do so or because there is no one else to do it (Piercy & Chapman, 2001).

Many other factors influence who becomes a caregiver, with gender at the forefront. As with the Gomez family, featured in this chapter's vignette, caregiving responsibilities frequently fall to the women in families. Although increasing numbers of men have become caregivers in recent years, most families follow a gendered family pattern in which women are more likely than men to take on caregiving roles (e.g., if a wife is not available, a daughter or daughter-in-law takes over rather than a son) (Lai, Luk, & Andruske, 2007; Uhlenberg & Cheuk, 2008). The extent of the disability, potential caregivers' geographic proximity to the care recipient, work schedule flexibility, physical health, and available resources influence who will provide care. The relationship history between family members is important, for instance stepfamilies and divorce may make intergenerational support to aging parents less certain (Silverstein & Giarrusso, 2010). Culture also influences how families approach caregiving responsibilities; *familismo* in Latino families and *filial piety* in Asian cultures encourage dedication and loyalty to one's family, thus encouraging family caregiving (Lai et al., 2007; Radina, Gibbons, & Li, 2009).

Caregiving can bring emotional closeness with the care recipient, a sense of accomplishment or purpose, and increased family cohesion (Coon, 2012). However, caregivers often face extensive demands on their time as well as difficulties that test their physical and mental endurance, referred to as *caregiver burden*. Caregiver burden is a "multidimensional response to the negative appraisal and perceived stress resulting from taking care of an ill individual, [and it] threatens the physical, psychological, emotional, and function health of caregivers" (Kim, Chang, Rose, & Kim, 2011, p. 864). Emotions commonly associated with caregiver burden are depression, loneliness, anger, and guilt. Caregivers frequently exhibit higher levels of depression, physical fatigue, and social isolation, compared to noncaregivers (Johnson, 2008). Having a strong sense of filial piety, which may be more present in certain non-Western cultures than Western cultures, does not exempt people from experiencing caregiver burden (Lai et al., 2007).

Those caring for loved ones with dementia experience the most severe stress because of challenges specific to cognitive decline—that is, behavior problems, the need for constant supervision, progressive deterioration, and lack of reciprocal expressions of affection and gratitude (Pinquart & Sörensen, 2003). Another unique challenge for dementia caregivers is *ambiguous loss* (Boss, 1999). Persons with dementia can eventually become psychologically absent (e.g., not remembering who their loved ones are) even though they are still physically present. This type of partial loss can be very difficult for caregivers who witness the gradual cognitive disappearance of their loved one on a daily basis.

As experienced by Carmen in the opening vignette, negotiating caregiving with other responsibilities can also be another source of caregiver stress. Similar to many caregiving adult children, Carmen is balancing her responsibilities to her parents with caring for her own family and working full-time. Eventually caregivers may become physically exhausted and emotionally drained, experiencing *role overload* as they try to manage multiple roles, which can increase their sense of caregiver burden. Others can also eventually experience *caregiver burnout* (e.g., a sense of emotional exhaustion and the feeling that one simply cannot continue in their caregiving role as they have been). At this stage, caregivers must make critical decisions about seeking assistance from others, scaling back their caregiving involvement, or reducing other commitments. Employed caregivers may be forced to reduce their hours or leave work entirely before they are financially and psychologically ready to do so (Johnson, 2008). Unfortunately, most caregivers wait until a crisis before asking for help. Moving a loved one into a long-term care facility may reduce some responsibilities, but it remains a stressful event in terms of locating optimal care, negotiating family involvement, and/or battling feelings of guilt (Caron, Ducharme, & Griffith, 2006). Moreover, such a move does not necessarily remove care-related stress. Unsatisfactory institutional care, for example, can lead to family members remaining involved and advocating for the older person (Rosenthal et al., 2007).

The stress associated with family caregiving goes beyond that experienced by caregivers. Although there is typically a primary caregiver, the entire family system may have to make accommodations and adjustments (Stephens, 1990). Feelings of inequity and conflict may also emerge among siblings as they negotiate their contributions to care (Connidis, 2010). Additionally, care recipients (i.e., the aging family members) encounter unique stressors related to their illness and increased dependence. Reduced self-esteem, frustration at their lack of autonomy, dealing with chronic or terminal illnesses, and institutionalization can result in considerable stress and depression (Brown, 2007). Furthermore, most caregiving situations are inequitable in that care recipients receive more support than they are able to reciprocate. This inequity contributes to reduced well-being as they experience feelings of being a burden to others (Brown, 2007).

Recall that, according to the ABC-X model of family stress, available resources (e.g., their own coping strategies and support services) are significant in influencing families' stress levels. In recognition of the stress associated with caregiving, numerous agencies and organizations at the exo and macrolevels have developed interventions, such as support groups, respite care services, adult day care services, and educational and resource information. These resources can assist families in dealing with stressful situations as well as provide valuable information about local, state, and federal resources.

Elder Abuse

Elder abuse is an unfortunate situation experienced by a minority of older adults that only recently has received increased attention (Mysyuk, Westendorp, & Lindenberg, 2013). According to the World Health Organization (WHO), *elder abuse* refers to "a single, or repeated act, or lack of appropriate action, occurring within any relationship where there is an expectation of trust which causes harm or distress to an older person" (WHO, 2002, p. 29). It is important to emphasize that elder abuse occurs within a *trust relationship* in which another person is responsible toward an older person (Goergen & Beaulieu, 2013); as such, it cannot be carried out by a stranger. In approximately 90% of elder abuse cases, family members are most typically the perpetrators (Eisokovits, Koren, & Band-Winterstein, 2013; Mysyuk et al., 2013). Not surprisingly, perpetrators often live with the elder they are abusing, and this is particularly true for older women (Amstadter et al., 2011). Paid caregivers in institutions, also in positions of trust toward the older person and responsible for their well-being, can be perpetrators, but little empirical research has been carried out in this area (Schiamberg et al., 2011).

Five types of elder abuse are typically recognized: (1) *physical* (e.g., hitting, choking, pinching, shaking, or using restraints); (2) *emotional* (e.g., isolating, insulting, humiliating, threatening, or treating the elder like an infant); (3) *financial* (e.g., illegal or improper use of an elder's funds, property, or assets); (d) *sexual* (e.g., unwanted touching); and (e) *neglect* (e.g., failure to provide food, water, or medication, or leaving them alone for long periods) (WHO, 2002).

Prevalence rates in countries such as the United States, Canada, and Great Britain range from 1% to 10% (Mysyuk et al., 2013), and prevalence differs based on the type of elder abuse being examined. Available data from adult protective services agencies in the United States emphasize that despite an increase in the reporting of elder abuse, it is suspected that a substantial number of elder abuse cases go undetected and untreated each year (Jirik & Sanders, 2014). Like the issue of family violence in general, abusive actions occurring within family homes are under reported because what happens in a home is considered private. Older individuals may face difficult decisions regarding whether or not to openly report elder abuse (those who are cognitively and physically able to do so), considering the costs and rewards. On one hand, for example, reporting the abuse could stop it; on the other hand, it might remove a person from their lives who still was important to them for various reasons and change the older person's life in unanticipated ways (e.g., he or she might now have to move into a long-term care facility if an important source of support is lost). As noted earlier, ambivalence can often be a part of relationships later in life (Silverstein & Giarrusso, 2010), contributing to the challenge of reporting elder abuse.

Older Latino immigrants and other groups, particularly those who live with their abusers, may hide such mistreatment because they want to protect their families: "*La familia* to avoid *vergüenza*, or shame, promotes tolerance of family violence and suppresses reporting" (DeLiema, Gassoumis, Homeirer, & Wilber, 2012, p. 1333). English language difficulties, citizenship status, and fear or mistrust of authorities may further decrease the likelihood that older Latinos report abuse (DeLiema et al., 2012).

Typical factors associated with an elder's vulnerability are "age, sex, race and ethnicity, socioeconomic status, cognitive impairment, physical disability, depressive symptoms, social network, and social participation" (Dong & Simon, 2014, p. 10). For example, individuals who are over age 80, female, African American, have more than two health issues, or have little social support are at a high risk of elder abuse. Those with dementia (particularly late-stage dementia) are also at a much higher risk as compared to the general population of older adults due to their greater dependence (Dong, Chen, & Simon, 2014). Finally, though incidences regarding elder abuse in the LGBT population are difficult to determine, this group may have additional vulnerabilities (National Resource Centre on LGBT Aging, n.d.). They are at risk of certain types of emotional abuse such as being "outed." Outing occurs when a person's sexual orientation or gender identity is revealed to someone else who was previously unaware of the fact. In this context, the outing is maliciously done by someone else and without the LGBT person's consent. Due to a history of "misunderstanding, neglect, and mistreatment" (De Vries, 2005, p. 64), many older LGBT individuals hide their sexual orientation for relevant reasons (National Resource Centre on LGBT Aging, n.d.), such as fear of rejection or discrimination from others. Being in control of how, when, and who they reveal their sexual orientation or gender identity to is important for their psychological well-being, and threatening to take that control away or using the threat of outing as a way to control the older person is a form of psychological abuse.

Many people assume that elder abuse emerges out of caregiver burden—a person caring for the dependent older person becomes too stressed with his or her responsibilities and thus lashes out in some way at the older person. This can certainly be the situation in some cases; however, this explanation has its limitations (Brandl & Raymond, 2012; Harbison et al., 2012). Specifically, this justification for abuse places blame on the older person (e.g., if they were easier to provide care for the caregiver would not feel overwhelmed) and attempts to excuse the abuser (Brandl & Raymond, 2012). Instead of the care receiver's dependency on the caregiver being a risk factor, some have argued that it is the caregiver's dependency on the care receiver for things such as housing and income that leads to the abuse (Brandl & Raymond, 2012). Additionally, substance abuse and mental illnesses may be contributing factors (Pickering & Phillips, 2014).

Family dynamics are important to examine, as families can have complicated patterns of interaction influencing how they cope with challenges later in life (Eisokovits et al., 2013). Subscribing strongly to *familism* may put older adults at greater risk of abuse since their abusers know they are unlikely to report them. Additionally, because in many cases elder abuse may be an extension of earlier abusive patterns (McDonald & Thomas, 2013), reaching out for assistance within a dysfunctional family system is unlikely. Pickering and Phillips (2014) criticize many theories of elder abuse for ignoring the fact that psychological and verbal patterns of abuse by adult children toward cognitively intact parents, for example, may be long-standing interactional patterns that have simply persisted into later life.

To fully understand and prevent elder abuse, an ecological approach is necessary. Multiple intervention opportunities (e.g., substance abuse treatment programs and caregiver respite programs) can contribute to strengthening family systems in the long term. Researchers, practitioners, and policy makers must also go beyond immediate family contexts and community resources to examine how factors such as societal values about aging and who is expected to take on unpaid caregiving in families, employment conditions for paid care providers, and government policies and laws play a role in elder abuse (Norris, Fancey, Power, & Ross, 2013).

MODELS OF COPING AND ADAPTATION

Because older individuals frequently experience simultaneous multiple stressors (i.e., failing health, increased dependence, and reduced resources), their coping methods are critical to their adjustment. *Problem-focused coping* occurs when individuals attempt to establish a semblance of control within an uncontrollable situation, by identifying specific and attainable goals they can reach. Older persons worried about their driving, for example, may decide to only drive during the day time, avoid driving on busy streets, or seek rides from family members and friends (Choi, Adams, & Mezuk, 2012). Such behaviors provide a retained sense of control and a method for overcoming feelings of helplessness (Lazarus & Folkman, 1984). In contrast, *emotion-focused coping* involves a more cognitive response to stress through denial, detachment, the reinterpretation of events, and the application of humor or religious/spiritual faith. With regard to driving, such coping may involve an acceptance of the inevitability of having to reduce or stop one's driving, or it could involve denial of the problem (Choi et al., 2012).

Related to emotional regulation is the coping process of *positive reappraisal*. In this type of coping, the individual reframes a stressful situation to see positive characteristics also present. This helps with managing feelings of despair and countering increasingly negative emotions (Folkman, 1997). Older individuals may engage in helpful processes that "minimize negative feelings, ignore unpleasant events, and process emotions less deeply" (Labouvie-Vief, 2005, cited in Tschanz et al., 2013, pp. 826–827).

Why do some older adults adapt to change with relatively minor difficulty and others cope much less effectively? The *principle of selective optimization with compensation* (Baltes & Baltes, 1990) describes a process of adaptation that older adults implement when faced with declines in their functional abilities or threats to their continued social and physical involvement. The retirement transition is an example of when this adaptation process can take place due to the reduced social involvement and lost worker role. This principle is based on three key interacting components: selection, optimization, and compensation. *Selection* refers to individuals' conscious reduction in domains of functioning because of age-related constraints. For example, an older woman diagnosed with a hearing loss may choose to give up certain activities to focus more time on those that cause her little discomfort and still provide her pleasure. *Optimization* occurs when individuals work to improve their performance on the activities they have selected. By focusing their energies on fewer interests, they can experience greater satisfaction and success in those areas. For instance, an older man who can no longer play the piano due to arthritis may choose to focus his energies on sharing his expertise with promising young piano players. *Compensation* refers to individuals' use of psychological, technological, and environmental aids to assist them in maintaining their social and physical involvement with the world (Baltes & Baltes, 1990). The piano teacher with severe arthritis may use audio or video recordings of earlier performances to demonstrate certain techniques to students. The point of this theory is that older adults do not passively accept increasing limitations or functional decline; rather, they combine specific strategies that enable them to maintain enough functional capacity to continue enjoying and participating in life. The value of these coping processes is the ability for older adults to retain a sense of purpose and meaning in their lives.

In addition to older adults' individual coping strategies, family members can have considerable influence on older adults' adaptations to age-related changes and their responses to stress. Families' positive influences usually take the form of social support. Three key types of behaviors constitute social support: aid, affect, and affirmation (Antonucci, 2001). *Aid* consists of tangible types of assistance, such as transportation, help with personal care tasks, or direction regarding where to obtain information about elder abuse. *Affect* refers to emotional support, provided through expressions of care and concern for an aging family member.

Finally, *affirmation* involves the sharing of values and the affirmation of the aging family member's importance and the decisions he or she makes, such as the decision to stop driving.

Most social support scholars view social relationships as critical to how older adults cope with the challenges of aging (Antonucci, Jackson, & Biggs, 2007; Silverstein et al., 2006). In fact, much research supports the assertion that social support has a positive influence on the health and well-being of older adults. The presence of social support, and even the anticipation of future support, appears to have a buffering effect on stress, mitigating its negative impacts. Anticipated support (believing that support will be provided in the future if needed) also appears to have a more significant impact on health and well-being than support already received or the frequency of contact with others (Antonucci et al., 2007). This finding emphasizes the importance of the perception of one's support situation (the C factor in the ABC-X model) in addition to the actual amount or quality of support available (the B factor) within a family. Accessing one's social support network in times of need, however, may depend on the type of stressor as well as the maintenance of quality relationships (Birditt, Antonucci, & Tighe, 2012).

Once again, from an ecological standpoint (Bronfenbrenner, 1979), it is important to recognize that larger social systems play a role in affecting aging individuals' and families' responses to stress. For example, at the macrolevel, many government and social policies contribute to the circumstances of individuals' retirements such as what retirement benefits and resources are available and when they are available (Calasanti, 2000). Similarly, for caregiving, exosystem features such as flex time, family leave time, and shared jobs can assist employed caregivers to remain at work. Finally, at the microlevel, aging families can significantly influence how older adult members cope with age-associated changes in terms of family interaction patterns and support provided. It is also important to recognize that older adults are resilient and often employ creative approaches to adapt to the social and functional limitations they encounter as they age. Rather than view aging adults as only passive and dependent participants, it is critical that they are recognized as active and influential family members who contribute significantly to the changing, aging family system.

CONCLUSION

Demographic changes that have taken place over the past century have significantly affected the structure, nature, and resources of aging families in the United States, Canada, and other developed and developing countries. Later life is frequently associated with stressful life events and transitions, and given our expanding aging populations and the implications of this growth, it is important for researchers and practitioners to understand the strategies that older adults use to cope effectively and the role of family systems and other systems in the positive adjustment of older adults. Due to the heterogeneity that exists among older adults and their families, perceptions of particular events and how individuals and families cope with these changes will continue to vary. Researchers documenting aging families' adaptive strategies may benefit from exploring more fully the inherent ability of seniors to grow and develop despite advancing age and characteristics of the broader environment that help to facilitate such resilience.

REFERENCES

Aldwin, C. M. (1990). The elders life stress inventory: Egocentric and nonegocentric stress. In M. A. P. Stephens, J. H. Crowther, S. E. Hobfoll, & D. L. Tennenbaum (Eds.), *Stress and coping in later-life families* (pp. 49–69). New York, NY: Hemisphere.

Aldwin, C., & Igarashi, H. (2012). An ecological model of resilience in later life. *Annual Review of Gerontology & Geriatrics, 32,* 115–130.

Aldwin, C. M., Sutton, K. J., Chiara, G., & Spiro, A., III. (1996). Age differences in stress, coping, and appraisal: Findings from the normative aging study. *Journal of Gerontology: Psychological Sciences, 51B,* 179–188.

Aldwin, C. M., Yancura, L. A., & Boeninger, D. K. (2007). Coping, health, and aging. In C. M. Aldwin, C. L. Park, & A. Spiro III (Eds.), *Handbook of health psychology and aging* (pp. 210–226). New York. NY: Guilford Press.

Amstadter, A. B., Cisler, J. M., McCauley, J. L., Hernandez, M. A., Muzzy, W., & Acierno, R. (2011). Do incident and perpetrator characteristics of elder mistreatment differ by gender of the victim? Results from the National Elder Mistreatment Study. *Journal of Elder Abuse and Neglect, 23,* 43–57.

Antonucci, T. C. (2001). Social relations: An examination of social networks, social support, and sense of control. In J. E. Birren & K. W. Schaie (Eds.), *Handbook of the psychology of aging* (5th ed., pp. 427–453). San Diego, CA: Academic.

Antonucci, T. C., Jackson, J. S., & Biggs, S. (2007). Intergenerational relations: Theory, research, and policy. *Journal of Social Issues, 63,* 679–693.

Baltes, P. B., & Baltes, M. M. (1990). Psychological perspectives on successful aging: The model of selective optimization with compensation. In P. B. Baltes & M. M. Baltes (Eds.), *Successful aging: Perspectives from the behavioral sciences* (pp. 1–34). Cambridge, England: Cambridge University Press.

Birditt, K. S., Antonucci, T. C., & Tighe, L. (2012). Enacted support during stressful life events in middle and older adulthood: An examination of the interpersonal context. *Psychology and Aging, 27,* 728–741.

Blieszner, R., & Bedford, V. H. (1995). The family context of aging: Trends and challenges. In R. Blieszner & V. H. Bedford (Eds.), *Handbook of aging and the family* (pp. 3–12). Westport, CT: Greenwood.

Boss, P. G. (1987). Family stress. In M. B. Sussman & S. K. Steinmetz (Eds.), *Handbook of marriage and the family* (pp. 695–723). New York, NY: Plenum.

Boss, P. (1999). *Ambiguous loss: Learning to live with unresolved grief.* Cambridge, MA: Harvard University Press.

Brandl, B., & Raymond, J. A. (2012). Policy implications of recognizing that caregiver stress is *not* the primary cause of elder abuse. *Generations, 36*(3), 32–39.

Bronfenbrenner, U. (1979). *The ecology of human development.* Cambridge, MA: Harvard University Press.

Brown, E. (2007). Recipients' psychological well-being: The role of sense of control and caregiver type. *Aging and Mental Health, 11,* 405–414.

Butrica, B. A., & Smith, K. E. (2012). The retirement prospects of divorced women. *Social Security Bulletin, 71*(1), 11–22.

Calasanti, T. M. (2000). Incorporating diversity. In E. W. Markson & L. A. Hollis-Sawyer (Eds.), *Intersections of aging* (pp. 188–202). Los Angeles, CA: Roxbury.

Caron, C. D., Ducharme, F., & Griffith, J. (2006). Deciding on institutionalization for a relative with dementia: The most difficult decision for caregivers. *Canadian Journal on Aging, 25,* 193–205.

Choi, M., Adams, K. B., & Mezuk, B. (2012). Examining the aging process through the stress-coping framework: Application to driving cessation later in life. *Aging & Mental Health, 16,* 75–83.

Colby, S. L., & Ortman, J. M. (2014). *The baby boom cohort in the United States: 2012 to 2060. Current Population Reports.* Washington, DC: U.S. Bureau of the Census. Retrieved October 3, 2014, from http://www.census.gov/prod/2014pubs/p25-1141.pdf

Connidis, I. A. (2010). *Family ties & aging* (2nd ed.). Los Angeles, CA: Pine Forge.

Connidis, I. A., & McMullin, J. A. (2002). Sociological ambivalence and family ties: A critical perspective. *Journal of Marriage and Family, 64,* 558–567.

Coon, D. W. (2012). Resilience and family caregiving. In B. Hayslip and C. G. Smith (Eds.), *Annual Review of Gerontology and Geriatrics: Emerging perspectives on resilience in adulthood and later life* (pp. 231–249). New York, NY: Springer.

Davey, A., & Szinovacz, M. E. (2004). Dimensions of marital quality and retirement. *Journal of Family Issues, 25,* 431–464.

DeLiema, M., Gassoumis, Z. D., Homeirer, D. C., & Wilber, K. H. (2012). Determining prevalence and correlates of elder abuse using *promotores*: Low-income immigrant Latinos report high rates of abuse and neglect. *Journal of the American Geriatrics Society, 60,* 1333–1339.

Denton, F. T., & Spencer, B. G. (2009). What is retirement? A review and assessment of alternative concepts and measures. *Canadian Journal on Aging, 28,* 63–76.

De Vries, B. (2005/2006). Home at the end of the rainbow. *Generations, 29,* 64–69.

Dew, J., & Yorgason, J. (2010). Economic pressure and marital conflict in retirement-aged couples. *Journal of Family Issues, 31,* 164–188.

Dong, X., Chen, R., & Simon, M. A. (2014). Elder abuse and dementia: A review of the research and health policy. *Health Affairs, 33,* 642–649.

Dong, X., & Simon, M. A. (2014). Vulnerability risk index profile for elder abuse in a community-dwelling population. *Journal of the American Geriatrics Society, 62,* 10–15.

Eisokovits, Z., Koren, C., & Band-Winterstein, T. (2013). The social construction of social problems: The case of elder abuse and neglect. *International Psychogeriatrics, 25,* 1291–1298.

Fehr, R. (2012). Is retirement always stressful? The potential impact of creativity. *American Psychologist, 67,* 76–77.

Ferrini, R. L., & Ferrini, A. F. (2013). *Health in the later years* (5th ed.). New York, NY: McGraw-Hill.

Flatt, M. A., Settersten, R. A. Jr., Ponsaran, R., & Fishman, J. R. (2013). Are "anti-aging medicine" and "successful aging" two sides of the same coin? Views of anti-aging practitioners. *Journals of Gerontology, Series B: Psychological Sciences and Social Sciences, 68,* 944–955.

Folkman, S. (1997). Positive psychological stress and coping with severe stress. *Social Science & Medicine, 45,* 1207–1221.

Fredriksen-Goldsen, K. I., & Muraco, A. (2010). Aging and sexual orientation: A 25-year review of the literature. *Research on Aging, 32,* 372–413.

Goergen, T., & Beaulieu, M. (2013). Critical concepts in elder abuse research. *International Psychogeriatrics, 25,* 1217–1228.

He, W., Sengupta, M., Velkoff, V. A., & DeBarros, K. A. (2005). *65+ in the United States: 2005. Current Population Reports.* Washington, DC: U.S. Bureau of the Census. Retrieved June 5, 2008, from http://www.census.gov/prod/2006pubs/p23-209.pdf

Harbison, J., Couglan, S., Beaulieu, M., Karabonow, J., vanderPlaat, M., Wildeman, S., & Wexler, E. (2012). Understanding "elder abuse and neglect": A critique of assumptions underpinning responses to the mistreatment and neglect of older people. *Journal of Elder Abuse and Neglect, 24,* 88–103.

Hooyman, N. R., & Kiyak, H. A. (2011). *Social gerontology: A multidisciplinary perspective* (9th ed.). Boston, MA: Pearson.

Humble, A. M. (2013). Moving from ambivalence to certainty: Older same-sex couples marry in Canada. *Canadian Journal on Aging, 32,* 131–144.

Jirik, S., & Sanders, S. (2014). Analysis of elder abuse statutes across the United States, 2011–2012. *Journal of Gerontological Social Work, 57,* 478–497.

Johnson, R. W. (2008). Choosing between paid elder care and unpaid help from adult children: The role of relative prices in the care decision. In M. E. Szinovacz & A. Davey (Eds.), *Caregiving contexts: Cultural, familial, and societal implications* (pp. 35–69). New York, NY: Springer.

Kim, H., Chang, M., Rose, K., & Kim, S. (2011). Predictors of caregiver burden in caregivers of individuals with dementia. *Journal of Advanced Nursing, 68,* 846–855.

Krause, N. (2007). Evaluating the stress-buffering function of meaning in life among older people. *Journal of Aging and Health, 19,* 792–812.

Lai, D. W. L., Luk, P. K. F., & Andruske, C. L. (2007). Gender differences in caregiving: A case in Chinese Canadian caregivers. *Journal of Women & Aging, 19,* 161–178.

Lawrence, A. R., & Schigelone, A. R. S. (2002). Reciprocity beyond dyadic relationships. *Research on Aging, 24,* 684–704.

Lazarus, R. S., & Folkman, S. (1984). *Stress, appraisal, and coping.* New York, NY: Springer.

Leach, M. (2009). America's older immigrants: A profile. *Generations, 32,* 343–349.

McDonald, L., & Thomas, C. (2013). Elder abuse through a life course lens. *International Psychogeriatrics, 25,* 1235–1243.

Mock, S. E., Sedlovskaya, A., & Purdie-Vaughns, V. (2011). Gay and bisexual men's disclosure of sexual orientation in the workplace: Associations with retirement planning. *Journal of Applied Gerontology, 30,* 123–132.

Mysyuk, Y., Westendorp, R. G., & Lindenberg, J. (2013). Added value of elder abuse definitions: A review. *Aging Research Reviews, 12,* 50–57.

National Alliance for Caregiving & AARP. (2009). A focused look at those caring for someone age 50 and older: Caregiving in the U.S. Washington, DC: Author. Retrieved August 19, 2014, from http://www.caregiving.org/pdf/research/FINALRegularExSum50plus.pdf

National Resource Centre on LGBT Aging. (n.d.). *A self-help guide for LGBT older adults and their care-givers and loved ones: Preventing, recognizing, and addressing elder abuse.* Retrieved August 16, 2014, from http://www.lgbtagingcenter.org/resources/pdfs/SELF-HELP_elderAbuse_Guide.pdf

Norris, D., Fancey, P., Power, E., & Ross, P. (2013). The critical-ecological framework: Advancing knowledge, practice, and policy on older adult abuse. *Journal of Elder Abuse & Neglect, 25,* 40–55.

Ortman, J. M., Velkoff, V. A., & Hogan, H. (2014). *An aging nation: The older population in the United States. Current Population Reports.* Washington, DC: U.S. Bureau of the Census. Retrieved August 15, 2014, from http://www.census.gov/prod/2014pubs/p25-1140.pdf

Pearlin, L. I., Aneshensel, C. S., Mullan, J. T., & Whitlatch, C. J. (1995). Caregiving and its social support. In R. H. Binstock & L. K. George (Eds.), *Handbook of aging and the social sciences* (4th ed., pp. 283–302). San Diego, CA: Academic.

Pickering, C. E. Z., & Phillips, L. R. (2014). Development of a causal model for elder mistreatment. *Public Health Nursing, 31,* 363–372.

Piercy, K. W., & Chapman, J. G. (2001). Adopting the caregiver role: A family legacy. *Family Relations, 50,* 386-393.

Pinquart, M., & Sörensen, S. (2003). Differences between caregivers and noncaregivers in psychological health and physical health: A meta-analysis. *Psychology and Aging, 18,* 250–267.

Radina, M. E., Gibbons, H. M., & Li, J-Y. (2009). Explicit versus implicit family decision-making strategies among Mexican American caregiving adult children. *Marriage & Family Review, 45,* 392–411.

Roberto, K. A., Blieszner, R., & Allen, K. R. (2006). Theorizing in family gerontology: New opportunities for research and practice. *Family Relations, 55,* 513–525.

Rosenthal, C. J., Martin-Matthews, A., & Keefe, J. M. (2007). Care management and care provision for older adults amongst employed informal care-givers. *Ageing and Society, 27,* 755–778.

Schiamberg, L. B., Barboza, G. G., Oehmke, J., Zhang, Z., Griffore, R. J., Weatherill, R. P., von Heydrich, L., & Post, L. A. (2011). Elder abuse in nursing homes: An ecological perspective. *Journal of Elder Abuse and Neglect, 23,* 190–211.

Shultz, K. S., & Wang, M. (2011). Psychological perspectives on the changing nature of retirement. *American Psychologist, 66,* 170–179.

Silverstein, M., Gans, D., & Yang, F. M. (2006). Intergenerational support to aging parents: The role of norms and needs. *Journal of Family Issues, 27,* 1068–1084.

Silverstein, M., & Bengtson, V. L. (2001). Intergenerational solidarity and the structure of adult child-parent relationships in American families. In A. J. Walker, M. Manoogian-O'Dell, L. A. McGraw, & D. L. G. White (Eds.), *Families in later life* (pp. 53–61). Thousand Oaks, CA: Pine Forge Press.

Silverstein, M., & Giarrusso, R. (2010). Aging and family life: A decade review. *Journal of Marriage and Family, 72,* 1039–1058.

Solinge, H. V., & Henkens, K. (2005). Couples' adjustment to retirement: A multi-actor panel study. *Journals of Gerontology: Social Sciences, 60B,* S11–S20.

Stawski, R. S., Sliwinski, M. J., Almeida, D. M., & Smyth, J. M. (2008). Reported exposure and emotional reactivity to daily stressors: The roles of adult age and global perceived stress. *Psychology and Aging, 23,* 52–61.

Stephens, M. A. P. (1990). Social relationships as coping resources in later-life families. In M. A. P. Stephens, J. H. Crowther, S. E. Hobfoll, & D. L. Tennenbaum (Eds.), *Stress and coping in later-life families* (pp. 1–20). New York, NY: Hemisphere.

Sutin, A. R., Costa, P. T. Jr., Wethington, E., & Eaton, W. (2010). Turning points and lessons learned: Stressful life events and personality trait development across middle adulthood. *Psychology and Aging, 25,* 524–533.

Szinovacz, M. (2003). Contexts and pathways: Retirement as institution, process, and experience. In G. A. Adams & T. A. Beehr (Eds.), *Retirement: Reasons, processes, and results* (pp. 6–52). New York, NY: Springer.

Szinovacz, M. (2013). A multilevel perspective for retirement research. In M. Wang (Ed.), *The Oxford handbook of retirement* (pp. 152–173). New York, NY: Oxford University Press.

Szinovacz, M. E., & Davey, A. (2005a). Predictors of perceptions of involuntary retirement. *The Gerontologist, 45,* 36–47.

Szinovacz, M., & Davey, A. (2005b). Retirement and marital decision making: Effects on retirement satisfaction. *Journal of Marriage and Family, 67,* 387–398.

Toossi, M. (2012). *Labor force projections to 2020: A more slowly growing workforce. Monthly Labor Review.* U.S. Bureau of Labor Statistics. Retrieved September 16, 2014, from http://www.bls.gov/opub/mlr/2012/01/art3full.pdf

Tschanz, J. T., Pfister, R., Wanzek, J., Corcoran, C., Smith, K., Tschanz, B. T., Steffens, D. C., Østbye, T., Welsh-Bohmer, K. A., & Norton, M. C. (2013). Stressful life events and cognitive decline in late life: Moderation by education and age. The Cache County Study. *International Journal of Geriatric Psychiatry, 28,* 821–830.

Uhlenberg, P., & Cheuk, M. (2008). Demographic change and the future of informal caregiving. In M. E. Szinovacz & A. Davey (Eds.), *Caregiving contexts: Cultural, familial, and societal implications* (pp. 9–33). New York, NY: Springer.

U.S. Census Bureau. (2014). *65 + in the United States: 2010.* Washington, DC: U.S. Government Printing Office.

Wang, M. (2007). Profiling retirees in the retirement transition and adjustment period: Examining the longitudinal change patterns of retirees' psychological well-being. *Journal of Applied Psychology, 92,* 455–474.

World Health Organization. (2002). *Active ageing: A policy framework.* Geneva. Retrieved September 2, 2014, from http://whqlibdoc.who.int/hq/2002/who_nmh_nph_02.8.pdf

Yancura, L., & Aldwin, C. M. (2010). Does psychosocial stress accelerate the aging process? In J. C. Cavanaugh & C. K. Cavanaugh (Eds.), *Aging in America. Vol. 2, Physical and mental health* (pp. 100–118). Washington, DC: American Psychological Association Press.

Zimmerman, L., Mitchell, B., Wister, A., & Gutman, G. (2000). Unanticipated consequences: A comparison of expected and actual retirement timing among older women. *Journal of Women & Aging, 12,* 109–128.

SECTION IV

Transitional Family Forms

CHAPTER 7

Divorce: Variation and Fluidity

David H. Demo and Mark Fine

The word *divorce* conjures up images of divided families, vulnerable children, failed marriages, unmet or unfulfilled commitments, long and expensive legal battles, resentment, hostility, bitterness, and economic hardship. It is understandable that people do not think positively about divorce. Adults do not marry with the expectation, and certainly not the hope, that their marriages will one day be dissolved, nor do most children hope that their parents will divorce and live apart. Nevertheless, large proportions of American families have experienced or are experiencing parental divorce, a phenomenon that cuts across racial and ethnic groups, albeit to varying degrees.

There are two primary ways that the divorce rate has typically been defined. First, the divorce rate is often defined as the number of divorces per 1,000 adults in a particular region in a particular year (the "crude divorce rate"). A second way to think about the divorce rate is the percentage of married adults who are projected to divorce at any point in the future. Although a smaller proportion of African Americans marry than do European Americans, using this second definition of the divorce rate, a much higher percentage of African American marriages are projected to end in divorce than is the case for European Americans (Orbuch & Brown, 2006). Approximately 70% of current African American marriages are projected to end in divorce, compared with 47% of European American marriages (Cherlin, 2009). For Latinos, this percentage is lower than that for both European Americans and African Americans (Umaña-Taylor & Alfaro, 2006). Partly because of these ethnic differences in divorce rates, but also because of other factors such as increases in cohabitation rates, many children do not live with two parents. In 2004, 78% of White children, 87% of Asian-American children, 68% of Hispanic children, and 38% of African American children lived with two parents (including stepparents). A higher percentage of African American children lived with a single parent in 2004 than did White non-Hispanic or Hispanic children (54% compared with 20% and 28%, respectively).

Note: The authors acknowledge the important contributions of Lawrence H. Ganong on previous versions of this chapter.

In this chapter, we provide an overview of what we know about divorce, the consequences it has on family members, and interventions designed to help those who are experiencing this family stressor. To accomplish these goals, we first provide a theoretical model that illuminates processes and outcomes relevant to divorce, with an emphasis on factors contributing to variation and fluidity in how individuals experience divorce (Demo & Fine, 2010). Second, to illuminate the context in which the model is embedded, we describe historical trends and patterns that place recent trends into context. Third, we present information on factors that predict and that may cause divorce. Fourth, using our theoretical model as a foundation, we review the literature on the consequences of divorce for parents and children, emphasizing risk and protective factors that predict how family members will adjust to this stressor. Finally, we describe and evaluate interventions that may facilitate divorce adjustment, focusing on parenting education for divorcing parents and divorce mediation.

THEORETICAL PERSPECTIVE

The divorce variation and fluidity model (DVFM; Demo & Fine, 2010) illustrated in Figure 7.1 highlights two central features of the divorce process: (1) There is considerable *variability* in how family members experience and adjust to divorce, and (2) children's and adults' adjustment during and following divorce is typically *fluid*, or changes, over time. Although divorce is generally associated with stresses and compromised adjustment among both children and adults, as we describe in more detail later, there is extensive variability. Some children and adults suffer dramatic setbacks to their well-being during and following divorce; some experience relatively minor or short-term deficits; some retain their predivorce adjustment level; and still others rebound quickly from divorce with improved adjustment. Which factors account for this variation? Why do some adults feel relieved and function quite well following divorce while others feel defeated and depressed? Similarly, why do some children and adolescents adjust successfully to parental divorce, reduced contact with one or more parents, and other changes accompanying marital disruption, while some of their peers are devastated?

In examining these questions, we also direct attention to the related issue of change over time, or fluidity, in individual adjustment. As the divorce process unfolds, both children and adults experience ebbs and flows in their adjustment, which are related to numerous changes that accompany divorce, including residential changes, neighborhood and geographic changes, and changes in family relationships, schools, friends, jobs, and standard of living.

The DVFM is an integrated process model of adjustment that outlines key factors influencing child and adult adjustment to divorce. The model is designed to be illustrative rather than exhaustive, and it is intended to demonstrate the highly dynamic nature of the divorce process. Divorce does not occur in a vacuum but is embedded within a complex set of interrelated contexts identified in the outer margins of Figure 1, including the legal climate, economic conditions, cultural values, gender, race, and sociohistorical context.

Figure 7.1   Divorce Variation and Fluidity Model

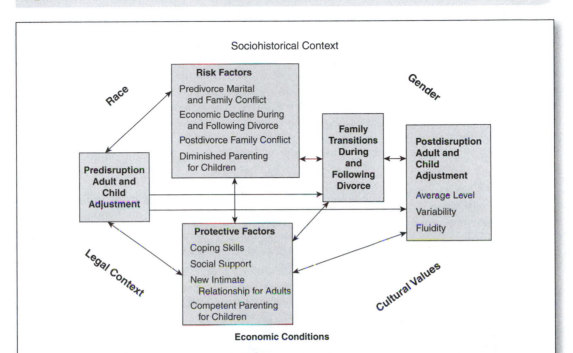

Source: Demo, D. H., & Fine, M. A. (2010). *Beyond the average divorce*. Thousand Oaks, CA: SAGE Publications.

At the far left side of Figure 1, predisruption levels of adult and child adjustment are posited to influence how the divorce process unfolds. Individuals who are functioning well prior to family disruption should be better prepared for, or even protected from, some of the stresses associated with divorce, whereas individuals with lower adjustment levels prior to divorce are more vulnerable to subsequent risks and transitions. Longitudinal studies indicate that children and adults who are better adjusted prior to divorce have better outcomes following divorce (Hetherington & Kelly, 2002; Sun, 2001).

The two large boxes in the center of Figure 7.1 illuminate the mediating influence of risk factors and protective factors in understanding resilience to divorce. Risk factors increase the likelihood of negative outcomes, whereas resilience refers to processes by which an individual (or group) overcomes difficult circumstances, "bounces back" from adversity, and becomes stronger in the face of a crisis (Walsh, 2002). The risk and resilience framework addresses why some parents and children in divorced families cope relatively well with this transition, whereas others do not adapt as successfully. For example,

factors that increase the risk of divorce include child maladjustment before the divorce, financial difficulties, conflict between the ex-spouses, and reduced involvement by the nonresidential parent (Demo & Buehler, 2013). By contrast, resilience is thought to be enhanced by such factors as family members receiving support from close friends, children not blaming themselves for their parents' divorce, and family members retaining an optimistic stance toward the changes that they will experience following divorce (Demo & Buehler, 2013).

The DVFM places the research focus on understanding *variation* in responses to the challenges posed by divorce and life in a single-parent household. For example, research has suggested that experiencing parental divorce increases the risk of children experiencing social, emotional, academic, or behavioral problems from 10% (in first marriage families) to 20% (Hetherington & Kelly, 2002). Although this suggests a heightened risk, this finding also indicates that *most* children in divorced families do *not* develop such problems. The DVFM attempts to identify factors that account for these differential outcomes to the same stressor.

In this framework, outcomes depend on the interplay among risk and protective factors and mechanisms (Margolin, Oliver, & Medina, 2001). Risk factors increase the likelihood of undesirable outcomes, whereas risk mechanisms are the processes by which a particular stressor (e.g., parental divorce) leads to adjustment difficulties. Protective factors are characteristics that promote adaptation to difficult circumstances, as well as family and contextual factors that buffer the effects of severe risk. Protective mechanisms are the ways in which protective factors have their positive effects. One type of protective factor—coping resources—refers to the social, economic, psychological, emotional, and physical assets on which family members can draw (Ahrons, 1994). Adaptation is facilitated to the extent that there are protective factors that are strong enough to help individuals and families cope with the risks that accompany stressors such as divorce.

Borrowing from life-course theory (Elder, 1998), the DVFM recognizes that family transitions during and following divorce play a critical role in shaping life trajectories, developmental change, and postdivorce adjustment. Family transitions refer to changes in family structure or household living arrangements associated with beginning or ending cohabiting, marital, or remarital relationships. For example, parents or other adults may move into or out of the household following divorce, thereby forming or disrupting relationships with children. Some adults pursue new romantic relationships but remain single, while others cohabit or remarry, perhaps multiple times, and many form stepfamilies. The DVFM directs attention to these transitions and the timing, duration, and quality of these relationships in moderating the impact of divorce on individual adjustment.

HISTORY AND CONTEXT

Although it is commonly believed that the divorce rate was low through the 1950s and then soared in recent decades, the divorce rate actually increased steadily from the mid-19th century through the 1970s (Teachman, Tedrow, & Hall, 2006). The divorce rate then stabilized at a high level in the early 1980s and declined modestly since then (Amato & Irving, 2006; Hurley, 2005; Teachman et al., 2006).

The cultural climate in the United States during the 1960s and 1970s featured an increasing emphasis on individualism (Cherlin, 2009). From the late 1950s to the late 1980s, singlehood, cohabitation, childlessness, and nonmarital sexual relations became more acceptable, while opposition to abortion and divorce weakened (Amato, 2004; Demo & Fine, 2010). For many, concerns with self-fulfillment and career development diminished their commitment to family, rendering marriage and other intimate relationships vulnerable.

Economic factors also contributed to rising divorce rates. Changing work patterns, diminished occupational opportunities, men's declining labor force involvement, stagnant wages for White men and declining wages for African American men, and massive underemployment for millions of lower-income wage earners created domestic turmoil for many families (Coleman, Ganong, & Warzinik, 2007; Teachman, 2000). Although women earn less than men for the same work, their reduced economic dependence on men made divorce a more acceptable alternative for women in unhappy marriages.

Many observers have argued that higher divorce rates are a result of declining levels of marital satisfaction in recent decades (Amato, Johnson, Booth, & Rogers, 2003; Bradbury, Fincham, & Beach, 2000). However, although overall levels of marital satisfaction have declined, there is little evidence that this decline led to an increase in the divorce rate (Amato et al., 2003). Perhaps a more plausible explanation of the increase in the divorce rate in the late 1960s and 1970s is that many individuals, especially women, recognized that marriage was not meeting their personal needs (Amato, 2004; Cherlin, 2004). In this context, it is perhaps not surprising that two thirds of divorces are initiated by women (Amato & Irving, 2006; Sweeney, 2002).

Other factors serve to undermine marital stability. Individuals often have unrealistic, idealistic, and romanticized notions about marriage. These conditions—personal fulfillment being strongly valued, lofty expectations not being satisfied, declines in marital satisfaction, and the perception that acceptable alternatives are available—increase the probability of divorce. Because it is unlikely that there will be substantial changes in these conditions in the near future, the divorce rate in the United States is likely to remain at or near current levels.

FACTORS THAT PREDICT AND CAUSE DIVORCE

The divorce variation and fluidity model encourages us to explore the complicated issues of which factors are predictive of some couples staying together while others dissolve their relationship and the causal mechanisms underlying *why* these factors are predictive of marital (in)stability. There is consistent evidence that several demographic, individual difference, and relationship variables contribute to a higher probability of divorce (i.e., they constitute risk factors) (Rodrigues, Hall, & Fincham, 2006). Unfortunately, we know much less about how relationship processes relate to the likelihood of divorce than we do about the influence of demographic and individual difference factors (Amato, 2004; Rodrigues et al., 2006).

Demographic risks include (a) being African American, (b) living in the western and southern parts of the United States, (c) living in an urban area, (d) cohabiting premaritally, (e) having a premarital birth, (f) being young at the time of marriage, (g) having less education, (h) being married for a shorter amount of time, (i) being remarried, (j) having divorced parents, and (k) being less religious. In terms of individual difference variables, divorce risk is positively related to neuroticism (i.e., a generalized tendency to experience negative emotions, such as sadness, anger, guilt, fear, and embarrassment), psychopathology, thinking of divorce, and higher levels of self-monitoring (i.e., the ability and motivation to control one's presentation to others). Finally, with respect to relationship variables, divorce risk is related to dissatisfaction with marriage, lower levels of commitment to the relationship, marital aggression, and more negativity than positivity in marital interactions (Rodrigues et al., 2006).

Identifying risk factors is considerably easier to do than identifying the *causes* of divorce. Determining the causes of relationship dissolution is extremely difficult because there are important distinctions between what people report to be the cause of their breakup and what may have actually caused the breakup (Powell & Fine, 2009). Hopper (1993, 2001) has suggested that people who are going through a divorce typically construct a public account of what happened in their relationship that led to its termination. These narrative accounts often present the individual in a positive light, minimizing his or her role and attributing the dissolution to either one's ex-spouse/partner or to circumstances beyond one's control. Thus, these stories may be both incomplete and inaccurate with respect to how the events surrounding the divorce actually unfolded. In addition, individuals may come to actually believe their stories, even if they were distortions of the truth.

By contrast, researchers attempt to identify the causes of divorce when they look for regularities in factors that lead to divorce across a population. Whereas the divorced individual's perspective identifies his or her subjective view of what caused the dissolution of the relationship, the researcher's perspective uses empirical investigations to identify factors that seem to account for divorce in the general population. Thus, the divorced individual's account and the researcher's perspective have different goals and may reach seemingly divergent conclusions. For example, many individuals blame the termination of their relationship on infidelity. However, because many relationships survive instances of infidelity, the researcher perspective suggests that infidelity is seldom the primary cause of dissolution. Each perspective taps a different, but important, aspect of the complex picture of why dissolution occurs.

What do ex-spouses typically report when asked "what went wrong" in their marriages? Wives report more dissatisfaction with marriage than do husbands (Amato et al., 2003). Common complaints by wives include husbands' authoritarianism, mental cruelty, verbal and physical abuse, excessive drinking, lack of love, neglect of children, emotional and personality problems, and extramarital sex. Men describe their former wives as nagging, whining, faultfinding, and immature (Hetherington & Kelly, 2002). It is common for women and men to share the views that communication problems, unhappiness, and incompatibility led to the divorce. Former spouses' descriptions of their marriages underscore that traditional gender scripts and power imbalances in marriage, work, and parenthood often have undesirable, even harsh, consequences for family members. However, as Hopper's (1993, 2001) work suggests, partners' accounts of the end of their romantic relationships are socially constructed to create a story that is acceptable to themselves as well as to those in their family and social networks. Thus, such accounts should be interpreted cautiously, as they may not accurately portray the events as they actually occurred.

DIVORCE AND ITS AFTERMATH

Research using large and representative samples has found moderate, mostly short-term effects on adult (Braver, Shapiro, & Goodman, 2006) and child adjustment (Amato & Anthony, 2014). Regarding children, Emery (1999) concluded that (a) divorce is a stressful experience; (b) divorce leads to higher levels of clinically significant adjustment and mental health problems; (c) most children are resilient and adjust well to divorce over time; (d) children whose parents divorce report considerable pain, unhappy memories, and continued distress; and (e) postdivorce family interaction patterns greatly influence adjustment following divorce.

There is also considerable variability in the nature of adjustment to divorce (Amato & Anthony, 2014; Demo & Fine, 2010). Individuals differ, sometimes considerably, in how they respond to divorce and in their *perceptions* of their adjustment to divorce. As feminist researchers emphasize, family life is perceived, defined, and experienced differently by each family member (e.g., McGraw & Walker, 2004). Rather than a unitary or "core" family reality, there are multiple and sometimes conflicting realities. Understanding divorce requires us to understand the perspectives of all family members regarding their pre and postdivorce family histories, relationships, and experiences.

It is important to note that adjustment to divorce occurs within a society that typically has held negative views of divorce. Although public disapproval of divorce has softened, divorced individuals still confront stigma, and members of single-parent families continue to feel deficient (Usdansky, 2009; Zartler, 2014). In response, divorced individuals develop elaborate accounts to explain the divorce to themselves and others (Hopper, 1993, 2001).

The circumstances associated with social disapproval are different for women than for men. Gerstel (1990) found that, compared to childless women, divorced mothers experienced harsher disapproval, particularly if they had young children, whereas divorced men did not perceive any differences in social reactions based on whether or not they were parents. Men who had been sexually involved outside the marriage prior to separation reported experiencing greater disapproval from others than did other men. Gerstel concluded that the processes associated with social rejection and stigma reflect "a gender-based ideology of divorce—and marriage" (1990, p. 464). More recent research has indicated that the stigma associated with being divorced has declined for both men and women, but Gerstel's work is still valuable in highlighting that men and women experience *different types* of social disapproval in ways that are consistent with a gender-based perspective of marriage (and divorce).

With this in mind, we now consider the specific consequences of divorce in several important life domains. To illustrate some key points, we present brief vignettes from interviews with college students who have experienced parental divorce (Harvey & Fine, 2010). The vignettes are not designed to be representative but to highlight variability in children's responses.

Economic Consequences

Women are more likely to be economically disadvantaged after divorce than are men. Of course, some women and men fare better financially than others, and having a high predivorce standard of living is a protective factor that lessens the negative economic impact of divorce. Nevertheless, despite this individual variation, a clear pattern is that the economic well-being of divorced women and their children plunges in comparison to predivorce levels, while divorced men often enjoy a *better* financial situation postdivorce (Sayer, 2006).

The economic costs of divorce are greater for women because most marriages and divorces involve children, and mothers continue to devote substantially more time and money than fathers to caring for children (Walzer, 2004). The time women invest in child care and other unpaid family labor restricts not only their income but also their educational and occupational opportunities. Women are less likely to work if they have young children, and family demands prompt many employed women to reduce time spent in paid work (Garey, 1999). Another major reason why women suffer more financially after divorce than men is that fathers tend not to comply fully with child support awards. Many mothers receive irregular or incomplete child support payments, and a substantial minority receives nothing (Manning & Smock, 2000; Pirog & Ziol-Guest, 2006). Even when fathers comply fully, child support awards are typically too low to meet the costs of raising children, and they are typically not indexed for inflation. One college student described the changes this way:

> Before the divorce, we were fairly well off, living in a nice house and getting most of what we wanted. After the divorce, my mother, my sister, and I moved into a small 2-bedroom apartment that was not even close to as nice as our former house. My parents argued a lot about the financial aspects of the divorce settlement and many of these arguments were in front of me. As a result, I became more aware than I wanted to of how child support was determined in Missouri. After the settlement, both my parents felt that they had been treated unfairly and both claimed to be "poor." All I cared about was that it seemed that there wasn't any money to buy things with, and this was all that much harder to deal with because, before the divorce, I had gotten used to getting what I wanted. The biggest changes I noticed following divorce were in the kind of place we lived in and the lack of having enough money to go around. (Republished with permission of Taylor and Francis/Routledge, from Harvey, J. H., & Fine, M. A. [2010].

Children of divorce: Stories of loss and growth [2nd ed., pp. 43–44]. New York, NY: Taylor and Francis/Routledge; permission conveyed through Copyright Clearance Center, Inc.)

Institutionalized sexism and gender discrimination in the wage workplace also contribute to women's sustained postdivorce economic decline. Most employment opportunities for women are in low-paying or temporary work, which offers little opportunity for advancement. Women's lower earnings relative to men's, when combined with the inadequacies of child support payments and the lack of affordable child care, doom many women and their families to long periods of economic hardship following divorce.

Psychological Adjustment

In some cases, it is fairly straightforward to think of changes associated with divorce as *consequences* of divorce, such as changes in the size or composition of friendship networks or income. But some changes may predate the divorce, and the timing of other changes is more difficult to assess. For example, how do we determine whether an adult's postdivorce adjustment problems are attributable to chronic strains associated with single parenting, to long-term mental or physical health problems, to family conflict or abuse that occurred prior to the divorce, or to some combination of these (and perhaps other) factors? It is extremely difficult to tease apart these varying possibilities.

Although several studies have examined the course of adult psychological adjustment following divorce, many have involved cross-sectional designs, have relied on clinical or convenience samples, or have failed to include comparison groups. Still, there are some consistent findings. As reviewed in Demo and Fine (2010), longitudinal studies have consistently shown that an important predictor of both women's and men's postdivorce psychological adjustment was their *pre*divorce adjustment. For both sexes, better coping and emotional functioning prior to divorce were associated with more effective coping and less anger and emotional distress after divorce. Preseparation communication and shared decision-making regarding child rearing also were associated with more cooperative involvement between parents after divorce. It should be noted, however, that individuals from ethnic/racial minority groups are underrepresented in the samples of these longitudinal (and other) studies.

There are interesting similarities and differences in the ways that women and men respond to family experiences preceding and following divorce. Both divorced women and divorced men who are involved in relationships with new partners adjust better psychologically and emotionally than others without such relationships (i.e., having a new romantic relationship served as a protective factor) (Hetherington & Kelly, 2002; Wang & Amato, 2000). Yet women appear to be bothered more by pre- and postdivorce family issues, tensions, and conflicts. For men, "new relationships were able to undo, with surprising rapidity, the narcissistic injury engendered by the divorce" (Coysh, Johnston, Tschann, Wallerstein, & Kline, 1989, p. 68). In contrast, "women appear to be more affected by the residual hostility from the past marriage and problematic relations between partners and children in their new marriages or relationships" (p. 68). A 22-year-old woman described her mother's struggles during and following divorce:

> While this was going on, my mother's self-esteem plummeted as she slipped into a deep depression. This was probably the most difficult part. For various reasons, all of her friends deserted her at once. This simply increased her feeling of loneliness and anger, and isolation. Because we were around, we bore most of my mom's frustrations. My mother would become angry and lash out at us. As the oldest child and the one with the shortest fuse, I caught the worst. . . . She was going through a period of regression, acting like a teenager with her newfound freedom. I felt the need to let her know that her immature, reckless behavior was not acceptable with me. (Republished with permission of Taylor and Francis/Routledge, from Harvey, J. H., & Fine, M. A. [2010]. *Children of divorce: Stories of loss and growth* [2nd ed., p. 46]. New York, NY: Taylor and Francis/Routledge; permission conveyed through Copyright Clearance Center, Inc.)

There are a number of possible explanations for gender differences in postdivorce adjustment. Women, in general, are more deeply committed to marriage, parenthood, and family life than men are; women devote substantially more time and energy to these activities than men do; and women are better attuned than men to family members' needs, the emotional climate of the marriage, and marital problems (Hetherington, 2003; Hochschild, 2003). Having invested more in the relationship, it is reasonable that the dissolution of the relationship inflicts greater emotional pain on women than on men. Other factors certainly contribute to women's postdivorce distress, including their worsened economic position and the chronic stresses associated with coordinating employment and single-parenting (Braver et al., 2006; Sayer, 2006).

As bleak a picture as this paints for many divorced women, there is considerable evidence to suggest that divorce is a short-term crisis, with stress increasing as the divorce approaches, then subsiding postdivorce as life is reorganized and individuals adjust to new routines and lifestyles (Demo & Fine, 2010). Many divorced women may feel that even with the demands placed on them following divorce, they prefer their current situation to the lives they had when they were married.

The evidence on race differences in adjustment to divorce is limited, but it appears that compared to their White counterparts, African American women receive more social support postdivorce (Orbuch & Brown, 2006). Kitson (1992) suggested that although African Americans view divorce as regrettable, the higher divorce rate among African Americans prompts greater acceptance and less stigma. Social, emotional, and financial adjustment to divorce appears to be very similar among Whites and African Americans (Amato, 2000b; Barrett, 2003).

Children's Adjustment

Perhaps no issue surrounding divorce generates more concern or stirs more controversy than children's adjustment to divorce, and the research literature on the subject is voluminous (e.g., see Amato, 2010; Barber & Demo, 2006). Here, we briefly summarize what we know about how children are influenced by processes associated with divorce, highlight the variability found in children's ability to adapt to divorce, and offer some explanations for these patterns.

As is the case for most adults, the evidence suggests that most children and adolescents experience adjustment difficulties (but not necessarily at *clinical* levels) for 1 to 2 years during the period leading up to and immediately following parental separation and divorce (Hetherington & Kelly, 2002). This is usually the period when marital and family conflicts intensify, when legal battles are fought, and when relationships with residential and nonresidential parents are restructured and renegotiated. On average, however, the adjustment of children and adolescents following divorce is only moderately lower than that of their counterparts in continuously intact first-marriage families (Demo & Fine, 2010). Recent analyses of two national samples reported "a substantial degree of variability in children's outcomes following parental divorce, with some children declining, others improving, and most not changing at all" (Amato & Anthony, 2014, p. 370).

Factors that are protective of children's postdivorce adjustment are the provision of economic resources; having positive, nurturing relationships with both parents; low levels of interparental and family conflict (Barber & Demo, 2006; Demo & Fine, 2010); and higher levels of predivorce adjustment (Strohschein, 2005). It is widely speculated that reduced involvement with nonresidential parents is damaging to children's well-being. Heightening this concern are studies showing that in many cases, paternal involvement following divorce is infrequent (McNamee, Amato, & King, 2014) and that fathers' contact typically diminishes over time (King, Harris, & Heard, 2004). A 20-year-old woman described how her relationship with her father deteriorated:

> Eventually he "became too busy," according to my father, to take our visits any longer. He still sent us birthday and Christmas cards with money enclosed and stopped by every once in a while. Then everything stopped for a few years. Neither my brother nor I had any contact with him, and he never saw us. The next time that I did see him I was probably 15 or 16 years old and was with my friends at the supermarket. I ran into him in the parking lot and all he could say was things to belittle me. He asked if I was pregnant, if I was still working fast food, or if I had flunked out of school by now. He made me feel about one inch tall and embarrassed me so much in front of my friends. He wasn't even happy to see me. Luckily, my friends stuck up for me and told him to "fuck off" and took me away from him.
>
> The next time I saw him was at Wal-Mart my junior year in college, where I endured the same treatment. This time, though, I had a lot more to say for myself and told him exactly what had gone on in my life concerning college, and my career just to prove to him that I was going somewhere in life. Both times I've run into him at the store, he was buying beer. So much for AA. (Republished with permission of Taylor and Francis/Routledge, from Harvey, J. H., & Fine, M. A. [2010]. *Children of divorce: Stories of loss and growth* [2nd ed., p. 95]. New York, NY: Taylor and Francis/Routledge; permission conveyed through Copyright Clearance Center, Inc.)

But the broader picture on children's relationships with parents following divorce is both more complex and more encouraging. Children live in a wide variety of family situations postdivorce, including arrangements in which nonresidential fathers (especially African American fathers) maintain regular contact with their children (King & Heard, 1999). Many children change residences (some several times) to live with a different parent (Amato, 2000a), children living with their fathers typically have relatively frequent contact with nonresidential mothers (Maccoby & Mnookin, 1992), and most children and adolescents adapt well to diverse forms of postdivorce family life (Demo & Fine, 2010; King & Heard, 1999). These patterns demonstrate that traditional definitions of family structure (e.g., father present or father absent) and broad generalizations of postdivorce parenting (e.g., "deadbeat dads") obscure substantial temporal and cultural variation in residential and visitation processes (King & Heard, 1999).

Following divorce, the *quality* of children's relationships with both parents affects their adjustment to divorce (Marsiglio, Amato, Day, & Lamb, 2000). There is also consistent evidence that children's adjustment is enhanced if they have a good relationship with at least one (but not necessarily both) of their parents (Hetherington, Bridges, & Insabella, 1998). Following divorce, conflicts between parents may lessen in frequency and intensity, and children benefit most when parents insulate children from these tensions, as this 20-year-old woman describes:

> Although I was very upset when my parents told me that they were getting a divorce, after a few years I knew that it was for the best. In fact, I couldn't even imagine how my parents had been able to get along as good as they did. After the divorce, my parents really tried to keep me out of the middle. I know that they were angry with each other, particularly my father being mad at my mom, but they always seemed to be able to put aside their differences so that they could do what was best for me. In fact, in the past few years, they have even become sort of like friends again. I don't want to put my kids through a divorce, but if it has to happen, I hope I can put their needs first like my parents did for me. (Republished with permission of Taylor and Francis/Routledge, from Harvey, J. H., & Fine, M. A. [2010]. *Children of divorce: Stories of loss and growth* [2nd ed., p. 63]. New York, NY: Taylor and Francis/Routledge; permission conveyed through Copyright Clearance Center, Inc.)

A serious problem confronting many children following divorce is prolonged economic hardship. Although children's postdivorce residential arrangements are variable and change over time, roughly two thirds of children live with their mother, 10% live with their father, and the remainder have dual residences or live in other arrangements (Amato, 2000a; King et al., 2004). As we have seen, most women and children experience a sharp, long-term decline in their standard of living following divorce. Economic hardship is associated with lowered parental well-being, less effective and less supportive parenting, inconsistent and harsh discipline, and distressed and impaired socioemotional functioning in children (Pong & Ju, 2000; Sun & Li, 2002, 2007). It should be clear, however, that these adverse effects are products of chronic financial stress and can be experienced by children in divorced and nondivorced families alike.

Multiple Family Transitions and Children's and Parents' Adjustment

Although research indicates that most children and adolescents who experience their parents' divorce score in the normal (or nonclinical) range on measures of adjustment, a small but growing minority may be at prolonged risk because of multiple transitions in family living arrangements. Transitions in family living arrangements refer to changes in family structure, marital status, or household living arrangements that mark the beginning or the end of cohabiting, marital, or remarried relationships. As children age, the likelihood increases that they will experience family structure change, as does the probability that they will experience more than one family transition. According to Cavanagh and Huston (2008), more than one in four children in the NICHD Study of Early Child Care and Youth Development experienced two or more family transitions by the end of fourth grade.

Consequences for Children

What effects do multiple family transitions have on children? Each family structure transition can be emotionally stressful, so there is the potential that the cumulative effect of multiple transitions across childhood and adolescence may be quite harmful. When parents and their romantic partners move into and out of the household, there are disruptions in adult sources of support, nurturance, supervision, and discipline. Changes in parenting behaviors, family routines, and emotional attachments are often accompanied by changes in residences, schools, neighborhoods, and peer groups. The changes can be confusing and bothersome to children, especially at the beginning, but over time many children and parents report happier relationships. An illustration of how these complex family structures can improve is described by a 22-year-old man:

> Eventually both of my parents remarried around the time of my pre-teen and young teenage years. I definitely had a hard time accepting these remarriages, especially my mom's. When I was in seventh grade I had to move to Indiana with my mom because my stepdad had trouble finding a job in Chicago where both my mom and dad lived. I was angry and bitter that I was essentially being taken away from my dad, my friends, and my hometown. My relationship with my stepdad struggled for a long time after the move. My real dad and I had always had a close relationship and so the distance between us was extremely hard on both of us and suffered in the long run. My dad remarried last although he had dated my stepmom for many years beforehand. Even though I only saw my dad and stepmom on alternating holidays and for a month each summer, my stepmom and I also had a rocky relationship. Looking back, I was jealous and bitter at my two stepparents for altering the life that I had gotten used to after the divorce.

The main positive aspect that I gained from my stepparents though was my stepsiblings whom I now consider my own brothers and sisters. I was an only child and since it wasn't possible anymore to have biological siblings, stepsiblings were the next best thing. I have four older siblings on my mom's side and two younger siblings on my dad's side now. I love them all very much and have a unique and special relationship with each of them. Another advantage of my parents' divorce and remarriages, besides the gain of family, would be all the friends and people that I have met. They have each had a strong impact in my life and will remain friends for life. I am very thankful for their presence in my life. Another positive aspect of the remarriages is of course my parents' happiness. They are both very happy with their new partners and have each been married for over a decade now. I seriously doubt that either one will divorce again, which of course pleases me. (Republished with permission of Taylor and Francis/Routledge, from Harvey, J. H., & Fine, M. A. [2010]. *Children of divorce: Stories of loss and growth* [2nd ed., pp. 67–68]. New York, NY: Taylor and Francis/Routledge; permission conveyed through Copyright Clearance Center, Inc.)

Analyses of data from three waves of the Fragile Families Study found that the frequency of mothers' partnership transitions was associated with increases in children's aggressive and anxious/depressive behavior at age 3 (Osborne & McLanahan, 2007). Although a single partnership change was associated with only a modest detrimental effect, the effects were additive, resulting in large effects for children who experienced multiple transitions. Furthermore, the pattern of accumulating effects of multiple transitions was obtained across White, Black, and Hispanic children.

Consequences for Adults

For adults, given the relatively high divorce rates for first marriages and the even higher rates for subsequent marriages, multiple divorces continue to be quite common; in 2004, for example, approximately 17% of adults experienced two or more divorces (Amato, 2004). This rate may have gone down slightly in the last decade because of slightly declining marriage rates, increases in cohabitation, and modest declines in the divorce rate since 1980 (Demo & Buehler, 2013). Furthermore, there is some evidence that the frequency of family transitions (i.e., marriage, divorce, cohabitation, singlehood) is related to higher levels of depression for women (Cavanagh & Huston, 2006).

In sum, multiple family structure transitions have modest detrimental effects for women, and perhaps men, but these negative consequences for adults are smaller in magnitude than are the comparable effects for children. Perhaps the effects on adults are smaller because adults (to varying degrees) choose to make these transitions whereas — children's transitions are often decided for them, because many adults have more sophisticated and effective coping skills than children, and/or because some adults may become more accustomed to divorce stressors (and presumably less affected by them) with each subsequent divorce.

INTERVENTIONS

In this section, we consider two types of interventions that attempt to improve the lives of those who have experienced divorce: parenting education for divorcing parents and family mediation. These two were selected because they have become institutionalized in the "divorce industry," have achieved a high level of popularity, have already affected large numbers of divorced families, and involve some degree of collaboration between legal and nonlegal professionals.

Parenting Education for Divorcing Parents

In no arena is the divorce industry more apparent than in the area of parenting education for divorcing parents. Partly because of an increased awareness of the stresses that divorce places on children, attention has been focused on helping children adjust more effectively to divorce. In recent years, the most frequent way this has been addressed is through educational programs that prepare parents to help their children cope with divorce. Parent education for separated and divorced parents is available in the vast majority of the states (46 as of 2008; Pollet & Lombreglia, 2008), and most of these programs are court-mandated (Blaisure & Geasler, 2006). These programs are offered in schools, universities, community agencies, and family courts (Salem, Sandler, & Wolchik, 2013), and they range widely in length and number of sessions, instructional methods, and educational goals. In general, these programs address child-focused, parent-focused, and/or court-focused content, including (a) postdivorce reactions of children and parents, (b) children's needs and reactions to divorce at different ages, (c) the benefits of cooperative postdivorce parenting, and (d) the emotional costs of placing children in the middle of parental disputes (Blaisure & Geasler, 2006).

The quality of the evaluations of these programs has lagged far behind programmatic development (Blaisure & Geasler, 2006; Pollet & Lombreglia, 2008). When evaluations of these programs are conducted, they have primarily consisted of "consumer satisfaction" questionnaires that ask participants how satisfied they were with various aspects of the program (Blaisure & Geasler, 2006). Results from these questionnaires typically show that consumers are very satisfied with the programs (Pollet & Lombreglia, 2008), which is not surprising given that clients usually report having positive experiences with a wide range of interventions.

However, client satisfaction does not necessarily mean that the programs are successful in achieving their primary goal—fostering behavioral change. Unfortunately, we know relatively little about the short- and long-term effectiveness of these parenting education programs in affecting behavior change. The few studies examining such change have yielded mixed results. Some have reported that compared to parents who do not attend such programs, parents in divorce education programs were more willing to seek outside help, litigated less often, and engaged in less conflict with coparents (Arbuthnot & Gordon, 1996; Bacon & McKenzie, 2004). Not all evaluation studies report success, however; several researchers have reported no differences between program participants and controls

(Douglas, 2004), and often findings are mixed, with program parents benefiting on some outcomes but not others (Bacon & McKenzie, 2004; Salem et al., 2013). Although there has been some improvement in the quality of and frequency of program evaluations of these programs, there is still a great deal of work to do before we can conclude with confidence that these programs are effective.

These educational programs have political and intuitive appeal, so the absence of supportive evidence of effectiveness has not deterred their widespread use and dissemination. However, without sound evaluation findings, courts and legislatures will find it increasingly difficult to justify mandating such programs. Thus, evaluations of these programs that extend beyond consumer satisfaction are very much needed.

Given that the primary targets of parent education for divorcing parents are *children*, one might wonder why children themselves are not the direct recipients of intervention. There are a number of reasons why parents are the direct recipients of these educational sessions, including that (a) they are more amenable to such interventions, (b) they perhaps have the insight and motivation to benefit from the material presented, and (c) it is logistically easier to require adults than children to attend such a session. Nevertheless, there are a number of programs developed for children whose parents are divorced or divorcing (Pedro-Carroll, 1997). Many of these are school-based programs that focus on helping children adapt socially and emotionally; becoming aware of their feelings about themselves, their parents, and the divorce; expressing feelings in appropriate ways; learning to cope with frustration; learning to get along with others; and enhancing self-esteem. There is some evidence that these group interventions are effective (Barber & Demo, 2006), but few programs have been adequately evaluated in controlled studies, and findings from the evaluation studies that have been conducted are not consistent or clear-cut.

Divorce Mediation

Mediation is one of a class of alternative dispute resolution approaches—they are considered "alternative" because they are less adversarial than traditional legal procedures and seek to reach agreements in a more cooperative manner. Divorce mediation consists of an impartial third party helping a divorcing or divorced couple identify, discuss, and, hopefully, resolve disagreements related to the divorce. Mediation has grown rapidly and is mandated in several states (Sbarra & Emery, 2006). Mediation usually addresses some or all of five areas of potential conflict: (1) property division, (2) spousal support, (3) child support, (4) custody, and (5) visitation (Beck & Sales, 2001; Sbarra & Emery, 2006). Successful mediation allows the divorcing couple to maintain control of decisions in these domains and results in each party feeling some ownership over the divorce agreement (Sbarra & Emery, 2006).

Mediation is based on the principle of cooperative negotiation, which is unlike the typically adversarial nature of the U.S. legal system, which views the parties as disputants who compete with each other for limited resources. In contrast to psychotherapy, mediation targets more specific, pragmatic, concrete, and immediate issues. Emery (1999) described the core of mediation as "renegotiating family relationships" (p. 379). The negotiation of relationships is not achieved by exploring psychological issues but rather by helping the (ex)partners agree on issues regarding child rearing.

Although early evidence was promising, subsequent research has led to less optimistic conclusions. Several studies suggested there are no short-term differences between mediation and more traditional adversarial approaches in enhancing psychological well-being and/or the quality of coparenting (Beck & Sales, 2001; Sbarra & Emery, 2006). The lack of positive short-term effects of mediation may be due to overly high expectations about what a brief intervention such as mediation can reasonably accomplish or a lack of measures that are sensitive to the nuanced ways that mediation may be helpful.

Nevertheless, mediation has been shown to be effective on some dimensions. In the Charlottesville Mediation Study (Sbarra & Emery, 2006), parents consistently preferred mediation over litigation in terms of both the process (e.g., feeling understood) and perceived outcomes (e.g., one's rights being protected) of the intervention. Furthermore, in a long-term (12-year) follow-up, nonresidential parents who went through mediation had considerably more contact (both face-to-face and by telephone) with their children than did those who had litigated settlements (Sbarra & Emery, 2006). However, a potential drawback of this additional contact is that ex-partners reported being more attached to each other than partners who went through litigation.

Mediation has its critics. First, as early as 25 years ago, Menzel (1991) expressed concern that men's greater power places women at a disadvantage in negotiating, and that mediators do not take these power differentials into account. Clearly, the potentially negative consequences of such power differentials are still present. On the other hand, noting that women are more satisfied than are men with both litigated and mediated settlements, Emery (1995) suggested that it is not that women are disadvantaged in mediation, but rather that men are disadvantaged in litigation. Thus, according to this view, men have more to gain in mediation than they often do in litigation, which leads them to be more satisfied with mediated agreements.

Second, mediation is not an appropriate strategy for some couples. Spouses who cannot communicate and problem solve with each other, whether because one or both spouses have personality characteristics that prohibit cooperative problem solving or because the couple has dysfunctional interactional patterns, are inappropriate candidates for mediation. As noted by Beck, Walsh, Mechanic, and Taylor (2010), mediation is generally considered to be counterindicated when there is interpersonal violence in the family.

Third, there has been controversy regarding who can be effective mediators. Mediators generally fall into one of two groups: lawyers and mental health professionals. Some have argued that lawyers are best suited to be mediators because of their knowledge of the law, whereas others have suggested that mental health professionals have greater knowledge of the psychological and emotional aspects of how children, parents, and families cope with divorce. Consistent with Emery's (1995) prediction, mediation has not and probably will not become a separate profession, but it has developed within both the mental health and legal professions.

Finally, there is some controversy pertaining to whether mediation should be mandated, used only in select cases, or voluntary. As Sbarra and Emery (2006) noted, there are some cases when mediation may be inappropriate, such as when a child and/or a spouse has been abused. Nevertheless, because mandating mediation typically requires that a couple attend and participate in a session but does not mean that the parties must reach a settlement, there are strong reasons to require mediation except in selected cases.

CONCLUSION

Divorce has become almost a normative experience in the 21st century. Although there is considerable variation in children's and adults' emotional adjustment to divorce (see Demo & Fine, 2010), most children and adults adapt well to a variety of postdivorce family forms and function in the normal ranges of adjustment. Among the small percentage who experience lingering difficulties, the problems can often be traced to poor adjustment preceding the divorce; predivorce family tension, stress, conflict, and hostility; postdivorce economic decline; postdivorce conflict between the ex-spouses; and multiple transitions in family living arrangements.

Divorce is more widely accepted and less stigmatized today than in the past, but it still tends to be viewed negatively and is often blamed for many individual and societal problems. Opposition to divorce also has legal and political implications as, from time to time, there have been efforts to make it more difficult for married couples to obtain divorces, such as longer waiting periods and requiring participation in counseling before the divorce is granted. The evidence reviewed in this chapter suggests that divorce is a prevalent (and sometimes even necessary) aspect of family life, and we believe that little is likely to be gained by restricting divorce and further stigmatizing divorce. Our position is that it makes more sense for family researchers, practitioners, and policy makers to focus attention and resources on identifying risk and protective factors and processes that are related to how effectively people adjust to divorce. For example, what can be done to help parents keep their children out of the middle of their conflicts? What are the best ways for parents to communicate their impending divorce to their children? How do support networks facilitate the adjustment of divorcing parents? In our opinion, exploring these and other issues from research, practice, and policy perspectives will be more helpful than devoting resources to trying to prevent divorce.

With specific reference to interventions, attention also needs to be devoted to designing programs that better prepare and educate divorcing adults—parents and nonparents alike—for the financial, coparenting, and personal stresses; transitions; and challenges they will face in a variety of postdivorce family forms. Client satisfaction with educational programs for divorcing parents is impressive, but little research has evaluated the short- and long-term impact of these programs on parenting effectiveness, parent–child relationships, or child well-being. Programs designed specifically for children are also needed. Finally, while there is a growing body of evidence suggesting that divorce mediation has numerous advantages over conventional adversarial divorces, more research is needed that evaluates when mediation is most effective and for which groups it is particularly well suited. The challenge will be to explore these and other interventions as ways of normalizing divorce and facilitating healthy adjustment to this stressor.

REFERENCES

Ahrons, C. (1994). *The good divorce: Keeping your family together when your marriage comes apart.* New York, NY: Harper Collins.

Amato, P. R. (2000a). Diversity within single-parent families. In D. H. Demo, K. R. Allen, & M. A. Fine (Eds.), *The handbook of family diversity* (pp. 149–172). New York, NY: Oxford University Press.

Amato, P. R. (2000b). The consequences of divorce for adults and children. *Journal of Marriage and the Family, 62,* 1269–1287.

Amato, P. R. (2004). Divorce in social and historical context: Changing scientific perspectives on children and marital dissolution. In M. Coleman & L. Ganong (Eds.), *Handbook of contemporary families: Considering the past, contemplating the future* (pp. 265–281). Thousand Oaks, CA: Sage.

Amato, P. R. (2010). Research on divorce: Continuing trends and new developments. *Journal of Marriage and Family, 72,* 650–666.

Amato, P. R., & Anthony, C. J. (2014). Estimating the effects of parental divorce and death with fixed effects models. *Journal of Marriage and Family, 76,* 370–386.

Amato, P. R., & Irving, S. (2006). Historical trends in divorce and dissolution in the United States. In M. A. Fine & J. H. Harvey (Eds.), *Handbook of divorce and relationship dissolution* (pp. 41–57). Mahwah, NJ: Lawrence Erlbaum.

Amato, P. R., Johnson, D., Booth, A., & Rogers, S. (2003). Continuity and change in marital quality between 1980 and 2000. *Journal of Marriage and Family, 65,* 1–22.

Arbuthnot, J., & Gordon, D. A. (1996). Does mandatory divorce education for parents work?: A six-month outcome evaluation. *Family and Conciliation Courts Review, 34,* 60–81.

Bacon, B. L., & McKenzie, B. (2004). Parent education after separation/divorce: Impact of the level of parental conflict on outcomes. *Family Court Review, 42,* 85–98.

Barber, B. L., & Demo, D. H. (2006). The kids are alright (at least, most of them): Links between divorce and dissolution and child well-being. In M. A. Fine & J. H. Harvey (Eds.), *Handbook of divorce and relationship dissolution* (pp. 289–311). Mahwah, NJ: Lawrence Erlbaum.

Barrett, A. E. (2003). Race differences in the mental health effects of divorce: A reexamination incorporating temporal dimensions of the dissolution process. *Journal of Family Issues, 24,* 995–1019.

Beck, C. J. A., & Sales, B. D. (2001). *Family mediation: Facts, myths, and future prospects.* Washington, DC: American Psychological Association.

Beck, C. J. A., Walsh, M. E., Mechanic, M. B., & Taylor, C. S. (2010). Mediator assessment, documentation, and disposition of child custody cases involving intimate partner abuse: A naturalistic evaluation of one county's practices. *Law and Human Behavior, 34,* 227–240.

Blaisure, K. R., & Geasler, M. J. (2006). Educational interventions for separating and divorcing parents. In M. A. Fine & J. H. Harvey (Eds.), *Handbook of divorce and relationship dissolution* (pp. 575–602). Mahwah, NJ: Lawrence Erlbaum.

Bradbury, T. N., Fincham, F. D., & Beach, S. R. H. (2000). Research on the nature and determinants of marital satisfaction: A decade in review. *Journal of Marriage and the Family, 62,* 964–980

Braver, S. L., Shapiro, J. R., & Goodman, M. R. (2006). Consequences of divorce for parents. In M. A. Fine & J. H. Harvey (Eds.), *Handbook of divorce and relationship dissolution* (pp. 313–337). Mahwah, NJ: Lawrence Erlbaum.

Cavanagh, S. E., & Huston, A. C. (2006). Family instability and children's early problem behavior. *Social Forces, 85,* 551–581.

Cavanagh, S. E., & Huston, A. C. (2008). The timing of family instability and children's social development. *Journal of Marriage and Family, 70,* 1258-1269.

Cherlin, A. J. (2004). The deinstitutionalization of American marriage. *Journal of Marriage and Family, 66,* 848–861.

Cherlin, A. J. (2009). *The marriage-go-round.* New York, NY: Vintage.

Coleman, M., Ganong, L., & Warzinik, K. (2007). *Family life in 20th century America.* Westport, CT: Greenwood.

Coysh, W. S., Johnston, J. R., Tschann, J. M., Wallerstein, J. S., & Kline, M. (1989). Parental postdivorce adjustment in joint and sole physical custody families. *Journal of Family Issues, 10,* 52–71.

Demo, D., H., & Buehler, C. (2013). Theoretical approaches to studying divorce. In M. A. Fine & F. D. Fincham (Eds.), *Handbook of family theories: A content-based approach* (pp. 263–279). New York, NY: Taylor and Francis.

Demo, D. H., & Fine, M. A. (2010). *Beyond the average divorce.* Thousand Oaks, CA: Sage.

Douglas, E. M. (2004). The effectiveness of a divorce education program on father involvement. *Journal of Divorce & Remarriage, 40,* 91–101.

Elder, G. H., Jr. (1998). The life course as developmental theory. *Child Development, 69,* 1–12.

Emery, R. E. (1995). Divorce mediation: Negotiating agreements and renegotiating relationships. *Family Relations, 44,* 377–383.

Emery, R. E. (1999). *Marriage, divorce, and children's adjustment* (2nd ed.). Thousand Oaks, CA: Sage.

Garey, A. I. (1999). *Weaving motherhood and work.* Philadelphia, PA: Temple University Press.

Gerstel, N. (1990). Divorce and stigma. In C. Carlson (Ed.), *Perspectives on the family: History, class, and feminism* (pp. 460–478). Belmont, CA: Wadsworth.

Harvey, J. H., & Fine, M. A. (2010). *Children of divorce: Stories of loss and growth* (2nd ed.). New York, NY: Taylor and Francis/Routledge.

Hetherington, E. M. (2003). Intimate pathways: Changing patterns in close personal relationships across time. *Family Relations, 52,* 318–331.

Hetherington, E. M., Bridges, M., & Insabella, G. M. (1998). What matters? What does not? Five perspectives on the association between marital transitions and children's adjustment. *American Psychologist, 53,* 167–184.

Hetherington, E. M., & Kelly, J. (2002). *For better or for worse.* New York, NY: Norton.

Hochschild, A. (with Machung, A.). (2003). *The second shift: Working parents and the revolution at home* (Rev. ed.). New York, NY: Viking/Penguin.

Hopper, J. (1993). The rhetoric of motives in divorce. *Journal of Marriage and the Family, 55,* 801–813.

Hopper, J. (2001). The symbolic origins of conflict in divorce. *Journal of Marriage and Family, 63,* 430–445.

Hurley, D. (2005, April 19). Divorce rate: It's not as high as you think. *The New York Times.*

King, V., Harris, K. M., & Heard, H. E. (2004). Racial and ethnic diversity in nonresident father involvement. *Journal of Marriage and Family, 66,* 1–21.

King, V., & Heard, H. E. (1999). Nonresident father visitation, parental conflict, and mothers' satisfaction: What's best for child well-being? *Journal of Marriage and the Family, 61,* 385–396.

Kitson, G. C. (1992). *Portrait of divorce: Adjustment to marital breakdown.* New York, NY: Guilford.

Maccoby, E. E., & Mnookin, R. H. (1992). *Dividing the child: Social and legal dilemmas of custody.* Cambridge, MA: Harvard University Press.

Manning, W. D., & Smock, P. J. (2000). Swapping families: Serial parenting and economic support for children. *Journal of Marriage and the Family, 62,* 111–122.

Margolin, G., Oliver, P. H., & Medina, A. M. (2001). Conceptual issues in understanding the relation between interparental conflict and child adjustment. In J. H. Grych & F. D. Fincham (Eds.), *Interparental conflict and child development* (pp. 9–38). Cambridge, England: Cambridge University Press.

Marsiglio, W., Amato, P. R., Day, R. D., & Lamb, M. E. (2000). Scholarship on fatherhood in the 1990s and beyond. *Journal of Marriage and the Family, 62,* 1173–1191.

McGraw, L., & Walker, A. (2004). Gendered family relations: The more things change, the more they stay the same. In M. Coleman & L. Ganong (Eds.), *Handbook of contemporary families: Considering the past, contemplating the future* (pp. 174–191). Thousand Oaks, CA: Sage.

McNamee, C. B., Amato, P., & King, V. (2014). Nonresident father involvement with children and divorced women's likelihood of remarriage. *Journal of Marriage and Family, 76,* 862–874.

Menzel, K. E. (1991). Judging the fairness of mediation: A critical framework. *Mediation Quarterly, 9,* 3-20.

Orbuch, T. L., & Brown, E. (2006). Divorce in the context of being African American. In M. A. Fine & J. H. Harvey (Eds.), *Handbook of divorce and relationship dissolution* (pp. 481–498). Mahwah, NJ: Lawrence Erlbaum.

Osborne, C., & McLanahan, S. (2007). Partnership instability and child well-being. *Journal of Marriage and Family, 69,* 1065–1083.

Pedro-Carroll, J. (1997). The Children of Divorce Intervention Program: Fostering resilient outcomes for school-aged children. In G. W. Albee & T. P. Gullotta (Eds.), *Primary prevention works* (pp. 213–238). Thousand Oaks, CA: Sage.

Pirog, M. A., & Ziol-Guest, M (2006). Child support enforcement: Programs and policies, impacts and questions. *Journal of Policy Analysis and Management, 25,* 943–990.

Pollet, S. L., & Lombreglia, M. (2008). A nationwide survey of mandatory parent education. *Family Court Review, 46,* 375–394.

Pong, S., & Ju, D. (2000). The effects of change in family structure and income on dropping out of middle and high school. *Journal of Family Issues, 21,* 147–169.

Powell, D., & Fine, M. A. (2009). Relationship dissolution, causes. In Harry T. Reis & Susan Sprecher (Eds.), *Encyclopedia of human relationships.* Thousand Oaks, CA: Sage.

Rodrigues, A. E., Hall, J. H., & Fincham, F. D. (2006). What predicts divorce and relationship dissolution. In M. A. Fine & J. H. Harvey (Eds.), *Handbook of divorce and relationship dissolution* (pp. 85–112). Mahwah, NJ: Lawrence Erlbaum.

Salem, P., Sandler, I., & Wolchik, S. (2013). Taking stock of parent education in the family courts: Envisioning a public health model. *Family Court Review, 51,* 131–148.

Sayer, L. C. (2006). Economic aspects of divorce and relationship dissolution. In M. A. Fine & J. H. Harvey (Eds.), *Handbook of divorce and relationship dissolution* (pp. 385–406). Mahwah, NJ: Lawrence Erlbaum.

Sbarra, D. A., & Emery, R. E. (2006). In the presence of grief: The role of cognitive emotional adaptation in contemporary divorce mediation. In M. A. Fine & J. H. Harvey (Eds.), *Handbook of divorce and relationship dissolution* (pp. 553–573). Mahwah, NJ: Lawrence Erlbaum.

Strohschein, L. (2005). Parental divorce and child mental health trajectories. *Journal of Marriage and Family, 67,* 1286–1300.

Sun, Y. (2001). Family environment and adolescents' well-being before and after parents' marital disruption: A longitudinal analysis. *Journal of Marriage and Family, 63,* 697–713.

Sun, Y., & Li, Y. (2002). Children's well-being during parents' marital disruption process: A pooled time-series analysis. *Journal of Marriage and Family, 64,* 472–488.

Sun, Y., & Li, Y. (2007). Racial and ethnic differences in experiencing parents' marital disruption during late adolescence. *Journal of Marriage and Family, 69,* 742–762.

Sweeney, M. (2002). Remarriage and the nature of divorce. *Journal of Family Issues, 23,* 410–440.

Teachman, J. D. (2000). Diversity of family structure: Economic and social influences. In D. H. Demo, K. R. Allen, & M. A. Fine (Eds.), *The handbook of family diversity* (pp. 32–58). New York, NY: Oxford University Press.

Teachman, J. D., Tedrow, L., & Hall, M. (2006). The demographic future of divorce. In M. A. Fine & J. H. Harvey (Eds.), *Handbook of divorce and relationship dissolution* (pp. 59–82). Mahwah, NJ: Lawrence Erlbaum.

Umaña-Taylor, A. J., & Alfaro, E. C. (2006). Divorce and relationship dissolution among Latino populations in the United States. In M. A. Fine & J. H. Harvey (Eds.), *Handbook of divorce and relationship dissolution* (pp. 515–530). Mahwah, NJ: Lawrence Erlbaum.

Usdansky, M. L. (2009). A weak embrace: Popular and scholarly depictions of single-parent families, 1900-1998. *Journal of Marriage and Family, 71,* 209–225.

Walsh, F. (2002). A family resilience framework: Innovative practice applications. *Family Relations, 51,* 130–137.

Walzer, S. (2004). Encountering oppositions: A review of scholarship about motherhood. In M. Coleman & L. H. Ganong (Eds.), *Handbook of contemporary families: Considering the past, contemplating the future* (pp. 209–223). Thousand Oaks, CA: Sage.

Wang, H., & Amato, P. R. (2000). Predictors of divorce adjustment: Stressors, resources, and definitions. *Journal of Marriage and the Family, 62*, 655–668.

Zartler, U. (2014). How to deal with moral tales: Constructions and strategies of single-parent families. *Journal of Marriage and Family, 76*, 604–619.

CHAPTER 8

Stress and Resilience in Stepfamilies Today

Chelsea Garneau and Kay Pasley

_____ Vignette _____

Nick was single when he met Adina and gave little thought to how her 10-year-old son, Jared, would affect their relationship. When they married a year later, they had never discussed his role in their new stepfamily. Nick expected the transition would be smooth, and he would act like a "regular father" after the marriage, partly because Jared's father had not been around for 9 years. It soon became clear, however, that neither Jared nor Adina shared this expectation. Nick and Jared had screaming matches every time Nick enforced a household rule or told Jared what to do. Frequently, Adina came to the defense of her son. Over time, Nick began to feel like he did not have a place in the family and felt betrayed by Adina's loyalty to her son. Often, when the three of them were together, it ended in a fight or in silence.

• • •

Stepfamilies have long been the focus of research (see Coleman & Ganong, 1990, as an example) with an emphasis on traditionally defined stepfamilies—families in which at least one adult was remarried and brought children from a prior union into the current one. A majority of these families were formed following divorce rather than the death of a spouse. However, much has changed in family life, and scholars are now more inclusive in defining stepfamilies to reflect the diversity of pathways that lead to them. For example, although stepfamilies consistently include children from prior unions, we also recognize those formed when never-married individuals with children go on to cohabit with or marry a partner who is not their child's biological parent. The typical pathway continues to be from one marriage to another marriage; however, stepfamilies are also recognized as forming after the dissolution and repartnering of nonmarital relationships involving both same-sex and heterosexual pairings. It is the children that link prior and current unions, regardless of whether these unions result from marriages.

The labels used to describe stepfamilies have also evolved over time. For example, earlier research and scholarly writing on stepfamilies frequently used terms such as *reconstituted* or *merged* families, whereas *blended* is a more common label. Other current terms reflect the diversity in pathways to stepfamilies and their structure by distinguishing between *married* and *cohabiting*, or unmarried, stepfamilies and those that are *simple* versus *complex*. A simple stepfamily includes two adults of which only one is a parent, whereas a complex stepfamily includes two adults who are both parents, regardless of where the children reside. The terms *resident* and *nonresident* account for whether the stepfamily household is the primary home of the child, which is often determined by residing in the home at least half of the time. It is important to note that although attempts have been made more recently to recognize various aspects of stepfamily diversity, much of what is known about stepfamily relationships continues to be based primarily on research with samples of married, resident stepfather families.

We begin this chapter by addressing the prevalence and demographic characteristics of stepfamilies in general. Then we discuss stepfamily stress from a family systems perspective to identify sources of stress within the various subsystems and the most common characteristics of resilient stepfamilies. We end with a brief description of psychoeducational and clinical approaches to easing stepfamily adjustment.

PREVALENCE AND DEMOGRAPHIC CHARACTERISTICS OF STEPFAMILIES

Estimates of the prevalence of stepfamilies in the United States today are often drawn from national surveys, such as the U.S. Census or the American Community Survey (ACS), and the results may vary (see Kreider & Lofquist, 2014, for a discussion). Some estimates focus on children of the householder (e.g., Census), whereas other estimates reference children by the type of relationship to both coresident parents (e.g., Current Population Reports [CPR]). However, all sources typically underestimate the number of stepfamilies by excluding (a) stepchildren who are nonresident and live elsewhere (often with a single parent and are counted as children in single-parent families) and (b) resident and nonresident children who are 18 years and older. Regardless of these and other limitations, these data provide the best information currently available.

The most recent estimates using data from 2001 (Kreider, 2005) show that less than 30 % of all marriages were remarriages, and of these remarriage unions, about 65 % form stepfamilies. This estimate is lower than past ones, likely due to the increase in cohabitation and decrease in marriages overall (Cherlin, 2010). Of these stepfamilies, children are most likely to reside in one of two types of stepfamilies. One type is a simple stepfamily that consists of their biological mother and a stepfather, as in the case of Nick, Adina, and Jared. Another type is a complex stepfamily, where children live with their mother and a stepfather, and the mother is a nonresident stepmother to his children. Other estimates from an urban sample (Carlson & Furstenberg, 2006) show that about 60 % of unmarried couples had at least one child from a prior union, forming cohabiting stepfamilies.

More information comes from examining children's living arrangements. Using data from 2010, Kreider and Lofquist (2014) report about 10% of children live with a stepparent, including 4.3% of children under 18 and 5.7% 18 years and older. Recall that children who reside with a single parent (usually a mother) and whose nonresident parent has repartnered or remarried are omitted from these numbers. Of the 10% of children who live with a stepparent, the majority are adolescents or older children (37% are 12–17 and 33% are 18+ years), with another 23.5% between 6 and 11 years and only 6.8% under 6. Most are living in married stepfamilies: 64% with a mother and stepfather (14% in unmarried couples) and 20% with a father and a stepmother (18% in unmarried couples). Unfortunately these data do not allow us to know how many of these stepparents also have children living elsewhere, but our best estimates suggest that about half of stepfather families do. The majority of children in stepfamilies are White (61%), 21% are Hispanic, and 12.5% are African American; this is similar to children in nonstepfamily households (Kreider & Lofquist, 2014). Stepchildren are more likely to have at least one disability and less likely to live in poverty than children living with two biological parents, whether married or cohabiting. Additionally, there is a higher incidence of racial difference between adults and children in stepfamilies, and stepchildren are more likely to reside with married or repartnered parents, in households with more members and higher median incomes, and with householders in the labor force but are less likely to have a college education (Kreider & Lofquist, 2014) compared with biological children, which includes those living with one or both biological parent. Compared with married stepfamilies, the adults in cohabiting stepfamilies are younger, more likely African American or Hispanic, and have lower incomes with both adults in the labor force and more children from prior partnerships (Kreider & Lofquist, 2014). Cohabiting stepfamilies are less stable than those formed through remarriage, and they typically include younger children.

A FAMILY SYSTEMS APPROACH TO STRESS AND RESILIENCE IN STEPFAMILIES

The unique family dynamics and potential sources of stress in stepfamilies are best understood and examined from a family systems perspective (Cox & Paley, 1997). This theoretical approach considers families as complex operating systems of individuals and groups of individuals, or subsystems (i.e., relationships among individuals within a family, such as the couple subsystem, parenting subsystem or sibling subsystem). Importantly, when an individual or subsystem experiences stress, other individuals or subsystems within the family are affected and vice versa, and this is often referred to as the "ripple effect." Subsystems are an appropriate unit of analysis for understanding stepfamilies, because stress in these families results from highly complex processes that cannot be thoroughly understood by focusing on the perspective of a single member.

Stress in the Larger Family System

The complexities of stepfamily relationships put them at greater risk for more family-level stress compared to traditional two-biological-parent families. Generally, common sources of stress in stepfamilies include more family transitions and instability, less clarity regarding member roles and family boundaries, and unrealistic expectations based on comparisons to the traditional two-biological-parent model. These sources of stress result primarily from the complex stepfamily structure and, thus, are unique to these families. The development of a stepfamily involves many transitions for all family members, and these can lead to significant family stress. Transitions include changes in household membership, residence (often motivated by needing a "fresh start" and new home to call their own), neighborhoods and schools, children's friendships, and adult relationships, as well as familiar routines. Stepfamilies must also decide how to distribute resources within the new family structure, including resources of money, space, time, and even affection. Particularly for children who previously lived with a single parent, the addition of a stepparent can mean an increase in financial resources in the family, but new stepsiblings can mean having to share a bedroom and making space throughout the house for more toys and belongings. Parents must find time to spend with their children and a new partner or spouse and, in some cases, devote energy to developing a relationship with new stepchildren.

In the face of multiple transitions and changes, stepfamilies must negotiate new expectations, roles, rules, routines, and rituals which meet the needs of all family members. Basic patterns of family interaction may be interrupted when roles in the family change. For example, an oldest child may be displaced by an older stepsibling, which can lead to role confusion for someone who has always been seen as the leader or most responsible sibling in the family due to his or her birth order. Expectations regarding daily family patterns, such as understanding how and when chores should be completed or who decides what to watch on television, are no longer a given and must be discussed or renegotiated. Different subsystems of biologically related family members may have family rituals that conflict with each other. For example, for the parent and child subsystem Friday night is considered "family movie night," whereas for the stepparent and his or her child subsystem Fridays are "family game night."

Although adjusting to some new roles may be difficult, stepparents especially struggle to determine their place in the new family system. Compared to parenting biological children, stepparenting lacks clear guidelines/social norms, and many stepparents at least initially experience ambivalence about interacting with stepchildren. Expectations may vary from doing little in child rearing to playing primary disciplinarian and nurturing roles similar to a parent. The resulting role ambiguity is a source of stress for several reasons. First, with uncertainty and the resulting frustration (Martin-Uzzi & Duval-Tsioles, 2013) stepparents often experience another layer of ambiguity at the family level, where other members hold different expectations for them (Coleman, Ganong, & Fine, 2000). Ganong and Coleman (2004) reported that stepfamilies in which family members are unable to agree on the stepparent's role tend to be more poorly adjusted, and when they are unable to meet the role expectations, stepparents report poorer individual adjustment.

Like role ambiguity, boundaries are less clear in stepfamilies than nonstepfamilies. Clear boundaries are important to healthy family functioning according to family systems theory, as internal boundaries help to better define stepparent roles in relation to other family members, and external boundaries allow families to establish their family identity. In stepfamilies, internal boundary ambiguity results in role ambiguity, as is evident in the case of Nick's confusion regarding how to enforce household rules. Also, external boundary ambiguity often results in disagreements within families over who is and is not a member, especially when nonresident parents are actively involved with children. Findings from one study indicate that mothers and their adolescents disagreed on their family structure, and those in more complex family structures (e.g., stepfamilies) are less clear about who constitutes a legitimate family member (Brown & Manning, 2009). In fact, nonresident stepmothers were likely to use a biological definition of family and frequently excluded stepchildren when defining their families (Doodson & Morley, 2006). Other research (Stewart, 2005) reported that greater boundary ambiguity was linked with living in a non-resident stepfamily, adolescent reports of lower family closeness and connectedness, and women reporting more spousal disagreement and greater risk for separation. Stepchildren are more likely to consider stepparents as family members when they have resided together or were younger at the time of stepfamily formation (Schmeeckle, Giarrusso, Feng, & Bengtson, 2006). Last, some evidence shows that the level of boundary ambiguity in stepfamilies may decrease overtime (Suanet, VanDer Pas, & van Tillburg, 2013); this may be due to their increasing prevalence and acceptance as a legitimate family form.

The final family-level source of stress in stepfamilies comes from holding unrealistic or stereotypically negative expectations for stepfamily life. Stepfamily scholars suggest that holding misguided beliefs or expectations can be harmful to family relationships, and evidence supports this assertion. Frequently stepfamily members turn to the familiar rules and roles of traditional two-biological-parent models, only to experience even greater distress when their attempts to implement similar rules and roles backfire (e.g., Ganong & Coleman, 2004). Many stepfamilies fall prey to the "social stigma perspective," which identifies stepfamilies as inferior to the traditional two-biological-parent family model and as an undesirable family form (Ganong & Coleman, 1997). Tied into this social stigma is "wicked stepmother" ideology and the view that stepparents cannot be loving and nurturing to stepchildren. On the other end of the range of expectations lies the unrealistic belief that adjustment will occur quickly following remarriage or cohabitation, and family members will easily develop close relationships resembling those in two-biological-parent families. As Nick learned in the opening vignette, overly optimistic expectations can increase stress in stepfamilies due to frustration and conflict once the realities of stepfamily life set in. Although many stepfamilies are able to successfully adjust to their new family and build strong, satisfying relationships, the process often takes time, and relationships must be allowed to develop differently than expected in nonstepfamilies.

Stress in the Couple Subsystem

Within stepfamilies, parents and stepparents belong to two related but distinct subsystems, the couple subsystem and the coparenting subsystem, each with unique opportunities for stress. The couple subsystem is particularly vulnerable due to the stress originating in other family subsystems (e.g., stepparent–stepchild), the continued presence of former partners (i.e., children's other biological parent), and lingering relational concerns from previous marriages or relationships. Importantly, many stepcouples also lack the strong couple bond or conflict management skills necessary to effectively overcome this stress.

Research shows that remarriages are at greater risk for dissolution than first marriages, and that cohabiting partnerships are at even greater risk for dissolution than are marriages (Sassler, 2010). However, little is known about the source of this risk, although some suggest a selectivity hypothesis: persons who divorce and remarry forming stepfamilies have unique characteristics that predispose them to dissolution (e.g., history of divorce in their family of origin) (Amato, 2000). There is evidence that the presence of children from a previous relationship is a primary source of stress and associated with greater likelihood of divorce (Teachman, 2008), and that stepfamilies with complex structures (e.g., his/hers/ours) are more prone to dramatic declines in marital quality (Slattery, Bruce, Halford, & Nicholson, 2011), which is linked with dissolution. Still other research shows that the quality of the couple relationship is affected by the quality of the stepparent–stepchild relationship rather than the reverse which is true in two-biological-parent families. In fact, clinical stepfamily experts have long emphasized the importance of building strong couple bonds (e.g., Visher & Visher, 1979). Because the parent–child relationship precedes that of the stepcouple, couple/spousal relationships must develop concurrently with stepparent–stepchild relationships. Because the children's needs take precedence over adults' needs, the stepcouple relationship is often neglected due to the demands of fostering relationships with stepchildren. Juggling these competing relationship demands can be stressful and negatively affect relationship quality (Slattery et al., 2011).

Lingering influences of a previous marriage and divorce can also be a source of stress for many stepcouples. Divorced adults may be coping with feelings of loss related to the dissolution of the prior marriage or unresolved emotional problems from the relationship (Visher & Visher, 1979). As such, partners may approach the new relationship with greater caution or anxiety, especially following divorce from a long-term relationship, and it is common to hold high expectations for the new partner to be "perfect." Thus, new stepcouples often experience pressure to meet high expectations while handling the competing demands of fostering multiple new stepfamily relationships. Findings from one study suggest that individuals who have unresolved issues from their previous marriage may put less effort into their remarriage, which in turn is linked with lower relationship satisfaction and greater risk for instability (Shafer, Jensen, Pace, & Larson, 2013).

Some have posited that stepcouples experience greater conflict and are less likely to use effective conflict management strategies than couples in nonstepfamilies; however, research findings are mixed. Although they likely experience more opportunities for conflict due to their complex family relationships, some evidence suggests that stepcouples experience both less positive and less negative interactions (Halford, Nicholson, & Sanders, 2007). Stepcouples also report more open expressions of anger, irritation, and criticism during conflict. However, these potentially negative behaviors appear to be diminished by other demonstrations of spousal support and use of affirming communication strategies (e.g., Brown & Robinson, 2012), such as communicating respect and acceptance.

Much less is known about couple relationships involving nonresident parents and stepparents, and many such couples must also negotiate living as a part-time stepfamily household with the associated stress. Overall, nonresident stepcouples tend to be more couple focused and formed with the primary goal of fulfilling the parent's desire for a partner with less emphasis on the new partner's role of stepparent (Ganong & Coleman, 2004). However, these couples still report tension in their relationship, as well as the parent–child and stepparent–stepchild relationships. Among other sources, some of this tension results from loyalty binds (DeGreef & Burnett, 2009) or feeling caught between one's love and commitment to a child and one's love and commitment to a new partner. In a small sample of nonresident stepmothers, a lack of control over matters involving the stepchild led to feelings of powerlessness and combined with anger and resentment had a negative impact on the marital relationship (Henry & McCue, 2009). Other results found that nonresident stepcouples have no more difficulty with triangulation and developing clear boundaries within the family or with increased exclusion of the stepparent than do resident stepcouples (Gosseline & David, 2007). Regardless of residence status, stepcouple relationship quality overall is lower when there are problems in the stepparent–stepchild relationship.

Stress in the Stepcouple Coparenting Subsystem

In addition to the couple/spousal subsystem, stepcouples also relate to one another as coparents. Few clear social norms regarding stepparenting leave stepcouples with the complicated task of determining how to best parent the children together. Similar to Nick and Adina, few stepcouples discuss issues of coparenting prior to cohabiting (e.g., Cartwright, 2010). Evidence shows, however, that when stepcouples are unable to come to an agreement or gain clarity regarding the stepparents' role, stepparent well-being suffers (Felker, Fromme, Arnaut, & Stoll, 2002). Because one of the greatest sources of stress within stepfamilies is conflict in the stepparent–stepchild relationship, this often spills over into the stepcouple coparenting relationship. In fact, the functioning of the stepparent–stepchild subsystem may be more important to stepcouple relationship stability than is the functioning of their subsystem. Couples in stepfamilies report greater tension and more disagreement than those in two-biological-parent families with child rearing being one of the most frequent topics of conflict (Hetherington & Kelly, 2002). In fact, child rearing is the most common topic of conflict in remarried families with finances ranking second compared to the reverse ranking of these two topics in first marriages (Stanley, Markman, & Whitton, 2002). Also, the structure of stepfamilies is such that at least one biological parent–child subsystem comes into the newly formed stepfamily with established family rules, routine, and culture. As coparents, stepcouples must come to terms with possible differences in their parenting styles and expectations for household rules and management, and this negotiation process can be a significant source of stress, particularly when differences are large and the couple struggles to compromise.

Because the structure of a stepfamily creates opportunities for loyalty binds, or situations where one family member feels torn between the competing wants and needs of two or more family members, they can be a significant source of stress in the coparenting subsystem. Adina felt torn between a desire to defend Jared when conflict arose between him and Nick; yet, she simultaneously wished to avoid conflict with Nick and to support his stepparenting. Weaver and Coleman (2010) interviewed biological mothers in step-families and found that they often try to negotiate the relationship between their children and new spouse, more frequently siding with their children when conflict intensified, using four primary strategies. *Defenders* protected their children and perceived stepparent–stepchild conflict as a result of the stepparent's "attacks." *Gatekeepers* pro-tected their children by controlling and limiting the development of a close stepparent-stepchild relationship, either resulting from a lack of trust that the relationship would be stable or in an attempt to separate their roles as mothers and wives. *Mediators* aimed to reduce stepparent–stepchild conflict and foster relationship development by stepping in to help solve problems, increasing stress for many mothers. Last, some mothers were *interpreters*, interrupting disagreements/conflict and using detailed explanations to help stepparents and children better understand one another. As was the case with Nick, loy-alty binds can cause stepparents to feel that their needs come last, and the resulting sense of exclusion can negatively affect the couple relationship. Because stepchildren often continue their contact with a nonresident parent, usually their father, they can experi-ence loyalty binds feeling torn between their love and commitment to the nonresident parent and the resident parent or stepparent. Thus, the coparenting that occurs across households and involves resident parents, nonresident parents, and stepparents is also a source of stress and requires negotiation of child-related issues and financial concerns.

Given the frequency of child- and finance-related conflict, child support issues are particularly difficult to manage (Gold, 2009). Such issues suggest that decisions related to money management are complicated in these families. Money is more likely to be managed separately in stepfamilies than in nonstepfamilies, often with each partner taking primary financial responsibility for their own children (e.g., Raijas, 2011). The numerous transitions that often precede stepfamily formation (e.g., separation/divorce, establishing child sup-port, moving residences, cohabitation with a new partner) are accompanied by financial transitions, which can increase financial stress going into the new stepfamily. Research indicates that remarried women who manage their money jointly tend to be more finan-cially secure than those who manage a portion of their finances separately (van Eeden-Moorefield, Pasley, Dolan, & Engel, 2007), and this is linked with better child outcomes. Other research shows that the decision to pool financial resources is considered by some stepfamily members to be symbolic of greater commitment to the new family and more family cohesion (Burgoyne & Morrison, 1997).

Stress in the Parent–Child Subsystem

In stepfamilies, the biological parent–child subsystem has the longest duration or shared history together. Even so, numerous opportunities for stress are present in this subsystem due to shifts in the parent's time and attention that result from the addition of new stepmembers and the increased complexities of family interactions.

Roughly 80% of parents begin dating within a year of filing for divorce, 50% identify a new relationship as "serious" (Anderson et al., 2004), and the majority go on to repartner or remarry quickly (Kreider & Ellis, 2011). Little is known about the dating processes of postdivorce parents; however, their courtship can be a significant source of stress for both parents and children. For example, Anderson and Greene (2005) identified nine transitions couples and families experience as part of the repartnering process leading to remarriage. These included initiation of dating, introducing the new partner to the children, identification of relationship as "serious," sleeping over when the child is present, cohabitation, breakup of the relationship, nonmarital pregnancy, engagement, and remarriage. These transitions can be stressful in part because there are few social norms on how best to handle them. When a parent begins dating, children who have been holding out hope for their parents' reconciliation may experience a renewed sense of loss, although for some this may not come until one parent remarries. The introduction of a new dating partner can cause even greater stress for children who spent a significant amount of time in a single-parent household or who developed a close relationship as the parent's confidant, as the introduction of a new partner/stepparent means a loss of time and attention from the biological parent. In families with multiple children, older siblings may take on some of the care-taking responsibilities over their younger siblings, which is also likely to be renegotiated when a new adult joins the household.

Opportunities for conflict also increase in the parent–child relationship when stepfamilies form, especially when children are adolescents—a period often marked by more intensive parent–child conflict (Hetherington & Kelly 2002). Although parents tend to side with their children, children may experience a coalition or agreement between parent and stepparent as lack of parental support or a threat to the parent–child bond. Additionally, parent–child relationships are especially difficult when stepchildren resist accepting the stepparent into the family. Overall, findings show that a mother's parenting stress increases when she moves in with a stepfather more so than when a previously single mother moves in with a child's biological father (Cooper, McLanahan, Meadows, & Brooks-Gunn, 2009), suggesting that increase in stress is related to the more complex nature of the parent–child–stepparent triadic relationship wherein stepparents are the outsider to an already established parent–child relationship.

Stress in the Stepparent–Stepchild Subsystem

The stepparent–stepchild relationship is perhaps the most fragile of subsystems in the new family, partly because it has the shortest shared history and experience. Thus, it is not surprising that this relationship is considered the greatest source of stress in stepfamilies. Two primary sources of stress in this subsystem are disagreements regarding the stepparent's role and stepchildren's loyalty to their other biological parent.

Research in this area is limited in that most of what is known about stepparent–stepchild relationships comes from research of resident stepfathers and stepchildren. Findings show that, on average, stepchildren rate their relationships with stepfathers more poorly than those with biological fathers (e.g., Hofferth et al., 2007). Developing a relationship with a stepchild often does not come easy for stepparents, and it is even more difficult when the stepparent lacks a clear understanding of what his or her role should be. Often, stepparents and parents expect the stepparent to play a more active parenting role unlike stepchildren, who are seeking more of a "friendship-like" relationship with stepparents (Ganong & Coleman, 2004). Overwhelmingly, research suggests that stress is greater in stepfamilies when stepparents attempt to adopt a disciplinary role with step-children too quickly, and these relationships are more positive when stepparents engage in more one-on-one affinity-seeking strategies early on, such as engaging in fun activities, communicating, and completing other tasks (e.g., chores or homework). Mothers often play an important role in the development of stepfather–stepchild relationships. Some mothers help to encourage and facilitate the development of closer relationships, whereas others discourage stepfathers from adopting an active stepparenting role. In general, and at least early on, opportunities for stress and conflict in the stepparent–stepchild relation-ship tend to be greater and opportunities for bonding fewer when spending time in the context of the whole family.

Stepchildren also play an important role in the development of relationships with stepparents, engaging in various behaviors that influence how stepparents attempt to relate to them. Stepchildren make intentional choices to express their love and affection for stepparents, to accept their influence, and have fun with them. For many children, the decision to accept a new stepparent is complicated by feelings of loyalty toward the biological parent of the same gender. They worry that becoming close to their stepfather will diminish their closeness with their father. In high conflict stepfamilies, the parent may reinforce or encourage these concerns to thwart the development of the stepparent–stepchild relationship. What is clear here is that the stress associated with stepfamily development increases significantly for children who are placed in the middle of adult conflict.

The stress experienced in the stepparent–stepchild relationship depends on a variety of factors discussed in a recent review (see van Eeden-Moorefield & Pasley, 2012). For exam-ple, younger children are more accepting of a stepparent than are older children. Also, because relationships take time to develop, stepparent–stepchild relationships of shorter duration are often less positive than those of longer duration, and they are more positive in resident compared to nonresident stepfamilies. Gender also makes a difference, such that stepfathers and stepsons adjust better than stepfathers and stepdaughters. Still other research shows that child temperament affects the nature of the stepparent–stepchild relationship; specifically, stepfathers express more warmth toward stepchildren who are more active and sociable rather than those less active and shy. Finally, compared to simple stepfamilies, in complex stepfamilies, stepparents may have greater difficulty determining how to engage as stepparents in ways that are different from their roles as parents to their children.

Stress in the Sibling Subsystem

Of the primary subsystems in stepfamilies, the sibling subsystem is perhaps the least understood. The composition of this subsystem can be exceedingly complex, with a vari-ety of combinations of full, half, and stepsibling relationships. More complex sibling con-stellations may increase opportunities for stress in stepfamilies, as alliances and loyalties can develop with biological relatedness as a dividing factor. Conflict among siblings in stepfamilies is a source of potential stress, but surprisingly little research attention has been paid to these relationship dynamics.

Some findings indicate that stepsiblings tend to have the lowest levels of negativity compared to half siblings and full siblings within and outside of stepfamilies (Anderson, 1999). However, stress may be present even when levels of overt conflict or negativity are low, because relationships among half siblings and stepsiblings are influenced by differential parenting along biological lines. Parents tend to feel closest to their own children, so differential parenting, which is more common in stepfamilies than nonstepfamilies (O'Connor, Dunn, Jenkins, & Rashbash, 2006), is associated with increased risk for poorer prosocial behavior and quality in social relations (Meunier, Wade, & Jenkins, 2012). However, sibling relationship quality is more strongly associated with internalizing and externalizing problem behaviors among nonstepsiblings (Baham, Weimer, Braver, & Fabricius, 2008). Half-sibling relationships tend to develop in a similar manner to those of full siblings, and although the birth of a half sibling into a stepfamily can lead to the feelings of displacement among school-aged stepchildren, this is not unlike children in two-biological-parent families.

Stress in the Binuclear Family Context

Stepfamilies are often formed in the context of a shared custody arrangement between former partners (and continuing relationships with extended family members especially paternal grandparents), which results in children having membership in at least two households. The level of stress associated with interactions across households varies greatly according to the quality of coparenting relationships. High levels of postdivorce/separation conflict between former partners likely spills over into the coparenting relationship, increasing stress in other subsystems and ultimately putting children at greater risk for poor outcomes.

Although 50/50 joint custody arrangements are becoming more common today, most children in stepfamilies spend more time in one parent's household than the other (Cancian, Meyer, Brown, & Cook, 2014). In stepfamilies where one parent maintains primary residential custody, it is not uncommon for this parent to try to control child-rearing practices when the child is in the other parent's care; this is often not well received by the nonresident parent (DeGreef & Burnett, 2009).

In the stepfamily context, "coparenting teams" become more complex, as the adults must not only negotiate the parenting roles of each biological parent but also the role that the stepparent will play in child-rearing. Mothers have been found to play complex roles in fostering family cohesion through simultaneously managing active coparenting relationships with their children's nonresident biological fathers and stepfathers (Favez, Widmer, Doan, & Tissot, 2015). Children suffer when parents are unable to develop a cooperative coparenting relationship following the end of their relationship (Dunn, O'Connor, & Cheng, 2005), as parents may send messages through the child, exposing them to undesirable information and negativity, so a child's relationship with a nonresident parent is another possible source of stress.

STEPFAMILY RESILIENCE

_____ **Vignette** _____

Vanessa and David moved in together 6 months ago, along with Vanessa's two teenage daughters, Elle (13) and Kate (15), from her previous marriage, and David's daughter, Julia (6), who lives with them every other week. The couple started dating a year earlier, soon after David's divorce was finalized and 5 years after Vanessa's divorce. Both David and Vanessa experienced difficult divorces and were aware of the impact it had on their children. From the beginning, they spent a lot of time discussing concerns about how their relationship would affect their daughters and even sought support from friends and Vanessa's pastor. When they decided to remarry, their expectations were realistic. They knew that they would have to create new family rituals and traditions with a lot of input from their children. The couple also decided early on that they would not play a disciplinary role with each other's children but would support each other in the efforts to discipline their own children. Vanessa's daughters enjoy having a younger sister in the house, and everyone looks forward to family movie night when Julia is present.

• • •

As is evident in this vignette, many stepfamilies adjust well to their new life and demonstrate resilience to confronting what are common sources of stress. Here we address the characteristics of these resilient stepfamilies:

1. **Realistic and positive expectations.** Like Vanessa and David, stepfamilies who identify as "successful" report having realistic expectations about their remarriages. For example, some individuals expect immediate feelings of love and affection among family members; however, stepfamily relationships become closer overtime when allowed to develop more slowly and naturally (van Eeden-Moorefield & Pasley, 2012). Also, beliefs that finances should be pooled and that adjustment should not come quickly are associated with reports of more family cohesion (Higginbotham & Agee, 2013) and higher marital quality and positive couple interaction (Garneau, Higginbotham, & Adler-Baeder, 2015).

2. **Clear roles and boundaries.** Stepfamilies adjust better when roles and boundaries are clear (Brown & Robinson, 2012). David and Vanessa established guidelines for their roles as parents and stepparents, allowing each to carry out their expected duties without fear of being undermined by the other. Everyone in the family understands and agrees upon their relationships, as well as the expected rules and roles that accompany these relationships.

3. **Open, clear communication and empathy.** Schrodt (2006) identified five different types of stepfamilies based on their ability to communicate effectively. Overall, those

in stepfamilies with more involvement, flexibility, and expressiveness, and less dissension and avoidance were closer, reported greater family cohesion and had more positive stepparent–stepchild relationships. When the decision to cohabit or remarry is discussed openly with children, and they are given the opportunity to express their concerns or feelings, an easier transition with greater acceptance results (Cartwright, 2012). Successful stepfamilies use affirming communication strategies and communicate respect and acceptance (e.g., Brown & Robinson, 2012). Also, stepfamilies tend to fare better when stepchildren are able to express themselves and communicate openly with both resident parents and stepparents, which results in stepchildren feeling like they are in a "real family" (Baxter, Braithwaite, & Bryant, 2006). They also feel closer to their stepfathers when they can talk about them with their mothers and when the mother and stepfather agree more on parenting and argue less (Jensen & Shafer, 2013).

4. **Flexibility.** Resilient stepfamilies are able to adapt and adjust to the numerous changes that accompany stepfamily formation (Brown & Robinson, 2012). They can renegotiate family boundaries to accept new members and develop relationships. Successful stepfamilies create an environment that allows members to adjust to their new roles and are open to revising old routines and rituals and establishing new ones. David and Vanessa and their daughters were open-minded when it came to merging their two family cultures, and each family member contributed to the development of new family rituals and traditions.

5. **Bonding and relationship building.** Well-adjusted stepfamilies emphasize the importance of spending time together as a family (Brown & Robinson, 2012) and use family activities and routines to promote bonding. Spending quality time together increases feeling like a family. Importantly, recommendations for successful relationship building in stepfamilies are to start slowly and spend more time getting to know one another in dyads rather than as a whole family initially (Metts et al., 2013). When stepparents and stepchildren reside together, they are more likely to develop trust in their relationship, which increases the likelihood of stepchildren considering stepfathers as "family." Vanessa and David's new family established a family movie night ritual, which helped build a sense of togetherness on the weekends when Julia was present.

6. **Strong social support systems.** Social support from multiple sources is a key to adjustment in stepfamilies, and this can come from former spouses, friends, relatives, and the broader community. For example, when stepparents and nonresident parents have more supportive relationships, stepparents are more satisfied with their partners (Schrodt, 2010). Social support in the community context may be especially important for the well-being of the stepfamily adults (van Eeden-Moorefield & Pasley, 2012).

7. **Positive coparenting relationships.** Positive relationships with nonresident parents and more cooperative coparenting across households are important sources of resilience in stepfamilies. Nonresident fathers who are remarried tend to be more involved with their children, and involved fathers provide another source of support (Aquilino, 2006). Closeness to a nonresident parent may be particularly important for older stepchildren, when stress increases in the stepfamily. Even when children have positive relationships with stepfathers, the relationship quality with nonresident fathers remains important for their well-being (Pryor, 2008).

WORKING PROFESSIONALLY WITH STEPFAMILIES

In recent years, more focus has been directed toward prevention and intervention strategies that reduce stress and increase stepfamily resilience. This focus has taken primarily two forms: the design, implementation, and evaluation of psychoeducation/relationship education programs and clinical interventions directed to the specific needs of stepfamilies.

Psychoeducation/Relationship Education

Clinical scholarship on the effectiveness of education-based interventions for stepfamilies began in the late 1970s, but attempts to develop empirically based programs are more recent (see Whitton, Nicholson, & Markman, 2008). Since 2000, efforts have increased to adapt psychoeducational interventions and develop new ones specifically targeting the needs of individuals and couples in complex family structures, such as stepfamilies. Although a variety of in-person and online programs are available to stepfamilies, many are sold commercially, are self-lead, and have not been empirically evaluated.

Focusing on the strengths of stepfamilies as a unique family structure instead of "broken" families, Adler-Baeder, Robertson, and Schramm (2010) outlined a conceptual model to aid in the evaluation of existing programs and the development of new relationship education programs for stepfamilies. Key to this model is a combination of psychoeducation and skills-based activities that address aspects of family functioning unique to stepfamilies and the core relationship skills essential to any healthy couple relationship. Several educational programs for stepfamilies have been evaluated using rigorous methodology (e.g., inclusion of control or comparison groups) and are shown to improve various aspects of stepfamily well-being (e.g., effective parenting/stepparenting, family cohesion, and marital quality) (e.g., DeGarmo & Forgatch, 2007; Lucier-Greer, Adler-Baeder, Harcourt, & Gregson, 2014). Importantly, general relationship education programs targeting basic but not stepfamily-specific interpersonal skills also are effective in improving individual-, couple-, and family-level well-being in stepfamilies (see Lucier-Greer, Adler-Baeder, Ketring, Harcourt, & Smith, 2012). However, qualitative findings indicate that participants in a stepfamily-specific program following Adler-Baeder and colleagues' (2010) proposed model report specific benefits from normalizing common stepfamily challenges and learning effective solutions to manage unique challenges in stepfamilies (Skogrand, Torres, & Higginbotham, 2010).

Clinical Intervention

For some stepfamilies, psychoeducational interventions may be enough to improve family functioning, whereas others may require a more focused intervention by a trained mental health professional. Much of the early published work on the complex relationship dynamics of stepfamilies came from scholars who drew heavily upon their own experiences working with stepfamilies in clinical settings (e.g., Visher & Visher, 1979). Over time, many of the assertions and recommendations made by these scholars were supported by research findings. As a result, strategies for addressing the unique challenges facing stepfamilies who seek help through counseling and family therapy were refined into a 10-step clinical approach to stepfamily therapy (Browning & Artelt, 2012).

As with psychoeducational interventions, clinical strategies for working with stepfamilies stem from the idea that issues are primarily rooted in their complex structure, and that stepfamilies' needs and relationship dynamics are different from those in nonstepfamilies. However, many of the strategies that developed were based on the functioning in biological-two-parent families and needed to be adjusted or avoided when working with stepfamilies. Browning and Artelt's (2012) model identifies steps for stepfamily therapy organized into three phases. First, *diagnostic steps* guide clinicians to more effectively identify the structure, subsystems, and concerns of the family within the unique context of their stepfamily dynamics. Next, *primary clinical interventions* are used to help normalize the stepfamily's experiences, increase empathy, and use a subsystems approach to help the family begin to understand issues of miscommunication and adjust their systemic functioning. Finally, during the *stepfamily integration* phase, practitioners help strengthen the coparenting relationships in the stepfamily, improve communication, and better integrate the various subsystems into the stepfamily. This proposed model is helpful in addressing the needs of stepfamilies in clinical settings as it combines the use of psychoeducation about normal, healthy stepfamily functioning with a systems approach to family therapy.

CONCLUSION

The information we presented here suggests that although stepfamilies are likely to experience greater stress than traditional, two-biological-parent families, there is also evidence that many of these families overcome or successfully cope with stress and adapt well to their more complicated family lives. Using a family systems approach, we have discussed some of the unique stresses that are part of living in a stepfamily while emphasizing the diversity across them. There is much variation in the nature of family life and the various relationships among family members. Much of the variations stems from the complexity of the family configurations and the linkages with those outside the immediate household, including nonresident parents and their spouses/partners and the broader social context in which they are embedded. Inherent in any discussion of stress is the opportunity for stepfamilies to demonstrate resilience, and we ended with a presentation of the characteristics of stepfamilies which lend themselves to success.

REFERENCES

Adler-Baeder, F., Robertson, A., & Schramm, D. G. (2010). Conceptual framework for marriage education programs for stepfamily couples with consideration for socioeconomic context. *Marriage & Family Review, 46*, 300–322.

Amato, P. R. (2000). The consequences of divorce for adults and children. *Journal of Marriage and Family, 62*, 1269–1287.

Anderson, E. R. (1999). Sibling, half sibling, and stepsibling relationships in remarried families. *Monographs of the Society for Research in Child Development, 64*, 101–126.

Anderson, E. R., & Green, S. M. (2005). Transitions in parental repartnering after divorce. *Journal of Divorce & Remarriage, 4*(3/4), 47–62.

Anderson, E. R., Greene, S. M., Walker, L., Malerba, C. A., Forgatch, M. S., & Degarmo, D. S. (2004). Ready to take a chance again: Transitions into dating among divorced parents. *Journal of Divorce & Remarriage, 40*(3–4), 61–75.

Aquilino, W. S. (2006). The noncustodial father–child relationship from adolescence into young adulthood. *Journal of Marriage and Family, 68*, 929–946.

Baham, M. E., Weimer, A. A., Braver, S. L., & Fabricius, W. V. (2008). Sibling relationships in blended families. In J. Pryor (Ed.), *The international handbook of stepfamilies: Policy and practice in legal, research, and clinical environments* (pp. 175-207). Hoboken, NJ: John Wiley & Sons.

Baxter, L. A., Braithwaite, D. O., & Bryant, L. E. (2006). Types of communication triads perceived by young-adult stepchildren in established stepfamilies. *Communication Studies, 57*, 381–400.

Brown, S. L., & Manning, W. D. (2009). Family boundary ambiguity and the measurement of family structure: The significance of cohabitation. *Demography, 46*, 85–101.

Brown, O., & Robinson, J. (2012). Resilience in remarried families. *South African Journal of Psychology, 42*, 114–126.

Browning, S., & Artelt, E. (2012). *Stepfamily therapy: A 10-step clinical approach*. Washington, DC: American Psychological Association.

Burgoyne, C. B., & Morrison, V. (1997). Money in remarriage: Keeping things simple—and separate. *The Sociological Review. 45*, 364–395.

Cancian, M., Meyer, D. R., Brown, P. R., & Cook, S. T. (2014). Who gets custody now? Dramatic changes in children's living arrangements after divorce. *Demography, 51*, 1381–1396.

Carlson, M. J., & Furstenberg, F. F. (2006). The prevalence and correlates of multipartnered fertility among urban US parents. *Journal of Marriage and Family, 68*, 718–732.

Cartwright, C. (2010). Preparing to repartner and live in a stepfamily: An exploratory investigation. *Journal of Family Studies, 16*, 237 –250.

Cartwright, C. (2012). The challenges of being a mother in a stepfamily. *Journal of Divorce & Remarriage, 53*, 503–513.

Cherlin, A. J. (2010). Demographic trends in the United States: A review of research in the 2000s. *Journal of Marriage and Family, 72*, 403–419.

Coleman, M., & Ganong, L. H. (1990). Remarriage and stepfamily research in the 1980s: Increased interest in an old family form. *Journal of Marriage and the Family, 52*, 925–941.

Coleman, M., Ganong, L., & Fine, M. (2000). Reinvestigating remarriage: Another decade of progress. *Journal of Marriage and Family, 62*, 1288–1307.

Cooper, C. E., McLanahan, S. S., Meadows, S. O., & Brooks-Gunn, J. (2009). Family structure transitions and parenting stress. *Journal of Marriage and Family, 71,* 558–574.

Cox, M. J., & Paley, B. (1997). Families as systems. *Annual Review of Psychology, 48,* 243–267.

DeGarmo, D. S., & Forgatch, M. S. (2007). Efficacy of parent training for stepfathers: From playful spectator and polite stranger to effective stepfathering. *Parenting: Science and Practice, 7*, 331–355.

DeGreef, B. L., & Brunett, A. (2009). Weekend warriors: Autonomy-connection, openness-closedness, and coping strategies of marital partners in nonresidential stepfamilies. *The Qualitative Report, 14*, 604–628.

Doodson, L., & Morley, D. (2006). Understanding the roles of non-residential stepmothers. *Journal of Divorce & Remarriage, 45*(3/4), 109–126.

Dunn, J., O'Connor, T. G., & Cheng, H. (2005). Children's responses to conflict between their different parents: Mothers, stepfathers, nonresident fathers, and nonresident stepmothers. *Journal of Clinical Child and Adolescent Psychology, 34*, 223–234.

Favez, N., Widmer, E. D., Doan, M., & Herve, T. (2015). Coparenting in stepfamilies: Maternal promotion of family cohesiveness with partner and with father. *Journal of Child and Family Studies.* Early view. doi:10.1007/s10826-015-0130-x

Felker, J. A., Fromme, D. K., Arnaut, G. L., & Stoll, B. M. (2002). A qualitative analysis of stepfamilies. *Journal of Divorce & Remarriage, 38,* 125–142.

Ganong, L. H., & Coleman, M. (1997). How society views stepfamilies. *Marriage & Family Review, 26,* 85–106.

Ganong, L. H., & Coleman, M. (2004). *Stepfamily relationships: Development, dynamics, and interventions.* New York, NY: Kluwer.

Gold, J. M. (2009). Negotiating the financial concerns of stepfamilies: Directions for family counselors. *The Family Journal, 17*(2), 185–188.

Garneau, C. L., Higginbotham, B., & Adler-Baeder, F. (2015). Remarriage beliefs as predictors of marital quality and positive interaction in stepcouples: An actor-partner interdependence model. *Family Process.* Advanced online publication. doi:10.1111/famp.12153

Gosseline, J., & David, H. (2007). Risk and resilience factors linked with the psychosocial adjustment of adolescents, stepparents and biological parents. *Journal of Divorce & Remarriage, 48,* 29–51.

Halford, K., Nicholson, J., & Sanders, M. (2007). Couple communication in stepfamilies. *Family Process, 46,* 471–783.

Henry, P. J., & McCue, J. (2009). The experience of nonresidential stepmothers. *Journal of Divorce & Remarriage, 50,* 185–205.

Hetherington, E. M., & Kelly, J. (2002). *For better or worse: Divorce reconsidered.* New York, NY: Norton.

Higginbotham, B., & Agee, L. (2013). Endorsement of remarriage beliefs, spousal consistency, and remarital adjustment. *Marriage & Family Review, 49,* 177–190.

Hofferth, S., Cabrera, N., Carlson. M., Coley, M., Day, R.L., & Schindler, H. (2007). Resident father involvement and social fathering. In S. Hofferth & L. Casper (Eds.), *Handbook of measurement issues in family research* (pp. 335–374). Mahwah, NJ: Lawrence Erlbaum Associates.

Jensen, T. M., & Shafter, K. (2013). Stepfamily functioning and closeness: Children's views on second marriages and stepfather relationships. *Social Work, 58,* 127–136.

Kreider, R. M. (2005). *Numbering, timing, and duration of marriages and divorces: 2001* (Current Population Reports, P70-97). Washington, DC: U.S. Census Bureau.

Kreider, R. M., & Ellis, R. (2011). *Number, timing, and duration of marriage and divorce: 2009* (Current Population Reports, P70–125). Washington, DC: Government Printing Office.

Kreider, R., & Lofquist, D. A. (2014). *Adopted children and stepchildren: 2010* (Current Population Reports, P220–572). Washington, DC: U.S. Government Printing Office.

Lucier-Greer, M., Adler-Baeder, F., Harcourt, K. T., & Gregson, K. D. (2014). Relationship education for stepcouples reporting relationship instability—Evaluation of the Smart Steps: Embrace the Journey curriculum. *Journal of Marital & Family Therapy, 40,* 454–469.

Lucier-Greer, M., Adler-Baeder, F., Ketring, S. A., Harcourt, K. T., & Smith, T. (2012). Comparing the experiences of couples in first marriages and remarriages in couple and relationship education. *Journal of Divorce & Remarriage, 53,* 55–75.

Martin-Uzzi, M., & Duval-Tsioles, D. (2013). The experiences of remarried couples in blended families. *Journal of Divorce & Remarriage, 54,* 43–57.

Metts, S., Braitwaith, D. O., Schrodt, P., Wang, T. R., Holman, A. J., Nuru, A. K., & Abetz, J. S. (2013). The experience and expression of stepchildren's emotions at critical events in stepfamily life. *Journal of Divorce & Remarriage, 54,* 414–437.

Meunier, J. C., Wade, M., & Jenkins, J. M. (2012). Mothers' differential parenting and children's behavioral outcomes: Exploring the moderating role of family and social context. *Infant and Child Development, 21,* 107–133.

O'Connor, T. G., Dunn, J., Jenkins, J. M., Rashbash, J. (2006). Predictors of between-family and within-family variation in parent-child relationships. *Journal of Child Psychology and Psychiatry, 47,* 498–510.

Pryor, J. (2008). Children in stepfamilies: Relationships with nonresident parents. In J. Prior (Ed.), *The international handbook of stepfamilies: Policies and practices in legal, research and clinical environments* (pp. 345–368). Hoboken, NJ: John Wiley & Sons.

Raijas, A. (2011). Money management in blended and nuclear families. *Journal of Economic Psychology, 32,* 556–563.

Sassler, S. (2010). Partnering across the life course: Sex, relationships and mate selection. *Journal of Marriage and Family, 72,* 557–575.

Schmeeckle, M., Giarrusso, R., Feng, D., Bengtson, V. L. (2006). What makes someone family? Adult children's perceptions of current and former stepparents. *Journal of Marriage and Family, 68,* 595–610.

Schrodt, P. (2006). A typological examination of communication competence and mental health in stepchildren. *Communication Monographs, 73,* 309–333.

Schrodt, P. (2010). Coparental communication with nonresidential parents as a predictor of couples' relational satisfaction and mental health in stepfamilies. *Western Journal of Communication, 74,* 484–503.

Shafer, K., Jensen, T. M., Pace, G. T., & Larson, J. H. (2013). Former spouse ties and postdivorce relationship quality: Relationship effect as a mediator. *Journal of Social Service Research, 39,* 629–645.

Skogrand, L., Torres, E., & Hibbingbotham, B. J. (2010). Stepfamily education: Benefits of a group-formatted intervention. *The Family Journal, 18,* 234–240.

Slattery, M. E., Bruce, V., Halford, W. K., & Nicholson, J. M. (2011). Predicting married and cohabitation couples' futures from their descriptions of stepfamily life. *Journal of Family Psychology, 25,* 560–569.

Stanley, S. M., Markman, H. J., & Whitton, S. W. (2002). Communication, conflict, and commitment: Insights on the foundations of relationship success from a national survey. *Family Process, 41,* 659–675.

Stewart, S. D. (2005). Boundary ambiguity in stepfamilies. *Journal of Family Issues, 26,* 1002–1029.

Suanet, B., VanDer Pas, S., & van Tilburg, T. G. (2013). Who is in the stepfamily? Changes in stepparents' family boundaries between 1992–2009. *Journal of Marriage and Family, 75,* 1070–1083.

Teachman, J. (2008). Complex life course patterns and the risk of divorce in second marriages. *Journal of Marriage and Family, 70,* 294–305.

van Eeden-Moorefield, B., & Pasley, K. (2012). Remarriage and stepfamilies. In G. Peterson & K. Bush (Eds.), *Handbook of marriage and the family* (3rd ed., pp. 517–547). New York, NY: Springer.

van Eeden-Moorefield, B., Pasley, K., Dolan, E. M., & Engel, M. (2007). From divorce to remarriage. *Journal of Divorce & Remarriage, 47*(3/4), 21–42.

Visher, E. B., & Visher, J. S. (1979). *A guide to working with stepparents and stepchildren.* New York, NY: Bruner/Mazel

Weaver, S. E., & Coleman, M. (2010). Caught in the middle: Mothers in stepfamilies. *Journal of Social and Personal Relationships, 27,* 305–326.

Whitton, S. W., Nicholson, J. M., & Markman, H. J. (2008). Research on interventions for stepfamily couples: The state of the field. In J. Pryor (Ed.), *The international handbook of stepfamilies: Policy and practice in legal, research, and clinical environments* (pp. 455–484). New York, NY: John Wiley & Sons.

CHAPTER 9

Adaptation Among Immigrant Families:
Resources and Barriers

Kevin Ray Bush, Bertranna A. Abrams-Muruthi,
Stephanie A. Bohon, and Hyoun K. Kim

IMMIGRANT FAMILIES IN THE UNITED STATES

According to estimates based on 2010 data from the U.S. Census Bureau, almost 40 million immigrants are living in the United States, accounting for approximately 12.5% of the total population (Grieco et al., 2012). The majority of foreign-born individuals living in the United States were born in Latin America and the Caribbean (53.1%), Asia (28.2%), and Europe (12.1%); the remaining are from African countries, Canada, Australia, and elsewhere (Grieco et al., 2012). These estimates do not include the estimated 12 million immigrants who are assumed to be living in the United States without proper documentation (Passel, 2006).

Immigrants to the United States include foreign-born individuals who plan to settle permanently as well as those who plan long-term but temporary stays, including students in U.S. universities. Immigrants can be categorized as economic migrants (i.e., those who come to the United States seeking better jobs and pay), family migrants (i.e., those who come to join family members already living here), or involuntary migrants (i.e., refugees who are fleeing political violence or extreme environmental devastation in their home countries). The term *first-generation immigrant* is typically used to refer to a foreign-born individual who has immigrated to the United States. The children of first-generation immigrants who are born in the United States (and, therefore, are U.S. citizens) are thus referred to as *second-generation immigrants,* and their children (the grandchildren of first-generation immigrants) as *third-generation immigrants.* In this chapter, we discuss families living in the United States in which at least some members are foreign-born.

For most immigrants, the decision to move to the United States is heavily influenced by family events and processes (Landale, 1997; Landale, Oropesa, & Noah, 2014; Rumbaut, 1997; Suarez-Orozco, Suarez-Orozco, & Todorova, 2008). This is true even when individuals—rather than families—immigrate. In places such as Mexico, families often select one or two members to immigrate, in order to maximize their household resources (Massey, Durand, & Malone 2002).

U.S. officials decide whether or not to approve visa applications on a case-by-case basis, but most migration decisions are made within the contexts of families or at least take family considerations into account. Therefore, the phenomenon of migration, whether of individuals or of families, needs to be understood at the family level (Landale, 1997; Landale et al., 2014). Unfortunately, most of the research on immigrants to date has tended to focus on individuals. As a result, traditional examinations of this process provide only a partial analysis.

Because of the wide diversity among immigrant families in general, it is impossible to describe one profile or set of experiences that is common to every immigrant family (L. D. McCubbin & McCubbin, 2013; Rumbaut, 1997). At the macro level, immigration policies and the broader social, historical, political, and economic contexts of the United States and immigrants' home countries influence the migration process and experience (Landale et al., 2014; Rumbaut, 1997). For example, over the years, U.S. immigration policies have changed, affecting the eligibility and capability of individuals and families who wish to immigrate. The 1965 amendments to the Immigration and Nationality Act of 1952 created a "family reunification" category of immigrants whereby applicants for visas who had family members already living in the United States were given preferential application status. The 1986 Refugee Act made it easier for families facing dire circumstances because of political violence or extreme environmental conditions in their home countries to immigrate as refugees.

Beginning in 1990, however, policies shifted that made family migration more difficult. The Immigration Act of 1990 shifted the balance of visa applicants away from family reunification in favor of work-related criteria (Sorenson, Bean, Ku, & Zimmerman, 1992). More specifically, the 1990 act gave preference to individuals who have education and credentials in particular fields (e.g., the biological and physical sciences) and those willing to invest large sums of money in the U.S. economy. Two additional laws passed in 1996, the Illegal Immigration Reform and Immigrant Responsibility Act and the Personal Responsibility and Work Opportunity Reconciliation Act, also limited legal family reunification migration and led to an increase in unauthorized immigration (Massey et al., 2002).

Immigrant families in the United States tend to be more diverse than ever before in terms of country of origin, language, socioeconomic status, and other social and demographic characteristics. Because of this diversity, we cannot discuss each distinct immigrant group here, but rather we focus on the general barriers, stressors, resources, and patterns of adaptation common among most immigrant families, with emphasis on the largest (Latinos), fastest growing (Asians), and largest Black (Afro-Caribbean) immigrant groups in the United States. Given this focus, we want to be careful to underscore the fact that great variation exists within each of these broad categories (e.g., Asians) as well as within specific cultural/ethnic groups of immigrants within each of these categories (e.g., Chinese, Japanese, Koreans, Laotian, East Indian, and Filipino). The vignette presented below will be referenced throughout the chapter to help illustrate examples of key points and concepts.

_____ Vignette _____

Maria migrated from Juarez, Mexico, to Atlanta with her three children to join her husband, Jaime, who has been living in the United States for 5 years. Although Jaime has a work permit ("green card"), Maria and the children are undocumented. They live in a poor neighborhood and share a small trailer with Jaime's brother, Jose; his wife; and their two young children. Because they cannot afford a car, Jose and Jaime share a ride to work with other men who work for the same construction company. Jose's wife works as a maid in a hotel. Each morning she catches a bus at 6:00 a.m., leaving her two toddlers in Maria's care until she returns in the evening. Maria spends her days caring for her own toddler and her niece and nephew while her two older children go to school. Sometimes Jaime goes with his coworkers to the store after work. Maria is embarrassed that her husband has to shop "like a wife." Maria and Jaime are saving money to buy a home, but it is hard to save much on Jaime's income. Maria wants to get a job, but there are not many jobs available for women without green cards that she could reach by bus. Additionally it would be difficult to work with her toddler and the fact that her sister-in-law relies on her to provide child care. She knows that her children will have a better life in the United States than they would have had in Mexico, but she worries that she is a burden to her husband and that he might leave her because she has little to contribute to the household.

• • •

ACCULTURATION AND ADAPTATION

The United States is a nation of immigrants, and the patterns of immigration as well as the reasons people immigrate vary substantially. A common characteristic among the majority of immigrant families, however, is stress associated with immigration. Many of the values, beliefs, and strategies that immigrant families and individuals have followed in order to function successfully in their home cultures differ from U.S. norms. An immigrant family's system will experience stress to the extent that members find that strategies (e.g., rules and roles relating to established patterns of interaction) they have used in the past to accomplish family tasks (e.g., providing for family, establishing and maintaining rules, facilitating identity development and socialization) are not as effective in the social, economic, and political contexts of the United States. Therefore, in addition to the normative (e.g., family transitions) and nonnormative (e.g., natural disasters) stressors that families encounter, immigrant families experience unique stress and change related to migration and acculturation.

Acculturation—that is, the process of adjusting to a new culture or society—involves potential changes in identity, values, behaviors, attitudes, interactions, and relationships (Berry, 2001). All family systems have their own unique rules that define appropriate behaviors and interactions that are influenced by cultural and ethnic values as well as socioeconomic status and other sociodemographic factors (Boss, 2002; H. I. McCubbin, Thompson, Thompson, & Fromer, 1998; Walsh, 2013). As family members encounter stress or pressure to change, the family system also experiences pressure to change. Family systems theory highlights the importance of interactions among individuals and family subsystems (e.g., parental, marital, and child) and the resultant meanings and structures that emerge out of these interactions (Anderson, Sabatelli & Kosutic, 2013). Thus, changes within a family are viewed as being processed by the entire family system, rather than by a single member. Moreover, stress is viewed as an agent of change rather than as inherently negative.

As a family system changes, individual family members change their ways of interacting in accordance with the new rules for interaction. For example, it is fairly common for Mexican immigrants to the United States to experience "family stage migration" (Hondagneu-Sotelo, 1994; Soto, 2009) in which one or two family members immigrate at a time. For example, in the vignette, Jaime immigrated first, leaving Maria and children behind, thus creating the need for changes in family strategies. As a man on his own, Jaime had accomplished many tasks—such as laundry, cooking, and other chores—typically performed by his wife. In turn, Maria, who was the de facto head of the family's household while in Mexico, had to perform many of the roles she previously shared with her husband (e.g., socialization and discipline of children) alone, as well as family tasks that had been her husband's sole responsibility (e.g., managing the family's finances). When Maria and the children eventually arrived in the United States, Jaime's and Maria's roles had to be renegotiated, resulting in something entirely new.

The effects of acculturation are complicated by other factors as well, including family members being at different stages in the acculturation process. Some members (particularly children) may assimilate rapidly, adopting values and beliefs of the mainstream U.S. culture (Berry, 2001). Some members may experience separation; that is, they may retain the values and beliefs of their cultures of origin and reject those of the mainstream U.S. culture. The most common form of adaptation among immigrants is integration, or the blending of aspects of both the home culture and the new culture (Berry, 2001), as most immigrants find it impractical to ignore the practices of their host country and find it comforting to retain some of the traditions of their homelands.

COMMON BARRIERS AND STRESSORS EXPERIENCED BY IMMIGRANT FAMILIES

Scholars have identified a wide variety of stressors that immigrant families may experience. The salience and impact of particular stressors, however, vary depending on these families' ethnicities, cultures, reasons for immigrating, and other social and contextual factors. Stressors exist at the community or society level (e.g., immigration policies and discrimination), the family level (e.g., change and conflict within intergenerational and marital relationships), and the individual level (e.g., depression, isolation, identity development). Immigrant families face various barriers (i.e., hindering structural factors and individual characteristics) in the adaptation process, including (a) lack of English-language fluency, (b) diminished social support networks, (c) intergenerational conflict, (d) lowered socioeconomic status, (e) poor housing conditions, (f) lack of familiarity with U.S. norms, (g) family separation/reunification, (h) fear of deportation, and (i) discrimination. Such barriers can be sources of stress for families and their individual members, creating change within family systems.

Language Barriers

Lack of fluency in English can lead to difficulties in establishing social support networks in the United States and accessing resources as well as discrimination. According to the Pew Hispanic Center, 68.2% of first-generation Hispanic immigrants and 39.1% of the Asian population speak little to no English (P. Taylor, Lopez, Martinez, & Velasco, 2012). The ability to speak English is closely related to daily functioning in U.S. society; it is likely to determine employment opportunities as well as an individual's level of social participation in the mainstream culture (Bhattacharya & Schoppelrey, 2004). Immigrant parents with school-age children often have trouble navigating the educational system and thus find it difficult to advocate for their children (Plata-Potter & de Guzman, 2012), which can lead to low levels of parental involvement in their child's education and subsequently negatively impact children's educational outcomes. For example, Maria has never seen the buildings where her children attend the sixth and tenth grades, and she worries because she hears that there are gangs at the high school, but language (as well as transportation and child-care) barriers make it difficult for her to get involved.

The inability to understand the prevalent language is a frustrating experience for many immigrants and can lead to increased pressure to learn English. However, adult family members are often unable to attend classes to learn English due to the lack of child care and transportation and time intensive employment/inflexible work hours or related barriers (Atiles & Bohon, 2002; Bhattacharya & Schoppelrey, 2004). All of these factors serve as barriers for Maria. For example, she would like to learn English, but there are few opportunities, as there are no English-speaking people in her neighborhood. Although she has heard that some churches offer free English classes, it is too expensive for her to take three children along on the bus. Communication barriers have also been cited as a hindrance to obtaining full citizenship for permanent residents in the United States who cannot speak English (Gonzalez-Barrera, Lopez, Passel, & Taylor, 2013).

Diminished Social Support Networks

When families move to the United States they leave behind most of their extended family members and friends; therefore they are faced with the task of navigating a new culture without familiar social supports. This lack of social support is detrimental to family functioning. Immigrant families need to establish new support networks in the United States; they may also need to redefine family relationships, such as changes in roles, boundaries, and patterns of interaction (Falicov, 2003).

In the absence of extended family members, immigrant families are likely to solicit support from different surrogate kin networks (Baptiste, 1987). Surrogate kin networks can consist of those individuals or groups from churches/spiritual communities, social service agencies, ethnic communities, or other social affiliations that support immigrants (Jamieson, 2008). These social networks facilitate acculturation by enhancing the immigration and adaptation of newcomers to host cultures by perpetuating communal support systems (Chioneso, 2008).

Immigrant women from cultures that adhere to traditional gender roles (e.g., where women's roles are restricted primarily to the socialization and nurturance of children and to family relationships) may find themselves at a distinct disadvantage in the United States (Chung, Tucker, & Takeuchi, 2008). In traditional Asian cultures, for example, extrafamilial relationships are not considered necessary for women, as women have multiple supports available to them within the extended family structure (Serafica, Weng, & Kim, 2000). Furthermore, in cases where women do have extrafamilial relationships, these relationships are mediated through family/kin system interactions rather than through the women's individual efforts. When women from such Asian cultures immigrate to the United States, they are not prepared for establishing and maintaining interpersonal relationships outside their families (Serafica et al., 2000).

Conflict in Intergenerational Relationships

Maintaining harmony in intergenerational relationships can be a major challenge for immigrant families. As family members adjust to their host country, their levels of acculturation may vary across age and gender. Staggered acculturation among family members, for example, can lead to acculturation stress, which in turn can lead to lower family functioning and changes within intergenerational relationships (Kwak, 2003; Roche, Lambert, Ghazarian, & Little, 2015). Scholars define acculturation stress as the stress experienced by immigrants during the process of adjusting and adapting to host cultures (Berry, 2001; Driscoll & Torres, 2013; Kwak, 2003). Children usually acculturate at a faster rate than their parents, which can lead to conflict as parents try to instill values and practices from their culture of origin, while children integrate more values and practices from the mainstream host culture (Suarez-Orozco et al., 2008). These cultural lessons from their parents may conflict with those they receive from their U.S.-born peers and teachers. For example, second- and third-generation immigrants are more likely to engage in behaviors and practices associated with individualistic cultures (e.g., premarital sex, cohabitation, later age at marriage) compared to first-generation immigrants (e.g., Driscoll & Torres, 2013; Kwak, 2003).

As immigrant children become more acculturated than their parents, the likelihood of intergenerational conflict and communication problems increases. Such conflict may result in children rejecting some or all of the values of the family's culture of origin (Kwak, 2003), leading to higher levels of stress for the family. Immigrant children often find themselves serving as translators for other less acculturated family members; many take on the role of family liaison or "cultural broker" between their families and the new society (Roche et al., 2015). In such situations, children are likely to feel the stress of adult responsibilities, whereas their parents may feel the stress of role reversal that comes from relying on children for their survival and well-being (Bhattacharya & Schoppelrey, 2004; Kwak, 2003; Roche et al., 2015).

Conflict and Change in Marital Relationships

Previous studies have found acculturation to be related to marital conflict (e.g., Flores, Tschann, Marin, & Pantoja, 2004) and marital satisfaction (Cruz et al., 2014). Immigrant families from a traditionally patriarchal society may find it difficult to carry out the family and spousal roles they learned in their cultures of origin. For example, immigrant wives are often forced to work outside the home in order to supplement family income. This change in economic status for women boosts their social status thus disturbing existing power dynamics in the couple dyad (Chun & Akutsu, 2003; Chung et al., 2008).

Cultural values impact couple and family interaction, roles, and how conflict is perceived and expressed. Higher levels of acculturation are associated with more direct communication and conflict negotiation, whereas lower levels of acculturation are associated with more use of conflict avoidance strategies and less acceptance of open expressions of conflict (Flores et al., 2004).

Similar levels of acculturation within couples are related to positive marital quality (Cruz et al., 2014), while different levels of acculturation between spouses are related to lower marital satisfaction and communication (Chia, Moore, Lam, Chuang, & Cheng, 1994; Cruz et al., 2014). For example, some researchers suggest that Asian immigrant men are more traditional and tend to assimilate into U.S. culture less readily than do Asian immigrant women, who tend to show more egalitarian attitudes (e.g., Chia et al., 1994); such differences can create significant tension and conflict between spouses.

Poor Housing Conditions

For the first few years they are in the United States, many immigrants live in housing that is, by most U.S. standards, inferior (Bhattacharya & Schoppelrey, 2004; Kearney et al., 2014). In addition to environmental hazards (e.g., mold, pesticides, rodents, cockroaches) that pose obvious health concerns (e.g., Kearney et al., 2014), a major family stressor related to immigrants' living conditions is overcrowding (Bhattacharya & Schoppelrey, 2004; Evans, 2006). In fact, immigrant children are approximately four times as likely to be living in crowded housing conditions compared to native-born children (Capps, 2001). It is not uncommon for many new immigrants to live in residences with more than one person per room.

Families in the United States also tend to spend more time inside their houses than do families in developing countries, which intensifies the feeling of overcrowding when occupancy levels are high. In addition, immigrant families often discover that it is not always safe to let children play outdoors because of limited common green space and dangerous motor vehicle traffic. This is illustrated in Maria's case. In Mexico, Maria had a small garden, and her children would play nearby while she tended it. She would walk with the children to the village to buy things the family needed. In Atlanta, however, she is afraid to walk to the store. There are no sidewalks, and she worries that the toddlers will run into the street.

When children (as well as adults) must spend most of their time crowded indoors, particularly in housing of inferior construction quality and cleanliness (e.g., mold, rodents, etc.), they can develop illnesses such as asthma (e.g., Kearney et al., 2014). Moreover, residential overcrowding has been linked with negative parenting behaviors (less responsiveness and lower levels of monitoring), increased chances of child maltreatment, and poorer child outcomes including psychological distress and lower social and cognitive competence (Evans, 2006).

Lack of Familiarity With U.S. Norms

Immigrant families often experience stress as they adjust to life in the United States because they do not fully understand American social norms, including those related to child care and child rearing. Violating these norms results in a variety of sanctions, ranging from ridicule to having their children removed from their homes (Johnson, Radesky & Zuckerman, 2013; Look & Look, 1997). For example, immigrant parents may not be aware of laws requiring that small children be restrained in special seats when riding in cars (Atiles & Bohon, 2002). Moreover, parents following traditional cultural practices of child rearing (e.g., cosleeping) or folk medicine (e.g., "cupping" or "coining") might be perceived as meeting criteria for neglect or abuse by child protection authorities in the United States (Johnson et al., 2013; Look & Look, 1997).

A related barrier to immigrant adjustment is lack of familiarity with the U.S. educational system (Bhattacharya & Schoppelrey, 2004; Plata-Potter & De Guzman, 2012). New immigrants from developing countries may not understand that children are required to attend school or that children enrolled in school must attend every weekday unless they are excused (Bohon, Macpherson, & Atiles, 2005). Moreover, immigrant parents may not understand the expectation of parental involvement in children's education.

Separation and Reunification

In the majority of immigrant families, members do not migrate at the same time, thus it is very common for children and parents, as well as spouses to endure long periods of separation. Reunification of the entire family can sometimes span many years (e.g., Rusch & Reyes, 2013) and many families run into unexpected delays including those related to finances, immigration laws/processes, housing issues, divorces, and remarriages (Suarez-Orozco et al., 2008).

During the separation, stress experienced by the loss of a family member leads to changes in the family system as family roles must be renegotiated. Often separation is experienced as ambiguous loss, thus adjustment can take more time and is difficult to accomplish (Boss, 2002). Since the parent, child, or other family member is not gone permanently, the family members' loss may go unacknowledged or unsupported (Boss, 2002). Moreover, family members who are not willing or able to renegotiate roles are thus less likely to accomplish necessary tasks, at least with the same level of competence as prior to the separation.

Family disruptions can also have implications for the well-being of immigrants. For example, research on Caribbean and Latino families in the United States indicates that immigrant youth who are separated from their families experience significant negative psychological repercussions (Suarez-Orozco, Todorova, & Louie 2002). Poor family attachment and reduced academic performance are typical products of such negative psychological problems. Members of the immigrant families are also more likely to feel increased impacts of stress and anxiety provoked by the process of immigration because of a limited family support network (Glasgow & Gouse-Shees, 1995). Reduced family support can therefore lead to increased risks of developing somatic complications and illnesses (Reynolds, 2005). In addition, disjointed family relationships reduce opportunities for intergenerational transfer of cultural beliefs and practices, a process that is vital in the preservation of many immigrant cultures (Chamberlain, 2003).

Reunification can also be stressful for family members. Successful reunification between children and parents depends on many factors including the coparenting between the caregiver in the country of origin and the immigrant parent(s). That is, the quality of the relationships among the caregiver in the country of origin, the child, and the immigrant parent contribute to the quality of parent child relationships and well-being upon reunification (e.g., Rusch & Reyes, 2013). The quality of communication (e.g., letters, e-mails, phone calls, remittances) between separated family members is also highly predictive of adjustment at reunification (Suarez-Orozco et al., 2008).

Fear of Deportation

Families often consist of mixed immigration statuses, such as being citizens (e.g., children who were born in the United States), legal immigrants with work permits, or undocumented immigrants. The legal or citizenship status of immigrants in the United States varies considerably. Although a majority of immigrants in the United States are legal through various types of immigration statuses (e.g., work permits, citizenship, etc.), it is estimated that approximately 12 million immigrants in the United States are undocumented (Passel, 2006). With immigrants from Mexico, for example, of the 12.5 million living in the United States in 2007, it is estimated that over half of them are undocumented (Passel & Cohn, 2010). Besides serving as a constant stressor, the fear of deportation can also hinder integration with the host culture, such as discouraging interaction with nonimmigrants as well as social institutions. For example, parents may not communicate with schools/teachers or seek medical or legal help (e.g., domestic violence, unfair/illegal treatment by employer or landlord) for fear of deportation. For Maria and Jaime, they would like to call the local authorities to complain about their landlord charging them more rent for each person in their trailer, since this is contrary to their agreement. However, since Maria and the rest of the family are undocumented, they cannot risk being deported.

Discrimination

Immigrant families often experience barriers to adjustment as the result of discrimination based on factors such as, race, ethnicity, immigrant status, and religion (e.g., FitzGerald & Cook-Martin, 2014). In more than two centuries of U.S. history, discrimination against immigrants has persisted unceasingly, with little changing except the group being defamed (FitzGerald & Cook-Martin, 2014). Over time, Irish, Chinese, Italian, Japanese, Eastern

European, and Latino immigrants have all been subjected to public resentment and official sanctions (Espenshade, 1995). One of the very first U.S. immigration laws—the Chinese Exclusion Act of 1882—barred Chinese immigrants from becoming U.S. citizens and effectively halted Chinese immigration for more than 60 years, breaking apart many Chinese families (Gyory, 1998). In the 1940s, approximately 110,000 Japanese-origin men, women, and children—the majority of whom were U.S. citizens—were forcibly evacuated from their homes and relocated to concentration camps. As a result, many lost their family farms/businesses and other important family resources (Hakim, 1995). After the attacks on the Pentagon and World Trade Center on September 11, 2001, hate crimes against persons of Middle Eastern descent increased precipitously, and the U.S. government instituted "antiterror" policies that made Middle Eastern and South Asian immigrants even greater targets for discrimination and prejudice (Bozorgmehr & Bakalian, 2004). Discrimination-related stressors often combine with other stressors to place immigrant families at increased risk for poor adaptation.

The issues of illegal immigration in the United States and concern regarding the negative impact on U.S. society has sparked debates, protests, and hurried inadequate legislation without much concern for immigrants who are already in the United States (e.g., Speiglman, Castaneda, Brown & Capps, 2013; Suarez-Orozco et al., 2008). Issues such as whether and how to deport illegal immigrants and their families, some of whom might be U.S. citizens, inadvertently place them in a tenuous position. As a result, many immigrants face daily discrimination ranging from verbal abuse to physical abuse, as well as barriers related to employment, education, and other opportunities that most people in the United States take for granted.

Inadequate Public Policies and Programs

One of the most problematic barriers that immigrant families face is the failure of U.S. social policies to address the needs of immigrants (FitzGerald & Cook-Martin, 2014; Speiglman et al., 2013; Suarez-Orozco et al., 2008). The only forms of government assistance that are available to immigrants (with the exception of refugees) are mainstream public assistance programs such as Temporary Assistance to Needy Families (TANF) (Broder & Blazer, 2011; Capps & Fix, 2013). The 1996 Personal Responsibility and Work Opportunity Reconciliation Act (commonly known as "welfare reform") increased restrictions on immigrants' ability to receive public assistance, extending the amount of time in the United States necessary for eligibility for most programs for the poor from 3 to 5 years. The law also bars immigrants from receiving benefits through the Supplemental Nutrition Assistance Program (SNAP; formally known as food stamps) or Supplemental Security Income (SSI) (Broder & Blazer, 2011; Massey et al., 2002). The federal government closely monitors immigrants' enrollment in public assistance programs, and attempting to enroll before the end of the 5-year waiting period is grounds for deportation. This level of punishment may discourage many immigrants from ever applying for assistance; immigrant enrollment in public assistance programs is far lower than enrollment among the U.S.-born (Broder & Blazer, 2011). The 1996 changes to the laws governing public assistance also definitively barred unauthorized immigrants from nearly all income-based assistance programs (Massey et al., 2002). Some progress has been made in this area during the reauthorization of the Children's Health Insurance Program (CHIP) in 2009. Close to half of all states opted to provide Medicaid and CHIP to "lawfully residing" children and pregnant women, regardless of their length of time in the country (Broder & Blazer, 2011). Moreover, with federal funds through CHIP, over a dozen states provide prenatal care to women regardless of status (i.e., citizenship/immigration, length in country) (Broder & Blazer, 2011).

Refugee families have considerably more financial and other resources available to them than do other immigrant families in the United States. Unfortunately, only immigrants who have been officially recognized by the U.S. government as refugees are eligible to receive such assistance (Tienda & Sanchez, 2013). Too often, for political reasons, the federal government grants only *economic immigrant* status to immigrant families who flee their homelands to escape violence, thereby cutting them off from refugee assistance programs (Broder & Blazer, 2011; Speiglman et al., 2013; Tienda & Sanchez, 2013).

Lack of Economic Resources

Socioeconomic status is both a predictor and an indicator of acculturation and adaptation. Although immigrant families exist across the socioeconomic continuum, many are at the lower levels, with children in immigrant families experiencing twice the poverty rate of native-born families in the United States (Van Hook, 2003). Often the work experience and training that immigrants have had in their countries of origin are not recognized in the United States, and so many educated professional immigrants are forced to take jobs for which they are overqualified (Austria, 2003; Bhattacharya & Schoppelrey, 2004; FitzGerald & Cook-Martin, 2014). Whether such employment is temporary or long term, it is typically less financially and psychologically rewarding than the work for which these immigrants are trained. Many immigrants who were professionals (e.g., lawyers, architects, accountants) in their home countries are unable to find employment in their fields and instead become owners of small businesses (Austria, 2003), taxi drivers (Bhattacharya & Schoppelrey, 2004), or take other types of jobs, typically lower paying, unrelated to their professional background.

Immigrant families with greater economic resources have more options regarding the neighborhoods and communities in which they choose to live; this, in turn, is related to the educational and occupational opportunities of family members (Suarez-Orozco et al., 2008). Poor immigrant families, of course, have fewer choices, and this can increase the amount of stress these families face and affect their family systems' ability to make the adjustments necessary for them to achieve a good quality of life in the United States.

COMMON RESOURCES AND ADAPTATION AMONG IMMIGRANT FAMILIES

Family adaptation is defined as the extent to which the internal functions of a family system (e.g., roles and perceptions) and/or external reality (e.g., social and economic contexts) are altered to achieve a system-environment fit (e.g., Boss, 2002; H. I. McCubbin et al., 1998; see Bush, Price, Price, & McHenry, Chapter 1, this volume). Adaptation involves long-term change, whereas adjustment is short-term change the family system makes in order to function successfully in different contexts (Boss, 2002). Although few scholars have examined migration and acculturation processes at the family level, a discussion of the various resources and patterns of adaptation seen among immigrant families will help to illustrate the process of change.

Resources that can aid immigrant family's adaptation exist at the society, community, family, and individual levels (e.g., L. D. McCubbin & McCubbin, 2013). Society- and community-level resources include immigration policies and programs and social support networks and services, such as those provided by religious institutions, ethnic enclaves, and communities in general. Family-level resources include shared family values and traditions, such as religion and familism, which can assist in maintaining effective family cohesion and communication and in establishing new social support networks. Individual-level resources include the ability to speak English, education, monetary resources, and familiarity with U.S. norms. Immigrant families' use of any of these resources depends on their perceptions of stressors as well as on their definitions of and goals for adaptation.

Perceptions of Barriers and Stressors

Immigration leads to changes in the events that individuals and families perceive as stressful, as well as changes in methods of coping with stressors (Boss, 2002). Obviously, when families encounter barriers, they experience these barriers as stressors. However, what any given family considers a barrier (and, therefore, a stressor) depends not only on the perception and meaning the family attaches to particular events but also on how the family defines adaptation (L. D. McCubbin & McCubbin, 2013; Yeh, Arora & Wu, 2006). For example, some immigrant families may perceive their children's increasing fluency in the English language as an asset to the family, whereas others might perceive it as a threat to the stability of the family. Culture, religion, education, resources, and prior experience are all important influences on families' perceptions of stressors and their subsequent responses (L. D. McCubbin & McCubbin, 2013; Walsh, 2013; Yeh et al., 2006).

Cultural Values

Value systems and associated behaviors serve as important influences within families. Shared values such as family cohesion, respect for elders, filial piety, and emphasizing family goals over individual goals can greatly increase the ability of a family system to maintain coherence during change by facilitating clear communication and similar definitions of stressors and adaptation goals among family members. That is, shared cultural values serve to maintain a cohesive and familiar family environment, thus facilitating support and effective coping (L. D. McCubbin & McCubbin, 2013; Walsh, 2013; Yeh et al., 2006; see Chapter 1, this volume). In Maria's family, the emphasis on family goals is apparent in Maria's provision of child care and the other three adults working in the paid labor force; all working toward the common goal of improving their family's well-being.

Shared family values such as self-sufficiency, perseverance, and familism bolster family adaptation by guiding the reframing of stressors into more manageable challenges. For example, an immigrant family that followed patriarchal norms in their home country may find that the wife has better employment opportunities than the husband. Viewing this stressor as a great opportunity for the wife to enter the workforce and for the husband to spend more time with the children would be consistent with values that emphasize the importance of the family unit over the individual. By reframing the stressor in this way, the family facilitates change in the family system that allows the family to meet its needs through the reversal of some spousal roles. The likelihood of such a change is dependent on the acculturation level of both spouses and the relative importance and flexibility of roles and values (e.g., patriarchy) within the family system.

Immigration Policies and Programs

Qualified legal immigrants to the United States are entitled to participate in mainstream public assistance programs such as TANF (Capps & Fix, 2013; Speiglman et al., 2013). Additionally, immigrants officially recognized as political asylum refugees by the U.S. government are very likely to take advantage of special government assistance programs for refugees (Bohon, 2001; Tienda & Sanchez, 2013). These include family resettlement programs, special language classes, and work training. Cities such as Atlanta, Georgia, and Portland, Oregon, are attractive destinations for refugee families, as many nongovernment refugee assistance agencies have been established in these locations to help families adjust to life in the United States. Refugees are also eligible for college financial aid, TANF, SNAP, and other assistance without going through the waiting periods required of other immigrants.

There are also government programs that help immigrants, regardless of their income (Speiglman et al., 2013). For example, the Civil Rights Act of 1964 and subsequent legislation requires that all public schools teach English to children who are not native English speakers. Therefore, all immigrant families with school age children should have at least one English speaker or an English learner in their home, provided that the children are in school. Some cities, such as Portland, Oregon, have also established day labor centers to ensure that workers, usually immigrants, have a safe place to wait for temporary work and are fairly paid for their labor (Ten Eyck, 2008).

Religion and Spirituality

Religious and spiritual beliefs and activities can serve as important resources for immigrants by fostering social support, adaptive coping strategies, self-efficacy, family cohesion, and community closeness (e.g., Finch & Vega, 2003; Kamya, 1997; Min, 2005; Walsh, 2013). Among African immigrants, for example, spiritual well-being has been found to be related to lower levels of stress, higher levels of family hardiness (ability to resist stress and cope effectively), and higher levels of coping resources (Kamya, 1997). Similarly, seeking religious support has been found to serve as a protective factor for health outcomes among Mexican immigrants, with those experiencing higher levels of discrimination benefiting the most from religious support seeking (Finch & Vega, 2003). Religious and spiritual organizations can also facilitate the formation of friendships and support networks with individuals and families from their native cultures (e.g., Min, 2005; Walsh, 2013). For example, the church is an important aspect of life for most Korean immigrants, fostering social support, a sense of belonging, and preservation of Korean cultural traditions (Min, 2005).

Ethnic Communities and Enclaves

Ethnic communities—that is, neighborhoods populated primarily by individuals and families from the same culture—can play very significant roles in the lives of immigrants. They provide the opportunity to adjust to life in a new country while living in somewhat familiar surroundings (e.g., language, food, and other customs) (Reynolds, 2005). Ethnic communities can also provide new immigrant families with social support in that they make it relatively easy for family members to form new friendships with individuals who have similar backgrounds but more experience and knowledge of their new country (Sanders & Nee, 1987). In Maria's family, living in an ethnic community has provided access to jobs and transportation for Jaime and Jose, without the need for English fluency.

Ethnic enclaves are extreme forms of ethnic communities in that they are larger and many of their economic activities are separated from those of the larger surrounding city (Bohon, 2001). The most famous ethnic enclaves are Little Havana in Miami, Little Tokyo in Honolulu, and the Chinatowns of San Francisco, Los Angeles, and New York. Immigrants who live in ethnic enclaves rarely have to venture outside the enclave boundaries to provide for their daily needs (Portes & Manning, 1986), unlike those who live in ethnic neighborhoods, most of whom work outside their neighborhoods in the larger community.

Living and working in ethnic enclaves is one method by which immigrant families cope with the problems of prejudice and discrimination (e.g., Fernandez-Kelly & Schauffler, 1994). Immigrants are not minorities within the enclave, and they are likely to have skills and work habits that are valued in the production of goods within ethnic enclaves. Many of the employers in ethnic enclaves also allow women to bring their children with them to work, so these women can simultaneously fulfill the role of both homemaker and wage earner (Fernandez-Kelly & Schauffler, 1994).

LATINO, ASIAN, AND AFRO-CARIBBEAN IMMIGRANT FAMILIES

Latino Immigrant Families

Latinos constitute the largest minority group in the United States. The U.S. Census Bureau uses the terms *Hispanic* and *Latino* interchangeably, both referring to persons of Cuban, Mexican, Puerto Rican, South or Central American, or other Spanish culture or origin regardless of race (Humes, Jones, & Ramirez, 2011). According to the Pew Hispanic Center, Hispanics accounted for approximately 17% of the country's population, at almost 54 million people in 2013 (Stepler & Brown, 2015). These immigrants accounted for almost half of the total foreign-born population, at almost 19 million, or 6% of the total U.S. population in 2013 (Stepler & Brown, 2015). A majority of the Hispanics or Latinos living in the United States have their origins in Mexico, with a total population of over 34.5 million, of which over 33% (11.5 million) are foreign born (Stepler & Brown, 2015). The next largest group of Latinos have their origins in Puerto Rico (although few are immigrants), with a total population of almost 4.7 million, followed by Cubans with a population of 1.9 million (Velasco & Dockterman, 2010).

Although these groups share similarities, Latinos are not a monolithic group, as there are unique characteristics within Latino subgroups. Cuban Americans, for example, are more likely than other Latino groups to have "more desirable" features commonly considered to be "Anglo," including blond or red hair and blue eyes, while Mexican Americans are much more likely to have features that accord with common stereotypes of Latinos, such as dark hair and eyes and darkish skin (Murguia & Telles, 1996). Thus, Mexican immigrants are more likely to experience within group marginalization as well as stigmatization for not being able to blend in with the White dominant group. This can create differential experiences of oppression and marginalization across Latino immigrant groups.

Socioeconomic status of Latino immigrants (e.g., income, housing values, and educational attainment) show trends that are typically below those of nonimmigrant Whites. According to the Pew Hispanic Center, Ecuadorians are the most well-off of all Latino immigrants, reporting average incomes of $50,000, higher than those of non-Latino Blacks ($33,300), yet still below the average income of non-Latino Whites ($54,000) (Velasco & Dockterman, 2010). Dominicans, who were ranked as the most impoverished of the Latino American immigrants, make an average income of $34,000, lower than that of Mexicans ($38,700), Guatamalans ($39,000), and Puerto Ricans ($36,000). Yet, the median household income of Hispanics overall dropped by more than $3,000 between the 2000 and 2010 census reports (Velasco & Dockterman, 2010).

The Latino population has access to large extended family support networks that have proven to be a positive resource for Latino immigrant families living in the United States (Landale et al., 2014). These networks serve as practical resources (i.e., instrumental support) to families (e.g., allowing for communal child-care arrangements, car-sharing options, financial support), as well as emotional support. However, the large number of Latino immigrants in the United States also sometimes works to this group's disadvantage. As M. Taylor (2000) notes, the size of an out-group is usually the biggest predictor of prejudicial attitudes among members of the in-group. Where minority groups are small, prejudice against members of those groups is less prevalent. Where minority groups are large, the reverse is true. This helps to account for the long history of discrimination against members of the two largest minority groups in the United States, African Americans and Latinos (Spain, 1999).

Asian Immigrant Families

Asians (including Pacific Islanders) are the fastest growing minority group in the United States., with a population of over 16.5 million in 2013, this group makes up 5.3% of the total population (Stepler & Brown, 2015). Asians account for approximately 28.2% of the total foreign-born population and 57.7% of the foreign born population who are naturalized U.S. citizens (Grieco et al., 2012). Although Asians are often treated as a monolithic group, great diversity exists within this population. Individuals with origins in at least 60 different Asian groups live in the United States; most of these groups have their own languages, religious traditions, and political, cultural, and migration histories (Austria, 2003; Lin & Cheung, 1999). The largest subgroup within the Asian population living in the

United States is Chinese (4 million), followed by Filipino (3.4 million), and Asian Indian (3.2 million) (Pew Research Center, 2013).

One of the inherent problems in understanding the experiences of Asian immigrants in the United States is that researchers have often paid little attention to sociocultural differences within distinct Asian groups, thus failing to recognize the potential influences of such differences on acculturation processes (Chun & Akutsu, 2003). For example, unlike Chinese, Japanese, and Korean immigrants, most of whom left their home countries voluntarily to seek better economic and educational opportunities, a majority of Southeast Asians arrived in the United States after being "forced" to leave their countries. Consequently, compared with other Asian immigrants, Southeast Asians are often less prepared for the new environment (e.g., poor English ability) and had limited exposure to Western culture at the time of their immigration (Ying & Akutsu, 1997). Given the wide diversity among Asian immigrants, each subgroup may face unique barriers and stressors in the process of adaptation.

Asian Americans have the highest income and educational attainment of any racial group; with a 2010 median family income of $66,000, compared to $54,000 and $33,000 for non-Hispanic-White and non-Hispanic Black households, respectively (Pew Research Center, 2013). Asian Americans are considered successful when examining other domains of social life such as low rates of divorce, crime, and violence (Sue, 2002). However, according to the U.S. Department of Labor (2011), although Asians are less likely to be unemployed, those who are unemployed face longer durations of unemployment and are more likely to experience long-term unemployment when compared to Whites or Hispanics. In addition, and to illustrate within group diversity, poverty rates were higher than the U.S. average (14.3%) for Vietnamese (14.7%) and Korean (15 %) immigrants (Macartney, Bishaw, & Fontenot, 2013).

One unique barrier that Asian immigrants face is the myth of Asian Americans as the "model minority" (Austria, 2003; Kim & Lee, 2014; Min, 2005). That is, Asians are often perceived as the most highly educated and economically successful ethnic minority group in the United States. Scholars have argued that this can lead to overgeneralizations that can hinder provision of assistance (e.g., needs not acknowledged), as well as Asians seeking help (e.g., Kim & Lee, 2014). More specifically, the model minority image exacerbates several problems that Asian immigrants may face, such as physical and psychological adjustment problems, because it leads educational and social service providers to virtually ignore the needs of Asians (Alvarez, Juang, & Liang, 2006; Austria, 2003). For example, because Asian American children, on average, tend to have higher levels of educational achievement than European American children (Pew Research Center, 2013), many policy makers assume that all Asian youth are academically successful and psychologically healthy (Austria, 2003; Kim & Lee, 2014).

Another issue in the adaptation process for Asian immigrants is their tendency to underutilize mainstream health services (Kim & Lee, 2014). For example, only 25.8% of the Asian population participated in government health insurance in 2013, this was lower than utilization from the Latino (36.4%), non-Hispanic Black (43.8%) and non-Hispanic White (33.2%) populations (Smith & Medalia, 2013). Yet, epidemiological surveys show that the rates of mental disorders among Asian Americans are comparable to other ethnic groups (Sue, 2002). Asians tend to emphasize coping mechanisms that rely on interdependent relationships and familial commitment and tend to delay seeking professional help until they exhaust all other personal resources (Lin & Cheung, 1999; Yeh et al., 2006). Costs, location, availability, limited knowledge of resources/services, and English-language proficiency have been proposed to explain "underutilization" of services (Sue, 2002).

Afro-Caribbean Immigrant Families

Afro-Caribbean people make up the largest population of immigrants of African descent in the United States (McCabe, 2011; Thomas, 2012). Compared to other immigrant groups in the United States, Caribbean immigrants are less likely to be new arrivals and more likely to have family already living in the host country (Chioneso, 2008). Contemporary patterns of migration indicate that there was an influx of Black immigrants to the United States between 1990 and 2000, and nearly 25% of the growth of the Black population in the United States is due to the African and Caribbean population (Logan, 2007). Compared to other regions of the world, the Caribbean has the greatest percentage of its population immigrating to the United States (Chioneso, 2008; Prachi, 2007). Reports by the Migration Policy Institute show that the overall Caribbean-born population made up 39.8% of all immigrants residing in Florida in 2009 (4 out of 10) and 24.1% of all immigrants residing in New York (McCabe, 2011). Additionally, more than one in ten immigrants in Connecticut (17.2%), Massachusetts (14.5%), New Jersey (14.4%), and Pennsylvania (11.2%) were born in the Caribbean. Currently, the foreign born from the Caribbean account for 9% of the total immigrant population (McCabe, 2011).

Afro-Caribbean immigrants live in close proximity to African Americans and also use formal English (McCabe, 2011; Thomas, 2012), making it easier for them to blend in with that population despite their unique cultural practices (Blau, 1960). It is important to note that this poses a new challenge for immigrants since the Black community in America historically faces different forms of oppression and marginalization (Kasinitz, Battle & Miyares, 2001). According to Bradatan, Melton and Popan (2010, p. 175),

> Being a part of a stigmatized group is a challenge, and people from that group (in our case, immigrants) can fight against the stigma either by disassociating themselves from that community, by trying to get quickly assimilated into the majority, or trying to change the status of their group, by emphasizing their belonging to the origin country national group.

The added weight of being a minority within a minority (Black and immigrant) makes it difficult for Afro-Caribbean immigrants to experience assimilation or integration within the acculturation process (Lopez, 2002). The challenges of immigration (e.g., citizenship status) intersect with products of racial marginalization (e.g., racial profiling) to make it harder for this group to assimilate or integrate to U.S. norms (Matthews & Mahoney, 2005).

Black minority groups are traditionally more likely to live in poverty than their White counterparts (Manuel, Taylor, & Jackson, 2012). However, within Black groups, researchers find that Afro-Caribbean immigrants are more likely to have better financial stability than other Black ethnic groups, such as African Americans and Africans (Manuel et al., 2012). Although educational attainment and employment for Afro-Caribbean immigrants is the highest within the Black immigrant groups (Thomas, 2012), they still have lower average earnings when compared to White and Asian Americans.

CONCLUSION

As an immigrant family faces social contexts in the United States that differ from those of their home country, the family system experiences stress, which can lead to changes in family strategies. In turn, changes in the family system can establish more adaptive rules, roles, and corresponding patterns of interaction within the family. That is, despite the long list of barriers and potential stressors that an immigrant family may face, stress is not necessarily negative. Stress on the family system can lead to change that is positive and increases adaptation. Religion, spirituality, ethnic communities and enclaves, shared cultural values, and informal and formal social support can serve as resources that aid immigrant families in adaptation.

Intervention efforts aimed at assisting immigrant families must consider the perspectives and social contexts of the target families (Flores et al., 2004; Santisteban & Mitrani, 2003). Interventions that violate the families' belief systems or that are not applicable to the families' particular social contexts will likely fail. Prior to beginning treatment with an immigrant family, it is important to assess characteristics and strategies of the family system, such as boundary hierarchies and methods of communication and conflict negotiation (Santisteban & Mitrani, 2003). For example, in a family that views children's open disagreement with parents as disrespectful, the parents are not likely to respond well to an intervention approach that instructs the children to tell the parents about their perceptions of parental and/or family rules. In such a case, the parents are likely to view the intervention as increasing the problem. Interventions that are less direct and that build on the strengths of the family's hierarchical values are likely to be more successful for such a family.

In addition, it is equally important to assess acculturation levels of each member as these influence values and interactions with the family system. For example, among immigrants from Mexico, interventions with more acculturated individuals and families require a different focus than less acculturated individuals and families because of the different perceptions and expression of conflict (Flores et al., 2004). That is, interventions with more acculturated individuals and families must be sensitive to more direct power struggles as the individual or family attempts to integrate cultural expectations from both their home and host cultures. In contrast, interventions with less acculturated individuals and families must be sensitive to the values, roles, and expectations from the home-country culture that influence the family system (e.g., less acceptance of open conflict). Needless to say, when there are individuals at different levels of acculturation within the family, interventions need to be more complex and tailored to fit the needs of the family and its members.

Currently, some human service programs exist to aid immigrant families, but many more are needed, especially for nonrefugee immigrant families (Speiglman et al., 2013;

Tienda & Sanchez, 2013). Decreasing the 5-year waiting period for eligibility in mainstream public assistance programs like Medicaid, food stamps, and Social Security Income may be a good starting point. Although, some states provide Medicaid and CHIP to "lawfully residing" children and pregnant women, regardless of their date of entry into the United States (Broder & Blazer, 2011), broader support would be beneficial. Bilingual programs are also needed to assist immigrant families in navigating their new country; such programs could raise immigrants' awareness and knowledge of the services and resources available to them and also help them to gain familiarity with U.S. cultural and legal norms (e.g., those concerning the educational system, child care, and domestic violence).

REFERENCES

Alvarez, A. N., Juang, L., & Liang, C. T. H. (2006). Asian Americans and racism: When bad things happened to "model minorities." *Cultural Diversity and Ethnic Minority Psychology, 12,* 477–492.

Anderson, S. A., Sabatelli, R. M., & Kosutic, I. (2013). Systemic and ecological qualities of families. In G. W. Peterson & K. R. Bush (Eds.), *Handbook of marriage and the family* (3rd ed., pp. 121–138). New York, NY: Springer

Atiles, J. H., & Bohon, S. A. (2002). The needs of Georgia's new Latinos: A policy agenda for the decade ahead. *Public Policy Research, 3,* 1–51.

Austria, A. M. (2003). People of Asian descent: Beyond myths and stereotypes. In J. D. Robinson & L. C. James (Eds.), *Diversity in human interactions: The tapestry of America* (pp. 63–75). New York, NY: Oxford University Press.

Baptiste, J. D. (1987). Family therapy with Spanish-heritage immigrant families in cultural transition. *Contemporary Family Therapy, 9*(4), 229–251.

Berry, J. W. (2001). A psychology of immigration. *Journal of Social Issues, 57,* 615–631.

Bhattacharya, G., & Schoppelrey, S. L. (2004). Preimmigration beliefs of life success, postimmigration experiences, and acculturative stress: South Asian immigrants in the United States. *Journal of Immigrant Health, 6,* 83–92.

Blau, P. M. (1960). Theory of Social Integration. *American Journal of Sociology, 65*(6), 545-556.

Bohon, S. A. (2001). *Latinos in ethnic enclaves: Immigrant workers and the competition for jobs.* New York, NY: Routledge.

Bohon, S. A., Macpherson, H., & Atiles, J. H. (2005). Educational barriers for new Latinos in Georgia. *Journal of Latinos and Education, 4,* 43–58.

Boss, P. G. (2002). *Family stress management: A contextual approach* (2nd ed.). Thousand Oaks, CA: Sage.

Bozorgmehr, M., & Bakalian, A. (2004, August). *Post-9/11 anti immigrant government initiatives: The response of Middle Eastern and South Asian American organizations.* Paper presented at the annual meetings of the American Sociological Association, San Francisco, CA.

Bradatan, C., Melton, R., & Popan, A. (2010). Transnationality as a fluid social identity. *Social Identities, 16*(2), 169–178.

Broder, T., & Blazer, J. (2011, October). *Overview of immigrant eligibility for federal programs.* Washington, DC: National Immigration Law Center. Retrieved from http://nilc.org/overview-immeligfedprograms.html

Capps, R. (2001). *Hardship among children of immigrants: Findings for the 1999 National Survey of America's Families.* Washington, DC: Urban Institute.

Capps, R., & Fix, M. (2013). Immigration reform: A long road to citizenship and insurance coverage. *Health Affairs, 32*(4), 639–642. doi:10.1377/hlthaff.2013.0187

Chamberlain, M. (2003). Rethinking Caribbean families: Extending the links. *Community, Work & Family, 6*(1), 63–76. doi:10.1080/1366880032000063905

Chia, R. C., Moore, J. L., Lam, K., Chuang, C. J., & Cheng, B. S. (1994). Cultural differences in gender role attitudes between Chinese and American students. *Sex Roles, 31,* 3–30.

Chioneso, N. A. (2008). (Re)Expressions of African/Caribbean cultural roots in Canada. *Journal of Black Studies, 39*(1), 69–84.

Chun, K. M., & Akutsu, P. D. (2003). Acculturation among ethnic minority families. In K. M. Chun, P. B. Organista, & G. Marín (Eds.), *Acculturation: Advances in theory, measurement, and applied research* (pp. 95–119). Washington, DC: APA.

Chung, G. H., Tucker, M. B., & Takeuchi, D. (2008). Wives' relative income production and household male dominance: Examining violence among Asian American enduring couples, *Family Relations, 57,* 227–238.

Cruz, R. A., Gonzales, N. A., Corona, M., King. K. M., Cauce, A. M., Robins, R. W., Widaman, K. F., & Conger, R. D. (2014). Cultural dynamics and marital relationship quality in Mexican-origin families. *Journal of Family Psychology, 28*(6), 844–854. doi:10.1037/a0038123

Driscoll, M. W., & Torres, L. (2013). Acculturative stress and Latino depression: The mediating role of behavioral and cognitive resources. *Cultural Diversity and Ethnic Minority Psychology, 19*(4), 373–382. doi:10.1037/a0032821

Espenshade, T. J. (1995). Unauthorized immigration to the United States. *Annual Review of Sociology 21,* 195–216.

Evans, G. W. (2006). Child development and the physical environment. *Annual Review of Psychology, 57,* 423–451.

Falicov, C. J. (2003). Immigrant family processes. In F. Walsh (Ed.), *Normal family processes: Growing diversity and complexity* (pp. 280–300). New York, NY: Guilford.

Fernandez-Kelly, P. M., & Schauffler, R. (1994). Divided fates: Immigrant children in a restructured U.S. economy. *International Migration Review, 28,* 662–690.

Finch, B. K., & Vega, W. A. (2003). Acculturation stress, social support, and self-rated health among Latinos in California. *Journal of Immigrant Health, 5,* 109–117.

FitzGerald, D. S., & Cook-Martin, D. (2014). *Culling the masses: The democratic origins of racist immigration policy in the Americas.* Cambridge, MA: Harvard University Press.

Flores, E., Tschann, J. M., Marin, B. V., & Pantoja, P. (2004). Marital conflict and acculturation among Mexican American husbands and wives. *Cultural Diversity and Ethnic Minority Psychology, 10*(1), 39–52.

Glasgow, G. F., & Gouse-Sheese, J. (1995). Themes of rejection and abandonment in group work with Caribbean adolescents. *Social Work With Groups, 17*(4), 3–27.

Gonzalez-Barrera, A., Lopez, M. H., Passel, J. S., & Taylor, P. (2013). *The path not taken: Two-thirds of legal Mexican immigrants are not US citizens.* Washington DC: Pew Hispanic Center. Retrieved from http://www.pewhispanic.org/files/2013/02/Naturalizations_Jan_2013_FINAL.pdf

Grieco, E. M., Acosta, Y. D., de la Cruz, G. P., Gambino, C., Gryn, T., Larsen, L. J., . . . Trevelyan, E. N. (2012). *The foreign-born population in the United States: 2010. American Community Survey Reports.* U.S. Census Bureau. Retrieved from https://www.census.gov/prod/2012pubs/acs-19.pdf

Gyory, A. (1998). *Closing the gate: Race, politics, and the Chinese Exclusion Act.* Chapel Hill: University of North Carolina Press.

Hakim, J. (1995). *A history of us: War, peace and all that jazz.* New York, NY: Oxford University Press.

Hondagneu-Sotelo, P. (1994). *Gendered transitions: Mexican experiences of migration.* Berkeley: University of California Press.

Humes, K., Jones, N. A., & Ramirez, R. R., (2011). *Overview of race and Hispanic origin, 2010.* Washington, DC: U.S. Dept. of Commerce, Economics and Statistics Administration, U.S. Census Bureau. Retrieved from http://www.census.gov/prod/cen2010/briefs/c2010br-02.pdf

Jamieson, L. (2008). Obligatory friends, surrogate kin: some questions for mentoring. *Youth & Policy, 99*, 55–66.

Johnson, L., Radesky, J., & Zuckerman, B. (2013). Cross-cultural parenting: Reflections on autonomy and interdependence. *Pediatrics, 131*(4), 631–633.

Kamya, H. A. (1997). African immigrants in the United States: The challenge for research and practice. *Social Work, 42,* 154–165.

Kasinitz, P., Battle, J., & Miyares, I. (2001). Fade to black? The children of West Indian immigrants in South Florida. In Rumbaut, R. G., & Portes, A., *Ethnicities: Children of immigrants in America.* Berkeley: University of California Press.

Kearney, G. D., Chatterjee, A. B., Talton, J., Chen, H., Quandt, S. A., Summers, P., & Arcury, T. A. (2014). The association of respiratory symptoms and indoor housing conditions among migrant farmworkers in Eastern North Carolina. *Jounral of Agromedicine, 19*(4), 395–405. doi:10.1080/1059924X.2014.947458.

Kim, P. Y., & Lee, D. (2014). Internalized model minority myth, Asian values, and help-seeking attitudes among Asian American students. *Cultural Diversity and Ethnic Minority Psychology, 20*(1), 98–106.

Kwak, K. (2003). Adolescents and their parents: A review of intergenerational family relations for immigrant and non-immigrant families. *Human Development, 46,* 115–136.

Landale, N. S. (1997). Immigration and the family: An overview. In A. Booth, A. C. Crouter, & N. S. Landale (Eds.), *Immigration and the family: Research and policy on U.S. immigrants* (pp. 281–291). Mahwah, NJ: Lawrence Erlbaum.

Landale, N. S., Oropesa, R. S., & Noah, A. J. (2014). Immigration and the family circumstances of Mexican-origin children: A binational longitudinal analysis. *Journal of Marriage and Family, 76*(1), 24–36.

Lin, K.-M., & Cheung, F. (1999). Mental health issues for Asian Americans. *Psychiatric Services, 50,* 774–780.

Look, K. M., & Look, R. M. (1997). Skin scraping, cupping, and moxibustion that may mimic physical abuse. *Journal of Forensic Sciences, 42*(1), 103–105.

Logan, J. R. (2007). Who are the other African Americans? Contemporary African American and Caribbean immigrants in the United States. In Y. Shaw-Taylor & S. A. Tuch (Eds.), *The other African Americans: Contemporary African and Caribbean immigrants in the United States.* Lanham, MD: Rowman & Littlefield Publishers.

Lopez, N. (2002). Race-Gender experiences and schooling: Second generation Dominican, West Indian and Haitian youth in New York City. *Race Ethnicity and Education, 5*(1), 69–89. doi:10.1080/13613320120117207

Macartney, S., Bishaw, A., & Fontenot, K. (2013). Poverty rates for selected detailed race and Hispanic groups by state and place: 2007–2011. *American Community Survey Briefs*, U.S. Census Bureau. Retrieved from http://www.census.gov/prod/2013pubs/acsbr11-17.pdf

Manuel, R. C., Taylor, R. J., & Jackson, J. S. (2012). Race and ethnic group differences in socioeconomic status: Black Caribbeans, African Americans and Non-Hispanic Whites in the United States. *Western Journal of Black Studies, 36*(3), 228–239.

Massey, D. S., Durand, J., & Malone, N. J. (2002). *Beyond Smoke and Mirrors: Mexican Immigration in an Era of Economic Integration.* New York, NY: Russell Sage.

Matthews, L., & Mahoney, A. (2005). Facilitating a smooth transitional process for immigrant Caribbean Children: The role of teachers, social workers, and related professional staff. *Journal of Ethnic & Cultural Diversity in Social Work, 14*(1/2), 69–92. doi:10.1300/J051v14n0104

McCabe, K. (2011). Caribbean immigrants in the United States. *Migration Policy Institute.* Retrieved from http://www.migrationpolicy.org/article/caribbean-immigrants-united-states

McCubbin, L. D., & McCubbin, H. I. (2013). Resilience in ethnic family systems: A relational theory for research and practice. In D. S. Becvar (Ed.), *Handbook of family resilience* (pp. 175–195). New York, NY: Springer

McCubbin, H. I., Thompson, E. A., Thompson, A. I., & Fromer, J. E. (Eds.). (1998). *Resiliency in Native American and immigrant families.* Thousand Oaks, CA: Sage.

Min, P. G. (2005). *Asian Americans: Contemporary Trends and Issues.* Newbury Park, CA: Pine Forge Press.

Murguia, E., & Telles, E. E. (1996). Phenotype and schooling among Mexican Americans. *Sociology of Education, 69,* 276–289.

Passel, J. S. (2006). *Size and characteristics of the unauthorized migrant population in the U.S.* Washington, DC: Pew Hispanic Center.

Passel, J. S., & Cohn, D. (2010). *U.S. unauthorized immigrant flows are down sharply since mid-decade.* Washington, DC: Pew Hispanic Center. Retrieved from http://pewhispanic.org/files/reports/126.pdf

Pew Research Center. (2013). The rise of Asian Americans. *Social and Demographics Trends,* Washington, DC: Pew Research Center. Retrieved from http://www.pewsocialtrends.org/files/2013/04/Asian-Americans-new-full-report-04-2013.pdf

Plata-Potter, S. I., & De Guzman, M. T. (2012). Mexican immigrant families crossing the education border: A phenomenological study. *Journal of Latinos and Education, 11*(2), 94–106. doi:10.1080/15348431.2012.659563

Portes, A., & Manning, R. (1986). The immigrant enclave: Theory and empirical examples. In S. Olzak & J. Nagel (Eds.), *Competitive ethnic relations* (pp. 47–68). Orlando, FL: Academic Press.

Prachi, M. (2007). Emigration and brain drain: Evidence from the Caribbean. *The BE Journal of Economic Analysis & Policy, 7*(1), 1–44.

Reynolds, T. (2005). *Caribbean mothers: Identity and experience in the U.K.* London, England: Tufnell Press.

Roche, K. M., Lambert, S. F., Ghazarian, S. R., & Little, T. D. (2015). Adolescent language brokering in diverse contexts: Associations with parenting and parent-youth relationships in a new immigrant destination area. *Journal of Youth and Adolescence, 44*(1), 77–89. doi:10.1007/s10964-014-0154-3

Rusch, D., & Reyes, K. (2013). Examining the effects of Mexican serial migration and family separations on acculturative stress, depression, and family functioning. *Hispanic Journal of Behavioral Sciences, 35*(2), 139–158.

Rumbaut, R. G. (1997). Ties that bind: Immigration and immigrant families in the United States. In A. Booth, A. C. Crouter, & N. S. Landale (Eds.), *Immigration and the family: Research and policy on U.S. immigrants* (pp. 3–46). Mahwah, NJ: Lawrence Erlbaum.

Sanders, J., & Nee, V. (1987). Limits of ethnic solidarity in the enclave economy. *American Sociological Review, 52,* 745–773.

Santisteban, D. A., & Mitrani, V. B. (2003). The influences of acculturation processes on the family. In K. M. Chun, P. B. Organista, & G. Marín (Eds.), *Acculturation: Advances in theory, measurement, and applied research* (pp. 121–135). Washington, DC: APA.

Serafica, F. C., Weng, A., & Kim, H. K. (2000). Asian American women's friendships and social networks. In J. L. Chin (Ed.), *Relationships among Asian American women* (pp. 151–175). Washington, DC: APA.

Smith, J. C., & Medalia, C. (2014). *Health insurance coverage in the United States: 2013.* Washington, DC: U.S. Department of Commerce, Economics and Statistics Administration, Bureau of the Census.

Sorenson, E., Bean, F. D., Ku, L., & Zimmerman, W. (1992). *Immigrant categories and the U.S. job market: Do they make a difference?* (Urban Institute Report No. 92-1). Washington, DC: Urban Institute Press.

Soto, L. (2009). Migration as a matter of time: Perspectives from Mexican immigrant adolescent girls in California's Napa Valley. *Dissertation Abstracts International Section A, 70,* 1385

Spain, D. (1999). America's diversity: On the edge of two centuries. *Population Reference Bureau Reports on America, 1*(2), 1–12.

Speiglman, R., Castaneda, R., Brown, H., & Capps, R. (2013). Welfare reform's ineligible immigrant parents: Program reach and enrollment barriers. *Journal of Children & Poverty, 19*(2), 91–106. doi:10.1080/10796126.2013.845144

Stepler, R., & Brown, A. (2015). *Statistical portrait of Hispanics in the United States, 1980–2013.* Washington DC: Pew Hispanic Center. Retrieved from http://www.pewhispanic.org/2015/05/12/statistical-portrait-of-hispanics-in-the-united-states-1980-2013

Suarez-Orozco, C., Todorova, I. L., & Louie, J. (2002). Making up for lost time: The experience of separation and reunification among immigrant families. *Family Process, 41,* 4, 625–43.

Suarez-Orozco, C., Suarez-Orozco, M. M., Todorova, I. (2008). *Learning a new land: Immigrant students in American society*. Cambridge, MA: Belknap Press.

Sue, S. (2002). Asian American mental health: What we know and what we don't know. In W. J. Lonner, D. L. Dinnel, S. A. Hayes, & D. N. Sattler (Eds.), *Online readings in psychology and culture* (Unit 3, Chapter 4; http://www.wwu.eud/ ~ culture). Bellingham, WA: Center for Cross-Cultural Research, Western Washington University.

Taylor, M. C. (2000). The significance of racial context. In D. O. Sears, J. Sidanius, & L. Bobo (Eds.), *Racialized politics: The debate about racism in America* (pp. 118–136). Chicago, IL: University of Chicago Press.

Taylor, P., Lopez, M. H., Martinez, J. H., & Velasco, G. (2012). *When labels don't fit: Hispanics and their views of identity*. Washington, DC: Pew Hispanic Center. Retrieved from http://www.pewhispanic.org/files/2012/04/PHC-Hispanic-Identity.pdf

Ten Eyck, T. (2008). "Uneasy reception for Portland day labor center." *Labor Notes*. Retrieved from http://labornotes.org/2008/07/uneasy-reception-portland-day-labor-center

Thomas, K. J. A. (2012). *A demographic profile of Black Caribbean immigrants in the United States.* Washington DC: Migration Policy Institute.

Tienda, M., & Sanchez, S. M. (2013). Latin American immigration to the United States. *Daedalus, 142*(3), 48–64. doi:10.1162/DAED_a_00218

U.S. Department of Labor. (2011). *The Asian-American labor force in the recovery*. Retrieved from http://purl.fdlp.gov/GPO/gpo10845

Van Hook, J. (2003). *Poverty grows among children of immigrants in the U.S.* Retrieved from http://www.migrationinformation.org/USfocus/display.cfm?ID = 188

Velasco, G., & Dockterman, D. (2010). *Statistical portrait of the foreign-born population in the United States, 2008*. Washington, DC: Pew Hispanic Center. Retrieved from http://www.pewhispanic.org/2010/01/21/statistical-portrait-of-the-foreign-born-population-in-the-united-states-2008

Walsh, F. (2013). Religion and spirituality: A family systems perspective in clinical practice. In K. I. Pargament, A., Mahoney, & E. P., Shafranske (Eds.), *APA handbook of psychology religion, and spirituality (Vol 2): An applied psychology of religion and spirituality* (pp. 189–205). Washington, DC: American Psychological Association.

Yeh, C. J., Arora, A. K., & Wu, K. A. (2006). A new theoretical model of collectivistic coping. In P. P. Wong, & L. J. Wong (Eds.), *Handbook of multicultural perspectives on stress and coping* (pp. 55–72). New York, NY: Springer.

Ying, Y., & Akutsu, P. D. (1997). Psychological adjustment of Southeast Asian refugees: The contribution of sense of coherence. *Journal of Community Psychology, 25,* 125–139.

The Newest Generation of U.S. Veterans and Their Families

Kyung-Hee Lee and
Shelley MacDermid Wadsworth

More than 2.5 million U.S. service members have been deployed in the past 14 years, creating a new generation of veterans (Institute of Medicine, 2013). This chapter discusses challenges these new veterans and their families may face, guided by the life-course perspective, which conceptualizes human development as unfolding over time, shaped by the choices and actions of individuals within constraints imposed by historical and social contexts. The chapter first situates the current wars and veterans in historical context (*historical time*). Next, individual *transitions* and challenges for veterans, their spouses, and their children are discussed, followed by a discussion of family transitions (*linked lives*). Finally, three interventions targeting challenges facing veterans and their families are introduced.

More than 2.5 million service members have been deployed during Operations Enduring Freedom (OEF), Iraqi Freedom (OIF), and New Dawn (OND) (Institute of Medicine, 2013). As these conflicts wind down and the U.S. military shrinks, a new generation of combat-exposed veterans is joining veterans of previous wars in U.S. society. The experiences of OEF/OIF/OND veterans are distinct from those of veterans of previous wars in a variety of ways. For example, during these wars, many service members experienced multiple deployments with little "dwell time" at home in between (Chandra et al., 2010). In addition, the nature of combat during OEF/OIF/OND produced different patterns of injuries than those from previous wars. As a result, the consequences of wartime deployment are also likely to be somewhat different for this generation than for veterans of previous wars.

As has historically been the case, most OEF/OIF/OND veterans served in enlisted ranks (85%) and are White (77%) and male (88%). Unlike some previous conflicts, such as Vietnam, more than half (59%) are married, and half have children (Institute of Medicine, 2013). Both service members and their families have been influenced by deployments to the most recent wars. In this chapter, we discuss the challenges faced by OEF/OIF/OND veterans and their families after deployments and during transitions to civilian life, using life-course perspectives (Elder, 1998). The term *veteran* is used in a variety of ways, but in this chapter we use it to refer to a person who served in the military in the past. We begin by discussing the experiences of individual family members, followed by the experiences of families as a whole. Finally, information regarding policy and prevention programs for military and veteran families is provided. It is important to acknowledge that this chapter has an important bias: We focus almost exclusively on family challenges and problems, even though most veteran families do *not* experience long-term negative consequences (Chandra, Burns, Tanielian, Jaycox, & Scott, 2008). We do this because readers of this text are likely to enter helping professions where they may encounter families struggling with challenges.

THEORETICAL FRAMEWORK: LIFE COURSE

_____ Vignette _____

Alvaro Ramos is a 27-year-old Hispanic male with a wife, Victoria (age 27), and a 3-year-old son, Jesus. After 4 years in the military and two deployments to Iraq as a medical specialist, he decided not to reenlist. Upon entering civilian life, he wanted to stay in the medical field both for job security and his passion for the field. He decided to go to a vocational college and get a stable job as a licensed practical nurse as soon as possible. They moved close to Alvaro's school away from their military community. His wife who had stayed at home taking care of their son while he was deployed agreed to take a job at a floral shop to help support the family while he was in school. Still, he needed to find a part-time job to make ends meet and now works in the evenings and some weekends. Jesus started going to a child-care facility during the day.

• • •

Life course perspectives (Elder, 1998) provide useful concepts such as *historical time*, *transitions*, *timing*, and *linked lives* that help us to understand veterans and their family lives. Life course perspectives conceptualize human development as a process that unfolds over time, shaped by choices individuals make and actions they take within constraints imposed by historical and social contexts. The concept of historical time helps us to understand events in the context of social conditions occurring at that time. For example, as discussed briefly above, veterans' experiences of the most recent wars are very different from those during the Vietnam War, and as a consequence, the new generation of veterans and their families may face different challenges in the future. Thus, it is important to consider *historical time* in understanding each generation of veterans and their families.

Individual and family lives are marked by both minor and major *transitions*. Some transitions are very common and experienced by most people, such as starting school or retiring, while other transitions are rare, such as being deployed to a combat zone or experiencing the sudden death of a family member. Transitions bring changes in roles and statuses to the individuals involved, such as when a job transition for one spouse means that the other becomes the primary economic provider for the family. Common transitions are usually easier to cope with than rare ones, because people generally are more likely to have prior knowledge of or experience with similar transitions and thus know what to expect in their new roles. Another important aspect of transitions is when they occur (the *timing* of the transition). Even common transitions can cause negative stress when they happen unexpectedly or at a time in life that does not conform to societal expectations. For example, in the previous vignette, Alvaro is a veteran and older than the traditional college student. He also has family responsibilities that many single students do not. Thus, his college experience differs from that of a young student right out of high school, and he may experience some challenges as a result.

Life course perspectives also emphasize the importance of *linked lives*. The concept of linked lives refers to connections people have not only to one another but also to larger contexts such as other generations in their family, other people in the society, and historical events. The concept helps to explain why and how a service member's experiences during combat deployment are connected to historic timing of the war and social and military support for the war. For example, many individuals joined the U.S. military in the aftermath of September 11, 2001. The concept is also useful in explaining how service members' family members are affected by military service and deployments, because it emphasizes the connections between the transitions of one family member and the experiences of other family members. In the Ramos family's case, Alvaro's decision to separate from the military changed many aspects of his family's life. Individually, Alvaro started a school and a job, and Victoria now has a new job, which means Jesus has to start going to a day-care facility during the day. Moreover, the move was a transition for the family as a whole. Separating from the military and moving away from their military community meant losing informal support from friends as well as formal military supports such military health care and housing.

Historical Time: The New Context

Placing the recent wars into the context of *historical time* helps us to understand the challenges being faced by OEF/OIF/OND veterans and their families. Every war is distinct. Like the first Gulf War, but unlike World War II or the Vietnam War, the recent wars were fought by an all-volunteer force. Because retaining service members is important in an all-volunteer force, service members now are more likely to serve for longer periods and to have families while still serving. For example, half of OEF/OIF/OND veterans were married with children, compared to 16% among Vietnam War veterans. Second, due to the long duration of the conflicts, OEF/OIF/OND veterans tend to have experienced higher numbers of deployments and longer cumulative durations of deployments than veterans of previous wars (Chandra et al., 2010). By the end of 2010, the average number of deployments was 1.72 with an average of 17.63 cumulative months of deployment for service members with multiple deployments (Institute of Medicine, 2013). Thus, service members experienced longer separations from their families and greater risk of exposure to combat and injuries. Third, despite the large number of OEF/OIF/OND veterans, their proportion in the general population is smaller than veterans of previous wars. For example, only 12% of male and 3% of female Americans under the age of 35 are OEF/OIF/OND veterans compared to 50% of male and 15% of female Americans under the age of 35 in the post-World War II veteran population (Castro & Kintzle, 2014). The implication is that OEF/OIF/OND veterans are entering predominantly civilian communities where there may be limited familiarity with their experiences, which may make it more difficult for them to find the support they need. Fourth, due to the nature of combat and advances in protective equipment and medical treatment during the recent wars, the types and prognoses of injuries differ from prior conflicts. For example, the estimated survival rate from injuries in the recent wars is 90%, compared to 70% during the Vietnam War. Injuries sustained in the recent wars are most often due to explosives (75%), which tend to cause multiple injuries, especially in the head and neck regions of the body. In contrast, most injuries during the Vietnam war were due to gunshots (Belmont et al., 2010).

Individual Transitions: Veterans

For most service members, military service incorporates a series of transitions, from one rank or role to another, as well as to and from deployments and, eventually, separation from military service. Many veterans pursue higher education following deployments or military service or enter or return to the civilian labor force. Others may return home with wounds or injuries. In this section, some of the transitions and related challenges veterans may experience are discussed, including education, employment, and wounds or injuries.

Education

After returning from deployment or completing military service, many veterans enter or return to colleges or universities to continue their educations. Historically, veterans have been successful in pursuing higher education, in part because of financial assistance provided by various versions of the GI Bill. For example, almost 8 million World War II veterans earned degrees in postsecondary schools or finished vocational trainings. In 2005, 65.7% of male veterans between the ages of 25 and 64 who were in the labor force had at least some college or an associate's degree, compared to 58% of nonveterans. The difference was larger for female veterans (79.8% vs. 64.9%; Holder, 2007).

By 2010, almost 1 million OEF/OIF/OND veterans had used GI Bill benefits for education. Approximately 60% (59.4) of the OEF/OIF/OND veterans who used GI Bill benefits between 2002 and 2010 earned a bachelor's degree within 6 years (Student Veterans of America, 2014). This rate compared favorably to the national graduation rate, which was 57% for first-time students who enrolled in 2002 and completed a bachelor's degree within 6 years (Aud et al., 2011).

Despite their educational successes, student veterans may encounter a variety of challenges including navigating benefit procedures, adjusting to the nonmilitary environment (e.g., managing their own schedule and duties), being older than other students, and coping with the insensitivities of others to war-related issues (Rumann & Hamrick, 2010). Combat exposure and posttraumatic stress disorder (PTSD) symptoms are also negatively related to the educational performance and social functioning of student veterans. Compared to civilian students, student veterans tend to have lower GPAs (Durdella & Kim, 2012).

Employment

In general, the employment situations of veterans have compared favorably to those of their civilian counterparts. According to the Bureau of Labor Statistics (2014), the unemployment rate of all veterans in 2013 was 6.6%, compared to 7.2% for nonveterans. The unemployment rates of OEF/OIF/OND veterans have been higher, however, than those of nonveterans. In 2013, the unemployment rate of male OEF/OIF/OND veterans was 8.8% compared to 7.7% of male nonveterans, and for female veterans, the difference was more pronounced (9.6% vs. 6.8%). Moreover, female veterans were 38% more likely to be unemployed than male veterans. When examined by ethnicity, veterans of all ethnicity groups except Black veterans had higher unemployment rates than their counterpart nonveterans. The differences between OEF/OIF/OND veterans and nonveterans seemed to be driven by the unemployment rates of younger veterans. The unemployment rates of male OEF/OIF/OND veterans between 18 to 24 years (24.3%) and 25 to 34 years (9.2%) were higher than similarly aged male nonveterans (15.8% and 7.5% respectively), while the unemployment rates for male veterans and nonveterans aged 35 and older did not differ (5.5% to 6.4%; Bureau of Labor Statistics, 2014).

Military service also influences veterans' earnings in the civilian job market. Historically, veterans of World War II outperformed nonveterans in education attainment and earnings, while Vietnam War veterans did not do as well as their civilian counterparts (MacLean & Elder, 2007). A recent study (Holder, 2007) found that, among people in the labor force aged between 25 and 64 years, median earnings were higher for veterans than nonveterans, and this was true for both males ($42,128 vs. $39,880) and females ($32,217 vs. $27,272).

Injuries

Over, 50,000 OEF/OIF/OND veterans (approximately 2%) have been physically injured in OEF/OIF/OND (Institute of Medicine, 2013). The percentage of the injured in OEF/OIF/OND is similar to that in the Korean and Vietnam Wars but smaller than 4% in World War II. The most common injuries (75%) are from explosives, compared to 35% in World War I, 73% in World War II, 69% in Korea, and 64% in Vietnam (Belmont et al., 2010).

It is estimated that Traumatic Brain Injury (TBI) accounted for 22% of the injuries during the recent wars. TBI is defined by the U.S. Department of Defense (2009) as structural injury and/or physiological disruption of brain function caused by an external force. The severity of TBI is determined by the extent of the loss of consciousness and posttraumatic amnesia; most TBIs in OEF/OIF/OND veterans (76.8%) are classified as mild (Institute of Medicine, 2013). According to an Institute of Medicine report (2008), TBIs are related to impairment in cognitive functioning such as attention, concentration, reaction time, memory, processing speed, and decision making. People with mild or moderate TBIs typically recover fully from the cognitive impairment within 6 months, but impairment from severe TBIs lasts longer. Long-term prognosis of TBI is complicated because veterans with a TBI have a higher risk of having other psychological problems such as PTSD, depression, or anxiety, which can delay recovery and make it difficult to isolate the effects of TBI. TBI is also related to increases in aggressive behaviors, unemployment, and relationship problems.

Mental health problems such as PTSD and depression, sometimes called invisible injuries, are some of the most common injuries among OEF/OIF/OND veterans (Institute of Medicine, 2008). The estimated prevalence rate of PTSD in OEF/OIF/OND veterans ranges from 5% to 15% (Tanielian & Jaycox, 2008) compared to 6.8% in the general population (Kessler et al., 2005). The rate is higher in service members with combat experience, severe injuries, and military sexual trauma (Institute of Medicine, 2013). PTSD is related to other mental disorders such as depression and psychosocial problems such as relationship problems, legal problems, and violence (Institute of Medicine, 2008). The estimated prevalence rate of major depression among OEF/OIF/OND veterans ranges from 5% to 37%, and the chance of being diagnosed with major depression increases with combat exposure (Tanielian & Jaycox, 2008). In the general population, the rate is 18.4% or more (Kessler et al., 2005).

Suicide

Suicide is the third-leading cause of death among U.S. active duty military members and has been rising (Armed Forces Health Surveillance Center, 2012). Before 2001, military suicide rates were 20% lower than those among civilians. According to the Department of Defense Suicide Event Report (Smolenski et al., 2013), however, the suicide rate was 22.7 per 100,000 for those serving on active duty and 24.2 per 100,000 for those in the Reserve component in 2012, much higher than the rate of 12.5 per 100,000 in the general population in the same year (Xu, Kochanek, Murphy, & Arias, 2014). Firearms were the most frequently used method of suicide (65.1%). Risk factors included being male and White, having mental health problems including PTSD and substance abuse, and relationship problems (Kaplan, McFarland, Huguet, & Valenstein, 2012). However, the importance of risk factors seems to change over the life course of veterans. For example, Kaplan and colleagues (2012) found that for younger veterans (aged 18 to 34) who committed suicide, relationship problems and alcohol use were more common than for middle-aged veterans (aged 35 to 44 and 45 to 64), for whom mental health problems were more common.

Recent research suggests that veterans of OEF/OIF/OND are at greater risk of suicide than veterans of previous wars (Bruce, 2010), as well as never-deployed active service members (Black, Gallaway, Bell, & Ritchie, 2011). Unique aspects of the OEF/OIF/OND conflicts may contribute to the elevated levels of risk. First, as discussed above, TBI is more common among OEF/OIF/OND veterans than others, and TBI is a risk factor for suicide in military populations (Institute of Medicine, 2013). Second, due to the volunteer nature of the current military force, new generations of veterans may enter a general population in which only a small percentage of citizens has served in the military, possibly resulting in lack of understanding (Castro & Kintzle, 2014). As a result, veterans may not find social and community support they need. Third, OEF/OIF/OND veterans tend to have experienced more and longer deployments than veterans of previous wars (Chandra et al., 2010); prolonged combat experiences are related to suicide risk (Bruce, 2010).

Individual Transitions: Spouses

_____ **Vignette** _____

Steve Mosier (age 37), a medically retired OEF veteran, came back from his last deployment with a severe TBI from a roadside bomb in Afghanistan. He also suffers from PTSD. Although Steve has made significant progress in his cognitive functioning, he still has problems with memory, concentration, and fatigue after a year of treatment. These symptoms, combined with symptoms of PTSD, make it hard for him to hold a steady job. His wife, Dana (age 37), manages most of the household and parenting responsibilities, Steve's medical and rehabilitation appointments, and her part-time job with help from their teenage son, Kevin (age 15). Dana often reports being overwhelmed with all the responsibilities and feeling depressed. Kevin misses the time spent with his dad before the injury. They used to build model planes together, which is harder now because his dad gets tired very quickly and has trouble concentrating on things. Their 10-year-old daughter, Tina, does not feel really close to Steve because Steve had been in and out of her life due to three deployments. Most of the time, she avoids interacting with him.

• • •

Military service dictates many aspects of families' lives. For example, many military families move frequently and experience many separations, both short and long for training or deployments. The demands of military life on families fall heavily on spouses. For example, frequent relocations have negative impacts on the careers of military spouses. Compared to civilian wives, military wives in one large national study were 9% less likely to be employed and, when employed, tended to earn 14% less than civilian wives of similar background between 2005 and 2011 (Hosek & MacDermid Wadsworth, 2013).

Deployments pose additional challenges to spouses of service members. During deployment, spouses assume additional household and parenting responsibilities. Furthermore, spouses may constantly worry about the safety of deployed service members while also trying to provide emotional support for them, as well as children or other family members. Thus, it is not surprising that spouses of service members reported depression (12.2%) and anxiety disorders (17.4%) during deployment at rates similar to rates among service members following deployment (depression, 14.2% to 14.7%, and anxiety, 15.7% to 17.5%; Eaton et al., 2008) and higher than spouses not experiencing deployment (23.7% vs. 19.1% for depression and 13.6% vs. 10.8% for anxiety; Mansfield et al., 2010).

After service members return from deployment, new challenges can arise for spouses. Family tasks minor and major, from taking out the garbage to disciplining children, need to be redefined, renegotiated, and redistributed. Some spouses may find it difficult to relinquish their newly acquired autonomy to make decisions (Gambardella, 2008). In addition, partners in some couples struggle to reconnect and communicate with each other following deployment (Knobloch & Theiss, 2012). Spouses report elevated rates of depression, anxiety, PTSD, and relationship difficulties during the reunion period. The challenges are even greater for spouses with injured service members (Institute of Medicine, 2013); these are discussed later.

Deployments may have additional negative implications for spouses' employment. Spouses often report deployments as a major factor in employment-related difficulties, especially when they have children. Juggling work and family while functioning as a single parent during deployment can be difficult. Moreover, their earnings may not be enough to cover increased child-care expenses, although the special combat pay provided during deployments is helpful. Thus, many spouses leave paid employment during deployment (Institute of Medicine, 2013). Finding a job after service members return home may not be easy.

In summary, military spouses share many aspects of military transitions with service members. Often, military spouses must shoulder the bulk of family responsibilities with limited help from service members. The challenges of the military lifestyle may become more intense during and after deployments, sometimes with negative implications for the psychological well-being of military spouses. Disruption in military spouses' employment while service members are in the military may have long-lasting effects on their career trajectories.

Individual Transitions: Children

In general, military children function as well as or better than civilian children in many respects (Park, 2011). For example, military children report similar rates of psychological and physical health problems as civilian children (Jeffereys & Leitzel, 2000). Moreover, one study found lower percentages of military adolescents engaging in risky behaviors such as sexual activity and use of alcohol and cigarettes than among civilian adolescents (Hutchinson, 2006).

Many studies report negative impacts of parental deployments during OIF/OEF/OND on children. Similar to spouses, children's well-being is negatively related to cumulative duration of deployments (Chandra et al., 2010). In general, children with a deployed parent displayed higher levels of emotional and social difficulties than the general population of children (Lester et al., 2010). A recent study (Card et al., 2011) reviewed 16 studies and concluded that deployment had small negative effects ($r = 0.08$) on children's overall adjustment and academic performance. However, the magnitude of the negative effects varied by age. The negative effects were strongest during middle childhood (6 to 11 years, $r = 16$ to 22) and weakest for adolescents (12 to 18 years).

Research findings consistently demonstrate that children's emotional, social, and academic problems in the context of deployment and reintegration depend on the well-being of the nondeployed parent at home. When nondeployed parents experience higher levels of distress, their children often do exhibit more social and emotional problems (Chandra et al., 2010).

New challenges after deployed parents return home include fitting the returning parent back into family routines, re-establishing closeness in the parents' relationship, and reconnecting with the returning parent (Chandra et al., 2010). In Tina's case in the second vignette, her dad had been gone for a great portion of her life, possibly making it more difficult to establish a secure relationship with her. Tina was having a harder time connecting with her dad than was her brother, who had developed a secure bond with his dad before the deployments started.

In summary, there is evidence that parental deployments have negative effects on children's outcomes. However, most research on the effects of parental deployments on children has examined short-term outcomes (Lester et al., 2010). It is hard to determine how parental deployments during childhood influence trajectories of educational achievement or well-being over the life course without longitudinal evidence. Moreover, it is important to note that military children have many protective factors through the military benefits provided to their parents, including access to health care and allowances for housing and child care when their parents are serving on active duty.

Linked Lives: Family Transitions

In general, military service has positive long-term effects on families, especially ethnic minority families (Burland & Lundquist, 2013). However, wartime deployments and subsequent combat exposure may have negative impacts on some families (Paley, Lester, & Mogil, 2013). In the following sections, we discuss some transitions that affect family relationships.

Couple Relationships

Deployment presents many challenges to marital relationships. During deployments, spouses at home have to deal with daily family and parenting responsibilities with limited help from their spouse, as well as loneliness and worries about the safety of the service member (SteelFisher, Zaslavsky, & Blendon, 2008). Both at-home spouses and service members report challenges of maintaining connections with each other and experiencing uncertainty about their relationship during deployment (Sahlstein, Maguire, & Timmerman, 2009). Service members' return home also creates new challenges. For example, couples sometimes have trouble renegotiating roles and responsibilities (Baptist et al., 2011).

Communication during and after deployment also impacts marital relationships (Baptist et al., 2011; Carter et al., 2011). During deployment, both spouses and service members struggle to balance their need to communicate in order to feel connected and their need to limit the information they share with their spouse in order to keep them from worrying (Baptist et al., 2011). A study of wives of deployed service members who limited information sharing to protect their husbands showed that they reported lower physical and mental health, whereas wives who disclosed stressful situations to their husbands reported higher marital satisfaction after deployment (Joseph & Afifi, 2010).

Some studies examine frequencies and methods of communication during deployment to determine which are most beneficial to postdeployment adjustment. Ponder and Aguirre (2012) found that service members who communicated daily with their spouses reported higher marital satisfaction after deployment than those who communicated with their spouses less than once per week. They also found that use of traditional mail was related to higher marital satisfaction compared to other methods of communication such as emails and telephone calls. It may be because letters provide a sense of privacy and security that other methods do not. Moreover, hand-written messages may appear as more tangible evidence of love and support (Carter et al., 2011). However, the benefits of frequent communication also depend on marital quality prior to deployment. Carter and colleagues (2011) found that more frequent communication during deployment was related to lower PTSD symptoms only for service members with higher marital satisfaction prior to deployment.

The relationship between deployment and marital quality is complex, and deployment does not affect every marriage in the same way. For example, a retrospective study of wives whose husbands had been deployed found five different trajectories of marital satisfaction across the deployment cycle (steady, decreasing, increasing, turbulent, and dipped) (Parcell & Maguire, 2014). Deployment itself did not necessarily reduce marital quality. Rather, the nature of the deployment and the marital relationship were more influential for marital quality following deployment. Studies consistently report strong negative associations of marital problems with combat experiences and PTSD (Institute of Medicine, 2013). In addition, long cumulative durations of deployments (Chandra et al., 2011), rather than their frequencies, and unexpected deployment extensions (SteelFisher et al., 2008) also seem to negatively impact marital relationships. Regarding the nature of marriages, marital quality prior to deployment, the ability to exchange mutual support during deployment, and having religious beliefs (Baptist et al., 2011) seem important to marital relationships after deployment.

Findings about the impact of deployment on divorce are not yet conclusive. Using data from the Defense Manpower Data Center (DMDC) that depict service members' marital and deployment histories, Karney and Crown (2007) examined divorce trends between 2002 and 2005 among service members who married during that period and found that longer deployments were related to lower risk of divorce. However, in another study, also using the data from the DMDC, Negrusa, Negrusa, and Hosek (2014) expanded the time frame to between 1999 and 2008 and found that longer cumulative months of deployments were related to increased risk of divorce. The predicted divorce rate within 2 years of marriage for service members returning from 6-month deployments was 1.4%, increasing to 1.5%, 1.8%, and above 2% with each 6-month increase. So, for example, by 3 years beyond the start of their marriages, 12.4% of couples who had experienced 6 months of deployment had divorced, compared to 8.4% of couples who had not experienced deployment. Both studies (Karney & Crown, 2007; Negrusa et al., 2014) found, however, that the negative impact of deployment on divorce risk was stronger for female service members.

Child Maltreatment

The estimated rate of child maltreatment rate in military families in 2012 was 6.1 per 1,000 children (U.S. Department of Defense, 2013), which was less than the 9.2 per

1,000 children in the U.S. civilian population (U.S. Department of Health & Human Services, 2013). Although there is as yet no explanation, one possible reason for the lower rate is that the military provides many child maltreatment prevention programs. The rate of child maltreatment in the military has fluctuated, however. Specifically, rates steadily increased from 5.8 % in 2001 to 6.4 % in 2004, followed by a decrease to 4.3 % in 2009. Currently the rates are again rising. The reason for the fluctuation is not clear yet. To understand the changing trend, more studies are needed examining the impact of different aspects of deployment such as number and duration of deployments and the effectiveness of the prevention programs the military offers (McCarroll, Fan, Newby, & Ursano, 2008).

Parental deployment is a significant risk factor for child maltreatment. Between 2001 and 2004, the rate of child maltreatment in families of Army solders with at least one combat deployment overall increased about 60 %. Moreover, the rate of physical abuse by nondeployed parents doubled, and the rate of neglect quadrupled during the same period (Gibbs, Martin, Kupper, & Johnson, 2007). Service members' departures to, as well as return from, deployments have been found to be related to increases in military child maltreatment (Rentz et al., 2007). In a recent study of Air Force families where maltreatment had previously occurred, there were more maltreatment cases by deploying parents prior to than following deployment, however (Thomsen et al., 2014), and the rate of child maltreatment by at-home parents was highest during deployment (McCarthy et al., 2013). These findings illustrate how the transition-related stressors may influence family members differently.

Families of Injured Veterans

Service members' injuries may have significant effects on family relationships, and family members may need to adjust their lives to changing needs of the injured veterans as they recover. In most cases, like in the Mosier family of Vignette 2, family members are the primary sources of practical support (e.g., managing doctors' appointments and household tasks, assisting the injured veteran with daily activities, etc.) and providing emotional support. Many military family caregivers face unique challenges, such as dealing with multiple injuries and navigating complex care systems, sometimes for many years. In the Mosier family, Dana takes on all these responsibilities herself while managing her part-time job and caring for the children.

Spouses of injured veterans often become the primary caregiver, placing them at risk for high stress. In general, spouses of injured veterans, like Dana, report higher levels of distress and depression. They also report relationship distress and, in the cases of PTSD especially, physical and psychological intimate partner violence (Institute of Medicine, 2013).

Service members' injuries also have direct and indirect impacts on children. Some injuries prevent service members from actively participating in parenting or joining certain family activities, thus spending less time with their children. Some service members may return home substantially changed by their experiences. Many mental disorders such as depression, PTSD, and TBI are related to changes in mood, personality, or cognitive function. In these cases, children may feel uncertain about their parents or even avoid them (Sayers, 2011), as Tina in the Mosier family does. When changes are drastic or permanent, children have to deal with the loss of the parents they used to know. Children also may experience sadness or confusion over the changes. The effects of parental injury differ depending on the developmental status of the children. Younger children may exhibit behavior problems or revert to behaviors they have outgrown (e.g., sucking a thumb) while teenagers may withdraw from the family (Cozza, Chun, & Polo, 2005). Older children, like Kevin in the Mosier family in the vignette, also may need to help with taking care of the injured parent, resulting in caregiving challenges for themselves.

As discussed previously, children are very susceptible to their parents' distress. Family life disruptions, including disturbances in routines, changes in discipline, and reduced time spent with children, have been related to higher distress in children (Cozza et al., 2010). In the Mosier family, Steve's participation in family and parenting activities is limited, and Dana's caregiver burden and stress levels are high, potentially making their children more vulnerable to distress.

Families Coping With Loss

As of September 2014, more than 6,800 service members (approximately 0.3%) had died as a result of injuries acquired during OEF, OIF, and OND (U.S. Department of Defense, 2014), and the suicide rate among members of the Armed Forces also had increased substantially. Although many scholars agree that the grieving processes in military families are similar to those in civilian families, Cohen and Mannarino (2004) identified some aspects unique to military death that may make grief more complicated. First, death by injury or suicide may occur during as well as following deployment. Second, during a deployment, families are constantly aware of the danger service members are facing and hopeful that they will never receive an unexpected knock on the door, notifying them of injury or death of their loved ones. Third, with combat death, there are chances that the family may recover only parts of the remains or may not have remains at all. Fourth, with the death of the service member, families who were living in military installations may have to move away from their friends and social support. In contrast, military families also receive a variety of supports after the injury or death of a service member. In particular, families may receive a military funeral, financial support, and health care, depending upon their service member's status and military rules regarding family eligibility (i.e., spouses and children are more likely to receive supports than are parents or adult siblings). Moreover, some family members take great pride and attribute great meaning to their loved one's combat death (Cozza, 2011).

The grieving process of spouses or partners of deceased service members is important for themselves as well as for their children. Children seem to adjust better after a service member parent's death when the surviving parent is doing better and parenting more effectively. Too much emotional disturbance on the part of the surviving parent (Cozza et al., 2005) may lead to more problems for children as they grieve. In summary, some family transitions after deployment are challenging to military families. Although it will be some time before we fully understand the long-term effects of the current wars on family trajectories, some of the transitions we have discussed have the potential to alter veteran families' lives enormously. For this reason, it may be important to identify more vulnerable families and their needs in order to be able to provide appropriate support.

Prevention and Intervention

There are many prevention and intervention programs available to military families, made possible by the efforts of government and military leaders, employers, universities, philanthropic organizations, and others. Three examples from different sources with strong evidence of success are discussed here. The GI Bill is a government and military effort with a long history. The 100,000 Jobs Mission is an effort led by civilian employers to help veterans. Families Overcoming Under Stress (FOCUS) is a partnership between military organizations and a university.

GI Bill

Military service can interrupt or delay service members' pursuit of higher education. Since the end of World War II, a series of "GI Bills" has addressed these interruptions or delays by providing financial support for the pursuit of higher education. GI Bills also have provided many veterans with educational opportunities they otherwise could not have afforded. For example, approximately 7.8 million World War II veterans and 3 million Korean War veterans have used GI Bill benefits for education, and these veterans have higher levels of education and earnings than those who did not use GI Bill benefits (Stanley, 2003). More than 8 million Vietnam veterans used GI Bill benefits for education (Bound & Turner, 2002).

The 2009 Post-9/11 GI Bill provides more financial aid for education than its predecessors. For example, compared to the Montgomery GI Bill, the most recent predecessor, the Post-9/11 GI Bill added a stipend for housing and books. Moreover, it allows veterans to transfer their educational benefits to their spouses or children (U.S. Department of Veterans Affairs, 2014). Information on the effects of the Post-9/11 GI Bill is still preliminary and expected to change over time, as the first 4-year graduates have just completed their educations. Approximately 1 million OEF/OIF/OND veterans used the GI bill between 2002 and 2010, and 51.7% of them earned a degree or certificate they were pursuing within 8 years, a rate similar to nonveteran students (Student Veterans of America, 2014).

100,000 Jobs Mission

The 100,000 Jobs Mission (www.veteranjobsmission.com) is an effort led by civilian employers to help veterans successfully reintegrate into civilian society. In 2011, 11 large companies formed a coalition with the goal of hiring 100,000 veterans by 2020. They also committed to sharing information regarding quarterly hiring numbers and best practices. At of the end of September, 2014, they had hired 190,046 veterans, and the coalition had grown to include more than 170 companies. After exceeding their original goal, they set a new goal of hiring 200,000 by 2020. The 100,000 Jobs Mission website serves as a place where veterans and employers can connect by providing resources and tools for both veterans and employers, including job listings, interview tips, and best practices.

Families Overcoming Under Stress (FOCUS)

FOCUS was originally developed by the University of California, Los Angeles (UCLA) and Harvard Medical School to help children and their families dealing with high stress. Since being adapted for military families dealing with deployment, FOCUS has been implemented at the Army, Navy, Marine Corps, and Air Force installations. Responding to diverse family needs, FOCUS now has been adapted for families with children between the ages of 3 and 5, families without children, and families dealing with wounds and injuries (Mogil et al., 2010).

FOCUS is an evidence-based and standardized prevention program for families. The training focuses on psychoeducation, emotional regulation skills, goal setting and problem-solving skills, techniques for managing traumatic stress reminders, and family communication skills (Lester et al., 2011). An evaluation of the effectiveness of FOCUS (Lester et al., 2012) found significant improvement in psychological distress of both service members and nonservice member parents, family functioning, children's behavioral problems and prosocial behaviors, and children's use of positive coping strategies. Participants' satisfaction with the program was also high.

CONCLUSION AND RECOMMENDATIONS

Despite the challenges that deployments and separating from the military pose for families, research suggests that most families successfully adjust to these transitions and changes. However, research also finds that some challenges are more stressful than others, and some individuals and families are at higher risk than others. Therefore, individual challenges and adjustments need to be understood in their historical and relational contexts. When comparing veterans of the current wars to veterans of previous wars, there are both similarities (e.g., education attainment) and differences (e.g., unemployment rate and suicide rate). Furthermore, veterans' deployment history and adjustment are related to the adjustment of spouses and children. It is still too early to draw conclusions about the effects of recent deployments on military families. Some challenges such as physical and psychological injuries may have long-term consequences. Thus, more longitudinal research is needed to determine how, if any, deployments change life trajectories of veteran families over time and why some families adjust better after deployment than others. Last, more attention is needed about families of same sex couples. Despite the recent repeal of "Don't Ask, Don't Tell," there are few studies on families of same sex couples in the military. Their experiences and challenges of transitioning after deployment may be different from other families.

As mentioned at the beginning of this chapter, OEF/OIF/OND veterans and their families are entering civilian communities that may lack understanding of military culture and, most of all, deployment experiences. Helping veterans and their families during this transition period may require concerted efforts from various sources. First of all, raising awareness about the challenges of veteran families in the community as a whole is necessary for successful reintegration. Communities can provide resources such as job placement, housing information, and treatment services. Second, colleges and universities can support the success of student veterans in higher education settings by identifying veterans early in the enrollment process and making and providing available resources. Third, employers in the community can reduce barriers to hiring veterans. Employers can be made aware of how military skills can be transferred into civilian jobs. Creating work environments that are sensitive to military culture, where veterans feel respected and understood may help to increase veterans' commitment to the employer. Finally, helping professionals need to be trained in military culture and challenges of veteran families to effectively assist them. Moreover, they need to be aware of community resources available to veteran families in order to refer the families to appropriate resources when needed.

REFERENCES

Armed Forces Health Surveillance Center. (2012). Death by suicide while on active duty, active and reserve components, US Armed Forces, 1998–2011. *Medical Surveillance Monthly Report, 19*(6), 2–11.

Aud, S., Hussar, W., Kena, G., Bianco, K., Frohlich, L., Kemp, J., & Tahan, K. (2011). *The condition of education 2011* (NCES 2011-033). Washington, DC: National Center for Education Statistics.

Baptist, J. A., Amanor-Boadu, Y., Garrett, K., Goff, B. S. N., Collum, J., Gamble, P., . . . Wick, S. (2011). Military marriages: The aftermath of Operation Iraqi Freedom (OIF) and Operation Enduring Freedom (OEF) deployments. *Contemporary Family Therapy, 33*(3), 199–214.

Belmont, P. J., Goodman, G. P., Zacchilli, M., Posner, M., Evans, C., & Owens, B. D. (2010). Incidence and epidemiology of combat injuries sustained during "the surge" portion of Operation Iraqi Freedom by a U.S. Army brigade combat team. *The Journal of Trauma: Injury, Infection, and Critical Care, 68*(1), 204–210.

Black, S. A., Gallaway, M. S., Bell, M. R., & Ritchie, E. C. (2011). Prevalence and risk factors associated with suicides of Army soldiers 2001–2009. *Military Psychology, 23*(4), 433–451.

Bound, J., & Turner, S. (2002). Going to war and going to college: Did World War II and the G.I. Bill increase educational attainment for returning veterans? *Journal of Labor Economics, 20*(4), 784–815.

Bruce, M. L. (2010). Suicide risk and prevention in veteran populations. *Annals of the New York Academy of Sciences, 1208*(1), 98–103.

Bureau of Labor Statistics (2014). *Employment situation of veterans summary*. Retrieved from http://www.bls.gov/news.release/vet.nr0.htm

Burland, D., & Lundquist, J. H. (2013). The best years of our lives: Military service and family relationships-A life-course perspective. In J. M. Wilmoth & A. S. London (Eds.), *Life course perspectives on military service* (pp. 165–184). New York, NY: Routledge.

Card, N. A., Bosch, L., Casper, D. M., Wiggs, C. B., Hawkins, S. A., Schlomer, G. L., & Borden, L. M. (2011). A meta-analytic review of internalizing, externalizing, and academic adjustment among children of deployed military service members. *Journal of Family Psychology, 25*(4), 508–520.

Carter, S., Loew, B., Allen, E., Stanley, S., Rhoades, G., & Markman, H. (2011). Relationships between soldiers' PTSD symptoms and spousal communication during deployment. *Journal of Traumatic Stress, 24*(3), 352–355.

Castro, C. A., & Kintzle, S. (2014). Suicides in the military: The post-modern combat veteran and the Hemingway effect. *Current Psychiatry Reports, 16*(8), 1–9.

Chandra, A., Burns, R. M., Tanielian, T., Jaycox, L. H., & Scott, M. M. (2008). *Understanding the impact of deployment on children and families*. Santa Monica, CA: Rand.

Chandra, A., Lara-Cinisomo, S., Jaycox, L. H., Tanielian, T., Burns, R. M., Ruder, T., & Han, B. (2010). Children on the homefront: The experience of children from military families. *Pediatrics, 125*(1), 16–25.

Chandra, A., Lara-Cinisomo, S., Jaycox, L. H., Tanielian, T., Han, B., Burns, R. M., & Ruder, T. (2011). *Views from the homefront*. Santa Monica, CA: Rand.

Cohen, J. A., & Mannarino, A. P. (2004). Treatment of childhood traumatic grief. *Journal of Clinical Child & Adolescent Psychology, 33*(4), 819–831.

Cozza, S. J. (2011). Meeting the wartime needs of military children and adolescents. In J. Ruzek, P. Schnurr, J. Vasterling, & M. Friedman (Eds.), *Caring for veterans with deployment-related stress disorders* (pp. 171–190). Washington, DC: American Psychological Association.

Cozza, S. J., Chun, R. S., & Polo, J. A. (2005). Military families and children during Operation Iraqi Freedom. *Psychiatric Quarterly, 76*(4), 371–378.

Cozza, S. J., Guimond, J. M., McKibben, J. B. A., Chun, R. S., Arata-Maiers, T. L., Schneider, B., Ursano, R. J. (2010). Combat-injured service members and their families: The relationship of child distress and spouse-perceived family distress and disruption. *Journal of Traumatic Stress, 23*(1), 112–115.

Durdella, N. R., & Kim, Y. K. (2012). Understanding patterns of college outcomes among student veterans. *Journal of Studies in Education, 2*(2), 109–129.

Eaton, K. M., Hoge, C. W., Messer, S. C., Whitt, A. A., Cabrera, O. A., McGurk, D., Castro, C. A. (2008). Prevalence of mental health problems, treatment need, and barriers to care among primary care-seeking spouses of military service members involved in Iraq and Afghanistan deployments. *Military Medicine, 173*(11), 1051–1056.

Elder, G. H. (1998). The life course as developmental theory. *Child Development, 69*(1), 1–12.

Gambardella, L. C. (2008). Role-exit theory and marital discord following extended military deployment. *Perspectives in Psychiatric Care, 44*(3), 169–174.

Gibbs, D. A., Martin, S. L., Kupper, L.L., & Johnson, R.E. (2007). Child maltreatment in enlisted soldiers' families during combat-related deployments. *JAMA, 298*(5), 528–535.

Holder, K. A. (2007). Exploring the veteran-nonveteran earnings differential in the 2005 American Community Survey. Paper presented at American Sociological Association annual meeting, New York, NY.

Hosek, J., & MacDermid Wadsworth, S. M. (2013). Economic conditions of military families. *The Future of Children, 23*(2), 41–59.

Hutchinson, J. W. (2006). Evaluating risk-taking behaviors of youth in military families. *Journal of Adolescent Health, 39*(6), 927–928.

Institute of Medicine. (2008). *Gulf War and health: Volume 6. Physiologic, psychologic, and psychosocial effects of deployment-related stress*. Washington, DC: The National Academic Press.

Institute of Medicine. (2013). *Returning home from Iraq and Afghanistan: Assessment of readjustment needs of veterans, service members, and their families*. Washington, DC: The National Academies Press.

Jeffereys, D. J., & Leitzel, J. D. (2000). The strengths and vulnerabilities of adolescents in military families. In J. A. Martin, L. N. Rosen, & L. R. Sparacino (Eds.), *The military family: A practice guide for human service providers* (pp. 225–240). Westport, CT: Praeger.

Joseph, A. L., & Afifi, T. D. (2010). Military wives' stressful disclosures to their deployed husbands: The role of protective buffering. *Journal of Applied Communication Research, 38*(4), 412–434.

Kaplan, M. S., McFarland, B. H., Huguet, N., & Valenstein, M. (2012). Suicide risk and precipitating circumstances among young, middle-aged, and older male veterans. *American Journal of Public Health, 102*(S1), S131–7.

Karney, B. R., & Crown, J. S. (2007). *Families under stress: an assessment of data, theory, and research on marriage and divorce in the military* (Vol. 599). Santa Monica, CA: Rand.

Kessler, R. C., Berglund, P, Demler, O., Jin R., Merikangas, K. R., & Walters, E. E. (2005). Lifetime prevalence and age-of-onset distributions of DSM-IV disorders in the national comorbidity survey replication. *Archives of General Psychiatry, 62*(6), 593–602.

Knobloch, L. K., & Theiss, J. A. (2012). Experiences of U.S. military couples during the post-deployment transition: Applying the relational turbulence model. *Journal of Social and Personal Relationships, 29*(4), 423–450.

Lester, P., Mogil, C., Saltzman, W., Woodward, K., Nash, W., Leskin, G., Beardslee, W. (2011). Families overcoming under stress: Implementing family-centered prevention for military families facing wartime deployments and combat operational stress. *Military Medicine, 176*(1), 19–25.

Lester, P., Peterson, K., Reeves, J., Knauss, L., Glover, D., Mogil, C., Beardslee, W. (2010). The long war and parental combat deployment: Effects on military children and at-home spouses. *Journal of the American Academy of Child & Adolescent Psychiatry, 49*(4), 310–320.

Lester, P., Saltzman, W. R., Woodward, K., Glover, D., Leskin, G. A., Bursch, B., Beardslee, W. (2012). Evaluation of a family-centered prevention intervention for military children and families facing wartime deployments. *American Journal of Public Health, 102*(S1), S48–S54.

MacLean, A., & Elder, G. H. (2007). Military service in the life course. *Annual Review of Sociology, 33*(1), 175–196.

Mansfield, A. J., Kaufman, J. S., Marshall, S. W., Gaynes, B. N., Morrissey, J. P., & Engel, C. C. (2010). Deployment and the use of mental health services among U.S. Army wives. *New England Journal of Medicine, 362*(2), 101–109.

McCarroll, J. E., Fan, Z., Newby, J. H., & Ursano, R. J. (2008). Trends in U.S. Army child maltreatment reports: 1990–2004. *Child Abuse Review, 17*, 108–118.

McCarthy, R. J., Rabenhorst, M. M., Thomsen, C. J., Milner, J. S., Travis, W. J., Copeland, C. W., & Foster, R. E. (2013). Child maltreatment among civilian parents before, during, and after deployment in United States Air Force Families. *Psychology of Violence*. Advance online publication.

Mogil, C., Paley, B., Doud, T. D., Havens, L., Moore-Tyson, J., Beardslee, W. R., & Lester, P. (2010). Families Overcoming Under Stress (FOCUS) for early childhood. *Zero to Three*, September, 10–16.

Negrusa, S., Negrusa, B., & Hosek, J. (2014). Gone to war: Have deployments increased divorces? *Journal of Population Economics, 27*(2), 473–496.

Paley, B., Lester, P., & Mogil, C. (2013). Family systems and ecological perspectives on the impact of deployment on military families. *Clinical Child and Family Psychology Review, 16*, 245–265.

Parcell, E. S., & Maguire, K. C. (2014). Turning points and trajectories in military deployment. *Journal of Family Communication, 14*(2), 129–148.

Park, N. (2011). Military children and families: Strengths and challenges during peace and war. *American Psychologist, 66*(1), 65–72.

Ponder, W. N., & Aguirre, R. T. P. (2012). Internet-based spousal communication during deployment: Does it increase post-deployment marital satisfaction? *Advances in Social Work, 13*(1), 216–228.

Rentz, E. D., Marshall, S. W., Loomis, D., Casteel, C., Martin, S. L., & Gibbs, D. A. (2007). Effect of deployment on the occurrence of child maltreatment in military and nonmilitary families. *American Journal of Epidemiology, 165*(10), 1199–1206.

Rumann, C. B., & Hamrick, F. A. (2010). Student veterans in transition: Re-enrolling after war zone deployments. *The Journal of Higher Education, 81*(4), 431–458.

Sahlstein, E., Maguire, K. C., & Timmerman, L. (2009). Contradictions and praxis contextualized by wartime deployment: Wives' perspectives revealed through relational dialectics. *Communication Monographs, 76*(4), 421–442.

Sayers, S. L. (2011). Family reintegration difficulties and couples therapy for military veterans and their spouses. *Cognitive and Behavioral Practice, 18*(1), 108–119.

Smolenski, D. J., Reger, M. A., Alexander, C. L., Skopp, N. A., Bush, N. E., Luxton, D. D., & Gahm, G. A. (2013). *Department of Defense suicide event report (DoDSER) calendar year 2012 annual report*. Tacoma, WA: National Center for Telehealth and Technology.

Stanley, M. (2003). College education and the midcentury GI Bills. *The Quarterly Journal of Economics, 118*(2), 671–708.

SteelFisher, G. K., Zaslavsky, A. M., & Blendon, R. J. (2008). Health-related impact of deployment extensions on spouses of active duty Army personnel. *Military Medicine, 173*(3), 221–229.

Student Veterans of America. (2014). *Million record project: A review of veteran achievement in higher education*. Retrieved from http://studentveterans.org/images/Reingold_Materials/mrp/download-materials/mrp_Full_report.pdf

Tanielian, T. L., & Jaycox, L. (2008). *Invisible wounds of war: Psychological and cognitive injuries, their consequences, and services to assist recovery*. Santa Monica, CA: Rand.

Thomsen, C. J., Rabenhorst, M. M., McCarthy, R. J., Milner, J. S., Travis, W. J., Foster, R. E., & Copeland, C. W. (2014). Child maltreatment before and after combat-related deployment among active-duty United States Air Force maltreating parents. *Psychology of Violence, 4*(2), 143–155.

U.S. Department of Defense. (2009). *DOD/VA code proposal final*. Washington, DC: Author.

U.S. Department of Defense. (2013). *Department of Defense family advocacy program child abuse/neglect (CAN) data FY12 report*. Washington, DC: Author.

U.S. Department of Defense. (2014). *U.S. casualty status*. Washington DC: Author. Retrieved from http://www.defense.gov/NEWS/casualty.pdf

U.S. Department of Health & Human Services. (2013). *Child maltreatment* 2012. Washington, DC: Author.

U.S. Department of Veterans Affairs. (2014). *Education and training*. Retrieved October 9, 2014, from http://www.benefits.va.gov/gibill

Xu, J., Kochanek, K. D., Murphy, S. L., & Arias, E. (2014). *Mortality in the United States, 2012* (NCHS data brief, No. 168). Hyattsville, MD: National Center for Health Statistics.

Violence in a Family and Community Context

Promoting Pathways to Resilient Outcomes for Maltreated Children

Margaret O'Dougherty Wright and
Lucy Allbaugh

Several decades of research have clearly demonstrated the negative and enduring consequences of child abuse and neglect on cognitive, emotional, behavioral, social, and physical health outcomes for children over the course of their lives (Cicchetti & Toth, 2005; Gilbert et al., 2009). However, while past research often neglected to study heterogeneity in outcomes among maltreated children, there has been growing interest in examining the processes that might underlie resilient outcomes for some members of this high-risk group (Cicchetti, 2013; Haskett, Nears, Ward, & McPherson, 2006; Jaffee, Caspi, Moffitt, Polo-Tomas, & Taylor, 2007). To gain a better understanding of what might predict these divergent life pathways, this chapter focuses on data gleaned from longitudinal studies that have examined a wide range of developmental outcomes. The chapter highlights what is known about factors that heighten risk for psychopathology and behavioral dysfunction following child maltreatment, as well as factors that promote positive adaptation and that protect or mitigate against adverse, enduring effects. Promising interventions to foster resilience and recovery following child maltreatment are also reviewed.

Resilience following child maltreatment is conceptualized as a dynamic, multilevel process, potentially changing over time depending on a variety of contextual factors and relational transactions. Since resilience is typically considered to be a multidetermined process, its presence is inferred in research studies, not measured directly, based on an assessment of both exposure to a risk condition/traumatic experience and subsequent positive adaptation. Our conceptualization of resilience is informed by ecological (Bronfenbrenner, 1979; Cicchetti & Lynch, 1993; Ungar, Ghazinour, & Richter, 2013); family systems (Goldenberg & Goldenberg, 2013; Walsh, 2006); and developmental, organizational, and attachment perspectives (Cicchetti, 2013; Masten, 2014; Sroufe, Egeland, Carlson, & Collins, 2005; Wright, Masten, & Narayan, 2013). We embrace a relational and developmental systems perspective, using the definition of resilience provided by Masten:

> The capacity of a dynamic system to adapt successfully to disturbances that threaten system function, viability, or development. (2014, p. 10)

We view this capacity to adapt as influenced by many interactions within the individual system and with other systems surrounding the individual, ranging from biological and psychological processes within the individual, to the levels of family, community, physical environment, and the broader cultural group in which the individual is embedded (Wright & Masten, 2015). As a result of these dynamic interactions, an individual's adaptive capacity for responding successfully to threat or challenge also depends on other systems' responses to the individual. This is the essence of a dynamic systems model of development. All adaptive (and maladaptive) behavior emerges from continual interactions of systems within the individual (e.g., genes, physiological, and psychological functioning) with systems in the environment, including other people (e.g., family members, extended kin, peers, teachers) and contexts (e.g., physical ecology, educational system, spiritual community, employment opportunities for the family, health care resources). This complexity highlights the importance of adopting an ecological, transactional, life span perspective.

Because of this dynamic interplay between multiple systemic levels, there are many challenges in conducting research on resilience following child maltreatment. Notably, since resilient outcomes reflect dynamic transactions between the person and his or her familial and community support systems, an individual's capacity for resilience can change over time with changing circumstances, the emergence of new threats and challenges, and alterations in access to and availability of social and organizational support (Masten, 2014; Wright & Masten, 2015). Consequently, longitudinal study of adjustment over time is critical in identifying the processes that help to maintain or that disrupt resilient functioning. In addition, given the multidimensional nature of resilience, it is critical to assess a range of outcomes across a variety of domains (e.g., cognitive, emotional, behavioral, social, and health). An individual may be resilient with respect to some adaptive outcomes and not to others, and may be more affected by particular types of stressors and challenges than others. How resilient outcomes are defined and the threshold for determining resilience that is used (e.g., the comparison sample and cutoff scores employed) also needs to be stated explicitly so that findings across studies can be compared. For example, Cicchetti and Rogosch (1997) determined resilience for their maltreated sample in comparison to the functioning assessed in their full sample of at-risk and maltreated individuals. Other studies have assessed success in meeting developmental tasks (Farber & Egeland, 1987) or used normed measures of psychopathology and/or positive adjustment (Kaufman, Cook, Arny, Jones, & Pittinsky, 1994; Sagy & Dotan, 2001). Such methodological differences can significantly impact reported rates of resilience (Haskett et al., 2006). Finally, it would be particularly helpful if studies documented whether the child or family had access to and used interventions that might have significantly altered the family's functioning. This would help to identify important protective influences altering the child's or family's trajectory in a positive direction that might account for some of the diversity in adjustment observed within the group.

RATES OF RESILIENCE AMONG MALTREATED CHILDREN

Longitudinal studies that have examined resilience following severe maltreatment have found evidence for adaptive functioning for some individuals across specific domains of functioning, but unfortunately only a small proportion of individuals consistently demonstrate resilience across a variety of different domains. Rates of resilience vary considerably depending on the definition of resilience, specific assessment measures, and breadth of domains assessed. In a recent prospective study of a nationally representative sample of children who had been involved with child protective services, Jaffee and Gallop (2007) reported that between 37% and 49% of the children demonstrated resilience in at least one domain (i.e., obtained an average score on normed mental health, social functioning, or academic achievement measures) over a 3-year assessment period. However, only 11% to 14% of children were resilient across all three domains at any point in time, and only 2% were consistently resilient across all domains at all assessment periods. These findings are similar to those of other researchers who have used longitudinal designs, multiple indicators of resilience, and sampled children with significant maltreatment histories (e.g., Cicchetti & Rogosch, 1997; DuMont, Widom, & Czaja, 2007; Egeland, Carlson, & Sroufe, 1993; Herrenkohl, Herrenkohl, & Egolf, 1994; Topitzes, Mersky, Dezen, & Reynolds, 2013). When these criteria for resilience are met, typically only 10% to 22% of children with maltreatment histories are classified as resilient. When a high threshold for resilient functioning is employed (e.g., global competence across multiple domains across time), very few maltreated children (0% to 5%) meet the criteria. Many children with severe maltreatment histories, while able to function well in some domains, typically struggle in others and often demonstrate fluctuations in functioning over time and across domains. Of note, rates of resilience in maltreated children tend to be lower than those for children who have experienced other types of family adversity such as parental drug abuse (35%; Luthar, D'Avanzo & Hites, 2003) and poverty (40%; Owens & Shaw, 2003). Since child maltreatment often occurs in the context of both of these types of family stress, the very low rates of resilience in maltreated children may be related to their cumulative exposure to adversity.

There are many reasons why stability in resilient functioning may be difficult to achieve for children with severe maltreatment histories. Their abuse and/or neglect is often characterized by an early onset and enduring nature, which heightens negative consequences (Cicchetti & Toth, 2005). Child maltreatment often occurs in the context of an ongoing relationship, which, particularly those with other family members, typically continues following the incident, allowing for further instances of abuse and neglect. Maltreatment by family members who are supposed to love, protect, and care for you is particularly difficult to understand and assimilate. Such treatment is antithetical to widely held societal values that the family should be a safe, dependable, and nurturing place (American Psychological Association [APA], 1996; Centers for Disease Control [CDC], 2014). Prior research has shown that familial child maltreatment can significantly disrupt the development of secure attachment (Bernard et al., 2012). In such families, the child's source of safety and protection is also a source of danger and distress (Charuvastra & Cloitre, 2008), which can lead to difficulty regulating emotions and internalizing secure expectations of support and assistance (Bowlby, 1988; Sroufe, 2005). In describing the challenges to successful adjustment a child in a maltreating family faces, Cicchetti highlights how dramatically such a home departs from the "average expectable environment" a child needs:

> Child maltreatment constitutes a severe, if not the most severe, environmental hazard to children's adaptive and healthy development. Deprived of many of the experiences believed to promote adaptive functioning across the lifespan, maltreated children traverse a probabilistic pathway characterized by an increased likelihood for a compromised resolution of stage-salient developmental tasks. (2013, pp. 402–403)

In addition, children who experience maltreatment can also be confronted with multiple stressful life experiences, rather than an isolated instance of abuse or neglect. Recent research suggests that it is this cumulative exposure to risk that most strongly predicts negative outcomes (Evans, Li & Whipple, 2013). For example, a child who is abused or neglected by his or her parents might also live in poverty, reside with a parent who struggles with significant psychopathology and/or addiction, live in substandard housing in a dangerous neighborhood, attend a school with inadequate resources and inexperienced teachers, have poor access to medical care, and have limited support outside his or her family. Each of these risk factors might impact different aspects of the child's physical health, psychological well-being, educational achievement, social relationships, and behavioral functioning and/or may interact in a nonadditive fashion to account for the uneven pattern of adaptation often observed in survivors of child maltreatment. This highlights the importance of assessing intensity, timing, and pattern of multiple risk exposure in determining developmental outcomes (Evans et al., 2013).

It is important to note that typically as the number of risk factors rise, assets and/or resources decline (Cicchetti, Rogosch, Lynch, & Holt, 1993; Masten, 2014). This reflects the fact that risk factors and resources are often inversely related to each other and in some cases reflect opposite ends of the same continuum (e.g., low and high IQ; poor- and high-quality parenting; Wright & Masten, 2015). Followikng, a case example from

Another reason resilience may be rare among maltreated children is the absence of protective factors in their life. Children's access to and ability to draw from resources, assets, and protective factors within themselves, their relationships, and their connections to other adaptive systems (Masten, 2014; Wright et al., 2013) are critical in understanding variability in adaptive outcomes following maltreatment. The availability of such resources can significantly influence, ameliorate, and/or alter the impact of maltreatment. Promotive influences (i.e., factors with equally beneficial effects regardless of risk level) and protective factors (i.e., variables that play a special role when risk or adversity is high) that have empirical evidence of acting as either a correlate, mediator, or moderator of resilience following maltreatment are listed in Table 11.1.

Table 11.1   Factors Related to Resilience Following Child Maltreatment

Child Factors
• Positive emotion and good self-regulatory ability
• High self-esteem and feelings of self-worth
• Internal perceptions of control
• Interpersonal reserve and self-reliance
• Good cognitive ability and reading skills
• Academic engagement and motivation
• Active coping skills and ability to process the traumatic experiences
• Good social problem-solving ability
• Abuse specific attributions that are not blaming of self, shaming of self, or excessively hostile toward other peers
Parent Factors
• Strong parent–child attachment with at least one parental figure
• Positive parental perceptions of the child
• Parent knowledge of child development; parental competence
• High levels of positive parenting
• Belief of child's disclosure and support following disclosure
• No continuation of abuse behaviors; abuse incident time limited
• Absence of parental psychopathology
• Adequate income
Family Factors
• Positive family communication and problem solving
• Adequate conflict resolution skills
• Adaptability, flexibility, stability, and cohesion
• Affective involvement and family engagement
Peer and Community Factors
• Presence of a close reciprocal friendship
• Presence of at least one supportive adult
• Stable love relationship history
• Strong educational system available
• Opportunities for parental employment
• Safe neighborhood housing and recreational areas
• Availability of and access to good medical and mental health care
• Social and organizational support available to the family

our longitudinal study (Wright, Allbaugh, Kaufman, Folger, & Noll, 2015) focusing on girls with significant maltreatment histories illustrates the potential importance of understanding multiple risk and protective factors that might be influential in determining outcome.

_____ **Vignette** _____

Janelle (a pseudonym) endured sexual abuse by her stepfather, which began when she was 5 years old and continued until she disclosed the abuse at age 13. She lived with her mother, stepfather, and three siblings and does not believe that others in her family were aware of the abuse until it was revealed to a younger sister and then her mother. To Janelle's relief, her mother was immediately supportive, fully believed the details of the abuse, and quickly alerted the authorities. These parental responses represent significant protective factors that may have helped to ameliorate Janelle's internalization of self-blame, shame, or feelings of powerlessness. Despite her fear, Janelle spoke with police and provided them with the information necessary to arrest her stepfather and send him to jail. She spoke with a counselor shortly after disclosure, and this further helped her understand that the abuse was not her fault. Her siblings supported her by distancing themselves from their stepfather. Janelle later faced additional stressors, including the death of extended family members, violence in her neighborhood, and an adolescent pregnancy. Despite the traumas she endured, she graduated from high school, is currently enrolled in college, and has not struggled with significant psychopathology. She has significant concerns about her daughter becoming a victim of abuse but has developed a range of strategies for keeping her child safe and managing her own anxiety to avoid becoming overwhelmed. While she has struggled at times with maintaining developmentally appropriate expectations of her child, they appear to have a warm, secure bond.

• • •

LONGITUDINAL STUDIES EXAMINING RESILIENT OUTCOMES FOR MALTREATED CHILDREN

Most of the existing research has identified correlates of resilience as opposed to processes involved in resilience. Because we view resilience as a dynamic, transactional process, we believe that longitudinal studies have the greatest potential for identifying protective and mitigating influences, as well as the interactions between individual and environment factors that foster or impede resilience. Protective factors likely vary depending on the child's age and developmental stage, with different variables predicting resilience over time (Haskett et al., 2006). There has also been little attention paid to processes that lead to sustained resilience over time, which can only be accomplished through longitudinal research. Consequently, in this section we focus primarily, although not exclusively, on studies that examine resilience in maltreated children over time and use an ecological multisystems approach. For clarity, we highlight factors that have been identified within the maltreated child, as well as features of the family environment and factors within the broader social context and community (see Table 11.1 for an overview). Wherever possible, interactions across these systems will be reviewed since the manner in which the child responds to and interacts with risk and protective factors at each level of the ecology is what accounts for the diversity in outcomes found among maltreated children.

Characteristics of the Child That Predict Resilience

The child's personal characteristics have been among the most frequently examined factors in research attempting to account for later resilience following child maltreatment (e.g., in Janelle's case, her patience and easy temperament fostered positive coping following additional ongoing stressors). Of note, self-system processes and personality characteristics have often emerged as more central factors in predicting resilient outcomes for maltreated children than have the relationship variables that have been assessed (Cicchetti, 2013). Whereas these latter factors (e.g., perceived emotional availability of mother) have been critical in predicting resilient outcomes in matched comparison samples of nonmaltreated children, they have not always been as salient for children with significant maltreatment histories. In part, this may relate to the large proportion of maltreated children who develop insecure or disorganized attachment relationships with their caregivers (Cyr, Euser, Bakermans-Kranenburg, & Van IJzendoorn, 2010). Consequently, these children might not trust that they can turn to caregivers for support and assistance and so develop alternative, independent means of coping. Personality factors that have emerged as significantly related to later resilience include self-reliance, self-confidence and high self-esteem, ego-control and a more reserved way of interacting with others, and ego-resilience characterized by flexible use of problem-solving strategies (Cicchetti & Rogosch, 1997; Kim & Cicchetti, 2003). Upon reflection, it is not so surprising that these personal characteristics might be more adaptive in the context of a high stress, maltreating home environment where staying attuned to danger, not being demanding, and being cautious and interpersonally reserved might help protect the child from being the target of continued abuse (Cicchetti et al., 1993; Cicchetti & Rogosch, 1997). In a longitudinal investigation exploring personality characteristics associated with resilience, Rogosch and Cicchetti (2004) found two distinct adaptive personality patterns that they labeled "gregarious" and "reserved." Children who had been maltreated, as well as comparison children, who were characterized by these patterns had more adaptive peer relationships than those who were characterized as "dysphoric," "undercontrolled," or "overcontrolled." These findings highlighted the importance of understanding the psychological and biological underpinnings of positive emotion and self-regulation, which have been consistent correlates of resilient outcomes (Cicchetti, 2013; Curtis & Cicchetti, 2007). Prolonged stress, which often results when child maltreatment is severe and chronic, has been related to increased allostatic load, characterized by dysregulated physiological functioning across multiple biological systems. Current research is examining how the regulation of physiological stress response systems is disrupted by abuse and neglect, resulting in vulnerability in other stress sensitive systems (e.g., the sympathetic nervous system, limbic and endocrine systems, and the immune system; Charney, 2004; Cicchetti & Rogosch, 2012).

Many children who have experienced maltreatment have difficulties in school and with peers (Jaffee & Gallop, 2007; Shonk & Cicchetti, 2001; Topitzes et al., 2013). Consequently, cognitive ability and social problem-solving skills have been explored as factors that might be associated with resilient outcomes. There has been inconsistency in the findings and stability of the effects over time with respect to measures of cognitive ability, with some studies not finding IQ or receptive vocabulary assessments predictive of later resilience (Cicchetti et al., 1993; Flores, Cicchetti, & Rogosch, 2005). However, success in school and strong academic motivation can provide a protective buffer for maltreated children and have been correlated with high self-esteem, feelings of self-efficacy, and vocational success (Shonk & Cicchetti, 2001). Traditional indicators of school success, such as high IQ and good receptive vocabulary skills, as well as academic engagement and motivation, help children to function successfully in the school environment (Shonk & Cicchetti, 2001). In the Lehigh longitudinal study (E. Herrenkohl, Herrenkohl, Rupert, Egolf, & Lutz, 1995), maltreated children with higher cognitive functioning in elementary school were more likely to be successful at high school follow-up, although IQ was a less powerful predictor than socioeconomic status (SES) or parenting behaviors. In the Chicago Longitudinal Study, which followed low-income minority participants for 24 years, reading achievement scores in eighth grade were significant mediators of adult resilience (Topitzes et al., 2013). Lower cognitive functioning in maltreated children has also been linked with subsequent antisocial behavior and mental health difficulties (Topitzes, Mersky, & Reynolds, 2011), which suggests that cognitive impairments might impact later resilience through noncognitive domains, in a cascading effect (Masten et al., 2005). Research in this area has also highlighted the importance of interactions between cognitive ability and other contextual influences. For example, in DuMont and colleagues' study (2007), a significant interaction occurred between the maltreated child's cognitive ability and the level of advantage in the child's neighborhood of origin in predicting adult resilience. Participants who had high cognitive ability and grew up in advantaged neighborhoods were three times more likely to be resilient than those from the same type of neighborhood who had lower cognitive ability. However, in less advantaged neighborhoods, these variables were not related.

In Jaffee and colleagues' (2007) longitudinal study, child strengths at ages 5 and 7 played a more important role in distinguishing resilient from nonresilient outcomes for boys than for girls. Boys, but not girls, who demonstrated high IQ had a greater probability of being resilient. The authors speculated that bright boys who were sociable and well-controlled might elicit more positive attention from teachers and other adults than girls with similar strengths, as such behaviors may be less expected in boys, particularly those who come from difficult home environments (Jaffee et al., 2007). However, other research exploring gender differences in adult resilience among abused children has revealed that more women met criteria for resilience, across more domains of functioning, than did men (DuMont et al., 2007). The factors impacting the trajectory of resilience are likely complex and context dependent and influenced by a variety of family and social factors discussed below. How these dynamics change over time for men and women and impact their trajectories has received little attention.

Social competence and good social problem-solving skills also enhance the likelihood that a maltreated child will be successful in forming close peer relationships, an important contributor to a resilient outcome. Child characteristics such as good emotion regulation and high sociability (e.g., extraversion) likely help in the formation and continuation of supportive relationships with both peers and other adult mentors (T. Herrenkohl, 2013). In the Chicago Longitudinal Study (Topitzes et al., 2013), peer social skills directly mediated later adult resilience, and the absence of positive peer social skills, coupled with acting out behaviors at ages 10 to 13, were strong contributors to later juvenile delinquency in adolescence and negative adjustment in adulthood.

In addition, children's internalized schemas, or internal working models, regarding evaluations of the self, others, and expectations for future events and interactions also likely contribute to their adjustment and to the quality of their relationships with others. When children have been exposed to a family environment in which their needs are met, they are more likely to develop positive self-regard and positive expectations of others, while negative evaluations of themselves, others, and the future are more likely in the context of a maltreating environment (see Cicchetti & Lynch, 1995). Evidence has demonstrated the relationship between social-information processing biases and both internalizing symptoms and externalizing behavioral problems (Dodge, 1993; Price & Landsverk, 1998). Processing patterns that reflect biased, hostile, inaccurate, or inept ways of perceiving the social world have been related to peer rejection, aggression, and other psychopathology (Dodge, 1993; Dodge & Coie, 1987).

The social cognitive processes that have received the most research attention have been attributional style and generation of adaptive social response strategies. Research that examined attributions of self-blame for the abuse experience found that self-blaming and self-shaming attributions do contribute unique variance to internalizing problems, even when controlling for abuse severity (McGee, Wolfe, & Wilson, 1997). In Janelle's case, support from her mother and siblings enabled her to access appropriate legal and mental health services. Their support and these resources may have helped her to process and understand this experience, decreasing the likelihood of internalized self-blame for the sexual abuse. Brown and Kolko (1999) also examined the relationship between physical abuse experiences; global and abuse-specific attributions; and level of anxiety, depression, and behavior problems. Both global and abuse specific attributional assessments accounted for significant variance in outcome, beyond that accounted for by abusive parenting. These findings highlight the salience of attributions, which may be as important as the abuse experience itself, in accounting for the development of psychopathology. Price and Landsverk (1998) found that caregiver report of the child's social competence, but not general degree of behavioral problems, was predicted by the degree to which children attributed hostile intent to peer behavior. Maltreated children who processed social information in an unbiased and competent manner were more likely to develop adaptive and competent forms of social responses than children who processed the information in a more biased manner. In contrast to the Brown and Kolko study, Price and Landsverk (1998) found that social problem-solving skills were predictive of both social competence and behavioral problems. Seeking adult assistance, ineffective strategies, and aggressive responses were related to externalizing problems, and ineffective problem-solving strategies predicted internalizing problems. Overall, the findings across these studies suggest the importance of examining attributional style and social problem-solving responses as potential mediating mechanisms linked to later functioning. If attributions and subsequent social responses are a driving force for positive or adverse outcomes for maltreated children, treatment approaches should emphasize social information processing, social problem-solving skills, and cognitive restructuring of attributions as key treatment intervention targets.

Protective Factors Within the Family Environment

While individual child factors have been widely explored with respect to fostering resilience, there are robust findings regarding the importance of parenting practices and the parent–child relationship, individual parent characteristics, and factors related to the larger family context. Interaction between individual child characteristics and the family context are also crucial to consider, as individual level protective factors may function differently within the context of certain family dynamics or parenting practices. A strong longitudinal study (Jaffee et al., 2007) examined individual factors in the context of cumulative life stress (a variable comprised of a range of stressful parenting, family, and community factors). Findings revealed that having fewer stressors differentiated resilient from nonresilient maltreated children with respect to antisocial symptoms, and that individual strengths (i.e., high IQ) predicted increased resilience only in the context of few (less than 4) cumulative stressors. With a high number of stressors, these same strengths actually detracted from later resilience. Thus, it is of utmost importance to understand not only parent and family factors that may promote resilience but also for whom these factors are most salient.

The importance of the parent–child relationship has been widely studied, and specifically it has been established as critical that a child have a strong attachment relationship with at least one stable parental figure (Banyard, Williams, Siegel, & West, 2002; E. Herrenkohl et al., 1994; Siegel, 2000). In Janelle's case, support from her mother and siblings was a key factor in determining her resilient outcome. Strong attachment among child sexual abuse (CSA) survivors to a nonmaltreating mother predicted lower rates of abuse in adult relationships (Siegel, 2000) and high scores on a multidimensional measure of resilience (Banyard et al., 2002). Presence of an affectionate and supportive nonabusing parent was associated with better school achievement among adolescent survivors of child physical abuse (E. Herrenkohl et al., 1994). It is important to note that seemingly contradictory findings suggest that acknowledging a parent's rejection and seeking alternative sources of support and affection also promotes resilience (E. Herrenkohl et al., 1994). This highlights the importance of distinguishing between a bond with a parent who is and one who is not capable of providing warmth and support. In some cases, seeking alternative relationships may be a better strategy for meeting emotional and developmental needs. Those who are able to recognize and accept their situation and feelings, or are more self-reliant generally, may be better poised to seek alternative stable attachment relationships (Cicchetti & Rogosch, 1997).

There are a range of parenting factors associated with increased rates of resilience (likely because they strengthen the attachment bond between parent and child), including the extent to which the parent holds positive perceptions of the child. Such perceptions may include accurate knowledge of child developmental milestones and needs or accurate expectations of the child with respect to both successes and limitations. In particular, the expectation that the child be capable of self-sufficiency was associated with goal setting, determination, and ultimately academic achievement in one small sample longitudinal study (E. Herrenkohl et al., 1994). Smith Slep and O'Leary (2007) found realistic expectations to be correlated with, though not predictive of, a broad measure of child resilience. Attributing blame to the child and use of overly negative discipline strategies has also been associated with aggression by both mother and fathers (Smith Slep & O'Leary, 2007), which is itself associated with less resilient outcomes.

Ongoing parental aggression, particularly ongoing abuse, or any abuse that occurs when the child is relatively older, is related to lower rates of resilience in adult romantic relationships and risk for revictimization (Banyard et al., 2002) and poorer school achievement (E. Herrenkohl et al., 1994). Such findings highlight the importance of positive rather than harsh or aggressive parenting strategies. Emotionally responsive caregiving in particular is a salient protective factor (Egeland et al., 1993). A crucial parenting response for nonmaltreating parents is support following disclosure of the abuse, which includes belief in the child's experiences and nonjudgment and nonblame for the abuse (Elliott & Carnes, 2001). A longitudinal study of female CSA survivors has established that blame, punishment, or disbelief following disclosure of abuse is associated with later dissociative symptoms (Banyard et al., 2002). Children whose parents react with blame to their disclosure of abuse may have a more difficult time coping with their experience and may also have a more difficult time accessing other necessary resources, such as legal intervention, medical, or mental health services. However, having a parent who is supportive and believes the child (as Janelle's mother did) and who can be a secure base from which he or she can embark on recovery, is a significant protective factor. Research findings have indicated that parent support following disclosure may be a better predictor of the child's later adjustment than the specific nature of the abuse experience (Tremblay, Hébert, & Piché, 1999).

With respect to individual parent characteristics, lower rates of parental psychopathology have been associated with greater resilience among maltreated children. Longitudinal data has indicated that parents with fewer antisocial personality traits (Jaffee et al., 2007) and absence of substance use disorders (Banyard et al., 2002; Jaffee et al., 2007) were more able to provide stability to their children, which fostered resilience. However, it is important to note that findings regarding parental antisocial personality traits in the Jaffee and colleagues' (2007) study were only significant among maltreated boys; girls' resilience was somewhat surprisingly not impacted by parents' antisocial symptoms. This highlights the importance of child–environment fit and emphasizes the differential impact that parent and family factors can have on individual children. Other factors, including parent education, occupation, and socioeconomic status, may promote resilience for some survivors. Mersky and Topitzes (2010) found that lower utilization of government assistance predicted high school completion and college attendance among maltreated children. Conversely, among female sexual abuse survivors, Banyard and colleagues (2002) did not find that family income predicted resilience, again highlighting that such factors are far from universal.

Factors related to the overall family environment are also widely implicated in the development of resilience. In Banyard and colleagues' (2002) longitudinal study of female CSA survivors, family of origin difficulty was associated with revictimization in adulthood. Positive family communication, conflict resolution, and problem-solving skills can foster a safer and more stable environment, and overall stability and cohesion of the family unit is important for promoting later well-being in a range of domains (Banyard et al., 2002). Affective involvement of the parents and overall family engagement can be crucial. Physical stability is also important. More frequent moves or changes in foster care placement has predicted lower resilience in adolescence, and although it did not directly predict adult resilience, this type of stability also predicted stability of resilience from adolescence to adulthood (DuMont et al., 2007). Fewer placements predicted resilience among adult CSA survivors (Banyard et al., 2002), and the presence of at least one stable caretaker throughout childhood was protective for some adolescents with physical abuse histories; those with stable caretakers and fewer foster care placements were more likely to complete school and less likely to have serious mental health problems (E. Herrenkohl et al., 1994).

Protective Factors Within the Broader Community Context

Unfortunately, significantly less research has focused on community-level factors. One area that has emerged as significant focuses on the nature of relationships outside the family, particularly with peers and with supportive adult mentors, teachers, or camp counselors. High quality, positive, and reciprocal relationships with peers emerged as a protective factor bolstering self-esteem for maltreated children in the Virginia Longitudinal Study (Bolger, Patterson, & Kupersmidt, 1998). Maltreated children who had a reciprocal friendship were three times more likely to be classified as resilient, and this was particularly the case for children whose maltreatment was chronic and involved physical abuse. Peer acceptance and friendships have been linked to lower engagement in externalizing behaviors among children exposed to domestic violence and harsh discipline practices in the context of ecological disadvantage (Criss, Pettit, Bates, Dodge, & Lapp, 2002). More extensive peer friendships were also protective against later peer victimization for children exposed to harsh, punitive, and hostile family environments (Schwartz, Dodge, Pettit, Bates, 2000). Similarly, adolescents who experienced maltreatment early in their life but had positive peer relationships were also more resilient (Collishaw et al., 2007; Perkins & Jones, 2004). Such friendships might enhance maltreated children's sense of emotional security and provide a much needed context in which to both learn and practice social skills and receive support and affection from others. This opportunity might be especially valuable for maltreated children whose families lack a consistent setting for positive interactions and affirmations of self-worth. However, other research has revealed that close friends might not always be protective and in some circumstances might be associated with increased risk for negative outcomes. It is critical to assess the characteristics of the peers and whether they engage in predominantly prosocial or deviant behaviors. Interactions with peers can provide opportunities for learning antisocial behavior. For example, Perkins and Jones (2004) found that having close friends who engaged in risky behaviors was associated with poorer adjustment, which is consistent with other research indicating the influence of peer group norms on engaging in deviant behavior (Gifford-Smith, Dodge, Dishion, & McCord, 2005).

Evidence is also mixed regarding the protective influence of supportive relationships with adults outside the context of the immediate family. In work by Cicchetti and colleagues (Cicchetti & Rogosch, 1997; Flores et al., 2005), the ability to form a relationship with a camp counselor was associated with later resilience, but interpersonal relationship features were stronger predictors of resilience for similarly disadvantaged but not maltreated comparison children. Their research suggested that one of the deleterious effects of maltreatment might be difficulty in making use of relationships with other adults in order to help them surmount challenges. In the Perkins and Jones (2004) study, support from other adults acted contrary to predictions. Having a close relationship with an adult outside the family increased the maltreated child's risk of engaging in five risky behaviors (i.e., alcohol use, drug use, tobacco use, risky sexual behavior, and suicide) and was surprisingly associated with lower school success. Paralleling the findings obtained with peers, this suggests that for some maltreated individuals, the type of adult that is sought out when support is not available from the family may not provide adaptive guidance or foster success in meeting developmental goals. However, other research has provided some support for the role of outside adults in fostering resilience. In Banyard and colleagues' (2002) study of African American CSA survivors, receiving support from someone special in the women's lives was an important protective factor. Similarly, maltreated individuals involved with highly supportive partners were more likely to be resilient in young adulthood than those without such relationships (DuMont et al., 2007). Finally, in the Minnesota Parent-Child Interaction Project (Pianta, Egeland, & Erickson, 1989), women with a history of maltreatment who were functioning adequately as mothers did report that having had a supportive, caring, and nurturing adult present during their own development was beneficial.

In reflecting on these inconsistent and at times counterintuitive findings, what stands out is that these relational variables (i.e., with parents, peers, partners, other adults) have often been studied in relative isolation and not in interaction with each other over time. The various capacities required to develop well-functioning social relationships and a willingness to rely on others for support likely draw upon the individual's entire history of relational experiences. This includes early attachment and closeness to caregivers, the quality and reliability of ongoing parental and nonparental support, and one's history of social competence with peers (Sroufe et al., 2005). Surprisingly, how these different aspects of the maltreated child's relational history work together has received little attention. Future longitudinal research focusing on how a secure or insecure attachment history specifically impacts subsequent engagement, closeness, and willingness to rely on others would be very helpful in understanding how best to support adaptive pathways to resilient outcomes for these children.

Protective factors at the community level that have been studied in other high risk contexts (e.g., poverty) typically focus on the important role of high-quality schools, availability of extracurricular activities, safe neighborhoods, employment opportunities for parents, participation in religious organizations, and access to good medical and mental health services (Masten, 2014; Wright & Masten, 2015). Since success in school is a strong predictor of positive vocational and mental health outcomes generally, access to high quality schools and positive school climate has received some attention with respect to later resilience for maltreated children. Perkins and Jones (2004) found positive school climate to be associated with lower engagement in in six of seven risky behaviors. Moreover, Sagy and Dotan (2001) found that sense of school membership and support from adults in school and in the community were associated with greater competence and less psychological distress for maltreated children. However, counter to predictions, Perkins and Jones found that engagement in extracurricular activities was associated with more antisocial behaviors in their sample. Similar to their findings on friendships, the characteristics of the peers engaging in the extracurricular activities (e.g., aggressive and substance abusing, vs. conscientious and supportive) may be key to understanding whether participation will lead to problematic or prosocial behaviors.

Not surprisingly, children living in neighborhoods with high crime and low social cohesion and social control are less likely to be resilient, especially when also living within a maltreating family (Jaffee et al., 2007). In addition, cumulative risk models have been strong negative predictors of resilience and outweigh any single risk or protective factor in a number of studies (DuMont et al., 2007; Jaffee et al., 2007). In DuMont and colleagues' (2007) study, those who were continuously resilient over a 25-year period were more likely to be female, had lived with both parents or in a long-term placement as a child, had a supportive partner relationship, and had experienced a low number of additional stressful life events. Across studies in this area, when children faced multiple family and neighborhood stressors in addition to maltreatment, even the presence of individual strengths was not sufficient to protect against later difficulties. These findings support multisystemic interventions that target multiple levels within the child's ecology. As Ungar (2005) suggests, "protective processes are not one dimensional, but interact with the settings in which they appear" (p. xxv). The longitudinal research on resilience in maltreated children to date has advanced a more contextually relevant, transactional understanding of resilience. However, there is still much work to be done to understand how to foster resilience over time. In the next section we highlight clinical interventions that attempt to foster recovery for children and families who have experienced maltreatment and that aim to prevent the intergenerational continuity of maltreatment.

HOW INTERVENTIONS CAN FOSTER RESILIENCE IN MALTREATED CHILDREN

An ecological, transactional theory of resilience has also provided a way of thinking about interventions to foster recovery and promote resilience for maltreated children and their families (Asawa, Hansen, & Flood, 2008; Barlow, Simkiss, & Stewart-Brown, 2006; MacMillan et al., 2009). While the target(s) of intervention may differ, these programs typically focus on factors amenable to change that have been linked to later positive outcomes in empirical research and attempt to avoid decontextualized approaches that often have poor long-term outcomes. Because risk and resilience are determined by dynamic contexts and reciprocal relationships between the children and their environment, intervention models have been designed to intervene at the level of the individual (i.e., individual therapy with the child as the primary target of services), the parent–child dyad (i.e., therapy with the child and his or her parents), and/or the child's community (i.e., the school). Each of these types of intervention is described, and existing evidence of their efficacy is briefly reviewed. We begin with a case study of a highly vulnerable participant from our project (Wright et al., 2015) and highlight key areas of intervention that might serve to alter her high-risk trajectory.

Vignette

Ashley (a pseudonym) grew up in a chaotic and neglectful household in which violent fights between her often-intoxicated parents, emotional abuse from her father, hunger, and intermittent homelessness were common. She had multiple foster placements but always ended up back home in neighborhoods with high levels of poverty and violence. She also became pregnant as a teen, which interfered with high school graduation. She had two children with a partner who eventually left her to raise the children on her own. She had a series of low-paying jobs before being recently fired for unreliability and conflict with others. With nowhere to live and no income, Ashley was forced to choose between moving back with her father, still an active drug user and emotionally abusive, or surrendering her children to foster care. Unable to face such a separation, she moved in with her father who frequently threatened to file false reports of child abuse if she did not give him her meager earnings so that he could purchase drugs. A dearth of protective factors in her life has resulted in ongoing struggles for Ashley as a young adult. She alternately feels emotionally overwhelmed and numb and has frequent panic attacks. She relies on her daughter for emotional support, despite the child's very young age. Though she objects to harsh discipline, she has resorted to shouting at and spanking her children to keep them quiet for fear of eviction. Ashley is struggling significantly, both personally and as a parent. Given the precariousness of her own mental health, her significant current life stress, continuing emotionally abusive treatment by her father, and limited repertoire of coping skills, she may be at risk for abuse or neglect of her own children. There are several promising comprehensive interventions that could help her and that might alter her very high-risk trajectory. Individual therapy might be particularly beneficial in helping Ashley cope with distress related to her profound childhood neglect, abuse, and exposure to parental violence and may provide strategies for coping with significant emotion dysregulation. She might also benefit from an intervention that addresses the multiple aspects of her life that are overwhelming and provides assistance in addressing housing and employment needs. Finally, Ashley and her children might particularly benefit from a parent–child intervention program that bolsters her parenting skills, supports her children's development, and improves overall family functioning.

• • •

INTERVENTIONS AT SPECIFIC LEVELS OF THE ECOSYSTEM

Trauma-Focused Cognitive Behavioral Therapy (TF-CBT)

TF-CBT is a cognitive-behavioral intervention for children ages 3 to 18 with emotional problems following significant traumatic experiences like child maltreatment. While non-offending parents are typically involved, the primary target of services is the individual child. Through a series of modules, children learn skills for processing thoughts, feelings, and behaviors related to the event itself. Parents are simultaneously instructed in specific parenting skills aimed at enhancing safety and improving family communication (e.g., Deblinger, Mannarino, Cohen, Runyon, & Steer, 2011). An extensive literature demonstrates the effectiveness of TF-CBT for reducing child PTSD symptomatology, improving parent emotional well-being, and increasing positive parenting practices (e.g. Cohen, Deblinger, Mannarino, & Steer, 2005; King et al., 2000), and evidence suggests that gains are maintained through 2-year follow-up (Deblinger, Steer, & Lippman, 1999), including among ethnically and socioeconomically diverse samples (e.g., Cohen et al., 2005).

Alternative for Families: A Cognitive Behavioral Therapy (AF-CBT)

Like TF-CBT, AF-CBT is a cognitive-behavioral intervention involving the child and his or her parent(s). However, while TF-CBT considers the child as the target of services and involves primarily nonoffending parents, AF-CBT is an adult-focused, family-centered therapy for reducing child maltreatment by changing parent behavior through instruction of additional skills and changing the overall family environment by addressing family communication and parent symptomatology (e.g., Kolko, Iselin, & Gully 2011). Importantly, AF-CBT has been widely used with ethnically diverse samples of at-risk and maltreating families (Kolko et al., 2011). Both the CBT and family therapy (FT) components of AF-CBT have been found to be associated with reduced parent-to-child and child-to-parent violence; reduced parent–child abuse potential, physical discipline, threats, and anger; fewer overall family problems; improved child social competence; and reduced child symptomatology (Kolko, 1996; Kolko et al., 2011).

Child–Parent Psychotherapy (CPP)

Also known as Infant–Parent Psychotherapy (IPP), Toddler–Parent–Psychotherapy (TPP), and Preschooler–Parent Psychotherapy (PPP), depending on the age of the child), CPP is an intervention based on attachment theory that considers the parent–child relationship as the main recipient of therapeutic services. Through nondirective, nondidactic relational interactions with the parent and child, the therapist models use of reflective functioning, provides psychoeducation about child development, and explores the parent's own maltreatment history (e.g., Lieberman, Van Horn, & Ghosh Ippen, 2005). Given Ashley's significant history of abuse and neglect and continued exposure to very disturbed family of origin relational patterns, this type of intervention might be particularly beneficial for her and her children. It could help Ashley better understand and support her children's developmental needs, reduce her reliance on them to meet her pressing emotional needs, and provide the personal support and guidance to her that has been missing in her life. Other attachment-based, dyadic interventions have been developed, many of which are similar to CPP with respect to the provision of services and the proposed mechanisms of change (e.g., Bernard et al., 2012; Erickson & Egeland, 2004; Marvin, Cooper, Hoffman, & Powell, 2002). Extensive evidence among racially and socioeconomically diverse samples suggests that CPP can improve attachment security and organization (Cicchetti, Rogosch, & Toth, 2006; Stronach, Toth, Rogosch, & Cicchetti, 2013); reduce child internalizing and externalizing behaviors (Dozier et al., 2006; Lieberman et al., 2005; Lieberman, Ghosh Ippen, & Van Horn, 2006); reduce parent distress (Lieberman et al., 2005, 2006); and reduce maltreatment recidivism (Osofsky et al., 2007).

Parent–Child Interaction Therapy (PCIT)

PCIT is another intervention that considers the parent–child dyad as the target of clinical services and includes any important caregivers. PCIT is based on social learning theory, and clinicians teach parents alternative discipline and reward strategies that will help them bond with their child and shape the child's behavior without resorting to aggression or violence (e.g., Chaffin et al., 2004; Eyberg, 1988). This type of intervention might be very helpful to Ashley in teaching positive parenting responses and more effective discipline techniques. PCIT is typically provided in a clinic environment, and parents are asked to practice skills at home between sessions (Chaffin et al., 2004; Timmer et al., 2006). Extensive evidence suggests PCIT as an effective strategy for teaching positive parenting behaviors; reducing observed problematic parenting strategies (Chaffin et al., 2004; Hakman, Chaffin, Funderburk, & Silovsky, 2009); increasing parent emotional well-being (Timmer et al., 2006); and decreasing children's observed problem behaviors and internalizing and externalizing symptoms (e.g., Chaffin et al., 2004; Hakman et al., 2009). PCIT has been found to reduce maltreatment recidivism (Chaffin, Funderburk, Bard, Valle, & Gurwitch 2011; Chaffin et al., 2004), however, when explored separately, this effect was only found for physical abuse and not neglect (Chaffin et al., 2004).

Nurse–Family Partnership (NFP)

NFP is another home-visitation model, based in attachment-theory, targeting the parent–child dyad. It has demonstrated efficacy with individuals whose life circumstances are similar to those of Ashley. It also incorporates self-efficacy theory and an ecological model to conceptualize child developmental needs. Nurses visit first-time moms and their infants in their homes weekly starting during pregnancy and continue until the child is 2 years of age; fathers and other caregivers are included whenever possible. Nurses provide information and guidance on child development, maternal mental health, and the parent-child bond and help support the family in pursuing their educational and occupational goals and facilitate connection with case management (Olds et al., 1997). While NFP was not developed specifically to address maltreatment, it is routinely offered to maltreating and at-risk families, and extensive research has linked NFP to a range of improved outcomes among this population, including reductions in child abuse and neglect, improved parent financial stability, romantic partner stability, child academic functioning, and fewer child injuries due to preventable causes (Olds et al., 2007). Outcomes at 12 years' postintervention also revealed reduced likelihood of youth substance use and internalizing symptoms and increased educational success (Kitzman et al., 2010). Such robust findings have been obtained among racially and socioeconomically diverse samples (Olds et al., 2007).

Incredible Years (IY)

The Incredible Years (IY) series is a set of programs aimed at children, parents, and teachers, that seeks to support child social, emotional, and behavioral development (Webster-Stratton, 1981). Implemented primarily in schools to target classroom behaviors, IY was not designed to intervene specifically with maltreating or at-risk families but targets emotional problems that are commonly the outcome of maltreatment and promotes positive parenting behaviors that can take the place of harsh or violent discipline. Thus, such services can be of huge potential benefit to maltreated children, and IY has been associated with reduced problem behavior, inattention and hyperactivity, and increased social competence and problem-solving skills. The program has also been associated with reduced harsh or physical discipline by parents, increased family communication, parenting confidence, decreased parent psychopathology, and teacher positive verbalizations (Webster-Stratton & Reid, 2010). More recently, IY has been studied in maltreating and at-risk families with promising results including improved parenting practices (i.e., decreased harsh and physical discipline and increased positive verbalizations), improved parent perceptions of the child (Letarte, Normandeau, & Allard, 2010), and improved child behaviors (Hurlburt, Nguyen, Reid, Webster-Stratton, & Zhang, 2013).

INTERVENTIONS TARGETING MULTIPLE SYSTEMS

Multisystemic Therapy (MST)

As the name implies, MST is an intervention that targets multiple ecological systems, including the family, school, and other community groups. MST is based on a social-ecological framework in which all stakeholders (i.e., the child, family members, case workers) are involved in goal setting, selection of specific interventions to address identified target behaviors, and ongoing assessment of progress (e.g., Henggeler, Schoenwald, Borduin, Rowland, & Cunningham, 2009). An adaptation of MST specifically for maltreating and at-risk families (MST for Child Abuse and Neglect; MST-CAN) has been developed that incorporates expanded availability of on-call therapists, ongoing analysis of abuse, and development of a family safety plan (Swenson, Penman, Henggeler, & Rowland, 2010). MST was developed for use with adolescents and is thus a much-needed intervention to address the needs of somewhat older maltreatment survivors. It might have been a particularly helpful intervention for Ashley's family of origin. In trials of MST-CAN with physical abuse survivors (ages ranging 10 to 17), those in MST experienced a more significant decline in PTSD, internalizing, and dissociative symptoms (Schaeffer, Swenson, Tuerk, & Henggeler, 2013; Swenson, Schaeffer, Henggeler, Faldowski, & Mayhew, 2010). Reductions in parent distress and substance use have also been reported (Schaeffer et al., 2013; Swenson, Schaeffer et al., 2010). Importantly, decreased physical and emotional abuse and neglect have been reported by youths (Swenson, Schaeffer et al., 2010) and reflected in child welfare records (Schaeffer et al., 2013) following MST.

Positive Parenting Program (Triple P)

Triple P is another intervention that targets multiple ecological systems including the family, school, and wider community and is a tiered system of programs designed to support families and to prevent and treat child behavioral and emotional problems (e.g., Foster, Prinz, Sanders, & Shapiro, 2008). The first tier is community intervention; information about child developmental difficulties and intervention options is disseminated widely, and parenting discussion groups are formed. Depending on the family's needs, family therapy may be recommended and may include individual, group, or online sessions. Triple P is a program for families of children up to 12 years of age, and Teen Triple P is available for children ages 12 to 16. Triple P has been extensively researched, and a robust body of literature suggests that it can impact a wide variety of outcomes for a range of families. However, comparatively less work has been done with maltreating and at-risk families. Because of the importance of community level implementation, population-level data is perhaps the best way to assess the effects of this program. Such findings suggest that counties in which the Triple P system was implemented had fewer cases of substantiated child maltreatment and fewer reports of maltreatment-related injuries by hospital staff (Prinz, Sanders, Shapiro, Whitaker, & Lutzker, 2009).

CONCLUSION AND FUTURE DIRECTIONS

The case examples of Janelle and Ashley highlight the importance of a comprehensive assessment of risk and protective factors at multiple levels of the child's ecology in order to understand what influences each person's developmental trajectory and how to best intervene. Reflecting on Ashley's specific situation, in order for her trajectory to be effectively altered in a positive direction, the importance of reducing her risk of continued abuse in her current living situation by finding safe alternative housing; assisting in addressing her current mental health, parenting, and employment needs; and helping her to find ways to increase her resources and develop new protective systems and other forms of support stand out as potential points of intervention. Such a multilevel, ecologically informed perspective could be critical in maximizing Ashley's opportunity for a resilient outcome. Janelle's case study reveals the importance of a key turning point in a maltreated child's life, the response to disclosure of abuse. Her mother believed her and took immediate legal action which resulted in a cessation of the sexual abuse and prosecution of the stepfather. Janelle's siblings were also very supportive, and mental health services were provided to help Janelle and her family cope successfully with the aftermath of this traumatic experience. Each example illustrates how resilience is dynamic and is negotiated over time, with many possible turning points that can result in significant alterations in the developmental trajectory.

While we typically think of resilience as "bouncing back" from a crisis and resuming our "normal" life before the crisis, Walsh perceptively notes that it is also important that we understand the process as "bouncing forward," which involves constructing a new sense of oneself in relation to others and the world (Walsh, 2002, p. 35). Future research needs to attend more closely to this dynamic process unfolding over time and provide a more fine-grained analysis of the complex and interconnected factors (within the person, family, and community) that foster or limit the individual's response to adversity and that influence his or her hopes, expectations, and opportunities for the future. Qualitative research can be particularly invaluable in this regard in revealing the complex interactions between the child and his or her environment that are influential and in identifying important protective influences. In particular, far greater attention needs to be paid to the interactions between the child's personal characteristics (e.g., gender, ability, temperament and personality, coping style) and specific family and community risks, resources, and supports. The potential protective role of schools and other community contexts (e.g., religious institutions, parent support groups, hospitals, social service agencies) needs much more research attention as well. While it seems safe to assume that our intervention efforts might be more successful if they addressed multiple levels of the child's ecology, at the present time, significantly less is known about how to intervene effectively at the ecosystem level, such as family-school partnerships or other collaborative relationships that might promote resilient child and family outcomes (Haskett et al., 2006).

Our review of longitudinal research examining rates of resilience in maltreated children revealed that only a small percentage of children was consistently identified as resilient over time, particularly when resilience was defined across a variety of domains of functioning. While very disturbing, this low rate of resilience was not unexpected as the children's maltreatment experiences were often associated with a variety of other significant adversities (e.g., poverty, living in a high crime area) and significant life stressors (e.g., living with an antisocial, depressed, or substance abusing parent, experiencing the violent death of a family member). The findings highlighted the enduring and pervasive effects of child maltreatment and revealed that the majority of maltreated children did have a difficult time recovering from the cumulative adversity they had faced. In addition to the impact of these experiences on their overall mental health, significant physical health concerns, heightened risk of engaging in delinquent and criminal behavior, lower educational and occupational attainment, reduced competence as a parent, and an elevated risk of intergenerational continuity of abuse have been documented in their adult lives (DuMont et al., 2007; Topitzes et al., 2013; Trickett, Noll, & Putnam, 2011).

These findings emphasize the importance of effective prevention and intervention efforts. While the interventions described need more rigorous evaluation, examination across diverse cultural groups, and a longer term follow-up period to document continued effectiveness, the interventions reviewed represent promising avenues for intervening in the lives of these vulnerable children and their families. With continued validation research and evidence for effectiveness across various cultural groups, these approaches may offer new interventions that can be disseminated more widely at the community level. It would be very helpful for future research to explore the specific time points that are the most sensitive for effective intervention and to examine what resources are most culturally relevant for specific groups to foster resilient trajectories (Panter-Brick, 2015). There has been relatively little research on how patterns of coping with child maltreatment might differ across cultures and limited focus as well on cultural protective factors and processes, until recently (Theron, Liebenberg, & Unger, 2015). Such research is critically needed to advance our understanding of how to maximize resilient outcomes over time. A key factor identified as very important, is intervening early in the child's life to reduce cumulative risk exposure. This can also create opportunities for the child to develop important emotional, social, academic, and behavioral competencies that can foster personal protective resources. Early intervention with maltreating parents might also result in the creation of a more stable, responsive, and caring home environment (CDC, 2014) and provide a context for positive parent–child interactions. Intervention research to date supports the importance of transactional, dyadic models of intervention and highlights the need to address negative bidirectional parent–child interactions that increase risk for negative outcomes (Chaffin et al., 2004). A shift to a multilevel dynamic systems model of risk and resilience will provide a powerful direction for future research on intervention and help to tailor our interventions to the specific needs of each child and family. Due to the dynamic nature of development, there is much that we can do to promote resilience and help to alter life course trajectories in a positive direction. Our challenge is to discover what combination of support and resources are needed for each family we work with and how these factors work together to promote and maintain the family's well-being over the long term.

REFERENCES

American Psychological Association. (1996). *Violence and the family: Report of the American Psychological Association Presidential Task Force on violence and the family*. Washington, DC: APA.

Asawa, L. E., Hansen, D. J., & Flood, M. F. (2008). Early childhood intervention programs: Opportunities and challenges for preventing child maltreatment. *Education & Treatment of Children, 31,* 73–110.

Banyard, V. L., Williams, L. M., Siegel, J. A., & West, C. M. (2002). Childhood sexual abuse in the lives of Black women: Risk and resilience in a longitudinal study. *Women & Therapy, 25*(3–4), 45–58.

Barlow, J., Simkiss, D., & Stewart-Brown, S. (2006). Interventions to prevent or ameliorate child physical abuse and neglect: Findings from a systematic review. *Journal of Children's Services, 1,* 6–28.

Bernard, K., Dozier, M., Bick, J., Lewis-Morrarty, E., Lindhiem, O., & Carlson, E. (2012). Enhancing attachment organization among maltreated children: Results of a randomized clinical trial. *Child Development, 83,* 623–636.

Bolger, K. E., Patterson, C. J., & Kupersmidt, J. B. (1998). Peer relationships and self-esteem among children who have been maltreated. *Child Development, 69*(4), 1171–1197.

Bowlby, J. (1988). *A secure base.* New York, NY: Basic Books.

Bronfenbrenner, U. (1979). *The ecology of human development: Experiments by nature and design.* Cambridge, MA: Harvard University Press.

Brown, E. J., & Kolko, D. J. (1999). Child victims' attributions about being physically abused: An examination of factors associated with symptom severity. *Journal of Abnormal Child Psychology, 27,* 311–322.

Centers for Disease Control. (2014). *Promoting safe, stable and nurturing relationships: A strategic direction for child maltreatment prevention.* Retrieved from http://www.cdc.gov/violenceprevention/pdf/cm_strategic_direction--long-a.pdf

Chaffin, M., Funderburk, B., Bard, D., Valle, L.A., & Gurwitch, R. (2011). A combined motivation and Parent-Child Interaction Therapy package reduces child welfare recidivism in a randomized dismantling field trial. *Journal of Consulting and Clinical Psychology, 79,* 84–95.

Chaffin, M., Silovsky, J. F., Funderburk, B., Valle, L. A., Brestan, E. V., Balachova, T., . . . Bonner, B. L. (2004). Parent-Child Interaction Therapy with physically abusive parents: Efficacy for reducing future abuse reports. *Journal of Consulting and Clinical Psychology, 72,* 500–510.

Charney, D. S. (2004). Psychobiological mechanisms of resilience and vulnerability. *American Journal of Psychiatry, 161,* 195–216.

Charuvastra, A., & Cloitre, M. (2008). Social bonds and posttraumatic stress disorder. *Annual Review of Psychology, 59,* 301–328.

Cicchetti, D. (2013). Annual research review: Resilient functioning in maltreated children—past, present, and future perspectives. *The Journal of Child Psychology and Psychiatry, 54,* 402–422.

Cicchetti, D., & Lynch, M. (1993). Toward an ecological/transactional model of community violence and child maltreatment: Consequences for children's development. *Psychiatry, 56,* 96–117.

Cicchetti, D., & Lynch, M. (1995). Failures in the expectable environment and their impact on individual development: The case of child maltreatment. In D. Cicchetti, & D. J. Cohen (Eds.), *Developmental Psychopathology, Vol 2: Risk, disorder, and adaptation* (pp. 32–71). Oxford, England: John Wiley & Sons.

Cicchetti, D., & Rogosch, F. A. (1997). The role of self-organization in the promotion of resilience in maltreated children. *Development and Psychopathology, 9,* 797–815.

Cicchetti, D., & Rogosch, F. A. (2012). Gene × Environment interaction and resilience: Effects of child maltreatment and serotonin, corticotropin releasing hormone, dopamine, and oxytocin genes. *Development and Psychopathology, 24,* 411–427.

Cicchetti, D., Rogosch, F. A., Lynch, M., & Holt, K. D. (1993). Resilience in maltreated children: Processes leading to adaptive outcome. *Development and Psychopathology, 5,* 629–647.

Cicchetti, D., Rogosch, F. A., & Toth, S. L. (2006). Fostering secure attachment in infants in maltreating families through preventative interventions. *Development and Psychopathology, 3,* 623–649.

Cicchetti, D., & Toth, S. L. (2005). Child maltreatment. *Annual Review of Clinical Psychology, 1,* 409–438.

Cohen, J. A., Deblinger, E, Mannarino, A. P., & Steer, R. A. (2005). A multisite, randomized controlled trial for children with sexual abuse-related PTSD symptoms. *Journal of the American Academy of Child and Adolescent Psychiatry, 43,* 393–402.

Collishaw, S., Pickles, A., Messer, J., Rutter, M., Shearer, C., & Maughan, B. (2007). Resilience to adult psychopathology following childhood maltreatment: Evidence from a community sample. *Child Abuse & Neglect, 31,* 211–229.

Criss, M. M., Pettit, G. S., Bates, J. E., Dodge, K. A., & Lapp, A. L. (2002). Family adversity, positive peer relationships, and children's externalizing behavior: A longitudinal perspective on risk and resilience. *Child Development, 73,* 1220–1237.

Curtis, W. J., & Cicchetti, D. (2007). Emotion and resilience: A multilevel investigation of hemispheric electroencephalogram asymmetry and emotion regulation in maltreated and nonmaltreated children. *Development and Psychopathology, 19,* 811–840.

Cyr, C., Euser, E. M., Bakermans-Kranenburg, M. J., & Van IJzendoorn, M. H. (2010). Attachment security and disorganization in maltreating and high-risk families: A series of meta-analyses. *Development and Psychopathology, 22,* 87–108.

Deblinger, E., Mannarino, A. P., Cohen, J. A., Runyon, M. K., & Steer, R. A. (2011). Trauma-focused cognitive behavioral therapy for children: Impact of the trauma narrative and treatment length. *Depression and Anxiety, 28,* 67–75.

Deblinger, E., Steer, R., Lippmann, J. (1999). Two-year follow-up study of cognitive behavioral therapy for sexually abused children suffering posttraumatic stress symptoms. *Child Abuse & Neglect, 23,* 1371–1378.

Dodge, K. A. (1993). Social-cognitive mechanisms in the development of conduct disorder and depression. *Annual Review of Psychology, 44,* 559–584.

Dodge, K. A., & Coie, J. D. (1987). Social-information-processing factors in reactive and proactive aggression in children's peer groups. *Journal of Personality and Social Psychology, 53*(6), 1146.

Dozier, M., Peloso, E., Lindhiem, O., Gordon, M. K., Manni, M., Sepulveda, S., Ackerman, J., Bernier, A., & Levine, S. (2006). Developing evidence-based interventions for foster children: An example of a randomized clinical trial with infants and toddlers. *Journal of Social Issues, 62,* 767–785.

DuMont, K. A., Widom, C. S., & Czaja, S. J. (2007). Predictors of resilience in abused and neglected children grown-up: The role of individual and neighborhood characteristics. *Child Abuse & Neglect, 31,* 255–274.

Egeland, B., Carlson, E., & Sroufe, L. A. (1993). Resilience as process. *Development and Psychopathology, 5,* 517–528.

Elliott, A. N., & Carnes, C. N. (2001). Reactions of nonoffending parents to the sexual abuse of their child: A review of the literature. *Child Maltreatment, 6,* 314–331.

Erickson, M. F., & Egeland, B. (2004). Linking theory and research to practice: The Minnesota Longitudinal Study of Parents and Children and the STEEP Program. The *Clinical Psychologist, 8,* 5–9.

Evans, G. W., Li, D., & Whipple, S. S. (2013). Cumulative risk and child development. *Psychological Bulletin, 139,* 1342–1396.

Eyberg, S.M. (1988). Parent-Child Interaction Therapy: Integration of traditional and behavioral concerns. *Child & Family Behavior Therapy, 10,* 33–46.

Farber, E. A., & Egeland, B. (1987). Invulnerability among abused and neglected children. In E. J. Anthony & B. Cohen (Eds.), *The invulnerable child* (pp. 253–288). New York, NY: Guilford Press.

Flores, E., Cicchetti, D., & Rogosch, F. A. (2005). Predictors of resilience in maltreated and nonmaltreated Latino children. *Developmental Psychology, 41,* 338–351.

Foster, E. M., Prinz, R. J., Sanders, M. R., & Shapiro, C. J. (2008). The costs of a public health infrastructure for delivering parenting and family support. *Children and Youth Services Review, 30,* 493–501.

Gifford-Smith, M., Dodge, K. A., Dishion, T. J., & McCord, J. (2005). Peer influence in children and adolescents: Crossing the bridge from developmental to intervention science. *Journal of Abnormal Child Psychology, 33,* 255–265.

Gilbert, R., Widom, C. S., Browne, K., Fergusson, D., Webb, E., & Janson, S. (2009). Burden and consequences of child maltreatment in high-income countries. *Lancet, 373(8),* 68–81.

Goldenberg, H., & Goldenberg, I. (2013). *Family therapy: An overview* (8th ed.). Belmont, CA: Brooks/Cole.

Hakman, M., Chaffin, M., Funderburk, B., & Silovsky, J. F. (2009). Change trajectories for parent-child interaction sequences during Parent-Child Interaction Therapy for child physical abuse. *Child Abuse & Neglect, 33,* 461-470.

Haskett, M. E., Nears, K., Ward, C. S., & McPherson, A. V. (2006). Diversity in adjustment of maltreated children: Factors associated with resilient functioning. *Clinical Psychology Review, 26,* 796–812.

Henggeler, S. W., Schoenwald, S. K., Borduin, C. M., Rowland, M. D., & Cunningham, P. B. (2009). *Multisystemic therapy for antisocial behavior in children and adolescents.* New York, NY: Guilford Press.

Herrenkohl, E. C., Herrenkohl, R. C., & Egolf, B. (1994). Resilient early school-age children from maltreating homes: Outcomes in late adolescence. *American Journal of Orthopsychiatry, 64,* 301–309.

Herrenkohl, E. C., Herrenkohl, R. C., Rupert, L. J., Egolf, B. P., & Lutz, J. G. (1995). Risk factors for behavioral dysfunction: The relative impact of maltreatment, SES, physical health problems, cognitive ability, and quality of parent-child interaction. *Child Abuse & Neglect, 19,* 191–203.

Herrenkohl, T. I. (2013). Person-environment interactions and the shaping of resilience. *Trauma, Violence, & Abuse, 14,* 191–194.

Hurlburt, M., Nguyen, K., Reid, J., Webster-Stratton, C., & Zhang, J. (2013). Efficacy of the Incredible Years group parent program with families in Head Start who self-reported a history of child maltreatment. *Child Abuse & Neglect, 37,* 531–543.

Jaffee, S. R., Caspi, A., Moffitt, T. E., Polo-Tomas, M., & Taylor, A. (2007). Individual, family, and neighborhood factors distinguish resilient from non-resilient maltreated children: A cumulative stressors model. *Child Abuse & Neglect, 31,* 231–253.

Jaffee, S. R., & Gallop, R. (2007). Social, emotional, and academic competence among children who have had contact with child protective services: Prevalence and stability estimates. *Journal of the American Academy of Child and Adolescent Psychiatry, 46,* 757–765.

Kaufman, J., Cook, A., Arny, L., Jones, B., & Pittinsky, T. (1994). Problems defining resiliency: Illustrations from the study of maltreated children. *Development and Psychopathology, 6,* 215–229.

Kim, J., & Cicchetti, D. (2003). Social self-efficacy and behavior problems in maltreated and nonmaltreated children. *Journal of Clinical Child & Adolescent Psychology, 32,* 106–117.

King, N. J., Tange, B. J., Mullen, P., Myerson, N., Heyne, D., Rollings, S., Martin, R., & Ollendick, T. H. (2000). Treating sexually abused children with posttraumatic stress symptoms: A randomized clinical trial. *Journal of the American Academy of Child and Adolescent Psychiatry, 39,* 1347–1355.

Kitzman, H. J., Olds, D. L., Cole, R. E., Hanks, C. A., Anson, E. A., Arcoleo, K. J., . . . Holmberg, J. R. (2010). Enduring effects of prenatal and infancy home visiting by nurses on children: Follow-up of a randomized trial among children at age 12 years. *Archives of Pediatrics & Adolescent Medicine, 164,* 412–418.

Kolko, D. J. (1996). Individual cognitive behavioral treatment and family therapy for physically abused children and their offending parents: A comparison of clinical outcomes. *Child Maltreatment, 1,* 322–342.

Kolko, D. J., Iselin, A. M., & Gully, K. J. (2011). Evaluation of the sustainability and clinical outcome of Alternatives for Families: A Cognitive-Behavioral Therapy (AF-CBT) in a child protection center. *Child Abuse & Neglect, 35,* 105–116.

Letarte, M. J., Normandeau, S., & Allard, J. (2010). Effectiveness of a parent training program "Incredible Years" in a child protection program. *Child Abuse & Neglect, 34,* 253–261.

Lieberman, A. F., Ghosh Ippen, C., & Van Horn, P. (2006). Child-parent psychotherapy: 6-month follow-up of an RCT. *Journal of the Academy of Child and Adolescent Psychiatry, 45,* 913–918.

Lieberman, A. F., Van Horn, P., & Ghosh Ippen, C. (2005). Toward evidence-based treatment: Child-parent psychotherapy with preschoolers exposed to marital violence. *Journal of the American Academy of Child and Adolescent Psychiatry, 44,* 1241–1248.

Luthar, S. S., D'Avanzo, K., & Hites, S. (2003). Maternal drug abuse versus other psychological disturbances. In S. Luthar (Ed.), *Resilience and vulnerability: Adaptation in the context of childhood adversities* (pp. 104–130). New York, NY: Cambridge University Press.

MacMillan, H., Wathen, C. N., Barlow, J., Fergusson, D. M., Leventhal, J. M., & Taussig, H. N. (2009). Interventions to prevent child maltreatment and associated impairment. *Lancet, 373,* 250–266.

Marvin, R., Cooper, G., Hoffman, K., & Powell, B. (2002). The Circle of Security Project: Attachment-based intervention with caregiver-pre-school child dyads. *Attachment & Human Development, 4,* 107–124.

Masten, A. S. (2014). *Ordinary magic: Resilience in development.* New York, NY: Guilford Press.

Masten, A. S., Roisman, G. I., Long, J. D., Burt, K. B., Obradovi, J., Riley, J. R., . . . Tellegen, A. (2005). Developmental cascades: linking academic achievement and externalizing and internalizing symptoms over 20 years. *Developmental Psychology, 41,* 733.

McGee, R. A., Wolfe, D. A., & Wilson, S. K. (1997). Multiple maltreatment experiences and adolescent behavior problems: Adolescents' perspectives. *Development and Psychopathology, 9,* 131–149.

Mersky, J. P., & Topitzes, J. (2010). Comparing early adult outcomes of maltreated and non-maltreated children: A prospective longitudinal investigation. *Children and Youth Services Review, 32,* 1086–1096.

Olds, D., Eckenrode, J., Henderson, C., Kitzman, H., Powers, J., Cole, R., . . . Luckey, D. (1997). Long-term effects of home visitation on maternal life course and child abuse and neglect: A 15-year follow-up of a randomized trial. *Journal of the American Medical Association, 278,* 637–643.

Olds, D. L., Kitzman, H., Hanks, C., Cole, R., Anson, E., Sidora-Arcoleo, K., . . . Bondy, J. (2007). Effects of nurse home visiting on maternal and child functioning: Age-9 follow-up of a randomized trial. *Pediatrics, 120,* e832–e845.

Osofsky, J. D., Kronenberg, M., Hammer, J. H., Lederman, C., Katz, L., Adams, S., . . . Hogan, A. (2007). The development and evaluation of the intervention model for the Florida Infant Mental Health Pilot Program. *Infant Mental Health Journal, 28,* 259–280.

Owens, E. B., & Shaw, D. S. (2003). Predicting growth curves of externalizing behavior across the preschool years. *Journal of Abnormal Child Psychology, 31,* 575–590.

Panter-Brick, C. (2015). Culture and resilience: Next steps for theory and practice. In L. C. Theron, L. Liebenberg, & M. Ungar (Eds.), *Youth resilience and culture: Commonalities and complexities* (pp. 233–244). New York, NY: Springer.

Perkins, D. F., & Jones, K. R. (2004). Risk behaviors and resiliency within physically abused adolescents. *Child Abuse & Neglect, 28,* 547–563.

Pianta, R., Egeland, B., & Erickson, M. F. (1989). The antecedents of maltreatment: Results of the mother-child interaction research project. In D. Cicchetti & V. Carlson (Eds.), *Child maltreatment: Theory and research on the causes and consequences of child abuse and neglect* (pp. 203–253). New York, NY: Cambridge University Press.

Price, J. M., & Landsverk, J. (1998). Social information-processing patterns as predictors of social adaptation and behavior problems among maltreated children in foster care. *Child Abuse & Neglect, 22,* 845–858.

Prinz, R. J., Sanders, M. R., Shapiro, C. J., Whitaker, D. J., & Lutzker, J. R. (2009). Population-based prevention of child maltreatment: The U.S. Triple P system population trial. *Prevention Science, 10,* 1–12.

Rogosch, F. A., & Cicchetti, D. (2004). Child maltreatment and emergent personality organization: Perspectives from the five-factor model. *Journal of Abnormal Psychology, 32,* 123–145.

Sagy, S., & Dotan, N. (2001). Coping resources of maltreated children in the family: A salutogenic approach. *Child Abuse & Neglect, 25,* 1463–1480.

Schaeffer, C. M., Swenson, C. C., Tuerk, E. H., & Henggeler, S. W. (2013). Comprehensive treatment for co-occurring child maltreatment and parental substance abuse: Outcomes from a 24-month pilot study of the MST-Building Stronger Families program. *Child Abuse & Neglect, 37,* 596–607.

Schwartz, D., Dodge, K. A., Pettit, G. S., & Bates, J. E. (2000). Friendship as a moderating factor in the pathway between early harsh home environment and later victimization in the peer group. *Developmental Psychology, 36,* 646–662.

Shonk, S. M., & Cicchetti, D. (2001). Maltreatment, competency deficits, and risk for academic and behavioral maladjustment. *Developmental Psychology, 37,* 3–17.

Siegel, J. A. (2000). Aggressive behavior among women sexually abused as children. *Violence and Victims, 15,* 235–255.

Smith Slep, A. M., & O'Leary, S. G. (2007). Multivariate models of mothers' and fathers' aggression toward their children. *Journal of Consulting and Clinical Psychology, 75,* 739–751.

Sroufe, L. A. (2005). Attachment and development: A prospective, longitudinal study from birth to adulthood. *Attachment & Human Development, 7,* 349–367.

Sroufe, L. A., Egeland, B., Carlson, E. A., & Collins, W. A. (2005). *The development of the person: The Minnesota study of risk and adaptation from birth to adulthood.* New York, NY: Guilford.

Stronach, E. P., Toth, S. L., Rogosch, F., & Cichetti, D. (2013). Preventive interventions and sustained attachment security in maltreated children. *Development and Psychopathology, 25,* 919–930.

Swenson, C. C., Penman, J., Henggeler, S. W., & Rowland, M. D. (2010). *Multisystemic therapy for child abuse and neglect.* Charleston, SC: Family Services Research Center, MUSC.

Swenson, C. C., Schaeffer, C. M., Henggeler, S. W., Faldowski, R., & Mayhew, A. M. (2010). Multisystemic therapy for child abuse and neglect: A randomized effectiveness trial. *Journal of Family Psychology, 24,* 497–507.

Theron, L. C., Liebenberg, L., & Ungar, M. (Eds.). (2015). *Youth resilience and culture: Commonalities and complexities.* New York, NY: Springer.

Timmer, S. G., Urquiza, A. J., Herschell, A. D., McGrath, J. M., Zebell, N. M., Porter, A. L., & Vargas, E. C. (2006). Parent-Child Interaction Therapy: Application of an empirically supported treatment to maltreated children in foster care. *Child Welfare, 85(6),* 919–939.

Topitzes, J., Mersky, J. P., Dezen, K., & Reynolds, A. J. (2013). Adult resilience among maltreated children: A prospective investigation of main effect and mediating models. *Child and Youth Services Review, 35,* 937–949.

Topitzes, J., Mersky, J. P., & Reynolds, A. J. (2011). Child maltreatment and offending behavior: Gender specific effects and pathways. *Criminal Justice & Behavior, 38,* 492–510.

Tremblay, C., Hébert, M., & Piché, C. (1999). Coping strategies and social support as mediators of consequences in child sexual abuse victims. *Child Abuse & Neglect, 23,* 929–945.

Trickett, P. K., Noll, J. G., & Putnam, F. W. (2011). The impact of sexual abuse on female development: Lessons from a multigenerational, longitudinal research study. *Development and Psychopathology, 23,* 453–476.

Ungar, M. (2005). Introduction: Resilience across cultures and contexts. In M. Ungar (Eds.), *Handbook for working with children and youth: Pathways to resilience across cultures and contexts* (pp. xv–xxxix). Thousand Oaks, CA: Sage.

Ungar, M., Ghazinour, M., & Richter, J. (2013). Annual review of research: What is resilience within the social ecology of human development? *Journal of Child Psychology and Psychiatry, 54,* 348–366.

Walsh, F. (2002). Bouncing forward: Resilience in the aftermath of September 11. *Family Process, 41,* 34–36.

Walsh, F. (2006). *Strengthening family resilience* (2nd ed.). New York, NY: Guilford Press

Webster-Stratton, C. (1981). Modification of mothers' behaviors and attitudes through videotape modeling group discussion program. *Behavior Therapy, 12,* 634–642.

Webster-Stratton, C., & Reid, M. (2010). Adapting the Incredible Years, an evidence-based parenting programme, for families involved in the child welfare system. *Journal of Children's Services, 5,* 25–42.

Wright, M. O., Allbaugh, L. J., Kaufman, J., Folger, S. F., & Noll, J. G. (2015). *Understanding lives in context: The challenges and triumphs of teen mothers with a history of child maltreatment.* Manuscript in preparation.

Wright, M. O., & Masten, A. S. (2015). Pathways to resilience in context. In L. C. Theron, L. Liebenberg, & M. Ungar (Eds.), *Youth resilience and culture: Commonalities and complexities* (pp. 3–22). New York, NY: Springer.

Wright, M. O., Masten, A. S., & Narayan, A. J. (2013). Resilience processes in development: Four waves of research on positive adaptation in the context of adversity. In S. Goldstein & R. B. Brooks (Eds.), *Handbook of resilience in children* (pp. 15–37). New York, NY: Springer.

Stress and Coping With Intimate Partner Violence

Lyndal Khaw

──────────── **Vignette** ────────────

Lucy met Dylan at a party. They instantly hit it off and spent all evening talking. Dylan had many qualities that attracted Lucy; he was charming, smart, and witty. The couple started dating and soon moved in together. Lucy felt that life was perfect. But life did not stay perfect. After a few months of living together, Lucy noticed some changes in Dylan's demeanor. He was easily agitated and often blamed her when something went wrong. When Lucy accidentally burned his toast one morning, he slammed his fist on the table, yelling, "Only an imbecile would burn toast!" He would also act suspicious when she went out, questioning where she was going, whom she would see, and what time she would be back. At times he even insisted that she cancel her plans and stay home. One day, Lucy confronted Dylan in the bathroom when she found him looking through her phone. Immediately, Dylan accused her of snooping. They argued, and Dylan grabbed Lucy's arm, pushed her on the floor, and punched her in the face. As Lucy lay bruised and shaken on the bathroom floor, she heard Dylan say, "Next time it won't be just a punch in the face."

──────── • • • ────────

Every day, thousands of women like Lucy experience physical, sexual, or psychological abuse by their current or former intimate partners. The Centers for Disease Control (CDC; 2014) describes intimate partner violence (IPV) as a serious preventable health problem, a far departure from what was once considered a private family matter. According to the National Intimate Partner and Sexual Violence Survey, more than a third (35.6%) of women in the United States have reported being raped, physically abused, and/or stalked by an intimate partner at some point in their lives, and nearly half of all men and women have experienced some form of psychological aggression by an intimate partner (Black et al., 2011). IPV affects individuals and families of every race, age, socioeconomic class, and sexual orientation. Because of its far-reaching impact, IPV also poses a high economic cost to the United States. This cost is estimated to exceed $5.8 billion every year, most of which is used to provide medical and mental health services to victims, survivors, and their families (National Center for Injury Prevention and Control, 2003). Considering the social and financial costs involved, it is not surprising that IPV is a major physical, psychological, and economic stressor to individuals and families.

TYPES OF INTIMATE PARTNER VIOLENCE

As a family stressor, IPV comes in multiple forms and generates a wide range of effects on families and individuals. Boss (2002) describes the gravity of this stressor succinctly when she equates IPV to a "terrorist at work inside the family who overpowers . . . and erodes the self-esteem of family members, produces feelings of helplessness and inadequacy in them, and shatters their assumption of fairness in the world" (p. 165). Although both men and women perpetrate IPV, much of IPV research reports greater prevalence and injury rates of violence among female victims compared to males (Tjaden & Thoennes, 2000). For ease of reading, this chapter refers to heterosexual females as victims or survivors of IPV (e.g., Lucy in the chapter-opening vignette), but this should *not* be misconstrued as all IPV victims are female.

Physical Abuse

Also known as battering, the CDC (2014) defines physical abuse as the intentional use of physical force to inflict harm or injury to an intimate partner. Physical abuse includes a wide range of abusive behaviors such as hitting, kicking, slapping, shoving, choking, stabbing, sexual assault or rape, and intimate partner homicide. News and other media outlets primarily report on physical abuse because its effects are often more visible and severe, making it the most recognized form of IPV. In 2009, singer Chris Brown was arrested for physically abusing his girlfriend Rihanna. Pictures of Rihanna's injured lip and black eye quickly surfaced in the news and social media, highlighting the kinds of injuries that may be endured from physical IPV.

Worldwide, approximately 13% to 61% of women across various nations report experiencing physical or sexual violence by a current or former male intimate partner in their lifetime (Garcia-Moreno, Jansen, Ellsberg, Heise, & Watts, 2006). In the United States, data from the National Violence Against Women Survey indicate that there are more female than male victims of physical abuse (17.6% vs. 5.9%) and that females are much more likely than males to be victims of physical or sexual abuse (Coker, Davis, et al., 2002). This trend, however, is not fully reflected among same-sex relationships. Compared to heterosexual men and women, both gay men *and* lesbian women are more likely to be physically assaulted by all types of perpetrators, including intimate partners (Tjaden, Thoennes, & Allison, 1999). However, gay men seem to be perpetrating IPV at higher rates compared to lesbian women, supporting the notion that men are still the primary perpetrators of IPV, regardless of their sexual orientation (Tjaden et al., 1999).

Physical abuse victimization seems to differ along racial lines, with higher rates reported among non-White women. For example, the National Intimate Partner and Sexual Violence Survey reveals the highest prevalence rates for physical IPV were among multiracial women, followed by non-Hispanic Black and American Indian or Native Alaskan women (Black et al., 2011). Lower prevalence rates were reported for Hispanics and non-Hispanic White women, as well as Asian or Pacific Islanders. However, because victims and perpetrators often underreport IPV, these prevalence rates are likely underestimated (Barnett, Miller-Perrin, & Perrin, 2011).

The list of both short and long-term effects of physical IPV is exhaustive. A study comparing 201 physically abused and 240 never abused women found that physically abused women have a 50% to 70% increase in gynecological (e.g., vaginal infections), central nervous (e.g., persisting headaches), chronic stress-related (e.g., back pain, digestive problems), and overall health problems (Campbell et al., 2002). The effects were greater for women who had been sexually abused, with or without the presence of other physical IPV. Similarly, Bonomi, Anderson, Rivara, and Thompson (2007) reported deleterious health effects for women experiencing both physical and sexual IPV, such as higher rates of depression, compared to those experiencing no IPV or physical IPV only. Researchers have also explored the effects of physical IPV to pregnant women and the developing baby. In one study that examined data from over 100,000 new mothers in 26 U.S. states, physical IPV before or during a pregnancy is linked to a host of maternal and infant health risks, including high blood pressure, increased hospital visits, preterm delivery, and low infant birth weight (Silverman, Decker, Reed, & Raj, 2006). Health complications often persist for mothers and infants, even at 1 year postpartum (McMahon, Huang, Boxer, & Postmus, 2011). Finally, physical IPV can and often does result in death. Analysis of data from the National Violent Death Reporting System shows that 80% of IPV-related homicide victims were killed by intimate partners, 77% of whom were women (Smith, Fowler, & Niolon, 2014). The remaining 20% were corollary victims, killed simply because they were in the wrong place at the wrong time. Many of these victims were the target victims' own children (Smith et al., 2014).

Emotional Abuse

Emotional abuse is defined as verbal and psychological violence that inflicts emotional trauma using acts, threats of acts, or coercive tactics (CDC, 2014). This type of IPV may include humiliation, coercive control, isolation, and degradation of an intimate partner, as well as economic abuse, and psychological destabilization (i.e., making someone feel crazy; Tolman, 1989). Among same-sex couples, threats to disclose a partner's sexuality (i.e., to "out" someone) may be used to further isolate victims from their family and friends (West, 2002). Recently, stalking has also been included as a form of emotional abuse. A study by Diette, Goldsmith, Hamilton, Darity, and McFarland (2014) suggests that repeated harassments and threats through unwanted calls, visits, or e-mails can exude a serious mental and psychological toll on victims.

Previously, experts have surmised that emotional abuse only occurred when physical abuse was present. However, IPV researchers now claim that in many cases, emotional abuse occurs independently of physical IPV, and there is evidence to suggest that emotional abuse alone may be far more damaging than physical IPV (Stark, 2007). Emotional abuse has been reported to be the most common form of IPV (Tjaden & Thoennes, 2000). In a review of 204 studies, Carney and Barner (2012) indicate the average prevalence rate of emotional abuse across these studies is about 80%. However, the prevalence rates varied greatly across the studies (ranging from 4% to over 90%). This wide range in prevalence rates may be due to the inconsistencies in how researchers define and measure emotional abuse (Barnett et al., 2011).

Further contributing to the varying prevalence rates is the tendency for researchers to examine specific aspects of emotional abuse rather than the violence as a whole. For example, in the National Intimate Partner and Sexual Violence Survey, 40% of both men and women reported some form of coercive control by their intimate partners, and 40% of women and 32% of men reported experiencing verbal or emotional abuse by a partner (Black et al., 2011). Such trends may suggest that roughly equal rates of men and women perpetrate emotional IPV. However, women are still being victimized at higher rates by other forms of emotional abuse, such as stalking. Specifically, findings from the same survey indicate that more women than men (13 million vs. 2.4 million) report stalking by a current or former intimate partner (Black et al., 2011), substantiating trends discussed earlier (Tjaden & Thoennes, 2000).

Just like physical IPV, emotional abuse produces a host of short- and long-term physical, emotional, and psychological effects that are well documented. For example, Coker, Davis, et al. (2002) found that both men and women who report severe forms of psychological abuse are at increased risk of poor physical health and depressive symptoms, compared to those who reported physical IPV alone. Similarly, Diette et al. (2014) found that stalked women between ages 23 and 29 are 265% more likely than nonstalked women to have mental health issues, at levels comparable to having been sexually assaulted. Chronic exposure to psychological abuse also strongly predicts posttraumatic stress disorder (PTSD) experiences (Arias & Pape, 1999) and accelerated cellular aging (Humphreys et al., 2012). Specifically, Humphreys et al. (2012) discovered women with chronic IPV stress had shorter telomere lengths (parts of human cells that affect how cells age) as compared to those with no IPV, with shorter telomeres indicating poorer health or higher morbidity. Psychological IPV also interferes with effective strategies to cope with IPV. Coping difficulties may explain why victims of psychological IPV are less likely to leave their abusers (Arias & Pape, 1999), are more likely to have suicidal thoughts or attempted suicide (Pico-Alfonso et al., 2006), or use alcohol or drugs (Golding, 1999) to cope with the abuse.

Typologies of IPV: Making Distinctions

In addition to the disparities in definitions, methods, and measures to study emotional IPV, another issue IPV researchers cannot seem to agree on is the issue of gender differences in IPV. Using empirical findings from hundreds of studies, some IPV experts have argued that men are just as likely as women to be victimized and that women are just as violent as men (i.e., gender symmetry; Straus, 2006), if not *more* violent than men (Archer, 2000). This perspective is typically known as the family violence perspective. On the other side of the fence, many IPV scholars and women's advocates holding the feminist perspective reject these conclusions, citing methodological flaws in the gender symmetry studies (Kimmel, 2002). Rather, they defend the studies that show women being victimized at higher rates by men (i.e., gender asymmetry).

In an attempt to reconcile the opposing sides, Johnson (1995) proposed an important view that suggests both conclusions made by the family violence and feminist perspectives were neither completely right nor wrong. Due to the inconsistencies in how IPV is measured and the samples used, Johnson believes that research studies from both perspectives were actually measuring two different types of IPV, patriarchal terrorism (now known as *intimate terrorism*) and common couple violence (now known as *situational couple violence*) (Johnson, 2006).

Intimate Terrorism

According to Johnson (1995), intimate terrorism is a type of IPV where violence is a part of a general strategy to exert power and control over an intimate partner. The deliberate use of coercive control tactics (e.g., threats, economic control, isolation) is central in these relationships (Stark, 2007). In his 1995 review and in subsequent work, Johnson notes that most victims of intimate terrorism are women abused by men, consistent with the feminist perspective of gender asymmetry in IPV (Johnson, 2006). Intimate terrorism is discovered mostly in agency samples (e.g., shelters, courts, hospitals) that report more frequent and severe experiences of violence. Johnson argues that the frequency and severity of IPV may prompt victims to seek help from these agencies in the first place.

Situational Couple Violence

In contrast, situational couple violence is the type of IPV where a pattern of control is generally absent from the relationship. Rather, violence is situation-based; it escalates and erupts when couples are facing a conflict (Johnson, 1995). Johnson (2006) found that perpetrators of situational couple violence were roughly equal in terms of gender (56% men vs. 44% women), which is consistent with the family violence perspective of gender symmetry. Individuals who experience this type of IPV are more likely to be found in community samples (e.g., general surveys) rather than agency samples. Because situational couple violence is conflict provoked, contact with formal help-seeking agencies (e.g., police or hospital) is usually not warranted as compared to an intimate terrorism case.

EXPLAINING VIOLENCE BY AN INTIMATE PARTNER

Every day in the United States and worldwide, a woman is more likely to be abused or killed by her current or former husband or boyfriend than by an acquaintance or a stranger on the street (Catalano, Smith, Snyder, & Rand, 2009). Why are some intimate partners violent? There are no definitive answers, but IPV researchers offer three possible explanations focusing on social learning theory, abusers' individual characteristics, and patriarchal structures.

Social Learning Theory: *"His Dad Was Abusive, Too"*

According to social learning theory, almost all forms of human behavior can be mimicked or modeled, simply by observing and interacting with certain behaviors in the environment. Many researchers believe that perpetrators of IPV ultimately learned the behavior. In 1961, psychologist Alfred Bandura found that when children as young as

3 years old watch an adult behave aggressively toward an inflatable "Bobo Doll," they are likely to imitate these aggressive acts themselves (Bandura, Ross, & Ross, 1961). Interestingly, in this study, boys appeared to use more aggression toward the doll, especially if their observed adult was also male, suggesting the effects of same-sex modeling behaviors.

Bandura's groundbreaking work pioneered the way for researchers to continue exploring the strong link between exposure to violence (e.g., through video games and media) and aggressive thoughts and behaviors among children and young adults. When it comes to IPV, the notion of perpetrating violence as a learned behavior is also supported by research. In an extensive review of the literature, Delsol and Margolin (2004) found that approximately 60% of abusive men (vs. only 20% of nonabusive men) reported being exposed to some form of violence in their families of origin. Essentially, men raised in violent homes are more likely to use violence in their intimate relationships as compared to men raised in nonviolent homes (Cui, Durtschi, Donnelian, Lorenz, & Conger, 2010; Jankowski, Leitenberg, Hennig, & Coffey, 1999).

Abusers' Individual Characteristics: *"Something Wasn't Right About Her"*

Another body of research has pointed specifically at abusers' individual characteristics to explain their violent behaviors, for example, anger. For years, studies have shown that abusers have higher levels of anger and hostility compared to nonviolent individuals, with abusers committing more severe violence reporting more anger and hostility than those with less severe violence (Norlander & Eckhardt, 2005). Because anger is an emotion, it is believed that IPV abusers lack emotion regulation skills and, thus, seem to have more difficulty controlling their anger (Gardner, Moore, & Dettore, 2014). Nevertheless, some studies find intervention programs that focus on anger management for IPV abusers to have little to no effect, as many men continue to use violence beyond completion of the program (Babcock, Green, & Robie, 2004). Thus, while anger and hostility are indeed characteristics of some IPV abusers, the functional role of anger in an IPV relationship needs to be further examined (Norlander & Eckhardt, 2005).

Abusers' drug and alcohol usage and its connection to IPV have also been vastly researched. For example, Caetano, Schafer, and Cunradi (2001) reported that 30% to 40% of male abusers and 27% to 34% of female perpetrators had been drinking at the time of abuse. An abuser is 11 times more likely to be violent on a day that he or she had been drinking (Fals-Stewart, 2003) and tends to use more severe violence while abusing drugs or alcohol (Thomas, Bennett, & Stoops, 2013). While IPV and substance abuse use are *connected*, we must refrain from assuming consistent cause and effect. Research has determined that drugs and alcohol do not *cause* people to become violent. Indeed, the majority of heavy drinkers are not violent, and the majority of IPV perpetrators are not under the influence of substances at the time of abuse (Caetano et al., 2001). Rather, the abusers who are predisposed to violence exhibit more severe abusive behaviors when under the influence.

Patriarchal Structure: *"He Was the King of the Castle"*

Feminist researchers have long argued that the root of IPV lies in a patriarchal system where women are deemed inferior to men and therefore are at greater risk of being victims of IPV. Historically, marriage itself was seen as an institution that oppressed women. For example, it was a common expectation for women to honor and obey their husbands (think of traditional wedding vows that may have conveyed such expectations). In the United States, men were legally allowed to hit their wives until 1920; however, the problem was seen as a private family affair and not a social problem until the 1970s, when the battered women's movement gained its momentum (Barnett et al., 2011). Up to 1993, marital rape was still legal in some parts of the United States, thus exonerating men who raped their wives from legal prosecution (Erez, 2002).

Today, while IPV is outlawed in the United States, in many cultures and countries around the world, male violence against women is still considered a normal part of family life, particularly in Middle Eastern and South Asian cultures. For example, a study with Palestinian husbands revealed a tendency to justify wife beating as acceptable, including blaming the victim for the violence (Haj-Yahia, 1998). Similarly, Zakar, Zakar, and Kraemer (2013) reported how the notion of an ideal wife among Pakistani men includes being docile and "subject to control, discipline and violent punishment" (p. 246). Many women in these cultures also share these beliefs. Among a sample of 1,854 married Jordanian women, 98% reported being subjected to at least one form of IPV; notably, 93% of these women also believed that wives must oblige their husbands (Al-Badayneh, 2012). Likewise, South Asian women who strongly agree with patriarchal social norms often do not see IPV as wrong and are less likely to believe that a woman is a potential victim of IPV (Ahmad, Riaz, Barata, & Stewart, 2004).

Having set the stage for the types, effects, and explanations for IPV, let us now explore how IPV affects individuals and families as a stressor. Guided by Boss's (2002) contextual model of family stress, we discuss various stress factors using relevant information from IPV studies.

CONTEXTUAL MODEL OF FAMILY STRESS

In 1958, Hill proposed the ABC-X model of family stress, which is considered the basis of all family stress theories. The contextual model of family stress (CMFS) is a heuristic extension of the ABC-X model that includes internal and external contexts surrounding the family (see Boss, 2002). In this chapter, we adapt a simplified version of the CMFS. In the core, sits the classic ABC-X stress model factors, surrounded by the family's external context. Each factor is explicated in the following. See Figure 12.1 for a representation of the simplified model.

The ABC-X Model

Stressor Event (A)

The A-factor is the stressor event, or the incident or situation that has the *potential* to invoke change in the family system. Although the label implies that the event "produces" stress, Boss (2002) cautions that not all stressor events are stress inducing since what is perceived as stressful in one family may not be so in another. With numerous physical, psychological, and emotional effects that are well evidenced in research, it is clear that

Figure 12.1   Simplified Contextual Model of Family Stress

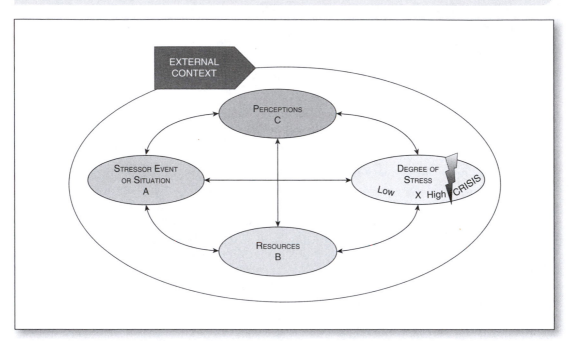

Source: Simplified Contextual Model of Family Stress. Adapted from Boss, P. G. (2002). *Family stress management: A contextual approach* (2nd ed.). Thousand Oaks, CA: SAGE Publications.

IPV is stressful to most families. However, the degree of stress produced in each family could vary, depending on the *source* (e.g., internal vs. external), *type* (e.g., normative/predictable vs. catastrophic/unexpected), *duration* (e.g., chronic vs. acute), and *density* (e.g., cumulative vs. isolated) of the stressor event. Thus, a woman who is physically abused by her husband for the first time after 5 years of marriage would likely perceive IPV differently from another woman who has been physically abused consistently for the past 5 years of her marriage.

Research suggests that the severity and type of abuse does influence a victim's response and help-seeking behaviors. Generally, the more severe and frequent the violence, the more likely IPV victims are to seek help (Duterte et al., 2008). For example, when IPV reaches a dangerous and potentially life-threatening point, physically and psychologically abused women most often seek help from legal and medical support systems such as the police or their family doctor (Vatnar & Bjørkly, 2013). Comparatively, victims of psychological or stalking-related IPV are more likely to disclose the violence to their informal support systems, such as family and friends (Sylaska & Edwards, 2014). These findings appear consistent with Johnson's two main types of IPV. Leone, Johnson, and Cohan (2007) found that women experiencing intimate terrorism relied more heavily on formal support systems whereas women experiencing situational couple violence frequently sought help from friends and neighbors. Indeed, the nature of the stressor event has a strong influence on the remaining factors in the model.

Resources (B)

The B-factor is defined as an individual's or a family's assets used to respond to or deal with the stressor event. Resources range from economic and tangible assets (e.g., money, education, social support) to emotional and psychological ones (e.g., coping skills). The absence or lack of resources may jeopardize a families' ability to manage the stressor event, placing them at risk for experiencing high levels of stress or crisis. IPV research has consistently identified the role of social support as a protective factor in mitigating the harmful mental health effects of IPV (e.g., depression) and increasing the quality of life for abused women over time (Beeble, Bybee, Sullivan, & Adams, 2009; Coker, Smith et al., 2002). Economic resources also play a comparable role. Historically, higher rates of IPV have been found among low-income and poor families (Rennison & Planty, 2003). Goodman, Smyth, Borges, and Singer (2009) theorized that when IPV and poverty intersect, the combination of stress, powerlessness, and social isolation puts victims at risk of developing emotional difficulties such as PTSD and depression. Indeed, the lack of economic resources and resulting social and structural conditions seem central in proliferating the cycle of violence for families in poverty.

Nonetheless, IPV also occurs in high-income families, albeit at slightly lower rates (Rennison & Planty, 2003). For these families, having economic resources does not guarantee an active response to the stressor event, as each individual perceives and uses their resources in different ways (Boss, 2002). Faced with the social pressure to preserve the family status, a high-income IPV victim may see her family's wealth as a barrier, rather than a resource, to cope with the violence. Consequently, she may be left relying on other available resources, such as family and friends. These trends were consistent with the findings reported in Haselschwerdt's (2013) study of affluent IPV survivors. Specifically, having substantial economic resources in the family meant having to "protect the status quo" (p. 57) by staying in the abusive marriage and maintaining the image of a happy family. In the end, what seemed most helpful to these women in coping with IPV was not their family's wealth but their formal and informal support systems.

Perception (C)

The C-factor is defined as the individual or collective assessment of the stressor event or situation and is hailed the most important factor in the CMFS by Boss (2002). How an individual or family perceives the stressor event can ultimately determine the degree of stress experienced by the family and subsequently, determine the outcome. Consider again the vignette at the start of this chapter: If Lucy believed that Dylan's actions were abusive and wrong, her subsequent response may be quite different than if she blamed herself for making Dylan angry. Indeed, perceptions of reality can be distorted (Boss, 2002), which is why so many victims' initial response to IPV is to deny its existence. Because they often view their relationships through rose-colored glasses, victims tend to minimize IPV and disengage from the current reality of their situation (Shir, 1999). However, as Boss puts it, "when even one family member begins to see things differently . . . change is on the way" (2002, p. 61). For example, in a study with 25 abused mothers, Khaw and Hardesty (2014) found that once mothers shifted their perception from prioritizing the family to prioritizing the safety of their children, they stopped efforts to keep the relationship together and focused on trying to leave their partners.

Stress or Crisis (X)

As shown in Figure 12.1, Boss (2002) modified the X-factor in the CMFS to illustrate low to high degrees of family stress, a construct that is distinct from family crisis. Family stress is considered as any kind of pressure, disturbance, or change to the family's equilibrium or state of stability. In many cases, individuals and families employ coping mechanisms to manage their lives so that the stress becomes tolerable. Such mechanisms are well illustrated in IPV research. Survivor theory contends that IPV victims actively engage in strategies to keep themselves safe in their relationships (Gondolf & Fisher, 1988). For example, to prevent violent episodes, women use placating strategies like avoiding the abuser, keeping the kids quiet when the abuser is home, and asking the abuser to calm down or seek counseling (Goodkind, Sullivan, & Bybee, 2004). Abused women also use personal strategies like relying on religion for strength and guidance (Brabeck & Guzman, 2008). For many personal, interpersonal, and societal reasons, IPV victims may use these strategies to tolerate the abuse for long periods of time before ever defining the abuse as unacceptable or intolerable (Liang, Goodman, Tummala-Narra, & Weintraub, 2005).

When the level of stress (and the abuse) becomes too overwhelming for the family, it can lead to a crisis. Boss (2002) describes family crisis as a state of "acute disequilibrium" (p. 67), where the family system hits a breaking point and is believed to have become dysfunctional. Qualitative studies of IPV suggest that the turning point from stress to crisis may be marked by an event or a series of events that lead to the realization the situation will never get better (Khaw & Hardesty, 2007). Some documented events include an escalation in IPV severity or frequency (e.g., abuser attempts to kill the victim), a major violation of trust (e.g., abuser commits infidelity), or a direct effect of IPV on children (e.g., abuser abuses his children). Once again, individual and family perception of this triggering situation may vary and determine the tipping point at which family stress actually becomes a crisis.

External Context

The external context surrounding the individual or family is one they have little control over. According to the CMFS, external contexts include any historical, cultural, economic, developmental, and hereditary/biological components that provide a "setting" within which families operate and manage stressor events (Boss, 2002). When exploring IPV, the external contexts of individuals and families must be considered, as perceptions of and responses to IPV depend on these settings. To illustrate, we once again consider the vignette at the start of this chapter. From the description, we know that Lucy is a heterosexual young female victim who is abused by a male partner. But what if the context of this abuse was a lesbian couple or a man abused by a female partner? Would the perceptions of IPV change? The answer is yes, and we briefly explore the external contexts affecting two distinct populations afflicted by IPV.

IPV in the Context of Same-Sex Relationships

Compared to heterosexual relationships, IPV in gay and lesbian relationships is relatively understudied. Rohrbaugh's (2006) review of same-sex IPV studies in the last 3 decades suggests that IPV occurs in approximately 12% of all same-sex relationships. Every day, same-sex IPV victims experience violence within the cultural and historical context of heterosexism, a belief system that favors and assumes heterosexuality. Coupled with homophobia, a negative prejudice toward gay and lesbian populations, individuals and families exposed to same-sex IPV find their experiences are minimized, ignored, or even used against them. In the United States, shelters designated for same-sex IPV are uncommon, thus explaining the notably low number of same-sex IPV victims who seek help from formal agencies (National Coalition of Anti-Violence Programs, 2013).

Another important external context to consider is the historical (and legal) context of same-sex partnerships in the United States. Because of heterosexism, the rights for same-sex couples to legally marry and have children have historically been limited. Prior to the June 26, 2015, ruling by the Supreme Court of the United States (SCOTUS) extending the right to marry to same-sex couples, only three states (Hawaii, Maine, and Washington) plus the District of Columbia had specified legal provisions for same-sex IPV. Two states (Louisiana and South Carolina) had explicitly excluded gays and lesbians from any legal recourse for IPV, such as getting an order of protection (American Bar Association, 2014). Even with the recent SCOTUS ruling, prejudice and discrimination against same-sex couples still exist nationwide. Given their precarious legal standing, many victims of same-sex IPV are unable to trust formal support systems and are forced to cope with IPV on their own (Hardesty, Oswald, Khaw, & Fonseca, 2011). For gay and lesbian parents, abusers may exploit their fear of losing legal custody of their children by threatening to "out" them in court (Rohrbaugh, 2006; West, 2002).

IPV in the Context of Male Victimization

The growing body of research on male victims of IPV suggests that the experiences of men and their responses to IPV occur within the sociocultural confines of rigid gender roles and expectations (Kimmel, 2002). In particular, our society assumes that men, being the physically larger sex, should have the ability to defend themselves in an IPV situation and thus, should not be victims. As Howard and Hollander (1996) surmised, "victimization, particularly in relation to physical abuse, seems so deeply coded as a female experience in contemporary Western society that a man who finds himself victimized is literally 'feminized'" (p. 86). Indeed, male IPV victims are socially isolated, stigmatized, and perceived as weak, vulnerable, or effeminate (Allen-Collinson, 2010).

Research suggests that these cultural and biological contexts play an important role in men's help-seeking patterns. For example, Tsui, Cheung, and Leung (2010) found that male IPV victims generally hide their victim identity, and very few use formal support resources because they do not meet male victims' needs (e.g., most shelters still primarily serve female victims). Consistent with the social stigma of being a male victim, men often cite shame and embarrassment as a prominent reason for not seeking help (Tsui et al., 2010). Studies also reveal the legal barriers to help-seeking for male IPV victims. In a review of the criminal justice literature, Shuler (2010) notes that male victims experience negative or unfair treatment from law enforcement and court systems, such as being arrested for IPV, disbelief of male victims' abuse allegations, and female abusers receiving lenient sentences or case dismissals by judges.

LEAVING ABUSIVE PARTNERS AND POSTSEPARATION COPING

In the final part of this chapter, I highlight the strength and resilience of IPV survivors in leaving their abusive relationships and maintaining separation from their former partners. We briefly discuss research on the process of leaving, followed by the coping strategies used by survivors to manage abusers' intrusion and maintain safety beyond separation. The chapter concludes with an overview of key interventions with abused IPV individuals and their families.

Leaving as a Process

Research suggests that most victims do eventually leave their abusers, often over multiple attempts (Khaw & Hardesty, 2014). This process is emotionally and physically exhausting, making it a stressor situation that potentially creates stress or incites a family crisis. Consistent with Boss's (2002) interpretation of the CMFS, external (e.g., cultural context) and internal stressors (e.g., fear of abusers) interact with coping resources to moderate and predict responses in the process of leaving (Anderson & Saunders, 2003). Leaving may also lead to crisis, for example, about two in five women report that IPV became worse when they tried to end the relationship (Goodkind et al., 2004), and the risk of intimate partner homicide actually increases at this point (Campbell et al., 2003). Over time, however, leaving an abusive partner is associated with better psychological well-being (Anderson & Saunders, 2003). As survivors regain a sense of agency and self-worth, they report better health outcomes compared to women who remain in IPV relationships (Campbell & Soeken, 1999).

Leaving an abusive partner is a process that involves multiple stages, rather than a single isolated event (Khaw & Hardesty, 2007). As shown in Table 12.1, a number of qualitative studies have found that the experience of leaving an abusive partner frequently takes place within a stage-based process. The first stage(s) usually consists of a woman initially coping with IPV by tolerating or denying the violence and trying to appease the abuser (Landenburger, 1989). However, once she recognizes the abuse or sees the effects of IPV on her family, she begins to emotionally and physically separate from her partner and the relationship (Merritt-Gray & Wuest, 1995; Moss, Pitula, Campbell, & Halstead, 1997). In postseparation, she attempts to carry on with her life by actively maintaining separation from her former abuser (Taylor, 2002).

Postseparation Coping

One common misconception is that after women leave their abusive partners, the abuse ends. Research shows this is *not* the case; even in postseparation, abused women are still at high risk for IPV (see Walker, Logan, Jordan, & Campbell, 2004). Fleury, Sullivan, and

Table 12.1   Research on the Process of Leaving

Study	Stages of Leaving	Description of Women's Responses
Landenburger (1989)	Binding Enduring Disengaging Recovering	Tries to make things work and appease abuser Tolerates abuse and self-blames Labels her situation as abusive and leaves Remains separated from the abuser
Merritt-Gray & Wuest (1995)	Counteracting Abuse Breaking Free Not Going Back Moving On	Refuses to leave Leaves the abuser and becomes a survivor Remains separated from the abuser Removed from the abuse but continues reclaiming self and her identity
Moss, Pitula, Campbell, & Halstead (1997)	Being In Getting Out Going On	Endures the abuse using several coping mechanisms (e.g., denial) Recognizes the abuse and leaves Grieves the loss of identities, relationships, and trust in others
Taylor (2002)	Defining Moments Moving Away Moving On	Disengages from the abuse and leaves Distances herself from the abuser Maintains separation from the abuser

Source: Adapted from Khaw, L., & Hardesty, J. L. (2007). Theorizing the process of leaving: Turning points and trajectories in the stages of change model. *Family Relations, 56*(4), 413–425.

Bybee (2000) noted that one in three women in their study had experienced an assault at least once by their ex-partner after leaving; about 72% of these assaults were severe and lethal, such as being kicked, choked, raped, or stabbed. Stalking is also a common tactic used by abusers during the separation period. Roberts (2005) found that 36% of women reported stalking violence (i.e., physical assault while being stalked) by an ex-partner. Stalking violence was more likely to occur if the abuser had made threats, abused drugs, or was jealous of a woman's new partner. Interestingly, the longer a woman stays separated from her ex-partner, the more stalking behaviors are reported. This finding suggests that IPV does not necessarily end and may in fact escalate after separation (Fleury et al., 2000).

Coping with the aftermath of IPV and with the process of leaving can be a significant challenge. Quite often, abusers maintain a presence in survivors' lives as a result of coparenting responsibilities (Walker et al., 2004). In a study involving 19 mothers who divorced their abusive husbands, Hardesty and Ganong (2006) found that fear of the abuser, pragmatic reasons (e.g., financial demands), and family ideology (e.g., belief that their children needed a father) drove mothers to settle for dual custody arrangements that allowed abusers to remain involved in family life. As a result, these abusers continued to exert control over their former partners (Hardesty & Ganong, 2006). Other studies, such as Wuest, Ford-Gilboe, Merritt-Gray, and Berman (2003) and Khaw and Hardesty (2014) report parallel observations of abusers controlling women's lives postseparation, either through direct (e.g., verbally abusing mothers while exchanging children for visitations) or indirect behaviors (e.g., making false allegations of mothers abusing their children in court). Wuest and colleagues (2003) identify this type of unwanted presence as intrusion, which interferes with mothers and children's physical, psychological, and mental health. Intrusion also impedes coping and hinders women's plans to move on and gain closure from their past (Khaw & Hardesty, 2014).

To manage and resist abusers' postseparation intrusion, women initiate strategies that center on either setting rigid family boundaries or renegotiating new ones. As reported by Khaw and Hardesty (2014), one strategy is to set rigid boundaries and exclude ex-partners from family life. Specifically, these women reinforce boundaries (e.g., telling the abuser to stay away), seek protective orders, and use third parties to avoid direct contact with ex-partners. Interestingly, those who set rigid boundaries also do not view abusers as good fathers and do not deem father involvement to be necessary (Khaw & Hardesty, 2014). More mothers in this study, though, did view father involvement as important for children's development and therefore continued coparenting with their ex-partners. These women renegotiated new family boundaries so that ex-partners continued as part of their children's lives but did not overlap with theirs. For example, separate birthday or holiday celebrations for children are organized in order to limit women's contact with their ex-partners. Taken together, efforts to either set rigid boundaries or renegotiate new boundaries help women regain a sense of control post-IPV as they actively keep their former partners out of their lives as much as possible (Hardesty & Ganong, 2006).

INTERVENTIONS FOR IPV

Given the scope and complexity of IPV, it is important to consider some key interventions that are available to victims and families. When an IPV victim seeks help from formal support systems, she may first contact a domestic violence shelter. According to the National Network to End Domestic Violence, in 2013, there were close to 2,000 shelters in the United States serving almost 67,000 victims (both adults and children). Shelters not only provide safety and refuge from an abusive home, but they also offer nonresidential services such as support and advocacy for legal cases, children's programs, and individual or group counseling. Research suggests that women who spend at least one night in a shelter and are exposed to ongoing advocacy and counseling services report less reabuse (i.e., repeat IPV incidents) and an improved quality of life (Wathen & McMillan, 2003). Furthermore, interactions with other shelter residents provide victims with valuable social support comprised of others who have also experienced IPV (Constantino, Kim, & Crane, 2005). Another important service commonly offered by shelters is safety planning, where IPV victims get help in developing an individualized plan to keep themselves and their children safe (Davies, Lyon, & Monti-Catania, 1998).

In situations where victims must make a spontaneous decision to leave, quick and appropriate emergency responses by "front line" professionals (e.g., law enforcement and medical staff) are crucial to ensuring the safety of victims and their families. In a nationwide study of over 14,000 law enforcement agencies, Townsend, Hunt, Kuck, and Baxter

(2005) reported most police departments in the United States have established written protocols for responding to emergency IPV calls, and increasingly, more law enforcement offices are requiring officers and emergency dispatchers to receive specialized IPV training. However, the same report also notes that many police departments do not include same-sex or dating relationships in their written protocols, which invariably excludes some victims from getting the help or protection they need. Similarly, medical professionals are in a unique position to detect IPV and respond to patients' disclosure (Cronholm, Fogarty, Ambuel, & Harrison, 2011). Whether a victim goes in for a routine physical examination or to seek medical treatment for IPV-related injuries, a physician or a nurse may be the first person to whom the victim has ever spoken about IPV. In this situation, it is critical that questioning and screening for IPV is performed in a nonjudgmental and respectful way, as an inappropriate response (or nonresponse) to disclosure may lead to victims' perpetual mistrust of formal support systems (Cronholm et al., 2011). A medical professional's non-response or lack of IPV screening can be viewed as a "missed opportunity" (p. 445) to document IPV and subsequently, provide resources and recommendations for victims to get help (Coker, Bethea, Smith, Fadden, & Brandt, 2002).

While IPV interventions play a crucial role in keeping individuals and families safe, focusing on IPV *prevention* is also a valuable goal (CDC, 2014). As discussed earlier in the chapter, many IPV scholars believe that violence is a socially learned behavior. Therefore, promoting a healthy, respectful, and nonviolent model of intimate relationships through prevention education should theoretically reduce the occurrence of IPV over time. For example, research indicates that prevention programs that target adolescents who are most at risk for IPV (e.g., inner-city adolescents) are successful in reducing the rates of both IPV perpetration and victimization (Langhinrichsen-Rohling & Turner, 2012). When it comes to addressing a social problem like IPV, prevention may indeed be the most effective cure.

REFERENCES

Ahmad, F., Riaz, S. Barata, P., & Stewart, D. E. (2004). Patriarchal beliefs and perceptions of abuse among South Asian immigrant women. *Violence Against Women, 10*(3), 262–282.

Al-Badayneh, D. M. (2012). Violence against women in Jordan. *Journal of Family Violence, 27,* 369–379.

Allen-Collinson, J. (2010). A marked man: Female-perpetrated intimate partner abuse. *International Journal of Men's Health, 8*(1), 22–40.

American Bar Association. (August 25, 2014). *Domestic violence civil protection orders.* Retrieved from http://www.americanbar.org/content/dam/aba/administrative/domestic_violence1/Resources/statutorysummarycharts/2014%20CPO%20Availability%20Chart.authcheckdam.pdf

Anderson, D. K., & Saunders, D. G. (2003). Leaving an abusive partner: An empirical review of predictors, the process of leaving, and psychological well-being. *Trauma, Violence, & Abuse, 4*(2), 163–191.

Archer, J. (2000). Sex differences in aggression between heterosexual partners: A meta-analytic review. *Psychological Bulletin, 126,* 651–680.

Arias, I., & Pape, K. T. (1999). Psychological abuse: Implications for adjustment and commitment to leave violent partners. *Violence & Victims, 14*(1), 55–67.

Babcock, J. C., Green, C. E., & Robie, C. (2004). Does batterers' treatment work? A meta-analytic review of domestic violence treatment. *Clinical Psychology Review, 23,* 1023–1053.

Bandura, A., Ross, D., & Ross, S. A. (1961). Transmission of aggression through imitation of aggressive models. *The Journal of Abnormal and Social Psychology, 63*(3), 575.

Barnett, O. W., Miller-Perrin, C. L., & Perrin, R. D. (2011). *Family violence across the lifespan: An introduction* (3rd ed.). Thousand Oaks, CA: Sage.

Beeble, M. L., Bybee, D., Sullivan, C. M., & Adams, A. E. (2009). Main, mediating, and moderating effects of social support on the well-being of survivors of intimate partner violence across 2 years. *Journal of Consulting and Clinical Psychology, 77*(4), 718–729.

Black, M. C., Basile, K. C., Breiding, M. J., Smith, S. G., Walters, M. L., Merrick, . . . M. R. (2011). *The National Intimate Partner and Sexual Violence Survey (NISVS): 2010 summary report.* Atlanta, GA: Centers for Disease Control and Prevention.

Bonomi, A. E., Anderson, M. L., Rivara, F. P., & Thompson, R. S. (2007). Health outcomes in women with physical and sexual intimate partner violence exposure. *Journal of Women's Health, 16*(7), 987–997.

Boss, P. G. (2002). *Family stress management: A contextual approach* (2nd ed.). Thousand Oaks, CA: Sage.

Brabeck, K. M., & Guzman, M. R. (2008). Frequency and perceived effectiveness of strategies to survive abuse employed by battered Mexican-origin women. *Violence Against Women, 14*(11), 1274–1294.

Caetano, R., Schafer, J., & Cunradi, C. B. (2001). Alcohol-related intimate partner violence among White, Black, and Hispanic couples in the United States. *Alcohol Research and Health, 25*(1), 58–65.

Campbell, J., Jones, A. S., Dienemann, J., Kub, J., Schollenberger, J., O'Campo, P., . . . Wynne, C. (2002). Intimate partner violence and physical health consequences. *Archives of Internal Medicine, 162*, 1157–1163.

Campbell, J. C., & Soeken, K. L. (1999). Women's responses to battering over time: An analysis of change. *Journal of Interpersonal Violence, 14*(1), 21–40.

Campbell, J. C., Webster, D., Koziol-McLain, J., Block, C., Campbell, D., Curry, M. A., . . . Laughon, K. (2003). Risk factors for femicide in abusive relationships: Results from a multisite case control study. *American Journal of Public Health, 93*(7), 1089–1097.

Carney, M. M., & Barner, J. R. (2012). Prevalence of partner abuse: Rates of emotional abuse and control. *Partner Abuse, 3*(3), 286–335.

Catalano, S., Smith, E., Snyder, H., & Rand, M. (2009). *Bureau of Justice Statistics selected findings: Female victims of violence.* Washington, DC: Bureau of Justice Statistics.

Center for Disease Control and Prevention. (2014, May 5). *Intimate partner violence.* Retrieved from http://www.cdc.gov/violenceprevention/intimatepartnerviolence

Coker, A. L., Bethea, L., Smith, P. H., Fadden, M. K., & Brandt, H. M. (2002). Missed opportunities: Intimate partner violence in family practice settings. *Preventive Medicine, 34*(4), 445–454.

Coker, A. L., Davis, K. E., Arias, I., Desai, S., Sanderson, M., Brandt, H. M., & Smith, P. H. (2002). Physical and mental health effects of intimate partner violence for men and women. *American Journal of Preventive Medicine, 23*(4), 260–268.

Coker, A. L., Smith, P. H., Thompson, M. P., McKeown, R. E., Bethea, L., & Davis, K. E. (2002). Social support protects against the negative effects of partner violence on mental health. *Journal of Women's Health & Gender-based Medicine, 11*(5), 465–476.

Constantino, R., Kim, Y., & Crane, P. A. (2005). Effects of a social support intervention on health outcomes in residents of a domestic violence shelter: A pilot study. *Issues in Mental Health Nursing, 26*(6), 575–590.

Cronholm, P. F., Fogarty, C. T., Ambuel, B., & Harrison, S. L. (2011). Intimate partner violence. *American Family Physician, 83*(10), 1165–1172.

Cui, M., Durtschi, J. A. Donnelian, B. M., Lorenz, F. O., & Conger, R. D. (2010). Intergenerational transmission of relationship aggression: A prospective longitudinal study. *Journal of Family Psychology, 24*(6), 688–697.

Davies, J. M., Lyon, E. J., & Monti-Catania, D. (1998). *Safety planning with battered women: Complex lives/difficult choices* (Vol. 7). Thousand Oaks, CA: Sage.

Delsol, C., & Margolin, G. (2004). The role of family-of-origin violence in men's marital violence perpetration. *Clinical Psychology Review, 24*(1), 99–122.

Diette, T. M., Goldsmith, A. H., Hamilton, D., Darity, W., & McFarland, K. (2014), Stalking: Does it leave a psychological footprint? *Social Science Quarterly, 95*(2), 563–580.

Duterte, E. E., Bonomi, A. E., Kernic, M. A., Schiff, M. A., Thompson, R. S., & Rivara, F. P. (2008). Correlates of medical and legal help seeking among women reporting intimate partner violence. *Journal of Women's Health, 17*(1), 85-95.

Erez, E. (2002). Domestic violence and the criminal justice system: An overview. *Online Journal of Issues in Nursing, 7*(1). Retrieved from www.nursingworld.org/ojin/MainMenuCategories/ANAMarketplace/ANAPeriodicals/OJIN/TableofContents/Volume72002/No1Jan2002/DomesticViolenceandCriminalJustice.aspx

Fals-Stewart W. (2003). The occurrence of partner physical aggression on days of alcohol consumption: A longitudinal diary study. *Journal of Consulting and Clinical Psychology, 71*(1), 41–52.

Fleury, R. E., Sullivan, C. M., & Bybee, D. I. (2000). When ending the relationship does not end the violence: Women's experiences of violence by former partners. *Violence Against Women, 6*(12), 1363–1383.

Garcia-Moreno, C., Jansen, H.A., Ellsberg, M., Heise, L., & Watts C. H. (2006). Prevalence of intimate partner violence: Findings from the WHO multi-country study on women's health and domestic violence. *The Lancet, 368*(9543), 1260—1269. doi:10.1016/S0140-6736(06)69523-8

Gardner, F. L., Moore, Z. E., & Dettore, M. (2014). The relationship between anger, childhood maltreatment, and emotion regulation difficulties in intimate partner and non-intimate partner violence offenders. *Behavior Modification 38*(4), 1–22.

Golding, J. M. (1999). Intimate partner violence as a risk factor for mental disorders: A meta-analysis. *Journal of Family Violence, 14*(2), 99–132.

Gondolf, E. W., & Fisher, E. R. (1988). *Battered women as survivors: An alternative to treating learned helplessness.* Lexington, MA: Lexington Books.

Goodkind, J. R., Sullivan, C. M., & Bybee, D. I. (2004). A contextual analysis of battered women's safety planning. *Violence Against Women, 10*(5), 514–533.

Goodman, L. A., Smyth, K. F., Borges, A. M., & Singer, R. (2009). When crises collide: How intimate partner violence and poverty intersect to shape women's mental health and coping? *Trauma, Violence and Abuse, 10*(4), 306–329.

Haj-Yahia, M. M. (1998). Beliefs about wife beating among Palestinian women: The influence of their patriarchal ideology. *Violence Against Women, 4*(5), 533–558.

Hardesty, J. L., & Ganong, L. H. (2006). How women make custody decisions and manage co-parenting with abusive former husbands. *Journal of Social and Personal Relationships, 23*(4), 543–563.

Hardesty, J. L., Oswald, R. F., Khaw, L., & Fonseca, C. (2011). Lesbian/bisexual mothers and intimate partner violence: Help seeking in the context of social and legal vulnerability. *Violence Against Women, 17*(1), 28–46.

Haselschwerdt, M. L. (2013). *Managing secrecy and disclosure of domestic violence in affluent communities: A grounded theory ethnography.* Retrieved from IDEALS Illinois, http://hdl.handle.net/2142/45362

Hill, R. (1958). Social stresses on the family: Generic features of families under stress. *Social Casework, 39,* 139–150.

Howard, J., & Hollander, J. (1996). *Gendered situations, gendered selves.* Thousand Oaks, CA: Sage.

Humphreys, J., Epel, E. S., Cooper, B. A., Lin, J., Blackburn, E. H., & Lee, K. A. (2012). Telomere shortening in formerly abused and never abused women. *Biological Research for Nursing, 14*(2), 115–123.

Jankowski, M. K., Leitenberg, H., Henning, K., & Coffey, P. (1999). Intergenerational transmission of dating aggression as a function of witnessing only same sex parents vs. opposite sex parents vs. both parents as perpetrators of domestic violence. *Journal of Family Violence, 14*(3), 267–279.

Johnson, M. P. (1995). Patriarchal terrorism and common couple violence: Two forms of violence against women. *Journal of Marriage and the Family, 57*, 283–294.

Johnson, M. P. (2006). Conflict and control: Gender symmetry and asymmetry in domestic violence. *Violence Against Women, 12*(11), 1003–1018.

Khaw, L., & Hardesty, J. L. (2007). Theorizing the process of leaving: Turning points and trajectories in the stages of change model. *Family Relations, 56*(4), 413–425.

Khaw, L., & Hardesty, J. L. (2014). Perceptions of boundary ambiguity in the process of leaving abusive partners. *Family Process.* doi:10.1111/famp.12104

Kimmel, M. S. (2002). "Gender symmetry" in domestic violence: A substantive and methodological research review. *Violence Against Women, 8*(11), 1332–1363.

Landenburger, K. M. (1989). A process of entrapment and recovery from an abusive relationship. *Issues in Mental Health Nursing, 10*(3–4), 209–227.

Langhinrichsen-Rohling, J., & Turner, L. A. (2012). The efficacy of an intimate partner violence prevention program with high-risk adolescent girls: A preliminary test. *Prevention Science, 13*(4), 384–394.

Leone, J. M., Johnson, M. P., & Cohan, C. L. (2007). Victim help seeking: Differences between intimate terrorism and situational couple violence. *Family Relations, 56*(5), 427–439.

Liang, B., Goodman, L., Tummala-Narra, P., & Weintraub, S. (2005). A theoretical framework for understanding help-seeking processes among survivors of intimate partner violence. *American Journal of Community Psychology, 36*(1/2), 71–84.

McMahon, S., Huang, C. C., Boxer, P., & Postmus, J. L. (2011). The impact of emotional and physical violence during pregnancy on maternal and child health at one year post-partum. *Children and Youth Services Review, 33*(11), 2103–2111.

Merritt-Gray, M., & Wuest, J. (1995). Counteracting abuse and breaking free: The process of leaving revealed through women's voices. *Health Care for Women International, 16*(5), 399–412.

Moss, V., Pitula, C., Campbell, J., & Halstead, L. (1997). The experiences of terminating an abusive relationship from an Anglo and African American perspective: A qualitative descriptive study. *Issues in Mental Health Nursing, 18*(5), 433–454.

National Center for Injury Prevention and Control (2003). *Costs of intimate partner violence against women in the United States.* New York, NY: New York City Anti-Violence Project.

National Coalition of Anti-Violence Programs (2013). *Lesbian, gay, bisexual, transgender, queer, and HIV-affected intimate partner violence in 2012.* Atlanta, GA: Centers for Disease Control and Prevention.

National Network to End Domestic Violence (2013). *2013 Domestic violence counts national summary.* Washington, DC: Author.

Norlander, B., & Eckhardt, C. (2005). Anger, hostility, and male perpetrators of intimate partner violence: A meta-analytic review. *Clinical Psychology Review, 25*(2), 119–152.

Pico-Alfonso, M. A., Garcia-Linares, I., Celda-Navarro, N., Blasco-Ros, C., Echeburua, E., & Martinez, M. (2006). The impact of physical, psychological, and sexual intimate male partner violence on women's mental health: Depressive symptoms, posttraumatic stress disorder, state anxiety, and suicide. *Journal of Women's Health, 15*(5), 599–611.

Rennison, C. M., & Planty, M. (2003). Nonlethal intimate partner violence: Examining race, gender, and income patterns. *Violence and Victims, 18*(4), 433–443.

Roberts, K. A. (2005). Women's experience of violence during stalking by former partners: Factors predictive of stalking violence. *Violence Against Women, 11*(1), 89–114.

Rohrbaugh, J. B. (2006). Domestic violence in same-gender relationships. *Family Court Review, 44*(2), 287–299.

Shir, J. S. (1999). Battered women's perceptions and expectations of their current and ideal marital relationship. *Journal of Family Violence, 14*(1), 71–82.

Shuler, A. C. (2010). Male victims of intimate partner violence in the United States: An examination of the review of literature through the critical theoretical perspective. *International Journal of Criminal Justice Sciences, 5*(1), 163–73.

Silverman, J. G., Decker, M. R., Reed, E., & Raj, A. (2006). Intimate partner violence victimization prior to and during pregnancy among women residing in 26 U.S. states: Associations with maternal and neonatal health. *American Journal of Obstetrics and Gynecology, 195*(1), 140–148.

Smith, S. G., Fowler, K. A., & Niolon, P. H. (2014). Intimate partner homicide and corollary victims in 16 states: National Violent Death Reporting System, 2003–2009. *American Journal of Public Health, 104*(3), 461–466.

Stark, E. (2007). *Coercive control: How men entrap women in personal life.* New York, NY: Oxford University Press.

Straus, M. (2006). Future research on gender symmetry in physical assaults on partners. *Violence Against Women, 12*(11), 1066–1097.

Sylaska, K. M., & Edwards, K. M. (2014). Disclosure of intimate partner violence to informal social support network members: A review of the literature. *Trauma, Violence, & Abuse, 15*(1), 3–21.

Taylor, J. Y. (2002). "The straw that broke the camel's back": African American women's strategies for disengaging from abusive relationships. *Women & Therapy, 25*(3/4), 145–161.

Tjaden, P., & Thoennes, N. (2000). Prevalence and consequences of male-to-female and female-to-male intimate partner violence as measured by the National Violence Against Women survey. *Violence Against Women, 6*(2), 142–161.

Tjaden, P., Thoennes, N., & Allison, C. J. (1999). Comparing violence over the lifespan in samples of same-sex and opposite-sex cohabitants. *Violence and Victims, 14*(4), 413–425.

Thomas, M. D., Bennett, L. W., & Stoops, C. (2013). The treatment needs of substance abusing batters: A comparison of men who batter their female partners. *Journal of Family Violence, 28*(2), 121–129.

Tolman, R. M. (1989). The development of a measure of psychological maltreatment of women by their male partners. *Violence and Victims, 4*(3), 159–177.

Townsend, M., Hunt, D., Kuck, S., & Baxter, C. (2005). *Law enforcement response to domestic violence calls for service.* Washington, DC: U.S. Department of Justice.

Tsui, V., Cheung, M., & Leung, P. (2010). Help-seeking among male victims of partner abuse: Men's hard times. *Journal of Community Psychology, 38*(6), 769–780.

Vatnar, S. K. B., & Bjørkly, S. (2013). Lethal intimate partner violence: An interactional perspective on women's perceptions of lethal incidents. *Violence and Victims, 28*(5), 772–789.

Walker, R., Logan, T. K., Jordan, C. E., & Campbell, J. C. (2004). An integrative review of separation in the context of victimization: Consequences and implications for women. *Trauma, Violence, & Abuse, 5*(2), 143–193.

Wathen, C. N., & MacMillan, H. L. (2003). Interventions for violence against women: Scientific review. *JAMA, 289*(5), 589–600.

West, C. M. (2002). Lesbian intimate partner violence: Prevalence and dynamics. *Journal of Lesbian Studies, 6*(1), 121–127.

Wuest, J., Ford-Gilboe, M., Merritt-Gray, M., & Berman, H. (2003). Intrusion: The central problem for family health promotion among children and single mothers after leaving an abusive partner. *Qualitative Health Research, 13*(5), 597–622.

Zakar, R., Zakar, M. Z., & Kraemer, A. (2013). Men's beliefs and attitudes toward intimate partner violence against women in Pakistan. *Violence Against Women, 19*(2), 246–268.

Family Responses to School and Community Mass Violence

Amity Noltemeyer, Courtney L. McLaughlin, and
Mark R. McGowan

Columbine. September 11. The Oklahoma City bombing. Sandy Hook. Whether directly or indirectly exposed, families are increasingly faced with the harsh reality associated with acts of mass violence in schools and communities. *Mass violence* is a term used to refer to a variety of events that typically include shootings, acts of terrorism, and other events that result in multiple fatalities and/or injuries (Fox & Levin, 2012; Substance Abuse and Mental Health Services Administration [SAMHSA], n.d.). Not only can exposure to mass violence contribute to transient feelings of posttraumatic distress (e.g., Rubin & Wessely, 2013), but long-term mental health and family functioning can also be significantly impaired (MacDermid & Wadsworth, 2010). Although individuals who personally experience the violence report the most profound adverse consequences, even those with no firsthand connection can report significant levels of psychological sequelae in response to these events (e.g., Galea et al., 2002; Norris et al., 2002; Yule et al., 2000).

Despite the deleterious consequences of community and school violence, the responses of families to these adverse situations are incredibly diverse. Some families demonstrate *resilience*, evidencing positive adaptation in the midst of tragedy. Considering the context in which families are situated, it is important to understand how families respond to mass violence and how professionals can foster family resilience. In this chapter, we begin with a hypothetical case study illustrating a family's experience with mass violence. Next, we describe the context of mass violence in the United States and delineate a theoretical framework to explain how it can impact families. Finally, we describe risk and protective factors that can influence family resilience, exploring implications for professionals working with families.

CASE STUDY

Two weeks ago, a 16-year-old adolescent entered Rivertown High School with a gun and fatally shot two students and one teacher and injured 26 others. Mr. Brown is a father to a 13-year-old daughter, Rory Brown, and they reside in a town 20 minutes from Rivertown in Mountain Top, where Rory attends Mountain Top High School. Even though the event did not occur in Rory's school, Mr. Brown and Rory are struggling to cope and have many concerns and fears. Mr. Brown is most concerned with providing the right supports for his daughter.

Immediately after the shooting, Rory's school, in collaboration with the Chamber of Commerce, the mayor, community mental health agencies, the hospital, and the police, disseminated information to community members. In addition to describing how key community agencies would communicate with community members, the documents provided resources for support. Additionally, one of the documents was designed to help adults understand warning signs for children and adolescents who may be struggling to cope with the traumatic event. Finally, families were encouraged to reflect on services that their family has previously used as initial resources for support. Because they had previously used the support network at the Mountain Top Community Church, Mr. Brown reached out to church professionals for assistance in the family's coping process.

Although Mr. Brown felt the supports from his church were helpful in guiding him and Rory to make meaning out of the event, he still saw signs that Rory and he were struggling. Rory's teacher expressed similar concerns, stating that since the event Rory had been more argumentative than usual, complaining of frequent stomachaches and displaying more inattention than usual. This prompted Mr. Brown to contact the school psychologist at Mountain Top High School. The school psychologist met with Mr. Brown and discussed his pre-event and post-event parenting style as well as his family's routines and roles. Mr. Brown felt this conversation was helpful since he did not recognize some of the changes that occurred since the event. The school psychologist also recommended minimizing certain types of media exposure, since the family's repeated revisiting of the event via the television appeared to trigger further anxiety. Finally, the school psychologist reminded Mr. Brown to continue to engage Rory in conversations about the event and monitor for additional signs of difficulty. At the end of the meeting, Mr. Brown was provided with a community and school resource guide for additional supports that he and Rory might use. Mr. Brown planned to seek out family counseling services in order to assist him and Rory in answering questions about why the event occurred and renew their feelings of security and hope.

MASS VIOLENCE: THE CONTEXT

Traumatic events, such as the shooting described in the case study, have a variety of social, psychological, physical, and economic consequences that disrupt numerous aspects of individual, family, and community functioning. Incidences of mass violence constitute one of the more poignant examples of human-made disasters in our society. In conceptualizing the impact of mass violence on our society, it is instructive to briefly explore the recent trends in violence in our country. Incidences of mass violence take on many forms in our communities, and adopting a nuanced view of these differences holds important clinical implications for guiding prevention or intervention efforts. In this century, examples have included community shootings (e.g., Aurora, Colorado, movie theater), school shootings (e.g., Sandy Hook Elementary School or Virginia Tech), and terrorist attacks (e.g., September 11 attacks or Boston Marathon bombings). For the purposes of this discussion, we will differentiate between community and school violence more broadly. Although this differentiation is useful for exploring the impact of mass violence on families, many of the current understandings of how individuals and communities react to these events are derived from the broader trauma literature, which includes events such as natural disasters. For example, in a meta-analysis conducted by Norris et al. (2002), the researchers differentiated between disasters and mass violence in their study of population outcomes. Their conclusions suggest that incidences of mass violence were significantly more likely to result in severe impairment than either technological (i.e., human produced event without intention, such as an unintentional airplane crash) or natural disasters.

Regardless of the specific nature of the traumatizing event, the subsequent maladaptive or adaptive responses that follow frequently form a common constellation of symptoms (Neria, Nandi, & Galea, 2007). From a clinical perspective, this presentation may manifest in individuals and families along a continuum of severity that ranges from mild distress to functionally limiting maladaptive responses resulting in the development of diagnosable psychiatric disorders (Galea, Nandi, & Vlahov, 2005; Galea & Resnick, 2005). In general, research has noted that those exposed to a traumatic event show increased rates of acute stress disorder, posttraumatic stress disorder (PTSD), major depression, panic disorder, generalized anxiety disorder, and substance use disorders (Neria, Gross & Marshall, 2006; Norris et al. 2002; Schuster et al., 2001). However, the likelihood for maladaptive outcomes has been found to be influenced by certain conditions. These include the directness of exposure to a traumatic experience, proximity to the trauma or threat, duration of exposure, fear response, premorbid functioning, prior trauma exposure, genetic predispositions, and other factors (Institute of Medicine, 2003; Ozer, Best, Lipsey, & Weiss, 2008). Familial maladaptive coping strategies may include denial, expressions of negative emotion, substance use, behavioral disengagement, and self-blame. Furthermore, familial responses to crisis have been suggested to contribute to functional changes in the family system (Myer et al., 2014). In light of the literature concerning the particularly deleterious impact of mass violence, specific instances of these events will be reviewed as a means of providing a context for discussing both adaptive and maladaptive responses to these events.

Despite heightened public attention, mass shootings in either the community or school setting are rare. However, the malicious intent and unpredictable nature of these violent acts in our communities produces a disproportionately adverse impact on those directly and indirectly affected (Hughes et al., 2011; Norris et al., 2002). According to a recent congressional report (Bjelopera, Bagalman, Caldwell, Finklea, & McCallion, 2013), there have been 78 public mass shootings between 1983 and 2012 that have resulted in 547 deaths. Among the 78 mass shootings, 26 occurred at workplaces of the identified shooter, while the next largest proportion of public mass shootings occurred at places of education.

Putting these statistics into perspective, the prevalence rate for murder in the United States has been declining. As illustrated in Figure 13.1, between the years of 1992 and 2011, the national murder rate dropped from 9.3 to 4.7 per 100,000 inhabitants (Federal Bureau of Investigation, 2012).

Consistent with national trends, the prevalence rate for violence in our nation's public schools has also demonstrated a decreasing trend between 1992 and 2006 (Modzeleski et al., 2008). Recent data trends indicate that from 2000–2001 to 2009–2010, 200 student homicides occurred in schools, with an average of 20 deaths per year. However, the student homicide rates have remained relatively stable since 2006 (Robers, Zhang, Truman, & Snyder, 2012). It is also relevant to note that the homicide rate in this setting is notably higher when adults are also taken into account (see Figure 13.2). When the annual homicide rate for youth ages 5 to 18 is taken into consideration, however, the average number of school homicides accounts for less than 1% of these deaths. In view of these data, the literature has consistently suggested that the perception of public safety has been negatively biased by the media publicizing horrific events (Duwe, 2005; Van Dyke & Schroeder, 2006) like the one at Sandy Hook Elementary School, where 20 students and six adults were killed by a lone gunman. In an effort to challenge these biased societal perceptions, researchers have provided rough estimates of the likelihood that a school will experience a student homicide based on the average number of deaths per year. They estimate the likelihood of a student homicide occurring at a school to be approximately "once every 6,000 years" (Borum, Cornell, Modzeleski, & Jimerson, 2010, p. 27).

Therefore, events like those described in the chapter case study are rare; rather, general trends in the data reinforce the notion that schools remain one of the safest places for children. However, unlike prevalence rates for mass shootings in community settings

Figure 13.1 Homicide Rates in the United States per 100,000 Inhabitants

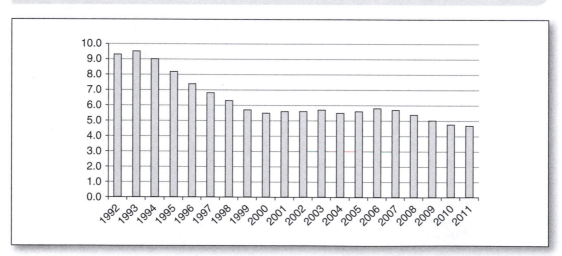

Source: Created with data obtained from *Uniform Crime Reports: Crime in the United States 2011* (Federal Bureau of Investigation, 2012).

Figure 13.2   Trends in Student and Total Homicides at School

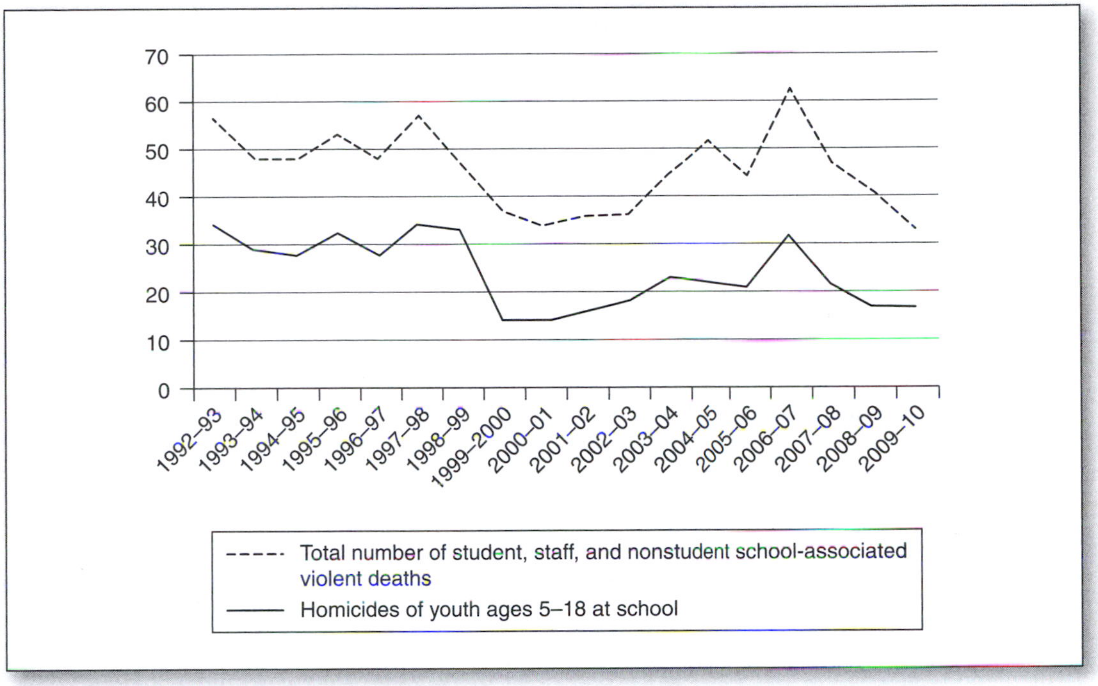

Source: Created with data obtained from the *Indicators of School Crime and Safety: 2011 report* by the National Center for Educational Statistics (Robers et al., 2012).

(see Duwe, 2005), the current frequency of acts of targeted violence in primary and secondary education settings is a relatively recent phenomenon. According to a joint report from the U.S. Secret Service and the Department of Education (Vossekuil, Fein, Reddy, Borum, & Modzeleski, 2002), there were 3 incidents of targeted school shootings in the 1970s, 5 in the 1980s, and 28 in the 1990s. Between 2000 and 2013, there have been 39 incidences of targeted school shootings in educational settings that have resulted in 117 deaths and 120 wounded individuals (Blair & Schweit, 2014). The significance of this evolving trend has fueled ongoing discussions concerning the psychological impact of these events on shaping our society's collective worldview (Warnick, Johnson, & Rocha, 2010). Considering the important role perceptions play in determining psychological outcomes, it is reasonable to expect that these trends will have important implications for exposed individual and families.

Recent research concerning the psychological impact of terrorism on perceptions of community safety also holds an increasingly important place when conceptualizing mass violence in this country. More specifically, when considering the relatively recent incidences of domestic terrorism that have been experienced since the turn of the century, researchers have suggested that there is a new sense of vulnerability in the country that contributes to increased levels of anxiety and stress concerning the possibility of another attack (Institute of Medicine, 2003). It is relevant to note that the genesis of much of the attention paid to this topic in the professional literature began in response to the terrorist attacks on September 11, 2001. The media coverage of these attacks has been noted to contribute significantly to the number of individuals exposed to the events as well as the duration of that exposure. Reactions of fear and horror can spread rapidly and are not limited to those experiencing the event directly. It also includes family members of victims and survivors and people who are exposed through broadcast images (Institute of Medicine, 2003).

The psychological consequences of mass violence involve a range of cognitive, emotional, physical, and behavioral responses that occur in individuals and families as the result of exposure to a traumatic event or threat of an event (see Table 13.1). As noted previously, these consequences vary in terms of both severity and duration. Stress reactions immediately following a traumatic event are quite common and typically resolve rapidly. However, in instances where symptoms continue for more than 3 days, a formal diagnosis of acute stress disorder may be warranted (American Psychiatric Association, 2013). Cognitive reactions include difficulties with memory and attention, confusion, or indecisiveness. Emotional responses include fear, horror, shock, and anger. Physical experiences associated with trauma include nausea, dizziness, hyperarousal, or increased heart rate. Traumatized individuals may also demonstrate atypical behavioral responses such as increased argumentativeness, avoidance of activities or places, and changes in eating or substance use patterns (Brock, Lazarus, & Jimerson, 2002). In the chapter case study, Rory was observed to have several of these responses—including physical symptoms, argumentativeness, and inattention.

It is important to note that the family system has been demonstrated to play a critical role in mediating or buffering a child's vulnerability to maladaptive responses to stressors

Table 13.1 Common Stress Reactions Following Traumatic Events

Physical	Cognitive	Emotional	Behavioral
Chest pain	Blaming others	Affective dysregulation	Avoidance of triggers
Chills	Confusion	Agitation	Antisocial acts
Difficulty breathing	Disorientation	Anxiety	Changes in appetite
Dizziness	Heightened or lowered	Apprehension	Changes in social
Elevated blood pressure	alertness	Denial	activity
Fatigue	Hypervigilance	Depression	Exaggerated startle
Headaches	Intrusive images	Emotional numbing	response
Muscle tremors	Nightmares	Fear	Restlessness
Nausea	Poor attention	Feeling overwhelmed	Substance use
Perspiration	Poor concentration	Grief	Withdrawal
Rapid heart rate	Suspiciousness	Guilt	
Shock symptoms		Irritability	
Thirst		Panic	

(Rutter, 1999). However, there is also a reciprocal interaction between the child and the family system that needs to be taken into consideration. For example, maladaptive responses to stressors may disrupt parenting practices by causing parents to be more irritable, controlling, and punitive. These maladaptive familial and parental responses have been demonstrated to increase the likelihood that a child will experience negative behavioral and mental health outcomes (Han & Shaffer, 2014; Shaffer, Lindhiem, & Kolko, 2013; Webster-Stratton, 1990).

THEORETICAL FRAMEWORK

The existence of mass violence in our society, and its unfavorable outcomes and correlates, is undeniable. However, individuals and families vary drastically in their responses to experienced or vicarious mass violence, with many demonstrating resilience in the midst of these stressors and adversities. Resilience has been defined as "patterns of desirable behavior in situations where adaptive functioning or development have been or currently are significantly threatened by adverse experiences" (Masten, 1999, p. 283). Rather than referring to a within-individual trait or characteristic, current ecological conceptualizations of the resilience construct recognize it as a dynamic and context-dependent process (e.g., Ungar, 2008). The study of resilience processes has historically occurred at the individual level. According to an interactive resilience model, resilience emerges for an individual when the relationship between an adversity and an unfavorable outcome is weakened by a protective factor (Fraser, Kirby, & Smokowski, 2004; Masten, Cutuli, Herbers, & Reed, 2002). Two types of interaction effects can occur: (1) an always-existing protective factor (e.g., individual temperament) moderates the impact of a risk, and/or (2) a risk-activated protective factor (e.g., involvement of child protective services in response to abuse) moderates the impact of a risk. Related to mass violence, an example of the former would be when an individual's personality characteristics buffer the psychological impact of a terrorist attack, whereas an example of the latter would be when a support group provided in response to the terrorist attack serves the same function. In both cases, the protective factor buffers the impact of mass violence on the development of psychopathology.

In addition to the importance of understanding individual resilience, resilience processes also occur at the family level. Family resilience refers to the successful coping of families in the midst of stress or adversity (Black & Lobo, 2008; McCubbin & McCubbin, 1988). According to Walsh (2012, p. 15), it is necessary to build families' capacity for resilience because "major stresses can derail the functioning of a family system, with ripple effects for all members and their relationships. . . . When families suffer, their children suffer." Integrating ecological and developmental perspectives, Walsh (2003) proposed a family resilience framework that recognizes three key processes for resilience: (1) family belief systems (e.g., making meaning of adversity, positive outlook, transcendence, and spirituality), (2) organizational patterns (e.g., flexibility, connectedness, and social/economic resources), and (3) communication/problem solving (e.g., clarity, open emotional expression, and collaborative problem solving). This strength-based framework recognizes that adversity and crises impact the entire family, and family processes mediate adaptation of all members of the family and the family unit (Walsh, 2003, 2012). This model builds upon McCubbin and Patterson's (1983) double ABCX model—recognizing the importance of minimizing stressors, managing hardships, maintaining the family system morale, developing resources needed to meet demands, and developing structures to accommodate new demands (McCubbin & Patterson, 1983; Walsh, 1996)—but also extends it by proposing key processes within family belief systems, organizational patterns, and communication processes that contribute to resilience.

Due to the interaction of individual and family processes in resilience, coupled with the limited empirical research on family resilience to mass violence specifically, we next examine research revealing possible risk and protective factors that can impact both individual and family adaptation to the stress of mass violence.

RESILIENCE IN THE MIDST OF MASS VIOLENCE

As previously mentioned, research has uncovered a variety of unfavorable outcomes associated with exposure to community and school mass violence. Only more recently, however, have investigations focused on the adaptive responses—both within-individual and situational—that buffer individuals and families from developing debilitating conditions such as PTSD and anxiety. Although research on mass violence has historically occurred in the context of war and military intervention outside of the United States (e.g., Keresteš, 2006; MacDermid Wadsworth, 2010; Qouta, Punamaki, & El Sarraj, 2008), the types of terrorism and mass shootings that have been occurring domestically are increasingly serving as fertile ground for expanding our understanding of resilience processes in the United States.

Resilience and Terrorism

In the United States, research following the 9/11 attacks has furthered our understanding of situational factors that promote or impede resilience. For example, Silver, Holman, McIntosh, Poulin, and Gil-Rivas (2002) found that the degree of exposure (i.e., proximity to the attack sites, presence at a site, contact with a victim, and degree of watching events live on television) to the attacks significantly predicted subsequent psychological distress. In fact, degree of exposure was noted to be more predictive of distress than the degree of loss. Further substantiating the exposure effect, Schlenger et al. (2002) found that the amount of time spent watching television coverage of the 9/11 attack predicted both PTSD symptomatology and general distress. Interestingly, Holman, Garfin, and Silver (2014) found that children who were exposed to daily media coverage of the Boston Marathon bombings (6 or more hours) had higher acute stress than did children directly exposed to the bombing events. Together, these results suggest that television exposure to mass violence may increase individuals' risk for maladaptation. Furthermore, regarding the chapter case study, these findings support the school psychologists' recommendation that Mr. Brown limit the amount of coverage he and Rory watched.

Surveying parents in New York City before and after 9/11, Stuber et al. (2005) also found that disaster experiences were associated with subsequent child behavior problems. Furthermore, family demographics (e.g., income, single-parent status, ethnicity) and parental reactions to the attacks were also related to behavioral problems. Parents who were unsure of how their child was responding to the attacks were also more likely to report behavior problems for that child following the attacks, and adolescents who observed a parent crying were more likely to evidence behavior problems 6 months following the attacks. Although youth may benefit from age-appropriate discussions about the attack, parental crying may communicate stress and therefore negatively impact child well-being in traumatic events when fear and uncertainty persist (as opposed to an isolated tragic event such as a natural disaster).

Bonanno, Galea, Bucciarelli, and Vlahov (2007) also studied resilience following the 9/11 attacks, with resilience being defined as having 1 or 0 posttraumatic stress symptoms along with lower levels of depression and substance use. Using data from a phone survey of 2,752 residents of the New York City area 6 months following the attacks, the researchers found that demographic variables, resources, and additional life stressors predicted resilience. Being male, Asian, and being over age 65 were demographic factors related to resilience. Furthermore, education was inversely related to resilience, suggesting education (or perhaps correlates of education such as work stress) hampered adaptation to the trauma in this sample. This finding contradicts some prior research and may be unique to the 9/11 attacks or similar types of large-scale violence. Resources positively related to resilience were lack of income loss, presence of social support, and the absence of chronic disease. Finally, the absence of additional life stressors was found to be most strongly related to resilience; participants with no prior trauma, no recent stressful events, and additional traumatic events since 9/11 were more likely to be resilient.

Resilience and Mass Shootings

Research subsequent to school and community mass shootings has also broadened our knowledge of factors contributing to long-term psychosocial outcomes. Hawdon, Räsänen, Oksanen, and Ryan (2012) studied three mass shootings and concluded that social solidarity emerging after the shootings decreased depressive symptoms and increased psychological well-being, even when controlling for other previously identified predictors of depression. Hawdon and Ryan's (2012) research following the Virginia Tech shooting further supports the importance of social connections with family and friends following a mass shooting. Using survey data from a sample of 460 students, they found that social solidarity, engaging in community events, and face-to-face interactions with family members all significantly enhanced well-being 5 months after the mass shooting that occurred on campus. Furthermore, virtual interactions with friends and family members were found to be beneficial provided they occurred along with face-to-face interactions. Together, these results reveal the important protective function families can serve in individual adaptation. In the chapter case study, these findings suggest that Mr. Brown's ongoing supportive interactions with Rory were likely beneficial to her well-being.

In another study following the Virginia Tech shooting, Littleton, Axsom, and Grills-Taquechel (2009) analyzed the degree to which interpersonal (e.g., companionship, loyalty of friends) and intrapersonal (e.g., optimism, life direction) resource loss and gain following the shooting predicted subsequent psychological distress in a sample of 193 female students at Virginia Tech. Structural equation modeling revealed that interpersonal and intrapersonal resource loss within the first 2 months following the shooting positively predicted greater psychological distress 6 months after the shooting. Furthermore, participants who experienced resource loss in the first 2 months after the shooting experienced an increased likelihood of further resource loss during the subsequent 4 months. Although resource gain was positively related to decreases in psychological distress, this relationship was weaker than it was between resource loss and psychological distress.

The impact of a secure attachment style on functioning after a school shooting has also been examined as an interpersonal resource that might mitigate the effects of trauma. Based on attachment theory, the manner in which an individual responds to a traumatic event, such as mass violence, may be rooted in that individual's attachment style that was established with the primary caregiver in infancy (Turunen, Haravuori, Punama, Suomalainen, & Marttunen, 2014). Turunen et al. (2014) studied the degree to which attachment style predicted PTSD and dissociative symptoms in a sample of survivors of a school shooting in Finland. Participants were administered multiple survey assessments 4, 16, and 28 months following the shooting. Analyses revealed that a secure attachment style provided the strongest protection against PTSD and dissociative symptoms. The more negative outcomes associated with the two insecure attachment types (avoidant and preoccupied) differed based on the amount of time since the shooting. When discussing the reasons for the protective advantage of a secure attachment style, the authors suggested that this could be explained in part by securely attached individuals' ability to recognize that other people are available for help and comfort and to appraise their own situation and seek this help when needed. These findings suggest early caregiver–child relationships may play a role in subsequent responses to trauma.

Systemic Reviews of Family Resilience and Mass Trauma

Whereas the preceding studies primarily focused on *individuals'* capacity for resilience, little research has specifically focused on *family* processes as predictors or outcomes of resilience specifically related to mass violence. However, drawing upon the broader traumatic loss literature, Walsh (2007) proposed that belief systems, organizational patterns, and communication processes can either serve as risk or protective factors for family resilience to trauma. For example, where shattered assumptions or a sense of hopelessness are risk factors for maladaptation, a belief system that can meaningfully manage the loss and maintain a positive outlook can serve to protect a family from negative outcomes. Related to organizational patterns, families should be supported to be flexible in roles to deal with the new challenges yet should provide security and stability to reduce chaos; they should also strive to remain connected and rely on family and community resources (Walsh, 2007). The latter is demonstrated in the chapter case study when Mr. Brown sought out community resources to help him and his daughter cope with the trauma. Finally, communication processes should be characterized by clarity and consistency, and individual differences in emotional expression should be recognized (Walsh, 2007).

Gewirtz, Forgatch, and Wieling (2008) also drew from the related mass trauma research to discuss the impact of parenting practices on child resilience. The researchers proposed that the quality of parenting subsequent to an instance of mass trauma mediates the relationship between the trauma and child adjustment and that the family is important given its role as "the most proximal social environment in which children learn patterns of adjustment" (p. 177). Gewirtz et al. proposed that exposure to mass trauma disrupts the family social system, and therefore recovery efforts after a traumatic event must strengthen parents' ability to promote positive family social interactions and draw upon available resources to facilitate posttraumatic functioning. For example, the authors suggested that parents who monitor, set limits, and problem solve after mass trauma are more likely have resilient children. Furthermore, the authors cited research suggesting that children use cues provided by parents to interpret whether a situation is safe or not; consequently, parental reactions to mass violence have the potential to influence child adaptation.

The more broadly defined adversity literature also reveals insights about the resilience of the family unit. For example, Black and Lobo (2008) conducted a literature review to identify recurrent and prominent factors that defined resilient families. They concluded that these factors included a positive outlook, spirituality or a shared value system, family member accord/cohesion, flexibility, harmonious family communication, sound financial management, family time, shared recreation, and routines and rituals, and a support network. These factors are consistent with Walsh's (2003) family resilience model, which focuses on enhancing communication processes (e.g., harmonious family communication), belief systems (e.g., positive outlook and spirituality or shared value system), and organizational patterns (e.g., routines and rituals and family member accord/cohesion).

Benzies and Mychasiuk (2009) also conducted an integrative review of research to identify risk and protective factors for family resilience at the individual, family, and community levels. At the individual level, malleable factors contributing to family resilience include an internal locus of control, an ability to regulate one's emotions, education, and coping skills. At the family level, being from a smaller family, having a mature mother, two-parent families, family cohesion, supportive parent–child interaction, social support, and stable/adequate income and housing have been shown to protect families from adversity. Finally, at the community level, involvement in the community, peer acceptance, supportive adult mentors, safe neighborhoods, and access to quality child-care and health care can serve a protective function for families. Although family resilience represents a complex interplay between protective factors like these and risk factors, Benzies and Mychasiuk contend that these identified factors offer an excellent starting point to inform family intervention.

Although these studies offer insights into factors that may help individuals and families adapt effectively, it is important to note that resilience is increasingly being viewed as a context- and culture-specific process. Therefore, factors that may contribute to the effective coping in one culture may not serve an equally protective role in another. Clauss-Ehlers and Lopez Levi (2002), for example, identified three cultural community resilience factors that may uniquely buffer community violence in Latino communities: *familismo* (i.e., putting family needs first, an obligation to family), *respeto* (i.e., acknowledging the authority of elders and people in positions of authority), *and personalismo* (i.e., recognizing the critical importance of positive relationships). Incorporating these values into support services could enhance psychosocial outcomes for Latino families (Clauss-Ehlers & Lopez Levi, 2002) and is consistent with the ecological nature of Walsh's (2003) family resilience model.

IMPLICATIONS FOR PROFESSIONALS WORKING WITH FAMILIES EXPOSED TO MASS VIOLENCE PREPAREDNESS

The National Child Traumatic Stress Network (2008) encourages professionals to ask three questions to assess their community's or school's preparedness to handle a violent event; however, in addition to professionals asking these important questions, they are also appropriate for families and communities to consider. First, if the violent event happened today, how ready is your family or community or school to respond? Second, what are your family, community, or school's resources and skills to respond to a violent event? And third, does your family, community, or school have the capacity to recover socially and emotionally?

In addition to giving consideration to these questions, professionals can preventatively help to prepare their system for the unfortunate circumstance of needing to support individuals and families in this capacity. Preparation should involve education, practice, and planning (Jimmerson, Brock, & Pletcher, 2005). In terms of education, there are a variety of crisis response trainings and resources available that provide appropriate models for families, communities, and schools to use. Although individual professionals may have training in this area, it is important that all members of the system are trained to respond within the specific family, community, or school environment. Furthermore, preventing mental health risk in the general population may help prevent future traumatic events. Mental Health First Aid (2014) and QPR Suicide Triage Training (2014) are two examples of trainings that are designed to assist professionals (i.e., counselors, teachers, administrators, etc.) and parents in recognizing risk factors in individuals and getting them the supports they need.

Enhancing protective factors is also key in the prevention of a traumatic event. Positive social relationships remain a key protective factor that can be enhanced through prosocial activities that encourage bonding and the development of positive peer and adult relationships. Families, schools, and communities can directly promote these interactions through structured after-school programs (i.e., youth groups, athletics, art/music groups, meditation or book clubs, etc.). Families have the opportunity to encourage these positive relationships by supporting children and adolescents when they engage appropriately with peers and adults by hosting an event or gathering at their home or transporting their child to an event or gathering. In the chapter case study, Mr. Brown reached out to his church network for social support that could be beneficial for him and Rory.

Beyond training and promoting prosocial relationships, professionals need to work together to practice the application of their skills. Professionals (i.e., counselors, teachers, administrators, etc.) should consider exploring Triage Assessment System (Myer, 2001), Seven-Stage Model of Crisis Intervention (Roberts, 2000), the National Incident Management System (Federal Emergency Management Agency, 2014), and/or PREPaRE (Brock et al., 2009). These resources provide frameworks and tools for prevention efforts prior to a crisis and support efforts after a crisis has occurred.

In addition to education and practice, professionals can plan ahead. For example, crisis response teams or interagency teams can be established to assist with response, a directory of resources can be created and maintained, methods for identifying and working with high-risk students and/or groups of students can be identified, a caregiver training and information guide can be compiled, and an information decimation system can be created (Jimmerson et al., 2005). Several of these preventative strategies were used in the case study presented at the beginning of the chapter. Planning may also entail establishing a system of mental health support that has a variety of levels of support for families. Additionally, consideration for the anniversary may be included as a part of planning. Although the specific event and circumstances will dictate what is done, preparations may include collecting resources/ideas to assist in making key decisions about a memorial, rescreening for families at risk, reactivating interagency supports, and so on. Table 13.2 contains some resources to consider when planning.

Table 13.2   Violent Event Resources for Communities and Schools

Organization	Resource Link	Description of Resource
Substance Abuse and Mental Health Services Administration (SAMHSA)	http://www.samhsa.gov/trauma-violence	Facts and resources
National Center for Crisis Management	http://www.nc-cm.org/index.htm	Membership and online training resources
The National Child Traumatic Stress Network	http://nctsn.org/sites/default/files/assets/pdfs/Child_Trauma_Toolkit_Final.pdf	Child Trauma Toolkit for Educators
National Institute of Mental Health (NIMH)	http://www.nimh.nih.gov/health/publications/helping-children-and-adolescents-cope-with-violence-and-disasters-community-members-trifold-2/index.shtml	What Community Members Can Do
National Education Association Health Information Network	http://neahealthyfutures.org/wpcproduct/school-crisis-guide/	School Crisis Guide
Center for Mental Health in School, UCLA Center	http://smhp.psych.ucla.edu/pdfdocs/crisis/crisis.pdf	Responding to Crisis at School
Office of Homeland Security	http://www.dhs.gov/topics	Relevant topics include preventing terrorism and resiliency
National Incident Management System (NIMS)	http://www.fema.gov/national-incident-management-system	Information on a systematic framework for interagency management of threats or hazards

Responding to Mass Violence: Enhancing Resilience

Individuals and families react differently to all types of violent events, regardless if they are directly or indirectly involved. Therefore, professionals should prepare for a wide variety of needs from families. As professionals work with individual family members, it is important for them to explore what resources an individual has previously accessed and to what extent those resources may be helpful to them as they begin the healing process (Walsh, 2007). For example, what connections does the individual have to family, community, cultural, and spiritual supports? Professionals must understand each individual's belief system to assist him or her in understanding perceptions and coping strategies within the context of the family system. Furthermore, professionals should be equipped to intervene with the family system to assist in making meaningful changes through counseling that focus on couple relationships, parenting roles and supports, and so on.

In terms of individual resilience, effective coping skills, belief systems, social support, emotional regulation, and internal loci of control have been found to be protective factors (Benzies & Mychasiuk, 2009; Bonanno et al., 2007). Therefore, professionals should consider preventatively encouraging individuals to continue to develop effective coping skills, establish a belief system, maintain and/or expand their social support system, practice social healthy responses to life events, and recognize to what extent they believe they can control an event. Professionals may consider identifying families in need of these individual supports by examining parenting subsystems that may be vulnerable (i.e., single parents, dual earning couples, financially unstable families).

At the family level, supportive parent–child interaction including secure attachment styles, family cohesion, and stable and adequate income are examples of family protective factors (Benzies & Mychasiuk, 2009; Black & Lobo, 2008; Turunen et al., 2014). Preventatively, professionals may consider offering education and intervention programs at both the family and community levels. Examples of preventative strategies may include improving relationships within the parenting subsystem (e.g., relationship between couples or single parent and his or her support system), parenting skills, family cohesion, and community family events and supports that encourage positive family interactions and cohesion. Additionally, professionals may consider compiling employment resources and/or creating a family resource room that is equipped with computers, printers, and other office materials to help support families in meeting their employment and income goals (Benzies & Mychasiuk, 2009; Black & Lobo, 2008; Turunen et al., 2014).

Community resilience, cohesion, and efficacy are essential factors in the prevention of a traumatic event. For example, safe neighborhoods; access to quality schools, child care, and health care; supportive mentors; and peer acceptance emerged as critical community protective factors within the literature (Benzies & Mychasiuk, 2009). Professionals may consider working with other community members to explore or enhance these factors within the community environment. Professionals may give consideration to using a community climate survey or creating a mentor program in the community.

In addition to these general recommendations regarding promoting family resilience in the aftermath of mass violence, the following are more specific recommendations to consider when working with families impacted by a violent event.

Mobilize Resources

Ideally, school and community teams will have engaged in planning prior to the occurrence of a violent event, which should include practice drills. If this has occurred, it is likely that teams have established interagency connections that are ready to be mobilized and have a mutual understanding of how the systems will be organized to support families. Mobilizing resources will likely involve a combination of emergency response for physical health needs (safe rooms, Kevlar blankets, etc.), basic resources (shelter, transportation, food), mental health supports, school and community agencies, and/or state and federal supports. Providing these types of outside resources is essential to counter the experience of loss often associated with a violent event (Hobfoll et al., 2007). It was evident in the case study at the beginning of the chapter that Mr. Brown and Rory were within a community that had prepared ahead of time and effectively mobilized resources after the traumatic event occurred.

Effective Parenting Style

It is reasonable to conclude that because violent events often create disruption to the family system, this in turn may threaten or compromise positive parenting within the family. According to Gewirtz et al. (2008), recovery efforts after a traumatic event must strengthen parents' ability to promote positive family social interactions. Therefore, professionals should encourage parents to effectively provide support, monitor, set limits, and problem solve after the event (Gewirtz et al., 2008), just like the school psychologist did in the chapter case study. Counseling supports should continue to be considered as a part of the efforts made to enhance effective parenting, as described in the case study.

Organization and Communication

Professionals can support their clients to establish a way to organize their response to the violent event (Walsh, 2007). How will the family maintain or change their routines? Are there any changes to the roles of individuals within the family? Are there changes to the rules the family previously followed? What levels of support will be most helpful to the family? Are they using all possible/needed supports? These questions relate to the notion in Walsh's (2012) family resilience model of enhancing family organizational patterns. In the case study, Mr. Brown likely asked himself several of these questions, as he engaged in effective organization and communication regarding his response to the violent event.

In addition to organization and communication within the family system, professionals must be aware of their own communication style. Hobfoll et al. (2007) cautions professionals against sharing rumors or "horror stories" as they are also working to process the event. Professionals may also consider working to support the community to prioritize efficient and accurate dissemination of information, which is helpful in supporting families with questions about their social support system (Hobfoll et al., 2007). This step is critical, because delays in linking individuals to their support networks have been found to increase the likelihood of symptoms associated with PTSD (Hobfoll et al., 2007).

Media Exposure

Research has found that frequency and duration of media exposure of the violent event is associated with negative outcomes, even when controlling for factors such as prior mental health status and media exposure prior to the violent event (e.g., Holman et al., 2014). Based on the research by Schlenger et al. (2002) reviewed earlier in this chapter, families should consider limiting the amount of time they spend watching television coverage of the violent event since it was found to predict both PTSD symptomatology and general distress. Although it is common to think of television when discussing media coverage, professionals are encouraged to help families examine all forms of media exposure, which also includes text messages, e-mail, Facebook, Twitter, YouTube, and so on. However, as revealed by Hawdon and Ryan's work (2012), virtual interactions with friends and family may be beneficial when concurrent with face-to-face interactions; thus, not all forms of media exposure are inherently negative. Consequently, professionals should help parents consider the effects of event media exposure, so that they can appropriately monitor exposure in themselves and their children. In the case study within this chapter, Mr. Brown recognized the need to set limits on Rory's television viewing related to the event.

Discover Meaning

Making meaning out of the violent event is considered a positive and adaptive response because it promotes resiliency and healing by making the event more comprehensible and manageable (Walsh, 2007). Therefore, professionals need to be prepared to support their clients to discover meaning of the violent experience (Walsh, 2007). It should be anticipated that clients may question their core beliefs, and guided discovery is essential to assist them in evaluating and possibly redefining them (Walsh, 2007). The examination of core beliefs is critical during this time since they are what individuals use to process the event as they provide people purpose and meaning in life (Walsh, 2007). Individuals may ask many "why" questions (i.e., "Why me?," "Why did this happen?," "Why did she do that?"). They may question their personal safety and the safety of their family, their personal legacy and/or mortality, the existence of a higher being such as God, and so on. (Walsh, 2007). Ultimately, the goal is for the professional to help guide the client to resolve these questions so that the client can positively cope and make meaning out of the experience for future events in life (Walsh, 2007). In the case study, Mr. Brown engaged in mental health supports to help Rory and himself discover meaning.

Therapy-Based Interventions

Cognitive Behavioral Therapy (CBT) has been found to be effective with individuals and family systems who are struggling to cope with a violent event (Follette & Ruzek, 2006). Some hypothesize CBT is effective because it encourages the individual and/or family system to use problem-solving skills that enhance self-efficacy and internal locus of control (Follette & Ruzek, 2006). Often individuals struggling to cope with a violent event display symptoms of PTSD. There has been some evidence in the literature for using exposure therapy and/or stress inoculation training with those struggling to cope with symptoms associated with PTSD (Hobfoll et al., 2007). As stated earlier, because the context of the violent event, and the population or culture impacted by it, are unique to each situation, the findings that are generalizable are limited.

CONCLUSION

Acts of mass violence are an unfortunate reality in our world. Although these events remain rare, they produce a range of unfavorable psychological consequences in exposed individuals and families. A resilience framework reveals preventative strategies and enhancing protective factors to promote adaptive functioning in the midst of the stress and anxiety caused by these violent events. Professionals working with families should consider their preparedness to respond to a violent event and should assist families in identifying and promoting prevention strategies and protective factors in the midst of trauma-induced stress. Although the recommendations outlined in this chapter may serve as a starting point for enhancing family functioning following an act of mass violence, resilience is a dynamic and context-dependent process; therefore, the type and intensity of the response should be adapted based on the unique characteristics of the family, the event, and the culture.

REFERENCES

American Psychiatric Association (2013). *Diagnostic and statistical manual of mental disorders* (5th ed.). Washington, DC: Author.

Benzies, K., & Mychasiuk, R. (2009). Fostering family resiliency: A review of the key protective factors. *Child & Family Social Work, 14,* 103–114. doi:10.1111/j.1365-2206.2008.00586.x

Bjelopera, J. P., Bagalman, E., Caldwell, S. W., Finklea, K. M., & McCallion, G. (2013). *Public mass shootings in the United States: Selected implications for federal public health and safety policy* (Congressional Report No. R43004). Washington, DC: Library of Congress Congressional Research Service.

Black, K., & Lobo, M. (2008). A conceptual review of family resilience factors. *Journal of Family Nursing, 14*(1), 33–55.

Blair, J. P., & Schweit, K. W. (2014). *A study of active shooter incidents, 2000-2013.* Washington, DC: Texas State University and Federal Bureau of Investigation, U.S. Department of Justice.

Bonanno, G. A., Galea, S., Bucciarelli, A., & Vlahov, D. (2007). What predicts psychological resilience after disaster? The role of demographics, resources and life stress. *Journal of Consulting and Clinical Psychology, 75*(5), 671–682. doi:10.1037/0022-006X.75.5.671

Borum, R., Cornell, D. G., Modzeleski, W., & Jimerson, S. R. (2010). What can be done about school shootings?: A review of the evidence. *Educational Researcher, 39,* 27–37. doi: 10.3102/0013189X09357620

Brock, S. E., Lazarus, P. J., & Jimerson, S. R. (2002). *Best practices in school crisis prevention and intervention.* Bethesda, MD: National Association of School Psychologists Press.

Brock, S. E., Nickerson, A. B., Reeves, M. A., Jimerson, S. R., Lieberman, R. A., & Feinberg, T.A. (2009). *School crisis prevention and intervention: The PREPaRE model.* Bethesda, MD: National Association of School Psychologists.

Center for Mental Health in Schools at UCLA. (2008). *Responding to a crisis at a school.* Los Angeles, CA: Author.

Clauss-Ehlers, C. S., & Lopez Levi, L. (2002). Violence and community, terms in conflict: An ecological approach to resilience. *Journal of Social Distress and the Homeless, 11*(4), 265–278. doi: 10.1023/A:1016804930977

Duwe, G. (2005). A circle of distortion: The social construction of mass murder in the United States. *Western Criminology Review, 6*(1), 59–78.

Federal Bureau of Investigation (2012). *Uniform crime reports: Crime in the United States 2011*. Retrieved from http://www.fbi.gov/about-us/cjis/ucr/crime-in-the-u.s/2011/crime-in-the-u.s.-2011/tables/table-1

Federal Emergency Management Agency. (2014). *National Incident Management System*. Retrieved from: http://www.fema.gov/national-incident-management-system

Follette, V. F., & Ruzek, J. I. (2006). *Cognitive-behavioral therapies for trauma* (2nd ed.). New York, NY: Guilford.

Fox, J. A., & Levin, J. (2012). *Extreme killing: Understanding serial and mass murder* (2nd ed.). Thousand Oaks, CA: Sage.

Fraser, M. W., Kirby, L. D., & Smokowski, P. R. (2004). Risk and resilience in childhood. In M.W. Fraser (Ed.), *Risk and resilience in childhood: An ecological perspective* (2nd ed., pp. 1–12). Washington, DC: National Association of Social Workers.

Galea, S., Ahern, J., Resnick, H., Kilpatrick, D., Bucuvalas, M., Gold, J., & Vlahov, D. (2002). Psychological sequelae of the September 11 terrorist attacks in New York City. *New England Journal of Medicine, 246*, 982–987. doi:10.1056/NEJMsa013404

Galea, S., Nandi, A., & Vlahov, D. (2005). The epidemiology of post-traumatic stress disorder after disasters. *Epidemiologic Reviews, 27*, 78–91.

Galea, S., & Resnick, H. (2005). Posttraumatic stress disorder in the general population after mass terrorist incidents: Considerations about the nature of exposure. *CNS Spectrums, 10*, 107–115.

Gewirtz, A., Forgatch, M., & Wieling, E. (2008). Parenting practices and potential mechanisms for child adjustment following mass trauma. *Journal of Marital and Family Therapy, 34*, 177–192.

Han, Z., & Shaffer, A. (2014). Maternal expressed emotion in relation to child behaviour problems: Differential and mediating effects. *Journal of Child & Family Studies, 23*, 1491–1500. doi:10.1007/s10826-014-9923-6

Hawdon, J., Räsänen, P., Oksanen, A., & Ryan, J. (2012). Social solidarity and wellbeing after critical incidents: Three cases of mass shootings. *Journal of Critical Incident Analysis, 3*, 2–25.

Hawdon, J., & Ryan, J. (2012). Well-being after the Virginia Tech mass murder: The relative effectiveness of face-to-face and virtual interactions in providing support to survivors. *Traumatology, 18*(4), 3–12. doi:10.1177/1534765612441096

Hobfoll, S. E., Watson, P., Bell, C. C., Bryant, R. A., Brymer, M. J., Friedman, M. J., . . . Ursano, R. J. (2007). Five essential elements of immediate and mid-term mass trauma intervention: Empirical evidence. *Psychiatry, 70*(4), 283–315.

Holman, E. A., Garfin, D. R., & Silver, R. C. (2014). Media's role in broadcasting acute stress following the Boston Marathon bombings. *Proceedings of the National Academy of Sciences of the United States of America, 111*(1), 93–98.

Hughes, M., Brymer, M., Chiu, W.T., Fairbank, J. A., Jones, R. T., Pynoos, R. S., . . . Kessler, R. C. (2011). Posttraumatic stress among students after the shootings at Virginia Tech. *Psychological Trauma: Theory, Research, Practice, and Policy, 3*, 403–411. doi:10.1037/a0024565

Institute of Medicine (2003). *Preparing for the psychological consequences of terrorism: A public health strategy*. Washington, DC: National Academic Press.

Jimmerson, S. R., Brock, S. E., & Pletcher, S. W. (2005). An integrated model of school crisis preparedness and intervention: A shared foundation to facilitate international crisis intervention. *School Psychology International, 26*(3), 275–296.

Kereteš, G. (2006). Children's aggressive and prosocial behavior in relation to war exposure: Testing the role of perceived parenting and child's gender. *International Journal of Behavioral Development, 30*(3), 227–239. doi:10.1177/0165025406066756

Littleton, H. L., Axsom, D., & Grills-Taquechel, A. (2009). Adjustment following the mass shooting at Virginia Tech: The roles of resource loss and gain. *Psychological Trauma: Theory, Research, Practice and Policy, 1*(3), 206–219. doi:10.1037/a0017468

MacDermid Wadsworth, S. M. (2010). Family risk and resilience in the context of war and terrorism. *Journal of Marriage and Family, 72,* 537–556. doi:10.1111/j.1741-3737.2010.00717.x

Masten, A. S. (1999). Resilience comes of age: Reflections on the past and outlook for the next generation of research. In M. D. Glantz & J. L. Johnson (Eds.), *Resilience and development: Positive life adaptations* (pp. 281–296). New York, NY: Klewer Academic/Plenum.

Masten, A. S., Cutuli, J. J., Herbers, J. E., & Reed, M. G. J. (2002). Resilience in development. In C. R. Snyder & S. J. Lopez (Eds.), *Handbook of positive psychology* (pp. 117–131). New York, NY: Oxford University Press.

McCubbin, H. I., & McCubbin, M. A. (1988). Typologies of resilient families: Emerging roles of social class and ethnicity. *Family Relations, 37*(3), 247–254.

McCubbin, H., & Patterson, J. M. (1983). The family stress process: The double ABCX model of adjustment and adaptation. *Marriage and Family Review, 6,* 7–37.

Mental Health First Aid. (2014, December 10). Retrieved from http://www.mentalhealthfirstaid.org/cs

Modzeleski, W., Feucht, T., Rand, M., Hall, J., Simon, T., & Butler, L., . . . Hertz, M. (2008). School-associated student homicides-United States, 1992–2006. *Morbidity and Mortality Weekly Report, 57*(2), 33–36.

Myer, R. A. (2001). *Assessment for crisis intervention: A triage assessment model.* Pacific Grove, CA: Brooks/Cole.

Myer, R. A., Williams, R. C., Haley, M., Brownfield, J. N., McNicols, K. B., & Pribozie, N. (2014). Crisis intervention with families: Assessing changes in family characteristics. *Family Journal, 22,* 179–185. doi:10.1177/1066480713513551

National Center for Crisis Management. (n.d.). Retrieved from http://www.nc-cm.org/index.htm

National Child Traumatic Stress Network Schools Committee. (2008). *Child trauma toolkit for educators.* Los Angeles, CA, & Durham, NC: National Center for Child Traumatic Stress.

National Education Association Health Information Network. (2007). *School crisis guide: Helping and healing in a time of crisis.* Retrieved from http://neahealthyfutures.org/wpcproduct/school-crisis-guide/

National Institute of Mental Health. (2006). *Helping children and adolescents with violence and disasters: What community members can do* (NIH Publication No. 07-3519). Retrieved from http://www.nimh.nih.gov/health/publications/helping-children-and-adolescents-cope-with-violence-and-disasters-community-members-trifold-2/index

Neria, Y., Gross, R., & Marshall, R. (2006). *9/11: Mental health in the wake of terrorist attacks.* New York, NY: Cambridge University Press.

Neria, Y. Nandi, A., & Galea, S. (2007). Post-traumatic stress disorder following disasters: A systematic review. *Psychological Medicine, 38,* 467–480. doi:10.1017/S0032391707001353

Norris F. H., Friedman M. J., Watson P. J., Byrne C. M., Diaz E., & Kaniasty K. (2002). 60,000 disaster victims speak: Part I. An empirical review of the empirical literature, 1981–2001. *Psychiatry, 65,* 207–239.

Ozer, E.J., Best, S.R., Lipsey, T.L., & Weiss, D.S. (2008). Predictors of posttraumatic stress disorder and symptoms in adults: A meta-analysis. *Psychological Trauma: Theory, Research, Practice, and Policy, 129*(1), 3–36. doi:10.1037/1942-9681.S.1.3

Qouta, S., Punamäki, R.-L., & El Sarraj, E. (2008). Child development and family mental health in war and military violence: The Palestinian experience. *International Journal of Behavioral Development, 32*(4), 310–321. doi:10.1177/0165025408090973

QPR Suicide Triage Training. (2014, December 10). Retrieved from http://www.qprinstitute.com/Triage.html

Robers, S., Zhang, J., Truman, J., & Snyder, T.D. (2012). *Indicators of School Crime and Safety: 2011* (NCES2012-002/NCJ236021). Washington, DC: National Center for Education Statistics, Institute of Education Sciences, U.S. Department of Education, and Bureau of Justice Statistics, Office of Justice Programs, U.S. Department of Justice.

Roberts, A. R. (Ed.). (2000). *Crisis intervention handbook: Assessment, treatment and research* (2nd ed.). New York, NY: Oxford University Press.

Rubin, G. J., & Wessely, S. (2013). The psychological and psychiatric effects of terrorism: Lessons from London. *The Psychiatric Clinics of North America, 36,* 339–350. doi:10.1016/j.psc.2013.05.008

Rutter, M. (1999). Resilience concepts and findings: Implications for family therapy. *Journal of Family Therapy, 21*(2), 119–144.

Schlenger, W. E., Caddell, J. M., Ebert, L., Jordan, B. K., Rourke, K. M., Wilson, D., . . . Kulka, R. A. (2002). Psychological reactions to terrorist attacks: Findings from the National Study of Americans' Reactions to September 11. *Journal of the American Medical Association, 288*(5), 581–588.

Schuster, M. A., Stein, B. D., Jaycox, L., Collins, R. L., Marshall, G. N., Elliott, M. N., . . . Berry, S. H. (2001). A national survey of stress reactions after the September 11, 2001, terrorist attacks. *New England Journal of Medicine, 345*(20), 1507–1512.

Shaffer, A., Liindhiem, O., & Kolko, D. J. (2013). Treatment effects of a modular intervention for early-onset child behavior problems on family contextual outcomes. *Journal of Emotional and Behavioral Disorders, 21,* 277–288. doi:10.1177/1063426612462742

Silver, R.C., Holman, E.A., McIntosh, D.N., Poulin, M., & Gil-Rivas, V. (2002). Nationwide longitudinal study of psychological responses to September 11. *Journal of the American Medical Association, 288*(10), 1235–1244.

Stuber, J., Galea, S., Pfefferbaum, B., Vandivere, S., Moore, K., & Fairbrother, G. (2005). Behavior problems in New York City's children after the September 11, 2001, terrorist attacks. *American Journal of Orthopsychiatry, 7*(2), 190–200. doi:10.1037/0002-9432.75.2.190

Substance Abuse and Mental Health Services Administration. (n.d.). *Incidents of mass violence.* Retrieved from http://www.disasterdistress.samhsa.gov/disasters/incidents-of-mass-violence.aspx

Turunen, T., Haravuori, H., Punama, R., Suomalainen, L., & Marttunen, M. (2014). The role of attachment in recovery after a school-shooting trauma. *European Journal of Psychotraumatology, 5,* 1–10. Retrieved from http://dx.doi.org/10.3402/ejpt.v5.22728

Ungar, M. (2008). Resilience across cultures. *British Journal of Social Work, 38,* 218–235. doi:10.1093/bjsw/bcl343

Van Dyke, R. B., & Schroeder, J. L. (2006). Implementation of the Dallas Threat of Violence Risk Assessment. In S. R. Jimerson & M. J. Furlong (Eds.), *The handbook of school violence and school safety* (pp. 603–616). Mahwah, NJ: Lawrence Erlbaum.

Vossekuil, B., Fein, R., Reddy, M., Borum, R., & Modzeleski, W. (2002). *The final report and findings of the safe school initiative: Implications for the prevention of school attacks in the United States.* Washington, DC: U.S. Department of Education, Office of Elementary and Secondary Education, Safe and Drug Free Schools Program, and U.S. Secret Service, National Threat Assessment Center.

Walsh, F. (1996). Family resilience: Crisis and Challenge. *Family Processes, 35,* 261–281.

Walsh, F. (2003). Family resilience: Strengths forged through adversity. In F. Walsh (Ed.), *Normal family processes* (3rd ed., pp. 399–423). New York, NY: Guilford Press.

Walsh, F. (2007). Traumatic loss and major disasters: Strengthening family and community resilience. *Family Processes, 46*(2), 207–227.

Walsh, F. (2012). Facilitating family resilience: Relational resources for positive youth development in conditions of adversity. In M. Ungar (Ed.). *The social ecology of resilience: A handbook of theory and practice* (pp. 173–185). New York, NY: Springer.

Warnick, B. R., Johnson, B. A., & Rocha, S. (2010). Tragedy and the meaning of school shootings. *Educational Theory, 60,* 371–390. doi:10.1111/j.1741-5446.2010.00364.x

Webster-Stratton, C. (1990). Stress: A potential disruptor of parent perceptions and family interactions. *Journal of Clinical Child Psychology, 19*(4), 302–312.

Yule, W., Bolton, D., Udwin, O., Boyle, S., O'Ryan, D., & Nurrish, J. (2000). The long-term psychological effects of a disaster experienced in adolescence: I: The incidence and course of PTSD. *Journal of Child Psychology and Psychiatry, 41*(4), 503–511.

Families Encountering Sickness, Poverty, and Death

Physical and Mental Illness and Family Stress

Jeremy Yorgason and Kevin Stott

Physical and mental illness share a number of common characteristics that can impact families. They are both often treated by professionals, treatment can involve the use of medications, and both types of illness may act as precursors to family relationship distress or as outcomes of that distress. Between 2011 and 2012, approximately 3% of the U.S. adult population reported experiencing serious psychological distress in the past 30 days, and around 23% of adults reported having a major chronic illness (National Center for Health Statistics, 2014). While these statistics represent adult experiences within a given year, most families will face physical and mental challenges at some point across the life course. Some face both simultaneously. For some, physical or mental illness is experienced in childhood or adolescence; others face these challenges during emerging adulthood or during midlife years. Still others face relapses of mental illness in later years and/or physical challenges associated with aging. Similar to other stressors addressed in this book, physical and mental illnesses typically occur within the context of family systems, where family members are seen as mutually influential. In this chapter, characteristics of physical and mental illness are addressed, a theoretical model for examining these stressors and family resilience is presented, and using this model, research findings relating to three situations, including childhood physical/mental illness, physical/mental illness in marriage, and physical/mental illness of aging parents, are discussed.

ILLNESS CHARACTERISTICS

Stressors associated with physical and mental illnesses often involve a complex interplay of illness characteristics and circumstances. These factors often include (a) type of illness, (b) amount of time since diagnosis or illness phase, (c) life course timing of illness onset, (d) illness intensity, (e) illness severity and threat, (f) illness uncertainty, and (g) projected duration of the illness (see Burman & Margolin, 1992; Rolland, 1994). To consider these characteristics, many studies on illness and families are carried out with small samples that are recruited with particular characteristics in mind, such as having a specific illness (which helps to control for illness intensity, threat, and projected duration to some degree; see Law, Fisher, Fales, Noel, & Eccleston, 2014; Murphy, Peters, Jackson, & Wilkes, 2011). Some studies recruit through medical arenas, allowing some uniformity in time since diagnosis (e.g., couples seeking treatment as a result of a diagnosis of cancer). Larger scale studies provide the benefit of tracking changes in health and family relationships across multiple years, with samples that generalize to larger populations. This chapter includes findings from both small and larger scale studies, drawing upon the strengths of each approach.

THEORETICAL FRAMEWORK

A broad range of theoretical frameworks has been applied to families and physical/mental health. In this chapter, a combination of H. McCubbin and Patterson's (1982) double ABC-X model, Walsh's (1998) family resilience model, and Karney and Bradbury's (1995) vulnerability-stress-adaptation model are presented. A representation integrating these approaches is shown in Figure 14.1.

Physical and mental health stressors (Figure 14.1) are linked to *individual and family outcomes* through *adaptive processes*. Health stressors are sometimes due to chance (e.g., brain injury resulting from a car accident) and sometimes caused or influenced by stable characteristics or behaviors called *enduring vulnerabilities* or *enduring characteristics* (e.g., poor eating habits, lack of exercise, and genetic predisposition leading to Type 2 diabetes). Health stressors and individual and family outcomes are also moderated by both positive and negative enduring characteristics. For example, when someone with the enduring vulnerability of depression experiences a physical health stressor (such as chronic back pain), the adaptive processes of the family can be different than if the person

Figure 14.1   Theoretical Model of Illness and Families Integrating Aspects of the Double ABC-X Model, Family Resilience, and the Vulnerability-Stress Adaptation Model

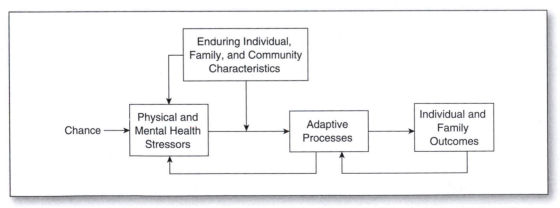

Source: Karney, B. R., & Bradbury, T. N. (1995). The longitudinal course of marital quality and stability: A review of theory, methods, and research. *Psychological Bulletin, 118*(1), 3–34.

Note: Model adapted from Karney and Bradbury (1995). Enduring characteristics also called risk and protective factors in the resilience literature and family demands and family capabilities in the family stress literature (see Patterson, 2002).

is not suffering from depression. Adaptive processes include family members' perceptions of the health stressors as well as their use of resources and the implementation of coping activities. The link between illness stressors and individual and family outcomes is also mediated by the adaptive processes that families undergo as they respond to stressors; that is, the ways that families adapt to illness stressors determine individual and family outcomes to a greater extent than the actual stressors. For example, marital outcomes when a wife has cancer depend on the effectiveness of coping behaviors, perceptions of prognosis, and knowledge about the illness, rather than the sole fact of being diagnosed with cancer. In the model, circular patterns are shown where adaptive processes feed back into stressors and where individual and family outcomes feed back into adaptive processes. For example, if a husband who is diagnosed with anxiety communicates openly with his wife, receives support from her, and works together with her against the anxiety (positive adaptive processes), additional stressors will likely be managed. In contrast, if couples communicate poorly, are not supportive, and live separate lives (poor adaptive processes), additional stressors are more likely to pile up.

Resilience can be identified in various parts of the model (Patterson, 2002). First, resilience could be examined by exploring enduring characteristics that lead to more positive family relationships and/or health outcomes. For example, cohesion may help families adapt more successfully to certain stressors. In this way, enduring characteristics are identified as risk and protective factors. Second, resilience could be identified in successful adaptive processes including an individual's or family's optimistic perceptions, helpful coping activities, and new resources that assist with family coping. Resilience could also be assessed by exploring various physical, psychological, and family relationship outcomes. As suggested by Coleman and Ganong (2002), however, resilience may be present in some individuals or family relationships but not in others. As a result, resilience does not necessarily include all family members.

WHEN A CHILD IS ILL

Vignette

Maria was diagnosed at age 7 with Type I diabetes. Rodney, a 12-year-old, recently received a mental illness diagnosis of depression. Maria and Rodney have received very different diagnoses, yet there are some common aspects of these challenges. Both are learning to manage chronic illness stressors. Both seek help from professional health care providers, and both use daily medications. Both have illnesses that can impact (for better or worse) other family members including parents, siblings, and sometimes extended family members. Last, both have the potential to live happy, productive, and resilient lives.

• • •

This vignette provides examples of potentially life-threatening and disabling childhood illnesses that require intense and ongoing treatment. The Federal Interagency Forum on Child and Family Statistics (2013) reported that in 2012 approximately 9% of children between the ages of 5 and 17 had some functional limitation resulting from a chronic illness, and 9% of youth between the ages of 12 and 17 had experienced a major depressive episode in the past year. The National Center for Health Statistics (2014) indicated that over 23% of children in the United States under 18 years of age had used prescriptions drugs within the past month from when the survey was taken. These percentages may seem small, but with more than 73 million children under the age of 18 in the United States in 2013 (Federal Interagency Forum on Child and Family Statistics, 2014), they suggest a substantial number of affected children and families.

Health Stressors

Childhood illness can present various individual and family stressors (for a review see Cohen, 1999) that are sometimes unique to specific types of illnesses. To date, many studies have focused on specific illnesses, thereby providing details about illness characteristics including onset, duration, and ways that a particular illness can impact families. Illnesses that have been the focus of research include general health problems/chronic illness, asthma, autism, cancer, cerebral palsy, cystic fibrosis, diabetes, Down syndrome, obesity, and Rett syndrome. Some efforts to understand the overall impact of childhood illnesses on families have used a "noncategorical" approach wherein stressors from a variety of illnesses reveal similar strains on families (see Gannoni & Shute, 2010; although illness-specific concerns may be more prevalent in the case of childhood cancer). This approach acknowledges differences, yet also emphasizes that there may be more similarities than differences involved when considering the impact of illness on the family.

Children with a chronic illness often encounter emotional, behavioral, and school-related problems (Silver, Westbrook, & Stein, 1998). For example, in a study of adults (age > 18) who had been diagnosed with cancer as children, Hovén, Lannering, Gustafsson, and Boman (2013) found that the illness in many cases was associated with personal strain, social/familial disruption, financial burden, and sibling impact. Some of these strains were reported by 20% of the sample to still be present 5 or more years after diagnosis.

Siblings of ill children can be affected by childhood illness. In a review of health-related quality of life (HRQOL), Limbers and Skipper (2014) report that siblings fare better than ill children, yet parents may underestimate illness effects of one child on the HRQOL of that child's sibling(s). Sharpe and Rossiter (2002) suggest that illnesses requiring daily management regimes put healthy siblings at greater risk than illnesses not requiring daily care. Indeed, childhood mental illness may impact siblings' life deeply and daily, including feelings of stigmatization (Lukens, Thorning, & Lohrer, 2004). In contrast, childhood illness may paradoxically be linked with greater sibling closeness, resulting in increased compassion and companionship (Sharpe & Rossiter, 2002).

Parents with a child who is chronically ill face stressors that are more intensive and pervasive than typical parental strains (Cohen, 1999). For example, research on childhood mental illness suggests that parents of such children experience a profound sense of loss, grief, and stress (Rasic, Hajek, Alda, & Uher, 2014). Childhood illness can have pervasive negative effects on various aspects of the lives of family members including their mood, lifestyle, education, self-esteem, social relations, physical well-being, and future concerns (Gannoni & Shute, 2010). In many cases, the compounded strains are so severe that parents experience symptoms common to posttraumatic stress (e.g., Manne, Hamel, Gallelli, Sorgen, & Redd, 1998). Mothers are often more involved in the daily care of the child and in interactions with medical professionals, while fathers often focus more on finances and their emotional closeness to the child (Cohen, 1999). Single parents face additional strain as they are often left to fill all of these roles alone.

Enduring Characteristics

Some characteristics of families protect them from or place them at an increased risk of experiencing illness stressors (e.g., socioeconomic status [SES], family structure, demographic factors). Studies indicate that the risk of children having a physical or mental illness varies by age, gender, race, and poverty status (Federal Interagency Forum on Child and Family Statistics, 2013). Furthermore, Newacheck and Halfon (1998) suggest that family structure (e.g., single-parent homes) is also predictive of increased risk, although this risk may simply be indicative of lower incomes.

Although age, race, and gender do not always moderate the link between illness and adaptive processes, SES, family structure, and parenting may. Lower SES is predictive of higher morbidity, higher percentage of income spent on health care, lower rates of insurance coverage, and higher rates of people not seeking medical care (Adler & Newman, 2002; National Center for Health Statistics, 2012). For example, when a child has asthma, lower family SES has been linked to having problems accessing health care services, lower parental understanding of the illness, less influence over environmental factors that may exacerbate an illness, and greater challenges in meeting family needs (Mansour, Lanphear, & DeWitt, 2000). Furthermore, among families with a child with autism, inability to pay for services was linked to higher parental burden (Vogan et al., 2014).

Adaptive Processes

Adaptive processes among parents and siblings surrounding children's health involve coping behaviors, perceptions, and resources. Regarding coping behaviors, family actions can be related to various health, mental health, and relationship outcomes. On the negative side, maternal depression and negative parenting, as well as family conflict, have been linked to dysfunctional child and adult emotional and health outcomes (Cohen, 1999; Lim, Wood, & Miller, 2008; Rasic et al., 2014). For example, the transfer of mental illness risk from parents to children may occur through parent/child interactions as indicated by more conflict with children, a more negative family environment, and lower parental monitoring (Van Loon, Van de Ven, Van Doesum, Witteman, & Hosman, 2014). In contrast, a strong indicator of positive outcomes is "balanced coping" (Cohen, 1999; Patterson, 1991). This occurs when illness demands are kept in perspective with other family needs. Balanced coping by parents becomes especially important in attending to the needs of both the ill child and healthy siblings. Other healthy family adaptive processes include (a) reorganizing and accessing resources as a family, (b) engaging in active coping (efforts to change the source of stress) and accommodating coping (efforts to adapt including reappraisal and positive thinking), (c) collaborating with medical professionals, (d) maintaining a positive outlook on life and hope for the future, and (e) providing emotional protection to the ill child (Compas, Jaser, Dunn, & Rodriguez, 2012; Kars, Duijnstee, Pool, van Delden, & Grypdonck, 2008; M. McCubbin, Balling, Possin, Frierdich, & Bryne, 2002; Mednick et al., 2007). A number of programs have been developed to assist families dealing with the chronic illness of a child (e.g., Kieckhefer et al., 2014). Family treatment programs may be received best by families when they are tailored to meet unique needs of families and in relation to specific illnesses, such as with the treatment of childhood obesity (see Banks, Cramer, Sharp, Shield, & Turner, 2014).

Illness Perceptions

Perceptions of childhood physical and mental health stressors often account for the link between illness and family resilience. However, perceptions likely differ over time and among family members (Cohen, 1999; Patterson, 1993; Patterson & Garwick, 1994). Families' views of stress resulting from childhood illnesses likely evolve across diagnosis, treatment, and management phases. Symptoms, diagnoses, and prognoses can be ambiguous, leaving families to deal with the unknown (see Berge & Holm, 2007; O'Brien, 2007; Roper & Jackson, 2007; Shpigner, Possick, & Buchbinder, 2013). Garwick, Kohrman, Titus, Wolman, and Blum (1999) indicate that shortly after diagnosis, many families ask the question of "why" the illness occurred. They report that most family members find some explanation for the childhood illness (e.g., biomedical cause, environmental cause, and so forth), but with time many stop asking why the illness happened and focus more on the needs of the child.

One demonstration of perceiving resilience is found in posttraumatic growth. Duran (2013) reviewed research literature on childhood cancer and found 35 studies between 1975 and 2010 that reported some positive effects of cancer. In that review, Duran defined posttraumatic growth as "the experience of positive change resulting from the struggle and/or cognitive engagement with the existential challenges of life events," (2013, p. 179). Duran suggested that the families of some children who survive cancer report being strengthened as a result of the experience, growing in areas that include meaning making, appreciation of life, self-awareness, closeness and family togetherness, and a desire to pay back society. Despite great physical or mental challenges, some families emerge stronger from their illness experiences.

Resources

A number of family resources have been linked to positive outcomes when childhood physical or mental illness occurs. Some resources are specific to family functioning, such as maintaining clear boundaries; communicating effectively; being flexible with rules, roles, and expectations; being committed to the family; maintaining a healthy marriage relationship; and maintaining family rituals and routines (Duran, 2013; Kars et al., 2008; Lee et al., 2004; Patterson, 1991; Retzlaff, 2007). These family resources provide stability for families during times of crisis, ambiguity, and change. Other resources consist of networks outside the family, such as integration in a social system and having social support from family, friends, religious groups, the workplace, and community agencies (I. Lee et al., 2004; M. McCubbin et al., 2002; Retzlaff, 2007; Rose, Joe, Shields, & Caldwell, 2014). Further resources may involve whole-family treatments for physical or mental illness of a child (see Banks et al., 2014; Keeton et al., 2013; Kieckhefer et al., 2014).

Outcomes

Typical outcomes examined in studies of childhood illness include individual (child, parent, sibling) psychological distress, health changes for better or worse in the ill child, and individual child and family functioning (Patterson, 1991). For example, Lim et al. (2008) examined the effect of maternal depression on parenting practices, which predicted higher child internalizing symptoms, followed by increased child asthma disease activity. Other studies have examined outcomes such as increasing chances for survival (Kars et al., 2008), diabetes metabolic control (Greene, Mandleco, Roper, Marshall, & Dyches, 2010), and individual functioning (M. McCubbin et al., 2002). Some research suggests that childhood illnesses can have negative impact on the achievement of developmental milestones in young adulthood (Pinquart, 2014). In contrast to individual outcomes, family functioning is more often viewed as part of the adaptive processes that feed into individual outcomes. In a study of Chinese family management of chronic childhood illness, various clusters of family functioning were identified (Zhang, Wei, Zhang, & Shen, 2014). In that study, family illness management styles were linked with levels of family and individual ill-child functioning. It is likely that these processes operate reciprocally.

WHEN A SPOUSE/PARTNER IS ILL

Vignette

Kyle had been married for 5 years when he officially received a diagnosis of posttraumatic stress disorder (PTSD) from his Veterans' Administration (VA) doctors. In his second tour of duty in Iraq, Kyle's patrol unit was attacked by an improvised explosive device (IED), and he was seriously injured. Thankfully, after months of grueling physical rehabilitation, Kyle regained much of the physical function he had lost. However, his wife, Felicia, noticed that he was now more prone to bouts of anger or depression, and she urged him to seek further help from the doctors at the local VA hospital. With the worst of Kyle's physical injuries behind them, both spouses wondered what the frightening new diagnosis of PTSD meant for their marriage. Could they adapt their lives around this challenge in a way that their relationship would not only remain intact but become stronger?

• • •

This vignette illustrates both physical and mental health challenges in the context of an intimate relationship that can result from military injuries. Although risks are associated with military action, such illnesses might still be considered as unexpected and can be chronic and sometimes progressive. These and other illnesses during adulthood can have a significant impact on marriage or committed partner relationships. These relationships are referred to hereafter as couple relationships though most research has been conducted in the context of traditional marriage.

Studies examining the impact of a general decline in health indicate a minor yet significant decrease in marital quality (Badr & Acitelli, 2005; Booth & Johnson, 1994). Studies investigating the impact of specific health problems sometimes report similar findings, yet other times they offer a more complex pattern between illness and marriage. Specific illnesses that have been studied in relation to couple relationships include (but are not limited to) alcohol dependence (Cranford, 2014), arthritis (Yorgason, Roper, Sandberg, & Berg, 2012), cancer (Morgan, Small, Donovan, Overcash, & McMillan, 2011), depression (Johnson, Galambos, & Krahn, 2014), dementia (Sherman, Webster, & Antonucci, 2013), diabetes (Trief et al., 2011), hearing loss (Yorgason, Piercy, & Piercy, 2007), heart problems (Sher et al., 2014), infertility (Onat & Beji, 2012), osteoporosis (Roberto, Gold, & Yorgason, 2004), and posttraumatic stress disorder (Gerlock, Grimesey, & Sayre, 2014).

Health Stressors

A growing body of literature examines the impact of physical illness within couple relationships (see Berg & Upchurch, 2007; Burman & Margolin, 1992) and, in general, finds that the amount of stress varies by type of illness. For example, hearing loss can result in difficulty in communication between spouses (see Yorgason et al., 2007), yet being diagnosed with cancer (see Norton & Manne, 2007) can present a greater life threat along with stress-laden treatments. Psychopathology in marriage has also received growing attention (see South, Krueger, & Iacono, 2011) with the type of mental illness differentially impacting marriage (e.g., mild depression vs. personality disorder; see South, Turkheimer, & Oltmanns, 2008).

Timing of illness onset can also influence the amount of stress experienced by a couple. First, if illness onset is somewhat expected, such as in later life or where a clear pattern of family history provided forewarning, couples may adjust better than if it is completely unexpected. Likewise, prior knowledge of illness before entering into marriage likely requires less adjustment. Finally, researchers have focused on stress at various points in the illness process, for example, at diagnosis, treatment, and during management (e.g., Kraemer, Stanton, Meyerowitz, Rowland, & Ganz, 2011).

Although the stress associated with an illness can be difficult for a couple, illness can also have a positive influence on marital quality. Yorgason, Booth, and Johnson (2008) found that a health decline was related to a *decrease* in marital quality, yet the onset of a disability was related to an *increase* in marital quality. A decline in self-rated health likely represents initial changes in health, while the onset of a disability may represent health declines that occur well after health problems have been in process, allowing time for couples to adapt. Similar to this finding, qualitative studies have found that some couples report an increase in couple positivity during times of health-related stress (Lingard & Court, 2014). For these reasons, it is important to consider illness conditions when interpreting findings.

Enduring Characteristics

The effects of physical and mental illness challenges may be stronger for younger couples than for older couples. The moderating effect of age is recognized in studies of couples dealing with illness during mid and later life (Berg & Upchurch, 2007). For example, Yorgason and colleagues (2008) found that general health declines are more strongly related to lower marital happiness for young and midlife adults than for older adults. Given that many health problems are age related and perhaps anticipated, marital quality may act as a buffer to physical and mental health concerns in later life couples (Bookwala, 2011; Bookwala & Franks, 2005). Despite this trend in the literature, studies describing the stressors of illness in both early and late marriage continue to emerge (see Berg et al., 2008; Kirchhoff, Yi, Wright, Warner, & Smith, 2012).

Whether the spouse is ill versus well and female versus male are also important enduring characteristics. Several studies indicate that marital quality is at greater risk for healthy spouses than for ill spouses (Burman & Margolin, 1992). For example, Checton, Greene, Magsamen-Conrad, and Venetis (2012) found that among "well" spouses, greater uncertainty about spousal illness prognosis was related to decreased communication efficacy and to increased perceptions that the illness was interfering in their lives. Similarly, Booth and Johnson (1994) found that spousal declines in health were related to lower marital happiness for the "well" spouse across a 3-year period. The effect of being the ill versus well spouse is further compounded by gender, with couples where husbands are ill and the wives are well reporting the greatest amount of distress. Rohrbaugh, Shoham, and Coyne (2006) also found that higher marital quality was linked to higher female patient survival rates. In contrast, when serious medical illnesses occur, female partners are more likely to be abandoned (i.e., get divorced) than when male partners are ill (Glantz et al., 2009). High marital quality prior to the onset of illness may be an enduring characteristic that can buffer the impact of illness-related stress. However, few studies have measured marital quality prior to illness onset; therefore, this characteristic is most often observed within the adaptive process that couples make in response to an illness.

Additional enduring characteristics that can moderate the link between illness and adaptive processes include SES, religiosity, and social support. Socioeconomic status, as measured by income, access to health care, and education, often results in resources that lead to more adaptive processes. Alternatively, poverty is a risk factor for many illnesses and often presents barriers to optimal health care, sometimes requiring a greater percentage of one's income to be spent on health care expenses (National Center for Health Statistics, 2007). Religiosity and spirituality have been associated with both lower levels of stress and higher levels of desirable outcomes within marriage (Ellison, Henderson, Glenn, & Harkrider, 2011; Yorgason, 2015). Benefits of religiosity are often attributed to the social support available through a faith community. Additionally, Clements and Ermakova (2012) showed that the religious construct of *surrender,* or self-denial for a divine purpose, can be an important stress buffer, which may indirectly have an impact on health.

Adaptive Processes and Outcomes

Adaptive processes that mediate the link between illness stressors and outcomes include illness mechanisms, illness-prompted resources, and couple coping and caregiving processes. Illness mechanisms, defined as life changes due to an illness, sometimes account for why illness is disruptive to families. Booth and Johnson (1994) reported that a decrease in finances, division of household labor, and marital problems account for some of the negative effects a health decline can have on marital happiness. Yorgason et al. (2008) also found that psychological distress was a consistent mediator between health decline and marital happiness. Negative effects of mental illness, such as treatment costs and medicinal side effects, have also been identified to have an impact on marital relationships (Seeman, 2013)

Stress-prompted resources, defined as resources that emerge as a result of an illness, can also influence couple relationships and influence couple interactions. In the case of diabetes, illness-prompted resources might include patient and spousal knowledge about the disease including how to manage it (Trief et al., 2011). Using that knowledge, activities such as meal planning and preparation, grocery shopping, having a shared diet plan, and the monitoring of blood sugar levels, when done together in a spirit of supportiveness and cooperation, have been shown to reduce stress and increase enjoyable marital interactions (August, Rook, Franks, & Parris Stephens, 2013). In other cases, medical professionals can provide knowledge that may help couples to prepare for caregiving roles (Henriksson, Årestedt, Benzein, Ternestedt, & Andershed, 2013).

Regarding couple adaptive processes, communication between spouses is paramount. Poor communication patterns, as illustrated by protective buffering (i.e., hiding negative feelings about the illness to avoid hurting the other spouse), can have negative consequences, such as lower life satisfaction and higher levels of depression and anxiety. In a study of couples in which one partner suffered from chronic obstructive pulmonary disease (COPD), Snippe, Maters, Wempe, Hagedoorn, and Sanderman (2012) reported that when a patient's perception of his or her partner's protective buffering was high, the patient's report of distress increased. Furthermore, when patient and partner perception levels of overprotection were not congruent, possibly because of poor communication about the illness and the patient's needs, the negative effects of the protective buffering were increased as patient distress levels increased.

Poor communication may also result from situations involving mental illness in marriage, such as PTSD symptoms, depression, and personality disorders. Gerlock and colleagues (2014) reported that among married military veterans with PTSD, couple communication was a challenge. They further suggested that couple mutuality (i.e., both spouses sharing of feelings, thoughts, and activities) may benefit couples managing PTSD symptoms of one spouse. Veterans with PTSD often experience emotional numbing, avoidance, the need for control, secrecy, and depression symptoms, all of which can impact couple communication negatively. With regard to depression, Harper and Sandberg (2009) found that higher depression among older couples (either one or both spouses) was associated with poorer affective communication and problem solving. Additionally, reports of personality disorder symptoms, by self or spouse, were linked with greater aggression and violence in the marriage relationship (South et al., 2008).

In comparison, good couple communication and supportive interactions can facilitate positive outcomes. For example, when one spouse is enduring painful arthritis, better outcomes result when the other spouse is aware of the level of pain being experienced by his or her partner (Martire et al., 2006). Good communication may also guard against the development or intensification of some mental illness conditions. For example, a greater frequency of communication between military spouses when one is deployed is linked with lower instances of PTSD symptoms (Carter et al., 2011). Thus, open communication not only about the specifics of an illness but also within the marital relationship in general may result in better couple relations.

The supportive practices couples develop can represent some of the most important adaptive processes to illness. It is common that when an individual is ill, a spouse is called on to provide at least some care. It is important for the caregiver to balance caring behavior while allowing autonomy in the recipient. For example, gaining knowledge about an illness in order to provide support to an ill spouse can be done in either controlling or supportive ways (Houston-Barrett & Wilson, 2014). Revenson, Schiaffino, Majerovitz, and Gibofsky (1991) describe this continuum of supportive behavior as the double-edged sword of social support. They report that positive support predicts lower depression, and problematic support predicts higher depression among rheumatoid arthritis patients.

WHEN AGING PARENTS ARE ILL

_____ **Vignette** _____

During the past 5 years, Diane has been caring for her mother, Thelma, who is diagnosed with Alzheimer's disease. Thelma also is bedridden due to hip problems that resulted from having multiple falls. As the primary caregiver, Diane has not been able to leave her mother's side for any extended amount of time. Diane's siblings are concerned because they have noticed that she is constantly tired and unusually anxious about future care options for her mother. Recently, Diane went to the emergency room to get help with irregular heart palpitations, which turned out to be an anxiety attack. Diane wonders how long she will be able to continue to provide this level of care for her mother.

• • •

As evidenced by the above vignette, when caring for an aging parent, there is often a strong connection between physical and mental health (e.g. Feng, Yap, & Ng, 2013). Older adults that experience physical health challenges often face comorbid mental distress due to decreased autonomy, increases in physical pain, and the development of other health complications. In some cases, comorbid mental and physical health challenges combine to have multiplicative negative effects on quality of life (Ho et al., 2014; Ryan et al., 2013). These combined mental and physical health challenges often translate into adult child caregivers providing both emotional and instrumental support to aging parents. Furthermore, caregivers commonly experience both physical and emotional stress as a result of their caregiving role. This section of the chapter deals mainly with literature addressing stressors, resources and perceptions, enduring characteristics, and adaptive processes related to caring for an aging parent.

Physical and Mental Health Stressors of Aging Parents

Physical health challenges in later life often include illnesses such as arthritis, heart disease, stroke, cancer, and diabetes. Due to these and other illnesses, approximately 30% of Medicare enrollees over age 65 report some level of difficulty performing activities necessary for daily living (Federal Interagency Forum on Aging-Related Statistics, 2012). Furthermore, in 2013, it was estimated that 5.2 million people in the United States were living with Alzheimer's disease (Hebert, Weuve, Scherr, & Evans, 2013). Regarding mental health, it's estimated that about 16% of people over age 50 experience mental health concerns (Substance Abuse and Mental Health Services Administration, 2013) with depression being the most prevalent (Volkert, Schulz, Härter, Wlodarczyk, & Andreas, 2013).

There are diverse pathways to becoming a caregiver for aging parents. For many, the process is gradual, with increasing care being linked to health deterioration and greater needs developing over time, for example, in cases of dementia. For others, becoming a caregiver occurs more rapidly due to a health crisis or emergency, such as with hospitalization due to having a stroke or being diagnosed with cancer. Regardless of how caregiving develops, physical and mental health concerns of aging parents can present difficult challenges for those providing care.

Enduring Characteristics

Several factors moderate the link between stress resulting from caring for an ill parent and adaptive processes. Gender is an important moderating factor because women are more likely to be caregivers. Pinquart and Sörensen (2006) reported that women "provided more caregiving hours, helped with more caregiving tasks, and assisted more with personal care" (p. 33). Furthermore, female caregivers often experience higher levels of burden than male caregivers (Rohr, Wagner, & Lang, 2013).

Marital status and having siblings also can influence caregiving of ill parents by adult children. Unmarried adult children are more likely to co-reside with a widowed mother (Seltzer & Friedman, 2014), and having a parent coreside with an adult child is linked to a lower likelihood of siblings becoming a caregiver (Pezzin, Pollak, & Schone, 2014). Some research suggests that aging parents with multiple children typically receive support from more than one child, although equality in care provided tends to occur only when siblings have similar levels of other commitments (i.e., employment and marital status; Tolkacheva, van Groenou, & van Tilburg, 2014). Generally, sibling support among adult children is generally beneficial, if siblings do not participate in caring for an ill parent, feelings of resentment and abandonment can occur (Barnes, Given, & Given, 1992).

Ethnicity and culture may influence the likelihood of caregiving, associated stressors, and outcomes. On one hand, ethnic or cultural identity may increase the likelihood of an adult child wanting to provide care (Anngela-Cole & Busch, 2011), actually providing care (Angel, Rote, Brown, Angel, & Markides, 2014), and having positive perceptions of the caregiver role (Vroman & Morency, 2011). On the other hand, ethnic or cultural influences may decrease the likelihood of care recipients using available formal services from which they might benefit (Brown, Friedemann, & Mauro, 2014). Culturally sensitive interventions for caregivers and aging care-recipients might enhance the quality of caregiving experiences of all involved.

Adaptive Processes

Adaptive processes that mediate the link between caring for an aging parent and the amount of stress experienced include perceptions, resources, and coping activities. From a stress and coping paradigm (Lazarus & Folkman, 1984), the adult-child caregiver's appraisal of the situation will influence outcomes. Resources related to social support are strong indicators of resilience for caregivers and can be helpful by reducing stress, encouraging good health behaviors, and pursuing effective coping activities (Pinquart & Sörensen, 2007). Regarding resources, having a network of supports (Koehly, Ashida, Schafer, & Ludden, 2014), access to formal services (Gaugler, Mittelman, Hepburn, & Newcomer, 2009), assistance from siblings (Tolkacheva et al., 2014), and financial resources (Sun, Hilgeman, Durkin, Allen, & Burgio, 2009) may be linked to better outcomes. Although support is generally viewed positively, receiving too little or too much support is sometimes linked with poorer outcomes (Djundeva, Mills, Wittek, & Steverink, 2014). Regarding perceptions, caregivers may experience more negative outcomes when they have high levels of guilt combined with low levels of personal leisure time (Romero-Moreno et al., 2014). Furthermore, caregivers' marriage relationship satisfaction may suffer when individuals perceive an unfair split of support for aging parents versus aging parents-in-law (J. Lee, Zarit, Rovine, Birditt, & Fingerman, 2012).

Outcomes

Adult children report both strains and gains as caregivers (Pinquart & Sörensen, 2003). The most consistent findings suggest that caregivers experience various burdens brought on by the care they provide, including increased depression, health symptoms, outpatient doctor visits (Chan, Malhotra, Malhotra, Rush, & Østbye, 2013), and even increased mortality (Perkins et al., 2013). Such challenges may be partially due to having restrictions on normal activities, increased health symptoms (Smith, Williamson, Miller, & Schulz, 2011), changing role demands (e.g., work plus the demands of caregiving; Wang, Shyu, Chen, & Yang, 2011), chronic stress (Leggett, Zarit, Kim, Almeida, & Klein, 2014), financial strain (Y. Lee, Tang, Kim, & Albert, 2014; Strauss, 2013), repetitive health crises (Sims-Gould, Martin-Matthews, & Gignac, 2008), grieving the loss of a parent (Anngela-Cole & Busch, 2011), and sometimes providing care in multiple arenas (DePasquale et al., 2014). The negative results of caregiver burden not only impact the life of the caregiver but also may result in care recipients receiving a lower quality of care (Smith et al., 2011). In contrast, gains related to being an adult-child caregiver include personal and spiritual growth, enhanced feelings of mastery, and emotional closeness to the care recipient (e.g. Pope, 2013; Sanders, 2005).

DISCUSSION AND CONCLUSION

Commonalities between childhood, spousal, and parental physical and mental illness provide a sense of what factors are most salient for families dealing with a chronic illness. Despite the stress created by illness, many families facing illness are drawn closer together. Furthermore, research suggests that families can experience strains and gains simultaneously.

Enduring characteristics can significantly influence the extent and duration of illness stress and can be used as a target for intervention. Enduring characteristics that cannot be changed, such as gender, age, family structure, and ethnic background, often strongly influence the illness experience of all family members and should be considered when assisting families. For example, mental and physical illness at any age is a challenge for families, although illness in later life may have less negative impact since it is more expected. Enduring characteristics that can be influenced, such as accessibility to health care, outside social support, and internal family interactions, also can be targeted by professionals as points of intervention. For instance, interacting in positive ways with the medical community and gaining knowledge about an illness can be important buffers to the stress associated with a specific illness. Finally, family patterns that are helpful when facing illness include effective family communication, "balanced" coping, family cohesion, and maintaining clear, yet flexible, boundaries.

Although perceptions of illness change with time, maintaining a positive outlook can be beneficial for individuals and families. This is not always easy, especially when a mental illness involves negative or unrealistic expectations. Furthermore different family members may have differing perceptions of the illness that are related to the roles that each family member carries out (i.e., parent, ill child, sibling). The outcomes of illness are often comorbid with or connected to psychological distress, indicating an important target for prevention and intervention.

Although a tremendous amount of research has been conducted in the areas reviewed in this chapter, there is much room for future study. While most researchers work to isolate effects of individual illness, comorbidity, especially across physical and mental health domains, needs further attention. From a methodological perspective, the study of illness in families includes a rich blend of qualitative and quantitative studies, yet future studies could use a mixed methods approach to explore resilience processes in greater depth. Many of the outcomes studied in research to date involve negative measures including psychological and relationship distress; hence, more measures of positive family functioning are needed. Although a growing number of studies are exploring illness longitudinally, the reality is that the windows of data collection often provide only a snapshot of the illness. Future research is needed to understand prediagnosis predictors of resilience, as well as family relationship processes across the different phases of illness. In addition, few studies have examined everyday physical and mental illnesses in families, such as colds, the flu, a broken limb, mononucleosis, and running a temperature, as well as fluctuations in depressive, anxious, and other psychological symptoms. More research is also needed to understand similarities in the effects of chronic illnesses in childhood, in adulthood, and in later life. Finally, literature exploring illness and families crosses many disciplines including nursing, medicine, and the social sciences. The influence of medical professionals interacting with families is such an integral aspect of experiencing illness that multidisciplinary research teams would enhance both the medical and the social arenas.

Research exploring childhood illness, illness of a marriage partner, and caring for an ill parent has dramatically increased in recent decades. Findings indicate (a) an increasing knowledge of the stressors that individuals and families face, (b) the enduring characteristics that predispose families to experience illness and act as protective and risk factors once a chronic illness occurs, (c) adaptive processes families often use, (d) and positive and negative outcomes commonly experienced. Research that has been carried out provides a strong base for future work, yet further effort is needed to better understand illness experiences within families.

REFERENCES

Adler, N. E., & Newman, K. (2002). Socioeconomic disparities in health: Pathways and policies. *Health Affairs*, *21*(2), 60–76.

Angel, J. L., Rote, S. M., Brown, D. C., Angel, R. J., & Markides, K. S. (2014). Nativity status and sources of care assistance among elderly Mexican-origin adults. *Journal of Cross-Cultural Gerontology*, *29*(3), 243–258.

Anngela-Cole, L., & Busch, M. (2011). Stress and grief among family caregivers of older adults with cancer: A multicultural comparison from Hawaii. *Journal of Social Work in End-Of-Life & Palliative Care*, *7*(4), 318–337.

August, K. J., Rook, K. S., Franks, M. M., & Parris Stephens, M. A. (2013). Spouses' involvement in their partners' diabetes management: Associations with spouse stress and perceived marital quality. *Journal of Family Psychology*, *27*(5), 712–721.

Badr, H., & Acitelli, L. K. (2005). Dyadic adjustment in chronic illness: Does relationship talk matter? *Journal of Family Psychology*, *19*(3), 465–469.

Banks, J., Cramer, H., Sharp, D. J., Shield, J. P., & Turner, K. M. (2014). Identifying families' reasons for engaging or not engaging with childhood obesity services: A qualitative study. *Journal of Child Health Care*, *18*(2), 101–110.

Barnes, C. L., Given, B. A., & Given, C. W. (1992). Caregivers of elderly relatives: Spouses and adult children. *Health & Social Work*, *17*(4), 282–289.

Berg, C. A., & Upchurch, R. (2007). A developmental-contextual model of couples coping with chronic illness across the adult life span. *Psychological Bulletin*, *133*(6), 920–954.

Berg, C. A., Wiebe, D. J., Bloor, L., Butner, J., Bradstreet, C., Upchurch, R., Patton, G. (2008). Collaborative coping and daily mood in couples dealing with prostate cancer. *Psychology and Aging*, *23*, 505–516.

Berge, J. M., & Holm, K. E. (2007). Boundary ambiguity in parents with chronically ill children: Integrating theory and research. *Family Relations*, *56*(2), 123–134.

Bookwala, J. (2011). Marital quality as a moderator of the effects of poor vision on quality of life among older adults. *The Journals of Gerontology Series B: Psychological Sciences and Social Sciences*, *66B*(5), 605–616.

Bookwala, J., & Franks, M. M. (2005). Moderating role of marital quality in older adults' depressed affect: Beyond the main-effects model. *The Journals of Gerontology Series B: Psychological Sciences and Social Sciences*, *60*(6), P338–P341.

Booth, A., & Johnson, D. R. (1994). Declining health and marital quality. *Journal of Marriage and the Family*, *56*(1), 218.

Brown, E. L., Friedemann, M.-L., & Mauro, A. C. (2014). Use of adult day care service centers in an ethnically diverse sample of older adults. *Journal of Applied Gerontology*, *33*(2), 189–206.

Burman, B., & Margolin, G. (1992). Analysis of the association between marital relationships and health problems: An interactional perspective. *Psychological Bulletin*, *112*(1), 39–63.

Carter, S., Loew, B., Allen, E., Stanley, S., Rhoades, G., & Markman, H. (2011). Relationships between soldiers' PTSD symptoms and spousal communication during deployment. *Journal of Traumatic Stress*, *24*(3), 352–355.

Chan, A., Malhotra, C., Malhotra, R., Rush, A. J., & Østbye, T. (2013). Health impacts of caregiving for older adults with functional limitations results from the Singapore Survey on Informal Caregiving. *Journal of Aging and Health*, *25*(6), 998–1012.

Checton, M. G., Greene, K., Magsamen-Conrad, K., & Venetis, M. K. (2012). Patients' and partners' perspectives of chronic illness and its management. *Families, Systems, & Health*, *30*(2), 114–129.

Clements, A. D., & Ermakova, A. V. (2012). Surrender to God and stress: A possible link between religiosity and health. *Psychology of Religion and Spirituality*, *4*(2), 93–107.

Cohen, M. S. (1999). Families coping with childhood chronic illness: A research review. *Families, Systems, & Health*, *17*(2), 149–164.

Coleman, M., & Ganong, L. (2002). Resilience and families. *Family Relations*, *51*(2), 101–102.

Compas, B. E., Jaser, S. S., Dunn, M. J., & Rodriguez, E. M. (2012). Coping with chronic illness in childhood and adolescence. *Annual Review of Clinical Psychology*, *8*(1), 455–480.

Cranford, J. A. (2014). DSM-IV alcohol dependence and marital dissolution: evidence from the National Epidemiologic Survey on Alcohol and Related Conditions. *Journal of Studies on Alcohol and Drugs*, *75*(3), 520.

DePasquale, N., Davis, K. D., Zarit, S. H., Moen, P., Hammer, L. B., & Almeida, D. M. (2014). Combining formal and informal caregiving roles: The psychosocial implications of double- and triple-duty Care. *The Journals of Gerontology Series B: Psychological Sciences and Social Sciences*. Advanced online publication Sept. 30, 2014; doi:10.1093/geronb/gbu139

Djundeva, M., Mills, M., Wittek, R., & Steverink, N. (2014). Receiving instrumental support in late parent-child relationships and parental depression. *The Journals of Gerontology Series B: Psychological Sciences and Social Sciences*. Advanced online publication Sept. 23, 2014; doi:10.1093/geronb/gbu136

Duran, B. (2013). Posttraumatic growth as experienced by childhood cancer survivors and their families: A narrative synthesis of qualitative and quantitative research. *Journal of Pediatric Oncology Nursing*, *30*(4), 179–197.

Ellison, C. G., Henderson, A. K., Glenn, N. D., & Harkrider, K. E. (2011). Sanctification, stress, and marital quality. *Family Relations: An Interdisciplinary Journal of Applied Family Studies*, *60*(4), 404–420.

Federal Interagency Forum on Aging-Related Statistics. (2012). *Older Americans 2012: Key indicators of well-being*. Washington, DC: U.S. Government Printing Office.

Federal Interagency Forum on Child and Family Statistics. (2013). *America's Children: Key national indicators of well-being*. Washington, DC: U.S. Government Printing Office.

Federal Interagency Forum on Child and Family Statistics. (2014). *At a glance for 2014, America's children: Key national indicators of well-being*. Washington, DC: U.S. Government Printing Office.

Feng, L., Yap, K. B., & Ng, T. P. (2013). Depressive symptoms in older adults with chronic kidney disease: Mortality, quality of life outcomes, and correlates. *The American Journal of Geriatric Psychiatry*, *21*(6), 570–9.

Gannoni, A. F., & Shute, R. H. (2010). Parental and child perspectives on adaptation to childhood chronic illness: A qualitative study. *Clinical Child Psychology and Psychiatry*, *15*(1), 39–53.

Garwick, A. W., Kohrman, C. H., Titus, J. C., Wolman, C., & Blum, R. W. (1999). Variations in families' explanations of childhood chronic conditions: A cross-cultural perspective. In H. I. McCubbin, E. A. Thompson, A. I. Thompson, & J. A. Futrell (Eds.), *The dynamics of resilient families* (pp. 165–202). Thousand Oaks, CA: Sage.

Gaugler, J. E., Mittelman, M. S., Hepburn, K., & Newcomer, R. (2009). Predictors of change in caregiver burden and depressive symptoms following nursing home admission. *Psychology and Aging*, *24*(2), 385–396.

Gerlock, A. A., Grimesey, J., & Sayre, G. (2014). Military-related posttraumatic stress disorder and intimate relationship behaviors: A developing dyadic relationship model. *Journal of Marital and Family Therapy*, *40*(3), 344–356.

Glantz, M. J., Chamberlain, M. C., Liu, Q., Hsieh, C.-C., Edwards, K. R., Van Horn, A., & Recht, L. (2009). Gender disparity in the rate of partner abandonment in patients with serious medical illness. *Cancer*, *115*(22), 5237–5242.

Greene, M. S., Mandleco, B., Roper, S. O., Marshall, E. S., & Dyches, T. (2010). Metabolic control, self-care behaviors, and parenting in adolescents with type 1 diabetes a correlational study. *The Diabetes Educator*, *36*(2), 326–336.

Harper, J. M., & Sandberg, J. G. (2009). Depression and communication processes in later life marriages. *Aging & Mental Health*, *13*(4), 546–556.

Hebert, L. E., Weuve, J., Scherr, P. A., & Evans, D. A. (2013). Alzheimer disease in the United States (2010-2050) estimated using the 2010 census. *Neurology*, *80*(19), 1778–1783.

Henriksson, A., Årestedt, K., Benzein, E., Ternestedt, B.-M., & Andershed, B. (2013). Effects of a support group programme for patients with life-threatening illness during ongoing palliative care. *Palliative Medicine*, *27*(3), 257–264.

Ho, C. S., Feng, L., Fam, J., Mahendran, R., Kua, E. H., & Ng, T. P. (2014). Coexisting medical comorbidity and depression: Multiplicative effects on health outcomes in older adults. *International Psychogeriatrics*, *26*(07), 1221–1229.

Houston-Barrett, R. A., & Wilson, C. M. (2014). Couple's relationship with diabetes: Means and meanings for management success. *Journal of Marital and Family Therapy*, *40*(1), 92–105.

Hovén, E. I., Lannering, B., Gustafsson, G., & Boman, K. K. (2013). Persistent impact of illness on families of adult survivors of childhood central nervous system tumors: A population-based cohort study: Persistent impact on families of childhood cancer survivors. *Psycho-Oncology*, *22*(1), 160–167.

Johnson, M. D., Galambos, N. L., & Krahn, H. J. (2014). Depression and anger across 25 years: Changing vulnerabilities in the VSA model. *Journal of Family Psychology*, *28*(2), 225–235.

Karney, B. R., & Bradbury, T. N. (1995). The longitudinal course of marital quality and stability: A review of theory, methods, and research. *Psychological Bulletin*, *118*(1), 3–34.

Kars, M. C., Duijnstee, M. S. H., Pool, A., van Delden, J. J. M., & Grypdonck, M. H. F. (2008). Being there: Parenting the child with acute lymphoblastic leukaemia. *Journal of Clinical Nursing*, *17*(12), 1553–1562.

Keeton, C. P., Ginsburg, G. S., Drake, K. L., Sakolsky, D., Kendall, P. C., Birmaher, B., Walkup, J. T. (2013). Benefits of child-focused anxiety treatments for parents and family functioning. *Depression and Anxiety*, *30*(9), 865–872.

Kieckhefer, G. M., Trahms, C. M., Churchill, S. S., Kratz, L., Uding, N., & Villareale, N. (2014). A randomized clinical trial of the building on family strengths program: An education program for parents of children with chronic health conditions. *Maternal and Child Health Journal*, *18*(3), 563–574.

Kirchhoff, A. C., Yi, J., Wright, J., Warner, E. L., & Smith, K. R. (2012). Marriage and divorce among young adult cancer survivors. *Journal of Cancer Survivorship*, *6*(4), 441–450.

Koehly, L. M., Ashida, S., Schafer, E. J., & Ludden, A. (2014). Caregiving networks—Using a network approach to identify missed opportunities. *The Journals of Gerontology Series B: Psychological Sciences and Social Sciences*. Advanced online publication Sept. 14, 2014; doi:10.1093/geronb/gbu111

Kraemer, L. M., Stanton, A. L., Meyerowitz, B. E., Rowland, J. H., & Ganz, P. A. (2011). A longitudinal examination of couples' coping strategies as predictors of adjustment to breast cancer. *Journal of Family Psychology*, *25*(6), 963–972.

Law, E. F., Fisher, E., Fales, J., Noel, M., & Eccleston, C. (2014). Systematic review and meta-analysis of parent and family-based interventions for children and adolescents with chronic medical conditions. *Journal of Pediatric Psychology*, *39*(8), 866–886.

Lazarus, R. S., & Folkman, S. (1984). *Stress, appraisal, and coping*. New York, NY: Springer.

Lee, I., Lee, E.-O., Kim, H. S., Park, Y. S., Song, M., & Park, Y. H. (2004). Concept development of family resilience: A study of Korean families with a chronically ill child. *Journal of Clinical Nursing*, *13*(5), 636–645.

Lee, J. E., Zarit, S. H., Rovine, M. J., Birditt, K. S., & Fingerman, K. L. (2012). Middle-aged couples' exchanges of support with aging parents: Patterns and association with marital satisfaction. *Gerontology*, *58*(1), 88–96.

Lee, Y., Tang, F., Kim, K. H., & Albert, S. M. (2014). The vicious cycle of parental caregiving and financial well-being: A longitudinal study of women. *The Journals of Gerontology Series B: Psychological Sciences and Social Sciences*, Vol. 70, 425-431. doi: 10.1093/geronb/gbu001

Leggett, A. N., Zarit, S. H., Kim, K., Almeida, D. M., & Klein, L. C. (2014). Depressive mood, anger, and daily cortisol of caregivers on high- and low-stress days. *The Journals of Gerontology Series B: Psychological Sciences and Social Sciences*.

Lim, J., Wood, B. L., & Miller, B. D. (2008). Maternal depression and parenting in relation to child internalizing symptoms and asthma disease activity. *Journal of Family Psychology*, *22*(2), 264–273.

Limbers, C. A., & Skipper, S. (2014). Health-related quality of life measurement in siblings of children with physical chronic illness: A systematic review. *Families, Systems, & Health*, *32*(4), 408–415.

Lingard, R. J., & Court, J. (2014). Can couples find a silver lining amid the dark cloud of ME/CFS a pilot study. *The Family Journal*, *22*(3), 304–310.

Lukens, E. P., Thorning, H., & Lohrer, S. (2004). Sibling perspectives on severe mental illness: Reflections on self and family. *American Journal of Orthopsychiatry*, *74*(4), 489–501.

Manne, S. L., Hamel, K. D., Gallelli, K., Sorgen, K., & Redd, W. H. (1998). Posttraumatic stress disorder among mothers of pediatric cancer survivors: diagnosis, comorbidity, and utility of the PTSD checklist as a screening instrument. *Journal of Pediatric Psychology*, *23*(6), 357–366.

Mansour, M. E., Lanphear, B. P., & DeWitt, T. G. (2000). Barriers to asthma care in urban children: Parent perspectives. *Pediatrics*, *106*(3), 512–519.

Martire, L. M., Keefe, F. J., Schulz, R., Ready, R., Beach, S. R., Rudy, T. E., & Starz, T. W. (2006). Older spouses' perceptions of partners' chronic arthritis pain: Implications for spousal responses, support provision, and caregiving experiences. *Psychology and Aging*, *21*(2), 222–230.

McCubbin, H. I., & Patterson, J. M. (1982). Family adaptation to crisis. In H. I. McCubbin, A. E. Cauble, & J. M. Patterson (Eds.), *Family stress, coping, and social support* (pp. 26–47). Springfield, IL: Thomas.

McCubbin, M., Balling, K., Possin, P., Frierdich, S., & Bryne, B. (2002). Family Resiliency in Childhood Cancer. *Family Relations*, *51*(2), 103–111.

Mednick, L., Cogen, F., Henderson, C., Rohrbeck, C., Kitessa, D., & Streisand, R. (2007). Hope more, worry less: Hope as a potential resilience factor in mothers of very young children with Type 1 diabetes. *Children's Health Care*, *36*(4), 385–396.

Morgan, M. A., Small, B. J., Donovan, K. A., Overcash, J., & McMillan, S. (2011). Cancer patients with pain: The spouse/partner relationship and quality of life. *Cancer Nursing*, *34*(1), 13–23.

Murphy, G., Peters, K., Jackson, D., & Wilkes, L. (2011). A qualitative meta-synthesis of adult children of parents with a mental illness. *Journal of Clinical Nursing*, *20*(23-24), 3430–3442.

National Center for Health Statistics. (2007). *Chartbook on trends in the health of Americans*. Hyattsville, MD: U.S. Government Printing Office.

National Center for Health Statistics. (2012). *Health, United States, 2011: With special feature on socio-economic status and health*. Hyattsville, MD: U.S. Government Printing Office.

National Center for Health Statistics (2014). *Health, United States, 2013: In brief*. Hyattsville, MD: U.S. Government Printing Office.

Newacheck, P. W., & Halfon, N. (1998). Prevalence and impact of disabling chronic conditions in childhood. *American Journal of Public Health*, *88*(4), 610–617.

Norton, T. R., & Manne, S. L. (2007). Support concordance among couples coping with cancer: Relationship, individual, and situational factors. *Journal of Social and Personal Relationships*, *24*(5), 675–692.

O'Brien, M. (2007). Ambiguous loss in families of children with autism spectrum disorders. *Family Relations*, *56*(2), 135–146.

Onat, G., & Beji, N. K. (2012). Marital relationship and quality of life among couples with infertility. *Sexuality and Disability*, *30*(1), 39–52.

Patterson, J. M. (1991). Family resilience to the challenge of a child's disability. *Pediatric Annals*, *20*(9), 491–492, 494–497, 499.

Patterson, J. M. (1993). The role of family meanings in adaptation to chronic illness and disability. In A. P. Turnbull, J. M. Patterson, S. K. Behr, D. L. Murphy, J. G. Marquis, & M. J. Blue-Banning (Eds.), *Cognitive coping, families, and disability* (pp. 221–238). Baltimore, MD: Paul H. Brookes.

Patterson, J. M. (2002). Integrating family resilience and family stress theory. *Journal of Marriage and Family, 64*(2), 349–360.

Patterson, J. M., & Garwick, A. W. (1994). Levels of meaning in family stress theory. *Family Process, 33*(3), 287–304.

Perkins, M., Howard, V. J., Wadley, V. G., Crowe, M., Safford, M. M., Haley, W. E., Howard, G., & Roth, D. L. (2013). Caregiving strain and all-cause mortality: Evidence from the REGARDS study. *The Journals of Gerontology Series B: Psychological Sciences and Social Sciences, 68*(4), 504–512.

Pezzin, L. E., Pollak, R. A., & Schone, B. S. (2014). Bargaining power, parental caregiving, and intergenerational coresidence. *The Journals of Gerontology Series B: Psychological Sciences and Social Sciences,* Vol. 70, 969-980. doi: 10.1093/geronb/gbu079

Pinquart, M. (2014). Achievement of developmental milestones in emerging and young adults with and without pediatric chronic illness—A meta-analysis. *Journal of Pediatric Psychology, 39*(6), 577–587.

Pinquart, M., & Sörensen, S. (2003). Associations of stressors and uplifts of caregiving with caregiver burden and depressive mood: A meta-analysis. *The Journals of Gerontology Series B: Psychological Sciences and Social Sciences, 58*(2), P112–P128.

Pinquart, M., & Sörensen, S. (2006). Gender differences in caregiver stressors, social resources, and health: An updated meta-analysis. *The Journals of Gerontology Series B: Psychological Sciences and Social Sciences, 61*(1), P33–P45.

Pinquart, M., & Sörensen, S. (2007). Correlates of physical health of informal caregivers: A meta-analysis. *The Journals of Gerontology Series B: Psychological Sciences and Social Sciences, 62*(2), P126–P137.

Pope, N. D. (2013). Views on aging: How caring for an aging parent influences adult daughters' perspectives on later life. *Journal of Adult Development, 20*(1), 46–56.

Rasic, D., Hajek, T., Alda, M., & Uher, R. (2014). Risk of mental illness in offspring of parents with schizophrenia, bipolar disorder, and major depressive disorder: A meta-analysis of family high-risk studies. *Schizophrenia Bulletin, 40*(1), 28–38.

Retzlaff, R. (2007). Families of children with Rett syndrome: Stories of coherence and resilience. *Families, Systems, & Health, 25*(3), 246–262.

Revenson, T. A., Schiaffino, K. M., Majerovitz, S.D., & Gibofsky, A. (1991). Social support as a double-edged sword: The relation of positive and problematic support to depression among rheumatoid arthritis patients. *Social Science & Medicine, 33*(7), 807–813.

Roberto, K. A., Gold, D. T., & Yorgason, J. B. (2004). The influence of osteoporosis on the marital relationship of older couples. *Journal of Applied Gerontology, 23*(4), 443–456.

Rohrbaugh, M. J., Shoham, V., & Coyne, J. C. (2006). Effect of marital quality on eight-year survival of patients with heart failure. *The American Journal of Cardiology, 98*(8), 1069–1072.

Rohr, M. K., Wagner, J., & Lang, F. R. (2013). Effects of personality on the transition into caregiving. *Psychology and Aging, 28*(3), 692–700.

Rolland, J. (1994). *Families, illness, and disability: An integrative treatment model.* New York, NY: Basic Books.

Romero-Moreno, R., Losada, A., Marquez, M., Laidlaw, K., Fernandez-Fernandez, V., Nogales-Gonzalez, C., & Lopez, J. (2014). Leisure, gender, and kinship in dementia caregiving: Psychological vulnerability of caregiving daughters with feelings of guilt. *The Journals of Gerontology Series B: Psychological Sciences and Social Sciences, 69*(4), 502–513.

Roper, S. O., & Jackson, J. B. (2007). The ambiguities of out-of-home care: Children with severe or profound disabilities. *Family Relations, 56*(2), 147–161.

Rose, T., Joe, S., Shields, J., & Caldwell, C. H. (2014). Social integration and the mental health of black adolescents. *Child Development*, *85*(3), 1003–1018.

Ryan, M., Merrick, E. L., Hodgkin, D., Horgan, C. M., Garnick, D. W., Panas, L., . . . Saitz, R. (2013). Drinking patterns of older adults with chronic medical conditions. *Journal of General Internal Medicine*, *28*(10), 1326–1332.

Sanders, S. (2005). Is the glass half empty or half full? *Social Work in Health Care*, *40*(3), 57–73.

Seeman, M. V. (2013). Bad, burdened or ill? Characterizing the spouses of women with schizophrenia. *International Journal of Social Psychiatry*, *59*(8), 805–810.

Seltzer, J. A., & Friedman, E. M. (2014). Widowed mothers' coresidence with adult children. *The Journals of Gerontology Series B: Psychological Sciences and Social Sciences*, *69B*(1), 63–74.

Sharpe, D., & Rossiter, L. (2002). Siblings of children with a chronic illness: A meta-analysis. *Journal of Pediatric Psychology*, *27*(8), 699–710.

Sher, T., Braun, L., Domas, A., Bellg, A., Baucom, D. H., & Houle, T. T. (2014). The partners for life program: A couples approach to cardiac risk reduction. *Family Process*, *53*(1), 131–149.

Sherman, C. W., Webster, N. J., & Antonucci, T. C. (2013). Dementia caregiving in the context of late-life remarriage: Support networks, relationship quality, and well-being. *Journal of Marriage and Family*, *75*(5), 1149–1163.

Shpigner, E., Possick, C., & Buchbinder, E. (2013). Parents' experience of their child's first psychiatric breakdown: "Welcome to hell." *Social Work in Health Care*, *52*(6), 538–557.

Silver, E. J., Westbrook, L. E., & Stein, R. E. K. (1998). Relationship of parental psychological distress to consequences of chronic health conditions in children. *Journal of Pediatric Psychology*, *23*(1), 5–15.

Sims-Gould, J., Martin-Matthews, A., & Gignac, M. A. M. (2008). Episodic crises in the provision of care to elderly relatives. *Journal of Applied Gerontology*, *27*(2), 123–140.

Smith, G. R., Williamson, G. M., Miller, L. S., & Schulz, R. (2011). Depression and quality of informal care: A longitudinal investigation of caregiving stressors. *Psychology and Aging*, *26*(3), 584–591.

Snippe, E., Maters, G. A., Wempe, J. B., Hagedoorn, M., & Sanderman, R. (2012). Discrepancies between patients' and partners' perceptions of unsupportive behavior in chronic obstructive pulmonary disease. *Journal of Family Psychology*, *26*(3), 464–469.

South, S. C., Krueger, R. F., & Iacono, W. G. (2011). Understanding general and specific connections between psychopathology and marital distress: A model based approach. *Journal of Abnormal Psychology*, *120*(4), 935–947.

South, S. C., Turkheimer, E., & Oltmanns, T. F. (2008). Personality disorder symptoms and marital functioning. *Journal of Consulting and Clinical Psychology*, *76*(5), 769–780.

Strauss, J. R. (2013). Caregiving for parents and in-laws: Commonalities and differences. *Journal of Gerontological Social Work*, *56*(1), 49–66.

Substance Abuse and Mental Health Services Administration (2013). *Results from the 2012 National Survey on Drug Use and Health: Mental health findings* (NSDUH Series H-47, HHS Publication No. [SMA] 13-4805). Rockville, MD: Author.

Sun, F., Hilgeman, M. M., Durkin, D. W., Allen, R. S., & Burgio, L. D. (2009). Perceived income inadequacy as a predictor of psychological distress in Alzheimer's caregivers. *Psychology and Aging*, *24*(1), 177–183.

Tolkacheva, N., van Groenou, M. B., & van Tilburg, T. (2014). Sibling similarities and sharing the care of older parents. *Journal of Family Issues*, *35*(3), 312–330.

Trief, P., Sandberg, J. G., Ploutz-Snyder, R., Brittain, R., Cibula, D., Scales, K., & Weinstock, R. S. (2011). Promoting couples collaboration in Type 2 diabetes: The diabetes support project pilot data. *Families, Systems, & Health*, *29*(3), 253–261.

Van Loon, L. M. A., Van de Ven, M. O. M., Van Doesum, K. T. M., Witteman, C. L. M., & Hosman, C. M. H. (2014). The relation between parental mental illness and adolescent mental health: The role of family factors. *Journal of Child and Family Studies*, *23*(7), 1201–1214.

Vogan, V., Lake, J. K., Weiss, J. A., Robinson, S., Tint, A., & Lunsky, Y. (2014). Factors associated with caregiver burden among parents of individuals with ASD: Differences across intellectual functioning: Caregiver burden in ASD. *Family Relations, 63*(4), 554–567.

Volkert, J., Schulz, H., Härter, M., Wlodarczyk, O., & Andreas, S. (2013). The prevalence of mental disorders in older people in Western countries—A meta-analysis. *Ageing Research Reviews, 12*(1), 339–353.

Vroman, K., & Morency, J. (2011). "I do the best I can": Caregivers' perceptions of informal caregiving for older adults in Belize. *The International Journal of Aging and Human Development, 72*(1), 1–25.

Walsh, F. (1998). *Strengthening family resilience.* New York, NY: Guilford.

Wang, Y.-N., Shyu, Y.-I. L., Chen, M.-C., & Yang, P.-S. (2011). Reconciling work and family caregiving among adult-child family caregivers of older people with dementia: Effects on role strain and depressive symptoms. *Journal of Advanced Nursing, 67*(4), 829–840.

Yorgason, J. B. (2015). Exploring daily religious/spiritual activities among older couples: Religious/spiritual influence moderating the effects of health symptoms on marital interactions. *Journal of Religion, Spirituality & Aging, 27*, 201–221.

Yorgason, J. B., Booth, A., & Johnson, D. (2008). Health, disability, and marital quality is the association different for younger versus older cohorts? *Research on Aging, 30*(6), 623–648.

Yorgason, J. B., Piercy, F. P., & Piercy, S. K. (2007). Acquired hearing impairment in older couple relationships: An exploration of couple resilience processes. *Journal of Aging Studies, 21*(3), 215–228.

Yorgason, J. B., Roper, S. O., Sandberg, J. G., & Berg, C. A. (2012). Stress spillover of health symptoms from healthy spouses to patient spouses in older married couples managing both diabetes and osteoarthritis. *Families, Systems, & Health, 30*(4), 330–343.

Zhang, Y., Wei, M., Zhang, Y., & Shen, N. (2014). Chinese family management of chronic childhood conditions: A cluster analysis: *Journal for Specialists in Pediatric Nursing, 19*(1), 39–53.

CHAPTER 15

Families Coping With Alcohol and Substance Abuse

Kevin P. Lyness and Judith Fischer

A prominent approach to the study of alcohol and families involves a biopsychosocial focus (Sher, Grekin, & Williams, 2005). This perspective organizes the prediction of pathological alcohol involvement (and, by extension, more general substance abuse) through consideration of biological contributions, psychological factors, and social influences. Conjoining this model with the family stress and coping model (see McKenry & Price, 2005) acknowledges the contribution of these biopsychosocial factors at each juncture: stressor, resource, perception, coping, and managing.

The purpose of this chapter is to review research on (1) children and adolescents and their parents coping with the challenges posed by substances and (2) intervention strategies. Throughout the chapter we put the emphasis on both the family stresses involved and the search for explanations of resilience in these situations of families coping with substance abuse. We pay particular attention to the mediating and moderating effects that intervene between two variables, such as those that occur when associations between parent drinking and offspring drinking are worked through (mediated) or altered (moderated) by other variables. The chapter begins with an illustrative vignette that highlights many of the findings summarized. Given limitations of space, we are unable to extend our discussion in this chapter beyond the contexts of families with children and adolescents. Information on other important topics related to families and substance misuse may be found in Arendt and Farkas (2007) for fetal alcohol spectrum disorder, Leonard and Eiden (2007) and Fischer and Wiersma (2012) for adult couples, and Stelle and Scott (2007) for elders in families.

Some definitions are in order. *Substance use,* as we use the term in this chapter, includes both experimental and regular use. *Substance misuse* refers to the excessive consumption of a substance. *Substance abuse* and *substance dependence* are clinical designations involving serious and persistent problems with substances. The recent revision to the *Diagnostic and Statistical Manual of Mental Disorders* (DSM-5; American Psychiatric Association, 2013) brings a significant departure from past editions in nomenclature. The only designation used is that of *substance use disorder* (with the substance name used, such as *alcohol use disorder*). The term *substance dependence* is no longer used; instead, the diagnosis includes a severity indicator (mild, moderate, severe). For all substance use disorders, there are four areas of behavior to assess: impaired control, social impairment, risky use, and pharmacological criteria (tolerance and withdrawal where applicable). Designations used in this chapter reflect those chosen by the authors cited.

In organizing the following literature review, we take a family developmental approach. Timing is an important part of the stress and coping model. Stressors may be time limited, but they may also extend over long periods. Particular situations may not be considered stressors at one developmental period but may be stressors at another. For example, Biederman, Faraone, Monuteaux, and Feighner (2000) found that *childhood* exposure to parental substance use disorders conferred a twofold risk on offspring, but *adolescent* exposure was associated with a threefold risk for the emergence of substance use disorders. Perceptions, resources, and problem solving may be greater or lesser depending on individual and family development. Coping that is effective in the short term may moderate the long-term impacts of a stressor or lead to a pileup of stressors over time. In any given family, the substance misuser(s) may be the parents, the offspring, or both. Treatments vary depending on whether the child in the family or the adult is the presenting patient. And when intervening with an alcoholic parent, the ages of the children in the family need to be taken into account (Kelley & Fals-Stewart, 2008).

Vignette

Karl is a 13-year-old boy who has been getting into trouble for drinking at school. This is not Karl's first time in trouble—he is often disruptive and aggressive and seems to lack impulse control. When he was younger, his parents (at the urging of the school) had him tested for attention deficit hyperactivity disorder (ADHD), but the results were inconclusive, and the psychiatrist did not recommend medication. Karl's parents are typically punitive and often use physical punishment, and Karl has reported not feeling supported by his parents. Moreover, Karl's parents have been considering getting a divorce. His father is a heavy drinker, although he has never been diagnosed with a substance abuse problem. Karl sees his father come home from work each night and drink five to six beers as he complains about his day. Recently, his father reports that the stress of dealing with Karl has led to increased drinking in order to cope. Karl has learned from this that drinking is a good way to relieve stress, and this reinforces his positive attitude toward alcohol. Karl's parents do not know most of his friends, but the school reports that Karl hangs out with a slightly older group of kids who are known to drink and party. Karl has never felt that he fits in very well with his peers, but this current group of friends seems more accepting of his impulsive nature. Karl has an older sister who has not gotten into trouble with substances and who has always been more controlled and inhibited. The school has recommended that the family see a therapist.

The family therapist, knowing some of the literature on stress and coping as well as alcohol and substance abuse, engaged a multifaceted approach. The therapist first addressed parental behaviors and coping, including the quality of the marriage, parenting styles, and Karl's father's drinking, with a focus on increasing self-regulation capacities in both parents and in Karl; with Karl by specifically focusing on developing positive goal structures and increasing his focus on choices he makes in coping. Partly as a result of increased self-awareness, Karl's father decided to cut down on his drinking and made a commitment to work on the marriage. Both parents agreed to specific behavioral interventions designed to interrupt Karl's disinhibited behavior patterns. The therapist also helped Karl find less maladaptive ways of coping, along with implementing interventions with Karl at the school that helped him develop a different peer group (particularly focusing on Karl's propensity for aggression). Finally, the therapist intervened with Karl directly about his drinking behavior, knowing that Karl's early onset of drinking places him at risk for later serious substance abuse problems.

• • •

CHILDREN AND SUBSTANCE ABUSE PROBLEMS

Most research on childhood substance abuse has focused on 8- to 11-year-olds. A number of scholars have documented the fact that children this young are using and even abusing substances (Acion, Ramirez, Jorge, & Arndt, 2013; Elkins, Fite, Moore, Lochman, & Wells, 2014). According to research conducted by Elkins et al. (2014), between 5% and 7% of fourth through sixth graders consumed alcohol, used marijuana, and/or used tobacco in the previous 30 days. Past 30-day binge drinking among sixth graders ranged from approximately 2% to 7%, values that depended upon the deployment status of a parent (Acion et al., 2013).

Child Characteristics

Research on substance abuse prior to adolescence tends to focus on childhood predictors of *later* adolescent and adult use and abuse (cf. Zucker, 2008) rather than correlates of *actual* substance use in childhood. Early alcohol initiation is strongly predicted by the presence of conduct disorders (Sartor, Lynskey, Heath, Jacob, & True, 2006). A considerable body of literature suggests that behavioral undercontrol or behavioral disinhibition (failure to inhibit behavioral impulses) in childhood, especially among males, is an important precursor of later adolescent problems with substance use and abuse (Chassin, Sher, Hussong, & Curran, 2013; Dubow, Boxer, & Huesmann, 2008; Zucker, 2008). Recent work has focused on socialization (a willingness to follow rules and endorse conventional values) and on boldness (including thrill seeking) in childhood. Longitudinal research has demonstrated a link between low socialization at ages 11 and 14 and boldness at age 11 to substance abuse at age 17 (Hicks et al., 2014).

Cognitions (expectancies, beliefs, and values) about alcohol use appear in children as young as 3 to 6 years old (Zucker, Fitzgerald, Refior, Pallas, & Ellis, 2000), particularly among children in alcoholic families. In a 4-year longitudinal study, Andrews and Peterson (2006) found that from first through fifth grade, children developed more favorable proto-typical views of substance use. Children's favorable attitudes toward alcohol and intentions to use alcohol at age 10 are associated with a higher probability of drug abuse and dependency at age 21 (Guo, Hawkins, Hill, & Abbott, 2001). Positive urgency (a personality trait reflecting the disposition to act in rash, impulsive ways when experiencing unusually positive moods) at the end of fifth grade was associated with increases in expectancies for social facilitation from alcohol at the start of sixth grade, which then predicted drinking status at the end of sixth grade, and alcohol expectancy and drinker status also predicted each other reciprocally across time (Settles, Zapolski, & Smith, 2014). Examining young children's cognitions and behaviors is important to understanding childhood and later substance use and misuse. McDermott, Clark-Alexander, Westhoff, and Eaton (1999) have suggested that emphasizing health concerns as a reason not to use alcohol is likely to be ineffective with children, but it may be useful to correct children's misconceptions about alcohol-related norms and risks before they begin active use.

The child characteristics that scholars have found to be related to *childhood* substance use include a mix of behavioral and cognitive variables: less competence (Jackson, Henriksen, & Dickinson, 1997), more tolerance to deviance, more deviant self-image, more susceptibility to peer pressure, and greater reported peer use (Loveland-Cherry, Leech, Laetz, & Dielman, 1996). In addition, childhood factors related to adolescent or young adult use include IQ and educational attainment (Dubow et al., 2008). Childhood antisocial behavior is a recurring and important correlate of later use (Dubow et al., 2008; Fitzgerald, Puttler, Refior, & Zucker, 2007; Leonard & Eiden, 2007).

Parent Factors

Jacob and Johnson (1997) conceptualize parenting influences on children as alcohol-specific effects and non-alcohol-specific effects. *Alcohol-specific effects* involve the behaviors of the parents with respect to alcohol and how these are related to the child's behavior and cognition. Frequently studied are the effects of being a child of an alcoholic (COA). Familial alcoholism has been linked to behavioral disinhibition and conduct problems in children, but this relationship is moderated by positive parenting practices (Molina, Donovan, & Belendiuk, 2010). Similarly, family functioning mediates the effects of parental psychopathology on adolescent externalizing behaviors (particularly fathers' perceptions of family functioning; Burstein, Stanger, & Dumenci, 2012). In general, parents' *substance-specific* influences on preadolescents have predictive utility for later adolescent and adult use and abuse (Dishion, Capaldi, & Yoerger, 1999). *Non-alcohol-specific effects* reflect the general aspects of the family environment that are related to children's deviant behavior, cognition, and substance use. Reflecting the operation of non-substance-specific influences are parenting practices and behaviors such as supervision, discipline, and nurturance of children; communication with children; parental divorce and remarriage; and clear family rules and monitoring (Guo et al., 2001).

Non-substance-specific factors are studied as operating alone, together with alcohol-specific factors, and as part of feedback loops. The non-substance-specific variables of low income and parental aggression are important correlates of child adjustment (Fals-Stewart, Kelley, Cooke, & Golden, 2003). In turn, childhood maladjustment is a predictor of greater harmful drinking at age 42 (24% more) (Maggs, Patrick, & Feinstein, 2008). The combination of parental alcoholism (alcohol-specific) with parental antisocial behavior (non-alcohol-specific) predicts child externalizing behavior, itself a predictor of more harmful drinking as an adult (Fals-Stewart et al., 2003; Fitzgerald et al., 2007; Maggs et al., 2008). A number of studies have provided evidence that parent reactions to children's difficult behaviors are followed by additional child maladaptation (Dishion et al., 1999).

Contextual Factors

In addition to personal and parental factors, there are a number of contextual factors that influence child substance abuse. For example, there are higher levels of substance use for children (age 10) living in a neighborhood with more trouble-making youth, antisocial friends, frequent alcohol use by best friends, frequent contact with antisocial friends, and high levels of bonding with antisocial friends (Guo et al., 2001). At the parental or familial level, low marital satisfaction can be a risk factor (Fals-Stewart et al. 2003). Parental divorce is a lesser risk factor for preadolescents than for adolescents (Needle, Su, & Doherty, 1990).

In sum, children with conduct problems, particularly in stressful homes, are at high risk for later substance use problems. Parenting responses that emphasize increased monitoring may make child externalizing problems worse. Clearly, help for parents in dealing with difficult children is warranted. In addition, the problems seem to extend beyond parenting to parents' own issues with substances, their relationships with each other, and their relationships with society.

ADOLESCENTS AND YOUTH AND SUBSTANCE ABUSE PROBLEMS

In the United States, the period of adolescence, roughly ages 13 to 19, is characterized by dramatic increases in substance use. The period of youth or young adulthood, up to age 25, is generally the time during which substance use and abuse peak (National Institute on Alcohol Abuse and Alcoholism, 2000). Monitoring the Future's annual surveys of 50,000 students in the 8th, 10th, and 12th grades document the latest figures. "Despite recent declining rates, two out of every three students (66%) have consumed alcohol (more than just a few sips) by the end of high school, and over a quarter (27%) have done so by 8th grade. In fact, half (50%) of 12th graders and one in nine (11%) of 8th graders in 2014 reported having been drunk at least once in their life" (Johnston, O'Malley, Miech, Bachman, & Schulenberg, 2015, p. 7).

Age of drinking onset in adolescence is a strong predictor of later alcohol abuse and disorder (Magid & Moreland, 2014; Tyler, Stone, & Bersani, 2006); adolescents who began drinking at 12 years or younger were at increased risk for developing later abuse and dependence compared with adolescents who held off until age 16 or older. Males reported drinking before age 12 at a rate almost three times that of females. Other factors influencing early alcohol initiation are conduct disorders, externalizing disorders, ADHD, parental alcohol dependence, and being male (Sartor et al., 2006). Associations between early drinking status and later problem behaviors remain even after controls are employed for a number of demographic and family variables (Ellickson, Tucker, & Klein, 2003). Findings such as these suggest that early drinking is an important risk in and of itself for later problems with alcohol.

From the late 1990s to 2014, substance use among adolescents generally declined, with many categories of substance use showing their lowest levels since 1991 in 2013 or 2014, though marijuana use has shown an increasing trend since 2007 (see Johnston et al., 2015, for an overview of the most recent Monitoring the Future surveys). Despite this decline, however, data from the Monitoring the Future surveys show large shifts in behavior from those in the 8th grade to those in the 12th grade. Scholars' attempts to account for these age-related changes, and to explain the use of substances in adolescence, have generated a substantial body of literature in which certain themes stand out. Researchers have looked at (a) adolescent characteristics, such as expectancies, achievements, moods, behaviors, stressors, personality, roles, and clinical diagnoses, as well as demographics of gender, ethnicity, school, and neighborhood; (b) substance-specific family characteristics, such as parent substance use and alcohol-specific parenting practices; and (c) non-substance-specific influences such as parenting styles, family dysfunction, family stressors, family socioeconomic status, and parent–adolescent communication. It should be noted that most of the research documents factors that are involved in greater risk. However, research on moderating variables highlights areas where there may be factors involved in resilience (doing well despite adversity). Recent research has also focused on looking at age-related trajectories, with four such trajectories typically emerging: (1) a low or nonusing trajectory, (2) a persistently high use trajectory, (3) a trajectory characterized by high initial use that declines over time, and (4) a trajectory that starts low and increases over time (Chassin et al., 2013). Study of these trajectories explores predictors of changing use.

Fitting primarily within the resources component of the stress and coping model, four important models link family history of alcoholism to adolescent pathological alcohol involvement: (1) positive affect regulation (produce positive feelings), (2) deviance proneness (demonstrate deficient socialization of which alcohol use is a part), (3) negative affect regulation (relieve negative emotions), and (4) pharmacological vulnerability (physical sensitivity to the effects of alcohol) (Sher et al., 2005). In research on moderators, scholars have sought to specify for whom and under what conditions associations hold between and among variables (Fischer & Wampler, 1994; Jacob & Johnson, 1997).

Adolescent Characteristics

Chassin et al. (2013) summarize research on the importance of the developmental periods of adolescence and emerging adulthood. There are several important considerations regarding adolescence that create increased risk for developing alcohol use disorders, including gaps in neurobiology between a rapidly developing reward system and the more slowly developing cognitive control systems. In addition, adolescents seem to be particularly sensitive to the neurotoxic effects of alcohol (Chassin et al., 2013).

Just as research has identified *childhood* behavioral disinhibition as an important factor in the prediction of early and later onset of substance use, there is a similar picture of the influence of *adolescent* behavioral disinhibition (Zucker, 2008). The relationship between high sensation seeking/impulsivity and substance use has been found to be moderated by gender, with a stronger association for males than for females (Baker & Yardley, 2002). The authors suggested that societal pressures and expectations placed upon females may help to explain this situation; such expectations may be protective for young women.

Researchers have examined problems related to both delinquency and substance use (deviance proneness) in adolescents over time, with mixed results (Chassin et al., 2013; Mason & Windle, 2002). Mason and Windle found that early delinquency appeared to have enduring consequences in adolescence for boys, whereas Merline, Jager, and Schulenberg (2008) reported that later alcohol use disorders among women were related to earlier theft and property damage behaviors. Among girls, apparent links between drug use and delinquency were based on the shared influences of third variables such as conduct problems (Mason & Windle, 2002).

Evidence for a negative emotion or internalizing pathway is mixed. For example, in the research of Englund, Egeland, Olivia, and Collins (2008), children with internalizing problems at age 7 reported less alcohol use in adulthood; however, at age 11, children with internalizing problems reported more alcohol use during young and middle adulthood for both genders and, for males, more alcohol use during adolescence. Parenting is related to offspring depression that is, in turn, related to alcohol abuse in college men and women (Patock-Peckham & Morgan-Lopez, 2007). Affect dysregulation has also been linked to substance abuse. James (2014) found that affect dysregulation mediated the relationship between childhood sexual abuse and substance abuse such that sexual abuse was associated with greater affect dysregulation, in turn, associated with more substance abuse.

Early positive alcohol expectancies are predictive of later heavy drinking in boys but not in girls (Griffin, Botvin, Epstein, Doyle, & Diaz, 2000). Neither mediating nor moderating effects of this association are well known. However, Barnow, Schuckit, and Lucht's (2002) research on German adolescents pulled together some of these threads. In their sample, adolescents with *alcohol problems* had more behavioral problems, more perceived parental rejection, less parental warmth, and more association with substance-using peers than did adolescents without alcohol problems. *Alcoholic* adolescents demonstrated all of these characteristics plus aggression/delinquency. Thus, adolescents lacking the self-control resource were more vulnerable to alcoholism. A review of general coping supports these conclusions: (a) adolescent coping is enhanced by warm, close relationships with parents; and (b) self-regulation plays an important role in adolescent coping (see Aldwin, 2007). Several recent studies have focused on specific coping mechanisms in adolescence and the link to substance misuse, generally finding that coping styles that involve avoidance, denial, or suppression are linked either directly to greater substance misuse or indirectly through increases in externalizing behaviors (Hotton, Garofalo, Kuhns, & Johnson, 2013; Lyness & Koehler, 2014; Wong et al., 2013).

Adolescent self-control forms a link between parental monitoring and adolescent substance use (Patock-Peckham, King, Morgan-Lopez, Ulloa, & Filson Moses, 2011). Regretfully, there is a reduced likelihood that stressed parents or those who themselves engage in deviant behavior will encourage or teach their children self-control.

There has been a recent focus on exploring the interaction of risks with other characteristics of the adolescent (e.g., race/ethnicity, sexual orientation, living arrangements, etc.). Rates of alcohol and other substance use have generally been lower for African American youth than for White or Hispanic youth (Johnston et al., 2015). For rural African American youth, family risk factors include having family members who use alcohol or drugs and being raised by nonfamily members, whereas being raised by family members and having parents who talk with the adolescent about the dangers of drug and alcohol use were protective (Myers, 2013). Acculturation in immigrant families has also been explored. For Asian American youth, acculturation was a risk factor for alcohol use only in the absence of attachment bonds to parents (Wang, Kviz, & Miller, 2012). Effective parenting in Latino families had direct effects on reducing alcohol use (Cox, Roblyer, Merten, Shreffler, & Schwerdfteger, 2013). Among Latino youth, findings suggest that the acculturation gap between child and parent may increase risk for alcohol use (Cox et al., 2013), and this relationship was found to be curvilinear. "It is predominantly youth who know English much better than their parents who are at risk of drinking substantially more than youth who are more similar to their parents" (Cox et al., 2013, p. 9). However, this risk was mediated by father involvement.

Sexual minority youth are at particular risk for alcohol and drug use, with this status conferring both direct risk and indirect risk through increased levels of depression (Pesola, Shelton, & van den Bree, 2014) and through higher levels of victimization (Drabble, Trocki, Hughes, Korcha, & Lown, 2013). Negative family interactions in the homes of sexual minority youth also increase risk for substance use and misuse (Rosario et al., 2014). Hotton et al. (2013) found a relationship between life stress, substance use, avoidant coping, and sexual risk behaviors in transgender women. Transgender men in substance treatment reported higher levels of family conflict than nontransgendered individuals in treatment (Flentje, Heck, & Sorensen, 2014).

Substance-Specific Parenting Factors

Associations between parental drinking and adolescent drinking are well documented (Sher et al., 2005; see Park & Schepp, 2014, for recent review). Involved in these associations are all the elements of the stress and coping model. Not only is there greater risk for alcohol problems among COAs and earlier initiation of drinking, but such children also show telescoped trajectories; that is, the interval from first using alcohol to the development of alcohol disorders is shorter (Hussong, Bauer, & Chassin, 2008). Peak age for first signs of an alcohol disorder is age 18. Considering the important transitions that accompany this age period (graduating high school, employment, romantic involvements), experiencing an alcohol disorder could disrupt the timing and success of these events and relationships. Fischer and colleagues have documented pathways from alcohol misuse of parents both to young adults' difficulties with particular romantic relationships (e.g., Fischer et al., 2005) and to the initiation and maintenance of dating relationships in general (Fischer & Wiersma, 2012). Another mediational pathway from parental alcohol use to adolescent use involves the effect on drinking motives, including social, enhancement, and coping motives (Müller & Kuntsche, 2011).

A family history of alcoholism is an important element in adolescent development of substance use problems. Children are thought to imitate behaviors modeled by their parents, but such an effect has failed to appear in studies of adopted children (Sher et al., 2005), and in an offspring-of-twin research design, such effects were modest at best (Slutske et al., 2008). Sibling modeling also interacts with peer influence. Whiteman, Jensen, and Maggs (2013) found that the association between sibling modeling and similarity in alcohol use was stronger when the siblings shared friends. In line with the results of parent drinking, it may be that the sibling effect is less about modeling and more about social influence and availability. As Pandina and Johnson (1990) cautioned, a family history of alcoholism does not inevitably produce an offspring with alcohol abuse or other problems, and a family without alcoholism does not necessarily protect offspring from developing substance use problems. Furthermore, siblings from the same family may be concordant or discordant for alcohol use. Fischer and Wiersma (2008) reported that 18% of siblings were different in alcohol use, primarily in adolescence, and that this difference appeared to reflect a niche-seeking strategy when there was more parental drinking.

If parental use of alcohol is associated with adolescent use, then parental recovery from alcoholism or cessation of alcohol-related problems should reflect a reduction in family stress and an alteration in children's expectancies and alcohol-related behaviors. However, researchers have found mixed outcomes in the offspring of recovering alcoholics (e.g., Pidcock & Fischer, 1998). Family recovery is a stressful endeavor, and attention needs to be given to children when other family members go through recovery (Lewis & Allen-Byrd, 2007). One positive effect of parents receiving treatment has been decreased child exposure to parental conflict (Rounsaville, O'Farrell, Andreas, Murphy, & Murphy, 2014).

Mediators

Mediators of associations between parental substance abuse and adolescent behavior identify mechanisms and processes in the transmission of adolescent alcoholism. Parenting styles represent one such mediator. Monitoring and supervision constitute one dimension of parenting style (Shorey et al, 2013); warmth and support constitute another. When parents abuse substances, their ability to provide appropriate levels of monitoring and support may be compromised, thereby providing a mediating pathway to adolescent substance use and abuse (Barnes, Reifman, Farrell, & Dintcheff, 2000). Furthermore, because parents are regarded as sources of information for children, it is important to consider what parents tell their children about substance use and abuse (i.e., alcohol-specific parenting practices). The effectiveness of parental communication about substance use varies. Although Chassin, Presson, Todd, Rose, and Sherman (1998) found that mothers' smoking-specific conversations with their adolescents were associated with lowered risk of adolescent smoking. Ennett, Bauman, Foshee, Pemberton, and Hicks (2001) indicated that for adolescents who were already using substances, parent–child communication on the topic actually made the situation worse. These researchers recommend that parents begin communicating with their children about substance use before the children initiate use. Nonnemaker, Silber-Ashley, Farrelly, and Dench (2012) also found that parent–child communication about drug use may actually increase likelihood of marijuana initiation, and Handley and Chassin (2013) concluded that "parental conversations about their own personal experiences with alcohol may not represent a form of parent-child communication about drinking that deters adolescent drinking" (p. 684). On the other hand, Haller and Chassin (2010) indicated that adolescents with alcoholic parents who perceived that they were then at risk for alcoholism reported lower levels of drinking over time. The authors suggest that beliefs about risk for alcoholism may be modifiable and could be a target for intervention. For younger children, talking with the child about harmful consequences of alcohol use only had an effect on later alcohol use initiation in families where the parents drank more frequently (Ennett, Jackson, Bowling, & Dickenson, 2013).

Alcohol-specific parenting strategies could be a mechanism through which monitoring and other parenting practices work, that is, a mediation effect. Parental provision of alcohol and access to alcohol in the home increases the likelihood that adolescents will express greater intent to use as well as greater actual alcohol use (Komro, Maldonado-Molina, Tobler, Bonds, & Muller, 2007). Parental approval of drinking or drug use is also consistently associated with greater adolescent drinking behavior, both directly and indirectly through effects on peers (Messler, Quevillon, & Simons, 2014). Nonetheless, the findings have not been consistent from study to study, suggesting the presence of moderating effects.

Moderators

Gender of the drinking parent (as well as of offspring) is an important moderator. Consistently, associations of predictors with drinking outcomes are stronger and more stable for males compared to females (Merline et al., 2008; Zucker, 2008). Greater male vulnerability may be genetic (Zucker, 2008). Maternal drinking is an often overlooked factor in offspring drinking but has been documented as playing an important role (Englund et al., 2008; White, Johnson, & Buyske, 2000). Tyler et al. (2006) attribute maternal influences to mothers' stronger role in child rearing. Recent research has more fully explored some of these associations. For example, maternal closeness has been found to partially mediate the association between maternal problem drinking and adolescent alcohol use (Shorey et al., 2013), and maternal closeness was protective when there was maternal problem drinking.

Other moderating factors that have been found to alter the association between parental drinking and offspring outcomes include expectations, peer orientations, ethnicity, family functioning, family structure, family cohesion, parental support, personality of the offspring, and family roles of the offspring (Fischer & Lyness, 2005). However, buffering effects by one parent of the negative effects of the other parent's drinking has not been one of the moderators (Curran & Chassin, 1996), and parental support loses its effectiveness among adolescents with higher levels of undercontrol (King & Chassin, 2004). With respect to resilience, Fischer and Wampler (1994) investigated the buffering effects of personality and family roles (hero, mascot, scapegoat/lost child) on the associations between offspring alcohol misuse and both family history of addictions and family dysfunction. They found that personality was a moderator of the association of family addictions with offspring drinking for both males and females, but family roles such as hero buffered offspring drinking only with respect to family dysfunction. Other research points to the importance of avoiding the role of parentified child in families with parental alcohol misuse. Such avoidance was related to higher self-concept, an indication of more resilience in these particular 10- to 18-year-old children (Godsall, Jurkovic, Emshoff, Anderson, & Stanwyck, 2004). The kind of coping a child engages in, such as active coping, is important to adjustment (C. Smith et al., 2006); unfortunately, parental alcoholism is more likely to lead to children using avoidant coping, a tactic associated with poorer adjustment. Adolescent depression also interacts with parental substance abuse, such that depressed adolescents with substance abusing parents develop substance use disorders earlier (Gorka, Shankman, Seeley, & Lewinsohn, 2013). Andrews, Hops, and Duncan (1997) concluded that although a good parent–child relationship is important to positive child adjustment, it may not always be protective in situations in which parents use substances.

Non-Substance-Specific Parenting Factors

Supervision and support are important parenting variables that operate regardless of parental substance use or abuse to influence adolescent outcomes (e.g., Coombs & Landsverk, 1988; Shorey et al., 2013). Among other benefits, these parenting practices may reduce stress, increase resources, and encourage active coping. Parental rules about alcohol are important in reducing adolescent alcohol use (Koning, van den Eijnden, & Vollenbergh, 2014). Koning et al. (2014) reported that stricter rules increased adolescent self-control and led to lower alcohol use only in families with high qualitative parent–child communication about alcohol. Abstaining youth have parents who convey warmth and do not use punishment to maintain control but instead clarify appropriate behavior and reinforce that behavior. However, parental overprotection has been linked to regular alcohol use in adolescence (Visser, de Winter, Vollebergh, Verhulst, & Reijneveld, 2013). Increased family involvement, support, and bonding during adolescence are protective factors that predict less problem alcohol use in adulthood (Vakalahi, 2002). Parental consistency has been found to be protective for Latino youth (West et al., 2013). On the other hand, White et al. (2000) failed to find an association of parental warmth/hostility toward their adolescent with later offspring adult drinking. The timing of the parenting behavior could be a factor in these differing findings.

Adolescent demands for autonomy may create parent–child stressors and disrupted parenting. Monitoring is a delicate balance during adolescence as parents weigh the need for youth to be become independent while providing enough guidance and control (Dishion & McMahon, 1998). Parental monitoring can be a protective factor against alcohol and other drug use; however, for this protection to emerge, adolescents had to report high levels of monitoring (Branstetter & Furman, 2013). Monitoring seems to be more protective in early adolescence, although family relationship quality continues to be protective across the transition to high school (Van Ryzin, Fosco, & Dishion, 2012). When middle school-aged children transitioned into a low monitoring situation from other modes of parental monitoring, there was an increased risk of substance initiation (Lippold, Greenberg, & Collins, 2014). There are also gender-specific effects—monitoring by the opposite-gender parent mediated the link between parenting styles and impulsiveness (Patock-Peckham et al., 2011) such that monitoring decreased impulsiveness (decreasing impulsive symptoms and increasing drinking control), which, in turn, was related to fewer alcohol-related problems.

Parental support is an important correlate of adolescent alcohol use, but the association is also mediated by other factors, such as religiosity, peer alcohol use, and school grades (Mason & Windle, 2002). Furthermore, students who received good grades elicited greater parental support. According to Bogenschneider, Wu, and Raffaelli (1998), mothers' responsiveness acted indirectly on adolescent alcohol use by helping to weaken adolescents' orientation to peers. Maternal depression, a condition that could reduce maternal support, contributed to adolescent and young adult problem drinking (Alati et al., 2005). There is also a complex interaction between genetic risk and family factors such as marital instability, alcoholism, and psychopathology in the home. Kendler et al. (2012), in a large-scale combination of data from adoption studies, found that the adverse environmental effects are stronger for those with high levels of genetic risk.

Wills and Cleary (1996) suggested that parent support buffers adolescent substance use by reducing the effects of risk factors and increasing the effects of protective factors. Family support moderates the effects of peers on adolescent substance use (Frauenglass, Routh, Pantin, & Mason, 1997). In a study of Hispanic eighth graders, Frauenglass et al. (1997) found that parent support was protective against the effects of peer modeling on tobacco and marijuana use whereas Cox et al. (2013) indicated that effective parenting in Latino families had direct links to lower probability of youth alcohol use. Van Ryzin et al. (2012) reported that parental knowledge about the child, such as his or her spending habits, activities, and who the child's friends were, had both direct effects on adolescent use as well as indirect effects through substance-using peers. The combination of supervision and acceptance, an *authoritative* parenting style, has been identified as a particularly important factor, both concurrently and longitudinally, in the reduced use of substances (Adalbjarnardottir & Hafsteinsson, 2001). Among older adolescents, having more indulgent and less controlling parents is more often associated with adolescent substance abuse than having authoritative parents. Tucker, Ellickson, and Klein (2008) indicated that adolescents living in permissive homes were nine times more likely to drink heavily in the ninth grade and three times more likely to drink heavily in the eleventh grade compared with children from nonpermissive homes. In general, the more the parent used alcohol, the more permissive were the alcohol rules for the adolescent. The more permissive the alcohol rules, the more the adolescent drank. Despite living in a permissive home environment, there were factors predicting less heavy drinking for these adolescents: social influences, alcohol beliefs, and resistance self-efficacy (Tucker et al., 2008). However, cross-cultural research has found that in Europe, both authoritative and indulgent (or permissive) parenting styles are protective (Calafat, Garcia, Juan, Becoña, & Fernández-Hermida, 2014), primarily because of the high levels of support present within the indulgent-permissive parenting styles.

In addition to parenting style, the quality of parent–child communication is important. Kafka and London (1991) established the value of an adolescent's having at least one parent with whom the adolescent has "open" communication. They found reduced levels of substance use among high school–age adolescents who had such a parent. However, openness of communication may not be enough; Humes and Humphrey (1994) suggested that parents also need to be sensitive to adolescents' needs.

Contextual Factors

There is quite a body of evidence that drinking or substance using peers influence adolescent use in various ways (e.g., see Shamblen, Ringwalt, Clark, & Hanley, 2014; on longitudinal growth trajectories), and there is evidence that parenting and peer factors interact (e.g., see Fagan, Van Horn, Hawkins, & Jaki, 2013). Kliewer and Zaharakis (2014) summarize the role of peers in family-based models of drug use progression, noting that multiple models support both the role of peers on drug use and interactions with family variables, including the quality of the parent–child relationship and identification with parents versus peers. They note that "although peers have significant influence on adolescent drug use . . . family processes affect the extent to which youth are drawn to affiliate with deviant peers" (Kliewer & Zaharakis, 2014, p. 61). Romantic relationships may also affect alcohol-related problems (Wiersma & Fischer, 2014). For example, both men and women who were in congruent heavy drinking relationships were at risk for serious alcohol-related problems in later adulthood, as were men in discrepant drinking relationships where they were the heavy drinkers (Wiersma & Fischer, 2014).

A number of factors operate directly and indirectly on adolescent substance use over time (Windle, 2000). Stressful life events were related to drinking to cope and directly to adolescent alcohol problems and may interact with a family history of alcoholism (i.e., those youth report higher levels of severe stressors; Charles et al., 2014). Specific stressful events linked to adolescent substance abuse include childhood sexual abuse (James, 2014); exposure to violence in families and communities (Schiff et al., 2014); and racial/ethnic discrimination (Sanders-Phillips et al., 2014) (although a cultural orientation serves as a protective factor, Unger, 2014). Adverse childhood experiences have a cumulative effect, with individuals exposed to multiple adverse events demonstrating higher risks for substance abuse (Mersky, Topitzes, & Reynolds, 2013).

Trauma is another important pathway to adolescent problem behavior (Chassin et al., 2013). The dual risks of COA status and sexual abuse in adolescence have been related to higher levels of adolescent problems, including chemical abuse, than that found in adolescents with only one risk factor (Fenton et al., 2013). Adolescents experiencing *current* abuse have been shown to have more problem behaviors, such as binge drinking, than adolescents with histories of *prior* abuse (Luster & Small, 1997). Employing a national data set, Kilpatrick et al. (2003) found connections between substance abuse and dependence during adolescence and (a) family alcohol problems, (b) having been a witness to violence, and (c) having been a victim of physical assault. Posttraumatic stress disorder (PTSD) occurred when sexual assault was added to the mix. Those who develop alcohol misuse subsequent to trauma are also more at risk for future assault (Mulsow, 2007). The effects of secondhand abuse (i.e., childhood abuse of parents of substance-abusing adolescents) may also be at work through its association with greater parental alcohol dependence (Peters, Malzman, & Villone, 1994). K. Smith, Smith, and Grekin (2014) reported on a moderated-mediation model in which distress mediated the relationship between childhood sexual abuse and alcohol consequences but only for those who reported coping motives for drinking, suggesting a tension-reduction model of alcohol use.

Some scholars have theorized that single-parent family structure creates distress in adolescents that may lead to greater affect and mood alteration through substance use. In addition, the lower levels of supervision and availability of parents in single-parent households may also lead to greater substance experimentation and abuse. Reflecting the stress approach, Jeynes's (2001) research of nationally representative U.S. 12th graders found that adolescents who had experienced more recent parental divorce drank more alcohol. Arkes (2013) reported that youth were more likely to use alcohol 2 to 4 years *before* parental divorce, and that effects persisted after divorce as well. The effect of divorce on alcohol use disorders was moderated by parental psychopathology; the effect of divorce was significant only in the presence of parental psychopathology (Thompson et al., 2014). But other variables, including parent unavailability, family quality, peer acceptance/self-esteem, and deviant peer involvement, serve as mediators between parental divorce and adolescent alcohol use (Curry, Fischer, Reifman, & Harris, 2004). In addition to the absence of the nonresident father, factors such as weak attachment and limited monitoring are also associated with adolescent alcohol use (K. Jones & Benda, 2004). The association between single-parent homes and alcohol use may hold only during adolescence (Merline et al., 2008). Divorce is not the only family structure risk factor; adolescents who transition from a single-parent family to a stepfamily increase their risk of initiating alcohol use (Kirby, 2006). There is some support, however, for the idea that instead of family structure, parent and peer relationships are better at explaining adolescent alcohol consumption (Crawford & Novak, 2008).

Homelessness is another particular risk for adolescent substance abuse (James, 2014), particularly for those with poorer coping skills (Nyamathi et al., 2010), as is living in foster care (Brook, Rifenbark, Boulton, Little, & McDonald, 2014). Brook et al. (2014) found that risk factors played a greater role in predicting drug use than protective factors in foster youth, highlighting the vulnerability of these youth. McDonald, Mariscal, Yan, and Brook (2014) reported that risks for foster care youth are amplified for females. Although homelessness is a risk factor, among those in intact families, *higher* socioeconomic status (SES) is actually a consistent risk factor for increased use (Melotti et al., 2013). On the other hand, economic hardships have an effect on parents' ability to provide supportive parenting, and this decrease in supportive parenting also indirectly affects problem drinking through a link to externalizing via maternal depression (Hardaway & Cornelius, 2014).

In sum, difficulties in making the transition from childhood to adolescence are compounded when alcohol and drugs enter the picture. Parents' use of substances gains added importance, creating stressors, influencing perceptions, detracting from resources, and hindering coping. Parents' flexibility in coping with adolescents' emerging needs for autonomy and independence should be gender sensitive, given that socialization pressures continue to differ for boys and girls. More resilient adolescents in the face of parental alcoholism, poorer parenting, and trauma tend to be female, less disinhibited, and more parentally supported and monitored.

BIDIRECTIONAL PROCESSES

Throughout this chapter, the studies we cited have primarily focused on a particular direction of effects from parent to child: alcohol abuse in parents *leads to* child and adolescent alcohol use and misuse; parenting practices help or hinder adolescent resistance to alcohol use. Other research suggests that bidirectional effects are at work. The title of one article put the issue as "Can Your Children Drive You to Drink?" (Pelham & Lang, 1999). A series of experimental studies documented an affirmative answer. Adoptive parents (Finley & Aguiar, 2002) of children whose biological parents had alcohol, antisocial, depressive, or other psychiatric disorders experienced double the risk of developing their own psychiatric or alcohol-related problems compared to adoptive parents of children without such a predisposition. Mezzich et al. (2007) found that, rather than parenting practices being a result of parental substance use disorders, parents' discipline was *elicited* by sons' neurobe-havioral disinhibition (ND); this ND was in turn related to sons' substance use disorders. Commenting on studies such as these, Leonard and Eiden (2007) stated, "Alcoholic parents are at higher risk for having children with behavior problems, and children's behavior problems may increase parental stress and lead to more drinking" (p. 299). Deater-Deckard (2004) suggested that parents may need family support, training in coping responses, and social policies such as parental leave to alleviate parenting stress. Elkins et al. (2014) looked at bidirectional effects of parenting and youth substance use during the transition to high school and found evidence for reciprocal effects for positive parenting (although youth substance use had effects on subsequent positive parenting, positive parenting did not affect youth substance use in this study), and for effective discipline, they stated that "find-ings indicated that higher effective discipline strategies decreased the likelihood of youth substance use in the subsequent grade, and engaging in substance use predicted lower perceived effectiveness of discipline in the subsequent year" (p. 481). According to Abar, Jackson, and Wood (2014), the quality of the parent–adolescent relationship moderates associations between parental knowledge and adolescent outcomes, such as heavy epi-sodic drinking.

ISSUES IN PREVENTION AND TREATMENT

Although we have focused on families coping with substance use and misuse in the discus-sion above, limiting prevention and treatment efforts to the individual in the family with the substance use problem is not sufficient to address the multiple levels of factors that are implicated in a person's substance use problem. There is no one place to start. In fact, alcohol misuse in families can extend back generations (Garrett & Landau, 2007). The substance-abusing parent certainly needs help, but so do the children in the family. As the preceding review illustrates, the stress and coping model highlights the importance of all the components—stressors, perceptions, resources, problem-solving skills, coping skills, and bidirectional effects—found in families dealing with substance abuse. Helping parents to effectively manage a behaviorally disinhibited child may interrupt the negative sequence of events from childhood to young adulthood. But helping children cope with a substance-abusing parent is also critical. Prevention of both early onset of substance use and early conduct disorder problems is a key factor in positive youth development. Fitzgerald et al. (2007) suggested that children from antisocial alcoholic families would benefit from inter-ventions that begin in infancy. Other pathways that children follow are sorted out in middle childhood, suggesting that interventions begin before this critical time. Bolstering the case for early intervention, Aldwin's (2007) developmental approach identifies coping as embedded in the social ecology of the family throughout the life span, beginning with infant and even prenatal coping behaviors.

Contradictory findings have emerged related to the utility of medicating children who have ADHD to prevent substance abuse (see Chang et al., 2014; Humphreys, Eng, & Lee, 2013), and not all behaviorally disinhibited children have ADHD. Nor is medication the sole answer for multifaceted family problems. If children and adults are dually diagnosed (e.g., alcohol abuse/dependence with PTSD), it is important to treat both (Mulsow, 2007). It is also necessary to deal with such family background issues as stresses surrounding grief, loss, and trauma (Garrett & Landau, 2007) for which alcohol abuse is a symptom. Parental monitoring of their children may be particularly important in parenting youth with ADHD (Walther et al., 2012).

Several reviews have demonstrated that family-based interventions are efficacious in treating adolescent substance abuse (e.g., O'Farrell & Clements, 2012). One target of effective treatment involves improvements in parenting practices (Henderson, Rowe, Dakof, Hawes, & Liddle, 2009). However, effective programs aimed at treating or preventing substance abuse involve multiple components and multiple points of entry (Boyd & Faden, 2002). These programs may be expensive; they may require commitments of time, energy, and other resources from schools and communities as well as the dedication of skilled leaders.

An important concomitant of recovery is the disruption of family dynamics, and programs need to address changes in family dynamics to prevent relapse and to prevent children in the family from experiencing additional difficulties (Lewis & Allen-Byrd, 2007). Fischer, Pidcock, and Fletcher-Stephens (2007) describe three evidence-based programs for alcohol-abusing adolescents that include the family as well as the adolescent. Dealing with family dynamics is only one goal of comprehensive intervention, however. As we noted in an earlier version of this chapter (Fischer & Lyness, 2005), to prevent relapse, programs must also consider settings and situations beyond the family itself, such as (a) effective aftercare services; (b) safe havens for children of addicted parents; (c) school, college, and community policies (Cleveland, Harris, & Wiebe, 2010); (d) cultural and subcultural norms and behaviors; and (e) support for recovery, important for singly diagnosed and dually diagnosed alike.

CONCLUSION

An encouraging aspect of recent studies examining how families cope with substance abuse is the inclusion of multiple variables, multiple perspectives, multiple waves of data collection spanning infancy to middle age, and sophisticated data analysis techniques. This very richness presents challenges to the scholars who report such research because the findings are embedded in complex webs of interrelated results. Studies that examine the changing nature of predictors across different developmental ages provide valuable information for prevention and risk reduction (e.g., Guo et al., 2001). With this information, programs can begin to focus on the key developmental periods specific to identified predictors.

With only a few exceptions, the literature we have reviewed in this chapter has largely reported on research with families of European heritage. However, the Monitoring the Future surveys repeatedly find lower rates of substance use among African American youth than among European American adolescents and higher rates among Hispanic youth (Johnston et al., 2015). Even when similar rates are reported across ethnic groups, as with marijuana use, researchers should not assume that predictors and pathways to substance use are analogous. Furthermore, the consequences of use are greater for African American than European American youth (D. Jones, Hussong, Manning, & Sterrett, 2008).

Future research must reflect the diversity of families coping with substance abuse, not just in terms of ethnicity and culture but also in terms of emerging understandings of the broad spectrum of close relationships covered by the term *families.* We have included in this review research on families with children and adolescents that we believe illuminates family scholars' understandings of families coping with substance abuse.

REFERENCES

Abar, C. C., Jackson, K. M., & Wood, M. (2014). Reciprocal relations between perceived parental knowledge and adolescent substance use and delinquency: The moderating role of parent–teen relationship quality. *Developmental Psychology, 50,* 2176–2187.

Acion, L., Ramirez, M. R., Jorge, R., & Arndt, S. (2013). Increased risk of alcohol and drug use among children from deployed military families. *Addiction, 108,* 1418–1425. doi:10.1111/add.12161

Adalbjarnardottir, S., & Hafsteinsson, L. G. (2001). Adolescents' perceived parenting styles and their substance use: Concurrent and longitudinal analyses. *Journal of Research on Adolescence, 11,* 401–423.

Alati, R., Kinner, S. A., Najman, J. M., Mamum, A. A., Williams, G. M., O'Callaghan, M., & Bor, W. (2005). Early predictors of adult drinking: A birth cohort study. *American Journal of Epidemiology, 162*(11), 1098–1107.

Aldwin, C. M. (2007). *Stress, coping, and development: An integrative perspective* (2nd ed.). New York, NY: Guilford.

American Psychiatric Association. (2013). *Diagnostic and statistical manual of mental disorders* (5th ed.). Washington, DC: Author.

Andrews, J. A., & Peterson, M. (2006). The development of social images of substance users in children: A Guttman unidimensional scaling approach. *Journal of Substance Use, 11,* 305–311. doi:10.1080/14659890500419774

Andrews, J. A., Hops, H., & Duncan, S. C. (1997). Adolescent modeling of parent substance use: The moderating effect of the relationship with the parent. *Journal of Family Psychology, 11,* 259–270.

Arendt, R. E., & Farkas, K. J. (2007). Maternal alcohol abuse and fetal alcohol spectrum disorder: A life-span perspective. *Alcoholism Quarterly, 25*(3), 3–20.

Arkes, J. (2013). The temporal effects of parental divorce on youth substance use. *Substance Use & Misuse, 48,* 290–297. doi:10.3109/10826084.2012.755703

Baker, J. R., & Yardley, J. K. (2002). Moderating effect of gender on the relationship between sensation seeking-impulsivity and substance use in adolescents. *Journal of Child and Adolescent Substance Abuse, 12*(1), 27–43.

Barnes, G. M., Reifman, A., Farrell, M. P., & Dintcheff, B. A. (2000). The effects of parenting on the development of adolescent alcohol misuse: A six-wave latent growth model. *Journal of Marriage and the Family, 62,* 175–186.

Barnow, S., Schuckit, M. A., & Lucht, M. (2002). The importance of a positive family history of alcoholism, parental rejection and emotional warmth, behavioral problems and peer substance use for alcohol problems in teenagers: A path analysis. *Journal of Studies on Alcohol, 63,* 305–312.

Biederman, J., Faraone, S. V., Monuteaux, M. C., & Feighner, J. A. (2000). Patterns of alcohol and drug use in adolescents can be predicted by parental substance use disorders. *Pediatrics, 106,* 792–797.

Bogenschneider, K., Wu, M., & Raffaelli, M. (1998). Parent influences on adolescent peer orientation and substance use: The interface of parenting practices and value. *Child Development, 69,* 1672–1688.

Boyd, G. M., & Faden, V. (2002). Overview. *Journal of Studies on Alcohol, 14*(Suppl.), 6–13.

Branstetter, S. A., & Furman, S. A. (2013). Buffering effect of parental monitoring knowledge and parent-adolescent relationships on consequences of adolescent substance use. *Journal of Child and Family Studies, 22,* 192–198. doi:10.1007/s10826-012-9568-2

Brook, J., Rifenbark, G. G., Boulton, A., Little, T. D., & McDonald, T. P. (2014). Risk and protective factors for drug use among youth living in foster care. *Child & Adolescent Social Work Journal.* Advanced online publication. doi:10.1007/s10560-014-0345-5

Burstein, M., Stanger, C., & Dumenci, L. (2012). Relations between parent psychopathology, family functioning, and adolescent problems in substance-abusing families: Disaggregating the effects of parent gender. *Child Psychiatry and Human Development, 43,* 631–647. doi:10.1007/s10578-012-0288-z

Calafat, A., Garcia, F., Juan, M., Becoña, E., & Fernández-Hermida, J. R. (2014). Which parenting style is more protective against adolescent substance use? Evidence within the European context. *Drug and Alcohol Dependence, 138,* 185–192. doi:10.1016/j.drugalcdep.2014.02.705

Chang, Z. Lichtenstein, P., Halidner, L., D'Onofrio, B., Serlachius, E., Fazel, S., Långström, N., & Larsson, H. (2014). Stimulant ADHD medication and risk for substance abuse. *Journal of Child Psychology and Psychiatry, 55,* 878–885. doi:10.1111/jcpp.12164

Charles, N. E., Ryan, S. R., Acheson, A., Mathias, C. W., Liang, Y., & Dougherty, D. M. (2014). Childhood stress exposure among preadolescents with and without family histories of substance use disorders. *Psychology of Addictive Behaviors.* Advanced online publication. doi:10.1037/adb0000020

Chassin, L., Presson, C. C., Todd, M., Rose, J. S., & Sherman, S. J. (1998). Maternal socialization of adolescent smoking: The intergenerational transmission of parenting and smoking. *Developmental Psychology, 34,* 1189–1201.

Chassin, L., Sher, K. J., Hussong, A., & Currant, P. (2013). The developmental psychopathology of alcohol use and alcohol disorders: Research achievements and future directions. *Development and Psychopathology, 25,* 1567–1584. doi:10.1017/S0954579413000771

Cleveland, H. H., Harris, K. S., & Wiebe, R. P. (Eds.). (2010). *Substance abuse recovery in college: Community supported abstinence.* New York, NY: Springer. doi:10.1007/978-1-4419-1767-6

Coombs, R. H., & Landsverk, J. (1988). Parenting styles and substance use during childhood and adolescence. *Journal of Marriage and Family, 50,* 473–482.

Cox, R. B., Roblyer, M. Z., Merten, M. J., Shreffler, K. M., & Schwerdtfeger, K. L. (2013). Do parent–child acculturation gaps affect early adolescent Latino alcohol use? A study of the probability and extent of use. *Substance Abuse Treatment, Prevention, and Policy, 8:4.* doi:10.1186/1747-597X-8-4

Crawford, L. A., & Novak, K. B. (2008). Parent-child relations and peer associations as mediators of the family structure-substance use relationship. *Journal of Family Issues, 29*(2), 155–184.

Curran, P. J., & Chassin, L. (1996). A longitudinal study of parenting as a protective factor for children of alcoholics. *Journal of Studies on Alcohol, 57*(3), 305–313.

Curry, L., Fischer, J., Reifman, A., & Harris, K. (2004, March). *Family factors, self-esteem, peer involvement, and adolescent alcohol misuse.* Poster presented at the biennial meeting of the Society for Research on Adolescence, Baltimore, MD.

Deater-Deckard, K. (2004). *Parenting stress.* New Haven, CT: Yale University Press.

Dishion, T. J., Capaldi, D. M., & Yoerger, K. (1999). Middle childhood antecedents to progressions in male adolescent substance use: An ecological analysis of risk and protection. *Journal of Adolescent Research, 14,* 175–205.

Dishion, T. J., & McMahon, R. J. (1998). Parental monitoring and the prevention of child and adolescent problem behavior: A conceptual and empirical formulation. *Clinical Child and Family Psychology Review, 1,* 61–75.

Drabble, L., Trocki, K. F., Hughes, T. L., Korcha, R. A., & Lown, A. E. (2013). Sexual orientation differences in the relationship between victimization and hazardous drinking among women in the National Alcohol Survey. *Psychology of Addictive Behaviors, 27,* 639–648. doi:10.1037/a0031486

Dubow, E. F., Boxer, P., & Huesmann, L. R. (2008). Childhood and adolescent predictors of early and middle adulthood alcohol use and problem drinking: The Columbia County Longitudinal Study. *Addiction, 103*(Suppl. 1), 36–47.

Elkins, S. R., Fite, P. J., Moore, T. M., Lochman, J. E., & Wells, K. C. (2014). Bidirectional effects of parenting and youth substance use during the transition to middle and high school. *Psychology of Addictive Behaviors, 28,* 475–286. doi:10.1037/a0036824

Ellickson, P. L., Tucker, J. S., & Klein, D. J. (2003). Ten-year prospective study of public health problems associated with early drinking. *Pediatrics, 111,* 949–955.

Englund, M. M., Egeland, B., Olivia, E. M., & Collins, W. A. (2008). Childhood and adolescent predictors of heavy drinking and alcohol use disorders in early adulthood: A longitudinal developmental analysis. *Addiction, 103*(Suppl. 1), 23–35.

Ennett, S. T., Bauman, K. E., Foshee, V. A., Pemberton, M., & Hicks, K. A. (2001). Parent-child communication about adolescent tobacco and alcohol use: What do parents say and does it affect youth behavior? *Journal of Marriage and Family, 63,* 48–63.

Ennett, S. T., Jackson, C., Bowling, J. M., & Dickinson, D. M. (2013). Parental socialization and children's susceptibility to alcohol use initiation. *Journal of Studies on Alcohol and Drugs, 74,* 694–702.

Fagan, A. A., Van Horn, M. L., Hawkins, J. D., & Jaki, T. (2013). Differential effects of parental controls on adolescent substance use: For whom is the family most important? *Journal of Quantitative Criminology, 29,* 347–368. doi:10.1007/s10940-012-9183-9

Fals-Stewart, W., Kelley, M. L., Cooke, C. G., & Golden, J. C. (2003). Predictors of the psychosocial adjustment of children living in households of parents in which fathers abuse drugs: The effects of postnatal parental exposure. *Addictive Behaviors, 28,* 1013–1031.

Fenton, M. C., Geier, T., Keyes, K., Skodol, A. E., Grant, B. F., & Hasin, D. S. (2013). Combined role of childhood maltreatment, family history, and gender in the risk for alcohol dependence. *Psychological Medicine, 43,* 1045–1057.

Finley, G. E., & Aguiar, L. J. (2002). The effects of children on parents: Adoptee genetic dispositions and adoptive parent psychopathology. *Journal of Genetic Psychology, 163*(4), 503–506.

Fischer, J. L., Fitzpatrick, J. A., Cleveland, B., Lee, J.-M., McKnight, A., & Miller, B., (2005). Binge drinking in the context of romantic relationships. *Addictive Behaviors, 30,* 1496–1516.

Fischer, J. L., & Lyness, K. P. (2005). Families coping with alcohol and substance abuse. In P. S. McKenry & S. J. Price (Eds.), *Families and change: Coping with stressful events and transitions* (3rd ed., pp. 155–178). Thousand Oaks, CA: Sage.

Fischer, J. L., Pidcock, B. W., & Fletcher-Stephens, B. J. (2007). Family response to adolescence, youth and alcohol. In J. L. Fischer, M. Mulsow, & A. W. Korinek (Eds.), *Familial responses to alcohol problems* (pp. 27–41). Binghamton, NY: The Haworth Press.

Fischer, J. L., & Wampler, R. S. (1994). Abusive drinking in young adults: Personality type and family role as moderators of family-of-origin influences. *Journal of Marriage and Family, 56,* 469–479.

Fischer, J. L., & Wiersma, J. D. (2008, November). *Patterns of sibling drinking in adolescence and young adulthood.* Presented at the National Council on Family Relations Annual Meeting, Little Rock, AR.

Fischer, J. L., & Wiersma, J. D. (2012). Romantic relationships and alcohol use. *Current Drug Abuse Reviews, 5,* 98–116.

Fitzgerald, H. E., Puttler, L. I., Refior, S., & Zucker, R. A. (2007). Family response to children and alcohol. In J. L. Fischer, M. Mulsow, & A. W. Korinek (Eds.), *Familial responses to alcohol problems* (pp. 11–25). Binghamton, NY: Haworth Press.

Flentje, A., Heck, N. C., & Sorensen, J. L. (2014). Characteristics of transgender individuals entering substance abuse treatment. *Addictive Behaviors, 39,* 969–975. doi:10.1016/j.addbeh.2014.01.011

Frauenglass, S., Routh, D. K., Pantin, H. M., & Mason, C. A. (1997). Family support decreases influence of deviant peers on Hispanic adolescents' substance use. *Journal of Clinical and Child Psychology, 26,* 15–23.

Garrett, J., & Landau, J. (2007). Family motivation to change: A major factor in engaging alcoholics in treatment. In J. L. Fischer, M. Mulsow, & A. W. Korinek (Eds.), *Familial responses to alcohol problems* (pp. 65–83). Binghamton, NY: Haworth Press.

Godsall, R. E., Jurkovic, G. J., Emshoff, J., Anderson, L., & Stanwyck, D. (2004). Why some kids do well in bad situations: Relation of parental alcohol misuse and parentification to children's self-concept. *Substance Use & Misuse, 39,* 789–809.

Gorka, S. M., Shankman, S. A., Seeley, J. R., & Lewinsohn, P. M. (2013). The moderating effect of parental illicit substance use disorders on the relation between adolescent depression and subsequent illicit substance use disorders. *Drug and Alcohol Dependence, 128,* 1–7. doi:10.1016/j.drugalcdep.2012.07.011

Griffin, K. W., Botvin, G. J., Epstein, J. A., Doyle, M. M., & Diaz, T. (2000). Psychosocial and behavioral factors in early adolescence as predictors of heavy drinking among high school seniors. *Journal of Studies on Alcohol, 61,* 603–606.

Guo, J., Hawkins, J. D., Hill, K. G., & Abbott, R. D. (2001). Childhood and adolescent predictors of alcohol abuse and dependence in young adulthood. *Journal of Studies on Alcohol and Drugs, 62,* 754–762.

Haller, M. M., & Chassin, L. (2010). The reciprocal influences of perceived risk for alcoholism and alcohol use over time: Evidence for aversive transmission of parental alcoholism. *Journal of Studies on Alcohol and Drugs, 71,* 588–596.

Handley, E. D., & Chassin, L. (2013). Alcohol-specific parenting as a mechanism of parental drinking and alcohol use disorder risk on adolescent alcohol use onset. *Journal of Studies on Alcohol and Drugs, 74,* 684–693.

Hardaway, C. R., & Cornelius, M. D. (2014). Economic hardship and adolescent problem drinking: Family processes as mediating influences. *Journal of Youth and Adolescence, 43,* 1191–1202. doi:10.1007/s10964-013-0063-x

Henderson, C. E., Rowe, C. L., Dakof, G. A., Hawes, S. W., & Liddle, H. A. (2009). Parenting practices as mediators of treatment effects in an early-intervention trial of multidimensional family therapy. *The American Journal of Drug and Alcohol Abuse, 35,* 220–226. doi:10.1080/00952990903005890

Hicks, B. M., Johnson, W., Durbin, C. E., Blonigen, D. M., Iacono, W. G., & McGue, M. (2014). Delineating selection and mediation effects among childhood personality and environmental risk factors in the development of adolescent substance abuse. *Journal of Abnormal Child Psychology, 42,* 845–859. doi:10.1007/s10802-013-9831-z

Hotton, A. L., Garofalo, R., Kuhns, L. M., & Johnson, A. K. (2013). Substance use as a mediator of the relationship between life stress and sexual risk among young transgender women. *AIDS Education and Prevention, 25*(1), 62–71.

Humes, D. L., & Humphrey, L. L. (1994). A multi-method analysis of families with a polydrug-dependent or normal adolescent daughter. *Journal of Abnormal Psychology, 103,* 676–685.

Humphreys, K. L., Eng, T., & Lee, S. S. (2013). Stimulant medication and substance use outcomes: A meta-analysis. *JAMA Psychiatry, 70,* 740-749. doi:10.1001/jamapsychiatry.2013.1273

Hussong, A. M., Bauer, D., & Chassin, L. (2008). Telescoped trajectories from alcohol initiation to disorder in children of alcoholic parents. *Journal of Abnormal Psychology, 117,* 63–78.

Jackson, C., Henriksen, L., & Dickinson, D. (1997). The early use of alcohol and tobacco: Its relation to children's competence and parents' behavior. *American Journal of Public Health, 87,* 359–364.

Jacob, T., & Johnson, S. (1997). Parenting influences on the development of alcohol abuse and dependence. *Alcohol Health and Research World, 21,* 204–210.

James, C. (2014). Childhood sexual abuse and adolescent substance abuse and sexual risk behaviours among homeless youth: The mediational roles of affect dysregulation and posttraumatic stress symptoms. *Dissertation Abstracts International: Section B: The Sciences and Engineering, 74(7-B)(E).*

Jeynes, W. H. (2001). The effects of recent parental divorce on their children's consumption of alcohol. *Journal of Youth and Adolescence, 30,* 305–319.

Johnston, L. D., O'Malley, P. M., Miech, R. A., Bachman, J. G., & Schulenberg, J. E. (2015). *Monitoring the Future national survey results on drug use: 1975–2014: Overview, key findings on adolescent drug use.* Ann Arbor: Institute for Social Research, University of Michigan.

Jones, D. J., Hussong, A. M., Manning, J., & Sterrett, E. (2008). Adolescent alcohol use in context: The role of parents and peers among African American and European American youth. *Cultural Diversity and Ethnic Minority Psychology, 14*(3), 266–273.

Jones, K. A., & Benda, B. B. (2004). Alcohol use among adolescents with non-residential fathers: A study of assets and deficits. *Alcoholism Treatment Quarterly, 22,* 3–25.

Kafka, R. R., & London, P. (1991). Communication in relationships and adolescent substance use: The influence of parents and friends. *Adolescence, 26,* 587–597.

Kelley, M. L., & Fals-Stewart, W. (2008). Treating parental drug abuse using learning sobriety together: Effects on adolescents versus children. *Drug and Alcohol Dependence, 92*(1–3), 228–238.

Kilpatrick, D. G., Ruggiero, K. J., Acierno, R., Saunders, B. E., Resnick, H. S., & Best, C. L. (2003). Violence and risk of PTSD, major depression, substance abuse/dependence, and comorbidity: Results from the national survey of adolescents. *Journal of Consulting and Clinical Psychology, 71,* 692–700.

Kendler, K. S., Sundquist, K., Ohlsson, H., Palmer, K., Maes, H., Winkleby, M. A., & Sundquist, J. (2012). Genetic and familial environmental influences on the risk for drug abuse: A national Swedish adoption study. *JAMA Psychiatry, 69,* 690–697.

King, K. M., & Chassin, L. (2004). Mediating and moderated effects of adolescent behavioral under-control and parenting in the prediction of drug use disorders in emerging adulthood. *Psychology of Addictive Behaviors, 18,* 239–249.

Kirby, J. B. (2006). From single-parent families to stepfamilies: Is the transition associated with adolescent alcohol initiation? *Journal of Family Issues, 27*(5), 685–711.

Kliewer, W., & Zaharakis, N. (2014). Family-based models of drug etiology. In L. M. Scheier & W. B. Hansen (Eds.), *Parenting and teen drug use: The most recent findings from research, prevention, and treatment* (pp. 37–61). New York, NY: Oxford University Press.

Komro, K. A., Maldonado-Molina, M. M., Tobler, A. L., Bonds, J. R., & Muller, K. E. (2007). Effects of home access and availability of alcohol on young adolescents' alcohol use. *Addiction, 102,* 1597–1608.

Koning, I. M., van den Eijnden, R. J. J. M., & Vollenberg, W. A. M. (2014). Alcohol-specific parenting, adolescents' self-control, and alcohol use: A moderated mediation model. *Journal of Studies on Alcohol and Drugs, 75,* 16–23.

Leonard, K. E., & Eiden, R. D. (2007). Marital and family processes in the context of alcohol use and alcohol disorders. *Annual Review of Clinical Psychology, 3,* 285–310.

Lewis, V., & Allen-Byrd, L. (2007). Coping strategies for the stages of family recovery. In J. L. Fischer, M. Mulsow, & A. W. Korinek (Eds.), *Familial responses to alcohol problems* (pp. 105–124). Binghamton, NY: Haworth Press.

Lippold, M. A., Greenberg, M. T., & Collins, L. M. (2014). Youths' substance use and changes in parental knowledge-related behaviors during middle school: A person-oriented approach. *Journal of Youth and Adolescence, 43,* 729–744. doi:10.1007/s10964-013-0010-x

Loveland-Cherry, C. J., Leech, S., Laetz, V. B., & Dielman, T. E. (1996). Correlates of alcohol use and misuse in fourth-grade children: Psychosocial, peer, parental, and family factors. *Health Education Quarterly, 23,* 497–577.

Luster, T., & Small, S. A. (1997). Sexual abuse history and problems in adolescence: Explaining the effects of moderating variables. *Journal of Marriage and Family, 59,* 131–142.

Lyness, K. P., & Koehler, A. M. (2014). Effect of coping on substance use in adolescent girls: A dyadic analysis of parent and adolescent perceptions. *International Journal of Adolescence and Youth.* Retrieved from http://dx.doi.org/10.1080/02673843.2013.866146. doi:10.1080/02673843.2013 .866146

Maggs, J. L., Patrick, M. E., & Feinstein, L. (2008). Childhood and adolescent predictors of alcohol use and problems in adolescence and adulthood in the National Child Development Study. *Addiction, 103*(Suppl. 1), 7–22.

Magid, V., & Moreland, A. D. (2014). The role of substance use initiation in adolescent development of subsequent substance-related problems. *Journal of Child & Adolescent Substance Abuse, 23,* 78-86. doi:10.1080/1067828X.2012.748595

Mason, W. A., & Windle, M. (2002). Reciprocal relations between adolescent substance use and delinquency: A longitudinal latent variable analysis. *Journal of Abnormal Psychology, 111,* 63–76.

McDermott, R. J., Clark-Alexander, B. J., Westhoff, W. W., & Eaton, D. K. (1999). Alcohol attitudes and beliefs related to actual alcohol experience in a fifth-grade cohort. *Journal of School Health, 69,* 356–361.

McDonald, T. P., Mariscal, E. S., Yan, Y., & Brook, J. (2014). Substance use and abuse for youths in foster care: Results from the communities that care normative database. *Journal of Child & Adolescent Substance Abuse, 23,* 262–268. doi:10.1080/1067828X.2014.912093

McKenry, P. C., & Price, S. J. (2005). Families coping with change. In P. S. McKenry & S. J. Price (Eds.), *Families and change: Coping with stressful events and transitions* (3rd ed., pp. 1–24). Thousand Oaks, CA: Sage.

Melotti, R., Lewis, G., Hickman, M., Heron, J., Araya, R., & Macleod, J. (2013). Early life socioeconomic position and later alcohol use: Birth cohort study. *Addiction, 108,* 516–525. doi: 10.1111/add.12018

Merline, A., Jager, J., & Schulenberg, J. E. (2008). Adolescent risk factors for adult alcohol use and abuse: Stability and change of predictive value across early and middle adulthood. *Addiction, 103*(Suppl. 1), 84–99.

Mersky, J. P., Topitzes, J., & Reynolds, A. J. (2013). Impacts of adverse childhood experiences on health, mental health, and substance use in early adulthood: A cohort study of an urban, minority sample in the U.S. *Child Abuse & Neglect, 37,* 917–925. doi:10.1016/j.chiabu .2013.07.011

Messler, E. C., Quevillon, R. P., & Simons, J. S., (2014). The effect of perceived parental approval of drinking on alcohol use and problems. *Journal of Alcohol and Drug Education, 58,* 44–59.

Mezzich, A. C., Tarter, R. E., Kirisci, L., Feske, U., Day, B., & Gao, Z. (2007). Reciprocal influence of parent discipline and child's behavior on risk for substance disorder: A nine-year prospective study. *American Journal of Drug and Alcohol Abuse, 33*(6), 851–867.

Molina, B. S. G., Donovan, J. E., & Belendiuk, K. A. (2010). Familial loading for alcoholism and offspring behavior: Mediating and moderating influences. *Alcoholism: Clinical & Experimental Research, 34,* 1972–1984.

Müller, S., & Kuntsche, E. (2011). Do the drinking motives of adolescents mediate the link between their parents' drinking habits and their own alcohol use? *Journal of Studies on Alcohol and Drugs, 72,* 429–437.

Mulsow, M. (2007). Treatment of co-morbidity in families. In J. L. Fischer, M. Mulsow, & A.W. Korinek (Eds.), *Familial responses to alcohol problems* (pp. 125–140). Binghamton, NY: Haworth Press.

Myers, L. L. (2013). Substance use among rural African American adolescents: Identifying risk and protective factors. *Child and Adolescent Social Work Journal, 30,* 79–93. doi:10.1007/s10560-012-0280-2

National Institute on Alcohol Abuse and Alcoholism. (2000). Drinking over the life span: Issues of biology, behavior, and risk. In *National Institute on Alcohol Abuse and Alcoholism, tenth special report to the U.S. Congress on alcohol and health: Highlights from current research.* Retrieved December 20, 2004, from http://www.niaaa.nih.gov/publications/10report/chap01.pdf

Needle, R. H., Su, S. S., & Doherty, W. J. (1990). Divorce, remarriage, and adolescent substance use: A prospective longitudinal study. *Journal of Marriage and the Family, 52,* 157–169.

Nonnemaker, J. M., Silber-Ashley, O., Farrelly, M. T., & Dench, D. (2012). Parent–child communication and marijuana initiation: Evidence using discrete-time survival analysis. *Addictive Behaviors, 37,* 1342–1348. doi:10.1016/j.addbeh.2012.07.006

Nyamathi, A., Hudson, A., Greengold, B., Slagle, A., Marfisee, M., Khalilifard, F., & Leake, B. (2010). Correlates of substance use severity among homeless youth. *Journal of Child and Adolescent Psychiatric Nursing, 23,* 214–222. doi:10.1111/j.1744-6171.2010.00247.x

O'Farrell, T. J., & Clements, K. (2012). Review of outcome research on marital and family therapy in treatment for alcoholism. *Journal of Marital and Family Therapy, 38,* 122–144. doi: 10.1111/j.1752-0606.2011.00242.x

Pandina, R. J., & Johnson, V. (1990). Serious alcohol and drug problems among adolescents with a family history of alcoholism. *Journal of Studies on Alcohol, 51,* 278–282.

Park. S., & Schepp, K. G. (2014). A systematic review of research on children of alcoholics: Their inherent resilience and vulnerability. *Journal of Child and Family Studies, 23*(2), 1–10. doi: 10.1007/s10826-014-9930-7

Patock-Peckham, J. A., King, K. M., Morgan-Lopez, A. A., Ulloa, E. C., & Filson Moses, J. M. (2011). Gender-specific mediational links between parenting styles, parental monitoring, impulsiveness, drinking control, and alcohol-related problems. *Journal of Studies on Alcohol and Drugs, 72,* 247–258.

Patock-Peckham, J. A., & Morgan-Lopez, A. A. (2007). College drinking behaviors: Mediational links between parenting styles, parental bonds, depression, and alcohol problems. *Psychology of Addictive Behaviors, 21*(3), 297–306.

Pelham, W. E., & Lang, A. R. (1999). Can your children drive you to drink? Stress and parenting in adults interacting with children with ADHD. *Alcohol Research and Health, 23*(4), 292–298.

Pesola, F., Shelton, K. H., & van den Bree, M. B. M. (2014). Sexual orientation and alcohol problem use among UK adolescents: An indirect link through depressed mood. *Addiction, 109,* 1072–1080. doi:10.1111/add.12528

Peters, K. R., Malzman, I., & Villone, K. (1994). Childhood abuse of parents of alcohol and other drug misusing adolescents. *International Journal of the Addictions, 29*(10), 1259–1268.

Pidcock, B. W., & Fischer, J. L. (1998). Parental recovery as a moderating variable of adult offspring problematic behaviors. *Alcoholism Treatment Quarterly, 16,* 45–57.

Rounsaville, D., O'Farrell, T. J., Andreas, J. B., Murphy, C. M., & Murphy, M. M. (2014). Children's exposure to parental conflict after father's treatment for alcoholism. *Addictive Behaviors, 39,* 1168–1171. doi:10.1016/j.addbeh.2014.03.017

Rosario, M., Reisner, S. L., Corliss, H. L., Wypji, D., Calzo, J., & Austin, S. B. (2014). Sexual-orientation disparities in substance use in emerging adults: A function of stress and attachment paradigms. *Psychology of Addictive Behaviors.* Advanced online publication. doi:10.1037/a0035499

Sanders-Phillips, K., Kliewer, W., Tirmazi, T., Nebbitt, V., Carter, T., & Key, H. (2014). Perceived racial discrimination, drug use, and psychological distress in African American youth: A pathway to child health disparities. *Journal of Social Issues, 70,* 279–297. doi:10.1111/josi.12060

Sartor, C. E., Lynskey, M. T., Heath, A. C., Jacob, T., & True, W. (2006). The role of childhood risk factors in initiation of alcohol use and progression to alcohol dependence. *Addiction, 102,* 216–225.

Schiff, M., Plotnikova, M., Dingle, K., Williams, G. M., Najman, J., & Clavarino, A. (2014). Does adolescent's exposure to parental intimate partner conflict and violence predict psychological distress and substance use in young adulthood? A longitudinal study. *Child Abuse & Neglect.* Advanced online publication. doi:10.1016/j.chiabu.2014.07.001

Settles, R. E., Zapolski, T. C. B., & Smith, G. T. (2014). Longitudinal test of a developmental model of the transition to early drinking. *Journal of Abnormal Psychology, 123,* 141–151. doi:10.1037/a0035670

Shamblen, S. R., Ringwalt, C. L., Clark, H. K., & Hanley, S. M. (2014). Alcohol use growth trajectories in young adolescence: Pathways and predictors. *Journal of Child & Adolescent Substance Abuse, 23,* 9–18. doi:10.1080/1067828.2012.747906

Sher, K. J., Grekin, E. R., & Williams, N. A. (2005). The development of alcohol use disorders. *Annual Review of Clinical Psychology, 1,* 493–523.

Shorey, R. C., Fite, P. J., Elkins, S. R., Frissell, K. C., Tortolero, S. R., Stuart, G. L., & Temple, J. R. (2013). The association between problematic parental substance use and adolescent substance use in an ethnically diverse sample of 9th and 10th graders. *The Journal of Primary Prevention, 34,* 381–393. doi:10.1007/s10935-013-0326-z

Slutske, W. S., D'Onofrio, B. M., Turkheimer, E., Emery, R. E., Harden, K. P., Heath, A. C., & Martin, N. G. (2008). Searching for an environmental effect of parental alcoholism on offspring alcohol use disorder: A genetically informed study of children of alcoholics. *Journal of Abnormal Psychology, 117*(3), 534–551.

Smith, C. L., Eisenberg, N., Spinrad, T. L., Chassin, L., Sheffield Morris, A., Kupfer, A., . . . Valiente, C. (2006). Children's coping strategies and coping efficacy: Relations to parent socialization, child adjustment, and familial alcoholism. *Development and Psychopathology, 18,* 445–469.

Smith, K. Z., Smith, P. H., & Grekin, E. R. (2014). Childhood sexual abuse, distress, and alcohol-related problems: Moderation by drinking to cope. *Psychology of Addictive Behaviors, 28,* 532–537. doi:10.1037/a0035381

Stelle, C. D., & Scott, J. P. (2007). Alcohol abuse by older family members: A family systems approach. In J. L. Fischer, M. Mulsow, & A. W. Korinek (Eds.), *Familial responses to alcohol problems* (pp. 43–63). Binghamton, NY: Haworth Press.

Thompson, R. J., Shmulewitz, D., Meyers, J. L., Stohl, M., Aharonovich, E., Spivak, B., . . . Hasina, D. S. (2014). Parental psychopathology moderates the influence of parental divorce on lifetime alcohol use disorders among Israeli adults. *Drug and Alcohol Dependence, 141,* 85–91. doi:10.1016/j.drugalcdep.2014.05.009

Tucker, J. S., Ellickson, P. L., & Klein, D. J. (2008). Growing up in a permissive household: What deters at-risk adolescents from heavy drinking? *Journal of Studies on Alcohol and Drugs, 69,* 528–534.

Tyler, K. A., Stone, R. T., & Bersani, B. (2006). Examining the changing influence of predictors on adolescent alcohol misuse. *Journal of Child and Adolescent Substance Abuse, 16*(2), 95–114.

Unger, J. B. (2014). Cultural influences on substance use among Hispanic adolescents and young adults: Findings from project RED. *Child Development Perspectives, 8*(1), 48-53.

Vakalahi, H. F. (2002). Family-based predictors of adolescent substance use. *Journal of Child and Adolescent Substance Abuse, 11*(3), 1–15.

Van Ryzin, M. J., Fosco, G. M., & Dishion, T. J. (2012). Family and peer predictors of substance use from early adolescence to early adulthood: An 11-year prospective analysis. *Addictive Behaviors, 37,* 1314–1324. doi:10.1016/j.addbeh.2012.06.020

Visser, L., de Winter, A. F., Vollebergh, W. A. M., Verhulst, F. C., & Reijneveld, S. A. (2013). The impact of parenting styles on adolescent alcohol use: The TRAILS study. *European Addiction Research, 19*(4), 165–172.

Walther, C. A. P., Cheong, J., Molina, B. S G., Pelham, W. E., Wymbs, B. T., Belendiuk, K., & Pedersen, S. L. (2012). Substance use and delinquency among adolescents with childhood ADHD: The protective role of parenting. *Psychology of Addictive Behaviors, 26,* 585–598. doi:10.1037/a0026818

Wang, M., Kviz, F. J., & Miller, A. M. (2012). The mediating role of parent–child bonding to prevent adolescent alcohol abuse among Asian American families. *Journal of Immigrant Minority Health, 14,* 831–840. doi:10.1007/s10903-012-9593-7

West, J. H., Blumberg, E. J., Kelley, N. J., Hill, L., Sipan, C. L., Schmitz, K. E., . . . Hovell, M. F. (2013). The role of parenting in alcohol and tobacco use among Latino adolescents. *Journal of Child & Adolescent Substance Abuse, 22,* 120–132. doi:10.1080/1067828X.2012.730359

White, H. R., Johnson, V., & Buyske, S. (2000). Parental modeling and parenting behavior effects on offspring alcohol and cigarette use: A growth curve analysis. *Journal of Substance Abuse, 12*(3), 287–310.

Whiteman, S. D., Jensen, A. C., & Maggs, J. L. (2013). Similarities in adolescent siblings' substance use: Testing competing pathways of influence. *Journal of Studies on Alcohol and Drugs, 74,* 104–113.

Wiersma, J. D., & Fischer, J. L. (2014). Young adult drinking partnerships: Alcohol-related consequences and relationship problems six years later. *Journal of Studies on Alcohol and Drugs, 75,* 704–712.

Wills, T. A., & Cleary, S. D. (1996). How are social support effects mediated? A test with parental support and adolescent substance use. *Journal of Personality and Social Psychology, 71,* 937–952.

Windle, M. (2000). Parental, sibling, and peer influences on adolescent substance use and alcohol problems. *Applied Developmental Science, 4,* 98–110.

Wong, C. F., Silva, K., Kecojevic, A., Schrager, S. M., Bloom, J. J., Iverson, E., & Landenau, S. E. (2013). Coping and emotion regulation profiles as predictors of nonmedical prescription drug and illicit drug use among high-risk young adults. *Drug and Alcohol Dependence, 132,* 165–171. doi: 10.1016/j.drugalcdep.2013.01.024

Zucker, R. A. (2008). Anticipating problem alcohol use developmentally from childhood into middle adulthood: What have we learned? *Addiction, 103,* 100–108.

Zucker, R. A., Fitzgerald, H. E., Refior, S. K., Pallas, D. M., & Ellis, D. A. (2000). The clinical and social ecology of childhood for children of alcoholics: Description of a study and implications for a differentiated social policy. In H. E. Fitzgerald, B. M. Lester, & B. S. Zuckerman (Eds.), *Children of addiction: Research, health, and policy issues* (pp. 109–141). New York, NY: Routledge/Falmer.

CHAPTER 16

Economic Stress and Families

Suzanne Bartholomae and Jonathon Fox

Vignette

Just after the financial crisis began in late 2007, James Jones, 51, was laid off from his job as a systems analyst from Citigroup. James was always a hard-working, dedicated employee who cared about his job. James has been married to Cecily for 13 years. They have 3 children. He made $60,000 a year and was the major breadwinner of the family. James receives a weekly unemployment check, but it isn't enough to cover his family's expenses, and unemployment benefits stop after 26 weeks. James and Cecily didn't have an emergency savings account, so they had to borrow some money from Cecily's mother. Their credit cards have also made up for some of the shortfall in income, and they will soon tap into the retirement savings James accumulated while working. James is becoming more and more withdrawn socially. Last week he ran into a former colleague at the park. He told Cecily how awkward the conversation was when he was asked what he has been up to; he said he felt like a "total loser." He doesn't sleep at night and seems to be irritable most of the time. He snaps at Cecily and the children. Cecily feels bad for James, but she is losing patience and just hopes that something good will happen soon.

• • •

James and Cecily's story is similar to many families who are just starting to recover from one of the longest and most severe economic downturns in American history, the Great Recession. Due to the Great Recession, families have sustained severe job losses, high unemployment, record-breaking long-term unemployment, significant job shortages, large declines in income, and a substantial rise in poverty (Bernstein, 2014). Research shows that during an economic recession, marriage, divorce, and fertility rates tend to decline and rates of family violence and suicide increase; when the economy is thriving, these indicators tend to work in the opposite direction (Blair, 2012).

As family scientists, we have long examined the link between adverse economic conditions and family processes and outcomes. A longitudinal study of children of the Great Depression published in the 1970s linked economic hardship to the reorganization of family roles and responsibilities (Elder, 1974). Similarly, rural farm families who experienced a severe economic downturn in the 1980s were the focus of several studies, showing the link between economic pressure and elevated depression, hostility, and marital distress (Conger & Conger, 2002; Conger & Elder, 1994). Recently, several studies have begun to exam of the effect of the Great Recession on families (e.g., Dew & Xiao, 2013; Landivar, 2012), with the current economic conditions providing a living laboratory to study economic stress. Taken together, there is a body of work that captures the importance of explaining how economic stress and financial problems influences family life.

DEFINING AND MEASURING ECONOMIC STRESS

Economic stress can be the by-product of conditions in the national, regional, or local economy, like the Great Recession. Economic stress can be described as either *normative* (resulting from expected milestones in the family life cycle, such as marriage or birth of a child) or *situational/nonnormative* (stemming from unexpected events, such as divorce, retirement, or illness). In addition, economic stress associated with life events may be *temporary* (e.g., a short-term drop in income due to job loss) or *chronic* (e.g., a long-term income loss because of a permanent work-limiting disability) (Voydanoff, 1983). With the Great Recession, which began in late 2007 and lasted through June 2009, James's economic stress started with the Great Recession, and if he had quickly rebounded by finding gainful employment it would have been characterized as temporary. His economic stress would be considered chronic if he continued to be unemployed, a more likely condition due to the slow recovery of the economy.

Family researchers often use the term *economic or financial stress* interchangeably with such terms as *economic or financial distress, hardship, pressure, and strain*. The concept of economic stress can be decomposed into employment and income-related stressors that can be described objectively (e.g., a lack of regular work and income) or subjectively (e.g., worrying about possible unemployment (Voydanoff & Donnelly, 1988). To assess objective economic stress, researchers examine patterns of employment and changes in income over time. For example, by comparing various individual, couple, and family outcomes (e.g., depression, marital satisfaction, and parenting) by employed versus unemployed status.

Financial strain represents the subjective, psychological aspects of economic stress and is thought to be related to but independent of one's income. Subjective measurement of economic strain or pressure can be defined as "the perceived adequacy of financial resources, financial concerns and worries, and expectations regarding one's future economic situation" (Voydanoff & Donnelly, 1988, p. 98). Families of similar income levels can have considerably different experiences based on their access to economic resources, like home ownership, and characteristics like family size and number of dependents. Researchers have generally assessed levels of financial strain by using Likert scale items. Family members rate how often they worry about their finances, how satisfied they are with their financial situation, their level of difficulty paying bills, and whether they have enough money to meet necessities and/or money left over at the end of the month. The components of economic stress are unique to each individual and family system, particularly the perception of the event. For James and Cecily, they had some resources to draw from and were able to make some adjustments; however, this combination is unique for each family.

In this chapter, we start by reviewing economic conditions and indicators of a family's financial status and economic stress. We use the family economic stress model as a framework. We then discuss the outcomes associated with economic stress, including a review of the research on economic stress and its interaction with resources and problem solving. Finally, using a family economic life cycle, we discuss coping strategies to combat negative economic events.

ECONOMIC CONDITIONS OF THE AMERICAN FAMILY

The United States is long heralded as one of the most affluent countries, with most families historically benefiting from a strong and prosperous economy. This distinction no longer holds. Relative to other nations, recent data show a decline in the number of Americans in the middle class, stagnant middle-class wages, a rise in income inequality, and the American middle class is no longer the world's wealthiest (Erickson, 2014). A shift has occurred; during recessionary periods income inequality typically shrinks, yet it widened during the Great Recession (Erickson, 2014). Currently families cannot keep up with the rising costs of being in the middle class and maintaining a middle-class standard of living. Erickson (2014) notes that "the costs of key elements of middle-class security—child care, higher education, health care, housing, and retirement—rose by more than $10,000 in the 12 years from 2000 to 2012, at a time when this family's income was stagnant" (p. 3). Economic security is at the core of being middle class. Whether measured objectively or subjectively, many low- and middle-income families are experiencing economic stress and financial pressures and are having difficulty recovering from the Great Recession (Mishel & Davis, 2014).

MEASURES OF FAMILY ECONOMIC WELL-BEING

For many families it takes just one crisis, such as a divorce or job loss, to devastate their economic well-being. Most measures of economic well-being vary substantially by demographic characteristics (e.g., gender, education, marital status, minority group status). We present a variety of economic indicators that family scientists use to measure and estimate the prevalence of economic stress in families. Studies by family scientists have documented the critical role economic resources play in the quality of family functioning (Conger & Elder, 1994; Rothwell & Han, 2010).

Employment Instability and Insecurity: A Threat to Family Life

The economic stressor most frequently studied by family researchers relates to employment—both job insecurity and unemployment. Job insecurity is the real or perceived threat of losing one's job. Both job insecurity and unemployment have been associated with poor physical health, high depressive symptoms, and lower life satisfaction (Cuyper, Makikangas, Kinnunen, Mauno, & De Witte, 2012; Meltzer et al., 2010). Symptoms commonly associated with job loss include a sense of helplessness, insecurity, depression, anxiety, strained family relationships, role anxiety, damaged self-esteem, and depletion of financial resources (Cuyper et al., 2012; McKee-Ryan, Song, Wanberg, & Kinicki, 2005; Voydanoff & Donnelly, 1988).

Unemployment might result from job dismissal, factory closing, or forced early retirement. Single-earner families, like James and Cecily's, are more vulnerable financially, in the case of illness or job loss they have no safety net from a backup earner. On the other hand, two income families budget both pay checks to meet financial obligations making job loss or illness potentially more serious than for a one-earner family where the other person can enter the labor market to make up for an income loss (Warren, 2007). With James's job loss came new constraints, disruptions, and stressors. The impact to his family was similar to what the research demonstrates, family relationships were strained and children experienced behavioral changes not previously seen (Morin & Kochhar, 2010; Warner, 2010). For James, there were also nonfinancial impacts, such as a loss of time structure, loss of social status associated with the job, disrupted social networks, reduced opportunities for social contact, and reduced goals and task demands (Creed & Klisch, 2005).

When the economy and labor market are healthy, families prosper. When the Great Recession began, the U.S. labor market had one of the worst records of job growth and sustained the most severe job loss in 7 decades (Mishel, Bivens, Gould, & Shierholz, 2012). In 2008, the number of unemployed Americans rose from 6.9 to 8.5 million compared to a year earlier (U.S. Bureau of Labor Statistics, 2014). Men experienced greater rates of unemployment, partially because of employment in industries hardest hit by the Great Recession, construction and manufacturing (Landivar, 2012). These labor market conditions, in hand with the Great Recession, quickly dismantled the financial security of many families, increasing feelings of stress.

Income: Family Livelihood

An important indicator used to measure family economic well-being is income. Income allows families to pay their mortgage, utility, and groceries bills, it allows parents to invest in their children's upbringing, and during tough economic times like a recession, it can ward off stress. Studies show a negative relationship between income and financial stress, with higher levels of income associated with lower economic stress (Amato, Booth, Johnson, & Rogers, 2007; Valentino, Moore, Cleveland, Greenberg, & Tan, 2014). Income has both a direct and indirect effect on marital outcomes, including an increase in conflict, problems, and thoughts of divorce, as well as lower marital happiness and interaction (Amato et al., 2007).

In 2013, family household median income before taxes was $65,587. Median income of all household types was $51,939, 8% lower than in 2007 (DeNavas-Walt & Proctor, 2014). Married couple households had the highest median income ($76,509) in 2013, followed by male-headed family households with no wife present ($50,625). In 2012, wives earned more than husbands in 29% of dual-earner marriages, an increase from 15.9% in 1988 (U.S. Census Bureau, 2012). Family households that were maintained by women with no husband present had the lowest income, $35,154 (DeNavas-Walt & Proctor, 2014). In

2013, households in the 95th percentile had incomes of $196,001, nine times more than households in the 20th percentile (DeNavas-Walt & Proctor, 2014).

Median household income is an imperfect measure of financial security because it only counts cash benefits and does not include the value of noncash benefits from employers (e.g., retirement plan contributions), food stamps (Supplemental Nutrition Assistance Program), health insurance (Medicare, Medicaid), public housing, or other income-support programs (DeNavas-Walt & Proctor, 2014). Household income and/or poverty level determines one's eligibility for benefits from public programs. Based on 2013 U.S. Census data, the poverty rate for families was 11.2%, and approximately 9.1 million families were in poverty; female-headed households represented the largest proportion (30.6%), followed by male-headed (15.9%) and married couple family households (5.8%) (DeNavas-Walt & Proctor, 2014). Many of the basics that most of us take for granted, families in poverty live without, including safe and quality living conditions, a healthy diet, and medical care.

Net Worth: A Measure of Family Wealth

Net worth is a tremendously important indicator of family economic well-being. Higher net worth denotes greater financial security and independence when times are tough, increased opportunities to further education and employment, and ability to move upward in terms of economic mobility and social class (McKernan, Ratcliffe, Steuerle, & Zhang, 2013). Net worth consists of a family's total assets (money accumulated in savings, checking, and retirement accounts including 401(k) plans and individual retirement accounts; real estate including home equity; stock holdings; and other assets such as cars, furniture, etc.) minus total liabilities (money owed on debts such as mortgages, credit cards, student loans). Net worth typically increases with income, age, education, housing status (home ownership), and marital status (marriage leading to increased net worth) (Bricker et al., 2014; Zagorsky, 2005).

Median household net worth was $81,200, and mean net worth was $534,600 in 2013 (Bricker et al., 2014). Inequality is strikingly evident in the distribution of net worth, the lowest income households (< 20 percentile) had a median net worth of $6,400 compared to $287,900 (80–89.9 percentile) and $1,275,700 (90–100 percentile) for households in the highest percentiles (Bricker et al., 2014). There is also alarming disparity in net worth levels among ethnic minority groups. In 2013, White only households had a median net worth of $142,000 compared to net worth of $18,100 for non-White or Hispanic households (Bricker et al., 2014). The types of assets held vary by household wealth and contribute to wealth disparity. Portfolios with stocks, bonds, and other investments generating financial assets tend to be held by wealthier households whereas lower income households hold most of their wealth in home equity through home ownership (Bricker et al., 2014).

Home Ownership: The American Dream

Families continue to maintain the American dream of home ownership. Since the 1960s, home ownership rates for the United States have ranged between 63% and 69%. In 2013, it was 64%, down from 69% in 2004 (Bricker et al., 2014). Several studies demonstrate the benefits of home ownership to individuals (e.g., better mental and physical health), children (e.g., greater educational attainment), and the community (higher civic engagement and social involvement) (Lindblad & Quercia, 2014). For American families, building home equity is fundamental to building wealth (Mishel et al., 2012). Home equity—the value of a home less the amount owed on the mortgage—constitutes a family's greatest financial asset and share of net worth. In 2013, mean home equity was $159,400, and the median home value was $170,000 (Bricker et al., 2014). Home ownership rates vary by family income—in 2013, the home ownership rate was 49.2% for families in the bottom half of the income distribution compared to 93.5% for families in the top 10% (Bricker et al., 2014).

The burst of the estimated $10.6 trillion housing bubble in 2007 was a contributing factor of the Great Recession (Howley, 2012). Subprime mortgages, a financial product developed for poor credit and/or low-income borrowers, precipitated the housing crisis by qualifying high-risk households. The burst in the housing bubble left almost one in four American homeowners "underwater," meaning their mortgage debt was worth more than the value of their home (Howley, 2012). The result was record home foreclosures, more than 8.2 million households started the foreclosure process, and 4 million completed the process between 2007 and 2011 (Blomquist, 2012). Home foreclosure signals severe financial distress in a family. James and Cecily might go into foreclosure if they cannot secure a steady income.

Household Debt and Families: Borrowing Against the Future

An increase in the ease of access to credit in the past decade created a credit boom, as a result there has been growing concern about increased indebtedness among families (Loonin & Renuart, 2007). Household debt becomes problematic when large amounts of unsecured debt are assumed or other financial obligations cannot be met. Faced with budget constraints due to rising prices and unfavorable economic conditions, families increasingly borrow against their future and use debt to support their consumption (Leicht & Fitzgerald, 2006).

Not all household debt is bad; debt is a financial instrument that can be used to create wealth and opportunities. For example, a mortgage is a secured debt where collateral (e.g., the house) is secured against the amount owed. A mortgage provides an opportunity for home ownership, which in turn contributes to increased wealth when families accumulate equity. Student loan debt creates human capital that has long-term returns. Secured debts are typically planned debts and increase family wealth. In 2013, 75% of families held some type of debt, the top three types were mortgages, education loans, and credit card debt (Bricker et al., 2014).

The most threatening type of debt to the long-term financial well-being of families is unsecured consumer credit—typically used to purchase items and services that usually do not last longer than the payment period, require interest payment to the lender, and yield no economic return while being held. In other words, it does not add to personal assets of a family; instead, it creates a burden of repayment. In 2013, about 38.1% of all family households carried a balance on their credit card, and the average family carried $5,700 in credit card debt (Bricker et al., 2014).

Credit card debt, worries about credit card debt repayment and meeting financial emergencies have been found to negatively impact perceived financial well-being (Porter &

Garman, 1993), physical health and mortality (Drentea & Lavrakas, 2000; Szanton, Thorpe, & Whitfield, 2010) and increased symptoms of depression, anxiety, anger (Drentea & Reynolds, 2012; Meltzer et al., 2010; Zurlo, Yoon, & Kim, 2014). If James and Cecily's credit card debt becomes unmanageable, there will be negative ramifications for them as individuals, as just noted, but they might also find it impacting their relationship.

Among married couples, consumer debt predicted more frequent marital conflict (Dew, 2008) and the likelihood of marital dissolution/divorce (Dew, 2011). The financial practices of married couples who believed their marriages were great, had little or no debt, had a goal of paying off debt, and lived within their means or were frugal (Skogrand, Johnson, Horrocks, & DeFrain, 2011). Couples whose home mortgage was paid off reported greater marital satisfaction (Nelson, Delgadillo, & Dew, 2013). Couples may recognize that consumer debt constrains future choices and may resent the time and money required to make debt payments (Dew, 2008).

When a family's debt becomes overwhelming, personal bankruptcy is an option and occurs when a person files a petition in federal court to declare their inability to repay their debts. The majority of bankruptcy filings occur because of reasons beyond the control of the family, such as job loss, divorce, or illness coupled with a lack of health insurance (Logan & Weller, 2008). Bankruptcy is a substantial indicator of a family experiencing severe economic stress, and it comes with long-term consequences. For example, a family's ability to secure low cost loans for housing or education are greatly diminished after filing for bankruptcy. During 2013, 1 million people filed for bankruptcy, largely due to unmanageable consumer debt (Administrative Office of the U.S. Courts, 2013), whereas more recently, unpaid medical bills were the cause of bankruptcy in three out of five petitions (LaMontagne, 2014).

Savings: Family Safety Net

Families can choose to save or spend household income left over after their expenses. If they don't spend it, they might choose to pay down their credit card debt or mortgage, or they can put it toward a savings goal such as retirement or education. In 2013, the proportion of American families that reported saving over the past year was 53% (Bricker et al., 2014). The top reasons for savings among Americans is for retirement (58%), unexpected expenses (53%), and just to save (49%). The median percentage of income saved by Americans was 2%, about 45% reported that they did not save any of their income in 2012 (Board of Governors of the Federal Reserve System, 2014). Americans are pessimistic about their ability to save, blaming credit card debt and impulsive spending as barriers (Bricker, Kennickell, Moore, & Sabelhaus, 2012). James is upset about not being able to save money toward a college savings fund.

The importance of savings is greater than ever because families are receiving fewer health and pension/retirement benefits from private employers (Weller, 2014). Families who maintain a cash reserve in an emergency savings account create a financial safety net that can help to avoid a financial crisis and enable them to meet financial obligations. Although financial professionals recommend a 3- to 6-month emergency savings fund, only half of Americans set aside this amount in an emergency or rainy day fund (Board of Governors of the Federal Reserve System, 2014). Asked to estimate how many months they could live at their current lifestyle if they had a sudden loss of income, 29.6 % of Americans could not maintain their lifestyle, with only 19.2 % agreeing they could maintain their lifestyle for a month. With no safety net, like in James's situation, American families hang on the precipice of financial disaster.

THE FAMILY ECONOMIC STRESS MODEL

The family economic stress model attributed to Conger and Elder (1994) predicts that economic hardship will lead to child and family outcomes through adverse changes in personal mental health, marital quality, and parenting. The process begins with external economic pressures such as involuntary job separation or a general countrywide economic downturn, such as the Great Recession, that lead to financial strains. These pressures result in declines in parental mental health, such as increased depression, which challenges both marital quality and parenting practices. Finally, compromised parenting yields negative family outcomes most often observed in child mental health and behavior. The family economic stress model has been applied to models of family and child outcomes in diverse economic systems and cultures (for review see Conger, Conger, & Martin, 2010); performing equally well in Finland's welfare state (Solantaus, Leinonen, & Punamaki, 2004), communist China (Shek, 2003), and capitalist economies such as the United States (Conger & Elder, 1994).

Economic stress in the family manifests itself directly by influencing individual well-being and indirectly by influencing family interaction (Conger et al., 1990; Elder & Caspi, 1988). Economic factors (e.g., unemployment, low income, excessive debt levels) have negative effects on the mental health and well-being of individuals (Drentea & Reynolds, 2012; McKee et al., 2005; Zurlo et al., 2014). Researchers have identified a relationship between economic stress and individual distress, such as increased levels of anger, hostility, depression, anxiety, somatic complaints, and poor physical health (Cuyper et al., 2012; Meltzer et al., 2010). In James's case, his ego and self-esteem have been greatly damaged by the layoff, he feels depressed and irritable. Even the association between economic strain and suicide has been linked (Ceccherini-Nelli & Priebe, 2011).

The adverse effect of economic stress on family functioning and family relationships is well documented (Conger et al., 2010). Studies show economic stress linked to decreased family satisfaction and cohesion (Voydanoff, 1990), forcing family members to adapt their roles and responsibilities. In James's case, Cecily is seeking work after being a stay-at-home mom, just as research shows, when a family experiences an income decline because of one member's job loss, other family members may be required to contribute to household resources by finding employment (Elder & Caspi, 1988). Economic stress can also lead to diminished relationship quality in the family through the strain and disruption caused by changes in social activities as well as changes in the support provided by social networks (Voydanoff, 1990). For example, James and Cecily are considering cutting back on the children's extracurricular activities because the added expense is causing stress.

The marital relationship is altered by economic stress, and several studies support the family economic stress model with respect to marital outcomes (Dew, 2007; Dew & Xiao, 2013; Kinnunen & Feldt, 2004). Specifically, a couple's adverse economic circumstances (e.g., loss of income), increases financial strain, which increases individual psychological distress, which in turn negatively impacts marital stability and adjustment (Kinnunen & Feldt, 2004). This process results in increased financial disputes and thus greater marital tension and discord (Dew, 2007; 2008; Gudmunson, Beutler, Israelsen, McCoy & Hill, 2007); increases husbands' hostility and explosiveness and decreases their supportiveness and warmth (Conger et al., 1990); and the overall the quality of the marital relationship declines (Conger & Conger, 2002; Dew, 2008).

Families facing economic stress may find that the quality of their parental well-being suffers, resulting in elevated anxiety, psychological distress, hostility, general life stress, depressive symptoms, somatization, and decreased feelings of efficacy (Conger & Conger, 2002; Gutman, McLoyd, & Tokoyawa, 2005; Mistry, Lowe, Benner, & Chien, 2008). Further, economic stress has been shown to affect parenting practices by reducing warmth and affective support (Mistry et al., 2008); reducing levels of sensitive, supportive behavior (Newland, Crnic, Cox, & Mills-Koonce, 2013); increasing inconsistent, controlling, and punitive discipline (Mistry et al., 2008); and lowering levels of parent involvement and supportiveness (Conger & Conger, 2002; Gutman et al., 2005). Levels of maternal warmth and social support and the provision of child learning experiences in the home are also affected negatively by economic stress (Klebanov, Brooks-Gunn, & Duncan, 1994).

Short- and long-term child outcomes have been associated with economic stress. Children who experience economic stress have been found to exhibit greater levels of depression, psychological distress, anxiety (Gutman et al., 2005); psychosomatic symptoms and chronic illness (Pederson, Madsen, & Kohler, 2005); more externalizing aggressive and antisocial problem behavior (Ponnet, 2014; Solantaus et al., 2004); decreased levels of self-esteem, self-efficacy, mastery, life satisfaction, and resourcefulness (Gutman et al., 2005; Shek, 2003); diminished school performance (Gutman et al., 2005); and increased substance abuse and psychiatric morbidity (Shek, 2003). Father's negativity resulting from economic pressure has been found to increase children's risk of depression and aggression (Elder, Conger, Foster, & Ardelt, 1992), whereas maternal financial stress has been shown to decrease the quality of the mother–child relationship, resulting in greater levels of depression and loneliness (Lempers & Clark-Lempers, 1997). Greater financial strain also reduces positive parent–adolescent relations—measured as shared activities and supportiveness— and increases negative parent–adolescent relations measured as frequency of conflict and aggressive interactions such as shouting or acting angry (Gutman et al., 2005).

COPING WITH ECONOMIC STRESS

The characteristics of financially challenged families—such as adaptability, cohesion, and authority patterns—that are in place both prior to and during a stressor event, like financial difficulties, are important in that they can alter the relationship between the event (such as unemployment and its associated hardships) and individual and family reactions. Families experiencing economic stress from their financial situation can draw on individual (e.g., education), psychological (e.g., self-efficacy), social (e.g., social support), relational (e.g., marital relationship), and financial (e.g., savings) resources to cope with their situation (Chen & Lim, 2012; Elder & Caspi, 1988; Valentino et al., 2014).

Individuals with positive self-evaluations, such as high self-esteem or self-worth and a strong sense of personal control or mastery over their situation are better prepared to manage their economic adversities and financial difficulties (Prawitz, Kalkowski, & Cohart, 2014). As such, these qualities can weaken the link between financial stress and mental health outcomes (McKee-Ryan et al., 2005; Zurlo et al., 2014). For example, self-efficacy and locus of control has been found to be an effective moderator in the context of economic stress (McKee-Ryan et al., 2005; Prawitz et al., 2014), influencing how an individual reacts to a given stressor event. Studies of unemployment have found that high self-efficacy successfully predicts reemployment (McGhee-Ryan et al., 2005), as does an individual's sense of employability (Cuyper et al., 2012), hope, optimism, and resilience (Chen & Lim, 2012). In James's case, being laid off was unexpected and quite damaging to his self-esteem. Financial resources, such as savings and unemployment compensation, are also important in mediating the effect economic stress has on individual and family outcomes (Dew, 2007; Rothwell & Han, 2010). The impact of job loss can be alleviated by income, liquid assets (e.g., money in bank accounts), public assistance (McKee-Ryan et al., 2005; Mistry et al., 2008), as well as the continuation of fringe benefits such as health insurance, severance pay, and pensions (Voydanoff, 1983).

As outlined in the family economic stress model, some social resources such as integration into family and social networks and quality of one's interpersonal relationships are weakened by financial strain. According to Elder and Caspi (1988), families respond to economic loss by restructuring resources and relationships. Restructuring may relieve the situation without improving it, or it may be an adaptive coping strategy. For those struggling with chronic economic issues, several coping strategies have been identified as effective in breaking the links established in the family economic stress model. For example, coping strategies such as problem solving, social support, acceptance of the situation, positive thinking, and distraction have been associated with fewer somatic complaints as well as anxious and depressive symptoms among families suffering from chronic economic stress (Wadsworth & Santiago, 2008).

FAMILY FINANCIAL PLANNING AS A COPING RESOURCE

Family financial planning can alleviate the psychological and social damage caused by economic stress, family vulnerability, and exposure to economic stress. The family life-cycle model developed by Ando and Modigliani (1963) is a common framework for understanding saving and consumption behavior of families. Over the family life cycle, spending is expected to be smooth and stable as the family maintains a standard of living with the use of savings during low-income periods. However, actual consumption patterns are often affected by changing family needs and wants, situational stressors, and significant historical events (Fox, 1995). Part of the gap between the theory of household resource allocation over time and actual resource allocation is explained by the nonnormative factors that are so prevalent among American families, including unanticipated unemployment, divorce, casualty losses, and unanticipated health care expenses (Fan, Chang, & Hanna, 1992; Finke & Pierce, 2006).

The family economic life cycle is composed of three key phases, identified by the relationship between expenditure and earning levels that define the life-cycle savings hypothesis. These phases, which we discuss in turn below, can serve as guidelines for addressing economic stress. When families employ systematic money management strategies, they can reduce or eliminate conflict during tough financial times. For example, research has shown that couples have fewer finance-related arguments when they use financial management strategies such as record keeping, goal-setting practices, and saving (Godwin, 1994). Couples under economic pressure who use effective problem-solving skills reduce marital conflict and thus marital distress (Conger et al., 1990).

Phase I. Family Formation: Starting a Credit and Debt Management Program

In the family formation phase, a family is expected to accumulate significant amounts of debt through the use of installment and consumer credit, largely as a result of the purchase of a home and expenses of child rearing for families with children. Planning for payment against this debt and worrying about possible default can easily become a source of stress within a family; however, by creating and following a debt management plan stress can be reduced. To make such a plan, the family needs to (a) establish credit goals or debt limits; (b) explore, understand, and make good choices among the various sources of credit; and (c) make fair comparisons between the costs of different types of credit (Garman & Forgue, 2007). Once family members have set their goals and tolerable debt levels, they can study their formal (banks or bank-like institutions) and informal (relatives and friends) credit options. Determining the actual cost of credit (the interest rate) should be most salient in the family's credit decision. Saving current income is a primary mechanism through which families achieve financial goals and prepare for financial emergencies. Saving provides a sense of economic control and serves as a safeguard or a coping resource in the event of economic stress (e.g., unemployment).

Phase II. Repaying Debt and Saving for Retirement

In the second phase of the family economic life cycle, the time at which most household heads reach their peak earning years, many families plan to accumulate wealth in anticipation of a substantial decrease in earned income in retirement. During this phase, families reduce or stabilize living expenses so they don't exceed income. As income increases with workplace experience and household formation nears completion, immediate financial demands are expected to subside, and the family has an opportunity to accumulate savings and pay off debt accumulated in the formation stage. However, during these peak earning years, many families are challenged by the repayment of accumulated debt, college education expenses, and deferral of the proper amount of consumption until retirement when reduced earnings are anticipated.

Families use tax planning, investment, and asset protection strategies to move assets from one point in the life cycle to another. Unfortunately, the complexity of these financial strategies can often become a source of additional economic stress in families (Aldana & Liljenquist, 1998). As a result, many families now seek the help of family financial managers to retire the debt accumulated in the previous phase and invest any surplus in financial assets. The most important action a family can take in this phase is to accurately determine their debt. Once the amount of debt is clear, they can allocate savings toward debt repayment, retire loans with the highest interest first, thus "investing" in the highest return assets earlier. This method of thinking about debt repayment, in similar terms as saving for future financial goals, helps financial managers justify an emphasis on debt repayment early in the financial life cycle, potentially relieving some of the stress involved in delaying savings for retirement and longer range financial goals.

Nonprofit organizations, such as Consumer Credit Counseling Services, have been established to assist families with the debt management process. Typically, such an organization will help a family reestablish more manageable payment terms for debt. The counseling service typically collects a lump sum payment from the family and redistributes the money to the creditors, thus relieving family members of the stress involved in direct contact with creditors. Research findings suggest that working with credit counselors can have positive impacts on individuals' financial well-being and health (Kim, Garman, & Sorhaindo, 2003; O'Neill, Sorhaindo, Xiao, & Garman, 2005). Clients who participated in a debt management program and reported improved health outcomes were more likely to engage in positive financial behaviors (O'Neill et al., 2005). However, using such a debt management system can also have significant drawbacks, the process itself is often reported as a negative event in credit bureau files, and participants must agree to discontinue any use of credit during the debt management process.

As families struggle to retire the debt they have accumulated in the formation stage, families with children may encounter significant additional educational expenses as offspring approach college age. Educational spending pressures have risen steadily in the United States as tuition increases have consistently outpaced increases in wages. The widespread perception of the hopelessness of this situation is expressed in most families' unwillingness to plan for or begin saving for children's education; one recent study found that parents plan to cover about 64% of their children's total college costs but are on track to save only 28% of that goal (Business Wire, 2014). Other surveys show about one quarter (24%) of parents with college bound children are taking advantage of plans, like Coverdell Savings Accounts or 529 plans, to save for their children's education (College Savings Foundation, 2010). Parents of college students face competing pressures, whether to save for their retirement or their children's education goals; the percentage of families who use retirement assets to pay for college expenses ranges from 7% to 25% (Brandon, 2014).

Studies consistently find that American families are underfinancing their retirement. These families will either need to increase their savings or reduce their living standards below expected levels upon retirement. Among those workers who save for retirement, 57% have accumulated less than $25,000 in savings and investments, excluding their home value and defined benefit plans, showing they are likely not on track for retirement at preretirement consumption levels (Employee Benefit Research Institute, 2015).

Garman and Forgue (2007) outline the formal process of retirement planning; families can use their guidelines to determine the levels of savings they need to meet their retirement spending needs. As with all financial planning prescriptions, the process begins with goal setting. Goals are set based on income needs in retirement. Anticipated retirement resources are then evaluated, these are subtracted from retirement needs, and a savings gap is estimated. Additional annual contributions needed to fill this gap are then calculated, and investment decisions are made to match individual investor risk tolerance levels and specific financial goals in retirement. In this final part of the retirement planning and saving process, a wide range of tax, investment, and insurance planning tools are available to families. It is at this point that many families rely on financial managers to cope with the complexities of the financial planning process. In fact, the sheer breadth of the field of financial planning appears to be a source of economic stress in families, one study found the lack of financial education and understanding about financial matters is a significant determinant of financial strain (Aldana & Liljenquist, 1998). Families who receive professional advice about finances and retirement have been found to be more satisfied with their current financial situation than are families who do not receive such advice (Kim et al., 2003).

Phase III. Living in Retirement and Planning for Intergenerational Transfers

In the third phase of the family economic life cycle, consumption expenditures are expected to outpace earnings as families tap savings and investment income for expenditures in retirement. At this end of the life cycle, some families face the problem of living on reduced incomes whereas others need to distribute excess assets among family members and/or favorite charities. These wealth transfers, and planning for them, can easily become an additional source of family stress and conflict through competition for assets.

The quality of the retirement experience relies on financial security. In a recent poll of Americans, the number one financial worry was adequately saving for retirement (Dugan, 2014). Most evidence indicates that Americans are not financially prepared for retirement. For example, retirees must plan to replace their income to support their standard of living and retirement plans, yet one estimate found more than half of U.S. households at risk of a reduced standard of living (Munnell, Webb, & Golub-Sass, 2009).

The average life expectancy for those reaching age 65 is 84.3 for males and 86.6 for females (Social Security Administration, 2015). American retirees reported retiring at age 62 (the highest age since 1991), and nonretired Americans reported 66 as their likely retirement age (Riffkin, 2014). Thus, most American can expect about 20 years to be spent in retirement. The uncertainty of Social Security, fewer employer-sponsored pension plans, and economic conditions, like the Great Recession are among the reasons for delayed expected retirement (Riffkin, 2014). When Americans say they will retire, a key factor is the value of their investments, followed by their health, the cost of health care, and inflation, (Jacobe, 2011).

In the simplest form of the family life-cycle savings model, families are assumed to hold no bequest motives, with every dollar spent during the lifetimes of the immediate family members. Clearly, an important extension of this life-cycle framework is consideration of the impact and process of passing wealth between generations (Modigliani, 1988). Stress resulting from the estate planning or intergenerational transfer portion of a family financial plan likely comes directly from (a) perceived legal complexities associated with asset transfers before and after death and (b) changing roles of family members in the financial management process (Edwards, 1991). The goal of estate planning is to maximize compliance with the descendants' wants while minimizing the erosion of wealth through taxes and transaction costs.

SUMMARY

Economic stress exacts social and psychological costs on the quality of family life, and family scientists are just beginning to uncover the toll the Great Recession has had on family functioning. Families have been shown to vary significantly in their vulnerability to changing economic events. Differing levels of resources and adoption of coping strategies explain family resilience under economic stress. In this chapter, we have offered the process of family financial planning over distinct life-cycle stages as a general preventive strategy, to help families reduce the social and psychological costs associated with economic stress. A robust literature supports the family economic stress model, however, further research investigating the strategies and coping mechanisms that help ameliorate the impact of economic stress on individuals and family relationships would benefit policy makers and practitioners.

Note: We want to express our gratitude to Shin Young Jeon for her research and editorial assistance.

REFERENCES

Administrative Office of the U.S. Courts. (2013). *2013 report of statistics required by the Bankruptcy Abuse Prevention and Consumer Protection Act of 2005*. Retrieved October 30, 2014 from http://www.uscourts.gov/Statistics/BankruptcyStatistics/bapcpa-report-archives/2013-bapcpa-report.aspx

Aldana, S. G., & Liljenquist, W. (1998). Validity and reliability of a financial strain survey. *Financial Counseling and Planning, 9*(2), 11–18.

Amato, P. R., Booth, A., Johnson, D., & Rogers, S. (2007). *Alone together: How marriage in America is changing*. Cambridge, MA: Harvard University Press.

Ando, A., & Modigliani, F. (1963). The life cycle hypothesis of saving. *American Economic Review, 53*(1), 55–84.

Bernstein, J. (2014). *Testimony of Jared Bernstein, senior fellow, Center on Budget and Policy Priorities, before the Joint Economic Committee*. Retrieved from http://www.cbpp.org/cms/?fa=view&id=4164

Blair, S.L. (2012). Economic stress and the family. *Contemporary perspectives in family research* (Vol. 6). Basingstoke, England: Emerald Group.

Blomquist, D. (2012). *2012 foreclosure market outlook* [Slideshow]. Retrieved from http://www.realty-trac.com/content/news-and-opinion/slideshow-2012-foreclosure-market-outlook-7021

Board of Governors of the Federal Reserve System (2014). *Household economic well-being. Report on the economic well-being of U.S. households in 2013*. Retrieved from http://www.federalreserve.gov/econresdata/2014-economic-well-being-of-us-households-in-2013-household-economic-well-being.htm

Brandon, E. (2014). *More parents use retirement accounts to pay for college*. Retrieved from http://money.usnews.com/money/retirement/articles/2014/09/02/more-parents-use-retirement-accounts-to-pay-for-college

Bricker, J., Dettling, L. J., Henriques, A., Hsu, J. W., Moore, K. B., Sabelhaus, J., Thompson, J., & Windle, R. A. (2014). Changes in U.S. family finances from 2010 to 2013: Evidence from the survey of consumer finances. *Federal Reserve Bulletin, 100*(4), 1–41.

Bricker, J., Kennickell, A. B., Moore, K. B., & Sabelhaus, J. (2012). Changes in U.S. family finances from 2007 to 2010: Evidence from the survey of consumer finances. *Federal Reserve Bulletin, 98*(2), 1–80.

Business Wire (2014, August 20). Time to break open the piggy bank: Parents expect kids to pay for more than one-third of college costs. Retrieved from http://www.businesswire.com/news/home/20140820005426/en#.VG2fmvnF-Ds

Ceccherini-Nelli, A., & Priebe, S. (2011). Economic factors and suicide rates: Associations over time in four countries. *Social Psychiatry and Psychiatric Epidemiology, 46*(10), 975–982.

Chen, D. J. Q., & Lim, V. K. G. (2012). Strength in adversity: The influence of psychological capital on job search. *Journal of Organizational Behavior, 33*(6), 811–839.

College Savings Foundation (2010). *2010 parent survey*. Retrieved from http://www.collegesavings-foundation.org/pdf/CollegeSurvey10V3-1.pdf

Conger, R. D., & Conger, K. J. (2002). Resilience in Midwestern families: Selected findings from the first decade of a prospective, longitudinal study. *Journal of Marriage and Family, 64*(2), 361–373.

Conger, R. D., Conger, K. J., & Martin, M. J. (2010). Socioeconomic status, family processes, and individual development. *Journal of Marriage and Family, 72*(3), 685–704.

Conger, R. D., & Elder, G. H., Jr., (1994). *Families in troubled times: Adapting to change in rural America.* New York, NY: Aldine.

Conger, R. D., Elder, G. H., Jr., Lorenz, F. O., Conger, K. J., Simons, R. L., Whitbeck, L. B., Huck, S., & Melby, J. N. (1990). Linking economic hardship to marital quality and instability. *Journal of Marriage and the Family, 52*(3), 643–656.

Creed, P. A., & Klisch, J. (2005). Future outlook and financial strain: Testing the personal agency and latent deprivation models of unemployment and well-being. *Journal of Occupational Healthy Psychology, 10*(3), 251–260.

Cuyper, N. D., Makikangas, A., Kinnunen, U., Mauno, S., & De Witte, H. (2012). Cross-lagged associations between perceived external employability, job insecurity, and exhaustion: Testing gain and loss spirals according to the Conservation of Resources Theory. *Journal of Organizational Behavior, 33*(6), 770–788.

DeNavas-Walt, C., & Proctor, B. D. (2014). *U.S. Census Bureau, current population reports, P60-249, income and poverty in the United States: 2013.* Washington, DC: U.S. Government Printing Office.

Dew, J. (2007).Two sides of the same coin? The differing roles of assets and consumer debt in marriage. *Journal of Family and Economic Issues, 28*(1), 89–104.

Dew, J. (2008). Debt change and marital satisfaction change in recently married couples. *Family Relations, 57*(1), 60–71.

Dew, J. (2011). The association between consumer debt and the likelihood of divorce. *Journal of Family and Economic Issues, 32*(4), 554-565.

Dew, J. P., & Xiao, J. J. (2013). Financial Declines, financial behaviors, and relationship satisfaction during the recession. *Journal of Financial Therapy, 4*(1). Retrieved from http://dx.doi.org/10.4148/jft.v4i1.1723

Drentea, P., & Lavrakas, P. J. (2000). Over the limit: The association among health, race and debt. *Social Science & Medicine, 50*(4), 517–529.

Drentea, P., & Reynolds, J. R. (2012). Neither a borrower nor a lender be: The relative importance of debt and SES for mental health among older adults. *Journal of Aging and Health, 24*(4), 673–695.

Dugan, A. (2014). *Retirement remains Americans' top financial worry*. Retrieved from http://www.gallup.com/poll/168626/retirement-remains-americans-top-financial-worry.aspx

Edwards, K. P. (1991). Planning for family asset transfers. *Financial Counseling and Planning, 2*(1), 55–78.

Employee Benefit Research Institute (2015). *Preparing for retirement in America.* Retrieved from http://www.ebri.org/pdf/surveys/rcs/2015/RCS15.FS-3.Preps.pdf

Elder, G. H., Jr. (1974). *Children of the Great Depression: Social change in life experience.* Chicago, IL: University of Chicago Press.

Elder, G. H., Jr., & Caspi, A. (1988). Economic stress in lives: Developmental perspectives. *Journal of Social Issues, 44*(2), 25–45.

Elder, G.H., Jr., Conger, R.D., Foster, E.M., & Ardelt, M. (1992). Families under economic pressure. *Journal of Family Issues, 13*(1), 5–37.

Erickson, J. (2014). The middle-class squeeze: A picture of stagnant incomes, rising costs, and what we can do to strengthen America's middle class. Washington, DC: Center for American Progress. Retrieved from http://cdn.americanprogress.org/wp-content/uploads/2014/09/MiddeClassSqueezeReport.pdf

Fan, X. J., Chang, Y. R., & Hanna, S. (1992). Optimal credit use with uncertain income. *Financial Counseling and Planning, 3*(3), 125–132.

Finke, M., & Pierce, N. L. (2006). Precautionary savings behavior of maritally stressed couples. *Family and Consumer Sciences Research Journal, 34*(3), 223–240.

Fox, J. J. (1995). Household demand system analysis: Implications of unit root econometrics for modeling, testing and policy analysis. *Consumer Interests Annual, 41,* 195–201.

Garman, E. T., & Forgue, R. E. (2007). *Personal finance, ninth edition.* Boston, MA: Houghton Mifflin.

Godwin, D. D. (1994). Antecedents and consequences of newlyweds' cash flow management. *Financial Counseling and Planning, 5*(4), 161–190.

Gudmunson, C. G., Beutler, I. F., Israelsen, C. L., McCoy, J. K., & Hill, E. J. (2007). Linking financial strain to marital instability: Examining the roles of emotional distress and marital interaction. *Journal of Family and Economic Issues, 28*(3), 357–376.

Gutman, L. M., McLoyd, V. C., & Tokoyawa, T. (2005). Financial strain, neighborhood stress, parenting behaviors, and adolescent adjustment in urban African American families. *Journal of Research on Adolescence, 15*(4), 425–449.

Howley, K. M. (2012). *Americans see biggest home equity jump in 60 years.* Retrieved from http://www.bloomberg.com/news/2012-06-14/americans-see-biggest-home-equity-jump-in-60-years-mortgages.html

Jacobe, D. (2011). Investors look beyond Social Security to fund retirement. Retrieved from http://www.gallup.com/poll/146807/Investors-Look-Beyond-Social-Security-Fund-Retirement.aspx

Kim, J., Garman, E. T., & Sorhaindo, S. (2003). Relationships among credit counseling clients' financial well-being, financial behaviors, financial stressor events, and health. *Financial Counseling and Planning, 14*(2), 75–87.

Kinnunen, U., & Feldt, T. (2004). Economic stress and marital adjustment among couples: Analyses at the dyadic level. *European Journal of Social Psychology, 34*(5), 519–532.

Klebanov, P. K., Brooks-Gunn, J., & Duncan, G. J. (1994). Does neighborhood and family poverty affect mothers' parenting, mental health, and social support? *Journal of Marriage and the Family, 56*(2), 441–455.

LaMontagne, C. (2014). *Nerd wallet health finds medical bankruptcy accounts for majority of personal bankruptcies.* Retrieved from http://www.nerdwallet.com/blog/health/2014/03/26/medical-bankruptcy/

Landivar, L. C. (2012). The impact of the great recession on mothers' employment. In S. L. Blair (Ed.), *Economic stress and the family* (Contemporary perspectives in family research Vol. 6, pp.163–185). Bingley, England: Emerald Group.

Leicht, K., & Fitzgerald, S. (2006). *Postindustrial peasants: The illusion of middle class prosperity.* New York, NY: Worth Publishers.

Lempers, J. D., & Clark-Lempers, D. S. (1997). Economic hardship, family relationships, and adolescent distress: An evaluation of a stress-distress mediation model in mother-daughter and mother-son dyads. *Adolescence, 32*(126), 339–356.

Lindblad, M. R., & Quercia, R. G. (2014). Why is homeownership associated with nonfinancial benefits? A path analysis of competing mechanisms. *Housing Policy Debate, 25*(2), 263-288. doi :10.1080/10511482.2014.956776

Logan, A., & Weller, C. E. (2008). *Bankruptcies back on the wrong track: Bankruptcy rates on the rise again despite the Bankruptcy Abuse Prevention and Consumer Protection Act of 2005.* Retrieved from www.americanprogress.org/issues/2008/06/bankruptcy_report.html

Loonin, D., & Renuart, E. (2007). The life and debt cycle: The growing debt burdens of older consumers and related policy recommendations. *Harvard Journal on Legislation, 44*, 167–203.

McKee-Ryan, F. M., Song, Z., Wanberg, C. R., & Kinicki, A. J. (2005). Psychological and physical well-being during unemployment: A meta-analytic study. *Journal of Applied Psychology, 90*(1), 53–76.

McKernan, S. M., Ratcliffe, C., Steuerle, E., & Zhang, S. (2013). *Less than equal: Racial disparities in wealth accumulation.* Urban Institute. Retrieved http://www.urban.org/uploadedpdf/412802-less-than-equal-racial-disparities-in-wealth-accumulation.pdf

Meltzer, H., Bebbington, P., Brugha, T., Jenkins, R., McManus, S., & Stansfeld, S. (2010). Job insecurity, socio-economic circumstances and depression. *Psychological Medicine, 40*(8), 1401–1407.

Mishel, L., Bivens. J., Gould. E., & Shierholz. H. (2012). *The state of working America, 12th Edition. An Economic Policy Institute book.* Ithaca, NY: Cornell University Press.

Mishel, L., & Davis, A. (2014, September 16). Modest income growth in 2013 puts slight dent in more than a decade of income losses [Blog Post]. Retrieved from http://www.epi.org/blog/modest-income-growth-2013-barely-begins

Mistry, R. S., Lowe, E. D., Benner, A. D., & Chien, N. (2008). Expanding the family economic stress model: Insights from a mixed-methods approach. *Journal of Marriage & Family, 70*(1), 196–209.

Modigliani, F. (1988). The role of intergenerational transfers and life cycle saving in the accumulation of wealth. *Journal of Economic Perspectives, 2*(2), 15–40.

Morin, R., & Kochhar, R. (2010, July 22). Lost income, lost friends—and loss of self-respect. Retrieved from http://www.pewsocialtrends.org/2010/07/22/hard-times-have-hit-nearly-everyone-and-hammered-the-long-term-unemployed/#

Munnell, A. H., Webb, A., & Golub-Sass, F. (2009). *The national retirement risk index: After the crash.* Chestnut Hill, MA: Center for Retirement Research at Boston College. Retrieved from http://crr.bc.edu/briefs/the-national-retirement-risk-index-after-the-crash

Nelson, S., Delgadillo, L., & Dew, J. (2013). Housing and marital satisfaction. *Marriage & Family Review, 49*, 546–561.

Newland, R. P., Crnic, K. A., Cox, M. J., & Mills-Koonce, R. W. (2013). The family model stress and maternal psychological symptoms: Mediated pathways from economic hardship to parenting. *Journal of Family Psychology, 27*(1), 96–105.

O'Neill, B., Sorhaindo, B., Xiao, J. J., & Garman, E. T. (2005). Financially distressed consumers: Their financial practices, financial well-being, and health. *Journal of Financial Counseling and Planning, 16*(1).

Pederson, R. C., Madsen, M., & Kohler, L. (2005). Does financial strain explain the association between children's morbidity and parental non-employment? *Journal of Epidemiology and Community Health, 59*(4), 316–321.

Ponnet, K. (2014). Financial stress, parent functioning and adolescent problem behavior: An actor–partner interdependence approach to family stress processes in low-, middle-, and high-income families. *Journal of Youth and Adolescence, 43*(10), 1752–1769.

Porter, N. M., & Garman, E. T. (1993). Testing a conceptual model of financial well-being. *Financial Counseling and Planning, 4*(3), 135–164.

Prawitz, A. D., Kalkowski, J. C., & Cohart, J. (2014). Responses to economic pressure by low-income families: Financial distress and hopefulness. *Journal of Family and Economic Issues, 34*(1), 29–40.

Riffkin, R. (2014). Average U.S. retirement age rises to 62. Retrieved from http://www.gallup.com/poll/168707/average-retirement-age-rises.aspx

Rothwell, D. W., & Han, C. K. (2010). Exploring the relationship between assets and family stress among low-income families. *Family Relations, 59*(4), 396–407.

Shek, D. T. L. (2003). Economic stress, psychological well-being and problem behavior in Chinese adolescents with economic disadvantage. *Journal of Youth and Adolescence, 32*(4), 259–266.

Skogrand, L., Johnson, A. C., Horrocks, A. M., & DeFrain, J. (2011). Financial management practices of couples with great marriages. *Journal of Family and Economic Issues, 32*(1), 27–35.

Social Security Administration. (2015). *Calculators: Life expectancy*. Retrieved from http://www.ssa.gov/planners/lifeexpectancy.html

Solantaus, T., Leinonen, J., & Punamaki, R. L. (2004). Children's mental health in times of economic recession: Replication and extension of the Family Economic Stress Model in Finland. *Developmental Psychology, 40*(3), 412–429.

Szanton, S. L., Thorpe, R. J., & Whitfield, K. (2010). Life-course financial strain and health in African-Americans. *Social Science & Medicine, 71*(2), 259–26.

U.S. Bureau of Labor Statistics. (2014). *Current employment statistics highlights*. Retrieved from http://www.bls.gov/ces/highlights052014.pdf

U.S. Census Bureau. (2012). *Table F-22.Married-couple families with wives' earnings greater than husbands' earnings: 1988 to 2012. Income-Families*. Retrieved from http://www.census.gov/hhes/www/income/data/historical/families

Valentino, S. W., Moore, J. E., Cleveland, M. J., Greenberg, M. T., & Tan, X. (2014). Profiles of financial stress over time using subgroup analysis. *Journal of Family and Economic Issues, 35*(1), 51–64.

Voydanoff, P. (1983). Unemployment: Family strategies for adaptation. In C. R. Figley & H. I. McCubbin (Eds.), *Stress in the Family: Vol. 2. Coping with catastrophe* (pp. 90–102). New York, NY: Brunner/Mazel.

Voydanoff, P. (1990). Economic distress and family relations: A review of the eighties. *Journal of Marriage and the Family, 52*(4), 1099–1115.

Voydanoff, P., & Donnelly, B. W. (1988). Economic distress, family coping, and quality of family life. In P. Voydanoff & L. C. Majka (Eds.), *Families and economic distress: Coping strategies and social policies* (pp. 97–116). Newbury Park, CA: Sage.

Wadsworth, M. E., & Santiago, C. D. (2008). Risk and resiliency processes in ethnically diverse families in poverty. *Journal of Family Psychology, 22*(3), 399–410.

Warner, J. (2010, August 6). What the great recession has done to family life. *The New York Times*. Retrieved from http://www.nytimes.com/2010/08/08/magazine/08FOB-wwln-t.html?_r = 0

Warren, E. (2007, May 10).*The new economics of the middle class: Why making ends meet has gotten harder, testimony before the finance committee of the United States senate*. Retrieved from http://finance.senate.gov/hearings/testimony/2007test/051007testew.pdf

Weller, C. E. (2014). *Economic snapshot: September 2014*. Retrieved from http://cdn.americanprogress.org/wp-content/uploads/2014/09/Sept14-econsnapshot.pdf

Zagorsky, J. L. (2005). Marriage and divorce's impact on wealth. *Journal of Sociology, 41*(4), 406–424.

Zurlo, K. A., Yoon, W., & Kim, H. (2014). Unsecured consumer debt and mental health outcomes in middle-aged and older Americans. *Journals of Gerontology, Series B: Psychological Sciences and Social Sciences, 69*(3), 461–469.

CHAPTER 17

Death, Dying, and Grief in Families

Colleen I. Murray

_____ **Vignette** _____

Ella is worried about her two children. Her husband died suddenly in a car accident 1 year ago, and her school-age daughter and teenage son are struggling with the loss. Her daughter has developed anxiety and fear of other loved ones leaving her and is having difficulty focusing on her schoolwork. Her son has withdrawn from family and friends, spending much of his time alone in his room. While she expects disengagement from a teenager, she is concerned because he refuses to talk about his father, and recently she found drug paraphernalia in his backpack. The children don't want to hurt their mother any further so they don't argue with her, but, instead, they fight more with each other than in the past. Her own grief recovery has been affected by her distance from family and a lack of community support; this has resulted in her feeling very isolated and alone. She has lost a great deal of weight and is unable to sleep more than a few hours at a time. In worrying about her children, she has neglected to address her many conflicting emotions including sadness, anger, and fear. She worries how she will keep their standard of living or send the children to college without her husband's income. Well-meaning coworkers tell her to read some popular psychology books and seek professional assistance in facilitating her children's grief as well as her own, but the resources she has found just don't seem right for her family.

• • •

The public images of death and grief that we see today are often those of terrorism, war, epidemics, natural disaster, or celebrity death. Many hold ambivalent views regarding displays of mourning for people one never knew in life or for publicizing one's grief, expressions Tony Walter (2008) calls the *new public mourning*. Although mourning may be a major source of social integration, most grieving is private and involves pain from personal relationships, even in cases where expression is vicariously triggered by a public tragedy. Most adults in industrialized countries today die from degenerative illnesses, and most young people die from sudden or violent causes. Overall, we live in an environment where death is invisible and denied, yet we have become desensitized to its vast media presence. These inconsistencies appear related to the extent we are personally affected by death—whether we define loss as happening to "one of us" or "one of them." This chapter addresses enduring processes and areas of change related to death in families.

Annually, there are more than 2.5 million deaths in the United States, affecting 8 to 10 million surviving immediate family members, including 2 million children and adolescents (Murphy, Xu, & Kochanek, 2013). Death is a crisis that *all* families encounter and is recognized as *the* most stressful life event families face, although most do not need counseling to cope (Shear, Ghesquiere, & Glickman, 2013). However, the study of loss as a family system phenomenon has received modest visibility.

ETIOLOGY OF "INVISIBLE DEATH" AND ITS CONSEQUENCES

From the Middle Ages through the 17th century, death was viewed as inevitable and natural (Aries, 1974). A movement to deny the realities of death began during the 18th century, and by the 20th century a lack of firsthand familiarity with death fostered an era in which death became sequestered, privatized, and invisible. Factors contributing to this lack of familiarity with death include increased life expectancy, changes in leading causes of death from communicable diseases to chronic and degenerative diseases (although there is renewed concern about increases in communicable diseases), redistribution of death from the young to old, decreased mortality rates, and increased duration of chronic illnesses. Geographic mobility and family social reorganization resulted in reduced intergenerational contact and fewer opportunities to participate in death-related experiences (Rando, 1993). As a result of the development of life-extending technologies, (a) most deaths occur in health care settings rather than at home, (b) care has become dominated by efforts to delay death by all means available, (c) we question our assumptions of what constitutes life and death, and (d) families are confronted with decisions of prolonging dying or terminating life of loved ones (Doka, 2005).

Although families have limited direct contact with death, they are bombarded with its presentation via news media (Murray & Gilbert, 1997). These frequent, violent portrayals of death as unnatural contribute to desensitization, as well as personal traumatization of the bereaved. Media-orchestrated emotional invigilation in reporting of celebrity death and mass tragedies leaves viewers with illusions of intimacy and grieving or concern that their behavior differs from what everyone else is doing (Walter, 2008). Private grief coexists with the public expression of grief which is increasingly visible on social media (Walter, Hourizi, Moncur & Pitsillides, 2012). Individuals who did not personally know the deceased can go through rituals of mourning, participate in Facebook memorials, and "virtually" attend celebrity funerals through television or the Internet, without feeling the depth of pain and depression of actual grief. Viewers may confuse their emotional response with the real grief experienced by loved ones of the deceased, and since their "recovery" is quick, they may be insensitive to the amount of time required to "return to normal" when they experience real grief.

These changes have increased the stress that families experience when coping with death. Those in industrialized countries do not view dying and bereavement as normal life-span experiences; rather, they compartmentalize death, frequently excluding children from family experiences. Adaption to loss has been hampered by lack of cultural supports that could assist families to integrate death into their ongoing life and the lack of instrumental social supports to help manage daily life disruptions in child care, housework, and finances (Walsh & McGoldrick, 1991). Often a minimum of rituals exists surrounding death, roles of the chronically ill or bereaved are not clearly defined, and geographic distance hinders completion of "unfinished business" and dealing with the loss (Shapiro, 2001).

As illustrated in the opening vignette, although death and grieving are normal, the bereaved can experience physical, psychological, and social consequences as a part of the coping process or as related stressors. Even though few studies use physiological measures, research suggests that bereavement can result in negative consequences for physical health, including illness, aggravation of existing medical conditions, increased use of medical facilities, and presence of new symptoms and complaints (Stroebe, Schut, & Stroebe, 2007). During anticipatory bereavement and the months following a loss, physiological changes are indicative of acute heightened arousal (i.e., increased levels of cortisol and cathecholamines, change in immune system competence, and sleep complaints) (Buckley et al, 2012). Sympatho-adrenal-medulla system changes during acute grief may even limit success of psychotherapy (O'Connor et al., 2013). There also are changes in neuroendocrine function, immune system competence, and sleep patterns that endure for years (Hall & Irwin, 2001). Intrusive thoughts and avoidance behaviors are correlated with sleep disturbances, which appear to intensify effects of grief, resulting in a decreased number and function of natural killer cells (Ironson et al., 1997). Although bereavement may be related to long-lasting changes, Rosenblatt (2000) found that the narratives of bereaved parents contained sparse reference to any personal health problems.

Epidemiologic studies cannot assess direct causal relationships between bereavement and illness, but researchers have suggested that bereavement is an antecedent of disease. Risk factors for increased morbidity and mortality include self-damaging or neglectful behaviors during bereavement, additional stress symptoms, elevated physiological arousal, and depression, as well as being male or Caucasian (Elwert & Christakis, 2006). Physiological resiliency appears to be related to coping strategies, social support networks, and healthy sleep.

Consequences of bereavement for mental health also are difficult to measure. Characteristics typically associated with grief are ones that would evoke concern in other circumstances. High rates of depression, insomnia, suicides, and anorexia may exist in conjunction with consumption of drugs, alcohol, and tobacco (Stroebe et al., 2007) as illustrated in the vignette of Ella's family. Lack of differentiation between grief and depression has been problematic as they represent distinct, although related reactions to bereavement.

The challenge of differentiating grief and depression is reflected in two contentious changes related to bereavement introduced in the American Psychiatric Association's (APA; 2013), *Fifth Edition Diagnostic and Statistical Manual of Mental Disorders* (DSM-5). One change is the elimination of the DSM-IV's bereavement exclusion (BE) that provided a 2 month window of bereavement before qualifying for a diagnosis of major depressive disorder (MDD), assuming that other criteria were not met. Scholars disagree as to whether the BE is valid (Wakefield & Schmitz, 2012; Zisook et al, 2012). In response to concerns, the DSM-5 includes the diagnosis of MDD for bereavement after 2 weeks of symptoms commonly found in intense normal grief. To avoid misdiagnosis the DSM-5 differentiates grief from MDD in three descriptive footnotes. The plan to remove BE met with sharp criticism and concerns that footnotes are inadequate, normal grief will be pathologized, and "for reasons of economic profit and clinical efficiency, people will often be prematurely diagnosed with depression and put on medication" that interferes with the pathway to recovery (Balk, Noppe, Sandler, & Werth, 2011, p. 208). Ironically, there is also concern that elimination of the BE may lead a counselor to view all grief as normal, missing those whose grief warrants additional treatment.

The second DSM-5 change added a single form of complicated grief, persistent complex bereavement disorder (PCBD), identified among trauma- and stressor-related disorders and included among conditions for further study. Validity and reliability of the criteria have been a focus of frequent criticism (Boelen & Prigerson, 2012). PCBD criteria include those from existing inventories that examine complicated grief (Shear et al., 2011) and prolonged grief disorder (Prigerson et al., 2009), as well as other criteria with less empirical support. These inventories have primarily been developed with samples of older, White, conjugally bereaved women and may not apply to other populations. Some of the criteria are so broadly defined that many bereaved persons, especially women and bereaved parents, may receive a false positive diagnosis for situations in which the normal grief response may be more intense and long-lasting than other losses (Thieleman & Cacciatore, 2014). Examples of these criteria include persistent yearning for the deceased, intense sorrow, frequent crying, difficulty accepting the death, feeling alone, or having anger related to the loss (APA, 2013). The list of symptoms results in 37,650 possible combinations by which a person could meet the diagnosis (Boelen & Prigerson, 2012). Although diagnostic criteria include symptoms that have persisted for at least 12 months for adults (6 months for children), there is no empirical evidence that this specific timing is warranted.

It also may be that yearning is more characteristic of grief than is depression (Klass, 2013), and bereaved who perceive a decline in their financial well-being are also at increased risk of psychological difficulties (Corden & Hirst, 2013). Research has suggested that individuals also identify bereavement as a social stressor, reporting lack of role clarity and support (Rando, 1993; Rosenblatt, 2000; Weiss, 2008). Changes in social status, conflicts in identity, disputes over family inheritance, and loss of roles, income, or retirement funds that may result from the death of a family member can contribute to social isolation. Changes in family communication patterns and relationships with people outside the family are common. Several of these factors are illustrated in Ella's situation.

Paradoxically, growth may also be an outcome of loss. *Posttraumatic growth* is both a process and outcome in which, following trauma, growth occurs *beyond* an individual's previous level of functioning (Tedeschi & Calhoun, 2008). Growth outcomes occur in *perception of self* (e.g., as survivor rather than victim, and self-reliant yet with heightened vulnerability), *interpersonal relationships* (e.g., increased ability to be compassionate or intimate, to self-disclose important information, and to express emotions), and *philosophy of life* (e.g., reorganization of priorities, greater appreciation of life, grappling with meaning and purpose of life, spiritual change, and sense of wisdom). In contrast, terror management theory (Pyszcznski, Solomon, & Greenberg, 2003) suggests that what appears to be growth is actually cognitive coping, which protects or distances us from traumatic events and buffers fear of death.

THEORIES OF GRIEVING

Theories are necessary for understanding complex response to loss and the sometimes counterintuitive phenomena that occur during bereavement (e.g., posttraumatic growth). They range from individualistic intrapersonal approaches to an interpersonal study of group influence. Scholars have proposed individual-based theories focusing on developmental stages or trajectories for the dying (e.g., Kübler-Ross, 1969) or survivors (e.g., Rando, 1993), derived from works of Freud (1917/1957) or Bowlby (1980). Such theories differ in number of stages identified, but they all assume that grief follows three basic phases, including periods of shock, denial, and disorganization; extremes including intense separation pain, volatile emotions, and active grief work; and resolution, acceptance, and withdrawal of energy from the deceased and reinvestment. Critics of these theories question the definition of "normal" grief and assumptions about how people "should" respond, including beliefs that (a) intense emotional distress or depression is inevitable, (b) failure to experience distress is indicative of pathology, (c) working through loss is important— intense distress will end with recovery, and (d) by working through loss, individuals can achieve resolution and intellectual acceptance (Wortman & Silver, 2001).

Others purport that stage theories have not been supported in research and view these theories as problematic because they are population-specific and misrepresent progress toward adjustment as linear (Weiss, 2008). Critics contend that progress is not always forward and that grief processes may have no definite ending (Rosenblatt, 2000). They argue that emphasis should not be on recovery or closure but on continuing bonds, relearning relationships, and renegotiating meaning of loss over time (Neimeyer, Klass & Dennis, 2014; Weiss, 2008).

Concern regarding developmental theories also deals with viewing grief as passive, with few choices for grievers. Critics contend that grieving is active, presenting the bereaved with challenges, choices, and opportunities, and that the bereaved are active participants relearning the world in terms of physical surroundings, relationships, and who they are (Weiss, 2008). They question the necessity of "grief work"—traditionally viewed as an essential cognitive process of confronting loss. Margaret Stroebe and her colleagues (2000) suggest that grief work is not a universal concept, its definitions and operationalizations are problematic, few studies have yielded substantial conclusions, and findings were intended for understanding of processes, rather than prescriptions for recovery. Archer (2008) suggests that it may be cognitive restructuring rather than grief work that is related to adjustment following loss.

Among individually centered process-based models is Rando's (1993) "Six R's" model, which assumes the need to accommodate loss. Processes include recognition of loss, reacting to separation, recollection and reexperiencing the deceased and the relationship, relinquishing old attachments and assumptive world, readjusting to move into a new world without forgetting the old, and reinvesting (p. 45). In contrast, the dual process model of coping (M. Stroebe & Schut, 2001) suggests that active confrontation of loss is not necessary for a positive outcome, and there may be circumstances when denial, avoidance of reminders, and repressive strategies are essential. Minimizing expression of negative emotions and using laughter as dissociation from distress may improve functioning (Bonanno, 2004). The dual process assumes that most individuals experience ongoing oscillation between *loss orientation* (coping with loss through grief work, dealing with denial, and avoiding changes) and *restoration orientation* (adjusting to various life changes triggered by death, changing routines, transitioning to a new equilibrium, avoiding or taking time off from grief). There is movement between coping with loss and moving forward with differences for individuals, type of loss, culture, and gender.

Although scholars have focused on dying or bereaved individuals, death does not occur in isolation. Individual process models have not been broadened to aid in understanding families, except for some psychoanalytic attempts. Archer (2008) suggests that rather than using Bowlby's work to look at the breaking of attachment bonds, it can instead be used to address the relationship between styles of attachment and grieving, thus going beyond the individual. Mikulincer and Shaver (2008) argue that Bowlby's work on the attachment behavioral system and pair bonds as related to bereavement has been misunderstood, and there is recent evidence from experiments and clinical observations in support of these psychodynamic processes. The bereaved form new attachment bonds while maintaining a symbolic attachment to the deceased, and they integrate that relationship into their new reality (i.e., a focus on both the loss and restoration). Those with insecure attachments have difficulty in oscillating between this hyperactivation and deactivation of the attachment system, overemphasizing one or the other.

Social constructionist theory has become an increasingly popular explanation as it accommodates integration of three approaches to explaining grief, including (1) continuing bonds and mental representations of the relationship, (2) meaning of the bereavement and maintenance of a meaningful world, and (3) loss of relationship supports from the deceased and the social network (Neimeyer et al., 2014). Work on grief from a family perspective has typically used elements of systems theories, particularly through integrative approaches to complex issues. Refined systemic models recognize that multiple griefs exist simultaneously for individuals, families, and communities, and although some thoughts and feelings are shared, others are not (Gilbert, 1996).

Family systems theory focuses on dynamics and provides concepts for describing relationships, offering a nonpathologizing conceptualization of grief as a natural process (Nadeau, 2008). The following premises of systems theory can be useful in examining families' adaptation to dying and death:

1. A family reacts to loss as a system. Although we grieve as individuals, the family system has qualities beyond those of individual members (Jackson, 1965), and all members participate in mutually reinforcing interactions (Walsh & McGoldrick, 1991).

2. Actions and reactions of a family member affect others and their functioning. Interdependence exists because causality is circular rather than linear (Shapiro, 2001).

3. Death disrupts a system's equilibrium, modifies the structure, and requires reorganization in feedback processes, role distribution, and functions (Bowen, 1976).

4. Death may produce an emotional shock wave of serious life events that can occur anywhere in the extended family in the years following loss (Bowen, 1976). Waves exist in an environment of denied emotional dependence and may seem unrelated

to the death. They may trigger additional stressor events or increase rigid strategies to maintain stability (Shapiro, 2001).

5. There is no single outcome from death of a member that characterizes all family systems. Various family characteristics, such as feedback processes (Jackson, 1965), patterns of relationships (Shapiro, 2001), family schema and family paradigm (Boss, 2006), influence the outcome.

Scholars have infrequently applied systems theory in examining death-related reorganization. Loss has traditionally been identified as a historical, individual, or content issue and inappropriate for traditional family systems work (which focused on process, homeostasis, differentiation of self from family, current interaction, and the present) (Nadeau, 2008; Walsh & McGoldrick, 1991). Recent versions of systems theory have focused on balance of change and continuity, as well as the negotiated inclusion of differences to balance self-assertion and cohesion. The family systems–based study of grief exists within a framework that includes intergenerational and family life-cycle perspectives (Walsh & McGoldrick, 1991), focusing on change in structural factors such as boundaries, and family dynamics such as roles and rules, as well as meaning making and communication (Nadeau, 2008). An examination of the relationship between individual grief and family system characteristics found that grief symptomatology at 4 to 5 weeks postloss did not predict any family system characteristics or grief symptomatology 6 months later (Traylor, Hayslip, Kaminski, & York, 2003). However, perception of family cohesion, expression of affect, and communication were predictors of later grief.

Particularly useful models are those that simultaneously consider individual, family, and cultural dimensions. Rather than relying on traditional family systems, these models integrate family systems' concepts with other perspectives. Rolland's (1994) family systems–illness model examines the interface of individual, family, illness, and health care team. Rather than identifying the ill individual as the central unit of care, it focuses on the family or caregiving system as a resource that is both affected by and influences the course of illness. This model can be useful for understanding experiences of the individual and family members during the terminal phase of chronic illness, in multiple contexts and across time. Shapiro (2001) applied a systemic developmental approach to examine grief as a family process. This clinical model views grief as a developmental crisis influenced by family history, sociocultural context, and family and individual life-cycle stages. Grief is a crisis of identity and attachment that disrupts family equilibrium but provides an opportunity for developing growth and stability.

Popular interactionist approaches account for context by incorporating life course, social constructionism, and systems concepts. These models recognize the unique interpretation of internal and external worlds of individuals and families dealing with loss (Harvey, Carlson, Huff, & Green, 2001; Rosenblatt, 2000). They use narrative methods, focus on meaning making or account making, and recognize intimate losses as part of a changing identity. These models assume that the accuracy of meaning given to any particular event is of limited importance because it is *meaning itself* that influences family interactions. Interactionist counseling would not help families to just understand and manage grief symptomatology but would also help to reconstruct a meaningful narrative of self, family, and world.

FACTORS RELATED TO FAMILY ADAPTATION TO DEATH

Characteristics of the Loss

Some characteristics of the death itself and societal interpretations of a loss can influence family adaptation. For example, when the duration of time before death is far longer or shorter than expected, or the sequence of death in a family differs from expected order, problems may occur. Elderly members are assumed to experience "timely" deaths. Early parental loss, death of a young spouse, and death of a child or grandchild of any age are considered tragic and evoke searches for explanations.

In addition, initial grief reaction to sudden or unexpected death may be more intense than death related to illness (Bowlby, 1980), with survivors experiencing a shattered normal world, a series of concurrent stressors and secondary losses, with unfinished business more likely to remain (Lindemann, 1944). Factors existing along a continuum that can affect coping include (a) perceptions of whether the loss was natural or human made; (b) degree of intentionality/premeditation; (c) degree of preventability; (d) amount of suffering, anxiety, or physical pain experienced while dying; (e) number of people killed or affected; (f) degree of expectedness (Doka, 1996, pp. 12–13); (g) senselessness; and (h) whether the survivor witnessed the death or its aftermath or found out about the loss through the media. Differences related to suddenness of death appear short term once internal control beliefs and self-esteem are considered (W. Stroebe & Schut, 2001) and are lessened when families are present during emergency medical procedures, such as during efforts to resuscitate (Kamienski, 2004).

According to the National Center for Health Statistics (Murphy et al., 2013), 80% of deaths of teens and young adults are sudden violent accidents, homicide, or suicide. A longitudinal study of parents surviving the sudden death of a child reported that marital satisfaction decreased during the first 5 years after the death; nearly 70% said it took 3 to 4 years to put their child's death in perspective; and at 5 years post death, 43% said they still had not found meaning in their child's death (Murphy, 2008).

Although popular works often discuss the suicide of an attachment figure as the most difficult loss, there is little empirical evidence to support this contention (Murphy, 2008). Homicide appears to be most directly related to posttraumatic stress disorder and grief marked by despair. In a mass trauma (a potentially life-threatening event experienced by a large number of people), adaptation appears to be influenced by whether it is a single event or recurring/ongoing; by emotional or geographic distance (with vicarious traumatization possible through media coverage, particularly for those who have experienced other unrelated losses); by attribution of causality; and by the interaction of personal, community, and symbolic losses (Webb, 2004).

Deaths following protracted illness can also be stressful. In such cases, family members have experienced a series of stressors before the death, including increased time commitments for caring, financial strain as a result of cost of care and lost employment, emotional exhaustion, interruption of career and family routines, sense of social isolation, and lack of time for self or other family members (Rabow, Hauser, & Adams, 2004). Although research findings on the existence, role, and multidimensionality of anticipatory grief are inconsistent, protracted illness appears to be associated with trauma and secondary morbidity—that is, difficulties in physical, emotional, cognitive, and social functioning of those closely involved with terminally ill persons (Rando, 1993). Deaths following chronic illness may still be perceived as sudden or unexpected by surviving adults who are not yet "ready," by children whose developmental stage inhibits their understanding that death is inevitable, and following multiple cycles of relapse and improvement. Deaths from trauma and illness have much in common. Similar to families who have witnessed or experienced death through violence, families experiencing prolonged or complicated grief, multiple deaths simultaneously, or a series of deaths in close proximity may display signs of posttraumatic stress disorder, with caregivers experiencing secondary traumatic stress (Anderson, Arnold, Angus, & Bryce, 2008).

Scholars have devoted increased attention to losses unacknowledged by society and *disenfranchised grief*—that is, grief that exists although society does not recognize one's right, need, or capacity to grieve (Doka, 2008). Examples include grief over the loss of unacknowledged personal relationships or those not recognized as significant, such as the death of a former spouse, lover, or extramarital lover; a foster child or foster parent; a stepparent or stepchild; a coworker; or a companion animal. In addition, deaths related to pregnancy (i.e., miscarriage, elective abortion, stillbirth, or neonatal death) may also be disenfranchised. Professional caretakers and first responders, especially those labeled as "heroes" or competently focused on tasks of rescue and recovery, also may suffer unacknowledged grief when they lose those for whom they provide care. Bereaved grandparents, men in general (Gilbert, 1996), and families of deceased addicts or death row inmates may also be disenfranchised. Many people see others, such as young children, older adults, and mentally disabled persons, as incapable of grief or without a need to grieve (Doka, 2008). Disenfranchisement also occurs when bereaved persons are told they are experiencing or expressing grief in inappropriate ways. Societal expectations of who is entitled to grieve change over time; losses that are gaining in recognition involve cohabitors and partners in a gay or lesbian relationship. However, Robson and Walter (2012) argue that disenfranchised grief is not binary (yes–no) but is hierarchical and complex.

People who are grieving various types of death report that they believe their grief has been stigmatized. They feel the discomfort of others who distance themselves, and they experience direct or indirect social pressure to become "invisible mourners" (Rosaldo, 1989). Disenfranchised grief often results from stigmatized losses, particularly when there is the assumption that the death was caused by an individual's disturbed or immoral behavior, or a fear of contagion, such as with AIDS, Ebola, or cancer-related deaths. Survivors of those who died from contagious diseases may experience multiple losses among family and friends and isolation. Stigma also occurs in families that have lost a member to suicide or homicide, resulting in altered identities, provoking feelings of anger and guilt, and experiencing isolation, blame, and injustice—characteristics of revictimization (Bucholz, 2002). Resulting secrecy and blame can distort family communication, isolate members, and diminish social support (Walsh & McGoldrick, 1991).

Factors Affecting Family Vulnerability

Death-related loss involves many secondary losses including personal, interpersonal, material, and symbolic losses. Families have more difficulty adapting to death if other stressors are present, as dealing with a loss does not abrogate other family needs. When normative events associated with family life cycle (e.g., new marriage, birth of child, or adolescent's move to increase independence) are concurrent with illness or death, they may pose incompatible tasks (Shapiro, 2001). In addition, the centrality of the deceased's role and the degree of the family's emotional dependence on that individual (i.e., function and position) influence adaptation. Shock waves rarely follow the deaths of well-liked people who played peripheral roles or of dysfunctional members unless dysfunction played a central role in maintaining family equilibrium (Bowen, 1976).

Complications in family adaptation can occur when there is intense and continuous ambivalence, estrangement, or conflict. Chronic mourning and depression have been reported by those with anxious-ambivalent attachments; somatization and cognitive suppression are more common among those with avoidant attachment styles (Mikulincer & Shaver, 2008). Grief after the death of an abuser can result in ambivalence, rage, secrecy, sadness, and shame (Monahan, 2003). During illness, there may be time to repair relationships, but family members may hesitate, fearing that confrontations increase risk of death.

Resources also influence the bereaved family's vulnerability and assist in meeting demands. They may be tangible (e.g., money or health) or intangible (e.g., friendship, self-esteem, role accumulation, or a sense of mastery). African American evacuees from the aftermath of Hurricane Katrina exhibited greater psychological distress (and a lower sense of recovery) if they were uninsured or experienced home destruction or a human loss (Lee, Shen, & Tran, 2009). The disruption that a bereaved family experiences is mediated by intensity and chronicity of family stress. Adaptation is facilitated by members' emotional regulation capacity, nonreactivity to emotional intensity in the system, cohesion and adaptability, and marital intimacy (Nadeau, 2008; Shapiro, 2001). Research findings on benefits of open communication about loss are mixed. Pennebaker, Zech, and Rime (2001) suggest that confiding in others is related to health after a loss. Others assert that the best predictor of emotional well-being is emotional regulation, not emotion-focused coping (Bonanno, 2004).

Social support networks appear to simultaneously complicate and facilitate grieving. Supporters may listen but hold unrealistic expectations. Availability of formal or informal networks does not guarantee support, especially in a society that does not sanction the expression of emotions surrounding loss. Some bereaved family members turn to face-to-face or online self-help groups composed of persons who have experienced a similar type of loss—a practice that may be predictive of finding meaning in death during the years that follow. However, rules of some family systems discourage members from sharing intimate information and feelings with persons outside the family. Religious belief also may simultaneously complicate and facilitate grieving. Belief in "God's plan" can help create meaning from loss, but it can create anger toward God for unfairly allowing the death and isolate the individual from familiar spiritual roots.

Family Belief System, Definition, and Appraisal

To understand how a family perceives a death or uses coping strategies, one must understand its assumptions about the world. A common paradigm is the "belief in a just world," which posits that the self is worthy and the world is benevolent, just, and meaning-ful (Janoff-Bulman, 1992; Lerner, 1980). This paradigm values control and mastery; it assumes fit between efforts and outcomes: One gets what one deserves. Such a view is functional only when something can be done to change a situation. Challenges to the just-world assumption make the world seem less predictable and can lead to cognitive efforts to manage fear of death. Such efforts can lead to blaming chronically ill persons for their conditions and lack of recovery, or to linking adolescent deaths to drug use or reckless behavior as a way of affirming, "It can't happen to my child." In contrast, for those dealing with loss, understanding the complexities, multiple levels of context, and short- or long-term effects of the event will facilitate grief.

Family members share some beliefs that are unintentionally but collectively con-structed. Family history and experiences with death provide a *legacy* (a way of looking at loss that has been received from ancestors) that is related to how the family will adapt to subsequent loss (Walsh & McGoldrick, 1991). Particularly in relation to several traumatic untimely deaths, a family may have a legacy of empowerment (i.e., family members see themselves as survivors who can be hurt but not defeated) or a legacy of trauma (i.e., family members feel "cursed" and unable to rise above their losses)—either of which can inhibit openness of the system. Families may not recognize transgenerational anniversary pat-terns or concurrence of a death with other life events, and members may lack emotional memory or have discrepant memories regarding a death (Shapiro, 2001). Members may make unconscious efforts to block, promote, or shift beliefs to maintain consistency with the legacy.

Grief can also be viewed as a process of *meaning construction* that evolves throughout the life of the bereaved. Several factors appear to influence families' construction of the meaning of their losses, including family schema, contact, cutoffs, interdependence, rituals, secrets, coherence, paradigms, divergent beliefs, tolerance for differences, rules about sharing, and situational and stressor appraisals (Nadeau, 2008; Rosenblatt, 2000). Researchers are increasingly noting the importance of making sense of the event, finding benefits from the experience, and shaping one's new identity to include the loss (Neimeyer et al., 2014). Irrational, violent death may result in meaning making expressed through activism or intense pursuit of numerous small actions.

Families may find additional challenges when experiencing a situation of family bound-ary ambiguity (i.e., confusion a family experiences when it is not clear who is in and who is out of the system) (Boss, 2006). Ambiguity rises when (a) the facts surrounding a death are unclear, (b) a person is missing but it is unclear if death has occurred, or (c) the family denies the loss. Degree of boundary ambiguity may be more important for explaining adaptation and coping than the presence of coping skills or resources. Both denial and boundary ambiguity initially may be functional because they give a shocked family time to deny the loss and then cognitively reorganize itself before it accepts the fact that the death is real. If a high degree of ambiguity exists over time, the family is at risk for malad-aptation. However, evidence that bonds continue to exist after death and that conversa-tions with the dead may be replacing rituals as the normative way bonds are maintained (Klass, 2013) may challenge the notion of boundary ambiguity, suggesting one can recog-nize loss while holding psychological, emotional, and spiritual connections to deceased loved ones.

Factors of Diversity

Despite Western cultural expectations, most couples experience incongruent grieving, often with one adult whose grief could be called *cognitive and solitary* and the other whose grief is more *social and emotional* (Gilbert, 1996). Perhaps this incongruence can be understood as a family system–level manifestation of M. Stroebe and Schut's (2001) dual process model. A functional system would require a *loss orientation* and *restoration orientation*. Studies of incongruent grieving have suggested that women often display an intuitive grieving style, with more sorrow, guilt, and depression than men (Doka & Martin, 2001). Men are socialized to manage instrumental tasks, such as those related to the funeral, burial, finances, and property. Women are more likely to take on caregiving roles, which require them to engage in both dual processes. However, men are more able to immerse themselves in work and block other intuitive tasks. Reasons for gender-related differences are not well understood but seem influenced by expectations and socialization. Research in this area has been hampered by reliance on studies completed during acute stages of grief and lack of nonbereaved control groups. Longitudinal studies of bereaved persons who have suffered violent or traumatic losses found few gender differences (Boelen & van den Bout, 2002/2003).

With gender controls, despite differences in social support, widowers experience greater depression and health consequences than widows (W. Stroebe & Schut, 2001). It has been thought that men have unrecognized problems because their socialization interferes with active grief processes (Doka & Martin, 2001). Men's responses to grief typically include coping styles that mask fear and insecurity, including remaining silent; taking physical or legal action in order to express anger and exert control; immersion in work, domestic, recreational, or sexual activity; engaging in solitary or secret mourning; and exhibiting addictive behavior, such as alcoholism. Cook (1988) identified a double bind that bereaved fathers experience: Societal expectations are that they will contain their emotions in order to protect and comfort their wives but that they cannot heal their own grief without the sharing of feelings. Similarly, Doka and Martin (2001) identified a third pattern of grief involving dissonance between the way one experiences grief and the manner it is expressed. For example, some males may experience internal grief feelings but are constrained from expressing them. Much of the problem may not be in men's grieving but rather in our understanding of the mourning process (Cook, 1988), which largely has been formulated through the study of women. As such, concepts of meaning making (Gilbert, 1996) and the dual process model (M. Stroebe & Schut, 2001) may be more relevant for men than concepts of grief work.

Grief is a socially constructed malleable phenomenon, and given current levels of immigration and contact among diverse groups, mourning patterns in the United States can be expected to change. In addition to commonalities, group differences in values and practices continue and present a wide range of normal responses to death. General areas in which differences exist include the following:

- Extent of ritual attached to death (e.g., importance of attending funerals, types of acceptable emotional displays, and degree to which these affairs should be costly)

- Need to see a dying relative

- Openness and type of display of emotion

- Emphasis on verbal expression of feelings and solitary or family expression of grief

- Appropriate length of mourning

- Importance of anniversary events

- Roles of men and women

- Role of extended family

- Beliefs about what happens after death, particularly related to suffering, fate, and destiny

- Value of autonomy/dependence in relation to bonds after death

- Coping strategies

- Social support for hospice patients

- Whether certain deaths are stigmatized

- Definition of when death actually occurs

- Barriers to trusting professionals

- Interweaving of religious and political narratives

- Appropriateness of the concept of recovery (Laurie & Neimeyer, 2008; McGoldrick et al., 1991; Rosenblatt, 2008)

Children's Grief

Children deal with many losses (e.g., death of pet, neighbor, peer, or grandparent; family move or divorce). From infancy onward, children recognize loss and do grieve, and their grief corresponds with the cognitive developmental stage that guides their other thinking processes (Essa & Murray, 1994). Like adults, they try to make sense of the situation and fit it into their understanding of the world. Also, like adults, they don't just "get over" a loss. Because of their cognitive development, children's understanding and remembrances of events and situations may seem fragmented and distorted to adults. They tend to be very concrete, focusing on physical and observable changes. Their understanding is further hindered by euphemisms that adults may use. For example, "going to see Grandma's body" may imply to the child that she has lost her head. "She is on vacation" or "went to sleep" can later manifest in a child who doesn't want to go to bed or worries when his parents plan a vacation. Similar to Ella's daughter in the vignette, children may fear losing other loved ones, and euphemisms may add to their confusion and fear of abandonment. Perhaps euphemisms serve a purpose in the denial of death that is existentially oriented

(Becker, 1973), and terror management theory scholars (Pyszcznski et al., 2003) say most adults need most of the time.

A death that may not appear to "affect" a child may be revisited later in life and expressed in a new way. As they move into new stages of cognitive development, children gain skills and resources for making sense of the world, they revisit their losses, and their meaning of events incorporates their new level of understanding (e.g., their understanding of what "permanent" means). Their grief is renegotiated, not resolved. Thus, adults need to be prepared to repeat things several times over the days, weeks, and years after a death.

The experience of dealing with death in childhood can have positive and negative outcomes. Children, like adolescents and adults, may regress to an earlier stage of cognitive development and behaviors. Bereaved children must also cope with grieving adults in their family, and their fears can be heightened by adult reactions that seem unclear and unusual (adults who are not their "normal" selves). Developmentally appropriate coping strategies may seem odd or frightening to adults. Children seem sad one minute and playing happily the next; adults may misinterpret that as a sign that the child isn't really grieving. In reality it is just a reflection of how children deal with change, stress, or crisis in general. Children grow and mature from opportunities to grapple with understanding loss. Depression and emotional withdrawal are not inevitable outcomes of childhood bereavement, and most children do not require counseling. Bereavement does not necessarily affect school functioning; for some, school is a refuge from other issues in family life, but for others it is not.

Factors that appear to influence childhood grieving include positive relationships and ample emotional and psychological support with a parent/caregiver, as well as open, honest, and developmentally appropriate communication about the death. Instead of insulating and isolating children from loss, encouraging (but not requiring) them to participate in family rituals and death-related activities allows them to develop skills for coping with loss. Generally, children who do best following the death of a loved one are those who experience the fewest additional changes and disruptions in their lives (Murray, 2001; Shapiro, 2001). Some children, including those who choose not to discuss loss with their parent for fear of adding to the adult's pain, may benefit from interacting with other bereaved children in support groups, grief camps, or Internet grief chat networks (Bachman, 2013; Metel & Barnes, 2011).

SPECIFIC LOSSES

The death of one's child is viewed as the most difficult loss, for it is contrary to expected developmental progression and thrusts one into a marginal social role that has unclear role expectations (Murphy, 2008). Deaths ranging from fetal loss to that of an adult child (who may also be a grandparent or a caregiver to older parents) can cause reactions similar to posttraumatic stress. From an Eriksonian perspective, young-adult parents grapple with death-related issues of identity as a parent and spousal intimacy, middle-aged parents deal with loss of generativity, and elderly parents deal with loss through a life review that includes wondering what it was worth and whether they have failed by outliving their children, resulting in either ego integrity or despair. Classic attachment and psychoanalytic models are inadequate to address experiences of bereaved parents. Newer models focus on integrating the deceased child into the parents' psychic and social worlds (Klass, 2013).

Society expects spouses to provide support and comfort during times of stress; however, this may not be possible for bereaved parents who are both experiencing intense grief as individuals, with unique timetables, and may not be "in sync" with each other (Rando, 1993). Sexual expression between bereaved parents can serve as a reminder of the child and elicit additional distress (Rosenblatt, 2000). However, previously reported high divorce rates of bereaved parents appear to be erroneous; research on which they were based is neither longitudinal nor representative and confuses marital distress and divorce.

Most research on sibling death is recent, focused on children and adolescents. Prior work on sibling loss generally was confined to clinical studies; recent work differentiates normal and complicated sibling grief patterns. Even in the same family, sibling grief reactions are not uniform or the same as parents, but they can be understood best in relation to individual characteristics (e.g., sex, developmental stage, relationship to the sibling). Scholars have not reported consistent behavioral or at-risk differences in school-age children who experienced parental death or sibling death, but they have found gender differences, with boys more affected by the loss of a parent and girls impacted more by the death of a sibling, especially a sister (Worden, Davies, & McCown, 1999).

Initial negative outcomes and grief reactions of siblings may include a drop in school performance, anger, a sense that parents are unreachable, survivor guilt, and guilt from sibling rivalry (even when siblings recognize the irrationality of their beliefs) (Rando, 1993; Schaefer & Moos, 2001). Adolescents who use religious coping ascribe more negative meaning to the death, especially when they try to reconcile belief in a loving God with a negative event such as sibling death (Hays & Hendrix, 2008). Although siblings report more family conflict than do parents, siblings rarely direct their anger toward parents, who they perceive to be vulnerable and hence in need of protection from additional pain. Long-term changes for bereaved siblings appear to be positive, especially in terms of maturity, which adolescents relate to appreciation for life, coping successfully, and negotiating role changes. Adults who lost siblings in childhood have reported that these losses fostered greater insights into life and death (Schaefer & Moos, 2001).

Siblings have unique bonds that continue following the death of a brother or sister (Packman, Horsley, & Davies, 2006). Deceased siblings also play an identity function for survivors who may feel a need to fulfill roles the deceased children played for parents or to act in an opposite manner in an attempt to show that they are different. In later adulthood, sibling death is the most frequent death of close family members, yet researchers have largely overlooked this loss. Surviving siblings appear to experience functioning and cognitive states similar to those of surviving spouses (Moss, Moss, & Hansson, 2001). Unfortunately, research on sibling grief to date has consisted primarily of cross-sectional investigations that rely on retrospective data, data no more than 2 years beyond the loss, and longitudinal data treated as cross-sectional due to small sample sizes.

The death of a parent can occur during childhood or adulthood. Children's reactions to parental death vary and are influenced by emotional and cognitive development, closeness to the deceased parent, responses of/interactions with the surviving parent, and perceptions of social support. Researchers have reported evidence of complicated grief, traumatic grief, and posttraumatic growth in parentally bereaved children and adolescents (Melhem, Moritz, Walker, Shear, & Brent, 2007; Wolchik, Coxe, Tein, Sandler, & Ayers, 2008). Adolescents grieving the death of a parent appear to have heightened interpersonal sensitivity, characterized by uneasiness and negative expectations regarding personal exchanges (Servaty-Sieb & Hayslip, 2003). Teens tend to flee a grieving peer; thus family support may be especially important for bereaved adolescents. Although many adolescents live in single-parent, divorced, or blended families, researchers have largely ignored the topic of parental death in those contexts or have focused on surviving parents' grief and adjustment.

The death of a parent is the most common form of family loss in middle age. Adult response to this loss is influenced by the meaning of the relationship, roles the parent played at the time of death, anticipation, disenfranchisement, circumstances of the death, impact on the surviving adult child, and maintenance of the parent–child bond while letting go (Moss et al., 2001). Adults whose parents experienced protracted illness or lived in nursing homes prior to death exhibit multidimensional responses to their parents' deaths, including sadness, grief, relief, persistence of memories about the parent, and a sense that the protection against death provided by the parents has vanished. Adults who become "orphaned" may find their identities and remaining relationships impacted.

Adults with mental disabilities who experience parental death have some aspects of grief in common with others but also have unique concerns. When individuals with psychiatric disabilities are faced in midlife with the death of a parent, they often have no preparation for this event. They may suddenly find themselves faced with making funeral arrangements, and dealing with financial repercussions of the death, as well as possible residential relocation (Jones et al., 2003).

Among the family losses during adulthood, the death of a spouse has been the most intensively studied; however, less attention has been given to spousal death in early or middle adulthood, widowed parents with dependent children, or death of other life partners such as committed homosexual couples. Loneliness and emotional adjustment are major concerns of spouses who lose a companion and source of emotional support, particularly in a long interdependent relationship in which there was a shared identity based on systems of roles and traditions (Moss et al., 2001). Conjugal bereavement can be especially difficult for individuals whose relationships assumed a sharp division of traditional sex roles, leaving them unprepared to assume the range of tasks required to maintain a household. The death of one's spouse brings up issues of self-definition and prompts the need to develop a new identity. Despite these problems, many bereaved spouses adjust very well, and the death of a partner does not always result in grief for the other (Watford, 2008). Some derive pleasure and independence from the new lifestyle, feeling more competent than when they were married.

An additional loss involves death and the multidimensional families of those in the military. Sacrificing one's life in military operations has historically been extolled as honorable. Generally, family members of a fallen soldier are embraced by their surrounding community, as well as the military organization, with intense support shortly after the loss, and a sense of meaning is constructed to account for, and help justify, the loss. The military's standard operating procedures help create a supportive environment for the surviving family (Bowen, Mancini, Ware, & Nelson, 2003). However, the prevalence and social legitimacy of military deaths have led to a general desensitization of communities to the length of time needed for grieving and impatience waiting for the family to move ahead. Survivors of military personnel who commit suicide may not receive the same support as other bereaved military families (Ramchand et al., 2015).

In addition, among service members, the lasting impact of combat losses on grieving is often overlooked or assumed to be posttraumatic stress disorder (Papa, Neria, & Litz, 2008). Yet war veterans often experience complicated grief as a result of the deaths of close friends, unit members, or leaders; survivor guilt; witnessing the death of other security forces and civilians; or their own killing of enemy insurgents. The close relationships that form within military units reflect attachment, and their losses are subject to grief as with loss of other attachment and family figures. Adjustment difficulties and suicide rates, especially of those with lengthy deployments, are indications that early evidence-based interventions are needed (Figley, 2007).

CONCLUSION AND SUMMARY

Dealing with death involves a process, not an event. It is an experience that all families *will* encounter and is inherent in the nature of close relationships. Despite its importance in the experiences of individuals and families, death still appears to be a taboo subject, and no comprehensive theory exists to account for the complexity and contexts in which grief occurs. Families' adaptation to death varies; factors that influence the process include characteristics of the death, family vulnerability, history of past losses, incompatible life-cycle demands, resources, belief systems, and the sociocultural context in which a family lives.

Although loss is a normal experience, it has been treated by theorists and researchers as a problem. More work needs to focus on processes and strengths, such as the process of coping (rather than problems) and factors that facilitate growth from loss (rather than those that inhibit growth). Examination of posttraumatic growth is a first step, but it warrants application beyond the individual to assess its applicability to families. Promising areas of study include the interface of grief with technology, including the role of social media, how the Internet is changing the way we die and mourn (from suicide bulletin boards to virtual grief therapy), and posthumous reproduction using cryopreserved gametes of a deceased partner.

REFERENCES

American Psychiatric Association. (2013). *Diagnostic and statistical manual of mental disorders* (5th ed.). Arlington, VA: Author.

Anderson, W. G., Arnold, R. M., Angus, D. C., & Bryce, C. L. (2008). Posttraumatic stress and complicated grief in family members of patients in the intensive care unit. *Journal of General Internal Medicine, 23,* 1871–1876.

Archer, J. (2008). Theories of grief: Past, present, and future perspectives. In M. S. Stroebe, R. O. Hansson, H. Schut, & W. Stroebe (Eds.), *Handbook of bereavement research and practice* (pp. 45–65). Washington, DC: American Psychological Association.

Aries, P. (1974). *Western attitudes toward death: From the Middle Ages to the present.* Baltimore, MD: Johns Hopkins University Press.

Bachman, B. (2013). The development of a sustainable, community-supported children's bereavement camp. *Omega, 67,* 21–35.

Balk, D.E., Noppe, I., Sandler, I., & Werth, J. (2011). Bereavement and depression: Possible changes to the Diagnostic and Statistical Manual of Mental Disorders: A report from the Scientific Advisory Committee of the Association for Death Education and Counseling. *Omega: Journal of Death and Dying, 63,* 199–220.

Becker, E. (1973). *The denial of death.* New York, NY: Free Press.

Boelen, P. A., & van den Bout, J. (2002/2003). Gender differences in traumatic grief symptom severity after the loss of a spouse. *Omega, 46,* 183–198.

Boelen, P.A., & Prigerson, H.G. (2012).Commentary on the inclusion of persistent complex bereavement-related disorder in DSM-5. *Death Studies, 36,* 771–794.

Bonanno, G. A. (2004). Loss, trauma, and human resilience: Have we underestimated the human capacity to thrive after extremely aversive events? *American Psychologist, 59,* 20–28.

Boss, P. (2006). *Loss, trauma, and resilience: Therapeutic work with ambiguous loss.* New York, NY: W. W. Norton.

Bowen, G., Mancini, J. A., Ware, W. B., & Nelson, J. P. (2003). Promoting the adaptation of military families: An empirical test of a community practice model. *Family Relations, 52,* 33–44.

Bowen, M. (1976). Family reaction to death. In P. J. Guerin (Ed.), *Family therapy: Theory and practice,* pp. 335-348. New York, NY: Gardner.

Bowlby, J. (1980). *Attachment and loss* (vol. 3), *Loss: Sadness and depression.* New York, NY: Basic.

Bucholz, J. A. (2002). *Homicide survivors: Misunderstood grievers.* Amityville, NY: Baywood.

Buckley, T., Morel-Kopp, M.C., Ward, C., Bartrop, R., McKinley, S., Mihailidou, . . . Tofler, G. (2012). Inflammatory and thrombotic changes in early bereavement: A prospective evaluation. *European Journal of Preventive Cardiology, 19,* 1145–1152.

Cook, J. A. (1988). Dad's double binds: Rethinking fathers' bereavement from a men's studies perspective. *Journal of Contemporary Ethnography, 17,* 285–308.

Corden, A., & Hirst, M. (2013). Economic components of grief. *Death Studies, 37,* 725–749.

Doka, K. J. (Ed.). (1996). Commentary. *In Living with grief after sudden loss: Suicide, homicide, accident, heart attack, stroke* (pp. 11–15). Bristol, PA: Taylor & Francis.

Doka, K. J. (2005). Ethics, end-of-life decisions and grief. *Mortality, 10*(1), 83–90.

Doka, K. J. (2008). Disenfranchised grief in historical and cultural perspective. In M. S. Stroebe, R. O. Hansson, H. Schut, & W. Stroebe (Eds.), *Handbook of bereavement research and practice* (pp. 223–240). Washington, DC: American Psychological Association.

Doka, K. J., & Martin, T. (2001). Take it like a man: Masculine response to loss. In D. A. Lund (Ed.), *Men coping with grief* (pp. 37–47). Amityville, NY: Baywood.

Elwert, F., & Christakis, N. (2006). Widowhood and race. *American Sociological Review, 71,* 16–41.

Essa, E.L., & Murray, C.I. (1994). Research in review: Young children's understanding and experience with death. *Young Children, 49,* 74–81.

Figley, C. R. (2007). An introduction to the special issue on the MHAT-IV. *Traumatology, 13,* 4–5.

Freud, S. (1917/1957). Mourning and melancholies. In J. Strachey (Ed. & Trans.), *The standard edition of the complete psychological works of Sigmund Freud* (Vol. 14, pp. 243–258). London, England: Hogarth Press.

Gilbert, K. R. (1996). "We've had the same loss, why don't we have the same grief?" Loss and differential grief in families. *Death Studies, 20,* 269–283.

Hall, M., & Irwin, M. (2001). Physiological indices of functioning in bereavement. In M. S. Stroebe, R. O. Hansson, W. Stroebe, & H. Schut (Eds.), *Handbook of bereavement research: Consequences, coping, and care* (pp. 473–492). Washington, DC: American Psychological Association.

Harvey, J. H., Carlson, H. R., Huff, T. M., & Green, M. A. (2001). Embracing their memory: The construction of accounts of loss and hope. In R. A. Neimeyer (Ed.), *Meaning reconstruction and the experience of loss* (pp. 231–243). Washington, DC: American Psychological Association.

Hays, J. C., & Hendrix, C. C. (2008). The role of religion in bereavement. In M. S. Stroebe, R. O. Hansson, H. Schut, & W. Stroebe (Eds.), *Handbook of bereavement research and practice* (pp. 327–348). Washington, DC: American Psychological Association.

Ironson, G., Wynings, C., Schneiderman, N., Baum, A., Rodriguez, M., Greenwood, D., . . . Fletcher, M. A. (1997). Posttraumatic stress symptoms, intrusive thoughts, loss, and immune function after Hurricane Andrew. *Psychosomatic Medicine, 59,* 128–141.

Jackson, D. (1965). The study of the family. *Family Process, 4,* 1–20.

Janoff-Bulman, R. (1992). *Shattered assumptions: Towards a new psychology of trauma.* New York, NY: Free Press.

Jones, D., Harvey, J., Giza, D., Rodican, C., Barreira, P. J., & Macias, C. (2003). Parental death in the lives of people with serious mental illness. *Journal of Loss and Trauma, 8,* 307–322.

Kamienski, M. C. (2004). Family-centered care in ED. *American Journal of Nursing, 104,* 59–62.

Klass, D. (2013). Sorrow and solace: Neglected areas of bereavement research. *Death Studies, 37,* 597-616.

Kübler-Ross, E. (1969). *On death and dying.* New York, NY: Macmillan.

Laurie, A., & Neimeyer, R. A. (2008). African Americans in bereavement: Grief as a function of ethnicity. *Omega, 57,* 173–193.

Lee, E.-K. O., Shen, C., & Tran, T.V. (2009). Coping with Hurricane Katrina: Psychological distress and resilience among African American evacuees. *Journal of Black Psychology, 35,* 5–23.

Lerner, M. (1980). When, why, and where people die. In E. S. Schneidman (Ed.), *Death: Current perspectives* (pp. 87–106). Palo Alto, CA: Mayfield.

Lindemann, E. (1944). Symptomology and management of acute grief. *American Journal of Psychiatry, 101,* 141–148.

McGoldrick, M., Almeida, R., Hines, P. M., Garcia Preto, N., Rosen, E., & Lee, E. (1991). Mourning in different cultures. In F. Walsh & M. McGoldrick (Eds.), *Living beyond loss* (pp. 176–206). New York, NY: Norton.

Melhem, N. M., Moritz, G., Walker, M., Shear, M. K., & Brent, D. (2007). Phenomenology and correlates of complicated grief in children and adolescents. *Journal of the American Academy of Child and Adolescent Psychiatry, 46,* 493–499.

Metel, M., & Barnes, J. (2011). Peer-group support for bereaved children: A qualitative interview study. *Child and Adolescent Mental Health, 16,* 201–207.

Mikulincer, M., & Shaver, P. R. (2008). An attachment perspective on bereavement. In M. S. Stroebe, R. O. Hansson, H. Schut, & W. Stroebe (Eds.), *Handbook of bereavement research and practice* (pp. 87–112). Washington, DC: American Psychological Association.

Monahan, K. (2003). Death of an abuser: Does the memory linger on? *Death Studies, 27,* 641–651.

Moss, M. S., Moss, S. Z., & Hansson, R. O. (2001). Bereavement and old age. In M. S. Stroebe, R. O. Hansson, W. Stroebe, & H. Schut (Eds.), *Handbook of bereavement research: Consequences, coping, and care* (pp. 241–260). Washington, DC: American Psychological Association.

Murphy, S. A. (2008). The loss of a child: Sudden death and extended illness perspectives. In M. S. Stroebe, R. O. Hansson, H. Schut, & W. Stroebe (Eds.), *Handbook of bereavement research and practice* (pp. 375–395). Washington, DC: American Psychological Association.

Murphy, S.L., Xu, J.Q., & Kochanek, K.D. (2013). Deaths: Final data for 2010. *National Vital Statistics Reports, 61*(4). Hyattsville. MD: National Center for Health Statistics.

Murray, C. I., & Gilbert, K. R. (1997, June). *British and U.S. reporting of the Dunblane school massacre.* Paper presented at the meeting of the 5th International Conference on Grief and Bereavement in Contemporary Society/Association for Death Education and Counseling. Washington, DC.

Murray, J. A. (2001). Loss as a university concept: A review of the literature to identify common aspects of loss in diverse situations. *Journal of Loss and Trauma, 6,* 219–241.

Nadeau, J. W. (2008). Meaning-making in bereaved families: Assessment, intervention, and future research. In M. S. Stroebe, R. O. Hansson, H. Schut, & W. Stroebe (Eds.), *Handbook of bereavement research and practice* (pp. 511–530). Washington, DC: American Psychological Association.

Neimeyer, R. A., Klass, D., & Dennis, M. R. (2014). A social constructionist account of grief: Loss and the narration of meaning. *Death Studies, 38,* 485–498.

O'Connor, M. F., Shear, M.K., Fox, R., Skirtskaya, N., Campbell, B., Ghesquiere, A., & Glickman, K. (2013). Catecholamine predictors of complicated grief treatment outcomes. *International Journal of Psychophysiology, 88,* 349–353.

Packman, W., Horsley, H., & Davies, B. (2006). Sibling bereavement and continuing bonds. *Death Studies, 30,* 817–841.

Papa, A., Neria, Y., & Litz, B. (2008). Traumatic bereavement in war veterans. *Psychiatric Annals, 38,* 686–691.

Pennebaker, J. W., Zech, E., & Rime, B. (2001). Disclosing and sharing emotion: Psychological, social, and health consequences. In M. S. Stroebe, R. O. Hansson, W. Stroebe, & H. Schut (Eds.), *Handbook of bereavement research: Consequences, coping, and care* (pp. 517–543). Washington, DC: American Psychological Association.

Prigerson, H.G., Horowitz, M. J., Jacobs, S. C., Parkes, C. M., Aslan, M., Goodkin, K. . . . Maciejewski, P. K. (2009). Prolonged grief disorder: Psychometric validation of criteria proposed for DSM-V and ICD-11. *PLoS Medicine 6*(8), e1000121.

Pyszcznski, T., Solomon, S., & Greenberg, J. (2003). *In the wake of September 11: The psychology of terror.* Washington, DC: American Psychological Association.

Rabow, M. W., Hauser, J. M., & Adams, J. (2004). Supporting family caregivers at the end of life: "They don't know what they don't know." *Journal of the American Medical Association, 291*(4), 483–491.

Ramchand, R., Ayer, L., Fisher, G., Osilla, K. C., Barnes-Proby, D., & Wertheimer, S. (2015). *Suicide postvention in the Department of Defense: Evidence, policies and procedures, and perspectives of loss survivors.* Santa Monica, CA: RAND Corporation.

Rando, T. A. (1993). *Treatment of complicated mourning.* Champaign, IL: Research Press.

Robson, P., & Walter, T. (2012). Hierarchies of loss: A critique of disenfranchised grief. *Omega, 66,* 97–119.

Rolland, J. S. (1994). *Families, illness, & disability: An integrative treatment model.* New York, NY: Basic Books.

Rosaldo, R. (1989). *Culture and truth: The remaking of social analysis.* Boston, MA: Beacon.

Rosenblatt, P. C. (2000). *Parent grief: Narratives of loss and relationship.* Philadelphia, PA: Brunner/Mazel.

Rosenblatt, P. C. (2008). Recovery following bereavement: Metaphor, phenomenology, and culture. *Death Studies, 32,* 6–16.

Schaefer, J. A., & Moos, R. H. (2001). Bereavement experiences and personal growth. In M. S. Stroebe, R. O. Hansson, W. Stroebe, & H. Schut (Eds.), *Handbook of bereavement research: Consequences, coping, and care* (pp. 145–167). Washington, DC: American Psychological Association.

Servaty-Sieb, H. L., & Hayslip, B. (2003). Post-loss adjustment and funeral perceptions of parentally bereaved adolescents and adults. *Omega, 46,* 251–261.

Shapiro, E. R. (2001). Grief in interpersonal perspective: Theories and their implications. In M. S. Stroebe, R. O. Hansson, W. Stroebe, & H. Schut (Eds.), *Handbook of bereavement research: Consequences, coping, and care* (pp. 301–327). Washington, DC: American Psychological Association.

Shear, M. K., Ghesquiere, A., & Glickman, K. (2013).Bereavement and complicated grief. *Current Psychiatry Reports, 15*, 406.

Shear, M. K., Simon, N., Wall, M., Zisook, S., Neimeyer, R. A., Duan, N., . . . Keshaviah, A. (2011). Complicated grief and related bereavement issues for DSM-5. *Depression and Anxiety, 28*, 103–117.

Stroebe, M., Schut, H., & Stroebe, W. (2007, December). Health outcomes of bereavement. *Lancet, 370*, 1960–1973.

Stroebe, M. S., & Schut, H. (2001). Models of coping with bereavement: A review. In M. S. Stroebe, R. O. Hansson, W. Stroebe, & H. Schut (Eds.), *Handbook of bereavement research: Consequences, coping, and care* (pp. 375–403). Washington, DC: American Psychological Association.

Stroebe, M. S., van Son, M., Stroebe, W., Kleber, R., Schut, H., & van den Bout, J. (2000). On the classification and diagnosis of pathological grief. *Clinical Psychology Review, 20*, 57–75.

Stroebe, W., & Schut, H. (2001). Risk factors in bereavement outcome: A methodological and empirical review. In M. S. Stroebe, R. O. Hansson, W. Stroebe, & H. Schut (Eds.), *Handbook of bereavement research: Consequences, coping, and care* (pp. 349–371). Washington, DC: American Psychological Association.

Tedeschi, R. G., & Calhoun, L. G. (2008). Beyond the concept of recovery: Growth and the experience of loss. *Death Studies, 32*, 27–39.

Thieleman, K., & Cacciatore, J. (2014). When a child dies: A critical analysis of grief-related controversies in DSM-5. *Research on Social Work Practice, 24*, 114–122.

Traylor, E. S., Hayslip, B., Kaminski, P. L., & York, C. (2003). Relationships between grief and family system characteristics: A cross lagged longitudinal analysis. *Death Studies, 27*, 575–601.

Wakefield, J. C., & Schmitz, M. F. (2012). Recurrence of depression after bereavement-related depression: Evidence for the validity of DSM-IV bereavement exclusion from the epidemiological catchment area study. *Journal of Nervous and Mental Disease, 200*, 480–485.

Walsh, F., & McGoldrick, M. (1991). Loss and the family: A systems perspective. In F. Walsh & M. McGoldrick (Eds.), *Living beyond loss* (pp.1–29). New York, NY: Norton.

Walter, T. (2008). The new public mourning. In M. S. Stroebe, R. O. Hansson, H. Schut, & W. Stroebe (Eds.), *Handbook of bereavement research and practice* (pp. 241–262). Washington, DC: American Psychological Association.

Walter, T., Hourizi, R., Moncur, W., & Pitsillides, S. (2012). Does the internet change how we die and mourn? Overview and analysis. *Omega, 64*, 275–302.

Watford, M. L. (2008). Bereavement of spousal suicide: A reflective self-exploration. *Qualitative Inquiry, 14*, 335–359.

Webb, N. B. (2004). The impact of traumatic stress and loss on children and families. In N. B. Webb (Ed.), *Mass trauma and violence: Helping families and children cope* (pp. 3–22). New York, NY: Guilford.

Weiss, R. S. (2008). The nature and causes of grief. In M. S. Stroebe, R. O. Hansson, H. Schut, & W. Stroebe (Eds.), *Handbook of bereavement research and practice* (pp. 29–44). Washington, DC: American Psychological Association.

Wolchik, S. A., Coxe, S., Tein, J. Y., Sandler, I. N., & Ayers, T. S. (2008). Six-year longitudinal predictors of posttraumatic growth in parentally bereaved adolescents and young adults. *Omega, 58*, 107–128.

Worden, J. W., Davies, B., & McCown, D. (1999). Comparing parent loss with sibling loss. *Death Studies, 23*, 1–15.

Wortman, C. B., & Silver, R. C. (2001). The myths of coping with loss revisited. In M. S. Stroebe, R. O. Hansson, W. Stroebe, & H. Schut (Eds.), *Handbook of bereavement research: Consequences, coping, and care* (pp. 405–429). Washington, DC: American Psychological Association.

Zisook, S., Corruble, E., Duan, N., Iglewicz, A., Karam, E.G., & Lanouette, N., . . . Young, T. (2012). The bereavement exclusion and DSM-5. *Depression and Anxiety, 29,* 425–443.

Index

About the Editors

Christine A. Price is an associate professor and coordinator for the Gerontology Program in the Department of Family and Child Studies at Montclair State University, Montclair, New Jersey. Her primary area of teaching is family gerontology, and her scholarly interests emphasize the transitional adjustment and psychosocial experiences of retired women. Her work has been published in several scholarly journals including *The International Journal of Aging and Human Development,* the *Journal of Women and Aging, Family Relations, and The Journal of Ethnographic and Qualitative Research*. She earned her master's and her PhD in Child and Family Development and graduate certificate in Gerontology from the University of Georgia.

Kevin Ray Bush is an associate dean, a professor of Family Studies and Social Work, and the codirector of the Doris Bergen Center for Human Development, Learning and Technology at Miami University in Oxford, Ohio. His research interests focus on child and adolescent development in the contexts of family, school, community, and culture. He has examined the relationships between parents, teachers, and child and adolescent development within diverse U.S. and international samples. Dr. Bush is also interested in program evaluation and has conducted evaluations of school, agency, and home-based child and family intervention programs. Dr. Bush has a master's degree in Marriage and Family Therapy from Arizona State University and a PhD in Human Development and Family Relations from the Ohio State University.

Sharon J. Price is professor emerita and former head of the department of Child and Family Development at the University of Georgia. She has published extensively in professional journals and coauthored or coedited several books. She won several teaching awards including the Osborne Award, presented by the National Council on Family Relations, and the highest honor for teaching at the University of Georgia, the Josiah Meigs Award. She was active in several professional organizations, serving in many capacities, including president of the National Council on Family Relations (NCFR), and is a fellow in NCFR. She earned her PhD from Iowa State University.

About the Contributors

Bertranna A. Abrams-Muruthi is a PhD candidate in Human Development and Family Sciences with a specialization in Marriage and Family Therapy at the University of Georgia. Her research centers on developing culturally responsive intervention and prevention programming for immigrant families. She received her MS in Family Studies from Miami University of Ohio.

Lucy Allbaugh is a doctoral student in Clinical Psychology at Miami University. Her research focuses on outcomes associated with trauma and on change in functioning across the life span, with a particular emphasis on resilient outcome and relational well-being. She is currently engaged in research to understand relational functioning among adolescents and young adults with experiences of maltreatment and other traumas, the experience of parenting as a survivor, and factors that contribute to continuity versus discontinuity in the intergenerational cycle of maltreatment.

Suzanne Bartholomae is an adjunct associate professor and state extension specialist in Family Finance in the Department of Human Sciences Extension and Outreach at Iowa State University. Her research interests include financial stress and coping and the financial socialization process, with a focus on parenting. She also studies the efficacy of financial education programs. Her work has been published in several scholarly journals including *Family Relations,* the *Journal of Family Issues,* the *Journal of Family and Economics Issues,* the *Journal of Adolescent Health,* and the *Journal of Consumer Affairs.* She earned her PhD from the Ohio State University.

Stephanie A. Bohon is the founder of the Center for Social Justice and associate professor of Sociology at the University of Tennessee at Knoxville. Her research focuses on the growth and needs of Latino migrants in the south, Latino immigration policy, and the difference between Latino migrant adjustment in established and emerging gateways. Her work has been published in several scholarly journals including *Social Problems, Social Science Quarterly, Rural Sociology, Population Research and Policy Review,* and the *Journal of Latinos and Education.* She is the author of *Latinos in Ethnic Enclaves* and *Immigration and Population.* She earned her PhD from Pennsylvania State University.

Adam Cless is a graduating senior in Family Studies and Human Services with a secondary major in Gerontology and minor in Conflict Analysis and Trauma Studies from Kansas State University. After graduation, he is planning to pursue a master's degree in Life Span Human Development at Kansas State University. His research interests address how families change and move through developmental transitions, including intergenerational transmission of family behaviors, parent–adolescent relationships, and the experiences of parents with a special needs child.

David H. Demo is associate dean for graduate programs in the School of Health and Human Sciences and professor in the Department of Human Development and Family Studies at the University of North Carolina at Greensboro. His research focuses on divorce and family transitions, changes in family relationships accompanying divorce, and the consequences of family transitions for family members' well-being. He has published widely in professional journals and has authored or edited several books, including *Beyond the Average Divorce* (with Mark Fine), *Handbook of Family Diversity* (with Katherine Allen and Mark Fine), *Parents and Adolescents in Changing Families* (with Anne Marie Ambert), and *Family Diversity and Well-Being* (with Alan Acock). He recently served as editor of the *Journal of Marriage and Family,* and he is a fellow of the National Council on Family Relations. He earned his PhD from Cornell University.

Mark Fine is professor and chair in the Department of Human Development and Family Studies at the University of North Carolina at Greensboro. He was editor of *Family Relations* from 1993 to 1996 and was editor of the *Journal of Social and Personal Relationships* from 1999 to 2004. His research interests lie in the areas of family transitions, such as divorce and remarriage; early intervention program evaluation; social cognition; and relationship stability. He was coeditor, along with David Demo and Katherine Allen, of the *Handbook of Family Diversity*, published in 2000. He coauthored, along with John Harvey, *Children of Divorce: Stories of Hope and Loss* in 2004; coedited, with John Harvey, *The Handbook of Divorce and Relationship Dissolution* in 2005; and coedited, with Jean Ispa and Kathy Thornburg, *Keepin' on: The Everyday Struggles of Young Families in Poverty*, published in 2006. In 2009, he coauthored with David Demo *Beyond the Average Divorce* and recently published a coedited volume on family theories with Frank Fincham, *Family Theories: A Content-Based Approach*. He has published almost 200 peer-reviewed journal articles, book chapters, and books. In 2000, he was selected as a fellow of the National Council on Family Relations. He earned his PhD from the Ohio State University.

Judith Fischer is professor emeritus of Human Development and Family Studies at Texas Tech University. She continues her research on family problems, addictions, and adult development. Her work has been published in addiction, family, and human development journals. She was coeditor of *Familial Responses to Alcohol Problems* and serves on the editorial board of *Journal of Marriage and Family.* She is a past president of the Groves Conference on Marriage and Family and was the first holder of the C. R. & Virginia Hutcheson Professorship in Human Development and Family Studies at Texas Tech University. She is a fellow of the National Council on Family Relations and a member of the Academy of the Groves Conference on Marriage and Family. She earned her PhD from the University of Colorado.

Jonathan Fox is the Ruth Whipp Sherwin Endowed Professor in the Department of Human Development and Family Studies; director of the Financial Counseling Clinic; and program leader in financial counseling and planning at Iowa State University. His research focuses on financial education and financial socialization. He has served as PI for several financial education evaluations, and his publications appear in journals such as *Financial Services Review, Financial Counseling and Planning,* the *Journal of Family Issues,* and the *Journal of Consumer Affairs.* From 2013 to 2014, Jonathan served as president of the American

Council on Consumer Interests. He teaches courses in personal and family finance and received his PhD in Consumer Economics from the University of Maryland.

Chelsea Garneau is an assistant professor in Human Development and Family Studies at the University of Missouri. Her research and publications relate to family processes (e.g., coparenting, parental monitoring, positive interaction, family cohesion) and individual, couple, and family well-being in complex family structures. Recent publications focus on the role of cognitions and marital and family relationship quality and interactions in stepfamilies. Dr. Garneau coauthored a book chapter on Stepfamilies for the 4th edition of *Normal Family Processes* and has written encyclopedia entries on various stepfamily-related topics for *The Social History of the American Family*, *The Encyclopedia of Family Studies*, and *Cultural Sociology of Divorce*. She is an active member of the National Council on Family Relations, the Population Association of America, and the International Association for Relationship Research. She earned her PhD from Florida State University.

Abbie E. Goldberg is associate professor of psychology at Clark University. Her research focuses on parenting in diverse families, including lesbian/gay parent families, adoptive families, and families formed through reproductive technologies. She has received grant funding for her work from a range of private and federal agencies, including the American Psychological Association, the Alfred P. Sloan Foundation, the Spencer Foundation, and the National Institutes of Health. She has over 60 peer-reviewed publications in journals such as the *Journal of Marriage and Family*, the *Journal of Family Psychology*, and *Adoption Quarterly*. She is the author of *Lesbian and Gay Parents and Their Children: Research on the Family Life Cycle* (2010) and *Gay Dads: Transitions to Adoptive Fatherhood* (2012). She earned her PhD from the University of Massachusetts Amherst.

Heather M. Helms is associate professor in the Department of Human Development and Family Studies at the University of North Carolina at Greensboro where she has been recognized with research, graduate mentoring, and teaching excellence awards. She teaches in the areas of work and family, family theory and research, and close relationships. Her research focuses on marital quality, parents' work and family relationships, and the sociocultural context of family relationships. Her work has been published in numerous scholarly journals including the *Journal of Marriage and the Family*, the *Journal of Family Psychology*, the *Journal of Family Theory and Review*, the *Journal of Family Issues*, and *Family Relations*. Her most recent research is funded by the National Center for Research on Hispanic Children and Families and focuses on the family experiences of Mexican immigrant couples with young children. She earned her PhD from Pennsylvania State University.

Natalie D. Hengstebeck is a doctoral candidate in the Department of Human Development and Family Studies at the University of North Carolina at Greensboro. With a particular emphasis on social inequality, her research focuses on how stress impacts individual well-being and couple relationships and ecologically informed strategies for improving couple functioning. Her work has been published in the *Journal of Family Issues* and the *Journal of Family Psychology*. Following a Fulbright Fellowship to the Netherlands to study family policies and couple relationships, she expects to complete her PhD in 2017.

Jessica D. High is a graduate student in Marriage and Family Therapy at Kansas State University, where she expects to earn degrees at both the master's and doctoral levels.

She earned a bachelor's degree in Family Studies and Human Services, as well as graduated with a minor in Conflict Analysis and Trauma Studies at Kansas State University. Clinically, Ms. High is interested in working with children and families who have experienced trauma or loss. She assists in teaching courses related to trauma, violence, and grief, which overlap with her research interests. Specifically, she is interested in the intersections of trauma and grief experiences in families and individuals across the life span. Ms. High currently works with Dr. Nelson Goff at Kansas State University on various teaching and research collaborations.

Áine M. Humble is an associate professor in the Department of Family Studies and Gerontology at Mount Saint Vincent University in Halifax, Nova Scotia, Canada. Her research interests focus on gender construction and family work, family rituals, women and healthy aging, same-sex couples, qualitative research methods, and feminist pedagogy. Her work has been published in scholarly journals such as *Family Relations*, the *Journal of Family Issues*, the *Journal of Women and Aging*, and *Canadian Journal on Aging*. She is a certified Family Life Educator through the National Council on Family Relations. She earned her PhD, with a minor in Women Studies, at Oregon State University.

Lyndal Khaw is an associate professor of Family and Child Studies at Montclair State University, Montclair, New Jersey. Her academic research focuses on intimate partner violence, specifically on women's process of leaving abusive partners and the impact of violence on family dynamics and relationships. Her work has been published in peer-reviewed journals including *Family Relations,* the *Journal of Family Theory and Review,* and *Family Process*. She has served on the board of directors of the National Council on Family Relations. She earned her PhD in Human Development and Family Studies from the University of Illinois at Urbana-Champaign.

Hyoun K. Kim is a senior scientist at the Oregon Social Learning Center, Eugene, Oregon and associate professor in the Department of Child and Family Studies at Yonsei University, Seoul, Korea. Her research interests center around the development of psychopathology in adolescents and young adults from at-risk backgrounds. Dr. Kim is co-investigator on multiple longitudinal studies of at-risk adolescents, including several randomized controlled trials to examine the efficacy of prevention programs aimed at facilitating the healthy development of at-risk youths. Her work has been published in more than 80 scholarly journals, including *Development and Psychopathology,* the *Journal of Family Psychology*, the *Journal of Marriage and Family*, *Prevention Science*, and *Psychoneuroendocrinology*. She earned her PhD from the Ohio State University.

Kelsey Koblitz is a senior undergraduate dual majoring in Psychology and Family Studies and Human Services with a minor in Conflict Analysis and Trauma Studies at Kansas State University. Upon her graduation in May 2015, she will be attending Oklahoma State University to pursue her Educational Specialist degree in School Psychology.

Kyung-Hee Lee is a postdoctoral research associate at the Military Family Research Institute at Purdue University. Her research interests include military families, work–family issues, dyadic and longitudinal processes of intimate relationships, and voluntary childlessness. She earned her PhD at Texas Tech and previously worked at Virginia Tech as a postdoctoral research associate and at Texas Tech as an adjunct professor.

Kevin P. Lyness is professor and director of the Marriage and Family Therapy PhD program in the Department of Applied Psychology at Antioch University New England. Previously he was on the faculty in Colorado State University's Marriage and Family Therapy program. He is a former assistant editor of the *Journal of Marital and Family Therapy* and serves on the editorial boards of the *Journal of Feminist Family Therapy* and the *Journal of Couple and Relationship Therapy*. He earned his PhD from Purdue University, and his initial training was in substance abuse counseling.

Shelley MacDermid Wadsworth is a professor in the Department of Human Development and Family Studies at Purdue University, where she also directs the Military Family Research Institute and the Center for Families. Her research focuses on relationships between job conditions and family life, with special focus on military families and organizational policies, programs, and practices. Dr. MacDermid Wadsworth is a fellow of the National Council on Family Relations, and a recipient of the Work Life Legacy Award from the Families and Work Institute. Dr. MacDermid Wadsworth served as the civilian cochair of the Department of Defense Task Force on Mental Health and also served on the Returning Veterans Committee of the Institute of Medicine and the Psychological Health External Advisory Committee to the Defense Health Board. In 2012, she received the Morrill Award from Purdue University for outstanding career achievements that have had an impact on society. She earned her PhD from Pennsylvania State University.

Mark R. McGowan is an associate professor of Educational and School Psychology at Indiana University of Pennsylvania. He is a licensed psychologist in Pennsylvania, a registrant of the National Register of Health Service Providers in Psychology, and a nationally certified school psychologist with over 10 years of experience working in both public and private settings. His research interests focus on the provision of mental health services in educational settings, violence risk and threat assessment, school-based neuropsychological assessment, supervision, and graduate training in psychology. Dr. McGowan earned a master's degree in School Psychology and a PhD in Counseling Psychology from Northern Arizona University.

Patrick C. McKenry was professor of Human Development and Family Science and African American and African Studies at The Ohio State University. His work focused on family stress and coping with particular interest in gender, cultural, and lifestyle variations. In addition to books, he published numerous articles in professional journals. He received his PhD from the University of Tennessee in Child and Family Studies and was a postdoctoral fellow at the University of Georgia in Child and Family Development. Pat and Sharon Price worked together for almost three decades and edited three previous editions of this book as well as the book *Divorce* (published by SAGE Publications). He died in 2004.

Courtney L. McLaughlin is an assistant professor in the Educational and School Psychology Department at Indiana University of Pennsylvania. Her primary professional interests are in the areas of school-based mental health, integrating cognitive-behavioral therapy into the school setting, preventing and intervening with children and adolescents struggling with depression in the school setting, and training school psychologists. She serves as an associate editor for the Alexander Graham Bell Association's Volta Review. Dr. McLaughlin earned her master's degree and PhD in School Psychology from Kent State University.

Colleen I. Murray is the director of the interdisciplinary PhD program in Social Psychology, professor of Sociology, and adjunct professor of Human Development and Family Studies at the University of Nevada, Reno. Her current research focuses on theories at the intersection of justice, culture, loss, and well-being, with particular emphasis on parent and sibling grief following sudden loss or mass tragedy, experiences of mixed migratory status immigrant families, and attitudes toward civilian use of drones. She has published numerous articles and chapters on family relationships, grief, adolescents, gender, and culture. She is a fellow in Thanatology with the Association for Death Education and Counseling and chairs the Grief and Families Focus Group of the National Council on Family Relations. She earned her PhD from the Ohio State University.

Briana S. Nelson Goff is a professor in the School of Family Studies and Human Services and director for the Institute for the Health and Security of Military Families, at Kansas State University. Dr. Nelson Goff's clinical experience and research specialization is with primary and secondary traumatic stress symptoms in trauma survivor couples, families, and children, with specific focus on military and disaster related traumatic events. Since 2010, Dr. Nelson Goff and Dr. Nicole Springer have collaborated on a national research study on the positive aspects of having a child with Down syndrome, which is both a personal and professional endeavor. She earned dual bachelor degrees in life science and psychology and a master's degree in marriage and family therapy, both from Kansas State University, and her PhD from Texas Tech University.

Amity Noltemeyer is an associate professor and coordinator of the School Psychology Program at Miami University of Ohio. Dr. Noltemeyer's research interests include school discipline disparities, resilience, multitiered systems of support, and school-based mental health services. She serves as co-PI to externally funded grants, past president of the Ohio School Psychologists Association, and coeditor of *School Psychology International* journal. She earned her master's and EdS degrees in School Psychology from Miami University and her PhD in School Psychology from Kent State University.

Kay Pasley is professor emeritus from Florida State University, where she was professor and chair of the department of Family and Child Sciences. She has studied remarriage and stepfamilies since 1977, writing extensively on the topic for both academic and popular audiences. Her research and publications pertain to relational processes in remarriages/repartnerships and fathering after divorce and remarriage. In addition to numerous journal articles, Dr. Pasley has coauthored the book *Remarriage* and coedited three books: *Stepfamilies: Issues in Research, Theory and Practice*; *Remarriage and Stepfamilies Today: Current Research and Theory*; and *Contemporary Families: Research Into Practice*. She is a fellow of the National Council on Family Relations and in 2012 received the Felix Berardo Mentoring Award. She served as the chair of the research committee and as a member of the board of directors of the Stepfamily Association of America until 2005. Dr. Pasley is a member of the Scientific Advisory Board for the National Resource Center for Stepfamilies. She earned her EdD from Indiana University.

Gary W. Peterson is professor emeritus for the Department of Family Studies and Social Work at the University of Miami in Oxford, Ohio. His areas of scholarly interest are parent–child/adolescent relations, cross-cultural influences on adolescent development, and family theory. His publications have appeared in numerous academic journals and edited book chapters. He is editor or coeditor of books on fatherhood, cross-cultural parent–adolescent relations, and adolescent development in families. Dr. Peterson's current research is concerned with how aspects of parent–adolescent relationships influence dimensions of adolescent social competence with a special focus on Mexican parent-adolescent relations. He is a past coeditor of the *Handbook of Marriage and the Family* (2nd ed.), the editor of the *Handbook of Marriage and the Family* (3rd ed.), and a previous editor of *Marriage and Family Review*. Dr. Peterson is a fellow of the National Council on Family Relations. He earned his PhD from Brigham Young University.

Nicole Springer is an associate professor of practice at Texas Tech University in the College of Human Sciences, director for the Center of Family Systems Research and Intervention, and director of the Family Therapy Clinic. She instructs undergraduate courses for students majoring in Community, Family, and Addiction Sciences as well as graduate courses in Marriage and Family Therapy. She has been licensed as a marriage and family therapist for over 15 years and is an approved supervisor and clinical member of AAMFT. Her research and clinical interests include medical family therapy, reproductive loss, as well as couple and family resilience. She has collaborated with Dr. Nelson Goff on a project examining hope and resilience in families raising a child with Down syndrome, which has resulted in numerous regional, state, and national presentations. She earned her PhD from Texas Tech University.

Natira Staats is a graduate student in the School of Family Studies and Human Services at Kansas State University. She earned an associate's degree in mathematics from Garden City Community College, a bachelor's degree in psychology from Kansas State University, and is currently pursuing a master's degree in marriage and family therapy at Kansas State University.

Kevin Stott is a graduate student in the School of Family Life at Brigham Young University. He is currently finishing his master's degree and will be continuing his education at the University of Missouri for PhD training. His research interests include the daily-life experiences of older adults and later life family relationships. He is especially interested in the mental, physical, and sexual health of older adults, especially among members of the baby-boom generation. He has presented original research at various professional conferences including the Gerontological Society of America and the Utah Council on Family Relations.

Margaret O'Dougherty Wright is a professor of psychology at Miami University of Ohio. Her research focuses on the long-term consequences of interpersonal trauma. She is interested in understanding what promotes positive resolution of abusive experiences as well as factors that lead to continued vulnerability. Her current research explores mothering as a survivor following childhood abuse or neglect, the identification of mediating and moderating factors that account for the link between childhood maltreatment and intergenerational continuity or discontinuity of abuse, and the exploration of protective processes that foster resilience in child abuse survivors, such as attachment relationships, social support, coping flexibility, and meaning making. She received her PhD in Clinical Psychology from the University of Minnesota and completed a clinical internship at UCLA's Neuropsychiatric Institute.

Jeremy Yorgason is an associate professor in the School of Family Life and director of the Family Studies Center at Brigham Young University. His research interests focus on later life family relationships, with an emphasis on marriage and health. His current research efforts explore ways that older couples manage age-associated health concerns. His work has been published in several professional journals including *Families, Systems, & Health; Family Relations;* the *Journal of Family Issues;* the *Journal of Aging Studies;* the *Journal of Applied Gerontology;* and *Research on Aging.* He received his PhD in Human Development from Virginia Tech University and was a postdoctoral fellow at the Gerontology Center of Pennsylvania State University.